W9-AVG-263

795

The Social Sciences
and American Civilization

The Social Sciences and American Civilization

BRUCE WATSON   WILLIAM TARR

Diablo Valley College

John Wiley & Sons, Inc.
NEW YORK, LONDON, SYDNEY

For Joyce and Joan

Preface

The title of this book, seemingly overambitious, is not meant to convey the scope of material covered but a point of view. That point of view is based on the interrelatedness of knowledge in the social sciences. Lest this bother some readers, let us hasten to add that we have avoided a piecemeal social science approach in which students are exposed to a morsel of each of the social sciences. Instead, we have selected what we feel to be some of the major themes and concepts from the behavioral sciences—sociology, anthropology, and psychology—and have applied these to the various trends and institutions of American civilization. The application of the themes and concepts to American life, although timely and interesting for beginning social science students, is above all a substantive peg upon which they can hang the abstractions to be learned. Moreover, the study of American trends and institutions has been placed in a historical context as a further aid to the application of concepts. For example, in the study of economic institutions the historical development of capitalism as a form of social organization and as an ideology are discussed before the strictly behavioral subject matter, such as socialization.

The concepts that we have introduced throughout the book are illustrated and elaborated by the frequent inclusion of the works of other authors. These essays have been chosen with care. The bases for selection were the pertinence and readability of the essays. Although theoretical consistency has been strived for, contrasting viewpoints have not been avoided.

We hope that our readers, instructors and students alike, find this to be a creative book. Although many textbooks are seemingly written to stand by themselves as instructional devices to be dryly regurgitated (even, perhaps, to replace the instructor), this book is written to be discussed and argued. Additional readings can be assigned to give any specific chapter more depth. Lists of readings at the end of each chapter, often containing many inexpensive paperback editions, allow for flexibility of approach.

The specific viewpoint of this book, of course, is our responsibility; that it was developed at all, however, has been the result of the contributions of many others. A two-year consultation program on the interrelatedness of the social sciences (1957–1959), drawing on scholars in residence at the Center for Advanced Study in the Behavioral Sciences, Palo Alto, California, did much to stimulate our thinking. We also gratefully acknowledge the aid of James Clark of Berkeley, California, without whose interest and enthusiasm the book might never have come into being: Otto Butz of San Francisco State College who, having read an early version of some of the first chapters, gave us pertinent suggestions for further development; our colleagues at Diablo Valley College—past and present—who provided the atmosphere and encouragement so necessary to us; and our families who have endured it all.

Bruce Watson
William Tarr

Concord, California
February 1964

Contents

Chapter 1
Tools for Social Analysis

Human behavior, the subject matter of the social sciences, is a highly controversial subject—but facts are accumulating. Many students approach it with ready-made explanations, such as "he's a Jew . . . a Frenchman . . . an artist . . . a redhead . . . a Republican . . ." or try to explain human behavior in such vague terms as human nature, instinct, or self-preservation. This is dead-end thinking which can never lead to answers about the real variations that exist in human conduct and why they exist.

The social sciences promise insight into human behavior, and with the development of understanding has come a necessary division of labor to facilitate deepest penetration into the complexities of man's behavior. The several disciplines of the social sciences, defined in the next section of this chapter, are results of that division of labor.

As specialization in the social sciences became more refined a feeling grew in some quarters that narrow specialists were not contributing a systematic, coherent body of knowledge about man. Out of this reaction came a technique consisting of "borrowed" methodologies and areas of special interest, revealing itself in such new subdisciplines as cultural history, social anthropology, and economic psychology. Despite opposition, this cross-fertilization—called integrated and interdisciplinary—continues to be one of the most promising avenues for a proper study of man.

The integration of knowledge can be exaggerated or oversimplified. On the one hand, integration may produce a grand synthesis of knowledge, such that a unified social science results. Or integration may simply list concepts in the hope that the student will be able to unify them. Both extremes are to be avoided. In this book the integration of knowledge is managed in two ways. First, appropriate concepts from various social sciences are brought to bear on a particular topic. Government, for example, not only is viewed from the usual historical and constitutional approach, but also is examined as a system of power, a system of value,

1

and a form of social organization. Second, certain themes developed in Part I of the book pervade the succeeding parts. The socialization process, for example, the means by which individuals acquire the beliefs, habits, and attitudes of their society, is extended beyond the family to other areas, such as the military and the economy.

The scope of this book is at once restricted and expanded by the words "American Civilization" in its title. "American" narrows our concern appreciably and justifies the exclusion of some remarkable research in the social sciences. "Civilization" on the other hand, broadens the arena for the study of human behavior more than some other concepts in current vogue in the social sciences such as "society" and "culture." Society refers to people and the ways in which they organize themselves and otherwise relate to each other. Culture refers to the products of the people in the society. This includes not only the material aspects of culture, such as tools or buildings, but also the nonmaterials, such as language, myth, or art. Society refers to the actors, culture to the action. The word civilization, however, encompasses both. But, as historians and anthropologists use the word civilization there is also included the degree of complexity in a given society. The Hottentots, the Plains Indians, and the Pygmies have not created civilizations; the ancient Egyptians, the Chinese, the Romans, and the Americans have. A written language, a high degree of division of labor, some say the presence of cities, organized religion, and a multigroup society are some of the factors that create the necessary complexity.

Although America is rooted in Europe, American civilization differs from the European in dress, language, manners, educational and political systems, and, to some degree, economic system. The particular configuration of beliefs and values, social groupings, and material products that comprise American civilization form the outer limits of this book.

THE NATURE OF SOCIAL SCIENCE

The social sciences are those disciplines that deal with human behavior and its results. Behavior is the concern of one or more of these sciences to the extent that individual or group behavior is affected by or affects some other group. It is also the concern of the social sciences that either type of behavior is affected by a creation of man or causes modification, destruction, or something to be created. The classification and interpretation of social phenomena constitute a social science. Social science has a vested interest in the whole field of inquiries relating to man's behavior and activities. It is likely, therefore, that there should be a considerable amount of overlapping of disciplines where the object of study is as complex, variable, and adaptable as man.

Given the great progress of social inquiry since the breaching of the traditional boundaries of the social disciplines, there is a specific contribution that each of the social sciences makes toward the greater knowledge of man. With the clear understanding that a growing number of subdisciplines and hybrids are adding significantly to our knowledge, the following list of basic social science disciplines will serve to demonstrate how each makes its distinctive contribution.

History. History is the oldest of the social sciences, although the least deserving of the designation "science." For centuries the writing of history was more art form and special pleading than objective study. In the past 100 years writers of history have worked to create a "new" history, that is, a branch of knowledge seriously devoted to the study of the interaction of factors and forces comprising man's past experiences. History today includes all the ramifications of human experience: the effects of man's geographic environment, his struggle for economic existence, his political relations with his fellows, and his cultural and spiritual achievements. All other social sciences draw on the materials of history.

Political Science. The State is the province of political science. Anything that has to do with the State can be included in the subject matter of political science in its broadest sense. It is concerned with the conditions under which variations of types of governments develop, with the distinguishing features of these types, with the relation of government to the governed in various historical situations, with political behavior, and with the peculiar methods each government employs to carry out its functions. Political facts are elements in the general structure of society. Fundamental to the understanding and interpretation of these facts is the concept of political power.

Economics. Economics studies who does, who will, and who should use which resources (including human labor), when, where, how, and for what purpose. In practice, economists study mainly the functioning of the institutions through which the allocation of resources is continually decided.

Anthropology. Concerned with man in a "sociocultural" sense, anthropology is devoted to the study of the interrelationships between man and culture. It draws heavily on biology, archaeology, geology, and geography, as well as on history, sociology, and psychology. When focused on culture, that part of his environment created by man, anthropology is clearly a social science.

Sociology. Also concerned with man in a sociocultural sense, sociology focuses on the general nature of human groups and on social processes. Broad in scope and methodology, sociology is perhaps the most vigorously "imperialist" of the social sciences because it expands its boundaries to cover all generalizations applicable to the structure and function of society.

Psychology. As a discipline pertaining to how the individual interacts with his environment, psychology is a social science when concerned with the individual's responses to culture and society. Like anthropology, psychology is related to several fields and can most legitimately be numbered among the social sciences when dealing with personality theory or social psychology.

There are other disciplines often considered to be social sciences or sciences with social implications: geography, linguistics, medicine, jurisprudence, criminology, education, eugenics, ethics, and art. Of the six basic social sciences, three are regarded more properly as behavioral sciences: sociology, anthropology, and psychology. This is a somewhat arbitrary distinction based on the emphasis in these disciplines on social actions rather than on chronological events. But as all six touch each other in one way or another we may not ignore the full range of social existence and social consequence.

VALUES AND THE SOCIAL SCIENCES

An even more important consideration than the division of labor is the inescapable problem of values. Value judgments simplify the task of the social scientist in that certain results can be measured against certain criteria, but the question persists: is the judgment valid? Is it true? Even complete objectivity, the essence of science, has at its base the ultimate value of truth. Should we, through improved techniques, arrive at highly objective findings, the application of such data will remain a value judgment. But the act of making a value judgment is not equivalent to a falsity. Value judgments and science are not antithetical, nor are they the same thing. The problem of objectivity and the danger of value judgments going awry is particulary acute in the social sciences for the reason that, in Julian Huxley's words, *the investigator is inside instead of outside his material.*

Writing in 1620, Francis Bacon understood the problems besetting the freeing of the natural sciences from prejudice and superstition. His *Novum Organum* stands as a landmark in the development of the scientific method.

xxxix

* There are four classes of idols which beset men's minds. To these for distinction's sake I have assigned names—calling the first class *Idols of the Tribe*; the second, *Idols of the Cave*; the third, *Idols of the Marketplace*; the fourth, *Idols of the Theater*.

xl

The formation of ideas and axioms by true induction is no doubt the proper remedy to be applied for the keeping off and clearing away of idols. To point them out, however, is of great use, for the doctrine of idols is to the interpretation of nature what the doctrine of the refutation of sophisms is to common logic.

xli

The Idols of the Tribe have their foundation in human nature itself, and in the tribe or race of men. For it is a false assertion that the sense of man is the measure of things. On the contrary, all perceptions, as well of the sense as of the mind, are according to the measure of the individual and not according to the measure of the universe. And the human understanding is like a false mirror, which, receiving rays irregularly, distorts and discolors the nature of things by mingling its own nature with it.

xlii

The Idols of the Cave are the idols of the individual man. For everyone (besides the errors common to human nature in general) has a cave or den of his own, which refracts and discolors the light of nature; owing either to his own proper and peculiar nature or to his education and conversation with others; or to the reading of books, and the authority of those whom he esteems and admires; or to the differences of impressions, accordingly as they take place in a mind preoccupied and predisposed or in a mind indifferent and settled; or the like. So that the spirit of man (according as it is meted out to different individuals) is in fact a thing variable and full of perturbation, and governed as it were by chance. Whence it was well observed by Heraclitus that men look for sciences in their own lesser worlds, and not in the greater or common world.

xliii

There are also idols formed by the intercourse and association of men with each other, which I call Idols of the Marketplace, on account of the commerce and consort of men there. For it is by discourse that men as-

---

* Francis Bacon, *Novum Organum*, as quoted in *The English Philosophers from Bacon to Mill*, pp. 34–35. Edwin A. Burtt, ed., New York: Random House, Inc., Modern Library Edition, 1939.

sociate; and words are imposed according to the apprehension of the vulgar. And therefore the ill and unfit choice of words wonderfully obstructs the understanding. Nor do the definitions or explanations where-with in some things learned men are wont to guard and defend themselves, by any means set the matter right. But words plainly force and overrule the understanding, and throw all into confusion, and lead men away into numberless empty controversies and idle fancies.

xliv

Lastly, there are idols which have immigrated into men's minds from the various dogmas of philosophies, and also from wrong laws of demonstration. These I call Idols of the Theater; because in my judgment all the received systems are but so many stage-plays, representing worlds of their own creation after an unreal and scenic fashion. Nor is it only of the systems now in vogue, or only of the ancient sects and philosophies, that I speak: for many more plays of the same kind may yet be composed and in like artificial manner set forth; seeing that errors the most widely different have nevertheless causes for the most part alike. Neither again do I mean this only of entire systems, but also of many principles and axioms in science, which by tradition, credulity, and negligence have come to be received.

After Bacon the methods of the natural sciences developed the hard way; that is, by a process of trial and error for a period of over 300 years, and the end is not yet in sight.

The social sciences, still closely entangled in human values, have not progressed apace with the natural sciences. Unable to conduct fully controlled experiments, the social scientist still must find the methods that will enable him to isolate social facts satisfactorily with the same facility as the natural scientist isolates his phenomena. Kingsley Davis, a contemporary sociologist, has made a brief but penetrating examination of the problems confronting social science.

*

Although everybody realizes that special obstacles impede the path of social science, not everyone has a clear notion of what they are. It is sometimes said that the social sciences are "youthful" and consequently have not yet had time to achieve scientific maturity. Such an explanation, however, merely poses the problem, for it does not tell why birth should come so much later or "adolescence" last so much longer in this field than in the study of chemistry, physics, or biology. Some say that social phenomena are more complex than other phenomena and that this makes them harder to

* Reprinted with permission of the publisher from *Human Society*, pp. 10–15, by Kingsley Davis. Copyright 1948, 1949 by The Macmillan Company.

understand. But as long as any branch of knowledge contains unknown frontiers (as every field does) its degree of complexity remains infinite. The mysteries of matter, organic life, and the astral universe are as deep and unsolved as the mysteries of social life. In fact, they seem to be more complex. Nearly everyone has some notion of social affairs, but the uninitiated are abysmally ignorant of the nature of the atom. Actually we have in social matters a special avenue of knowledge that is denied the natural scientist because we experience social and psychic realities subjectively and can therefore, simply by examining our own motives, gain some insight into why people behave as they do.

What, then, can the hazards of social science be? To understand them calls for an understanding of society itself. In other words, it is only through social science that the obstacles can be explained; and, in its attempt to explain them, paradoxically, social science is shackled by these very obstacles. It seems a hopeless circle, but let us try anyway. . . .

A social system is always normative. Its integration rests upon the fact that its members carry in their heads, as part of the cultural heritage, the notion that they *ought* or *ought not* to do certain things, that some actions are *right* or *good* and others *wrong* or *bad*. Each person judges himself and his fellows according to these subtle and ubiquitous rules; and any violation is punished by some negative reaction, be it slight or great. An evaluative attitude, an attitude of praise and blame, of accusation and justification, thus pervades every human society. To question the rules, or worse yet, to question the sentiments lying behind them, is to incur certain penalties, the least of which is controversy. The person who tries in his own thinking to escape entirely the moralistic system in order to study behavior objectively, who tries to analyze social norms and values as if they were amoebae or atoms, is quickly branded as an agnostic, cynic, traitor, or worse. Instead of public support for his work, he must count on public hostility.

To protect himself the social scientist usually accepts certain social values (the ones generally agreed upon in his society) and merely studies the means of attaining them. He thus eliminates from his inquiry the very phenomena that from a sociological point of view are the most fundamental bases of social existence. But his failure to adopt a scientific attitude may go still further. He may willingly or unwillingly get involved in controversies—i.e., disputes in which the public has taken sides—and espouse one set of values as against another. In this case he frequently winds up by becoming a special pleader, a propagandist or wishful thinker, the very opposite of a scientist. No one thinks ill of him for this, except those on the other side, because partisanship on public issues is the expected thing.

It is this dual role of the social scientist, the fact that on the one hand he is a member of a normative group and on the other an observer of this same group, that explains the main limitation on his scientific activity. It does no good to *blame* him for his limitations, to hold him responsible for his fuzzy definitions, his inexact methods, innocuous conclusions, erroneous predictions, and pompous vocabulary. These are simply the unconscious means by which he protects himself. He is expected to wear the garb of science, but is forbidden to perform its functions; therefore, he merely goes through a harmless abracadabra while reaching conclusions that everyone, or at least everyone on his side, wants to hear. If he is accused of being unscientific, he merely says that the social sciences are still in their youth and that social phenomena are very complex, or else he says that in social matters it is impossible to be neutral, not realizing, apparently, that such a statement, if taken in an epistemological sense, is self-contradictory.

In any society there are sentiments not to be questioned. They are not even to be studied dispassionately, because the mere mention of their violation in anything but a horrified tone may be taboo. More than one professor has been dismissed from an American university for inquiring into the sex life of the unmarried, for taking an open-minded attitude toward religious dogma, for teaching a course about socialism, or for adopting an unpatriotic attitude. Such subjects, if touched at all, must always be handled circumspectly, with the professor reiterating his devotion to the supreme values. The object of study should not be the values themselves, but violations of them, because violations call for action. Thus if the social scientist studies divorce, he is presumably doing so for the purpose of reducing this "evil." If he studies government, it is for the purpose of removing the obstacles to true democracy, true communism, or true fascism, depending on where he is. In any large and complex society, however, there are other matters on which public opinion is admittedly divided, and these may be discussed more freely. Yet such free discussion does not necessarily mean objective discussion. Every controversy has two sides, and both sides condemn anyone who attempts a purely dispassionate analysis. It is an ancient principle that he who does not agree, disagrees. The social scientist cannot afford to expose the assumptions, interests, and values of *both* sides alike. He must align himself with one or the other side, or risk becoming universally unpopular. If it is prohibition he must be either for or against it. If it is birth control, socialized medicine, Negro equality, labor unionization, woman's suffrage, literary censorship, legalized gambling, or higher taxes, he must find reasons why it ought or ought not to be. This is the first question the public asks— which side is he on?—and the public has an exceptional ability or compulsion to read evaluative attitudes into written or spoken statements. Indeed, ordinary language is so saturated with such attitudes that it is virtually impossible to use it without laying oneself open to the charge of partisanship. An attempted dispassionate analysis merely winds up by insulting both sides, or if it is not dealing with a controversial subject but simply with human behavior, it seems satirical.

Much of what passes for social analysis is merely an attempt to assess the blame for something. Who is responsible for crime? Who is responsible for World War II? Who is responsible for high prices? However necessary such assessment of moral responsibility may be for the operation of society, it is not the same thing as causal analysis and often, in fact, obscures the latter.

In some ways the sociologist is faced with more obstacles than other social scientists, precisely because in trying to see society as a whole he is forced to examine the nature of human values. He must subject the mores and the basic institutions to objective analysis. He must deal with religion and the family, for example, in a spirit of secular inquiry rather than in a spirit of awe and taboo. The economist and political scientist, assuming without question the institutional framework, can deal for the most part with rational conduct and popular issues, and so escape some of the sociologist's difficulties. These specialists run into other troubles, however. The literature of political science in particular is permeated by metaphysical and moralistic concepts; sometimes it seems to be more an exercise in ethical theory than in empirical knowledge.

In view of the obstacles confronting social science, some people say there is no such thing, that at best there are merely "social studies." Others believe that social science exists but inconsistently take the view that the practitioner of it cannot be neutral, that he must inevitably take sides. If this means taking sides with reference to the matter under investigation, then it is a denial of science. Without neutral analysis knowledge is impossible. All science is neutral in the sense that the emotions of the investigator do not influence the observation and explanation of the facts. True, there are plenty of scientific controversies. Such controversies are the very breath of science. But they are controversies with reference to theoretical issues, not with reference to moral or political issues; and they are settled by observation and logic, not by propaganda and obfuscation.

Social behavior does not represent some special category of reality intrinsically impervious to systematic study. It is just as amenable to scientific investigation as any other natural phenomenon. The obstacles come, not from the subject matter itself, but from the limitations placed on the investigator by his own society. Consequently, we may look for the greatest development of social science when certain conditions are fulfilled. The first is that the society be so large, complex, and diversified that its citizens require a great amount of exact social knowledge to keep the whole thing going. In such a society the activities that are regarded as sheer means, having only a fluid relation to the ultimate ends, are quite numerous—and so long as they are regarded as means they may be studied with impunity. In such a society, moreover, the division of labor is carried extremely far, so that it seems feasible to meet the need for exact social information through a special group (always small) of persons professionally engaged in social research and teaching. Such a group is given a sort of license to investigate objectively—i.e., is given a certain amount of academic freedom, security of tenure, and scholarly seclusion. In return it is supposed to observe the canons of scientific method and the ethic of unbiased teaching. If one of the group uses his mantle of scientist to give an air of authority to propaganda, or if he converts his classroom into a political platform, he is not acting as a scientist and has no right to demand special immunity from reprisal on the part of those who disagree with him. A democratic state, for example, does not want to give a protected platform to those advocating dictatorship. It may, however, support an objective inquiry into the nature of dictatorships. If, in the classroom or in research, there is any advocacy, it must on the whole be in favor of the established values; yet under certain circumstances and in a limited sense there may be no advocacy at all, but simply analysis.

Modern industrial society favors a certain amount of social science, sociology included. Before the industrial age there was plenty of speculation about social matters, but it was primarily moralistic. Confucius, Plato, Aristotle, Aquinas were concerned with what people ought to do rather than what they really do. It was not until the eighteenth and nineteenth centuries that anything like genuine social science arose. By that time the industrial revolution had created a more complicated society, forcing on scholars a new awareness of social phenomena. It had also led to a more secularized society permitting interpretations of social phenomena that were less religious and moralistic. Finally, the achievements of natural science had popularized scientific method and suggested the possibility that this approach might be applied to the data of society. For reasons mentioned, the success of the new social science was rather slight. The various branches had a slow and gradual development, and are now still limited in scope and achievement. Nevertheless, it is plain that in our type of society there can be, and is, some social science despite the obstacles.

ORGANIZATION OF THE BOOK

This volume has been designed to provide the student with a starting point from which to begin his understanding of the social processes that influence the behavior of man, particularly in an American setting. In this connection the student will find selected writings from social scientists and others interested in the affairs of man to provide essential concepts, facts, and points of view, as well as background materials and interpretation.

Part One is devoted to the four tools of analysis: (1) man as an organism, (2) personality, (3) the human group, and (4) culture. These tools, or concepts, form the analytic basis of the text. From them derive the themes woven throughout the topical chapters which follow.

In Part Two the nature of the human community is discussed. Its primary concerns are the processes that have brought about the change from small communities steeped in tradition to the contemporary urban explosion and its way of life.

Parts Three and Four deal with the socialization process, the means whereby individuals acquire the beliefs, habits, and attitudes of their society. Part Three concentrates on the institutions of initial socialization that function particularly in the socialization of the child. Some of the typical problems of the family, church, and school are explored in the setting of the human community. The effects of military experience on socialization occupy Part Four. In this sense the military is regarded as a transitional institution of socialization between boyhood and adult life.

Part Five centers on the economic institution. The development of Western capitalism is presented, followed by consideration of the changing nature of ideologies in the capitalistic system. Three examples of the way in which occupational roles are acquired figure in this study, and a final chapter deals with some of the problems of capitalism in contemporary America.

The study of political institutions comprises Part Six. Again, the historical and ideological backgrounds of the American system are discussed. These are followed by an analysis of power relationships and the socialization of political beliefs and their expression in voting. Another chapter of Part Six inspects selected problems of the American nation-state. The final chapter of Part Six takes up militarism in contemporary America.

Part Seven is concerned with certain unsolved problems in American civilization. That the book ends on this note is fitting, for the social sciences are themselves a frequent response to the problems and issues existent in social life.

The social sciences are not only an intellectual tool by which abstract processes and events can be analyzed. They are also a response to human need: the need, to paraphrase Kingsley Davis, to recognize the moral obligations of being human in a world that not only has become economically and politically interdependent but also is undergoing a profound revolution in social and cultural relationships. That revolution is symbolized by the quest for self-determination among former colonial peoples, by the persistent search for realization of the democratic ideology among the underprivileged and among the minorities within America itself, and by the ideological challenge presented by the Soviet Bloc. In a world of change, will American civilization meet its stated responsibilities as a democratic society? The social sciences provide a basis for understanding such social issues, a means for resolving them, and a spiritual commitment to man's rationality in an immense, complicated social world.

Selected Readings

Hoselitz, B. F. *A Reader's Guide to the Social Sciences*. Glencoe, Ill.: The Free Press, 1960.
*Lerner, Daniel. *The Human Meaning of the Social Sciences*. New York: Meridian Books, 1962.
Lynd, Robert. *Knoweldge for What?* Princeton: Princeton University Press, 1939.
*Mannheim, Karl. *Ideology and Utopia*. New York: Harvest Books, n.d.
*Stern, Fritz. *Varieties of History*. New York: Meridian Books, 1959.
*Teggart, Frederick J. *Theory and Processes of History*. Berkeley: University of California Press, 1960.
*Whitehead, Alfred North. *Science and the Modern World*. New York: New American Library, 1948.

* Paperback edition.

Part One
Introduction

The interrelatedness of knowledge is widely accepted in many fields of study. Perhaps the most dramatic acceptance has been in the physical and biological sciences. A research problem in one of these subjects often necessitates broad understandings of concepts and procedures in another. Recent studies in human heredity, for example, have made it necessary to understand both chemistry and physics. The explosion of a nuclear device leads to increased knowledge in chemistry and geology. It is clear that development in any one physical science depends more and more on developments in other physical sciences.

A similar interrelatedness among the social sciences is now becoming accepted. No one social science can provide a full explanation of human behavior. Many early writers attempted this feat which resulted in the development of various kinds of determinisms. A determinism is any theory that seeks to explain a social phenomenon through a single set of factors. Karl Marx was an economic determinist because he believed that all change in society could be linked to alterations in the economic system. Similarly there are psychological determinisms, cultural determinisms, and so on through the social sciences. In contrast to such determinisms, Part One of this book is devoted to the interrelationship of theories and concepts from a number of social sciences which may help to improve our understanding of human behavior. We are interested not only in *what* humans do, but also in *why* they do it.

Part One contains 4 chapters (2–5), each devoted to a particular set of interrelated concepts and theories. Chapter 2 deals with the human organism and the biological foundations of human behavior. As such, it helps us to understand what is and what is not inherited, and how inheritance influences the developing human organism. Chapter 3 is a survey of three theories of personality, from the Freudian theory, which is heavily oriented toward biology, to the theory of social interaction, which is more concerned with the social factors in personality development. Chapter 4 considers the human group—the setting within which the individual personality functions. Chapter 5 examines the concept of culture which is the values, beliefs, and attitudes that shape human behavior.

The chapters composing Part One are linked together by a central theme—the socialization process, whereby the biological being is transformed into the human being. This theme underlies the entire book. The broadly conceived concepts of organism, personality, society, and culture which follow provide clues to understanding the socialization process as it unfolds throughout life.

Chapter 2

Man as an Organism

In early America, the Calvinist doctrine of predestination implied that all human characteristics and behavior were inborn, the result of God's planning, and more or less immutable. No longer do we speak of "beating the devil out" of the small child in the literal sense of our Puritan forebears. A somewhat more modern attitude looks for environmental causes of abnormal behavior with little thought given to "inborn" traits. This is the *tabula rasa* idea of personality: Man enters the world a blank page to be inscribed by his physical and social environments. John B. Watson, a key figure in the environmental school of the 1920's, said, "Give me a dozen healthy infants, well-formed, and my own specific world to bring them up in and I'll guarantee to take any one at random and train him to become any type of specialist I might select—doctor, lawyer, artist, merchant-chief, and yes, even beggarman and thief, regardless of his talents, penchants, tendencies, abilities, vocations, and race of his ancestors." [1]

Environment was given further significance years later in Russia by Trofim D. Lysenko, the flower of Soviet science under Stalin. Lysenko insisted not only that environment determined behavior and was therefore controllable, but more importantly, that behavior could be transferred to succeeding generations. That is, learned behavior, conditioned by the proper communist environment would become part of the good communist's genetic material to be passed on to offspring. It is obvious that the reason for Lysenko's popularity with the inner circle of Russian leadership was the neat way in which his so-called theory fitted into Marxist dogma, which called for a withering away of the state—any bourgeois characteristics would simply be bred out of the stock.

Neither of these "schools" provides a satisfactory explanation of human behavior, but each has elements which, taken from context, seem to fit in a meaningful pattern. Most responsible scientists today regard man's behavior as a product of both heredity and environment. Differences among individuals and groups result from variations between and

15

within these two factors, although disagreement over the degree of contribution of each indicates that we do not know all there is to know about man.

In this chapter we shall begin with the physical basis of human personality as separable from the social and cultural factors. Much of the data on behavior comes from laboratory plants and animals; in many cases the application of these findings to man is by inference. Inference, of course, does not mean a lack of validity, but some mental reservations should be made by the reader where experiment on man is impossible or incomplete.

SOME IDEAS ON HEREDITY AND GROWTH

The science of genetics is relatively new and usually dates from 1866 when the work of Gregor Mendel, an Augustinian monk and naturalist, was first published.

The Abbé Mendel found that by breeding purebred white-flowered peas with purebred red-flowered peas the result was all red flowers in the first generation; the dominant red gene suppressed the white gene. When the red hybrids were mated, each plant in the second generation had a one-in-four chance of inheriting only white genes. When this occurred an all-white purebred pea emerged—the result of mating hybrids with recessive characteristics present in each. The one-in-four chance is known as the Mendelian ratio of inheritance. Statistically, because of random selection, this ratio will turn up only in a certain number of chances.

Little use was made of Mendel's discovery until the turn of the century. Today genetics is a rapidly growing science as demonstrated by the emergence of such new specialties as population biology, biostatistics, and biophysics. The stake is high: the secret of life.

Writing in the *Antioch Review*, Theodosius Dobzhansky stated the case this way: "The human body starts its existence as a fertilized egg cell, weighing about one-twentieth millionth of an ounce. An adult is some billion times heavier. The growth occurs through the assimilation of food. Quite literally, man is a conglomeration of transformed groceries. And yet, this conglomeration of transformed groceries is alive, feels joy and suffering, is conscious of self, and of other persons and of the universe." [2]

How does this happen? The nearest approach to an answer is that this all-important transformation of raw materials into human tissue is engineered by the action of the genes which man inherits from his ancestors.

That children often look remarkably like one parent or display certain family characteristics of a physical nature is a partial demonstration of the work of the genes. To bolster this argument from another side we might cite as evidence of heredity the 300 years of music written by various Bachs. Or we might mention Mozart's first minuet written at the age of five, undoubtedly the consequence of an innate aptitude, since Mozart's environment, at that age, could have had little opportunity to influence him. Many mathematical wizards were child prodigies. At six, Samuel Reshevsky, the American chess phenomenon, was giving pointers to men who had played the game for 50 years—and they listened! Thus not only is the color of hair and eyes sealed at the moment of conception, but so is the general level of mental capacity.

Both parents contribute approximately equal amounts of genetic material to the offspring through the media of sperm and egg cells. In the nuclei of both sex cells tiny bodies called *chromosomes* carry the genes or units of heredity. Literally thousands of genes line up on each of the 46 chromosomes in the fertilized egg cell, or *zygote*,[3] and the possible combinations of inherited characteristics in the new individual run into the hundreds of trillions. There seems to be sufficient basis, therefore, for the appearance now and then of a Bach, a Mozart, a Shakespeare, or an Einstein, as well as for differences among the rest of us.

The distribution of parental inheritance in the biological sense appears to be entirely at random. Moreover, because two sets of genes are inherited, two genes influence the same trait. Since one gene is dominant and the other recessive, and the dominant trait is expressed over the recessive one, we have an explanation of why a child might not look at all like the parents but instead be the image of a grandfather. In the case of an undesirable characteristic, such as the predisposition to schizophrenia, the condition must be present at least as a recessive gene in both parents.

Mutation, or sudden variation, in a gene is thought to be an actual rearrangement of the chemical composition of the gene, in turn giving rise to recessive characteristics. Most mutations are harmful—but the rare "good" ones are believed to account for evolution.

Though man does not lend himself to experiments in heredity as willingly as the garden pea, the hypothesis and theory which loom so large in human genetics are essentially correct for there have been no significant contradictions in the findings of geneticists. Modern technology is responsible for two giant strides in the field today: genes are now visible where once they had not been visible; and it is now possible to determine the molecular structure of a gene—*deoxyribonucleic acid* (DNA), the substance that carries the information of heredity and is believed to govern all cells.

In the latter phase, the work of Linus Pauling, James D. Watson, Francis H. C. Crick, and others has opened remarkable new vistas from which some believe it will be possible to glimpse the very origins of life. The chemical structure of DNA allows geneticists to make predictions about its function. The arrangement of the four bases of DNA (adenine, guanine, thymine, cytosine) into its characteristic, giant, double-helix molecule carries information in a four-symbol code, much like digits on the magnetic tape of an electronic computer. The thousands of steps on each molecule and the thousands of molecules in each chromosome permit a vast amount of coded information to be carried, telling how to develop particular organisms, ranging from a bacterium to a man. Yet the entire supply of DNA that *could* control the heredity of the next generation of man (several billion individuals) could be put in a cube one-twenty-fifth of an inch on each side!

*
There are ample, broad, and extremely diverse reasons for thinking that a knowledge of human heredity can contribute enormously and in many ways to the understanding of human beings with whom we deal continuously. Human genetics has potentialities for contributing to the understanding of the people not only from the standpoint of the diseases that afflict them, but also from the standpoint of their temperaments, their mental operations, their emotions, their motivations and drives, their diverse aptitudes and abilities, all of which greatly affect their functioning as members of society . . .

The function of human minds is without doubt closely correlated with brain anatomy and function. We know that a multitude of human troubles, including the devastating ever-present threat of war, start in men's minds. What could be more logical than for biological scientists to be interested in human brains and whatever genetic factors enter into their make-up?

We need desperately to understand men's minds better than we do, and on the basis of differences in brain structure alone there is ample reason for thinking that inheritance enters into the quality of everyone's mind.

Yet the most influential school of thought in psychology and particularly

* Roger J. Williams, "Why Human Genetics?" *Journal of Heredity*, Vol. 51, March–April 1960, pp. 91–98. By permission of the American Genetics Association.

psychiatry is one which traces the vagaries of individual minds back to environmental influences during infancy or even in some case to prenatal life. Walter C. Alvarez, the veteran physician, complains about the lack of attention to heredity in this field: "In most of the present day books on psychiatry, there is not even a short section on heredity. The book resembles a text on paleontology written for a fundamentalist college, but not one word on evolution." . . . We need to know far more than we do about the extent to which various human attributes and behavior are genotypical in origin. Do sleep patterns have predominantly environmental origin? Is liking for warm or cold climates merely based upon previous climatic experience? Are special gustatory likes and dislikes merely conditioned by previous experience? Is love of poetry (or a particular type of poetry) induced environmentally? Are histrionic leanings primarily the result of training? Are temperaments merely cultivated? Is creativity a natural endowment, or does it arise because of special nurture? Do emotional disorders arise primarily as a result of childhood experience or does inheritance contribute in an important way? To what extent are special aptitudes—mechanical, mathematical, musical, etc.—environmentally induced? These are some of the many questions which only human geneticists can answer.

The most important task of human genetics is to gain understanding of the potentialities of human genotypes so as to make possible the intelligent "manipulation of the environment." Many social scientists . . . [have] . . . the idea that an environment can be devised which, when applied generally to the human race, will yield the best phenotypes. Strictly from the genetic standpoint, nothing could be farther from the truth. Each genotype might be expected *a priori* to require for best results a distinctive environment patterned after its own needs. What human genetics can contribute is the vast amount of knowledge about genotypes which will make possible the intelligent manipulation of the specific environments to bring about the desired ends whatever they may be.

Roger J. Williams in the foregoing passage is not asking for intelligent manipulations of the environment in order that environmental change will feed back into the genetic structure. Rather he wants us to make the most of what we have.

And in the Soviet Union, where Lysenko is now politically and scientifically discredited, the idea that environmental change will produce behavioral change as a result of genetic mutation no longer persists, but the Soviets still are determined to make the most of what they have. Witness a statement in a recent issue of the Soviet journal *Novy Mir*: "All children are to be brought up in state run collectives. Parents will be permitted to visit their children and their living quarters as often as the rules allow. A children's collective, when directed by an experienced pedagogue, is incomparably better equipped to give greatest indoctrination to the child in the best social habits than the most loving and attentive mothers. Egoistic inclinations in the child will be snuffed out in the cradle. In place of these inclinations, all inborn social instincts and sympathies will be developed as the result of the new conditioned reflexes formed in the process of daily comradely relationships." [4]

Whereas Russian officialdom has dropped Lysenko, the Soviets may be over-extending Pavlov's theory of the conditioned reflex. But it is politically and scientifically important for the West to see what the Russians are doing. While the democratic conscience must and does shrink from thought control, we must address ourselves to counteracting the problem posed here and to implement the plea in Professor Williams' article. To accomplish the former we will need to understand ourselves better. What better place to begin than genetics?

THE CENTRAL NERVOUS SYSTEM

The chief obligation of personality is to create or maintain a design for living which permits both the harmonious appeasement of immediate needs and progress toward distant goals. Conflicts arise both inside and outside the individual. They must be resolved if balance is to be achieved and preserved, if the individual is to be considered "normal," and if he is to survive.

The brain, three pounds of "messy substance shut in a dark warm place," and its allied nervous tissue, the spinal cord, and its warning and motor nerves, are the structures charged with making adjustments to the external and internal environments. The nervous system might be termed a highly sophisticated *servomechanism*, but so infinitely more complex than any yet created by man that its behavior is of an entirely different order.

*

If we believe that genes are the determining cause in height, we cannot deny the same governing factors in deciding whether the brain will be large or small, with highly convoluted surfaces or smooth, with sensitive viable junctions called "synapses" between nerve cells or with resistant synapses. Should such an admission be made then we have every reason in studying the physical basis of personality to study, however briefly, the nervous system in

* Reprinted from V. H. Mottram, *The Physical Basis of Personality*, pp. 59–69. London: Penguin Books, Ltd., 1952, second revised edition. By permission of the publisher.

man, for upon the nature of the brain depends much of the personality. If this be doubted a quotation from almost any medical publication concerning the nervous system will prove convincing. Here is the account of an individual whose personality altered remarkably as the result of damage to one portion of his nervous system—"basal frontal atrophy" following a motor-cycle accident. The author labels the section "Post-concussional personality changes." (Paterson, *Lancet*, 1942, vol. ii, p. 717.)

The man was a soldier, ambitious, smart, and successful. By the age of 20 he had gained considerable promotion. After some time out of the Army he rejoined and again received rapid promotion. The background of army life modified his undoubted aggressive personality and made him a disciplined N.C.O. who could be entrusted with the responsibility of training soldiers. Proper respect and deference towards his superior officers had become automatic.

He suffered a severe injury to the head, presumably, from the context of the article, in a motor-bicycle accident, and this accident damaged a part of the forebrain and produced "basal frontal atrophy." It was seen that his character had undergone a change. He was now jovially familiar in his social attitude. He treated superior officers as equals and asked a ward sister her age as an opening remark in a conversation. His farewell salutation to his doctors was "Cheerio, okey-doke." On leaving the hospital he made light of his residual symptoms, wanted to return to work without sick leave, and was on a motor-bicycle again at once. He was without any fear whatever and very aggressive. Prompted by a casual and inoffensive remark from a colleague, he knocked him out.

The atrophy of the forebrain caused by the injury changed his character so that instead of a disciplined and useful member of the Army organization there appeared an undisciplined, aggressive, and euphoric personality whose value to such an organization would be less than zero. The man probably either inherited or developed in early days an aggressive attitude towards life. When the brain was normal this could be curbed, modified, and rendered useful. When a particular part of the brain was damaged this aggressive attitude lost the restraining influence from the forebrain and appeared as a caricature of itself.

(A less drastic, but efficacious, means of altering the apparent character of a person is to send a brief current of electricity through the forebrain. Persons suffering from melancholia or similar states of mind, such as pathological self-centeredness, can be brought to a much more normal condition by ten or a dozen weekly treatments. It is hardly too much to say that a conversion from selfishness to altruism can be effected by electric shocks acting, when added up, to six seconds! Many can testify to this and I have seen it in action. *Can* electricity take the place of a spiritual guide or the traditional much prayer and fasting?)

Modern psychiatrists now have recourse to surgery in desperate cases of psychological trouble when other less drastic methods of cure have failed. The connections between the forebrain and that deep-seated center of emotional life, the optic thalamus (see below), are severed, and in a considerable percentage of the cases the personality is so changed that the patient can thereafter lead a normal life.

Many similar changes of personality, due to damage of the brain by encephalitis lethargica (sleeping sickness), could be adduced by medical men who have come into contact with this disease. A cheerful, open-hearted, sociable being may be changed into a morose, secretive, and antisocial man.

Now a reasonable description of the nervous system requires a whole book or indeed a series of books, so that only the merest sketch is here possible or attempted.

The nervous system consists of nerve cells, their branches, and peculiar connective tissue which ties the whole together. The central part of the nervous system is buried away from harm within the skull and the backbone. It is thus highly centralized, and its central offices, so to speak, consist of hierarchies upon hierarchies of government. In man an enormous degree of centralization has taken place and a recently and highly developed portion, called by Sherrington the "roof-brain," has gathered much, though not all, of the governance into its hands.

The unit officers of these hierarchies of government are the nerve cells (better named "neurones"). There are some 2,000,000,000 of them—a huge government and civil service—whose tasks have to be co-ordinated, regulated, and rendered almost automatic. It is difficult in practical life to manage a small bureaucracy of a million or so. It becomes effete, out of touch, unprogressive. But here is a bureaucracy (one officer to each inhabitant of the earth in number) smoothly carrying on the government of the body— whereas in social affairs on this planet we are still several centuries away from efficient government or co-ordination.

The nervous system (unlike other organs such as the heart or liver) consists of units that differ in size, shape, and appearance as different plants differ among themselves. The cells of the liver are all alike. Moreover, the cells of a frog's liver are not very unlike those of a human being, though their cousinship is at very many removes. But the neurones of the nervous system are extraordinarily unlike each other in size and shape—much more so than the human liver cell and the frog's. Yet their cousinship is close. They may be spherical, spider-shaped, like fishing rods, like trees, or the seaweed laminaria, or even that of the Sargasso Sea. Their bodies may be tiny in diameter—some two fifty-thousandth parts of an inch across, or they may be just visible to the naked eye. Their branches may be tiny in extent, sufficient to keep two next-door neighbors among the packed nerve cells in touch with one another, or they may run from the roof brain down to the end of the spinal cord—a distance of about three feet.

The function of this amazing system "of lines and nodal points, gathered together at one end into a great ravelled knot, the brain, and at the other end trailing off to a sort of stalk, the spinal cord" (Sherrington, *Man on his Nature*, p. 223.) is to send messages to the muscles which will make the body move effectively as a whole. (Adrian, quoted by Sherrington.)

And as there are grades of activity from a single contraction of a set of muscles, as in the knee-jerk, to the manifoldly more complex reactions of the body as in running or the following of a line of print by the eyes, so we find (i) areas (or rather volumes) of nerve-cells grouped together to preside over some simple reaction, and (ii) tracts—long branches of nerve cells—linking up the activity of one group of nerve cells with that of another, so that their joint actions may be mutual and co-ordinated.

A simple reaction such as the knee-jerk—which takes effect almost inevitably if the tendon below the knee of a leg lightly thrown over the other knee as in sitting be tapped—is spoken of as a reflex. Other simple reflexes are the blinking of the eye when something, even a snowflake, threatens it; or the watering of the mouth when its mucous membrane is painfully disturbed. More complicated reflexes are those of sneezing, coughing, and breathing. Still more complicated are the co-ordinated movements of fore and hind limbs in animals or the arms and legs of a human being in walking and running. As complicated are the movements of the six muscles controlling the position of each eye so that the flight of a bird seen from a train—or that of an aeroplane seen from another aeroplane—may be effortlessly followed. All such reflexes are, in ultimate analysis, the reaction on the part of the body to a stimulus or group of stimuli playing upon the sense organs of the body. They carry on till they reach their goal or are interrupted by some other activity of the body. The nervous system reacts in a machine-like way, the parts of the machine being inherited according to patterns and styles determined, it may be supposed, by the genes.

The spinal cord controls mainly the reflexes of the limb movements. The lower end of the stalk of the brain controls those reflexes which have to do with breathing, with supply of blood to the various parts of the body, with the activities of the heart and the digestive system. Higher up we meet a compact group of nerve cells and their branches, the little brain, which guides and reinforces the activities of muscles. Still higher, in the optic thalamus, as it is called, we meet a structure whither all sensory impulses, started in whatever part of the body, run; where they are sorted out and whence are relayed impulses (a) to the big knots of motor nerve cells known as the corpora striata and (b) to the roof-brain (see below). This thalamus seems to be the seat of all emotional reactions, and beneath it, in the hypothalamus, is a center or group of centers, from which run nerves controlling the muscles, etc., which enable us to "register" emotion. (Of this more anon.) Above and beyond the thalamus lies a tremendous sheet of tissue called by Sherrington the "roof-brain" (the neopallium or cerebral cortex). This is enormously developed in man. It is rudimentary in the bird, the reptile, and the amphibians. It is small in the dog, much larger in the ape, but only in man does it reach an overwhelming development. Its functions, apart from acting (*i*) as an end station for all sensory messages, except those of pain which do not travel beyond the thalamus, (*ii*) as an originator of "willed" movements of muscles, and (*iii*) as centers for reflexes connected with vision, balance, and hearing, are those of (*iv*) guidance of the reflex actions under control of "lower" reflex centers, of (*v*) deciding upon the reactions to be made or the reflex actions to be suppressed. In addition to this we think of the roof-brain as the seat of the mind, that unanalysable, unplaceable constituent part of ourselves of which we are conscious though it seems to have no parts nor magnitude.

The anatomy of the parts of the nervous system does not so much concern us as its activities. No nerve cell is continued into its neighbor. There is a physiological separation between them, and this junctional tissue we term a synapse. Let us take a simple reflex such as the withdrawal of a part of the body when a painfully hot object is touched. There is sensory apparatus in the hand. This is awakened to activity by the hot object. Nervous impulses pass up a sensory nerve to the spinal cord. Here they break through the resistance of a synapse (really group of synapses) and rouse to activity a motor nerve cell (really a group of motor nerve cells). These nerve cells fire off a volley of nervous impulses along the motor nerves to the muscles (the flexor muscles) which draw the injured limb in towards the body and away from the hot object. The structures, thus working together—sensory organ, sensory nerve, synapse, motor nerve cell, motor nerve and muscle—we call a reflex arc. Upon such reflex arcs (never quite so simple as the one described) all the reactions of the body depend. The paths may be longer, the number of nerve cells and of the synapses between them be greater, and the motor side of the reaction be much more complicated. None the less the pattern is the same. We meet several places in the reflex arc where the nervous impulses must leap a gap in order to wake the next adjacent cells to activity.

Now this gap offers greater resistance at one time than another. Fatigue and drugs such as alcohol, opium, and chloroform increase the resistance. Other drugs such as caffeine, strychnine, and tetanin reduce the resistance. In some people the resistance is permanently high and in others permanently low. One person hardly moves at a sudden sound. Another jumps "half out of his skin." The first is a placid individual, the second "highly strung."

It is notorious that these differences can be seen from the moment of birth—there are placid babies and fretful babies. Is it not possible that these differences—differences in the reactivity of the nervous system—are inherited? Are not the genes concerned in the inheritance of highly irritable reflex arcs?

We have spoken above of a hierarchy of governing centers in the nervous system. There are the old-established ones which govern the ancient reflexes of standing, walking, running, breathing, and the circulation of the blood. There are later-developed centers coordinating the reactions of the body as a whole. And then, finally, there are those most recently developed sheets of nerve tissue called the roof-brain. As we proceed through these hierarchies we find them more and more easily put out of gear. Whereas it takes a large dose of chloroform to upset the breathing reflexes, quite a small dose will stop the activity of the roof-brain.

Again we have to recognize persons with highly resistant roof-brains and those with less resistant. Some people work under a concentration of alcohol, nicotine, and fatigue products which would render others useless members of society. It is exactly the reactions of these "higher" centers upon which so much of personality depends. A person with highly resistant roof-brain cells will show a different personality from that of one with less resistant cells. Is it not possible that the genes so endow one person with a resistant nervous system and another with a sensitive system?

Especially is the personality seen in emotional display. Reactions may be uncolored or colored with emotion; and as the color varies from person to person so the personality is different. The Oxonian walks along the street as if it belonged to him. The Cambridge man as if he doesn't care to whom it belongs. The difference in emotional reaction to the street gives them different personalities. (Of course this is an illustration of the effect of nurture rather than nature or inheritance, but it illustrates the point; that emotional reaction affects personality.)

Some natures are highly emotional, and in them either the optic thalamus is over-developed or the roof-brain has not been able to keep a sure hand and curb over the thalamus. Again, may it not be the genes which determine the relative sizes and efficiencies of the roof-brain and the thalamus?

Emotional life, as we have said, seems to depend on the thalamus, and just below the thalamus and in close connection with it are the supreme central offices which control the activities of the heart, blood vessels, alimentary tract, digestive secretions, and so on. It is a commonplace that these organs are affected in emotion. In painful emotion the face blanches, the hair stands on end, the pupils of the eyes dilate, the eyeballs protrude, the mouth is parched, the heart-beat increases in rate and force and there is an uncomfortable sensation in the pit of the stomach. X-ray shadows of the stomach show that in painful emotion it loses elasticity and the lower end drops below the line of the hips. All digestive movement ceases. Chemical analysis of the blood shows an increase in the sugar called glucose. One and all, these reactions are those given when the path of outflow from the central nervous system to the viscera, called the "sympathetic nervous system," is stimulated. It might be thought that the body has a special part of the nervous system specialized to "register" painful emotion, but the better theory is that this system has been developed to enable an animal to meet an emergency. All the physical and chemical reactions to an emergency make the animal more able to cope with the situation—by fight or by flight. The emotions accompany these reactions. None the less, emotional folk must use the sympathetic system more than placid people. There is another outflow to the viscera, which antagonizes the sympathetic. This is the parasympathetic (or false sympathetic) which arises from the nervous system in two places— the stem of the brain, and low in the spinal cord. As its main constituent is the vagus nerve, that vagabond nerve which wanders to and fro over the viscera seeking what it may control, the term "vagotonic" has been applied to those people in whom the parasympathetic gets the upper hand. Parts, if not the whole, of the parasympathetic system are active during pleasurable emotions, in particular during the prelude to and the consummation of res venerea.

Years ago it was proposed to divide people into two types, the vagotonic and the sympathicotonic, and although this classification has not been widely accepted, or rather was accepted and then dropped, the writer is convinced that there is much in it. Of course it must not be supposed that the two types are Mendelian allelomorphs or that there are not gradations between the two types. People, however, appear to belong to one group or to the other, but just as some people in this country are more democratic or social- istic than others, so are some more vagotonic than others. Vagotonicity and sympathicotonicity must ultimately depend upon the development of the hypothalamus, and the emotional tone of a person depends (i) on the development of the thalamus and (ii) the amount of control the roof-brain has acquired over the thalamus reactions. It is difficult not to believe that such characteristics are inherited, and, indeed, have proved of great im- portance in evolution.

One last topic, on which we are on surer ground, may be considered before we leave the nervous system. Size of brain matters and the surface area of the cerebral hemispheres—the roof-brain—matters. The enormous animals of geological ages had brains about the size of a walnut. But dominance in evo- lution has depended on centralization of government of the body in the brain. Moreover, the capacity for intelligence depends on the convolutions of the roof-brain rather than on its brute weight. Man has not only an enormous roof-brain as compared with even the highest apes, but intelligence is related not to mere size of the brain but to the intricacy of its convolutions. And just as the shape, say, of such superficial characters as the curve of an eyebrow or lip depend on inheritance, we can hardly doubt that the size of the roof-brain and the number of its convolutions depend upon inheritance. And as intelligence largely determines personality, one main basis of personality must be determined largely by inheritance. We are what we are largely because we inherit a definite type of nervous system.

An inviting avenue opens up here: whether the intense hierarchical development of control in the nervous system is not an argument for dictatorship in the body politic. The temptation to stroll or even give more than a glance along this avenue must be resisted. First: it is not in the least germane to our discussion; second, such an "argument" is no argument at all, but an appeal to analogy; third, the master mind of research into the activities of the nervous system gives this as his verdict on its Totalitarian possibilities:

"We might imagine this principle (convergence of control) pursued to culmination in final supreme convergence on one ultimate pontifical nerve-cell, a cell [which is] the climax of the whole system of integration. Such would be a spatial climax to a system of centralization. It would secure integration by receiving all and dispensing all as unitary arbiter of a totalitarian state. But convergence toward the brain offers in fact nothing of that kind. The brain region which we may call "mental" is not a concentration into one cell but an enormous expansion into millions of cells. They are it is true richly interconnected. Where it is a question of "mind" the nervous system does not integrate itself by centralization upon one pontifical cell. Rather it elaborates a million-fold democracy whose unit is a cell."

THE GLANDS OF PERSONALITY

Continuing the discussion of integrative devices, we turn to the endocrine system or the so-called "glands of personality." The hormones secreted by the endocrine glands regulate and correlate bodily activities chemically as contrasted with the electrical quality of the nervous impulses discussed in the last section. Hormones are potent substances. Very small amounts of them introduced into the system can produce marked effects. For instance, if the hormone *thyroxin* varies as little as one- or two-thousand-millionths of our body weight, thus resulting in a hypothyroid or hyperthyroid condition, the personality is altered dramatically. It is important to remember how fine is the knife-edge on which the personality balances, and how little chemical distinction there seems to be between the normal and the abnormal. Much of a person's behavior and many of his traits which, collectively, constitute personality are dependent on the normal functioning of the endocrine glands.

*

   If the genes establish the rough outlines of the individual's destiny in the first place, the endocrine glands become the executors or administrators of that destiny. Chemical or surgical interference with their work may alter the growth of the individual as effectively as though his original genetic endowment had been tampered with.

   As pacemakers for the whole growth process these secreting cells operate by throwing their chemical products into the blood stream. Carried to the growing cells, these chemicals accelerate some processes and retard others, producing varying effects upon the already chemically differentiated tissues, accelerating changes in the reproductive organs, vocal cords, hair cells, breasts. And since they have acted as pacemakers for the building of these characteristic structures, may we not also regard them as pacemakers for behavior? It is apparent from physiological studies that the growth spurt of adolescence is accompanied by changes in the endocrine system. Shall we not, therefore, look upon the characteristic changes in adolescent *behavior* as paced by these glands? Is it not possible that these pacemakers will furnish the key to many of the mysteries hidden under the term "sexual instinct?" [See discussion of sexual instinct under Freud in Chapter 3.]

   The relationship between the endocrines and the nervous system is not a simple one. In one sense the glands are primary, for they were in existence as secreting cells before the nervous system supplied them with inhibitory and excitatory fibers. They are known to influence the course of growth of the nervous system itself. The mentally defective cretin and the mongolian idiot are illustrations of defective development of the nervous system of endocrine origin, and the dramatic depression of development of all intellectual functions in these cases illustrates the potency of endocrine control. Both have been attributed to thyroid gland deficiency in the fetal period. In the case of the cretin the effect can be partially counteracted by thyroid medication; but in the case of the mongolian idiot the changes have proved irreversible.

   Sooner or later, however, the endocrine structures fall at least partially under the dominance of the organism as a whole, and the nervous system instigates and depresses their activity. Many of the details of the innervation of these glands are unknown at present; but it is generally understood that each of them is subject to two types of excitation. Direct evidence of nervous control of glandular tissue is familiar to all of us in the instance of salivation. When our mouth waters at the sight of an appetizing dish it is through neural excitation that the gland is thrown into operation. Similar neural connections (identified with certainty in the case of the adrenal

* From *Human Behavior*, by Lawrence Cole. Copyright 1953 by Harcourt, Brace and World, Inc. Reprinted with the permission of the publisher.

glands, which will no longer put out adrenalin when denervated) are believed to act upon each of the glands of internal secretion, either through direct nerve supply to the gland cells or indirectly through the control of rate of blood flow through the gland tissues. When we remember that some of the impulses flooding the nervous system originate in the external matrix and that glands (like other effectors) are subject to conditioning, we can see that external stimulation can alter internal chemistry and growth. Another indirect control is through food supply and dietary habits. Extreme undernourishment prevents the normal growth and functioning of the reproductive glands.

The pot-bellied, slow-growing, dwarfed, and mentally sluggish cretin is a vivid example of what severe and chronic deprivation of thyroid secretions can do to the process of growth and development. An equally dramatic demonstration of the effect of its secretions upon the maturation process is the fact that a few drops of iodine (the principal chemical component in the glandular product) added to the water in which tadpoles are developing will convert them into tiny frogs as small as flies within a two-week period (a transformation that does not ordinarily occur in the bullfrog until the second or third season of growth has been completed). In this case the metamorphosis is in both structure and behavior: the animal is transformed from dependence upon an aquatic-swimming action system to an air-breathing, hopping creature. Growth has been accelerated, and the maturation of structures produces suddenly a whole new set of action patterns. Deprived of thyroids, on the other hand, pollywogs remain at the pollywog stage though as large as mature frogs.

This contrast between the fast and slow growth, the alert and sluggish behavior, indicates something of the nature and range of thyroid effects. Like an open damper which permits an entering draught to quicken vital fires, the thyroid secretion speeds chemical change in almost every tissue. The basal metabolic rate rises and falls with thyroid output; and when the rate of transformation of energy falls too low, as in the hypothyroid individual who lacks the normal amount of glandular secretion, the individual will become fatigued rapidly and will respond sluggishly. Characteristically he will develop defenses against a too-demanding environment. A part of the difference in energy output between youth and age, between a lively youngster and a tired school teacher, can be traced to levels of thyroid output and to differences in metabolic rates. With the onset of age the thyroid output decreases, energy consumption falls, and the fat-and-forty waistline grows.

Over-secretion of the gland (hyperthyroidism) in adult human subjects may become excessive to the point of endangering health. These patients are, as a group, excitable, nervous, tense, quick to react and inclined to overreact. Heart and alimentary tract show accelerated contractions, blood pressure is elevated, and a fine tremor may be noted in the extended fingers. In the throat area above the gland the throbbing pulse is easily palpable. The characteristic protruded eyes of the hyperthyroid are a caricature of fright, and excitement. The proximate cause of this protrusion lies in the tension of the smooth muscles of the eye socket, a tension that exists in the musculature in general and gives a trigger-like character of the stimuli acting upon the patient. His tension is easily converted into the full-blown emotional response.

There is a temptation to extend this clear contrast between the sluggish and stupid cretin and the alert and excitable hyperthyroid patient into the middle ranges, and to make differences in gland physiology account for the whole scale of emotionality and intelligence; but the available evidence indicates that so many additional factors contribute to these differences that the simple and clear relationship between endocrine status and these mental traits is obscured.

One interesting parallel between the experimental animal and man is found in the sensitivity to heat loss. Richter and Eckert observed that removal of the thyroid glands of rats set them to work covering their bodies with the nesting materials. Dr. Charles Mayo has observations on human subjects which show an interesting parallel: he found the hypothyroid patient to be typically slow in speech, slow in reactions, *sensitive to cold* (watching the radiators and the thermometer and wearing shawls and sweaters, and protesting at every draught from open window or door.) Another clinician reported a patient who drove about in a closed automobile in midsummer, dressed in heavy overcoat. Feeding as little as two grains of thyroid extract "thawed him out" and induced a feeling of warmth and well-being he had not known before.

Other mental changes, accompanying extreme deviations in thyroid secretion, have been described by clinicians. The hypothyroid individual is described as suspicious, depressed, lacking in initiative, irritable, melancholy, forgetful, unable to concentrate, with slow (and even sing-song) speech. However, the consensus of psychiatric opinion would stress the fact that such a complex of traits is not the simple and direct product of glandular failure but rather that the lowering of vital reserves serves to bring out latent traits which have hitherto lain dormant in the personality. A mild degree of suspiciousness in the make-up of the person becomes exaggerated as the individual grows less capable of coping with interpersonal stresses, and may emerge as a more completely formed delusion of persecution. And the new life style may develop as a freshly-formed compensatory adjustment as the individual learns to husband his limited resources. Instead of meeting his stresses directly and liquidating his suspicions by direct actions, he may sit apathetically while his suspicions increase in dimension. It is doubtful, however, if the glandular deficit alone can determine the direction of the compensation.

The hyperthyroid is described as irritable, distractible, easily upset, with wide swings in mood. The hyperthyroid's "drive" is credited with diverse results. Dr. Crile, a well-known goiter specialist operating in the so-called "goiter belt" (the Great Lakes area), writes: "Pity the man who marries a hyperthyroid, for his nights will be filled with anguish and his days with remorse." Stockard, on the other hand, thinks that these tall, lean, rapidly-growing, intelligent individuals are ideally fitted for a role of active, energetic, leadership. Stockard believes that they are apt to be adventurous explorers, inventors, hewers of new paths. These last characteristics suggest that even sober scientists have their rhapsodic moments. Such an evaluation of this glandular type seems on a par with the comments of the biologist who ventured into the field of sociology with an explanation for the rise of Hitler in terms of the sluggish submissiveness of the Bavarian peasant group, which is known to be prone to hypothyroidism in certain districts.

The truth seems to be that the glandular secretion affects metabolic rates, energy output, temperature regulation; and as these functions rise and fall there will occur gross changes in adaptation. The specific form of the adaptation at the high level will depend upon the totality of forces that have conspired to form the personality; and the hyperthyroid's performance may take the form of the poetry of Shelley, the voyages of Columbus, or the irascibility of the terrible Mr. Bang. The low-level output may find expression in uncomplicated dullness, apathy, or if combined with other factors it may facilitate an introverted withdrawal, a defensive and hostile (but covert) suspiciousness. The relations with the personality in general are not those of a simple part which determines a totality but of a part-function arising in a *total setting*. It acts as a multiplier, a catalyzer, affecting all reaction-systems and not just one pattern in particular. Conversely, there are undoubtedly reverse effects: the total life style may serve to exaggerate the glandular action —as when the hyperthyroidism occurs in the energetic but anxious personality make-up, and the stimulations from the sympathetic nervous system, which are an essential part of all emergency emotions, still further exaggerate the excess of glandular action. Here a vicious cycle can be set up, the gland exaggerating the anxiety and the emotional reactions activating the thyroid secretion.

Utilizing Horney's tridimensional scheme [see Chapter 3 for a discussion of Karen Horney] for analyzing abnormal interpersonal behavior, we could imagine the following triad of changes in the personalities of hypothyroid patients.

1. In the aggressive, self-assertive, vindictive make-up—where the main line of motion has been consistently *against* people—the thyroid loss would lead to compensatory hostile and suspicious behavior. The most available

lines of action involve dominating, vindictive, destructive acts.

2. In the dependent one, already moving toward others and seeking solution to his problems through enlistment of aid, protection, love, the thyroid failure would intensify these claims and increase these needs.

3. In the withdrawn individual who has already taken the path of resignation as a means of lessening the conflicts too intense to bear, even more of life would be surrendered as the role of serene and integrated spectator (the man without desires) takes over more and more of life.

A single physiological occurrence, such as thyroid failure, produces changes in a system that has already developed coping and compensating mechanisms. It seems, therefore, that we must consider the self-in-action that is affected by these occurrences before we can speak of personality changes that are characteristic effects of specific glandular changes.

Two endocrine glands (the pituitary and the gonads) are so closely linked in function, and so intimately involved in the process of maturing, that we shall discuss them together. The pituitary has been known as the growth-regulating gland since 1886. When certain striking cases of gigantism and dwarfism were tracked to their source it was found that the abnormal growth was caused by abnormal function of the anterior portion of a small spherical mass of cells, no larger than a good-sized pea (1.2 to 1.5 centimeters in diameter). Suspended in a bony pocket underneath the central portion of the brain, and joined by a slender stalk of tissue to the nervous centers in the hypothalamus, the pituitary supplies the chemical regulators for at least a half-dozen bodily functions. In addition to regulating growth, the gland secretion stimulates the thyroid, gonads (ovaries and testes), adrenals, mammary glands, affects metabolism and regulates urinary output.

At present we are more certain of the range of pituitary functions than we are of the precise nature and number of chemical substances that mediate these functions, though biochemical research is rapidly making headway in identifying the active principles. Some of the work of the gland is stimulated by neural impulses which travel over the stalk connecting it with the hypothalamus, and some of its action is regulated by chemical agents in the blood with which the gland is richly supplied. There is a two-way exchange between ovarian cells and the pituitary, via the blood-stream, by means of which the oestrus cycle is regulated. The secretions of the pituitary also regulate the activity of the mammary glands in the nursing mother, and in return the suckling produces tactual stimuli which activate the pituitary via neural connections. In experimental animals whose spinal cords have been severed, such suckling does not maintain the pituitary substances that regulate milk-secretion if the nipples lie *below the cut;* but if some of the glands *above the cut* are stimulated by the suckling, *all* of the mammary glands will continue to secrete.

Early and persistent over-secretion of the growth hormone produces gigantism. The glandular hyperfunction may be accompanied by an actual deficiency of the gonad-stimulating hormone, particularly in the later stages, and an under-activity of the reproductive system is noted. Some endocrinologists have suggested that the secondary atrophy of the sex glands, the functioning of which normally serves to arrest the growth spurt, is responsible for the continuation of growth beyond puberty in this case. If the oversecretion of the pituitary occurs after mature growth has been achieved, a distorted growth of the extremities and internal organs (especially the liver) results. This latter condition is known as *acromegaly*. Personality changes have been reported in these patients. While some of these (sluggishness, apathy, drowsiness) may be due to the direct failure of the glandular secretion, others are probably indirect in their development and depend upon the person's reaction to his changed and unattractive appearance (enlarged arms, hands, feet, coarsened features, thickened lips, and the like).

The burst of growth and the increase of size and secretory activity of the reproductive glands which we associate with adolescence are matters of pituitary action. Timed by the genes, in the first instance, the pituitary serves as the final executor in regulating the developmental schedule. Experimental acceleration of pubescence can be induced by injections of the anterior pituitary hormone. Removal of the gland causes a slowing of growth, dwarfism, and a marked decline in activity. Experimental animals tend to remain infantile in bodily form.

In experimental animals, injections of pituitary hormones produce changes in behavior that are as pronounced as the structural transformations. Accompanying the growth spurt, which results in altered bodily proportions and the maturing of sexual organs, new activities emerge: males and females act as sexually mature animals. For example, copulatory behavior does not ordinarily appear in the albino rat before the 40th day, but if glandular injections are begun on the 22nd day the male may show the complete adult pattern within a week. This acceleration of pubescence can be brought about directly by the injections of the sexual hormone, or indirectly by the injection of the anterior pituitary hormone.

(An attempt to induce maturation in an undeveloped adult human subject was reported by Hamilton in 1937. A 27-year-old medical student complained of headache and many mental symptoms. His bodily status was that of an individual castrated before puberty and he was sexually impotent. Physical and mental virility was induced by injections of the male hormone. During the course of treatment these injections were replaced by injections of an inert substance without the knowledge of the subject. The patient then reported an immediate return of his pre-injection status.)

From the beginning, when we learned that the hen of the domestic fowl could be converted into a comb-bearing, crowing, hen-treading, pseudo-male by operative procedures which removed the ovaries and replaced their secretions either by grafts of testicular tissue or by injections of the male hormone, investigators have sought evidence for other cases of sex reversal. Canaries, mice, rats, guinea pigs, monkeys, have been subjected to this type of test. Sex reversals cannot be produced in all forms. Where they are most complete there is evidence of a pre-existing bisexuality. For example, the male toad (*Bufo americanus*) normally possesses rudimentary ovaries. When the testes are removed these ovarian tissues grow, and other reproductive structures change in form and function. Although the creature is genetically a male, it now behaves as a female, fully assuming the reversed sexual role. In this case we might more properly call the young toad neutral since he can be so easily driven toward either one of two divergent developmental goals through this interference with hormonal secretions. Lowering the temperature has been found to produce a differential action on the developmental process, also, causing the eggs of frogs and toads to develop in the female direction, suppressing testicular growth. High temperatures produce a preponderance of males. A similar, though not complete equipotentiality for growth and behavior exists in the domestic fowl. In the latter case, treating normal hens with androgens induces crowing, strutting, fighting, but the reversal is incomplete.

Clinical literature of recent years has contained numerous reports of attempts to treat the (human) homosexual with glandular products. The procedure is founded upon the same line of reasoning that has guided many of the investigators in the animal field: namely, that since both (gonadotropic) hormones are known to be present in both sexes, and since normally the androgen is dominant in the male, may it not be that the male homosexual is basically a case of estrogen dominance and may it not be possible to reverse the dominance of estrogens by testosterone injections? Inviting though the theory is in its simplicity, the clinical evidence does not support it. In the first place assays of blood and urine have failed to substantiate the hypothesis of estrogen dominance in the homosexual and the indicated treatment has not brought about the hoped for results. The cases of bisexuals whose behavior alternates between the two patterns (and sometimes within a few hours) offer a difficult problem for those who would explain the choice of a sex object on the basis of the *dominance* of one of the hormones. And there are clinical cases in which the endocrines produce a progressive masculinization (in the female) in secondary sexual characteristics without any corresponding changes in mental outlook or desires. It appears, therefore, that the data on human subjects (as well as those on rat and insect) argue against an endocrine determination of the precise pattern of sexual behavior. If the neural pattern is too fixed in the insect, it is too plastic in man.

In the lower forms of animal life two differences are worth emphasis: (1) there is a greater degree of stereotypy of behavior, and (2) the process of maturation prepares the way for the appearance of complete patterns which, in the higher forms, require the shaping impact of experience. Even in as humble a form as the rat this experience can overlay and modify the innate equipment; but barring such distorting action in the course of training, growth brings the complete pattern to fruition. In the chimpanzee and man experience plays a more important role, and the development of mature behavior is a gradual one. The sensory-motor elements of which the mature responses are built appear early in pre-pubertal life; yet observers agree that the first attempts of mature animals to copulate indicate much clumsiness and lack of organization of behavior, especially in the male. When the part-reactions appear in the prepubescent play of anthropoids they seem to have little, if any, sexual significance; and when biological maturity is achieved and the occasion (with attendant physiological readiness) is suddenly at hand, these earlier assemblages of action-systems do not organize themselves suddenly around the new biological drive. In the higher anthropoids, at least, experience has to shape expectancies.

CONCLUSION

From this brief treatment, it is hoped that the reader will be able to form a base for the discussion that follows. An attempt has been made merely to emphasize one aspect of man's personality—and it would be wise to remember that, until proven otherwise, man is greater than the sum of his parts. We are "converted groceries" plus—worth far more than the $2 price tag on our chemical constituents.

Nature has endowed the human race with inborn drives but not with the complex patterns for satisfying them. That the physical basis for personality is insufficient is borne out by the fact that an infant will not develop in a normal way physically or emotionally unless reared in a relatively receptive and absolutely human environment. This continuing human environment is really a process—the process of socialization. It begins with the mother, or mother substitute, fondling the child and ends with the transmission of the culture. In the next chapter the important process of socialization is examined from several angles.

Notes

1. John B. Watson, *Behaviorism*, New York: W. W. Norton & Co., 1925, p. 82.
2. Theodosius Dobzhansky, "Genetics and the Destiny of Man," *Antioch Review*, Spring 1959, p. 57.
3. The human cell normally contains 46 chromosomes. The sperm and egg cells of each parent contribute 23 chromosomes each to the new individual by means of a

process of *reduction* division, a vital step in sex cell production which insures the proper complement of genetic material in new individuals.

4. Quoted in Abram Kardiner, "When the State Brings Up the Child," *Saturday Review*, August 26, 1961, p. 9. See Chapter 3 for a discussion of social instincts.

Selected Readings

*Bates, Marston. *Man in Nature.* Englewood Cliffs: Prentice-Hall, 1961.

Dobzhansky, Theodosius. *Evolution, Genetics, and Man.* New York: John Wiley and Sons, Inc., 1955.

Fuller, John L., R. E. Jackson, and W. R. Thompson. *Behavior Genetics.* New York: John Wiley and Sons, Inc., 1960.

*Sherrington, Sir Charles. *Man on His Nature.* New York: Anchor Books, 1955.

*Sussman, Maurice. *Animal Growth and Development.* Englewood Cliffs: Prentice-Hall, 1960.

* Paperback edition.

Chapter 3

Personality

Human life is fundamentally biological. The infant is born with certain reflexes, certain drives, such as hunger and thirst, which he must satisfy or die. The particular way in which the nervous system and the endocrine system function will influence his behavior. But not everything that an infant is or will become as he matures is biologically determined at conception. There is inherent in each person the potentiality of growth—not merely of physical size—but also of intellect, capacities, and emotional response.

Whether or not an individual learns to play a concert grand piano or to beat a hollow log with a stick, what he eats, how and when he eats, the kinds of clothing he wears, and the importance he gives to these activities, whether he exhibits anger when he is frustrated or passively accepts the situation, the particular morality he displays—all these are dependent on other individuals and groups with which he comes into contact, together with their values, beliefs, and attitudes. These we shall learn in succeeding chapters to call a person's society and culture.

It is the interrelationships between the individual and his society and its culture that mold the human personality. Although personality rests on a biological base, it is shaped and given direction by other individuals and groups in the transmission of their values, beliefs, and attitudes. To what extent do biological and social factors contribute to the development of the human personality? The explanation of these contributions has become a major task of the social sciences, particularly of psychology. The result has been the development of a number of theories of personality. Some theories emphasize social and cultural factors. Others attempt to blend the biological and social science viewpoints. The following sections of this chapter are devoted to representations of each of these theoretical views. The first to be discussed is the psycho-analytic theory of Sigmund Freud, followed by a social theory of personality as developed in the works of George H. Mead. Finally, a synthesis of the

37

biological and social theories is presented in the work of the neo-Freudian theorist Karen Horney.

SIGMUND FREUD AND THE PSYCHO-ANALYTIC VIEWPOINT

Sigmund Freud lived most of his life in Vienna. He taught at the University of Vienna Medical School but, finding his path to promotion and recognition blocked by strong anti-Semitism, turned to private practice as a neurologist. Freud first went to Paris for about a year. There he studied under Jean Charcot, who had gained some success with hypnosis as a therapeutic device. Not long after he returned to Vienna, inspired by a colleague of his, Joseph Breuer, Freud perfected the technique of free association, a method by which a patient talks out his problems with an analyst.[1] Once engaged in a substantial therapeutic practice, Freud began to evolve his theory of personality.

Freud's view of personality was based on his belief that man had certain innate biological drives or, more literally, charges of energy, which continually sought to be expressed. The first of these drives is the *eros*, or life drive. The eros is expressed by the *libido*, or pleasure principle. It finds outlet through self-love, love of others, and the uninhibited pursuit of pleasure. The eros is located in that area of the mind Freud called the unconscious. The second drive is the *thanatos*, or death wish. It is expressed by the impulse toward self-destruction and the destruction of others. It, too, is located in the unconscious.

The two drives of life and death receive their energies from the unconscious *id*. The id is animalistic, amoral, irrational energy. It seeks to reduce through pleasure the pain of the tensions caused by unconscious conflicts. But the energies of the id which are to be expressed through pleasures are repressed by a moral force—the *superego*. This may be thought of as the innate morality of society.

The clash between the id and superego gives rise, in turn, to the expression of the ever present, but so far latent, potentialities of the *ego*. The ego is the accommodating part of the mind. It attempts to solve the problems presented by the conflicts between the clashing forces. In doing so, it operates according to a principle of reality. This is, in fact, a psychological compromise. As Freud said, ". . . the ego learns that it must inevitably go without immediate gratification, learn to endure a degree of pain, and altogether renounce certain sources of pleasure." [2]

The immediate social reality to which we must all adjust is the family. Through the mother and father, the family provides the child with the ingredients of the superego. But the child, of course, through the id, may attempt to rebel against the authority, discipline, and morality which the parents represent. Yet to rebel against the parents as figures of authority is also to rebel against them as objects of love and affection. The result for the child is intrapersonal conflict. The ego must find ways to minimize the pain caused by such conflict.

In the following essay, Freud described the interrelationships between the structures of the personality—id, ego, and superego—and the three levels of consciousness—conscious, preconscious, and unconscious. It will be noted that Freud cautioned the reader not to be tempted into the fallacy of equating each of the levels of the mind with the structures of the personality.

*
What is meant by "conscious," we need not discuss; it is beyond all doubt. The oldest and best meaning of the word "unconscious" is the descriptive one; we call "unconscious" any mental process the existence of which we are obliged to assume—because, for instance, we infer it in some way from its effects—but of which we are not directly aware. We have the same relation to that mental process as we have to a mental process in another person, except that it belongs to ourselves. If we want to be more accurate, we should modify the statement by saying that we call a process "unconscious" when we have to assume that it was active *at a certain time*, although *at that time* we knew nothing about it. This restriction reminds us that most conscious processes are conscious only for a short period; quite soon they become *latent*, though they can easily become conscious again. We could also say that they had become unconscious, if we were certain that they were still something mental when they were in the latent condition. So far we should have learnt nothing, and not even have earned the right to introduce the notion of the unconscious into psychology. But now we come across a new fact which we can already observe in the case of errors. We find that, in order to explain a slip of the tongue, for instance, we are obliged to assume that an intention to say some particular thing had formed itself in the mind of the person who made the slip. We can infer it with certainty from the occurrence of the speech-disturbance, but it was not able to obtain expression; it was, that is to say, unconscious. If we subsequently bring the intention to the speaker's notice, he may recognize it as a familiar one, in which case it was only temporarily unconscious, or he may repudiate it as foreign to him, in which case it was permanently unconscious. Such an observation as this justifies us in also regarding what we have called "latent" as something "unconscious." The consideration of these dynamic relations puts us in a

* Reprinted from *New Introductory Lectures in Psychoanalysis*, by Sigmund Freud, pp. 99–112. Trans., W. J. H. Sprott. Copyright 1933 by Sigmund Freud and 1961 by W. J. H. Sprott. By permission of W. W. Norton and Co., Inc.

position to distinguish two kinds of unconscious: one which is transformed into conscious material easily and under conditions which frequently arise, and another in the case of which such a transformation is difficult, can only come about with a considerable expenditure of energy, or may never occur at all. In order to avoid any ambiguity as to whether we are referring to the one or the other unconscious, whether we are using the word in the descriptive or dynamic sense, we make use of a legitimate and simple expedient. We call the unconscious which is only latent, and so can easily become conscious, the "preconscious," and keep the name "unconscious" for the other. We have now three terms, "conscious," "preconscious," and "unconscious," to serve our purposes in describing mental phenomena. Once again, from a purely descriptive point of view, the "preconscious" is also unconscious, but we do not give it that name, except when we are speaking loosely, or when we have to defend in general the existence of unconscious processes in mental life.

You will, I hope, grant that so far things are not so bad and that the scheme is a convenient one. That is all very well; unfortunately our psychoanalytic work has compelled us to used the word "unconscious" in yet another, third, sense; and this may very well have given rise to confusion. Psychoanalysis has impressed us very strongly with the new idea that large and important regions of the mind are normally removed from the knowledge of the ego, so that the processes which occur in them must be recognized as unconscious in the true dynamic sense of the term. We have consequently also attributed to the word "unconscious" a topographical or systematic meaning; we have talked of *systems* of the preconscious and of the unconscious, and of a conflict between the ego and the unconscious system; so that the word "unconscious" has more and more been made to mean a mental province rather than a quality which mental things have. At this point, the discovery, inconvenient at first sight, that parts of the ego and super-ego, too, are unconscious in the dynamic sense, has a facilitating effect and enables us to remove a complication. We evidently have no right to call that region of the mind which is neither ego nor super-ego the Ucs. system, since the character of unconsciousness is not exclusive to it. Very well; we will no longer use the word "unconscious" in the sense of a system, and to what we have hitherto called by that name we will give a better one, which will not give rise to misunderstandings. Borrowing, at G. Groddeck's suggestion, a term used by Nietzsche, we will call it henceforward the "id." This impersonal pronounce seems particularly suited to express the essential character of this province of the mind—the character of being foreign to the ego. Super-ego, ego, and id, then, are the three realms, regions, or provinces into which we divide the mental apparatus of the individual; and it is their mutual relations with which we shall be concerned in what follows. . . .

You must not expect me to tell you much that is new about the id, except its name. It is the obscure inaccessible part of our personality; the little we know about it we have learnt from the study of dream-work and the formation of neurotic symptoms, and most of that is of a negative character, and can only be described as being all that the ego is not. We can come nearer to the id with images, and call it a chaos, a cauldron of seething excitement. We suppose that it is somewhere in direct contact with somatic processes, and takes over from them instinctual needs and gives them mental expression, but we cannot say in what substratum this contact is made. These instincts fill it with energy, but it has no organization and no unified will, only an impulsion to obtain satisfaction for the instinctual needs, in accordance with the pleasure-principle. The laws of logic—above all, the law of contradiction—do not hold for processes in the id. Contradictory impulses exist side by side without neutralizing each other or drawing apart; at most they combine in compromise formations under the overpowering economic pressure toward discharging their energy. There is nothing in the id which can be compared to negation, and we are astonished to find in it an exception to the philosophers' assertion that space and time are necessary forms of our mental acts. In the id there is nothing corresponding to the idea of time, no recognition of the passage of time, and (a thing which is very remarkable and awaits adequate attention in philosophic thought) no alteration of mental processes by the passage of time. Conative impulses which have never got beyond the id, and even impressions which have been pushed down into the id by repression, are virtually immortal and are preserved for whole decades as though they had only recently occurred. They can only be recognized as belonging to the past, deprived of their significance, and robbed of their charge of energy, after they have been made conscious by the work of analysis, and no small part of the therapeutic effect of analytic treatment rests upon this fact.

It is constantly being borne in upon me that we have made far too little use of our theory of the indubitable fact that the repressed remains unaltered by the passage of time. This seems to offer us the possibility of an approach to some really profound truths. But I myself have made no further progress here.

Naturally, the id knows no values, no good and evil, no morality. The economic, or, if you prefer, the quantitative factor, which is so closely bound up with the pleasure-principle, dominates all its processes. Instinctual cathexes seeking discharge—that, in our view, is all that the id contains. It seems, indeed, as if the energy of these instinctual impulses is in a different condition from that in which it is found in the other regions of the mind. It must be far more fluid and more capable of being discharged, for otherwise we should not have those displacements and condensations which are so characteristic of the id and which are so completely independent of the qualities of what is cathected. (In the ego we should call it an idea.) What would one not give to understand these things better? You observe, in any case, that we can attribute to the id other characteristics than that of being unconscious, and you are aware of the possibility that parts of the ego and super-ego are unconscious without possessing the same primitive and irrational quality. As regards a characterization of the ego, in so far as it is to be distinguished from the id and the super-ego, we shall get on better if we turn our attention to the relation between it and the most superficial portion of the mental apparatus; which we call the Pcpt-cs (perceptual-conscious) system. This system is directed on to the external world, it mediates perceptions of it, and in it is generated, while it is functioning, the phenomenon of consciousness. It is the sense-organ of the whole apparatus, receptive, moreover, not only of excitations from without but also of such as proceed from the interior of the mind. One can hardly go wrong in regarding the ego as that part of the id which has been modified by its proximity to the external world and the influence that the latter has had on it, and which serves the purpose of receiving stimuli and protecting the organism from them, like the cortical layer with which a particle of living substance surrounds itself. This relation to the external world is decisive for the ego. The ego has taken over the task of representing the external world for the id, and so of saving it; for the id, blindly striving to gratify its instincts in complete disregard of the superior strength of outside forces, could not otherwise escape annihilation. In the fulfillment of this function, the ego has to observe the external world and preserve a true picture of it in the memory traces left by its perceptions, and, by means of the reality-test, it has to eliminate any element in this picture of the external world which is a contribution from internal sources of excitation. On behalf of the id, the ego controls the path of access to motility, but it interpolates between desire and action the procrastinating factor of thought, during which it makes use of the residues of experience stored up in memory. In this way it dethrones the pleasure-principle, which exerts undisputed sway over the processes in the id, and substitutes for it the reality-principle, which promises greater security and greater success.

The relation to time, too, which is so hard to describe, is communicated to the ego by the perceptual system; indeed it can hardly be doubted that the mode in which this system works is the source of the idea of time. What, however, especially marks the ego out, in contradistinction to the id, is a tendency to synthesize its contents, to bring together and unify its mental processes which is entirely absent from the id. When we come to deal presently with the instincts in mental life, I hope we shall succeed in tracing this fundamental characteristic of the ego to its source. It is this alone that produces that high degree of organization which the ego needs for its highest achievements. The ego advances from the function of perceiving instincts to that of controlling them, but the latter is only achieved through the mental representative of the instinct becoming subordinated to a larger organisation, and finding its place in a coherent unity. In popular language, we may say that the ego stands for reason and circumspection, while the id stands for the untamed passions.

So far we have allowed ourselves to dwell on the enumeration of the merits and capabilities of the ego; it is time now to look at the other side of the picture. The ego is after all only a part of the id, a part purposively modified by its proximity to the dangers of reality. From a dynamic point of view it is weak; it borrows its energy from the id, and we are not entirely ignorant of the methods—one might almost call them "tricks"—by means of which it draws further amounts of energy from the id. Such a method, for example, is the process of identification, whether the object is retained or given up. The object-cathexes proceed from the instinctual demands of the id. The first business of the ego is to take note of them. But by identifying itself with the object, it recommends itself to the id in the place of the object and seeks to attract the libido of the id on to itself. We have already seen that, in the course of a person's life, the ego takes into itself a large number of such precipitates of former object-cathexes. On the whole the ego has to carry out the intentions of the id; it fulfils its duty if it succeeds in creating the conditions under which these intentions can best be fulfilled. One might compare the relation of the ego to the id with that between a rider and his horse. The horse provides the locomotive energy, and the rider has the prerogative of determining the goal and of guiding the movements of his powerful mount toward it. But all too often in the relations between the ego and the id we find a picture of the less ideal situation in which the rider is obliged to guide his horse in the direction in which it itself wants to go.

The ego has separated itself off from one part of the id by means of repression-resistances. But the barrier of repression does not extend into the id; so that the repressed material merges into the rest of the id.

The proverb tells us that one cannot serve two masters at once. The poor ego has a still harder time of it; it has to serve three harsh masters, and has to do its best to reconcile the claims and demands of all three. These demands are always divergent and often seem quite incompatible; no wonder that the ego so frequently gives way under its task. The three tyrants are the external world, the super-ego and the id. When one watches the efforts of the ego to satisfy them all, or rather, to obey them all simultaneously, one cannot regret having personified the ego, and established it as a separate being. It feels itself hemmed in on three sides and threatened by three kinds of danger, toward which it reacts by developing anxiety when it is too hard pressed. Having originated in the experiences of the perceptual system, it is designed to represent the demands of the external world, but it also wishes to be a loyal servant of the id, to remain upon good terms with the id, to recommend itself to the id as an object, and to draw the id's libido on to itself. In its attempt to mediate between the id and reality, it is often forced to clothe the Ucs. commands of the id with its own Pcs. rationalizations, to gloss over the conflicts between the id and reality, and with diplomatic dishonesty to display a pretended regard for reality, even when the id persists in being stubborn and uncompromising. On the other hand, its every movement is watched by the severe super-ego, which holds up certain norms of behavior, without regard to any difficulties coming from the id and the external world; and if these norms are not acted up to, it punishes the ego with the feelings of tension which manifest themselves as a sense of inferiority and guilt. In this way, goaded on by the id, hemmed in by the super-ego, and rebuffed by reality, the ego struggles to cope with its economic task of reducing the forces and influences which work in it and upon it to some kind of harmony; and we may well understand how it is that we so often cannot repress the cry: "Life is not easy." When the ego is forced to acknowledge its weakness, it breaks out into anxiety: reality anxiety in face of the external world, normal anxiety in face of the super-ego, and neurotic anxiety in face of the strength of the passions in the id.

I have represented the structural relations within the mental personality, as I have explained them to you, in a simple diagram [reproduced below].

You will observe how the super-ego goes down into the id; as the heir to the Oedipus complex it has, after all, intimate connections with the id. It lies further from the perceptual system than the ego. The id only deals with the external world through the medium of the ego, at least in this

Structural Relations within the Mental Personality

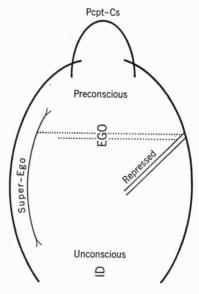

diagram. It is certainly still too early to say how far the drawing is correct; in one respect I know it is not. The space taken up by the unconscious id ought to be incomparably greater than that given to the ego or to the pre-conscious. You must, if you please, correct that in your imagination.

And now, in concluding this certainly rather exhausting and perhaps not very illuminating account, I must add a warning. When you think of this dividing up of the personality into ego, super-ego, and id, you must not imagine sharp dividing lines such as are artificially drawn in the field of political geography. We cannot do justice to the characteristics of the mind by means of linear contours, such as occur in a drawing or in a primitive painting, but we need rather the areas of color shading off into one another that are to be found in modern pictures. After we have made our separations, we must allow what we have separated to merge again. Do not judge too harshly of a first attempt at picturing a thing so elusive as the human mind. It is very probable that the extent of these differentiations varies very greatly from person to person; it is possible that their function itself may vary, and that they may at times undergo a process of involution. This seems to be particularly true of the most insecure and, from the phylogenetic point of view, the most recent of them, the differentiation between the ego and the super-ego. It is also incontestable that the same thing can come about as a result of mental disease. It can easily be imagined, too, that certain prac-tices of mystics may succeed in upsetting the normal relations between the different regions of the mind, so that, for example, the perceptual system becomes able to grasp relations in the deeper layers of the ego and in the id which would otherwise be inaccessible to it. Whether such a procedure can put one in possession of ultimate truths, from which all good will flow, may be safely doubted. All the same, we must admit that the therapeutic efforts of psychoanalysis have chosen much the same method of approach. For their object is to strengthen the ego, to make it more independent of the super-ego, to widen its field of vision, and so to extend its organisation that it can take over new portions of the id. Where id was, there shall ego be.

It is reclamation work, like the draining of the Zuyder Zee.

THE VIEWPOINT OF SOCIAL INTERACTION

The theory that personality stems not only from biological forces but also from an individual's social interactions with others has a different emphasis from the works of Freud. Not only does the emphasis differ, but so does the history of this theory of social interaction. It did not originate as a therapeutic device, but emerged as a description of the origin and function of the human personality in its social setting. In-stead of having been developed by one man, it has received contributions from many. And, instead of being a psychological theory of personality, stressing the individual, it is a sociological theory, stressing group factors.

One of those who contributed significantly to this theory in its early stages was Charles Horton Cooley, a professor of sociology at the University of Michigan. Cooley believed that the personality of the Self developed through social experience. As the individual interacts with others, he obtains from their responses an image of himself. Cooley called this process the "looking-glass Self." His analysis indicated that it was a process composed of three elements: (1) the imagined *image* of ourselves in others; (2) an imagined *judgment* of what that appearance is; and (3) a Self-feeling or response.[3]

We are correct in concluding that Cooley considered those intimate social relationships within families and between friends to be among the most important social experiences an individual could have.[4] These intimate forms of association transmit to the individual the values, beliefs, and attitudes that become the core of his personality structure.

Cooley's analysis was indeed penetrating, but the University of Chicago philosopher and psychologist George Herbert Mead elaborated and gave depth to the social interaction viewpoint. Mead's analysis demonstrated the importance of symbols—both physical gestures and language —as the mechanisms of interaction. For interaction to occur there must be an awareness of the presence of others followed by communication with them. Such communication necessarily is dependent on the symbols used; therefore, there must be an awareness of the meaning of the symbols on the part of the persons who are interacting with each other. Unless such awareness is present, there will not be a foundation for understanding, and communication will not have taken place. Those symbols conveying the same meaning to the persons making them as to the persons responding to them were called by Mead "significant symbols."[5]

An important addition must be made to this point. Mead not only emphasized the symbolic nature of interaction but also its creative qualities. In addition to man, many animals communicate. Their symbolic modes, or more properly, their modes of signals, are fixed by the nature of the beast. Dogs, for example, have been barking at each other in the same way for centuries. And they bark the same whether they live in the United States, Japan, or Nigeria. Man, in contrast, has the capacity to differentiate and enlarge his symbolic system. He can and has forgotten parts of it; he can stifle it; he can elaborate a gesture; he can, in short, make of his symbols what he will. There is, then, between man and other animals both quantitative distinctions based on size and complexity, and qualitative distinctions based on the symbolic nature of the existence which man has made for himself.[6]

The values, beliefs, and attitudes of others that are communicated by significant symbols are finally absorbed by the individual into the Self. Mead went on in his analysis to distinguish among levels of the Self. These arise out of the varying levels of social interaction that we experience: we may be aware of others as individuals or we may be aware of them as an organized group. However, lest we think of ourselves as mere sponges absorbing without choice or reflection the attitudes of others, Mead also indicated a level of Self which reflected the unique nature of the organism.

In the following selection, the social psychologist Kimball Young summarizes the complex statement of Mead concerning the levels of the Self—what Mead called the *I* and *me*. Young not only stated Mead's theory; he also suggested some relationships between the Self as Mead viewed it and the psychoanalytic view of Freud. These relationships will be elaborated further in the third, or neo-Freudian, theory to follow, and in the discussion at the end of this chapter.

*
. . . The self is born when we become an object to ourselves, that is, when we take the attitudes of others toward our own actions and respond, or tend to respond, to ourselves as others have reacted to us. We have already noted how the acts of an individual are qualified by what others expect of him. But, after all, the description so far has dealt largely with the static and structural aspects of the self. Hence the question naturally arises, is the individual in action purely the product of roles laid down by those around him? Is the self merely a collection and finally an integration of various specific or general "me's"—to use Mead's word again—that have emerged as overt roles? Despite all that others can do to us or for us, there remains the sense of individuality, of our own movement in relation to outer objects or persons, and of our activity in regard to these internalized "me's." In recognition of this dynamic qualty in activity, G. H. Mead, following William James, introduced the concept of the "I," which is set off against the "me" or "other"—either diverse or general in character. In fact, for Mead, the self in action must be considered as made up of both the "I" and the "me."

The "me" really consists of the roles and attitudes taken up by the individual from parents, siblings, and playmates, later from teachers, preach-

* Reprinted from *Personality and Problems of Adjustment* by Kimball Young. Copyright 1940, F. S. Crofts and Company, Inc. (including passages from George H. Mead) by permission of Appleton-Century-Crofts.

ers, and policemen, and even from imaginary characters, which are worked over into one's own action and thought. But, when the child does come to act, there is more to the matter than a mere duplication of the role which he has picked up from another. There is a dynamic item or feature in the whole interactive process. This is the "I," the self as actor. At the outset this is made up of the needs or impulses which carry the organism into a given cycle of behavior. But in the process of interaction with others the active "I" begins to be affected by the various "me's" which the individual takes over from others.

According to G. H. Mead, the simplest manner in which to describe the operation of the "I" is to recognize that we know it only in memory. It is always active in the present, but we are never quick enough to catch it except in retrospect. Yet, when we look back upon the "I" in memory, it has already taken on certain aspects of a "me" which has acted in relation to some social object. In other words, the "I" always appears as a historical item in behavior. It is the response of the individual to the attitudes of others, while the "me" is the more or less integrated set of attitudes and ideas of others which one has assumed as one basis for the overt action itself.

In gestural or linguistic (subovert) interaction there is no sharp distinction between the "I" and the "me," although logically the latter serves as a phase of the object toward which the "I" responds at the moment. That is, in responding to another we react to him as an external object and also to an internal image of him, or to him as a "me." But, as Mead points out, one cannot entirely predict what this response of the "I" to the "me" will be. *There is a degree of uncertainty in every overt act except purely reflex ones.* So, too, in reflective thought, which usually takes the form of internal conversation, the same mechanism operates. Thus in overt or covert activity the attitudes of other persons which one assumes as factors influencing his own behavior will constitute the immediate "me." But exactly what an individual is going to do about the situation—defined in terms of this "me"—he does not know completely in advance. True, he can take this situation into his own experience because he can and does assume the ideas and attitudes of other persons involved in it. But the "I" comes into play in his response. As G. H. Mead puts it, the "I" is "the answer which the individual makes to the attitude which others take toward him when he assumes an attitude toward them." Yet, after he has reacted, the "I" appears in the field of experience, as we said above, chiefly as a memory image.

Thus, although the attitude or incipient action which a person may take toward others may be partially known in terms of his previous responses, the actual overt response which follows is not entirely predictable. It contains a novel feature. It is something which even the individual cannot anticipate completely. He may be aware of himself and of the situation, but precisely how he will react he never knows, as Mead puts it, "until after the action takes place." *Thus the "I" is the unpredictable, the unique, the novel element in our thought processes and in overt action.* It represents, in short, the unanticipated, unpredictable feature of all activity more or less. This statement represents the logic of the matter. Actually, of course, there exist in most individuals levels of predictability. In highly automatic reactions the "I" factor does take on stability; in those involving any degree of choice, however, there is always this uncertain element. But in any case the "I" is constantly related to the "me" or "other." G. H. Mead thus summarizes the matter:

> The "me" does call for a certain sort of an "I" in so far as we meet the obligations that are given in conduct itself, but the "I" is always that distinction, if you like, between the "I" and the "me." The "I" both calls out the "me" and responds to it. Taken together they constitute a personality as it appears in social experience. The self is essentially a social process going on with these two distinguishable phases. If it did not have these two phases there could not be conscious responsibility, and there would be nothing novel in experience.

Though Mead's concept of the "I" provides recognition of the dynamic nature of all behavior and thought, we must not imagine from his discussion that the "I" is the same unchangeable element in every varied act. It is certainly not an unqualified factor in that sense. It is capable of modification by the various "me's," which in turn depend upon the social-cultural training and the configuration of the time and place. We would often act otherwise than we do were it not for the external restraints—the expectancies—which are laid upon us by others. And, when we act, there is an "I" or actor phase, quite as well as a "me" phase, in the totality of response. We have only to observe ourselves or listen to confidential remarks of our friends to understand this. A person remarks, "I wanted to give him a piece of my mind, but I thought better of it and said something else." This merely means that one combination of "I" and "me" was inhibited in its overt expression by another combination more in line with social approval. A further illustration from the drama comes to mind. The traditional "asides" indicate the operation of dual patterns of verbal expression—one communicated, one held to the level of subvocal thinking is made audible, so that the audience is "let in on" the thoughts and attitudes which the characters in the play are normally suppressing in their accepted conversations.

Thus, though the "I" and the "me" are structurally segregated, they fuse together in any given action—which action, however, is qualified by the situation. It often happens that there is a form of dissociation lying behind the communication itself. We say one thing but want to say another.

In everyday living this segmentalization—or even dissociation—of role-taking and acting is common. The act is qualified at many points by what we should like to do but can or dare not do. Men live so much in terms of half measures and compromises. Yet there are other situations in which we may get a more effective fusion of the "I" and the "me," that is, in which competing or conflicting combinations do not arise to inhibit or qualify our actions. This is illustrated neatly in the intensity of the teamwork in some joint and highly interesting cooperative activity. It is illustrated also in the exaltation of fighting or of sexual congress. It is seen in all-engrossing mystical, patriotic, aesthetic, and religious activities. Such fusion often occurs, of course, in creative work. We say, "A man loses himself in his work," meaning that there is a more or less complete combining of the "I" and the "me"—of the actor and the introjected social role to which he takes an attitude merging into a totality. As G. H. Mead remarks, "The self under these circumstances is the action of the 'I' in harmony with the taking of the role of others in the 'me.' " This convergence of the action and the introjected social object produces that unity of response which is the aim of integration. We shall see over and over again that mental conflicts or strain result largely from the conflict between the "me's"—with their associated "I's"—which societal demands lay upon us. The lack of sense of unity and solidarity which characterizes the secondary-group organization of modern society is but a sociological conception of this same phenomenon in the life of the individual.

The unique character of the "I" is a most important feature of the personality organization. Its roots appear to lie (1) in the organic or constitutional foundations of activity itself, the wants or impulses in connection with which feelings, emotions, fatigue, energy organization, and glandular and other bodily functions play a part; (2) in the so-called unconscious associations which have been so well exposed by psychoanalysis; and (3) in the conscious but uncontrolled mental associations depending upon exposure to a wide variety of social experiences. It represents the creative, flexible aspect of the personality. It serves as the basis of that autonomous, individualized form and activity which distinguish one person from another.

The concept of emergence applied to personality relates exactly to this novel aspect of thought and action. When this uniqueness concerns important additions to the culture, we call the individual a leader or a genius; but we all possess some of this novelty in behavior, or in thought, although in varying degrees and in different situations.

This factor of uniqueness in personality is difficult to describe and analyze objectively. Science, of course, emphasizes standardized categories, comparison of likenesses and differences among classified items or events, and hypotheses which lead to generalization and ultimately to prediction and control. Hence, when we admit uniqueness and hence unpredictability in personality, we must also raise the question whether these data may be dealt with objectively. But, this difficult problem aside, we must reckon with the fact that, on the basis of constitutional variations, of personal-social conditioning, and of cultural training, each individual does organize and reorganize his life in unique ways. Our responses themselves give witness to this fact. Despite rigid definitions of situations—aside from the most objective aspects of scientific procedure itself, where the responses are limited and specialized—the particular reaction of one individual will vary slightly from that of another. Even in matters of severe and closely controlled definitions of role, as in an army, though the overt conduct of the participants may be highly similar, it is never completely identical. And in other situations society and culture permit wide divergences in definition and in attitude and overt behavior.

In the social setting of group life it appears evident that the "me's" or roles of an individual represent the organization of interactional patterns and culture which call for more or less stable and predictable reactions on our part. But the "I," the internal or overt action of the individual in relation to these patterns, is never entirely calculable. In the make-up of the "me" both cultural and personal-social factors are introjected into the individual. The "me" therefore, as it enters into conduct, may be definite and controllable. The most certain features are those which arise in connection with objectives, scientific data. But also relatively stable are those aspects of the "me" which come to us from the laws, mores, and regulations of society. Less certain are those from the field of nonmoral conventions and fashion. Least definite would be those which come from the more or less unique and unpredictable behavior of others—which behavior is itself, from the standpoint of those others, characterized by the very uncertainty, the very uniqueness, of their "I" as it acts toward us. It is in these latter situations, in fact, that personal-social conditioning exercises its greatest influence.

It is the "I," then, as it is rooted in physiological drives and in early experiences, and as it has been influenced along the line of its development by "me's," that constitutes an important component of the growing and changing self. The purely "conventional" person is one whose adaptation within himself of the role of others has more or less tended to submerge the organic and early factors which might otherwise go into making a dominant and unique "I." Freud's concept of the "superego" helps us to understand this matter. The superego is constructed from the moral "me's" or roles which culture has foisted upon the growing individual. When the superego, the "me's" of moral behavior picked up from family and community, come to dominate us completely, we tend to fit neatly into the social order and to obey its mandates quite consistently. When the superego does not completely dominate the "id" impulses (still using Freud's term for basic impulses or needs) or modify the "ego" (perception and reason in Freud's sense), the individual makes adjustments to the societal demands more in keeping with his own wishes. The matter has bearing on certain types of leadership. The so-called strong-willed man who develops a new social theory or carries out a social reform, or the scientist who flies in the face of conventional "facts" and "findings" of his field, may be thought of as that person whose "I" is not completely dominated by the "me's" which society and culture have thrust upon him.

There are vast individual differences, of course, in the relative effectiveness or power of the "I" as against the various "me's" which one has acquired in interaction. Thus the genius stands out from the mass of people in his community by virtue of his important "I." On the other hand, the conventional person, in contrast with the deviate (whether the latter is socially accepted or not), is one in whom the *me-ness* far outweighs in importance the *I-ness*. But the very attention which even the conventionalized person gives the unique and "different" individual—whether to condemn or to praise him—affords considerable evidence of this novel trend in all of us; otherwise the necessary identification with the leader, with the unique person, would not be possible.

Thus, as important as the role of the "other" or "me" is in building the self, it is only one aspect of the process. The unique "I" is always at hand in our waking states to modify, add to, or subtract from these social influences which play upon us. This *I-ness* depends upon constitutional foundations, upon impulses, wants, and bodily perceptions, and upon the wide range of social-cultural conditioning to which we have been exposed, much of which comes to light through unconscious associations that apparently affect the actor, the "I" itself.

With this description of the rise of the self from the interacting of individuals and with some of the important structural and functional aspects of the self exposed, we shall now turn to discuss the broader problem of the relation of the self to social status and the sense of security.

A NEO-FREUDIAN VIEW OF PERSONALITY

The last theory of personality we shall review is a neo-Freudian viewpoint developed by Karen Horney. The phrase neo-Freudian refers to those theorists who have based many of their premises on the work of Freud, but who have emphasized different aspects of the processes of growth and maturation of personality. There is no neo-Freudian theory. Instead, each theorist has worked along the lines of his own interests.[7]

Karen Horney was a neo-Freudian theorist greatly influenced by the theory of social interaction. Her contribution indicated how social interaction developed the potentialities of man's biological nature. She did not accept the purely instinctive character of Freud's id concept but believed the biological nature of man comprised all the potentialities for growth within each of us: the particular collection of feelings, thoughts, capacities, and gifts that each of us possesses. Horney called this the Real Self.[8]

The growth of the Real Self's potentialities was a process of discovery which only the individual himself could accomplish. Although intrapersonal factors give rise to strains which may thwart the development of the Real Self, the social interaction experienced by an individual also may present Self-realization. Such extreme responses from others as overprotection or indifference, or dominance or passivity can be diverting. These result from neurotic needs and unfulfilled desires unconsciously possessed by the other persons. The neurotic responses of others do not fulfill the potentialities of the Real Self, but develop a neurotic image of what the individual believes he *should* be.[9] Horney called this the Idealized Self. She also indicated that there was a third level of Self, called the Actual Self, comprising everything that a person was at a given moment.

Because of the tyranny of the "should's" or the Idealized Self, the potentialities of the Real Self cannot unfold. They are repressed. The consequence of this is that basic anxiety emerges in the individual. As Horney said:

> It is his feeling of being isolated and helpless in a world conceived as potentially hostile. The cramping pressure of his basic anxiety prevents the child from relating himself to others with the spontaneity of his real feelings, and forces him to find ways to cope with them. He must (unconsciously) deal with them in ways which do not arouse, or increase, but rather allay his basic anxiety.[10]

This lack of harmony with oneself inevitably leads to alienation or Self-estrangement. This means that the individual is interacting with others in something less than a satisfying manner because of the domination of his personality by the Idealized Self. He cannot express himself in terms of his own capacities, but only in terms of what he believes are the demands of others. We shall see in a subsequent chapter that such alienation is a major problem of our time.[11]

The following selection describes the processes by which such alienation takes place:

*

. . . The loss of self, says Kierkegaard, is "sickness unto death"; it is despair —despair at not being conscious of having a self, or despair at not willing

* Reprinted from *Neurosis and Human Growth*, pp. 158–161, by Karen Horney, M.D. Copyright 1950 by W. W. Norton and Co., Inc. By permission of W. W. Norton and Co., Inc.

to be ourselves. But it is a despair (still following Kierkegaard) which does
not clamor or scream. People go on living as if they were still in immediate
contact with this alive center. Any other loss—that of a job, say, or a leg—
arouses far more concern. This statement of Kierkegaard's coincides with
clinical observations. Apart from the pronounced pathologic conditions mentioned above, its loss does not strike the eye directly or forcefully. Patients
coming for consultation complain of headaches, sexual disturbances, inhibi-
tions in work, or other symptoms; as a rule, they do not complain about having lost touch with the core of their psychic existence.

Let us now, without going into detail, obtain a comprehensive picture
of the forces responsible for the alienation from self. It is in part the consequence of the whole neurotic development, especially of *all that is compulsive in neurosis*. Of all that implies "I am driven instead of being the
driver." It does not matter in this context what the particular compulsive
factors are—whether they operate in relation to others (compliance, vin-
dictiveness, detachment, etc.) or in the relation to self, as in self-idealization.
The very compulsive character of these drives inevitably deprives the person
of his full autonomy and spontaneity. As soon as, for instance, his need to
be liked by everybody becomes compulsive, the genuineness of his feelings
diminishes; so does his power to discriminate. As soon as he is driven to do
a piece of work for the sake of glory, his spontaneous interest in the work
itself decreases. Conflicting compulsive drives, in addition, impair his integration, his faculty to decide and give direction. Last but not least, the
neurotic pseudo-solutions, though representing attempts at integration, also
deprive him of autonomy because they become a compulsive way of living.

Secondly, the alienation is furthered through processes, likewise compulsive, which can be described as *active moves away from* the real self. The
whole drive for glory is such a move, particularly through the neurotic's
determination to mold himself into something he is not. He feels what he
should feel, wishes what he *should* wish, likes what he *should* like. In other
words, the tyranny of the should drives him frantically to be something
different from what he is or could be. And in his imagination he *is* different
—so different, indeed, that his real self fades and pales still more. Neurotic
claims, in terms of self, mean the abandoning of the reservoir of spontaneous
energies. Instead of making his own efforts, for instance, with regard to human relations, the neurotic insists that others should adjust to him. Instead
of putting himself into his work, he feels entitled to having it done for him.
Instead of making his own decisions, he insists that others should be responsible for him. Therefore his constructive energies lie fallow, and he
actually *is* less and less a determining factor in his own life.

Neurotic pride removes him a step further from himself. Since he now
becomes ashamed of what he actually is—of his feelings, resources, activities
—he actively withdraws his interest from himself. The whole process of ex-

ternalization is another active moving away from his self, actual and real. It is astonishing, by the way, how closely this process coincides with Kierkegaard's "despair of not wanting to be oneself."

Finally, there are *active moves against* the real self, as expressed in self-hates. With the real self in exile, so to speak, one becomes a condemned convict, despised and threatened with destruction. The idea of being oneself even becomes loathsome and terrifying. The terror sometimes appears undisguised, as one patient felt it when thinking: "This is me." This appeared at a time when the neat distinction she made between "me" and "my neurosis" started to crumble. As a protection against this terror the neurotic "makes himself disappear." He has an unconscious interest in not having a clear perception of himself—in making himself, as it were, deaf, dumb, and blind. Not only does he blur the truth about himself but he has a vested interest in doing so—a process which blunts his sensitiveness to what is true and what is false not only inside but also outside himself. He has an interest in maintaining his haziness, although he may consciously suffer under it. One patient, for instance, in his associations often used the monsters of the Beowulf legend, who emerged at night from the lake, to symbolize his self-hate. And once he said: "If there is a fog, the monsters can't see me."

The result of all these moves is an alienation from self. When we use this term we must be aware that it focuses on only one aspect of the phenomenon. What it expresses accurately is the subjective feeling of the neurotic of being removed from himself. He may realize in analysis that all the intelligent things he has said about himself were in reality disconnected from him and his life, that they concerned some fellow with whom he had little if anything to do and the findings about whom were interesting but did not apply to his own life.

In fact, this analytic experience leads us straight into the core of the problem. For we must keep in mind that the patient does not talk about weather or television: he talks about his most intimate personal experiences. Yet they have lost their personal meaning. And, just as he may talk about himself without "being in it," so he may work, be with friends, take a walk, or sleep with a woman without being in it. His *relation to himself has become impersonal*; so has his relation to his whole life. If the word "depersonalization" did not already have a specific psychiatric meaning, it would be a good term for what alienation from self essentially is: it is a depersonalizing, and therefore, a devitalizing, process.

I have already said that the alienation from self does not show as directly and blatantly as its significance would suggest, except (speaking of neuroses only) in the state of depersonalization, feelings of unreality, or amnesia. While these conditions are temporary, they can occur only in people who are estranged from themselves anyhow. The factors precipitating the feelings of unreality are usually severe injuries to pride together with an acute increase of self-contempt, exceeding what is tolerable for the particular person. Conversely, when—with or without therapy—these acute conditions subside, his alienation from self is not thereby essentially changed. It is merely restrained within such limits that he can function without conspicuous disorientation. Otherwise the trained observer would be able to perceive certain general symptoms pointing to an existing alienation from self, such as deadness of the eyes, an aura of impersonality, an automatonlike behavior. Writers such as Camus, Marquand, and Sartre have described such symptoms excellently. For the analyst it is a source of never-ending astonishment how comparatively well a person can function with the core of himself not participating.

DISCUSSION

However opposed the theories presented here may appear to be, especially those of Freud and Mead, there is no doubt that they penetrate directly to the center of the theoretical problems they undertake to solve. Freud's conception of the workings of the unconscious impulses added a new dimension to the understanding of human motivation. Mead gave us great insight into the function of communication in the origin and development of the Self. The works of Horney blended the sociological concerns of those interested in general aspects of social structure with the therapeutic concerns of psychiatry.

But there is a pitfall that awaits the unwary student who mistakes the introduction of these theories for the final word on personality, and who does not attempt to go further in his understanding of them. Each theory is built upon a triad of relationships: id, ego, and superego; I, Me, and Generalized Other; Real Self, Idealized Self, and Actual Self. How convenient it would be if one system could be translated into the other. Does not the Real Self have similarities to the id? Cannot the superego and the Generalized Other be said to be synonymous? No, they cannot be translated in this way. The reason is that each of the theories is derived from different premises.

Review, for example, the nature of the superego and the Me. The superego has been defined as an anticathexis to the impulses of the id; it is the internal morality of society. The Me is the internalized attitudes of other individuals. Although they sound similar, they are not similar. The superego develops out of necessity to control the instincts in order to continue to gain love and affection from others; its initial social aspect is actually a manifestation of the sexual instincts of the eros. The Me, in contrast, is a totally social process; its setting is the social group, not the individual. It is an *inter*personal phenomenon, not an *intra*personal one. Although these differences are apparent, the Me nevertheless carries out functions Freud determined to be ego functions. Through adopting the attitude of others, the Me becomes for the individual a source of thought. The same differences occur with other points of the theories under examination. They appear superficially to have certain similarities, but exceptions to each soon render the similarities of little consequence.

It would appear, therefore, that the theories had little hope of being woven into a more systematic and cohesive general theory. Yet such was not the case. The neo-Freudian theorists, exemplified here by the work of Karen Horney, fused the social interaction and psychoanalytic viewpoints.[12] This neo-Freudian synthesis has been important in two respects. First, it has sought to settle some basic theoretical conflicts in psychology. Second, it has contributed to an advancement in the scientific study of personality. Both points will be elaborated in the following paragraphs.

Horney abandoned any notion that there was an opposition between the human organism and the social environment. The question she answered was not whether the organism was or was not more important than the environment in the formation of personality. She explicitly indicated what each had to contribute to that formation. This has great value for the science of personality. For when a decision has to be made about the relative importance of one set of data as against another, the temptation may be to defend the first decision reached regardless of what subsequent data may indicate. This results in the destruction of an objective attitude. What started as a scientific investigation ends as a personal feud and an academic popularity contest.

Horney stressed the notion that the innate potentialities of the Real Self were in a state of continuous growth within a social setting. This has two important implications. First, it relegates the Freudian sexual impulse to but one among other impulses. This enabled Horney to elaborate the growth factor which has been thought of as the *total* innate potentialities of the individual. Happily, such potentialities as intellect, achievement, and the direction of emotional responses have been subjected to close investigation by psychologists, culminating in the development of psychological testing. This means that potential can be identified and measured within the limits of the tests and can be verified under similar conditions. Second, and a corollary to the first implication, Horney's concepts can be used to stress the importance of understanding the nature of specific situations of social interaction. Freud, on the other hand, discussed social life only under the broadest categories—society, as a whole, or civilization; as a consequence, some of his work became quite speculative. Its value as a means for gathering sufficient data for the building of hypotheses became sorely minimized. Mead went in the opposite direction. His observations were of the intimate group life of families and of small town life. Only recently has his work been brought into the setting of the modern metropolis.[13]

The Real Self concept, to the contrary, applies to both the conditions of the intimate group and the more encompassing forms of human association. Any number and kind of specific situations can be studied. From these the psychological and social factors that lead either to the realization or thwarting of the innate potentialities of the individual can be developed to explain better the relationships between the individual and his society and its culture.

Closely related to the foregoing points was the realization by Horney that the functions of society and, more specifically, the process of social interaction could not be made to fit into Freud's biological scheme. If developed to their logical extremes, the concepts of Freud, the authors believe, would lead to the conclusion that the social and cultural world of man is a result of instinctive processes. Since man is biologically one, we should expect a consistency and uniformity in human actions and values. This is not the case. Actions differ from situation to situation as different values mold actions and circumstances. Human nature, as Cooley said, is group nature. The variations in the size, form, and function of human groups; the values, beliefs, and attitudes they transmit; and the changes they undergo contribute to the development of the organism from a biological animal to a human being and create the conditions for Self-realization. The process by which this takes place is the subject of the following two chapters on group life and culture.

Notes

1. Calvin Hall, A *Primer of Freudian Psychology*, New York: Mentor Books, 1954, p. 15.
2. Sigmund Freud, *A General Introduction to Psycho-Analysis*, Garden City: Garden City Publishing Company, 1943, p. 314.
3. *Human Nature and the Social Order*, in *The Two Major Works of Charles H. Cooley*, Glencoe, Ill.: The Fress Press, 1956, p. 152.
4. *Social Organization*, in *The Two Major Works of Charles H. Cooley*, Ch. 3. See also, Robert Gutman, "Cooley: A Perspective," *American Sociological Review*, Vol. 23, June 1958, pp. 251–256.
5. *Mind, Self and Society*, Chicago: University of Chicago Press, 1934, pp. 71–72, 268–269.

6. Cf., Ernst Cassirer, *An Essay on Man*, New Haven: Yale University Press, 1944, Chapters 2 and 3, *et passim*.
7. For other examples of neo-Freudian theories see: Alfred Adler, *Understanding Human Nature*, New York: Permabooks, 1946; Carl Jung, *The Integration of Personality*, New York: Farrar and Rinehart, 1939; Abram Kardiner, *The Individual and His Society*, New York: Columbia University Press, 1939; Erich Fromm, *Escape from Freedom*, New York: Rinehart, 1940.
8. Karen Horney, *Neurosis and Human Growth*, New York: W. W. Norton, 1950, pp. 17, 158, and 173.
9. Horney, *op. cit.*, Ch. 3.
10. Horney, *op. cit.*, p. 18.
11. For elaboration of the concept of alienation see: Erich Fromm, *The Sane Society*, New York: Rinehart, 1955; also, Melvin Seeman, "On the Meaning of Alienation," *American Sociological Review*, Vol. 24, December 1959, pp. 789 ff.
12. The following discussion is adapted from Louis Schneider, *The Freudian Psychology and Veblen's Social Theory*, New York: King's Crown Press, 1948, p. 52 ff. Only those points in Schneider's discussion that were applicable to the selections that have been used here were chosen for elaboration.
13. See the discussion of the presentation of the Self in Chapter 8.

Selected Readings

Dewey, John. *Human Nature and Conduct*. New York: Modern Library, 1922.

Erickson, Erick. *Childhood and Society*. New York: W. W. Norton, 1950.

*Freud, Sigmund. *A General Selection from the Works of Freud*. New York: Anchor Books, 1957.

*Freud, Sigmund. *The Origins of Psychoanalysis*. New York: Anchor Books, 1954.

*Hall, Calvin. *A Primer of Freudian Psychology*. New York: Mentor Books, 1954.

Horney, Karen. *New Ways in Psychoanalysis*. New York: W. W. Norton, 1939.

*Kohler, Wolfgang. *Gestalt Psychology*. New York: New American Library of World Literature, 1947.

Malinowski, Branislow. *Sex and Repression in Savage Society*. New York: Harcourt, Brace, 1927.

*Mead, George H. *The Social Psychology of George H. Mead*. Ed. Anselm Strauss. Chicago: University of Chicago Press, 1956.

Shibutani, Tamotsu. *Personality and Society*. Englewood Cliffs, N.J.: Prentice-Hall, 1960.

* Paperback edition.

Chapter 4

Human Groups

The last chapter reviewed three theories of personality. The neo-Freudian and social interaction theories necessitate a detailed understanding of our relations with others in social groups, relations which mold and give direction to human personality. Even Freud's biological approach to the development and expression of personality illustrated the impact of purely social relations upon the expression or, more characteristically, the repression of id impulses.

To understand our relationships with others we make three distinctions between those behaviors that have other persons as their point of reference and those that do not.[1] There are *nonsocial* reactions which are learned through direct and repeated contact with stimuli in the environment. These become habitual. The student, for example, leans his head on his hands as he reads; the outdoorsman squints in the bright sun; the teacher paces the floor as he lectures. These are distinctly individual behaviors. Then there are *social* reactions which are learned from the conscious or unconscious assimilation of the behaviors of others; these reactions, however, remain individual responses. Thus, the enjoyment of a beautiful picture or amusement over a humorous line in a book are individual reactions, although what is considered beautiful or humorous is something learned from others. Lastly, behavior consists of social interaction. In this kind of situation the behavior of someone else affects our own behavior, calling up a new set of responses on our part which in turn affect the behavior of the other person. It is the behavior of others that is the great variable in our lives.[2] Through significant symbols identical responses are elicited in the person making the symbol as well as in the other person responding to it.[3] The human personality does not develop in a vacuum; we are always aware of the presence of others.

Individuals act according to patterns of social interaction. Standards, or norms, of behavior influence their action as does the situation within which interaction occurs. On the other hand, social interaction sometimes develops under circumstances in which existing norms do not apply, or for which, because the situation is new in the experiences of the persons concerned, norms do not exist. The following sections of this chapter are devoted to explaining these considerations.

SOCIAL ROLES

It is through our relationships with others that we learn their attitudes and responses toward us which we then make our own. As we have seen, Charles H. Cooley understood the rudiments of this in what he called the "looking-glass Self." Mead, however, gave depth to Cooley's view by noting that when we make the attitudes and responses of others our own, when we adopt their habits, gestures, language and tones, we make possible the development of social roles.[4] Social roles are the behaviors employed by individuals to satisfy what others expect of them.

The first level of role-taking is seen in the adoption of *specific* roles. As a child grows he comes into contact with many different kinds of people. He sees them not only as separate personalities but as people who themselves are performing distinct and functional roles. The child is often captivated by these roles and seeks to play them himself—fireman, policeman, bus driver, mother, father, and so on. However, these roles are highly individualistic and specific in their references. They operate on the level of the Self that we have learned to call the "me." These specific roles may be acted out with others, as when children play house. They also may be acted out in privacy, with the child of necessity assuming a number of different, specific roles to complete the game. The child may also perform specific roles created in his own imagination, inventing and responding to them. A. A. Milne's poem *Binker* illustrates this:

> Binker—what I call him—is a secret of my own,
> And Binker is the reason why I never feel alone.
> Playing in the nursery, sitting on the stair,
> Whatever I am busy at, Binker will be there.
> Binker's always talking, 'cos I'm teaching him to speak:
> He sometimes likes to do it in a funny sort of squeak,
> And he sometimes likes to do it in a hoodling sort of roar . . .
> And I have to do it for him 'cos his throat is rather sore.[5]

Thus, through language and imagery the child develops multiple worlds within his own.[6]

Yet the personality of the individual is more than a series of specific roles. The roles become fused into a larger pattern on the level of the

Self, which Mead, as we saw in the last chapter, called the Generalized Other. At this level of Self a certain amount of continuity can be expected in the roles played, and differences in expectations vanish as similarities between situations emerge. The child soon learns literally to play the game of life. He discovers that he cannot always respond as he would wish, nor can he always change roles in the middle of the game. He discovers rules and, with them, the "normative expectations" of his society. This level of role-taking is called the *generalized* role. It is explained in the following statement by Kimball Young.

*
In time the introjections of the various individual roles around the child begin to get organized or integrated into larger patterns of response, perhaps because many of these imagined roles actually overlap. Thus a father at home has a certain function; as a business or professional man he has another and thus furnishes a different "copy" for the child to follow. Yet in his playing of the father's role, there is, for the child, a certain continuity and commonality between the two. G. H. Mead refers to this larger ordering of roles into a unity under the term "the generalized other." That is, out of a wide range of specific roles of "others" which he has played, there emerges in time a generalized and more or less integrated pattern of the total role of the child. This becomes a part of the integrated self which grows up in everyday interaction with hundreds of specific persons whose attitudes and habits get woven into the child's own. The development of the generalized pattern is well indicated by G. H. Mead when he draws a contrast between the early play life of the child and the activity of the older child or youth as a member of a team in a game with rules, differentiated roles, and standard practices.

By the time the child in our society is seven or eight years of age, he begins to play simple coordinated games of the type where the children choose up "sides" and make up a team. In such games each child performs the same task as his teammates, as in tossing quoits or shooting or throwing at a target, but the success of each are added together to make up the total score for one's team. Thus arises a rudimentary kind of teamwork. It is interesting to note in passing that this is about the age, too, when, according to Piaget, the child begins to shift from egocentric, self-centered remarks to more specialized speech.

But in the team game proper—which the child learns in the prepubertal and early adolescent years—each player, while he has a specialized function, discovers that his role is qualified by the special tasks of his teammates and that in order to play his own part he must be able to play the part of these

* Reprinted from *Personality and Problems of Adjustment* by Kimball Young. Copyright 1940, F. S. Crofts and Company, Inc. Reprinted by permission of Appleton-Century-Crofts.

others as well—overtly and especially in imagination. In other words, in an organized game where a number of individuals are involved, and where each has his own function to perform, the person in taking his own role must learn also to take the role of everyone else in the game as well. In the first games which the child plays the number of specialized roles is usually limited, but it increases as he learns to play basketball, baseball, football, hockey, and the like. But in any case, in order to carry out his part, he must know what every other member of his team is supposed to do or is going to do. He must also anticipate the actions of the opposing team's members. He does not, of course, have to carry all the possible patterns of action in mind at once, but he may have to have a dynamic picture of two, three, or four other individuals present in consciousness at the same time. Thus the first baseman's actions will be effective for making a particular play only if he can in imagination assume the ideas and attitudes of the pitcher, the catcher, and the man at bat. The successful ball player is just that one who is able to imagine the actions of others and thus in his own inner form of thought or imagination be able to anticipate what they will do. Mechanistically he does actually experience in his own neuromuscular system incipient responses like those of the other players, both those of his own team and those of the opposing side.

In complicated games many of a player's own functions as well as these anticipatory reactions to what the others will do are put into rules and standard practices. These serve to limit and to define closely the specific roles of each player in relation to all the others. It is interesting to observe that even in rudimentary games children themselves often make up rules on the spot to help define and thus objectify their varied behavior. As G. H. Mead remarks, "The rules are a set of responses which a particular attitude calls out." When a greenhorn at a game does not follow the rules—that is, the expected patterns of actions—he confuses his teammates as well as the opposing team. In short, the regulations and standard practices help the child to organize his various roles into something of a unity, in a generalized pattern.

The application of this illustration to other social activities is apparent. In order to participate with other members of the family the child has to obey the rules of the family game. He cannot forever decide on the spur of the moment to take a novel role; otherwise, he would acquire no regularity of habits and attitudes. In other words, he must, in the first years of life, learn his more general role as *child* in the family. Later he will be pupil, comrade, industrial worker, religious participant, voter, and the like. But more than that, he must carry over from family to the school, the church, the community, the factory, or business certain common elements in his primary roles, although, as he extends the range of his interactions outward from the family, each of these other groups will furnish him in addition some specific and general roles. . . .

G. H. Mead's concept of the generalized other is basic to an understanding of the integration of the self. It rests upon the ability of the individual to develop general attitudes and ideas out of a wide variety of specific and concrete experiences, which in turn raises the recurrent problems in psychology of general versus specific attitudes and of transfer of training. Apparently an individual may have a range from specific attitudes and habits to general attitudes and habits. So, too, the individual may play more or less specific roles in some instances and yet in others may develop the generalized or integrated self. The child is characterized by specific roles, the mature, integrated adult by a generalized self. More or less generalized roles may become linked to concepts of given primary or secondary groups, to those of a larger society or nation, or to humanity or mankind in general. Just how broad and all-inclusive the generalized other may become depends in part on one's capacity to identify himself with a participating role with reference to such human associations as may be considered units in themselves.

ROLE STRAIN

In the preceding section we have seen how the roles played by individuals in social intercourse enter our study. So far, the description of these social roles has been essentially theoretical, based on the assumption that most social relationships are normal.[7] However, as a practical matter, although most individuals want to do what is expected of them as members of society and play their roles according to the rules of the game,[8] society's expectations may be greater than the individual capacity. This results in *role strain*.[9]

Role strain may develop from four sources. Certain expectations, for example, may need to be met at specific times and places and it is unlikely that conformance to them will always be automatic and satisfying. This source of role strain suggests the theater adage, "the show must go on," regardless of the feelings of the performer. A second source results from the different kinds of roles we play in relationships with others, each having its own set of expectations which increase as we pass from childhood into the adult world. The differing expectations in this category of role strain stem from contradictory requirements of performance, from conflicts of time and place, or from disagreements over how much of the individual's resources should be expended. A third source of strain emerges from the varying activities related to any particular role. This is the source of strain found in large organizations in which a department head, for example, feels the necessity of befriending the employees as individuals but is faced with the managerial duty to maintain impersonal authority. The last form occurs when an individual, as a result of one role, enters into a number of relationships with other persons. This is called *role set*. It, too, is found in large organizations in which, through acceptance of a role in the bureaucracy, the individual enters relationships based on subservience, leadership, and forced congeniality.

The problem posed by role strain concerns the need of the individual to combine an entire system of roles.[10] The more extensive the society is, the more complicated the problem and the greater necessity to reduce role strain. One means by which this can be accomplished is the individual's decision to enter, or leave, a particular relationship.[11] He may seek to compartmentalize his roles, attempt to overlook inconsistencies, or control them by delegating the role to others. A wife may successfully delegate the housekeeping role to her daughter, but she cannot delegate her sex role. The individual may also seek to multiply the number of roles he plays. This multiplicity, called *extension*, allows the individual to curtail participation since any one role may become an excuse for ignoring the others. Extension, of course, is limited by real ceilings of time, energy, and talent; or through physical isolation the individual may seek to reduce role strain by placing bulwarks between himself and other persons in his environment. More often this is accomplished by placing intermediaries between himself and those whom he would seek to avoid. The ultimate means of reducing role strain is the most difficult—that is, eliminate the relationship entirely. But once a commitment to a relationship has been made the moral obligation to maintain it is not easy to avoid. If elimination is actually accomplished, it will generally be through ostracism of the persons making untenable demands, or by quitting the situation entirely. This, of course, destroys the possibility of receiving any rewards resulting from such relationships.

Another means of reducing role strain involves the individual's level of performance—which is a direct result of his resources—once he is committed to a relationship.[12] These resources include such things as time, energy, talent, money, and knowledge; and their employment in role-playing is determined by an interrelationship among three factors. The first is the desire of the individual to do what is expected of him. If he is thoroughly committed to the role, if he enjoys what he is doing, if he gains a sense of satisfaction from it, his level of performance will be close to the requirements of the situation. A second factor is the individual's judgment of the role's relative rewards and punishments. If there is a promise of high reward he is likely to go further toward meeting role requirements than if rewards are lacking. Punishment, although a negative factor, may have the same effect—the greater the threat of punishment for failure to perform as expected, the greater the possibility of conforming behavior. Finally, other persons in a social situation influence the interaction of any two individuals in a particular relationship; and these other persons form the third force influencing the performance of a role. They may seek either to modify the expected behavior of the two in the initial relationship if the expectations are too high, or to raise them if they judge the expectations to be too low. When the expected behavior of the initial two is so great that they cannot perform as required, the roles of the other persons are also affected. Higher expectations may be imposed on them, higher than they themselves are prepared to meet. When the expected behavior, on the other hand, is too low, the self-esteem of the other persons might very well be compromised.

From this discussion of role strain, we see that the expectations which govern the playing of a social role are neither inflexible nor absolute, but are influenced by the resources an individual brings to any social situation and by the techniques he employs to maximize those resources. For this reason no two social situations or social relationships are ever alike.

SOCIAL STATUS

A social role is to be understood as more than a measure of strain between expectation and resource. Every social role has its own prestige. Some roles are "significant," others "insignificant." Some are "high," "important," and "good"; others are "low," "unimportant," and "bad." The implied scale of values by which we rate a social role is called *social status*.

Social status is granted to an individual by others; it is also taken away by others—in contrast to social roles which are maintained whether we want them or not. A man would find it difficult, for example, to reject altogether the behavior expected of him as a man—but the *degree* to which he conforms to expectation is the criterion for his social status, ascribed by others. Thus, the greater his conformity to what is expected of him, the more likely he will be considered a "good" man, and social status then becomes one of the rewards and, potentially, if withdrawn, one of the punishments in social relationships.

Social status is a reward or punishment, as the case may be, contributing to an individual's definition of himself. The attitudes of others, adopted and made a part of the Self, are status attitudes. From the assessment of others we obtain a relative significance which we assign to these attitudes. Status attitudes on the whole are constant, although they may shift from time to time within a given role or from one situation to another. In the first instance, a husband is the breadwinner in his family; yet, due to prolonged illness, his status may become reduced when his wife takes on the role of major provider for the family. In the second instance, a teacher may be thought of by his students as "old Man Smith." In association with his colleagues he is viewed as "that young Smith fellow." Deep and prolonged uncertainty about status may give rise to anxiety and in extreme cases, according to Karen Horney, develop into alienation from the Self.[13] Uncertainty about status occurs if one feels that one is not adequate to anticipate the responses of others toward oneself—in short, an individual is placed in the highly uncomfortable position of not knowing "where he stands."

Social status may be ascribed, achieved, generic, or specific. In the passage that follows, Richard La Piere defines each of them. You will note that these kinds of social status are related to each other. In subsequent chapters on social class and social institutions these distinctions will become important.

*
The ascription of social status is, like the extension of credit by a merchant, an act of faith; but whereas the credit extended by the merchant is usually based upon some empirical experience with the customer, such as, for example, a report on the customer from the local credit bureau, "social credit" is generally given in accordance with either cultural formula or personal sentiment. Cultural formulas most commonly center around nativity. In all societies the status ascribed a male infant is different from that ascribed a female; in most societies parentage determines the complex of kinship status relationships which the infant is granted—e.g., that he is son to so-and-so, nephew to so-and-so, grandson to so-and-so, etc. Upon his parentage depends, further, his initial and often his permanent ethnic, class, national, and other status positions. Moreover, it is largely nativity that determines his particular status with his particular parents; thus if he is the first-born son he may be accorded quite different status from that which is accorded his younger brother. Finally, certain "accidents of birth," some of genetic determination, some not, may profoundly affect the status accorded him. Thus, a girl who, in terms of her society, is exceptionally beautiful may be ascribed by her parents and others quite different status from that ascribed a girl who by the same standards is ugly.

The status that is ascribed to an individual at or shortly after birth largely determines the direction his socialization will take—whether he will be brought up to be, in terms of his culture, masculine or feminine, a lower- or

* Reprinted from A *Theory of Social Control*, pp. 75–79, by Richard T. La Piere. Copyright 1954. McGraw-Hill Book Company, Inc. By permission.

upper-class person, etc. He will be, in sum, more or less effectively socialized to fit the status that has been ascribed to him. Once granted, ascribed status tends to endure, irrespective of the individual's own conduct; thus the individual may be able to enjoy throughout his life a status for which he never pays. The idolized son may, for example, remain a son to his parents—eventually, perhaps, inheriting their wealth—although he fails in every way to be a proper son to them. Conversely, the man with the ascribed ethnic status of Negro will most likely remain a Negro, although he may strive to escape the stigma, as he might come to view it, that was attached to him at birth.

In most instances ascribed status can be either modified or withdrawn for cause; for nothing social is ever final. Parents can, for example, disinherit their wayward son, although they seldom do. The status of a man may be modified should it become known that he is a homosexual. Even the hereditary and ascribed status of a king can be revoked through revolution; the wealthy aristocrat can be reduced to poverty, the landed gentry made landless, etc. But for the most part, the risk of losing an ascribed status is so slight that the possibility of such a loss has comparatively little direct effect upon the conduct of the individual. Ascribed status is, therefore, more important in the socialization of the individual than as a basis for social control of him.

Achieved status is status that is granted as a social reward for some sort of personal accomplishment and, usually but not invariably, on the assumption that the services rendered in the past will continue to be forthcoming in the future. Thus a man confers upon a certain girl the status of wife (and she upon him that of husband) on the assumption—not, of course, always valid—that because she was a pleasant companion during his courtship of her she will be equally pleasant and companionable in the future.

Since achieved status is granted as a reward for past conduct, the prospect of obtaining it is an inducement to the individual to behave in such ways as to earn it. Moreover, achieved status is always subject to withdrawal for failure to live up to the requirements of that status. A king may rule badly and still die on the throne; but the achieved status of President, like that of any elected politician, is subject to periodic review. Parents seldom disinherit a son for bad conduct; but in most societies the achieved status of wife is contingent upon continued good conduct. Achieved status is thus a far more effective basis for social control than is the ascribed variety. . . .

Ascribed status never determines the status that an individual will achieve; it does, however, usually limit the character and number of achieved status positions to which the individual is eligible. Obvious is the fact that anyone born a female cannot achieve a status that is limited exclusively to males and vice versa. No man can become a wife, no woman a husband; in most societies, including our own, the female is excluded from the status of priest and the male from that of nun. Although a woman may, in certain societies, gain the ascribed status of queen, none has as yet achieved that of President.

The relationship between ascribed and achieved status is seldom, however, as simple as the above illustrations might suggest. The only generalization that can be made is that nativity invariably determines in one way or another the *opportunities* that the individual will have to achieve status. Thus in contemporary American society the ethnic status of the individual—as indicated by such signs as name, accent, or skin color—sets fairly rigid limits upon the status positions he can secure. Negroes are discriminated against in politics, business, and many social affairs; in the political life of many of our cities only those with a certain ethnic background—e.g., the Irish in Boston —have much chance of success; in many Southern towns the man with Yankee manners and accent is forever precluded from attaining full social standing. . . .

The distinction between ascribed and achieved status hinges upon what constitutes the basis for the granting of the status *i.e.*, on whether status is granted on faith and in hope that the individual will in due course pay for it or whether it is granted on the basis of his past performance. Equally important is the distinction between generic and specific status grants. This distinction depends upon how many are involved in granting status and the nature of the individual's relations with them.

Any status, whether ascribed or achieved, that is granted by all, or at least by most, of the social population is *generic*. Ascribed ethnic, class, and sex statuses are invariably generic; and age status, especially the status of child and of elder, is ordinarily and for the most part generic. In some instances occupational, regional, or even family status is so widely recognized that it may be considered generic in type. In our own society, for example, a Negro is a Negro wherever he goes; a woman is a woman; a child is a child; and, if he makes himself known, a physician is a physician. It is true, of course, that the particular status granted a Negro, a woman, a child, or a physician, varies considerably from place to place, from class to class, and from circumstance to circumstance. Nevertheless, Negroes are still almost everywhere and regardless of their personal characteristics excluded from white hotels, restaurants, etc., and are welcomed—as whites are not—to Negro establishments. Women—provided that they belong to the right class and ethnic position—are almost everywhere eligible for admission to "ladies' rooms," dress shops, and many other places from which men may be excluded. And the achieved status of physician commands a certain amount of respect everywhere in the United States, as does that of magic man in most primitive societies.

Generic status is often an important initial determinant in situational interactions. Upon the individual's generic status may depend his eligibility to enter into a given situation and, to some extent, how he is defined by the other participants. Ascribed generic status—e.g., ethnic, class, or sex—may also, as has been indicated, preclude the individual's entering some of the achievable status positions provided by his society and predispose him to entering others. For the most part, however, generic status is never so highly esteemed by the individual as status which—whether ascribed or achieved —is specific in character.

Specific status is status that is granted by a comparatively small number of persons who know the individual personally, rather than just recognize him as a member of a category of persons, and whose regard for him is both intimate and detailed. Kinship status is the most common form of specific status; a boy is son to his father and mother and, as a rule, to no one else. To have the specific status of son to parents is, in most instances, far more important to the individual than simply to have the generic status of "white male, twenty-one years of age." Likewise, to be granted the specific status of friend by half a dozen well-known fellow students is usually more meaningful and highly valued than to be granted the generic status of student of such and such a college, although the latter is prerequisite to the former. On the whole, the value that the individual places on his generic status derives from the specific status which it enables him to secure.

TYPES OF SOCIAL ORGANIZATION: SOCIAL GROUPS

An individual's social environment encompasses all persons who interact with that individual in recognized types of relationships, that is, those relationships based on social roles and social status.[14] A social group is defined as two or more persons, aware of each other's presence, entering into social interaction through communication.[15]

Groups vary in size, duration, function, basis of organization, and social interaction.[16] The simplest group consists of two people, with complexity of interaction increasing as numbers grow. A group may live but a moment. Two people come together, exchange a few words, and move on. In contrast there are groups that endure for years and generations; the traditional family group is of this type.[17] Groups differ, of course, in function, depending on the particular goal, and also on the basis of organization. As an example of the latter, an organization may arise in response to a need predetermined by the culture, as in the case of a school system. Or the organization may come into being purely in response to individual needs and interests, as an athletic club. Finally, groups vary according to the nature of the social interaction they foster— from the rapid and direct, as in personal conversation, to the slow and indirect, as the interoffice memo.

Social groups are classified traditionally into four types: primary, secondary, in- or we-groups, and out- or other-groups. The concept of the primary group, to be elaborated in the subsequent selection, was first developed by Charles Cooley.[18] A primary group is characterized by intimate, daily, face-to-face contact. Many examples come to mind: the family, one's peers, some types of work groups, the playground group, and the neighborhood. These examples imply that no particular form of interaction characterized primary relationships.[19] Instead, any one may run the gamut from the most traditionally defined social relationship to deep feelings of emotion to highly rational calculations of choice.

The logical opposite of the primary group is the secondary group. As this type unfortunately did not receive Cooley's attention, it is a kind of sociological stepchild developed through the writings of a number of theorists.[20] Secondary groups may, and often do, possess two characteristics of primary groups. There may be face-to-face and daily relationships —but the requisite intimacy of the primary group is lacking, a consequence of the generally more rational basis for secondary group organization. A school class, work groups, church organizations, labor, business, and professional associations are characterized by the special interests typical of secondary groups. Again the factor of intimacy is lacking with a corresponding decline in the solidarity of the group. Communication is often indirect, as through newsletters and the mass media of communication. Roles tend to be highly functional and not always related to roles played outside the group. Hence, secondary group relationships tend to be transitory.

The relationship among the various groups within a society is generally cohesive since cooperation is needed if the work of the society is to be done. Yet, from time to time, antagonisms, suspicions, and conflicts emerge. When this happens the dominant force of the group—be it primary or secondary—will close ranks and shut out the antagonistic elements in a defensive action based on loyalty to the group, obedience to its wishes, and willingness to make any appropriate sacrifice. A group that closes ranks and experiences increased solidarity is called a *we*-group or an *in*-group. Those shunned are called the *other*-group or the *out*-group.[21] The sense of the *we*-group is felt first in the family among one's peers. It is extended through the socialization process to include school and community, and beyond to broader loyalties, as to the nation.

The following selection by Charles Cooley on the primary group illustrates many of the principles of the foregoing definitions.

*
By primary groups I mean those characterized by intimate face-to-face association and cooperation. They are primary in several senses, but chiefly in forming the social nature and ideals of the individual. The result of intimate association, psychologically, is a certain fusion of individualities in a common whole, so that one's very self, for many purposes at least, is the common life and purpose of the group. Perhaps the simplest way of describing this wholeness is by saying that it is a "we"; it involves the sort of sympathy and mutual identification for which "we" is the natural expression. One lives in the feeling of the whole and finds the chief aims of his will in that feeling.

It is not to be supposed that the unity of the primary group is one of mere harmony and love. It is always a differential and usually a competitive unity, admitting of self-assertion and various appropriative passions; but these passions are socialized by sympathy, and come, or tend to come, under the discipline of a common spirit. The individual will be ambitious, but the chief object of his ambition will be some desired place in the thought of the others, and he will feel allegiance to common standards of service and fair play. So the boy will dispute with his fellows a place on the team, but above such disputes will place the common glory of his class and school.

The most important spheres of this intimate association and cooperation —though by no means the only ones—are the family, the play-group of children, and the neighborhood or community group of elders. These are practically universal, belonging to all times and all stages of development; and are accordingly a chief basis of what is universal in human nature and human ideals. The best comparative studies of the family . . . show it to us as not only a universal institution, but as more alike the world over than the exaggeration of exceptional customs by an earlier school had led us to suppose. Nor can any one doubt the general prevalence of play-groups among children or of informal assemblies of various kinds among their elders. Such association is clearly the nursery of human nature in the world about us, and there is no apparent reason to suppose that the case has anywhere or at any time been essentially different. . . .

Primary groups are primary in the sense that they give the individual his earliest and completest experience of social unity, and also in the sense that they do not change in the same degree as more elaborate relations, but form a comparatively permanent source out of which the latter are ever springing. Of course they are not independent of the larger society, but to some extent reflect its spirit; as the German family and the German school bear somewhat distinctly the print of German militarism. But this, after all, is like the tide setting back into creeks, and does not commonly go very far. Among the

German, and still more among the Russian peasantry are found habits of free cooperation and discussion almost uninfluenced by the character of the state; and it is a familiar and well-supported view that the village commune, self-governing as regards local affairs and habituated to discussion, is a very widespread institution in settled communities, and the continuator of a similar autonomy previously existing in the clan. . . .

In our own cities the crowded tenements and the general economic and social confusion have sorely wounded the family and neighborhood, but it is remarkable, in view of these conditions, what vitality they show; and there is nothing upon which the conscience of the time is more determined than upon restoring them to health.

These groups, then, are springs of life, not only for the individual but for social institutions. They are only in part molded by special traditions, and, in larger degree, express a universal nature. The religion or government of other civilizations may seem alien to us, but the children or the family group wear the common life, and with them we can always make ourselves at home.

. . . the view here maintained is that human nature is not something existing separately in the individual, but a *group-nature or primary phase of society*, a relatively simple and general condition of the social mind. It is something more, on the one hand, than the mere instinct that is born in us . . . and something less, on the other, than the more elaborate development of ideas and sentiments that makes up institutions. It is the nature which is developed and expressed in those simple, face-to-face groups that are somewhat alike in all societies; groups of the family, the playground, and the neighborhood. In the essential similarity of these is to be found the basis, in experience, for similar ideas and sentiments in the human mind. In these, everywhere, human nature comes into existence. Man does not have it at birth; he cannot acquire it except through fellowship, and it decays in isolation.

TYPES OF SOCIAL ORGANIZATION: COLLECTIVE BEHAVIOR

Each of us participates in collective behavior of one kind or another as part of our daily lives.[22] Collective behavior may take the form of the uncontrolled, the bizarre, as in various types of crowds, mobs, or riots in which emotions are permitted free rein. Social interaction is intensified, and deep, though short-lived, loyalties are born on the spot. On the other hand, collective behavior is also manifested in socially acceptable forms —special interest publics, thoughtful audiences, and widespread social movements dedicated to the general welfare.

Regardless of the specific form of collective behavior, three conditions characterize its development.[23] The first is an absence of guide lines for behavior in a given situation. When crisis disrupts the normal channels of communication and the normal flow of activities, when people come together in a time of rapid change and do not know what to do about it, the situation ripens for the emergence of collective behavior. The second condition develops in those situations in which firm decision is lacking or in which decision is ambiguous, allowing for the free play of opinion and, indeed, emotion. Under these conditions a fortuitous leadership may emerge in an effort to guide discussion and influence the final decision. And third, changing perspectives and values give rise to circumstances favorable to the appearance of certain forms of collective behavior. For example, some members of the society may decide that the existing social order needs change; other members of the society resist change. The resultant behavior, on either side, is characterized by radical ideologies, intensive emotional appeals by the leadership, and high levels of personal commitment, all modes of behavior operating outside normal expected channels.

The ways in which these conditions unfold is illustrated in the following discussion of the nature and formation of publics, particularly important to our subsequent study of political institutions. We shall see fluid situations lacking norms, in which a particular type of collective behavior emerges, and how it contributes to the formation of public opinion.

*

. . . The term *public* is used to refer to a group of people (*a*) who are confronted by an issue, (*b*) who are divided in their ideas as to how to meet the issue, and (*c*) who engage in discussion over the issue. As such, it is to be distinguished from a public in the sense of a national people, as when one speaks of the public of the United States, and also from a *following*, as in the instance of the "public" of a motion picture star. The presence of an issue, of discussion, and of a collective opinion is the mark of the public.

We refer to the public as an elementary and spontaneous collective grouping because it comes into existence not as a result of design, but as a natural response to a certain kind of situation. That the public does not exist as an established group and that its behavior is not prescribed by traditions or cultural patterns is indicated by the very fact that its existence centers on the presence of an issue. As issues vary, so do the corresponding publics. And the fact that an issue exists signifies the presence of a situation which cannot be met on the basis of a cultural rule but which must be met by a collective decision arrived at through a process of discussion. In this sense, the public

* Reprinted from "Elementary Forms of Collective Groupings," *New Outline of Principles of Sociology*, pp. 189–91, by Herbert Blumer, ed. Alfred M. Lee. Copyright 1951. By permission of Barnes and Noble, Inc.

is a grouping that is natural and not conventional, one that is spontaneous and not preestablished.

This elementary and natural character of the public can be better appreciated by noticing that the public . . . is lacking in the characteristic features of a society. The existence of an issue means that the group has to act; yet there are no understandings, definitions, or rules prescribing what that action should be. If there were, there would be, of course, no issue. It is in this sense that we can speak of the public as having no culture—no traditions to dictate what its action shall be. Further, since a public comes into existence only with an issue it does not have the form or organization of a society. In it, people do not have fixed status roles. Nor does the public have any we-feeling or consciousness of its identity. Instead, the public is a kind of amorphous group whose size and membership varies with the issue; instead of having its activity prescribed, it is engaged in an effort to arrive at an act, and therefore forced to *create* its action.

The peculiarity of the public is that it is marked by disagreement and hence by *discussion* as to what should be done. This fact has a number of implications. For one thing, it indicates that the interaction that occurs in the public is markedly different from that which takes place in the crowd. A crowd mills, develops rapport, and reaches unanimity unmarred by disagreement. The public interacts on the basis of interpretation, enters into dispute, and consequently is characterized by conflict relations. Correspondingly, individuals in the public are likely to have their self-consciousness intensified and their critical powers heightened instead of losing self-awareness and critical ability as occurs in the crowd. In the public, arguments are advanced, are criticized, and are met by counter-arguments. The interaction, therefore, makes for opposition instead of the mutual support and unanimity that mark the crowd.

Another point of interest is that this discussion, which is based on difference, places some premium on facts and makes for rational consideration. While, as we shall see, the interaction may fall short by far of realizing these characteristics, the tendency is in their direction. The crowd means that rumor and spectacular suggestion predominate; but the presence of opposition and disagreement in the public means that contentions are challenged and become subject to criticism. In the face of attack that threatens to undermine their character, such contentions have to be bolstered or revised in the face of criticisms that cannot be ignored. Since facts can maintain their validity, they come to be valued; and since the discussion is argumentative, rational considerations come to occupy a role of some importance.

Now we can consider the question as to how a public acts. This question is interesting, particularly because the public does not act like a society, a crowd, or the mass. A society manages to act by following a prescribed rule of consensus; a crowd, by developing rapport; and the mass, by the convergence of individual selections. But the public faces, in a sense, the dilemma of how to become a unit when it is actually divided, of how to act concertedly when there is a disagreement as to what the action should be. The public acquires its particular type of unity and manages to act by arriving at a collective decision or by developing a collective opinion.

TYPES OF SOCIAL ORGANIZATION: TYPES OF SOCIETIES

Not only specific social groups but also the sum of related social groups, which we call society, may undergo change in structure and in function. Western civilization, in general, and American society, in particular, have undergone such changes. At one time the majority of the population lived in small towns engaged in limited forms of industry, or lived on farms; today the majority of the population lives in cities. Once our labor was devoted to supplying the essentials for survival; now we devote ourselves to the production and distribution of the abundance of an industrial economy.

These changes have been described as the traditional urban shift,[24] a consolidation of two polar types of societies. Unfortunately there is little agreement about the characteristics of each.[25] Many theorists concerned with this problem have attempted to establish patterns of behavior and types of values that are typically rural or typically urban. Examination reveals that a black and white distinction has little substance. Too often superficial observation mistakes purely cultural phenomena for valid differences between rural and urban society. Blue jeans, barn architecture, plaid shirts, and hill-billy music are discovered in an urban setting; ivy league suits, modern architecture, and jazz music are discovered in a rural setting.

The alternative is to attempt isolation of those basic characteristics that make true distinction between rural and urban polarities—the society having the *least* number of these traits may be considered traditional, and the society manifesting them in the *greatest* number, urban.

Five characteristics have been so identified. They are: anonymity, division of labor, heterogeneity, impersonal and formally prescribed relationships, and symbols of status that do not depend upon personal acquaintance.

Anonymity derives from social interaction within a society in the highest degree. In traditional society interaction is intimate and enduring, often encompassing a lifetime. The starting points for such intimate and enduring interaction are the family and one's peers. In urban society such relationships are more difficult to establish. Of course, there are families and peer groups, but often there is little relationship between the two. Contacts are transient in nature: the children grow up and leave home, make friends and enter occupations in a milieu with which the parents have little or no association. Friendships, themselves, may be fleeting as families move from one place to another. Children change schools; husbands change jobs. Anonymity of relations is furthered by those processes that tend to cause social and psychological distance between people in spite of their physical closeness. Thus, the mass media of communication create audience situations that make it difficult for interaction to take place among the audience members. The barriers of segregation create distances between people which increase social and psychological distance.

Traditional societies are often thought of as being entirely agricultural in their economy, but the economic system, as such, has little to do with the classification of a society. Some New England and Mid-Western communities, although abounding in industrial activity, are to be classified nevertheless as remnants of a traditional society. The quality that characterizes such a society, however, is the undifferentiated nature of its *division of labor*. Urban society, in contrast, has a highly differentiated division of labor, a vast complexity of interrelated, yet separate, agricultural, commercial, and industrial practices with a seemingly endless array of interdependent roles.

Heterogeneity develops from the division of labor. Heterogeneity is often discovered in traditional societies; it is inescapable throughout urban society. The trend toward greater occupational specialization, together with specifically urban residence, make almost a complete cycle: the heterogeneity of an urban society is maintained by the anonymity of social relations, reinforced, in turn, by the specialization of functions created by division of labor.

Impersonal relationships are an outgrowth of the above factors. In a traditional society relationships tend to be quite personal. An individual is known throughout the society in terms of the roles and statuses he possesses within his family. Such relationships are a generic status type, whether ascribed or achieved. In an urban society such status relationships are more specific. Who or what your father is, although important for some kinds of relationships, has minimal importance in relation to the need for certain types of skills and abilities regardless of birth or background. This is particularly true in regard to jobs and statuses. Such occupational skills as "heel seat scourer" and "gore stapler" are highly specific in nature. The result is that it becomes difficult to relate to another person in terms of his job status. Moreover, the movement of the population in an urban society, together with specialization of function, make for transient relationships only, at best.

What are the differences in the social solidarity of rural and urban societies? What are the social catalysts? In a traditional society the close interpersonal relationships make it possible for the society to attain solidarity through the operation of the folkways—or customs—and mores.[27] Folkways are patterns of behavior characteristic of a social group or society. Shaking hands, tipping a hat to a lady, manners, and conventions are examples of folkways. Mores are patterns of behavior considered necessary for the welfare of the group or society. Morality is one of these. The functioning of the mores and folkways depends on a continuity in the socialization process. The ideals implanted in the child by his family or peers must be reinforced by social relationships beyond the limits of these primary groups. The less differentiated more generic social relationships of a rural society are conducive to such reinforcement. In an urban society, although folkways and mores do exist, their function is compromised by the anonymity of social relations. In order to establish a continuity, to be able to anticipate the conduct of strangers, law has been developed as a rational means of ordering social relations.[28] The law formalized social relationships by placing some folkways and mores within a legal framework, such as making some of the Ten Commandments legalistic, and by creating laws to anticipate situations not covered by the folkways and mores.

Family and peer group associations loom large in social action especially in a traditional society. However, as the society moves away from this characteristic intimacy different bases emerge. *Status* depends less on personal relationships than on outward symbols. The less personal way of life in an urban society and the style of life portrayed to others—taste, manners, one's material possessions, and how all these are used in the manipulation of human relations—become the significant factor in the achievement of status.[29] Not always do we discover credibility beneath the façade of status symbols which accounts, perhaps, for the cynicism often attributed to the character of the urbanite.

These five factors are not absolute. Some societies, of course, stand closer to one pole than to the other. But no society changes all at once and completely. A particular community or a whole region may possess both rural and urban characteristics. The over-all trend in the United States, however, is toward an urban society, and the five characteristics of this development must be taken into account.[30] Nor does it appear feasible to reverse the trend to some romantic conception of the past. Attempts to do so by moving to suburbia have failed because the urbanites have carried the patterns of the city with them. Cape Cod architecture, the wagon wheel in the front gate, maple furniture in the living room are illusory. Instead we must understand the nature of community organization and development (see Part Two) and the nature of values, beliefs, and attitudes—or culture.

Notes

1. The following discussion is based upon Richard T. La Piere, *Collective Behavior*, New York: McGraw-Hill Book Co., 1938, pp. 7–9.
2. *Ibid.*, p. 8.
3. *George H. Mead, Mind, Self and Society*, Chicago: University of Chicago Press, 1934, pp. 71–72, and Chapter II, *supra*.
4. See Mead's supplementary essay "The Self and the Process of Reflection," in *op. cit.*, pp. 354–378.
5. From the book *Now We Are Six* by A. A. Milne. Copyright 1927 by E. P. Dutton and Company, Inc. Renewal, 1955, by A. A. Milne. Reprinted by permission of the publishers.
6. Cf., Kimball Young, *Personality and Problems of Adjustment*, New York: Crofts, 1947, p. 170.
7. Cf., Ralph Linton, *The Study of Man*, New York: Appleton-Century, 1936.
8. Talcott Parsons, *The Social System*, Glencoe, Ill.: The Free Press, 1949, pp. 36 ff.
9. William J. Goode, "A Theory of Role Strain," *American Sociological Review*, Vol. 25, August 1961, pp. 483–496.
10. *Ibid.*, p. 485.
11. *Ibid.*, p. 487 ff.
12. *Ibid.*
13. Karen Horney, *Neurosis and Human Growth*, New York: W. W. Norton, 1950.
14. Young, *op. cit.*, p. 4.
15. For an excellent treatment of social groups see George C. Homans, *The Human Group*, New York: Harcourt, Brace and Co., 1950.
16. Richard T. La Piere, *A Theory of Social Control*, New York: McGraw-Hill Book Co., 1954, p. 100 ff.
17. There is evidence to indicate that this may be changing. See Paul Glick, "The Life Cycle of the Family," *Marriage and Family Living*, Vol. 17, February 1955, pp. 3–9.
18. Charles H. Cooley, *Social Organization*, Glencoe, Ill.: The Free Press, 1956.
19. For a full statement of forms of social action see Max Weber, *The Theory of Social and Economic Organization*, New York: Oxford University Press, 1947, pp. 115 ff.
20. Cf., Louis Wirth, "Urbanism as a Way of Life," *American Journal of Sociology*, Vol. XLIV, July 1938, pp. 1–24.
21. William G. Sumner, *Folkways*, New York: Mentor Books, 1960, p. 27.
22. For a recent attempt to classify forms of collective behavior see Ralph Turner and L. M. Killian, *Collective Behavior*, Englewood Cliffs, N.J.: Prentice-Hall,

80 Human Groups

Inc., 1957. Also, Neil Smelser, *Theory of Collective Behavior*. New York; The Free Press, 1963.
23. Leonard Broom and Philip Selznick, *Sociology*, Evanston, Ill.: Row-Peterson and Co., 2nd ed., 1958, p. 251.
24. There have been a couple of dozen variations on the theme. Among the most useful have been: Ferdinand Toennies, *Community and Society*, trans. C. P. Loomis, East Lansing, Michigan: Michigan State University Press, 1957; Emile Durkheim, *The Division of Labor in Society*, trans. G. Simpson, Glencoe, Ill.: The Free Press, 1949; Weber, *op. cit.*; Wirth, *op. cit.*
25. Cf., Richard Dewey, "The Rural Urban Continuum," *American Journal of Sociology*, Vol. LXVI, July 1960, pp. 60–66.
26. Dewey, *ibid.*, p. 65.
27. Sumner, *op. cit.*, pp. 17 ff.
28. Cf., Max Weber, *Essays in Sociology*, trans. and ed. C. W. Mills and Hans Gerth, New York: Galaxy Books, 1958, p. 220 ff.
29. W. H. Form and G. P. Stone, "Urbanism, Anonymity, and Status Symbolism," *American Journal of Sociology*, Vol. LXII, March 1957, pp. 504–514.
30. Dewey, *op. cit.*, et passim.

Selected Readings

Duncan, Otis D., and Albert J. Riess, Jr. *Social Characteristics of Urban and Rural Communities, 1950*. New York: John Wiley and Sons, Inc., 1956.
Gans, Herbert. *The Urban Villagers*. New York: Free Press of Glencoe, 1962.
Homans, George C. *The Human Group*. New York: Harcourt, Brace and Company, 1950.
Nadel, S. F. *The Theory of Social Structure*. Glencoe, Ill.: The Free Press, 1957.
Redfield, Robert. *The Little Community*. Chicago: University of Chicago Press, 1955.
Sjoberg, Gideon. *The Pre-Industrial City*. Glencoe, Ill.: The Free Press, 1960.
Smelser, Neil. *Theory of Collective Behavior*. New York: The Free Press of Glencoe, 1963.
Smith, Thomas. *The Agrarian Origins of Modern Japan*. Stanford, Calif.: Stanford University Press, 1959.
Toennies, Ferdinand. *Community and Society*. Trans. and ed. Charles P. Loomis. East Lansing: Michigan State University Press, 1957.

Chapter 5

The Nature of Culture

The attitudes of human beings do not emerge from mere whim. Behavior just does not happen without cause. We have seen this in the concepts related to personality and the human group. Moreover, we have learned that groups do not exist without purpose or direction. Considering the concept of culture will add to our understanding of behavior.

What is culture? As seen by Alfred L. Kroeber and Talcott Parsons, culture is the sum of values, ideas, and other meaningful symbols created by man to shape human behavior, and the artifacts of that behavior as they are transmitted from one generation to the next.[1]

This means, first of all, that culture is created and transmitted. Man originates the beliefs, ideas, and values which govern his behavior. They are of his own doing, his own brainchildren. Similarly, through behavior man creates the artifacts by which he lives, passing his knowledge along to his heirs. Succeeding generations add the accumulated culture of their lifetimes, pass it along, and so on. Therefore, when we note a society's concern with material objects, when we meet a belief that competition is the basis of society, or when we hear an entire group speaking the English language, we know that these behaviors and attitudes are learned. They have been created and transmitted by man; they are cultural. That they are learned is evident from the diversity of cultures in the world. Were these behaviors biological, we should expect a greater uniformity among cultures, since man is, biologically, a single species.

We often hear that culture is the cause of one thing or another, or that culture does something or influences something. Culture, as such, neither causes, does, nor influences anything. Human beings composing the culture cause, do, and influence things. But they do so in relation to the attitudes, beliefs, and values handed down by others, which they share in common with their contemporaries. It is the members of the society who keep its culture alive; without people, the culture would die. In this sense, culture is an abstraction; it indicates that continuity exists in the pattern of behavior within one or more societies.[2]

The definition also says that culture is composed of material and non-

81

material elements. So far we have addressed ourselves to the nonmaterial aspects: values, beliefs, and attitudes. Each of these is an abstraction, understood only through some kind of symbol such as the arts, language, religion, myth, or even science. Unless we are able to create and renew these symbols, we find it quite impossible to maintain culture.[3] As to the material objects, or artifacts, of culture, they consist of everything that man has developed from the first paleolithic hatchet to the latest high-speed electronic computer. They include even those things that record the nonmaterial phases of culture. Material objects often reflect the needs, values, and beliefs of a society, although this occurs all too frequently by impression and implication. Yet material objects give important clues to culture—especially those cultures that do not survive.

There is still another aspect of culture to emphasize. We have indicated that any society may possess a culture of its own or share what it possesses with other societies. This observation contains an important implication: the sets of values and beliefs, the attitudes, the direction taken by behavior patterns, and the artifacts of any single culture will differ markedly from those of another. Consider how often people call a particular behavior—for instance, selfishness, a competitive urge, or aggression—"human nature" or "instinctive." There is nothing biologically innate about such behavior. Behaviors such as selfishness, competitiveness, and aggressiveness are learned as part of one's cultural experience. These and all other cultural phenomena vary in relation to time and place, and cultures themselves are relative. A normal aspect of American culture cannot be assumed to be normal in other cultures. No one can expect one's own cultural standards to be acceptable to others.

Unfortunately, this concept of cultural relativity has been grossly misunderstood. Clyde Kluckhohn, the anthropologist, explains the problem:

*
Cultural relativity is one of the most influential concepts of modern anthropology. In a vulgarized form it has been taken to mean that behavior which is customary among any people is therefore justified. On this basis, we should have to accept slavery or Nazism as morally acceptable. What anthropologists have wished to point out in this area of their work is the broad spectrum of variability in human values and the necessity for considering all values and items of behavior in their own context. However, it is true that for at least a generation anthropologists concentrated more upon cultural differences than upon the equally factual similarities. It is also clear that insufficient consideration has been given to values as such and to systems of values. If the essence of culture is the selection of certain paths of life from among two or more

* Reprinted from Clyde Kluckhohn, "Anthropology," What is Science?, ed., J. R. Newman, p. 343. Copyright 1955. By permission of Simon & Schuster, Inc.

that are objectively possible, the essence of this selectivity resides in the value system. Man is not only the tool-using animal; he is the valuing animal, constantly making judgments of "better" and "worse" and behaving in terms of preferences that are by no means altogether reducible to biological needs and to the immediate situation. Human life is a moral life precisely because it is a social life. In human society cooperation and the other necessities of group living are not taken care of by instinct as they are for the social insects. There must be standards.

To approach the study of other peoples and other cultures with an attitude of relativity, then, is to free our own thinking of prejudice.

CULTURE AND PERSONALITY

Although the concept of culture is an important analytical tool in its own right, its usefulness increases when applied to other concepts of the social sciences. The relationship between culture and personality is particularly significant in any discussion of the socialization process. The relationship itself, however, is indirect, since we do not have to come into contact with an immediately present aspect of culture for it to affect our personalities. Many points of knowledge, for example, are understood and shared by comparatively few persons. Nevertheless, the existence of that knowledge has great influence on all. This applies most obviously to the vast range of scientific and technical knowledge. The relationship of culture and personality helps us to understand the continuity of culture, for despite differences within a culture and individual ideas about values and beliefs, there is always agreement about the ideal.

Of course, the real situation may not live up to the ideal, giving rise to annoying inconsistencies, perhaps exposing cultural conflicts and anxieties. William Graham Sumner, a leading sociologist of the early part of this century, suggested that in the long run such inconsistencies tended to be ignored.[4] But he did not specify which cultural element was inconsistent, nor say whether new cultural elements necessarily emerged, nor whether one dominated another, nor whether a new system evolved in place of the inconsistent ones.

A further understanding obtained through the relationship of culture to personality concerns *basic personality*.[5] Primary groups, especially those met in childhood, initiate the socialization process. Within such groups, as we have seen, are formed the fundamental characteristics of personality. Those characteristics that recur more frequently than others form the basic personality. Within a given society children share a fairly common core of experiences engendered by such activities as feeding, toilet-training, weaning, brother and sister relationships, and the like. These experiences are reinforced by the common acceptance of specific sets of values and beliefs. Individual views, of course, will develop through differences in interpretation of experience and as a result of the child's capacity to perform as expected. Most persons, however, will cling to the basic personality type valued by the culture.

There is good evidence from the works of Ruth Benedict, Margaret Mead, and Abram Kardiner that the concept of basic personality is significant in the analysis of primitive or traditional societies, although some controversy surrounds its application to urban societies. This is particularly true of national character studies.[6] A major difficulty with the latter is that they do not take into account subcultural differences in interpreting the various values that exist in a heterogeneous society. Such heterogeneity (Chapter 4) is related to the extended division of labor in urban societies. It is possible, therefore, to expect a greater range of values and diversified personality types in an urban environment.

Whatever practical difficulties there may be in the relationship between culture and personality, theory permits some precise statements. The following study by Ralph Linton expresses two influences of culture on personality. As Linton notes, the obvious beginning of influence occurs in early childhood, at the start of the socialization process, but he adds another dimension—its continuation in the life of an adult. For this reason social science is interested in groups other than the family and peers as agencies of socialization.

*
The influences which culture exerts on the developing personality are of two quite different sorts. On the one hand we have those influences which derive from the culturally patterned behavior of other individuals *toward* the child. These begin to operate from the moment of birth and are of paramount importance during infancy. On the other hand we have those influences which derive from the individual's observation of, or instruction in, the patterns of behavior characteristic of his society. Many of these patterns do not affect him directly, but they provide him with models for the development of his own habitual responses to various situations. These influences are unimportant in early infancy but continue to affect him throughout life. The failure to distinguish between these two types of cultural influence has led to a good deal of confusion.

It must be admitted at once that the two types of influence overlap at certain points. Culturally patterned behavior directed toward the child may

* From the *Cultural Background of Personality*, pp. 139–146, by Ralph Linton. Copyright 1945, D. Appleton-Century-Crofts Company, Inc. Reprinted by permission of the publisher.

serve as a model for the development of some of his own behavior patterns. This factor becomes operative as soon as the child is old enough to observe and remember what other people are doing. When, as an adult, he finds himself confronted by the innumerable problems involved in rearing his own children, he turns to these childhood memories for guidance. Thus in almost any American community we find parents sending their children to Sunday School because they themselves were sent to Sunday School. The fact that, as adults, they greatly prefer golf to church attendance does little to weaken the pattern. However, this aspect of any society's patterns for child-rearing is rather incidental to the influence which such patterns exert upon personality formation. At most it insures that children born into a particular society will be reared in much the same way generation after generation. The real importance of the patterns for early care and child-training lies in their effects upon the deeper levels of the personalities of individuals reared according to them.

It is generally accepted that the first few years of the individual's life are crucial for the establishment of the highly generalized value-attitude systems which form the deeper levels of personality content. The first realization of this fact came from the study of atypical individuals in our own society and the discovery that certain of their peculiarities seemed to be rather consistently linked with certain sorts of atypical childhood experiences. The extension of personality studies to other societies in which both the normal patterns of child-rearing and the normal personality configurations for adults were different from our own only served to emphasize the importance of very early conditioning. Many of the "normal" aspects of European personalities which were accepted at first as due to instinctive factors are now recognized as results of our own particular patterns of child care. Although study of the relations between various societies' techniques for child-rearing and the basic personality types for adults in these societies has barely begun, we have already reached a point where certain correlations seem to be recognizable. Although a listing of all these correlations is impossible in a discussion as brief as the present one, a few examples may serve for illustration.

In societies in which the culture pattern prescribes absolute obedience from the child to the parent as a prerequisite for rewards of any sort, the normal adult will tend to be a submissive individual, dependent, and lacking in initiative. Even though he has largely forgotten the childhood experiences which led to the establishment of these attitudes, his first reaction to any new situation will be to look to someone in authority for support and direction. It is worth noting in this connection that there are many societies in which the patterns of child-rearing are so effective in producing adult personalities of this type that special techniques have been developed for training a few selected individuals for leadership. Thus, among the Tanala of Madagascar, eldest sons are given differential treatment from birth, this treatment being designed to develop initiative and willingness to assume responsibility, while other children are systematically disciplined and repressed. Again, individuals who are reared in very small family groups of our own type have a tendency to focus their emotions and their anticipations of reward or punishment on a few other individuals. In this they are harking back unconsciously to a childhood in which all satisfactions and frustrations derived from their own fathers and mothers. In societies where the child is reared in an extended family environment, with numerous adults about, any one of whom may either reward or punish, the normal personality will tend in the opposite direction. In such societies the average individual is incapable of strong or lasting attachments or hatreds toward particular persons. All personal interactions embody an unconscious attitude of: "Oh well, another will be along presently." It is difficult to conceive of such a society embodying in its culture such patterns as our concepts of romantic love, or of the necessity for finding the one and only partner without whom life will be meaningless.

Such examples could be multiplied indefinitely, but the above will serve to show the sort of correlations which are now emerging from studies of personality and culture. These correlations reflect linkages of a simple and obvious sort, and it is already plain that such one-to-one relationships between cause and effect are in the minority. In most cases we have to deal with complex configurations of child-training patterns which, as a whole, produce complex personality configurations in the adult. Nevertheless, no one who is familiar with the results which have already been obtained can doubt that here lies the key to most of the differences in basic personality type which have hitherto been ascribed to hereditary factors. The "normal" members of different societies owe their varying personality configurations much less to their genes than to their nurseries.

While the culture of any society determines the deeper levels of its members' personalities through the particular techniques of child-rearing to which it subjects them, its influence does not end with this. It goes on to shape the rest of their personalities by providing models for their specific responses as well. This latter process continues throughout life. As the individual matures and then ages, he constantly has to unlearn patterns of response which have ceased to be effective and to learn new ones more appropriate to his current place in the society. At every step in this process, culture serves as a guide. It not only provides him with models for his changing roles but also insures that these roles shall be, on the whole, compatible with his deep-seated value-attitude systems. All the patterns within a single culture tend to show a sort of psychological coherence quite aside from their functional interrelations. With rare exceptions, the "normal" individual who adheres to them will not be required to do anything which is incompatible with the deeper levels of his personality structure. Even when one society borrows patterns of behavior from another, these patterns will usually be modified and reworked until they become congruous with the basic personality type of the borrowers. Culture may compel the atypical individual to adhere to forms of behavior which are repugnant to him, but when such behavior is repugnant to the bulk of a society's members, it is culture which has to give way.

Turning to the other side of the picture, the acquisition of new behavior patterns which are congruous with the individual's generalized value-attitude systems tends to reinforce these systems and to establish them more firmly as time passes. The individual who spends his life in any society with a fairly stable culture finds his personality becoming more firmly integrated as he grows older. His adolescent doubts and questionings with respect to the attitudes implicit in his culture disappear as he reaffirms them in his adherence to the overt behavior which his culture prescribes. In time he emerges as a pillar of society, unable to understand how anyone can entertain such doubts. While this process may not make for progress, it certainly makes for individual contentment. The state of such a person is infinitely happier than that of one who finds himself compelled to adhere to patterns of overt behavior which are not congruous with the value-attitude systems established by his earliest experiences. The result of such incongruities can be seen in many individuals who have had to adapt to rapidly changing culture conditions such as those which obtain in our own society. It is even more evident in the case of those who, having begun life in one culture, are attempting to adjust to another. These are the "marginal men" whose plight is recognized by all who have worked with the phenomenon of acculturation. Lacking the reinforcement derived from constant expression in overt behavior, the early-established value-attitude systems of such individuals are weakened and overlaid. At the same time, it seems that they are rarely if ever eliminated, still less replaced by new systems congruous with the cultural milieu in which the individual has to operate. The acculturated individual can learn to act and even to think in terms of his new society's culture, but he cannot learn to feel in these terms. At each point where decision is required he finds himself adrift with no fixed points of reference.

In summary, the fact that personality norms differ for different societies can be explained on the basis of the different experience which the members of such societies acquire from contact with their cultures. In the case of a few small societies whose members have a homogeneous heredity, the influence of physiological factors in determining the psychological potentialities of the majority of these members cannot be ruled out, but the number of such cases is certainly small. Even when common hereditary factors may be present, they can affect only potentialities for response. They are never enough in themselves to account for the differing content and organization which we find in the basic personality types for different societies.

SOCIAL INSTITUTIONS

An integrated theory of individual, society, and culture is necessary for the study of human behavior, and the concept of the institution is helpful in the formulation of such theory. Popular misconceptions exist about the meaning of the term institution. To many people it refers to a building, such as a bank or a hospital. To others the term signifies any *single* folkway or the mores of a culture; in this sense, a curse word, or shaking hands, or cheating on examinations may be considered institutions. Actually, the term as used by the social scientist is more complex: institutions are neither specific buildings nor specific folkways, though each may operate within his concept of an institution.

What does the social scientist mean by institution? William Graham Sumner defined it as a concept, and a structure.[7] An institution is an interrelated system of values, beliefs, ideas, doctrines, and interests. The structure, in turn, is the means by which the institution is organized. The concept may be studied through the behavior of social groups created to achieve common ends.

Human need arises from three sources: biological, social, and cultural. Biological need is universal. Social and cultural needs are fixed by society. Thus, in a given society most members will share approximately the same needs, which may be satisfied expediently in association with others. Many of us could grow our own food, given a back yard or a window box; a few possess the skills required to hunt or fish. But how much easier it is to organize ourselves into a system whereby some people spend all of their time providing the goods and services. How much easier it is to have trained people guide us in our learning than attempt to go it alone. We might learn to read and write by ourselves, but in what direction would we move after these skills had been mastered? The organization of individuals into appropriate social groupings in pursuit of commonly shared values (goals) is by far more effective. Education, religion, politics, economics, marriage and family, and military are among the most important areas in which the individual, society, and culture are integrated.

This simplified explanation gives some idea of the ordinary organization of society. But there are also the social deviants who do not fit in the social system. We have already noted two personal or individual sources for deviation. The first was Horney's theory of self-alienation. The second was the theory of role strain.

Are there cultural sources of deviation? Are deviates from the society simply unable to behave as expected? Are they morally weak? One answer is given by Ruth Benedict: "those who function inadequately in any society are not those with certain fixed 'abnormal' traits, but may well be those whose responses have received no support in the institutions of their culture. The weakness of these aberrants is in great measure illusory. It springs, not from the fact that they are lacking in necessary vigor, but that they are individuals whose responses are not reaffirmed by society. They are, as Sapir phrases it, 'alienated from an impossible world.'" [8]

In a traditional society deviations may appear to be more serious and threatening than in urban society—a consequence of the more meaningful relationships that prevail in a rural setting. Therefore, the possibility of greater urban tolerance for deviation points up the need for better understanding of the nature of institutional behavior.

The following selection by Richard La Piere describes some of the more salient structural features of the institutional idea. The ideology of institutional behavior will be an important aspect of the study of political and economic institutions to be undertaken later in this book.

*   In the more stable and highly integrated societies of the past, group life was maintained and group membership was replenished largely through what are called institutions—the family, the feudal manor, the church, and so on. These institutions were not, of course, tangible entities, but were, rather, patterns of social organization which could be perceived in the behavior of many human beings. For example, the institution of the patriarchal family in China was a pattern which could be perceived in the behavior of millions of Chinese people for more than two thousand years.

Any specific institutional pattern, such as the Chinese patriarchal family, is manifest as a constellation of a multitude of distinct but related social situations. In the institution of the Chinese family these included, among the more colorful, the various ceremonies surrounding birth, death, and marriage.

How a constellation of situations goes to make up an institutional pattern may best be seen by analogy. Just as the plot of a play is conveyed by the enactment of a number of specific scenes, the pattern of the institution is revealed by the interaction which occurs in a number of separate situations. Each such situation builds upon the previous situation and contributes to the succeeding situation in much the same way as each stage scene adds to the previous one and contributes to the succeeding one. The full cycle of such situations constitutes the institutional constellation, just as the cycle of stage scenes constitutes the play.

Obviously, then, any given situation of an institutional constellation is significant only as a subordinate element of the total constellation. When, by way of illustration, a Chinese boy and girl of a century ago came together to go through the marriage ceremony, that situation was but one of a multitude of others which went to make up the Chinese institution of the family. In itself, the marriage was, therefore, unimportant. It was no more than an instrument of the institution. All aspects of the ceremony—the place

* Reprinted from *Collective Behavior*, pp. 63–69 and 76–77, by Richard T. La Piere. Copyright 1938, McGraw-Hill Book Company, Inc. By permission.

in which and the time at which the bride and groom met, the presence of others, and the interaction which occurred—were almost entirely determined by institutional factors. Any particular marriage ceremony had social significance, therefore, only as it, too, contributed to the making of the institutional constellation.

Like the stage scene, the institutional situation does, however, have a unity of its own. Each stage scene is a little playlet; it begins in the meeting of certain members of the cast. The characters may come on to an empty set, or the beginning of a scene may be marked simply by one character's leaving the stage or by some new character's coming on. The action of the scene unfolds. To mark the termination of the scene, the curtain falls; or some new character is introduced to change the "situation."

Likewise, each institutional situation has internal unity. Thus, the marriage ceremony begins with the meeting of the bride and groom and ends when they have completed the procedure which makes them man and wife. . . .

Institutions differ widely among societies, even as plays differ one from another. The situations which contribute to the making of a specific institution also differ, even as do the scenes of a specific play. All situations of all institutions have, however, certain common socio-psychological attributes, even as all scenes of all plays have certain common elements. The behavior which occurs in these situations falls into a comparatively distinct, although somewhat broad, category. Such behavior may for convenience be termed institutional behavior.

During some periods of social history, such as, for example, our Middle Ages, institutional behavior has been the predominant type of . . . behavior. Today, institutional behavior is so foreign to our experience that the analysis which follows may seem foreign to reality. Our age is one of rapid social change, in which older institutional patterns have lost their functional values and in which the remnants of those patterns persist as curious anachronisms. . . .

Sociologically and in terms of its functional consequences, a social institution might be described as originating in collective need for a long-run plan of action. A social group cannot maintain itself on the basis of day-by-day, trial-and-error adjustment. The activities of today must be planned in terms of their effects upon tomorrow. Consequently, a social plan must be devised. Such a plan serves to reduce human dependence upon trial and error and to make individual behavior a contribution to collective long-run welfare. In time the plan becomes an established institution, handed down more or less intact from generation to generation. Sociologically, therefore, the institution is to be considered as a behavior-controlling mechanism for the satisfaction of one or a number of group needs—economic, educational, religious, and the like.

Since each institutional situation is but an element in the institutional constellation, the origin and function of the institutional situation must be referred back to the institution itself. The origin and function of any particular situation cannot be deduced from study of that one situation any more than the origin and function of a cog of a machine can be discerned by examination of the cog itself. Nor can the origin and function of that situation be discerned from a study of the interests and initiative of the individuals involved, any more than the origin and function of the scene of a play can be explained as a consequence of the ambition of the players to display their talents.

Individual initiative and human interests do, of course, appear in the making of any specific institutional situation; e.g., in the making of a marriage ceremony, the wedding date is fixed by people, parents select the bride for their son, etc. But individual initiative is so highly channelized that it serves only to foster the fulfillment of the institutional plan, much in the sense that a minister by his efforts to encourage attendance at the Sunday morning service in a given church fosters the maintenance of religion. Without human beings who possess some initiative, no social situation, institutional or otherwise, would arise. But the origin and function of a given institutional situation are not to be explained as the consequence of individual initiative, any more than the fact that a religious service is held in a given church on a given Sunday is to be explained on the basis of the initiative of the minister who officiates.

Even more evident is the fact that, although interests may be antecedent to the coming together of people in an institutional situation, those interests are institutional rather than individual. Those interests are a part of the mechanism of the institutional constellation of which the given situation is simply one manifestation.

The forces which make for the meeting of a group of human beings in any particular institutional situation are complex and may never be completely understood. But it may be stated as a general principle that behind that situation is a series of social events, each building in accordance with the institutional pattern toward that situation and toward subsequent institutional situations. Those events and their effects upon the individuals involved constitute the forces of institutional life. In these forces lie the origin and function of the given institutional situation.

Even as the situation originates in the forces of institutional life, the pattern of the interaction resolves largely in accordance with the institutional formula. Without knowing the particular individuals involved, it would have been possible, for example, to describe in rather complete outline the various patterns of interaction which would appear in any Chinese wedding ceremony. This being true, it is quite evident that the individuals concerned simply enacted these patterns and had no part in their determination.

We can say, therefore, that the patterns of interaction which arise in institutional situations, like the situations themselves, originate in the forces of institutional life and function to institutional ends. Thus, when during the course of a Chinese marriage ceremony the bride and groom kowtow to the ancestral spirits, they do so because it has, as it were, been "written" and because this act in some way contributes to the operation of the family system. Individual initiative, self-interests, and trial and error play no greater part in the devising of the pattern of interaction than they do in the devising of the situation in which that interaction occurs. Thus, the interactions which occur during the course of the Chinese marriage ceremony, like the ceremony itself, are to be understood only in terms of the larger pattern of the Chinese family.

The origin and function of any particular institutional pattern of interaction can, therefore, be discerned only by a study of the institution and its place in the total social system. Institutional behavior has no significance, individual or collective, apart from the contest in which it appears.

To gain any comprehension of the origin and function of any given instance of institutional behavior, we must, therefore, refer to the findings of the anthropologist and sociologist, who can perhaps tell us something of the development of the social institution which forms the background of the particular behavior under consideration. Long, careful, objective study is necessary before the long-run collective significance of a given instance of institutional behavior can be explained. That explanation will never be simple, and seldom can it be clear.

For every institutional situation, however, there is a socially provided explanation. These explanations have no relation to objective fact; they are merely the ideological justifications of institutional behavior. They do not give the real reasons for the appearance of the situations or for the behavior which occurs therein, but they do serve to answer any question which might arise among the participants.

Ordinarily the members of an institutional situation do not feel called upon to question or to explain the reason why they behave as they do; they act their special roles with mechanical ease and with automatic unconcern. What they do is, for them, entirely normal and to be taken for granted. Thus, ethnologists have sometimes found it rather difficult to secure from their primitive informants the why of primitive practices. Apparently it does not occur to the primitive that any reason or explanation is necessary, although the primitive informant is usually able to provide some sort of explanation when it is required of him. Perhaps it is only, "We do this because, if we did not, the spirits would be offended."

In any event, the ideology is one which satisfies the participant; it justifies his role in terms of personal advantages accruing to him. Thus, burial practices may be explained as necessary to prevent the spirits of the dead from returning to annoy the living or, possibly, as necessary to assure that these spirits will be happy in the afterworld. In the former instance, the self-interest nature of the explanation to those who bury the dead is obvious.

In the latter case, proper burial affects only the welfare of the departed. Those who provide that burial have, however, a personal interest in it, in that, by setting a good example, they increase their own chances of being given a proper burial upon death.

To those who hold them, ideological explanations for any mode of institutional behavior are quite logical and intelligible. Evident to the scientist, however, is the fact that ideological explanations for participation in institutional behavior are sheer social fictions. The ideological reasons, for example, for the participation of an individual in situations of a religious order are always in terms of his personal interests—threat of punishment, promise of rewards, etc., in the afterlife. Actually, of course, the reason for the participation of an individual in religion is, under a going social order, that such participation contributes to the fulfillment of long-run, collective ends. It may be that in the long run and on the average, such participation is individually advantageous. But for any specific situation, participation is far more likely to run counter to actual self-interest.

Institutional ideologies normally are kept in the background. Only when the stresses of social change prevent the maintenance of a given institutional pattern do these ideologies loom large in the minds of people. In contemporary America many people cling to and constantly refer back to ideologies which surrounded the institution of the patriarchal family. This is particularly evident in regard to sex behavior and only less apparent in regard to the relationships between parent and child. It still happens occasionally that a father will stand upon his rights as a father to prevent his child from being taken to public school or from being given modern medical care. For such resistance to legal pressure he will advance explanations quite in keeping with a system of family life which began to go out of practice more than a century ago. It often happens, therefore, that ideologies outlive the institutional practices which they once served to justify. . . .

It must not be assumed . . . that institutional behavior is mechanical, as accurately predetermined as are the movements of the various parts of a fine watch. Whatever else they may be, human beings are never robots. Thus, although the actors in a given scene behave according to the script of the play, that scene will never be reenacted in exactly the same way. Even the same cast will give a variable performance from night to night. This variability may arise from one or both of two circumstances: although he endeavors to play his role as it is written, an actor may prove inept; although he knows his role well, the actor may display initiative and may thereby embellish his part by deviating from the script. It is by deviations of this latter order that the superlative performance is achieved. Mechanized exactitude kills the spirit of a play, just as meticulous rendering of a symphony makes dull music.

In much the same way, each institutional interaction is in some ways unique. Institutional factors set the basic patterns; but human beings play the roles—meticulously, blunderingly, or superlatively. No people have been human marionettes, responding automatically to the dictates of the social system under which they live and which makes possible the maintenance of their group life. Although study of a great number of comparable institutional situations may lead to the perception of a common social pattern, each situation in itself is in some small part the product of the individual initiative and the trial-and-error efforts of its members.

Furthermore, it must not be supposed that even in a stable society all . . . behavior is institutional in character. Thus, under the patriarchal family system, the members of a family do not necessarily behave in terms of their institutional roles all the time. The children of such a family might, for example, behave in their institutional roles during the family dinner, only to behave in ways quite improper for brothers and sisters the moment they leave the table. Upon their leaving, their father and mother might relax and indulge in banter more fitting to lovers than to stern parents.

In the highly integrated society, the basic collective needs are satisfied through institutional mechanisms. By these, the fundamental patterns of collective life are fixed. But it may be suspected that no social system yet devised has been so well equilibrated that it could mold all its incoming members to fit that system perfectly. Inevitably, some individuals will try to shape the system to suit their particular tastes.

CULTURAL CHANGE

In Western civilization we often make the mistake of attempting to account for cultural change in terms of material or technological change. That is, we point to the advent of satellites and space flight, and call it cultural change. The flaw in this thinking is the tendency to account for change by use of example only. Moreover, changes in the nonmaterial aspects of culture can never be explained by the "example" method. Finally, we run the risk of confusing change with progress.[9]

Progress has one major implication: that a culture of necessity is moving toward a particular goal. Political history demonstrates this idea in the White Man's Burden of the nineteenth century. The price for these historical "necessities" was high. But social science makes no claim for historical goals in its concept of change: it is rather a means of describing what is now taking place, not what ought to be.

A culture may change through the *discovery* of new knowledge.[10] Discovery, of course, is sometimes accidental but seldom do we simply stumble on an unknown piece of knowledge. More often new knowledge results from concentrated and rational research into a particular problem. A second way in which cultures change is through *invention*, the practical application of something that has been discovered. It is not unusual for a discovery to lie idle for years because there is no practical use for it. This is true, for example, in research in physics where the bombardment of a particular type of atom has resulted in the unexpected production of many elements whose uses remain completely unknown at this time. Discoveries, applied initially in one form, are often combined in newer forms, as in the automobile. Drive shafts, gears, wheels, electrodes, and internal combustion engines had all been known long before they were fused into the automobile. A third way in which cultures change is by diffusion, which literally means a borrowing between cultures. Diffusion increased the pace of life in the late Middle Ages as the Crusades broadened the world perspective of Europe; diffusion accounted for the rapidity of Japanese transition from a feudal way of life to an industrial order in less than 50 years. In short, diffusion releases any culture from the necessity of having to discover or invent everything it uses.

Although all cultures change to some degree, the rate of change within any one culture may vary. One aspect of the culture may develop much faster than another. For example, the development of the automobile has been much faster than our ability to create either roads or legislation to regulate the auto. William Ogburn, an American social scientist, called the differential rate of change *culture lag*.[11] Ogburn divided culture into two parts: material culture and adaptive culture. Material culture consists of those things wrought by invention and discovery. Adaptive culture is the institutions created by man and the values and beliefs around which such institutions are organized. To Ogburn, the material culture changes more rapidly than the adaptive culture; hence, the latter tends to "lag" behind the former.

The adaptive culture may lag behind the material for a number of reasons. There are, for instance, those persons who find that maintenance of existing conditions is to their own best advantage. As a consequence, they resist change in the areas of ideas and institutions. There are also those whose reaction is one of fear. They believe that any change in the adaptive culture would be a threat to their own security and, in their view, a threat to the entire society. They want institutions to act as a break on change. Education, for example, by accumulating the traditions of a society, may block change in the adaptive culture.

Whatever the reasons for culture lag, Ogburn believed the process to be a major cause of our social problems. This conclusion has been debated in the social sciences. Perspectives on this issue will be gained as we study human communities, their institutions, and their problems.

Notes

1. Alfred L. Kroeber and Talcott Parsons, "The Concepts of Culture and of Social System," *American Sociological Review*, Vol. 23, October 1958, p. 583. This is a narrower definition than often is used in anthropology. For a criticism see R. D. Gastil, "The Determinants of Human Behavior," *American Anthropologist*, Vol. 63, December 1961, pp. 1281–91.
2. Cf. Richard La Piere, A *Theory of Social Control*, New York: McGraw-Hill Book Company, 1954, p. 30.
3. Ernst Cassirer, An *Essay on Man*, New Haven: Yale University Press, 1944, *passim*.
4. Graham Sumner, *Folkways*, New York: Mentor Books, 1960, p. 21.
5. See Abram Kardiner, *The Psychological Frontiers of Society*, New York: Columbia University Press, 1945; Margaret Mead, *Sex and Temperament in Three Primitive Societies*, New York: Morrow and Company, 1935; Talcott Parsons, *The Social System*, Glencoe, Illinois: The Free Press, 1951, pp. 227 ff.
6. For a rather good evaluation of culture-personality studies see A. R. Lindemith and Anselm Strauss, "A Critique of Culture-Personality Writings," *American Sociological Review*, Vol. 15, pp. 587–600.
7. Sumner, *op. cit.*, pp. 61 ff.
8. Ruth Benedict, *Patterns of Culture*, New York: Mentor Books, 1946, pp. 249–250. The necessity of understanding the consequences of interrelationships in a social organization is pertinent. In the social sciences this is commonly referred to as "functional analysis." Some consequences are relevant in a meaningful or useful way whereas others may be harmful. The former category is called functional, the latter disfunctional. An abundant literature on this analysis exists— a system, incidentally, not without its difficulties. Central to the discussion are the following works: Talcott Parsons, *op. cit.*; Robert K. Merton, *Social Theory and Social Structure*, Glencoe, Illinois: The Free Press, 1957, Rev. Ed., pp. 19–84; and Kingsley Davis, "The Myth of Functional Analysis as a Special Method in Anthropology and Sociology," *American Sociological Review*, Vol. 24, December 1959, pp. 757–772.
9. From J. B. Bury, *The Idea of Progress*, London: The Macmillan Company, 1920.
10. Ralph Linton, *The Study of Man*, New York: D. Appleton-Century Company, 1936. For a recent review of theories see Wilbert Moore, "A Reconsideration of Theories of Social Change," *American Sociological Review*, Vol. 25, December 1960, pp. 810–818.
11. William Fielding Ogburn, *Social Change*, New York: Viking Press, 1922.

Selected Readings

*Du Bois, Cora. *The People of Alor*. New York: Harper Torchbooks, 1961. 2 vols.
*Kluckhohn, Clyde. *Mirror for Man*. Greenwich, Conn.: Premier Publications, 1962.
*Mead, Margaret. *Culture Patterns and Technical Change*. New York: Mentor Books, 1959.
*Sorokin, Pitirim. *Society, Culture, and Personality*. New York: Harper and Bros., 1947.
*Wallace, Anthony. *Culture and Personality*. New York: Random House, 1961.

* Paperback edition.

Part Two
Community Structure
and Processes

In the four chapters of Part One we developed some tools of analysis, a set of concepts and themes, by which to understand better the nature of human behavior. As we moved in our survey from the specific nature of the biological organism, through the study of personality and the human group, to the more general processes of culture there was the constant reminder that human beings do not live in so many vacuums. Human life is group life—more than that, human life is community life. Part Two is devoted to understanding the structure of human communities and the processes which operate within them.

The materials of Part Two necessarily draw upon those of Part One. Particular use will be made of such concepts as the distinction between primary groups and secondary groups, and the distinction between traditional societies and urban societies. These two distinctions will be helpful in indicating certain changes that have occurred in the communities within each type of society. Also of use will be the concept of institutions developed in Chapter 5. Although the nature of community life may seem rather broad, at first, for further understanding the nature of personality, we will find that further depth is added to our knowledge of the concept as we relate individual, group, and community to one another.

Part Two is comprised of three chapters. Chapter 6 deals with the concept of the human community. A survey is made of the spatial nature of community development and the implications of that development for group life. An institutional conception of the human community is also developed. The three aspects of community life—space, groups, and institutions—are then applied to communities in traditional societies. Chapter 7 traces the change from traditional societies to urban societies. Trends in population, the particular spatial qualities of communities in urban societies, and the recent surge of suburban development are discussed. Chapter 8 is concerned with social stratification in urban communities as it emerges from the increased complexity of role and status systems created, in turn, by changes in the division of labor.

With the completion of Part Two we turn to the study of specific institutions within urban communities.

Chapter 6

The Concept of Community

Man is a symbol and culture-making animal. He is also a *community-making* animal. From earliest paleolithic time man has lived a communal life. This chapter is concerned with the nature of that life.

Any community, irrespective of the society in which it exists, is composed of three basic systems.[1] First, a community contains an ecological system: the organization of community life based upon man's adaptation to the physical environment. Second, a community is a system of social organization: that is, the relationships of individuals and groups. Third, a community is a place within which values, beliefs, and attitudes are expressed.

THE ECOLOGY OF THE COMMUNITY [2]

The adaptation of organisms to their environment is seldom individual in character. Rather it is communal, based on the interdependency of the various organisms in the environment. Charles Darwin described such interdependence as a web of life. His classic example involved an interdependence of red clover, bees, field mice, and cats. Darwin noted that bees pollinated the clover in such a way that the greater number of bees in a given season the more red clover. He also observed that the number of bees depended on the number of field mice who lived by raiding the bee hives. In turn, the field mice population was related to the number of cats. Ultimately, the amount of red clover depended on the size of the cat population.

In his example, Darwin described two ecological processes. The first is *symbiosis* which refers to the mutual dependence of dissimilar organisms. Bees, mice, and cats are enemies but they constitute one another's food supply. This is an example of symbiosis. The relation between the clover and the bees is another. But symbiosis alone does not hold together the web of life. A second ecological process, *commensalism*, also serves as a force of cohesion. Commensalism refers to the competitive

99

relationship among members of a single species. The field mice provide a good example. If the cat population should diminish, there is the probability that the mouse population will increase, which may be stimulated further by uninterrupted raiding of the bees. Indiscriminate nest raiding, however, destroys the source of food for the next generation of mice. As a consequence, the now overplentiful mice compete with one another for a depleted source of food.

Every web of life exists within a habitat, that is, the inorganic part of the environment: weather, soil, and temperature. Organisms must adapt to the particular habitat in which they live or, as we shall see in the case of man, they must change it. Within any given habitat some organisms are able to survive; others are not. Those that do survive because of the particular web of life that has emerged among them in the habitat are said to live in a *biotic* community. This is a community in the sense that the common need of adaptation to the habitat has been achieved collectively through interdependencies within the web of life.

The web of life within a biotic community is constantly fluctuating. Change in one part of the community brings about change in other parts. The impact of change is determined by its relative importance in the over-all functioning of the community. The loss of one cat in a web of life is of greater significance to the biotic community than is the loss of one mouse or one bee. On the other hand, the addition of owls or hawks will dramatically affect the interdependencies and create new configurations within the web of life.

Man is the only organism in nature with the ability to adapt to any habitat in which he finds himself. Many animals swim in water. Man swims; he also floats down the river on a log. Many animals eat only vegetation; others only meat. Man eats both. Some animals perform in certain feats with greater power and agility than man. But no animal exercises dominance over both his habitat and web of life in which he finds himself. The degree of dominance, however, will depend on man's perception and awareness of the *nature* of the habitat and the web of life.

In many traditional societies, especially those characterized as primitive, there is a direct relation between the habitat, the web of life in the habitat, and man's place in the web. Primitive man must hunt his prey, often competing with lower forms of animal life for the same sources of food. The Hottentots of South Africa, for example, are known to hunt for the same types of vegetation eaten by baboons and other species.[3] Primitive man is also as susceptible to the vagaries of nature as any other organism. Drought, which sends game in search of water, makes it necessary for primitive man to follow the game. Fire and storm may find man and animal competing for the same refuge.

The commensalistic process also operates in a direct manner. In the search for food one group of people may find itself in competition with another group for the same source. Competition develops when the sustenance of one biotic community becomes inadequate to support its population, forcing the population to invade the territory of another biotic community. When, for example, the fishing waters of a clan of Northwest Coast Indians becomes depleted, that clan will likely move to a better site. Competition arising with another clan for the same site could lead to attempts at accommodation by cultural means as exemplified in Northwest Coast culture by the famous *potlatch* ceremony.[4] This is a rivalry of gift-giving in which one clan or tribe, by giving away and destroying its own property, attempts to shame another clan into submission. If the group originally claiming the fishing waters triumphs at the potlatch, the invading clan will have to withdraw. If attempts at accommodation fail, war could likely ensue.

In agrarian cultures the problems of adaptation revolve about the necessity for securing a bountiful crop. Again, the competition for space can give rise to forms of accommodation. In medieval Europe, for instance, a form of agriculture known as the three field system and strip tillage developed. The land was divided into three fields, two put into production while the remaining one lay fallow. The fields were rotated each year. Within each field the land was divided into strips, thereby preventing the likelihood of one or a few farmers possessing plots of highly arable land while others tilled rocky or sandy soil. All had a share in the land, good and bad.

A biotic community of man is a system of dynamic relationships, in which change may come about in a variety of ways: the discovery of new food; the invention of a new tool; a different distribution in the division of labor. Man's struggle to create a habitat totally his own is culminated in the urban community.[5] The city is the concrete manifestation of man's dominance over nature.

Symbiosis and commensalism continue to function as ecological processes within the urban community, with somewhat altered characteristics. In an urban community there remains the necessity for providing the means of survival; however, the fact of division of labor relegates sheer survival to minor concern. Agriculture itself has been subject to the division of labor, and industrialization with fewer people is now directly involved in the production of foods. Changes in the American farm population provide a striking example. In 1920 the farm population of the United States comprised 30.1 per cent of the total population of the United States. By 1960 it had fallen to only 8.7 per cent of the total.[6]

The process of symbiosis in an urban community is also rendered less rigid by advances in transportation. Indeed, the advent of the railroad, and later, interstate trucking, was a direct factor in the feeding, and hence the establishment of large urban communities. Hundreds of miles of freeway and new design in refrigerated trucking, especially, now make possible the long distance shipment of short-lived food products.

With an ever greater proportion of the population living in urban communities the process of symbiosis undergoes further change. *Inter*species symbiosis is supplanted by *intra*species symbiosis, still another consequence of the division of labor. A new, man-made web of life, a new system of interdependencies, emerges. This interdependence consists of a complexity of functions that must be performed to maintain life in the urban community, functions not only economic, but also political, religious, educational, familial, recreational, and esthetic. In one form or another, they are the universals of human life, with the difference that, in the urban community, order in these functions is obtained through the rational processes of law. (The traditional society, as we have seen, relies heavily on the folkways and mores for orderly function.) Moreover, the functions of an urban community soon reach a point of specialization which makes it difficult for any one individual to understand intimately, or participate in them all.

Commensalism, too, experiences change as the urban community develops. Competition for immediate sources of survival is minimized, at the same time that competition among the *related functions* within the community increases. The familiar example may be cited of competition for physical space between economic functions of a similar nature—say retail department stores. One store may purchase an adjacent office building and convert it into space for business. The added space means more stock, an increase in the variety of goods displayed, and expanded customer area within the store. As store number one shows a profit others soon follow the pattern. The result is an outward spatial movement of the business district.

An impetus to growth in any community arises from the nature and location of transportation. The presence of a harbor, the existence of a railway hub, or the bisecting of the community by major highways determines the location of economic activity and, in turn, the residential and subsidiary business functions.

As the means of transportation becomes extended, as land use within the urban community becomes concentrated (accompanied by rising land values), the city begins, literally, to sprawl. The result is the unplanned, unorganized fringe city, and the high density suburb.

From the viewpoint of human ecology, the man-made biotic community is able to be understood through the processes of symbiosis and commensalism. Modern urban man has achieved mightily in dealing with his habitat. His problem is to adapt to the environment that he has created for himself.

THE SOCIAL ORGANIZATION OF COMMUNITIES

The social organization of a community derives from the unique relationship existing between an individual and the group of which he is a member. Our discussion of ecology pointed up the close relationship between simple physical space and social organization. We have also noted a commonplace in traditional society: the individual's intimate knowledge of the space in which he lives. Indeed, in the most primitive communities, man is concerned not only with his tilled fields, but also the game trails, meadows, forest, and landmarks. These are all meaningful spatial relations. He depends on them for immediate survival.

In the spoken history of many primitive peoples we often discover an unbroken use of the land, sometimes reaching back through 20 or 30 generations. The land remains in the possession of the same families, in trust, so to speak, by each generation for the one to come after.[7] A village in one of these societies is often nothing more than a cluster of families, related by blood or marriage. The Yugoslavian *zadruga*, for example, is a joint family group, a village related through marriage. As a new family is founded, a new house is added to the village, so that the community itself serves as a kind of spatial patterning of generations.

Urban communities present a startling contrast to the communities of traditional societies. Seldom does an individual know with any intimacy the total physical space of the urban area—one reason being, of course, that the urban area comprises more differentiated uses of space than one person can hope to comprehend.[8]

The nature of property ownership has also changed. By and large, private individuals and corporations, rather than families, own urban property. Changed, too, is the attitude toward property. Instead of being held in trust for succeeding generations, urban property is consumed as a commodity and utilized as an investment. Sentiment is lost in the rational pursuit of profit. This is true not only of commercial and industrial properties but also of residential property. The realtor's assurance that the $18,950 house can be "fixed up" nicely to sell for $24,000 in five or six years makes an attractive sales appeal to the profit-minded prospect.

The change in the attitude toward property is given further impetus by two additional factors. One is the high rate of physical mobility among the urban population. The search for new and better occupational opportunities, job transfer by the company, and the migration of a rural population to urban communities suggest a physically unstable population. The second factor concerns the expectations regarding property ownership in the urban community. In an older, traditional setting, the father expected to pass the land on to his son. Today's expectation is that the son will acquire his own home and property. The rate of consumption of the father's property, the shared wish for a better life for the son, the anticipation of a new home with new conveniences all contribute to the newer view.

The difference in the individual's relation to the space within traditional and urban communities will markedly influence the nature of his social interaction. The homogeneous, closely knit character of the traditional society makes for direct interaction, intimate by virtue of duration through the years, meaningful because of the contexts in which it occurs.[9] It is not surprising that many writers emphasize the major role of primary group relationships in the solidarity of traditional societies.[10]

A diversified and constantly shifting urban population, on the other hand, fosters social interaction between individuals which tends to be secondary in nature.[11] Mutual claims are transitory. They relate to the one specific function shared within the urban setting and do not touch other segments of the individual's life. Indeed, urban man will often compartmentalize his life to prevent intrusion by a stranger.

The vast number of secondary relationships within urban communities does not mean that there are no primary groups. Families, peers, cliques, and some work groups are found in any type of community—but in the urban setting, more often than not, there is no interaction *between groups*. Those primary group relations pertaining to family membership illustrate this. It is not uncommon for parents and children to have separate sets of friends. Of course, there may be an acquaintance between the parents of the children who are friends, but this may be based on convenience rather than a bond of intimacy. Both parents and children may have sets of friends related only to specific situations. For the parents there are friends at work, friends in the neighborhood, and social friends —none of whom are the same people. There may also be sex differences:

the husband with his "Saturday morning golf chums"; the wife with her "Thursday evening bridge girls." Each is potentially a primary group, with none necessarily relating to the other.

Interaction within the urban community is indirect due to lack of group cohesion and the rapid tempo of life.[12] People respond to indirect interaction in three typical ways. The first response is delegation.[13] For the airing of opinions which, individually, might never be heard, people seek such forms of representation as interest groups, clubs, associations, and political parties. These voluntary associations again emphasize the secondary nature of urban group life because the values around which they are organized seldom encompass the entire life of the individual members.

The urbanites' second response to indirect interaction has been the formation of spontaneous, transitory social groupings in relation to some issue. The latter is not planned organization, as in delegation. Transitory groupings, as we learned in Chapter 4, are called publics. The total membership of a particular public is never known, hence, the members have a need to communicate as widely as possible in the hope of reaching a maximum number of interested persons and also the need for information on which to base a decision. This accounts, in part, for the development and popularity of the mass media of communication in urban communities.

The difficulties with the mass media are many, but this much can be said: the communication tends to be one way, with no reciprocity, no return communication. The nature of the interaction is indeed indirect. Nor is communication always certain about the composition of its publics. To counter these difficulties, which are multiplied by a vast competition for the eyes and ears of urban man, communicators frequently try to heighten their impact. Sudden increases in sound, bold colors, offbeat promotional schemes, anything that will interrupt the din of life and capture attention is considered a valid communication technique.

The third response to indirect interaction is completely contrary to the others; it is a feeling of powerlessness, a judgment by the individual that his behavior, despite his social associations, cannot influence the course of events.[14] Powerlessness is illustrated by the comment, "I am only one person. What can I do?" This response to indirect interaction stems from the fractional relations experienced within the urban community. It results also from the impact on the individual of the number and density of people in the community, and from the awe with which he views the existing and bewildering system of social relations.

INSTITUTIONS IN THE TRADITIONAL COMMUNITY

In the last chapter we reached the understanding that values and beliefs do not exist apart from people. Individuals living in society share their culture and transmit it to one another. The community is the setting in which the sharing and transmitting of values and beliefs takes place. The sharing and transmitting of culture occur, as we have seen, through institutions, for individuals possess common needs and aspirations which can be pursued most effectively together. With respect to the culture concept, any community—in addition to being an ecological system and a system of social organization—is a complex of institutions.[15]

In the primitive communities of traditional societies the institutions frequently are limited to those necessary for survival. Whether the economy is a nomadic hunting, pastoral, or sedentary agricultural type is immaterial. Within such a community, property tends to be owned by families; tools and weapons may be owned by the family or by the clan. Socialization and education are one and the same. Thus, when the individual reaches puberty in these communities he is considered an adult. Religion is not practiced so much for emotional comforts or the worship of an abstract deity as for a desire to control nature in order to aid the hunter or obtain a larger crop. Even art is bent to the problem of survival. Not infrequently, targets of the hunt are painted in the belief that by painting these animals, the artists can control the spirits.[16]

In traditional societies which are primitive, industrial, or completely commercial, the institutional pattern assumes a different character. It takes no one particular form because the bases of the varied cultural influences in these types of societies tend to be much broader than in primitive ones. What does appear to be common among these societies is that the immediate problem of survival seems reasonably well solved through a stabilization of the economy. Not all current production goes for current consumption. This is made possible by the discovery of new foods, the development of better grains, the improvement of animal husbandry, and the perfection of more efficient tools. The same factors that enable man to dominate his habitat contribute to changes in the institutional pattern of his community. Both religion and art are free here to seek new directions rather than remain bound to survival. Although there may be a distinction between the socialization of the child in the family and education as a special institution, there may be an awareness of roles other than those contributing directly to survival.

A good example of such a preindustrial community was the feudal village of medieval Europe,[17] a complex of institutions composed of family agriculture, Church, and feudal nobility. Although an obvious division of labor existed in these villages, there was also a strong web of interdependence. The three-field system of planting, mentioned earlier, was the economic base of feudalism. The serfs who tilled the fields were sometimes free men but more often were bound in servitude to the feudal lord. The feudal lord not only depended on the crop yield to maintain himself and his entourage; he also relied on such taxes as he could levy upon the serfs from time to time. The serfs, in addition to field work, constructed roads, bridges, canals, and the castle in time of peace, and acted as foot soldiers in time of war. The lord, in turn, fed the poor, cared for the sick and wounded as he might, kept order among his people through the offices of feudal law, and often tried to improve agriculture.

The system remained stable as long as it did because of the Catholic Church which laid the mantle of God's Will over all. Not only the moral order of the Church but also the entire social order was conceived to have been ordained by God. Divine ordination, of course, placed the Church in a powerful position in relation to the other institutions of feudal society. The power of the Church was compromised, to a degree, by its dependence on the two other major institutions, agriculture and nobility. The greater number of the clergy, with the exception of various monastic orders that were self-sustaining, depended on the work and will of the serfs for sustenance. The Church, itself, depended on the feudal nobility for the extension and support of Church power.

The well-knit web of life of feudal Europe was, after a fashion, the major source of its downfall. Any change in one phase of life automatically creates changes in all others. When new efficiencies and new directions arose in Europe, they had a drastic effect on the institutional pattern. The Crusades of the eleventh and twelfth centuries stimulated travel and trade with the Near East, ushering in the age of exploration. A revival of town life occurred in the late Middle Ages. These communities, politically, militarily, and economically independent of feudal ties, possessing the core of a commercial middle class, geared to market conditions rather than to feudal tradition, became a vital force in the growth and expansion of life in Europe (see Chapter 14).

INSTITUTIONS IN THE URBAN COMMUNITY

The early trends of change were given additional force in the seventeenth and eighteenth centuries. This period, known as the Enlightenment, was characterized by the growth of the physical and biological sciences and the political and economic philosophies which were expressions of the right of the individual and of property—in contrast to the rights of hereditary power. It was also a time of revolution, bringing political and social revolutions in England, America, and France, and the Industrial Revolution in England, soon to be diffused among the greater part of Western Civilization.

The industrial city which culminated these changes was a completely new complex of highly specialized institutions. The location of economic activity within the industrial city, as we shall see in greater detail, greatly influenced the density of population and spatial characteristics of the urban community. There is also evidence to indicate that the development of governmental functions has had similar influences.[18]

It would be easy to conclude that economic and political institutions, like the family in traditional communities, have been the binding force in urban communities. This is not the case. Neither institution has been a binding force.[19] In the economic institution, absentee ownership has often been a disruptive influence, lending itself to disinterest in the total welfare of the community in favor of the *status quo*. Direct influence has been exercised by corporation officials who obtain office, sit on the governing boards of recreation and sanitation districts, or become school trustees. Indirect influence has been derived through membership in service and social clubs, through financial control of the mass media of communication, and through graft.

Government in the urban community is a paradox. In the effort to extend more efficient services to rapidly expanding populations, urban governments have become proliferated to the point where they can actually break down, rather than integrate, the community. A study by Edward Banfield and Morton Grodzins indicated that in 1950 more than one-half of the total population of the United States lived in 168 metropolitan areas.[20] By 1960 nearly 70 per cent of the population was living in 212 metropolitan areas. There were 16,000 separate governments in those 168 metropolitan areas containing more than half the 1950 U.S. population.[21] Metropolitan New York alone had 1071 different local governments.[22] Water districts, light districts, recreational districts, special assessment districts for everything from sidewalks to urban renewal, school districts, library districts, and sewer districts are typical of the various kinds of urban governments. Each has the right to tax. Each has its own board of directors whose members, in most instances, are elected. None relates to any other in any coordinated fashion and all are separate from the functions of the central city government. Not one of the metropolitan areas has a single over-all governmental structure.[23]

The lack of integration within urban communities is related to the argument that modern man is in search of values, is rootless, alienated from himself and the world about him.[24] The viewpoint developed so far in this study of human behavior supports the bulk of this argument. Modern man *is* rootless and alienated in many ways from himself and the surrounding world. That he is searching for values is questionable. Value systems have existed, so far as is known, as long as man. They exist today. The real problem appears to be the quest for community.[25] For only within a meaningful system of community can any set of values become significant in the lives of the population. When both spatial and social relations are such that they foster the dissolution of community, no system of values is likely to be meaningful.

THE COMMUNITY IN TRADITIONAL SOCIETY

We turn now to the application of the elements of systems of community life. In America, traditional society has been synonymous with the rural past. This is quite different from Europe because in America we never experienced a true feudalism. A case has been made for the translation of the manorial system from Europe to the American South,[26] but there were too many differences between the systems. Rural America generally developed in semi-isolation. Farms were spatially separated. Villages were few and far between and their functions in the rural life about them were limited. Indeed, the vast spaces of the American wilderness and prairie appeared to consume the population as fast as it emigrated.

In the selection that follows, James Williams depicts some of the pronounced characteristics of traditional, rural life in America. Three factors stand out in his discussion: first, the relationship between individuals and space; second, the patterns of interaction formed by individuals and the institutions within which they function; and, third, the consciousness of individuals of the spatial relations and patterns of interaction within which they move.

Williams' selection begins the description of the three elements of community as developed in this chapter. The description continues in Chapter 7, which deals with the urban community, and in Chapter 8, concerned with social stratification. The analysis goes deeper in Part Three, in which specific institutions within traditional and urban societies are studied.

* The rural community, up to the time of the Civil War, remained comparatively isolated from the outside world. Canals and railroads had been built connecting the cities with the seaboard, but most of the rural villages still relied on stage routes. Traveling was slow and uncomfortable and was undertaken only in case of necessity. This isolation accentuated the group consciousness of the community.

Within the community the neighborhoods maintained their early distinctness. Even though not very congenial with his neighbors, the farmer was intensely conscious of them and curious about outsiders. Though hospitable he was apt to be a bit suspicious of outsiders. Many stories illustrate this. Several farmers were sitting in a country store when a young man, a stranger, came in. "Looks a little like rain," he ventured affably. No response. Finally one farmer queried, "What may your name be?"

"James Hammond. My grandfather used to live just a mile up the road."

"Oh, Bill Hammond! Ye-es, it does look a little like rain. . . ."

The attitude of familiar intercourse among the members of the rural neighborhood and of aloofness toward outsiders was pronounced in certain families of most of the neighborhoods of our typical community up to 1900. For instance, in that year Blankwell, which had a post office, was contemplating applying for a rural mail delivery service, which had already been installed at the Center, a neighborhood lying three miles nearer the village. But the leading citizen of Blankwell opposed the rural delivery and his influence prevailed for some time. He said, "We are a little community here by ourselves. We want the post office. We want the people to come here for their mail and meet one another and so perpetuate the good feeling of our hamlet."

This neighborhood consciousness was a consciousness of people living in the same small area. They might have no vital interests in common and might have different occupations. The point is that they lived in a small area on the roads of which they might meet one another at any time. So the characteristic reaction was the conventional salutation with which people greet those with whom they are familiar. The habit of "speaking to everybody" comes from the rural neighborhood where everybody is known to and speaks to everybody else. This habit sometimes persists when rural people settle in a larger place, where they are criticized for speaking to people whom they do not know. While the members of the neighborhood might have no vital interests in common, the neighborhood configuration of each member included many common ways of acting and believing and there was always a reaction against a new way. As the reaction against strangers was pronounced, so was that against strange ways of acting and thinking.

* From *The Expansion of Rural Life*, by James M. Williams, pp. 32–44. Published by Crofts, 1926. By permission of the author.

The neighborhood configuration of the individual included: (1) a conscious attitude of askance toward outsiders; (2) a conscious attitude of familiarity toward members; (3) a consciousness of being judged by outsiders, to a certain extent, as a member of a neighborhood, rather than as an individual; (4) a consciousness of being under the pressure of the neighborhood to follow its ways and profess its beliefs and sentiments, though this behavior might not always be personally agreeable. Families would not always submit to this pressure and more than one family moved from an uncongenial neighborhood to one more satisfying. In our typical community a family moved out of one section into another "to get out of that ungodly neighborhood." A family in an "ungodly" neighborhood feared the bad influences on its children and imagined that outsiders might "class" it with the other "ungodly" families. The individual got his meaning, to outsiders who did not know him personally, from the attitudes of the groups to which he belonged—from the attitudes of his family and his neighborhood—and the group influence in many cases tended to justify that meaning. That is, because of subservience to social pressure the character of the individual tended to be moulded after the pattern of the configurations that constituted his or her social environment. Loyalty was felt to require conformity to the attitudes and beliefs of one's family and community.

The we-feeling of the neighborhood was not at that time weakened by the differentiation of economic conditions and by the rise of distinctive agricultural industries that has since taken place. Even the professional man— the doctor, the lawyer—was not so distinct an individual as he is today in the village or city. Many stories that illustrate this common level of all individuals have for generations been current in the rural districts. For instance, a certain farmer, no matter how ill he was, would not permit his family to call a doctor; and, if one was called, he would not take the medicine prescribed. This averseness to having a doctor was a common rural trait, but the man in this case was particularly stubborn. To him the doctor knew little more about illness than anybody else and his remedies were no better than "home remedies." After getting over an illness in the course of which the doctor had been called and had left medicine, this farmer one day called to the doctor as he was passing and handed him the medicine with the words, "Here, Doc, I'll return your medicine and as soon as I get time I'll return your visits." Humor, fellow-feeling, and self-reliance were aspects of the behavior of the early neighborhood in which all were familiar, equal, much alike and similarly aloof toward outsiders.

The isolation of the neighborhood preserved the definiteness of that group. The village was a less definite group. Not only was there greater diversity in occupations but also each villager was less likely than the man in the country to meet all the others frequently. A stranger aroused somewhat less interest in the village than in a rural neighborhood because the villagers were less definitely known to one another and a stranger was by contrast less noticeable. But within some village populations there had developed, at the beginning of the first period of rural expansion, as definite groups as the neighborhood. One of these was the village aristocracy, that is, certain old families the ancestors of which had made money and which, though now no more wealthy than some newly rich families, had, for two generations, associated intimately and exclusively. They prided themselves not on their wealth for they sneered at the "new rich," and not on their culture for they regarded lightly an unusual family which had bright children away at college, but rather on their status. They were the aristocracy and they could become very much excited over a new rich family that presumed itself worthy to enter their circle. In their reaction against new ways of acting or thinking they showed a more extreme intolerance than that of the rural neighborhood.

The social pressure of the community was accentuated by the proneness of the rural mind to obsessions of dislike. As physical isolation conduces to a suspicious attitude toward strangers, so mental isolation conduces to a dislike of new ways and new ideas. One who behaved differently in a certain respect from his neighbors or had different ideas was disliked. The difference might be so insignificant that the person was not indignantly condemned but was called "just queer." A dislike made the mind susceptible to ideas that accentuated it, so that all sorts of stories might be circulated about the queer person. The isolation and monotony of rural life encouraged gossip and accentuated emotional states. Gossip gave the imagination free play, with little regard to the truth of what was expressed. The most interesting gossip was gossip against somebody so that people were quite likely to conform from "fear of what people would say." Of course this attribute, like the others we have mentioned in this chapter, is characteristic of all social configurations. One finds, even in groups of so-called educated people, a dislike of the nonconformist as such, a tendency to avoid dislike by conformity, and a tendency to gossip. The attributes are most pronounced in isolated groups because the latter are clearly defined, the distinctions between the group and outsiders are clearly seen, and isolation heightens the appreciation of the group ways and the aversion to other ways of doing and thinking.

The pressure exerted by a group proceeds especially from representative members. The exemplary citizen is expected to assume the attitude which the rank and file should take to any situation. In the rural family it was an axiom of behavior that the members should accept without question the attitude of the father to a particular situation. The father's customary attitude to his family was, "I expect you to respect my attitude." They were to accept it without dispute and even without asking his reasons. In the neighborhood the people expected one another to accept the attitude of leading citizens to a particular situation or issue; the leading citizens expected their "say-so" to be accepted without question. Of course the attitude of liberty frequently upset this expectation; the leading citizens themselves did not always agree, for instance on political questions, but there was a tendency for groups to form around leaders and for one—the Republican group—to "swear by what Squire Haven says" and another—the Democratic—to "swear by what Squire Williams says." These leaders were quite likely to be old-time rivals for some town office as, for example, justice of the peace. They expected their attitudes toward various questions to be accepted by their respective followings; and the people acquiesced in this expectation. Thus there was a strong tendency toward conformity in the isolated neighborhood. The minister exemplified this spirit. He was expected not to "side with" either party to a controversy, either in the church or in the community, but to confine himself to the lofty presentation of divine truth about which there could be no difference of opinion.

The smaller configurations, as families, rural neighborhoods, and village social sets are more definite than larger ones, because of the intimacy of the relations of the individual members and because of the many things they do in common. For this reason it is difficult to interest farmers in the entire rural community, or villagers in the entire village. In like manner among school boys those on the same street naturally run together and are less interested in their school group as a whole than in their own set. . . .

Social configurations overlap in their functioning. The family attitudes of early rural life were transmuted into neighborhood and church attitudes. On the other hand, religion was a means of increasing social pressure in the family and the neighborhood in that it provided a supernatural sanction of behavior. Thus the configurations were articulated in a general scheme of behavior that adapted the people to their conditions. When the configurations were well articulated, personal impulses, including individual rivalry, were subordinated to the common attitudes and beliefs. The desire for recognition was for recognition of loyalty to family, church, or neighborhood, by living true to the general behavior sponsored by each group and by having a part in the projects undertaken by the groups.

Notes

1. Louis Wirth, "Urbanism as a Way of Life," *American Journal of Sociology*, Vol. XLIV, July 1938, pp. 1–24.
2. The following discussion is taken from Amos Hawley, *Human Ecology*, New York: Ronald Press, 1950, and James Quinn, *Human Ecology*, Englewood Cliffs, N.J.: Prentice-Hall, 1950.
3. Cited in Hawley, *op. cit.*, p. 59.
4. Ruth Benedict, *Patterns of Culture*, New York: Mentor, 1946, Chapter VI.
5. The material specifically related to the growth of cities will be reviewed in Chapter 7.

6. United States Department of Commerce, *Statistical Abstracts of the United States*, 1961, Table 840, p. 613. Redefinition of the category "rural farm" affects the percentages a bit.
7. Oscar Handlin, *The Uprooted*, New York: Universal Library, 1951, Chapter 1.
8. Anselm Strauss, *Images of the American City*, New York; Free Press, 1961, p. 65.
9. Don Martindale, *American Society*, Princeton: D. Van Nostrand, 1960, p. 155.
10. Benedict, *op. cit.*
11. Wirth, *op. cit.*, p. 12.
12. *Ibid.*, p. 13.
13. *Ibid.*
14. Melvin Seeman, "On the Meaning of Alienation," *American Sociological Review*, Vol. 24, December 1959, pp. 784 f.
15. Hawley, *op. cit.*, Chapter 15.
16. Wirth, *op. cit.*, p. 22.
17. The Institutional theory of the city has been most fully developed by Max Weber in his work *The City*, ed. and trans. Don Martindale and Gertrude Neuwirth, Glencoe, Ill.: The Free Press, 1958. For other institutional theories of the community see: Fustel de Coulanges, *The Ancient City*, New York: Anchor Books, 1956; Henri Pirenne, *Medieval Cities*, New York: Anchor Books, 1956; and Henry Sumner Maine, *Ancient Law*, New York: Everyman's Library, 1931.
18. For a survey of functions of primitive art and their relation to style, especially among the Northwest Coast Indians, see Franz Boas, *Primitive Art*, New York: Dover Press, 1955.
19. What follows is a brief and general discussion. For a survey of feudal systems see Rushton Coulborn, *Feudalism in History*, Princeton: Princeton University Press, 1956. For a specific study of the English feudal village see George Coulton, *The Medieval Village*, Cambridge: Cambridge University Press, 1926.
20. O. D. Duncan and A. J. Reiss, *The Social Characteristics of Urban and Rural Communities, 1950*, New York: John Wiley and Sons, Inc., 1956, p. 9.
21. Martindale, *op. cit.*, pp. 194 ff.
22. Cited in *Ibid.*, p. 198.
23. *Ibid.*
24. Emile Durkheim, *Suicide*, Glencoe, Ill.: The Free Press, 1951; Elton Mayo, *The Social Problems of an Industrial Civilization*, Boston: Harvard University School of Business Administration, 1945; Karl Mannheim, *Man and Society in an Age of Reconstruction*, New York: Harcourt, Brace and Company, 1951; and T. S. Eliot, *Notes Toward a Definition of Culture*, New York: Harcourt, Brace and Company, 1949.
25. Robert Nisbet, *The Quest for Community*, New York: Oxford University Press, 1953.
26. Martindale, *op. cit.*, p. 122.

Selected Readings

Durkheim, Emile. *The Division of Labor in Society*. Trans. George Simpson. Glencoe, Ill.: The Free Press, 1933.

Hatt, Paul and A. J. Reiss (eds.). *Cities and Society*. Glencoe, Ill.: The Free Press, 1957.

Mumford, Lewis. *The Culture of Cities*. New York: Harcourt, Brace and Company, 1938.

Park, Robert E. *Human Communities*. Glencoe, Ill.: The Free Press, 1952.

Redfield, Robert. *The Little Community*. Chicago: University of Chicago Press, 1955.

Redfield, Robert. *Peasant Society and Culture*. Chicago: University of Chicago Press, 1956.

Sjoberg, Gideon. *The Preindustrial City*. Glencoe, Ill.: The Free Press, 1960.

Stein, Maurice. *The Eclipse of Community*. Princeton: Princeton University Press, 1960.

Theodorson, George A. (ed.). *Studies in Human Ecology*. Evanston, Ill.: Row-Peterson, 1961.

Chapter 7

The Shift from Traditional to Urban Society

Modern man, searching for personal identity in a world of rapid technological change, often finds himself torn between the old attitudes and beliefs and a new set of values. Either he subscribes to the new values or attempts to escape. The processes of urbanization, bureaucratization, industrialization—especially characteristic of today's world—also add complication and confusion to his "quest for community."

Man's habitat itself has responded most quickly to the acceleration in world change. The tenth century brought the end of the Dark Ages in Western Europe, and the emergence of an "urban development" as towns and cities gradually reappeared. But it was the Industrial Revolution in nineteenth-century England that quickened the pace of urbanization in the Western world, and more recently in Asia and the emergent nations of Africa.

Many city-dwellers feel little satisfaction or sense of fulfillment in the urban community. The image of the farm as opposed to the city, pastoral life versus asphalt jungle, may give rise to real misgivings about the wisdom of leaving the farm. In addition, the permissive nature of secondary association found in the city is a significant factor in the search for escape on the part of the maladjusted urbanite, escape which can include the ultimate choice of suicide.

The remarkable change in America's habitat is illustrated by the shift in the character of the population. In 1860, 80 per cent of America was rural; by 1960, 70 per cent of America lived in an urban environment, and a still greater percentage engaged in nonfarming occupations.

Although the trend toward urban concentration continues in the United States, the nature of the movement is somewhat changed. Many cities are still growing, others are experiencing a renaissance, but none is keeping pace with the general population increase; hence a marked tendency for urban populations to decentralize. The resulting confusion

117

of political, economic, and social structures in the welter of unincorporated subdivisions, school districts, fire districts, mosquito abatement districts, composing a new environmental phenomenon has been labeled megalopolis, interurbia, and exurbia.[1] The extent of countershift is revealed in the 23 million increase in U.S. population between 1950 and 1960; two-thirds of this growth took place on the outskirts of the American city.

A sharp increase in population density heightens the competition for living space—and, given the tendency of the middle class to move out, it is conceivable that some American cities will shortly resemble the foreign model of sharp contrast between the top and the bottom strata of society. As middle-income groups leave the central city, they seek a clearer sense of identity, primary association, and community in a marriage of farm wholesomeness and city convenience.

The future role of the central city is a problem of concern to large numbers of individuals and public and private agencies. How the central city is to be linked to its outlying areas, whether by private automobile or by mass rapid transit, is only one of the major questions surrounding the subject. In the sections that follow we examine more closely the nature of world urbanization, the ecology of the city, and the case for the city.

THE GROWTH OF WORLD URBANIZATION

What causes humans to congregate in increasing numbers once they leave the nomadic life? Does the answer lie simply in a social drive, or is the motivation complicated by economic, political, esthetic, and religious considerations? These questions must be asked because of the historical rural-urban shift, and because it is hard to decide whether the shift is good or bad until its causes are fully understood.

Cities do not rise full-blown on rural soil. They have a genesis and a development which is more or less common throughout the world. With the possible exception of Brasilia, the city, modern or ancient, emerges as a result of the needs felt in the surrounding areas, although in some cases the needs are imposed by outside force. A classic example of the latter is the railroad town of the American West. The railroads, building rapidly under the stimulus of government subsidies, established towns both as a spur to settlement of the investment, and as division points for the physical maintenance of the line.[2] Regardless of the origin of the city, it must continue to meet the needs of the immediate and surrounding population or it decays, and "urban blight" sets in.

We may speak of "urbanized societies," in which a high proportion of the population lives in cities, only in reference to the nineteenth and twentieth centuries. Over the years an increase in urbanization has slowed the rate in older industrial nations, but the acceleration of urban growth in underdeveloped areas keeps the total world rate high. Kingsley Davis, an urban sociologist, has traced this international phenomenon in the following article.

*

Urban phenomena attract sociological attention primarily for four reasons. First, such phenomena are relatively recent in human history. Compared to most other aspects of society—e.g., language, religion, stratification, or the family—cities appeared only yesterday, and urbanization, meaning that a sizable proportion of the population lives in cities, has developed only in the last few moments of man's existence. Second, urbanism represents a revolutionary change in the whole pattern of social life. Itself a product of basic economic and technological developments, it tends in turn, once it comes into being, to affect every aspect of existence. It exercises its pervasive influence not only within the urban milieu strictly defined but also in the rural hinterland. The third source of sociological interest in cities is the fact that, once established, they tend to be centers of power and influence throughout the whole society, no matter how agricultural and rural it may be. Finally, the process of urbanization is still occurring; many of the problems associated with it are unsolved; and, consequently, its future direction and potentialities are still a matter of uncertainty. This paper examines the first and last points: the origin, growth, and present rate of progress of urbanization in the world. Since good statistics on urban concentration do not exist even today for substantial parts of the world, and hardly exist for any part during most of the time since cities have been in existence, we are forced to rely on whatever credible evidence can be found and so can reach only broad conclusions concerning early periods and only approximations for recent times.

Because the archeological evidence is fragmentary, the role of cities in antiquity has often been exaggerated. Archeologists in particular are inclined to call any settlement a "city" which had a few streets and a public building or two. Yet there is surely some point in not mistaking a town for a city. Moreover, what is important is not only the appearance of a few towns or cities but also their place in the total society of which they were a part. Thus, even though in particular regions around the Mediterranean and in southern and western Asia many towns and a few cities arose prior to the Christian Era, there were severe limitations both on the size that such cities could

* Reprinted from "The Origin and Growth of Urbanization in the World," *American Journal of Sociology*, by Kingsley Davis, Vol. LX, March 1955, pp. 29–37. By permission of The University of Chicago Press.

reach and on the proportion of the total population that could live in them.

Speaking generally, one can agree with the dominant view that the diverse technological innovations constituting Neolithic culture were necessary for the existence of settled communities. Yet one should not infer that these innovations, which began some 8000–10,000 years ago, were sufficient to give rise to towns as distinct from villages. Even though the Neolithic population was more densely settled than the purely hunting or food-gathering peoples, it was nevertheless chiefly engaged in an occupation—agriculture—which requires a large amount of land per person. The Neolithic population density was therefore not a matter of town concentration but rather a matter of tiny villages scattered over the land.

What had to be added to the Neolithic complex to make possible the first towns? Between 6000 and 4000 B.C. certain inventions—such as the ox-drawn plow and wheeled cart, the sailboat, metallurgy, irrigation, and the domestication of new plants—facilitated, when taken together, a more intensive and more productive use of the Neolithic elements themselves. When this enriched technology was utilized in certain unusual regions where climate, soil, water, and topography were most favorable (broad river valleys with alluvial soil not exhausted by successive cropping, with a dry climate that minimized soil leaching, with plenty of sunshine, and with sediment-containing water for irrigation from the river itself), the result was a sufficiently productive economy to make possible the *sine qua non* of urban existence, the concentration in one place of people who do not grow their own food.

But a productive economy, though necessary, was not sufficient: high productivity per acre does not necessarily mean high per capita productivity. Instead of producing a surplus for town dwellers, the cultivators can, theoretically at least, multiply on the land until they end up producing just enough to sustain themselves. The rise of towns and cities therefore required, in addition to highly favorable agricultural conditions, a form of social organization in which certain strata could appropriate for themselves part of the produce grown by the cultivators. Such strata—religious and governing officials, traders, and artisans—could live in towns, because their power over goods did not depend on their presence on the land as such. They could thus realize the advantages of town living, which gave them additional power over the cultivators.

The first cities, doubtless small and hard to distinguish from towns, seem to have appeared in the most favorable places sometimes between 6000 and 5000 B.C. From that time on, it can be assumed that some of the inventions which made larger settlements possible were due to towns and cities themselves—viz., writing and accountancy, bronze, the beginnings of science, a solar calendar, bureaucracy. By 3000 B.C., when these innovations were all exercising an influence in Egypt, Mesopotamia, and India, there were in existence what may be called "true" cities. After that there appears to have been, for some 2000 years, a lull during which the most important innovations, toward the end of the period, were alphabetic writing and the smelting of iron. Curiously, the cities in the regions where city life had originated eventually went into eclipse, and it was not until Greco-Roman times that new principles made possible, in new regions, a marked gain in city existence. The fact that the greatest subsequent cultural developments did not occur primarily in the regions where the first cities arose suggests that cities are not always and everywhere a stimulant of economic and social advance. If anything, the first cities had a stultifying effect on cultural progress, due perhaps to the unproductive insulation and excessive power of the urban elite. There is no doubt that the religio-magical traditionalism of the early cities was profound. . . .

To the questions why even the largest cities prior to 1000 b.c. were small by modern standards, why even the small ones were relatively few, and why the degree of urbanization even in the most advanced regions was very slight, the answer seems as follows: Agriculture was so cumbersome, static, and labor-intensive that it took many cultivators to support one man in the city. The ox-drawn plow, the wooden plowshare, inundation irrigation, stone hoes, sickles, and axes were instruments of production, to be sure, but clumsy ones. Not until iron came into use in Asia Minor about 1300 b.c. could general improvement in agriculture be achieved. The static character of agriculture and of the economy generally was fostered perhaps by the insulation of the religio-political officials from the practical arts and the reduction of the peasant to virtually the status of a beast of burden. The technology of transport was as labor-intensive as that of agriculture. The only means of conveying bulky goods for mass consumption was by boat, and, though sails had been invented, the sailboat was so inefficient that rowing was still necessary. The oxcart, with its solid wheels and rigidly attached axle, the pack animal, and the human burden-bearer were all short-distance means of transport, the only exception being the camel caravan. Long-distance transport was reserved largely for goods which had high value and small bulk— i.e., goods for the elite—which could not maintain a large urban population. The size of the early cities was therefore limited by the amount of food, fibers, and other bulky materials that could be obtained from the immediate hinterland by labor-intensive methods, a severe limitation which the Greek cities of a later period, small as they remained, nevertheless had to escape before they could attain their full size.

There were political limitations as well. The difficulty of communication and transport and the existence of multifarious local tribal cultures made the formation of large national units virtually impossible. The first urban-centered units were city-states, and when so-called "empires" were formed, as in Egypt, in the Sumerian region, and later in Assyria, much local autonomy was left to the subordinated areas, and the constant danger of revolt prevented the extension of the hinterlands of the cities very far or very effectively. It is symptomatic of the weakness of the early cities that they were constantly threatened and frequently conquered not only by neighboring towns but also by nonurban barbarians. Each wave of barbarians tended to rebuild the urban centers and to become agricultural and sedentary, only to be eventually overwhelmed in turn by new invaders. Other limiting factors were the lack of scientific medicine (which made urban living deadly), the fixity of the peasant on the land (which minimized rural-urban migration), the absence of large-scale manufacturing (which would have derived more advantage from urban concentration than did handicraft), the bureaucratic control of the peasantry (which stifled free trade in the hinterland), and the traditionalism and religiosity of all classes (which hampered technological and economic advance).

The limitations explain why we find, when the sites furnish adequate evidence, that the earliest cities were small affairs, usually no more than towns. Whether in the new or in the old world, even the biggest places could scarcely have exceeded 200,000 inhabitants, and the proportion of the total population living in them must have been not more than 1 or 2 per cent. From 50 to 90 farmers must have been required to support one man in a city.

If urbanization was to escape its early limitations, it had to do so in a new region, a region more open to innovation and new conceptions. As it turned out, the region that saw a later and greater urban development was farther north, the Greco-Roman world of Europe, flourishing approximately during the period from 600 B.C. to A.D. 400. Iron tools and weapons, alphabetic writing, improved sailboats, cheap coinage, more democratic institutions, systematic colonization—all tended to increase production, stimulate trade, and expand the effective political unit. Towns and cities became more numerous, the degree of urbanization greater. A few cities reached a substantial size. Athens, at its peak in the fifth century B.C., achieved a population of between 120,000 and 180,000. Syracuse and Carthage were perhaps larger.

The full potentialities of the ancient world to support a large city were realized only with the Romans. Through their ability to conquer, organize, and govern an empire, to put the immediate Italian hinterland to fruitful cultivation, to use both force and trade to bring slaves, goods, food, and culture to the imperial capital, they were able to create in Rome (with the possible exception of Constantinople some centuries later) the largest city that was to be known in the world until the rise of London in the nineteenth century. Yet, despite the fact that Rome and Constantinople came to hold populations of several hundred thousand, they were not able to resist conquest by far less urbanized outsiders. The eclipse of cities in Europe was striking. Commerce declined to the barest minimum; each locale became isolated and virtually self-sufficient; the social system congealed into a hereditary system. When finally towns and cities began to revive, they were small, as the following estimates suggest: Florence (1338), 90,000; Venice (1422), 190,000; Antwerp (sixteenth century), 200,000; London (1377), 30,000; Nuremberg (1450), 20,165; Frankfort (1440), 8719.

Yet it was precisely in Western Europe, where cities and urbanization had reached a nadir during the Dark Ages, that the limitations that had characterized the ancient world were finally to be overcome. The cities of Mesopotamia, India, and Egypt, of Persia, Greece, and Rome had all been tied to an economy that was primarily agricultural, where handicraft played at best a secondary role and where the city was still attempting to supplement its economic weakness with military strength, to command its sustenance rather than to buy it honestly. In western Europe, starting at the zero point, the development of cities not only reached the stage that the ancient world had achieved but kept going after that. It kept going on the basis of improvements in agriculture and transport, the opening of new lands and new trade routes, and, above all, the rise in productive activity, first in highly organized handicraft and eventually in a revolutionary new form of production—the factory run by machinery and fossil fuel. The transformation thus achieved in the nineteenth century was the true urban revolution, for it meant not only the rise of a few scattered towns and cities but the appearance of genuine urbanization, in the sense that a substantial portion of the population lived in towns and cities.

URBANIZATION SINCE THE INDUSTRIAL REVOLUTION

Urbanization has, in fact, gone ahead much faster and reached proportions far greater during the last century and a half than at any previous time in world history. The tremendous growth in world trade during this period has enabled the urban population to draw its sustenance from an ever wider area. Indeed, it can truly be said that the hinterland of today's cities is the entire world. Contemporary Britain, Holland, and Japan, for example, could not maintain their urban population solely from their own territory. The number of rural inhabitants required to maintain one urban inhabitant is still great— greater than one would imagine from the rural-urban ratio *within* each of the highly urbanized countries. The reason is that much of agriculture around the world is still technologically and economically backward. Yet there can be no doubt that, whether for particular countries or for the entire globe, the ratio of urban dwellers to those who grow their food has risen remarkably. This is shown by the fact that the proportion of people living in cities in 1950 is higher than that found in any particular country prior to modern times and many times higher than that formerly characterizing the earth as a whole.

The rapidity of urbanization in recent times can be seen by looking at the most urbanized country, England. In 1801, although London had already reached nearly the million mark (865,000), England and Wales had less than 10 per cent of their population in cities of 100,000 or more. By 1901 no less than 35 per cent of the population of England and Wales was living in cities of 100,000 or more, and 58 per cent was living in cities of 20,000 or more. By 1951 these two proportions had risen to 38.4 and 69.3 per cent, respectively.

Britain was in the van of urban development. A degree of urbanization equal to that she had attained in 1801 was not achieved by any other country until after 1850. Thereafter the British rate of urbanization began slowly to decline, whereas that of most other countries continued at a high level. By assembling available data and preparing estimates where data were lacking, we have arrived at figures on urbanization in the world as a whole, beginning with 1800, the earliest date for which anything like a reasonable estimate can be obtained. It can be seen that the proportion has tended to do a bit better than double itself each half-century and that by 1950 the world as a whole was considerably more urbanized than Britain was in 1800. As everyone knows, the earth's total population has grown at an extremely rapid rate since 1800, reaching 2.4 billion by 1950. But the urban population has grown much faster. In 1800 there were about 15.6 million people living in cities of 100,000 or more. By 1950 it was 313.7 million, more than twenty times the earlier figure. Much of this increase has obviously come from rural-urban migration, clearly the most massive migration in modern times.

In 1800 there were apparently less than 50 cities with 100,000 or more inhabitants. This was less than the number in the million class today and less than the number of 100,000-plus cities currently found in many single countries. By 1950 there were close to 900 cities of 100,000 or more people, which is more than the number of towns and cities of 5000 or more in 1800.

As yet there is no indication of a slackening of the rate of urbanization in the world as a whole. If the present rate should continue, more than a fourth of the earth's people will be living in cities of 100,000 or more in the year 2000, and more than half in the year 2050. For places of 20,000 or more, the proportions at the two dates would be something like 45 per cent and 90 per cent. Whether such figures prove too low or too high, they nevertheless suggest that the human species is moving rapidly in the direction of an almost exclusively urban existence. We have used the proportion of the population in cities of 20,000 and 100,000 or more as a convenient index of differences and changes in degree of urbanization. Places of less than 20,000 also fit a demographic definition of "urban." When, therefore, more than a third of the population of a country lives in cities of the 100,000 class (38.4 per cent in England and Wales in 1951), the country can be described as almost completely urbanized (81 per cent being designated as "urban" in the English case in 1951). We thus have today what can be called "urbanized societies," nations in which the great majority of inhabitants live in cities. The prospect is that, as times goes on, a greater and greater proportion of humanity will be members of such societies.

The question may be raised as to how such an extreme degree of world urbanization will prove possible. Who will grow the food and fibers necessary for the enormous urban population? The answer is that agriculture may prove to be an archaic mode of production. Already, one of the great factors giving rise to urbanization, is the rather late and as yet very incomplete industrialization of agriculture. As farming becomes increasingly mechanized and rationalized, fewer people are needed on the land. On the average, the more urbanized a country, the lower is its rural density. If, in addition to industrialized agriculture, food and fiber come to be increasingly produced by manufacturing processes using materials that utilize the sun's energy more efficiently than plants do, there is no technological reason why nearly all of mankind could not live in conurbations of large size.

The highest levels of urbanization are found today in northwestern Europe and in those new regions where northwest Europeans have settled and extended their industrial civilization. Oceania is the most urbanized of the world's major regions, because Australia and New Zealand are its principal components. North America is next, if it is defined as including only Canada and the United States. The regions least urbanized are those least affected by northwest European culture, namely, Asia and Africa.

The figures for world regions are less valuable for purposes of analysis than are those for individual countries. The latter show clearly that urbanization has tended to reach its highest point wherever economic productivity has been greatest—that is, where the economy is industrialized and rationalized. This explains why urbanization is so closely associated with northwest Europeans and their culture, since they were mainly responsible for the industrial revolution. Of the fifteen most urbanized countries in the world, all but one, Japan, are European in culture, and all but four derive that culture from the northwest or central part of Europe.

The rate of urbanization in the older industrial countries, however, is slowing down. During the twenty years from 1870 to 1890 Germany's proportion in large cities more than doubled; it nearly doubled again from 1890 to 1910; but from 1910 to 1940 the increase was only 36 per cent. In Sweden the gain slowed down noticeably after 1920. In England and Wales the most rapid urbanization occurred between 1811 and 1851. Contrary to popular belief, the fastest rate in the United States occurred between 1861 and 1891. Since, as we noted earlier, there has been no slowing-down of urbanization in the world as a whole, it must be that, as the more established industrial countries have slackened, the less-developed countries have exhibited a faster rate. In fact, such historical evidence as we have for underdeveloped areas seems to show that their rates of urbanization have been rising in recent decades. This has been the case in Egypt, where the rate is higher after 1920 than before; in India, where the fastest urbanization has occurred since 1941; in Mexico, where the speed-up began in 1921; and in Greece, where the fastest period ran from 1900 to 1930. Asia, for example, had only 22 per cent of the world's city population in 1900 but 34 per cent of it in 1950, and Africa had 1.5 per cent in 1900 but 3.2 per cent at the later date.

With respect to urbanization, then, the gap between the industrial and the preindustrial nations is beginning to diminish. The less-developed parts of the world will eventually, it seems, begin in their turn to move gradually toward a saturation point. As the degree of urbanization rises, it of course becomes impossible for the rate of gain to continue. The growth in the urban proportion is made possible by the movement of people from rural areas to the cities. As the rural population becomes a progressively smaller percentage of the total, the cities no longer can draw on a noncity population of any size. Yet in no country can it be said that the process of urbanization is yet finished. Although there have been short periods in recent times in England, the United States, and Japan when the city population increased at a slightly slower rate than the rural, these were mere interludes in the ongoing but ever slower progress of urban concentration.

DECENTRALIZATION OF THE CENTRAL CITY

The continuance of urbanization in the world does not mean the persistence of something that remains the same in detail. A city of a million inhabitants today is not the sort of place that a city of the same number was in 1900 or in 1850. Moreover, with the emergence of giant cities of five to fifteen million, something new has been added. Such cities are creatures of the twentieth century. Their sheer quantitative difference means a qualitative change as well.

One of the most noticeable developments is the ever stronger tendency of cities to expand outward—a development already observed in the nineteenth century. Since 1861, the first date when the comparison can be made, the Outer Ring of Greater London has been growing more rapidly than London itself. There is no doubt that the process of metropolitan dispersion has increased with time. This fact is shown for the United States by comparing the percentage gains in population made by the central cities with those made by their satellite areas . . . *within the metropolitan area outside the central cities* it was the "rural" parts which gained faster than the urban parts. Clearly, the metropolitan districts were increasingly dependent on the areas outside the central cities, and especially upon the sparsely settled parts at the periphery of these areas, for their continued growth.

The same forces which have made extreme urbanization possible have also made metropolitan dispersion possible, and the dispersion itself has contributed to further urbanization by making large conurbations more efficient and more endurable. The outward movement of urban residences, of urban services and commercial establishments, and of light industry—all facilitated by improvements in motor transport and communications—has made it possible for huge agglomerations to keep on growing without the inconveniences of proportionate increases in density. In many ways the metropolis of three million today is an easier place to live and work in than the city of five hundred thousand yesterday. Granted that the economic advantages of urban concentration still push populations in the direction of urbanization, the effect of metropolitan dispersion is thus to minimize the disadvantages of this continued urban growth.

The new type of metropolitan expansion occurring in the highly industrial countries is not without its repercussions in less-developed lands as well. Most of the rapid urbanization now occurring in Africa and Asia, for example, is affected by direct contact with industrial nations and by a concomitant rise in consumption standards. Although private automobiles may not be available to the urban masses, bicycles and buses generally are. Hence Brazzaville and Abidjan, Takoradi and Nairobi, Jamshedpur and New Delhi, Ankara and Colombo are not evolving in the same manner as did the cities of the eighteenth and nineteenth centuries. Their ecological pattern, their technological base, their economic activity, all reflect the twentieth century, no matter how primitive or backward their hinterlands may be. Thus the fact that their main growth is occurring in the present century is not without significance for the kind of cities they are turning out to be.

Speculation concerning the future of urbanization is as hazardous as that concerning any other aspect of human society. Following the direction of modern trends, however, one may conclude that, with the industrial revolution, for the first time in history urbanization began to reach a stage from which there was no return. The cities of antiquity were vulnerable, and the degree of urbanization reached was so thin in many societies as to be transitory. Today virtually every part of the world is more urbanized than any region was in antiquity. Urbanization is so widespread, so much a part of industrial civilization, and gaining so rapidly, that any return to rurality, even with major catastrophes, appears unlikely. On the contrary, since every city is obsolescent to some degree—more obsolescent the older it is—the massive destruction of many would probably add eventually to the impetus of urban growth.

The fact that the rate of world urbanization has shown no slackening since 1800 suggests that we are far from the end of this process, perhaps not yet at the peak. Although the industrial countries have shown a decline in their rates, these countries, because they embrace only about a fourth of the world's population, have not dampened the world trend. The three-fourths of humanity who live in underdeveloped countries are still in the early stages of an urbanization that promises to be more rapid than that which occurred earlier in the areas of northwest European culture.

How urbanized the world will eventually become is an unanswerable question. As stated earlier, there is no apparent reason why it should not become as urbanized as the most urban countries today—with perhaps 85–90 per cent of the population living in cities and towns of 5000 or more and practicing urban occupations. Our present degree of urbanization in advanced countries is still so new that we have no clear idea of how such complete world urbanization would affect human society; but the chances are that the effects would be profound.

In visualizing the nature and effects of complete urbanization in the future, however, one must guard against assuming that cities will retain their present form. The tendency to form huge metropolitan aggregates which are increasingly decentralized will undoubtedly continue but probably will not go so far as to eliminate the central business district altogether, though it may greatly weaken it. At the periphery, it may well be that the metropolis and the countryside, as the one expands and the other shrinks, will merge together, until the boundaries of one sprawling conurbation will touch those of another, with no intervening pure countryside at all. The world's population doubles itself twice in a century, becoming at the same time highly urbanized, and as new sources of energy are tapped, the possibility of centrifugal metropolitan growth is enormously enhanced. If commuting to work could be done with the speed of sound and cheaply, one would not mind living two hundred miles from work. Almost any technological advance from now on is likely to contribute more to the centrifugal than to the centripetal tendency. It may turn out that urbanization in the sense of emptying the countryside and concentrating huge numbers in little space will reverse itself—not, however, in the direction of returning people to the farm but rather in that of spreading them more evenly over the land for purposes of residence and industrial work. "Rurality" would have disappeared, leaving only a new kind of urban existence.

THE URBAN COMMUNITY AS AN ECOLOGICAL SYSTEM

Cities are not homogeneous structures, but are, rather, amalgams of many diverse activities which require a high degree of specialization of manpower. Here then are two important considerations in the cities' utilization of land: downtown industrial districts and good and bad neighborhoods. Urban ecology is the sociological term that defines the study of spatial segregation or how the social organization of the city is distributed. "The inhabitants of a given area tend to have not only a general social station in common but also many other characteristics.

It is found that fertility, mortality, and migration; crime, delinquency, divorce, and suicide; insanity and morbidity; illegitimacy, illiteracy, vice, pauperism, and many other indices of social behavior differ sharply from one area of the city to another." [3]

Another urban sociologist, Nels Anderson, gives us some insights concerning this relationship of man to his physical environment in the following excerpt.

THE COMPETITION FOR SPACE

*
There tends to be order in the way in which people, whether in a village, town, or great city, occupy their land. As there is a semblance of order in the position, size, and arrangement of communities with respect to one another, so within any community there is a functional distribution in the uses of space. We may assume that all uses of space are competitive and that each use involves certain minimum conditions. All uses, however, tend to be based on one common characteristic: that they be as near as possible to the center of the community.

Uses of space differ widely in the minimum amount of space needed for adequate functioning. A furniture dealer needs more space than a tobacco seller; a manufacturer of dresses needs more space than a furrier, and a manufacturer of men's clothing needs even more. A hotel for transients is more compact for residence than a building of one-room apartments, and the latter in turn is more compact than the apartment buildings for housing families. Thus cost of land and rentals are selective factors. Occupiers who handle goods that are both compact and high priced (if turnover of goods is high) have an advantage in competition for the most-desired space.

Some occupiers must be near the railroads or ships, or if they use auto transport, they must have more room. They cannot locate near the urban center as can a lawyer or doctor who needs but two or three rooms. Thus access is a selective factor as well as land values and rents. But there are still other selective factors. Some types of spatial uses tend to cluster. Dress manufacturers must have their show rooms within a limited area. They must be near one another, and the area must be near the hotels. For reasons of competition they cannot scatter.

When these various factors that influence location have had their effect, the result is that the total occupancy of a habitat tends to have a related unity. The distribution of space users tends to form a pattern, the result of hundreds or thousands of individual choices. Occupiers tend to fall into groups, and the arrangement is not without logic. We may say that the pat-

* From *The Urban Community*, by Nels Anderson, pp. 112 ff., Copyright 1959, Holt, Rinehart and Winston, Inc. By permission.

tern centers at the point of most desired access at the community center and extends outward beyond the limits of the community.

In a competitive situation, especially if population in the community is increasing and economic activity expanding, the relationships between areas within the occupation tend to be in continuous change. This dynamic character of space occupancy is clearly visible in American cities, and it is somewhat the same in cities and towns of other new countries. Although the processes of change are not so evident in the older cities, some clustering of activities can be seen.

As competition for space in the urban community determines the location of occupiers and the relationships of areas into patterns, so does it influence the use of space inside the buildings. We are all familiar with the space-saving methods used in apartment buildings, but if we study the use of space in a great office building, say of an insurance company, or the arrangement of sections and counters in a department store, we will find in miniature space-use patterns not unlike those in the community itself. It is the work of a specialist, a "space-control" man, to arrange the offices in the insurance company building so there is a "flow" of the work. The arrangement must also take into account the authority structure of the company. In the department store, space-control experts must arrange the display of goods with the convenience of the customers in mind. Some goods "must" be on the ground floor near the front entrance. Other goods are more appropriately placed in the basement. House furnishings are usually on one of the upper floors. Areas of the floor space least in demand for merchandising are used for packaging or storing goods. The entire operation forms a pattern.

Ecological patterns in any community may or may not be clearly seen. A specialized activity, unique for a particular city, may give rise to specialized areas not found in other cities. However, the shape of the city, the flow of the traffic, the character of intersecting streets, and other physical conditions may give one city a pattern of space occupancy quite different from another. Not infrequently, the pattern of occupancy is due to a mixture of influences, two of which need special mention: the historical and the geographic.

Among other things, a study of the historical development of a city must deal with past efforts of the people to adapt to an inconvenient or threatening geographic site—an effort which for some cities has been heroic. New Orleans, for example, rests on an area of flat land which is lower than the level of the Mississippi River and which must continually be guarded against floods. Alexandria, Egypt, is built on a long, low sandbar and its shape has been so determined. San Francisco has been hampered in its growth by a rugged shore line and high hills. New York is stretched over three islands with water bodies limiting its shape and growth. Stockholm, Sweden, is also built on irregular bodies of land intersected by areas of water. Other examples could be cited; in fact, some of the great world cities are most inconveniently located as far as site is concerned.

It must be said, however, if the site on which a city rests is one that provides maximum access to the various hinterlands, and if there are good economic and other reasons for population and work to be centered at that point, then the city will adapt and thrive. We may say that it will fit itself into the "lay of the land." All the functions pertinent to any area of human habitation will find their place in whatever ecological pattern that develops, and special functions peculiar to the particular city will be more favorably situated than others in the pattern.

This task of adapting to the lay of the land is not a matter that concerns the city alone. In one way or another it concerns nearby areas which may be suburban to the city, since the pattern of occupancy extends outward with various networks of communication and access. A factory nearer to the urban center may need to locate its warehouses in a suburb; the in-town publisher may locate his printing plant in a distant suburb. The outer areas that are used and the way in which they are used also depends on what is possible and practicable.

ACCESSIBILITY AND COMPETITION

The uses of land are in many ways conditioned by its location with respect to other places, a thought that has already been expressed under the term "access." In a society where everyone walks and where four or five miles is the radius of convenient contact, the implications of distance are not so involved as in a community where different types of transportation are available and the time-money costs of moving goods or going places tend increasingly to decline. Thus access takes on a new meaning with each improvement in transportation, and changes resulting with respect to distance are reflected in the ecology of space occupancy.

It needs to be recognized that such changes in access which affect distances between places also affect adversely or favorably different areas and communities. The small town, the larger town, the small city, or the great city tend generally, although not always, to become more accessible to more people, ". . . hence," says Hawley, "the territorial scope of the community and, to a larger extent, the number of individuals who may live in close mutual dependence. Similarly, the distribution of units within the community varies with the time used in movement. A temporal pattern is implicit in each and every special pattern." [4]

The objective of facilities for reducing the time-money cost of distance is to make access to the community center easier for more people and more goods from a wider area, and to make these wider areas more accessible for the town or city. As Hawley indicates, this greater accessibility may affect space uses in the community itself. Thus it is to be expected that certain functions will expand and need more space. Other and weaker space occupiers will be squeezed and will need to find a new location. The direction of this expansion within the community is likely to be along the newly created lines of access or very much in relation to them. If a new superhighway enters a city, outward extension of the city will usually follow that highway, more so than along less well-improved roads to the city. Especially it is to be expected that new residential areas will locate along the new highway, relieving pressure on residential areas in the city.

Hawley mentions the temporal pattern as being implicit in the space pattern. The temporal pattern concerns distance in terms of cost in time and money, especially in time. If one were to draw a series of irregular circles from the urban center outward, called the 20-minute zone, the 30-minute zone, and so on up to an hour, such a temporal map of the city would show that some areas that are geographically near the urban center, say within a mile or so, may be more distant in terms of time than are other areas up to five miles away. Differences in time-distance, as they influence space occupancy, may result in areas within the city being isolated. In the same way, as Dickinson points out, areas and places outside the city may become isolated from one another, for, while each may be on a rapid transit line with the metropolis, local access networks tend to lose importance. Each village or town now acquires a niche in the city-hinterland relationship.[5]

From time to time students of community life have offered hypotheses describing the processes of urban growth and space occupancy. One very much debated formula was that offered by Burgess in 1925. Based on his studies in Chicago, Burgess concluded that areas of occupation, which he called "natural" areas, tend to be grouped into types in terms of distance (geographic) from the urban center. That the urban center has a character of its own and could be identified was not debated; difficulty arose in pinpointing areas of occupation just outside the urban center, or those two miles or five miles distant. Burgess undertook to group these areas into "zones." He concluded that a number of zones or "concentric circles" could be identified. These zones tend to be circular except as interrupted by topographical features, water bodies, or works of man such as railroads, parks, or major highways.

Outside the central area Burgess identified a zone of light manufacture and slum residence into which manufacturing and other nonresidential uses of space were spreading. The next ring included a better class of homes for workingmen. The third ring was occupied largely by heavy industry, although it also contained residential areas. Next came the suburban areas, which are likely to be mixed in character since suburbs tend to have their individual identities to some extent. Within the frame of the zonal arrangement Burgess noted the presence of special districts: "hobohemia" where homeless men gather, the "gold coast" where the rich concentrate, certain areas of vice, and finally, ethnic centers like "Chinatown." [6]

Enough has been said about the spatial relations of people in their use of land in the urban community to emphasize the role of competition between the occupants of land in the community. Although we will not examine more closely the characteristics of such competition, we do need to consider some of its implications. Property rights of many kinds are involved, and these often involve very expensive court cases. These contests relate not only to the rights over ownership, but also rights to a reasonably free use of land. There are rights regarding renting space as well as rights of access. These contests over rights in land are not peculiar to great cities alone but are common to all communities, even primitive villages, where the issues are judged on the basis of custom, and the rules of custom may be as complex as those of the law.

Contests about rights may affect individual occupancies here and there, but they do not prevent a type of collective competition between a cluster of occupants and different clusters surrounding them, in which a particular area occupied by a cluster of space users may be in process of contracting or expanding. If it is contracting, space may be yielded to adjacent clusters that may be expanding. If the cluster is expanding, it encroaches upon one, or another, or different areas around it. If it is not possible to expand in this manner, the entire cluster may move to a new location and there become stronger than before.

While adjustment to space problems involves individual choices, different individuals tend to make similar choices, since the realities that must be considered are similar or the same. An important automobile dealer may rent space for show rooms at an intersection not too distant from the urban center, a vicinity formerly occupied by old tenements. Owners of the new buildings conclude that high rentals can be had from the automobile dealers, already crowded by the building of a new hotel in the area they presently occupy. Other automobile dealers move to the new location. Auto-supply dealers follow. A used-car show room locates nearby. The result very soon is a cluster of like-interest occupants, and this area is identified as a specialized market.

Specialization in the production of goods generally develops as an adaptation to a competitive situation. It enables the maker of goods to operate on a larger scale, producing more goods at a lower price. Doctors, if they are specialists, need to be located near the urban center. A large number may concentrate in one or more office buildings, where the different specialists necessary to one another will be found. The X-ray laboratory will generally be here in the midst of its market where it is most needed rather than in an office building occupied by lawyers. Such a group of specialists cluster not alone for economic reasons; they constitute a service whose value to the community is greater if they are clustered and hence accessible to more people in a more effective way.

Not all urban space occupiers are so dependent on clustering. A mail-order firm may need to be near the urban center, perhaps in the first zone outside the center. It does not need to be accessible to customers, but to transport facilities—railroads, postal and express services. A junk yard, a specialty very necessary in the urban community, needs to be accessible to all areas, but it does not need to be clustered with other junk yards. It must, on the contrary, locate in an area where its presence is not resisted. However, the junk market (old metal, old clothing, paper, bottles, etc.) may cluster in areas that have become isolated in the space competition race.

The different specialities found in the urban community may be classified according to a number of major groups, somewhat as follows:

(1) *Financial group*, which may include banking, insurance, the stock market, export and import and shipping offices. These tend to cluster, although establishments of each type may be scattered.

(2) *Marketing group*, includes a variety of markets, some of which need to cluster, particularly wholesalers catering to wide markets or specialty shops, catering to exclusive customers. The less exclusive and expensive the merchandise, the more the market is spread out. While specialty shops may cluster, others such as fur or jewelry shops need to be near the urban center but do not need to cluster. Stores selling commonly used goods may be widely scattered.

(3) *Professional group*, includes a variety of specialists, some of whom cluster while others need not, although all need to be centralized. Besides lawyers and doctors, this group would include tax experts, accountants, advertisers, editors and publishers, fortune tellers, faith healers, and artists—the list is long.

(4) *Catering and social-life group*, found in every urban community and often centrally located, includes hotels and special restaurants, theaters and night clubs, exclusive- or not-so-exclusive membership social clubs or university clubs.

There are, of course, other groups, but his list is enough to indicate the relationship between urban space occupancy and specialized activities.

SUCCESSION IN LAND USE

In almost every city bronze plates may be found on the sides of buildings which report that "on this site stood the building" in which some man famous a hundred years or more ago was born. The old house was removed and perhaps another building used for another purpose took its place, and perhaps that building also was replaced by still another, the present one, which is used for still another purpose. In the course of a century this same bit of land may have been occupied by three different structures, each more modern and more economically productive than the previous. The different occupants, coming and going, have put this space to different uses. Such a parade of occupations is common to American urban life, but is not always so evident in Old World cities where space occupancies change much more slowly.

This process of occupancy change is generally known as "succession." It may refer either to a succession of occupants in a structure or to a succession of structures on the same plot of land, although both types of succession are evident when a particular land unit or area is seen in a long-term perspective. In American cities succession is conspicuously seen in the occupation of residences. A new apartment building intended for, and occupied by middle-class families may within a decade be regarded as "getting old" and therefore not a first choice of middle-class families; before another decade has passed it is receiving occupants of lower-middle-class status at comparatively lower rentals. Within another decade the building is no longer modern and the new occupants are of the upper lower class. Most of the people moving away are in search of better housing. The social and economic status of each new wave of occupants tends to be lower than the previous one. Ultimately the structure reaches the point at which it can no longer be profitably used for residence. It will be replaced by a more modern apartment or by a structure used for another purpose.

As this process of succession is evident in single buildings, so it can be seen in groups of buildings, not only in residences, but in stores, office buildings, hotels, theaters, and restaurants—any structure that may be outmoded with passing time and technological advance. . . .

Succession, ecologically speaking, is concerned with the change of use of a unit of land or the change of occupants within a use group, or it may be expressed in structural change to meet changing needs of the same use group. It is to be found, in one form or another, in all urban communities, although it will be most evident in rapidly growing communities. Succession can scarcely be absent in communities that are being stimulated by technological change. Even if technological change is at a minimum, succession may result from competition between space users. In such cases the displacements resulting from competition may be apparent only in occasional shifts and, seen at any one time, the local situation may appear to be in equilibrium. Equilibrium, however, is a highly relative term.

An approximate equilibrium is found between the existing order and pressures for change. These pressures may result from influences which intrude from the outside or from changes within, as when a group in some area increases in size and in activity. Such an equilibrium, continuing in its tendencies, also exists for regions as well as for whole communities, although each community has its own processes of change. Ecological changes are never total (except perhaps in disaster), but are distributed to different sectors of community life. Thus, each area is affected either by internal change or change in neighboring areas; only gradually are groups of areas affected. The wider community is not thrown out of equilibrium. Normally, life in the modern community is flexible and tolerant of change, and maintains balance.

Human ecology is the study of man in his community life, adjusting to his habitat. It concerns his spatial relations within the community, how the competing interests in the community manage to share the space available for such uses as residence, work, leisure, as well as for collective public or private purposes. All of these uses tend to be competitive and concern the use of land or space. Space has economic value and can be rented or sold, a source of profit. It is also limited, and hence multiple use, such as building into the air or digging into the earth, is encouraged. Space that is very accessible acquires high value, as in the urban center where it is compactly used; its value is low when it is least accessible.

In the use of the urban habitat man tends toward specialization in the occupation of space. Some areas are used for residence, others for industry, others for commerce, and so on. But there are different types of residence and industrial areas and many types of commercial areas, which may in the great city be called special markets. In different ways these areas are occupied by users who tend to cluster. In some cases these areas are expanding, in others contracting; but whether growing or declining, neighboring areas are affected. Changes in one area effect changes in other areas.

Seen in wider perspective, these different related uses of space tend to be interlocked from the urban center to the outer suburbs, and even beyond. Relations between points within this extended pattern are affected by distances between them and by the ease with which they may be made accessible to one another. It is being recognized that the extended region of occupancy from urban center to the remotest suburbs has a unity which can be graphically presented in terms of a series of occupation zones from the urban center outward.

One ever-present result of competition between occupiers is that any particular bit of land or area may witness a succession in users and uses as well as in structures. These changes tend to be continuous, although they may move faster in some urban communities (and in some countries) than in others. However, such change is never complete. The effects tend to be scattered, which permits the existing order to remain in equilibrium, although it is a moving equilibrium in communities of rapid change.

THE FUTURE OF THE URBAN COMMUNITY

Is the city in America breaking down? Has it outlived its usefulness? If not, how else can suburban migration be explained? The remarkable growth at the urban fringe since the Second World War might be likened to the effects of an overactive pituitary in the adult. This condition, known as *acromegaly*, brings a coarsening of the features caused by growth at the extremities. For a time there is increased strength in the afflicted person, but, if the disease is not arrested, death results. Is this what is in store for the city—increasing ugliness coupled with a kind of vitality which, in turn, leads to decay? A number of students of the city are concerned about this possibility.

There is a paradox in the desire to retain the qualities of the city while responding to the strong attraction to the suburbs. Downtown merchants follow the emigrants by establishing suburban branches, and then attempt to lure them back downtown to save the floundering main store. The middle classes who commute to work in the city object to conditions in the city, which made them decide to leave; but they have also removed their political, economic, and social strength, leaving the problems of the metropolis to those who can or must stay. The city is being decentralized against its will. Its shrinking industry represents a loss in the tax base, and the shrinking population represents a loss in political power.

Is the city necessary in this age of instantaneous communication and swift transportation? What role does the city play in our lives and can we get along just as well without it? The following article by James Marston Fitch, an architect, is an eloquent plea to do something for and about the city before the decay becomes too advanced.

* In recent years a whole literature has appeared on "the disappearing city." Following that special brand of Social Darwinism which is endemic to so much current thought, it argues that the metropolis is "doomed," "obsolete," its disappearance from the stage of history and from beneath our feet ineluctable. According to this interpretation of the "law" of survival of the fittest, the city is destined simply to dissolve, distributing its amenities in a thin, even film of suburban houses, shopping centers, and country day schools across the landscape.

It is perfectly true that the mechanization of American life in all its major aspects has almost equalized the historic disparity between the material conditions of urban and rural life. A whole range of amenities hitherto the monopoly of the city has in the past fifty years been extended into the countryside—amenities of which the public school, the paved road, the ambulance, and the powerline are merely symbols. Mechanization has also made possible the decentralization of manufacturing, thereby introducing

* Reprinted from "In Defense of the City," by James Marston Fitch, *Columbia University Forum*, Vol. III, Fall 1960, pp. 4–10. By permission of the author.

new modes of work and thought into the rural hinterland. And these same events have of course affected the function and the form of the metropolis. Mechanization makes possible the unprecedentedly fluid movement of people and goods, and this has meant that many of the commercial and industrial activities historically concentrated in the central city could be moved out of it. With those activities could go the population connected with them.

These shifting populations and processes have, especially in recent decades, left ugly vacuums and imposed dreadful strains upon the physical and social fabric of the central city—and the resulting confusion and squalor have driven further sectors of the population out to the suburbs, even though their economic and cultural focus remained in the central city. The result of all this has been the blurring of the physical and cultural distinctions between the city and the countryside and the birth of a whole set of misconceptions, as well-intentioned as they are misinformed, about the city. Not only is the countryside now described as a more pleasant place in which to live (the urban elite, Virgil no less than Vanderbilt, has often felt this was during epochs of social peace), but now, for the first time in Western history, it is seriously being argued that the city itself is no longer viable.

This is a grotesque misreading of the city's historic function. As the etymology of the word suggests, the city has always been not merely the vessel but the actual generator of civilization. It is not at all accidental that such words and concepts as Civil, Civilized, Citizen, Urbane, Urbanity, cluster around the word and concept City. For urban experience is their point of origin. They represent mankind's distilled experience with the city as a special instrument of social organization. It has always been the lodestar of farmer, herdsman, hunter, sailor. It offered them steady employment, and the food, clothing, and shelter that were statistically so chancy elsewhere. It offered them paved streets, lighted taverns, buzzing markets, instead of barnyard mud or storm-tossed ocean nights. It promised them music, dancing, theater, and spectacle. Even more precious, it gave them relative safety from war and sanctuary and asylum for dissent. But beneath all of these was the city's most splendid gift: *a range of choice*, an entire spectrum of possible lines of action. This was the lodestar that pulled them, the chance of escape from the routine idiocy of life on the farm, the steppe, the sea.

The attractive power of the city is somewhat obscured in contemporary America by the surface glitter of universal mechanization. But one need only visit such under-industrialized countries as Egypt or Greece to see the attraction still vividly at work. The peasantry flees the stupefying poverty and monotony of a countryside ravished by centuries of ignorance and neglect. And its instinct is correct, however inadequately or unevenly Cairo or Athens may live up to its promises. For the amelioration of the material conditions of life can be accomplished only by the science and technology of the city;

even the regeneration of agriculture and the countryside is, culturally, an urban task.

Of course, the advantages which the city offered the citizen were a kind of cultural superstructure erected upon its basic economic function. As an instrument of production, it was unique—the only conceivable habitat of merchant and banker, craftsman and artist, because it afforded them three conditions, critically important and available nowhere else: proximity, predictability, option. The city constituted a common reservoir of raw materials and finished goods, of manual and intellectual skills, upon which everyone engaged in production could draw. This was a reservoir of absolutely incalculable value, one which no individual could conceivably afford to maintain alone. And its concentration, in both time and space, meant that any producer had immediate *proximity* to all the goods and services upon which he depended as well as to those who, in turn, depended upon him. Because there was always duplication of every type of goods and skill, there was always *predictability* of supply. And, finally, because of both of the above conditions, the city offered the last essential of the market, *option*, a range of choice within a given type or category.

Out of such quantitative relationships grew the qualitative phenomena of civilization. And if such a process was true of the city of antiquity, how much more characteristic it is of the infinitely more complex fabric of modern industrial society. Today, when we speak of financial centers, garment centers, publishing centers in a great metropolis like New York; or when we refer to Detroit as the center of one industry or Hollywood of another, we are dealing not in metaphor but in the most concrete of social realities. Such a center represents a unique concentration of cultural forces. Personal, face-to-face contact; daily exposure to the friction of competitive ideas; continual exchange of information and opinion within related fields—these are the essential properties of the center. And this, precisely, is why the center cannot be decentralized. Modern technology may permit the dispersal of this or that phase of production. Modern telecommunications may make it possible for a single national center to control a national industry. But the creativity of the urban center will no more survive subdivision and dispersion across the countryside than would the human brain survive a similar distribution across the nervous system.

These are some of the fundamentals ignored by the literature of the "disappearing city." There are other considerations for those who think that paved roads and electric refrigerators are equivalent to urban culture. A law of urban development, analogous to those which operate in the physical sciences, dictates that human communities must pass beyond some quantitative minimum in order to effect that qualitative change which we call social invention. This qualitative difference is not directly (or at least not mechanically) proportional to simple physical magnitude. The Athens of Pericles was never larger than Yonkers. Renaissance Florence was smaller than New Haven. Chicago, on the other hand, is three times the size of Imperial Rome and has not a fiftieth of her power and substance. It seems logical to suppose that, for a given level of technological development, there must be an optimal size for the metropolis. But on the basis of present knowledge, it does not seem possible to say what that optimum size should be. It may well be that the great metropoli of the world are too large to function effectively. It may well be that the future will see a planned reduction in their size. But this is a far different thing from declaring them "obsolete" and rejoicing in their dissolution.

Yet that is what large and influential sectors of American opinion are doing today. They describe the desiccation of the central city (and the parallel urban sprawl which pollutes more of the landscape every day) as inevitable. Some of them go much further, hailing the process as good:

> We have been able to disperse our factories, our stores, our people; in short, to create a revolution in our living habits. Our cities have spread into suburbs . . . The automobile has restored (sic!) a way of life in which the individual may live in a friendly neighborhood, it has brought city and country closer together, it has made us one country and a united people. (Report of the Clay Committee on national highways, appointed by President Eisenhower in 1954.)

Insofar as the future of the city is the subject of any responsible thought, that thought seems dominated by a kind of mad *laissez-faire*-ism. Subjected to a whole set of anarchic and destructive forces, the city is expected to prove itself, medieval-style, in a trial by fire and water. If it survives, this theory seems to say, well and good; if it succumbs, good riddance. This preposterous policy of nonintervention permits the subsidy of all sorts of forces hostile to the city's well-being, yet forbids any defensive response.

This is especially clear in the field of transportation, where the dominant attitude is one of macabre non sequitur. Responsible men see nothing improper in the expenditure of tens of billions of dollars to build new highways to bring automobiles into the cities. Yet they are outraged at the obvious corollary—that there should be free, tax-supported parking garages to receive the cars that are thus dumped into the city. Respectable opinion finds it unobjectionable to subsidize the movement of people and goods by motor, plane and barge—none of which could move a mile without stupendous public expenditures on highways, airports, and rivers. Yet this same opinion boggles at the idea of subsidy to the railroads, grows apoplectic at the mention of nationalization (though the USA is the only nation on earth which still clings to the polite fiction that privately-owned railroads are consonant with national welfare). The central city is being throttled by such paradoxes. Its streets are drowning in a rising tide of vehicular traffic at the same time that public mass transportation systems are declining. Rail passenger service between cities, and especially commuter service into the city, is collapsing without a finger's being raised to prevent it. The large investment represented in interurban and trolley systems has been junked piecemeal, with no effort at rehabilitation. Side by side with this private bankruptcy, billions in public funds have been pumped into insatiable highway schemes which —whatever they may have accomplished in the countryside—have only led to steadily worsening traffic conditions in the central city.

Transportation is only one aspect of the urban problem but, like the circulatory function in the animal body, it is a critically important one. And our current irrational manipulation of it reveals our lack of understanding, at both national and local levels, of the cultural function of the central city and of the minimal conditions for its survival. The physical expression of this function (proximity, predictability, option) is the street. The street, and not the buildings on it, is the secret of the city. Unless the street is healthy, the city dies.

Part of the American mismanagement of the city is due to our persistent inability to see the difference between the street and the road. Our long exploitative experience with land as a commodity leads us to act as if every country lane was destined ultimately to become a profitable city street. Many have, of course; and this very process has served to conceal the essential difference between the two. For a road, properly speaking, is for moving people and goods from where they are to where they want to get to; while a street, properly speaking, is for people who are already where they want to be. Thus the road can be almost indefinitely widened or extended. Since transport is its only function, it can be designed to accept any type of vehicle, in any quantity, moving at any rate of speed. But a city street, to be successful, must meet the incomparably more subtle assignment of facilitating commerce in ideas and goods. It is therefore primarily a pedestrian facility and must be designed to the walker's scale in time and space.

Of course, the foot has always had to share the street with the wheel, and competition between the two is not new. Already in Cicero's Rome, wheeled traffic was so heavy on the main thoroughfares that it was restricted by law to late night hours (much to the annoyance of the tenants of the apartment houses on either side). This conflict has steadily sharpened, especially since the Industrial Revolution. Only Venice, with her unique separation of water-borne transport from all pedestrian traffic, has escaped: and it is to Venice that one must go today to comprehend how wonderful a space is a street without any wheels!

But what was merely conflict before the automobile appeared has become a mortal dichotomy since. Its impact upon the central city has been disastrous throughout the world but its most destructive effects have been most acutely felt in America. Not only have we made the widest use of the auto as a means of personal transport; but also we have greatly extended, if not indeed largely built, most of our cities since the introduction of the auto fifty years ago. Some of the newer metropolitan areas (Houston, Los Angeles) have been structured upon the private auto as the only form of transportation.

No other form of wheeled traffic has ever approached the auto in destructiveness. (No reference is here intended to its destruction of human life, though that is murderous enough; it is the nation's seventh most important cause of death and fourth highest cause of disability; and it is now coming under suspicion as contributing to the alarming rise of lung cancer.) For the auto has not merely taken over the street. It is dissolving all the connective tissue of the city. Its appetite for space is absolutely insatiable: moving and parked, it devours urban land. In Los Angeles, where the process is perhaps most advanced, the spectacle is frightening; the economist George H. Hildebrand, a long-time student of that city, says:

> Two-thirds of the land area of Los Angeles is now devoted to streets, freeways, and parking lots. A recent semi-official projection of future public investment, amounting to several billions for the next decade, commits over half to the motor car. Not one cent is set aside for public transportation. Between 1949 and 1951 an invaluable nucleus for a rapid transit rail system was deliberately abandoned in favor of exclusive dependence upon freeways and the private automobile.

It would be dismaying enough if these freeways, which cost from $3 to $15 millions per mile solved the problem. Unfortunately, says Professor Hildebrand, they do not:

> Already they are so clogged with traffic at peak hours that one can say of them: as a means of transportation they are always available except when you need them. The center of the city is dying. There are no proper facilities for opera, symphony, or theater . . . All civic energies are devoted to the sole purpose of "relieving" automobile congestion—by encouraging it further. Each day the atmosphere is poisoned by smog, two-thirds of which is attributable to automobiles. What has emerged is an endless waste of suburbs, yielding an impression of chaos and ugliness . . . if this is the image of American future, it is not a pleasant one.

Much the same picture may be seen (and with especial clarity from the air) in any American city. The public groundspace has been rendered largely uninhabitable. Esthetically it has been destroyed, lost beneath a tide of moving, stalled, and parked automobiles. Gas-filled, noisy, and hazardous, our streets have become the most inhumane landscapes in the world.

Under such circumstances, it is not surprising that the social and cultural effectiveness of the central city has dropped alarmingly. To restore it, the street must be redeemed. And this, as Louis Kahn, the famous Philadelphia architect and city planner, has pointed out, can only be done by unscrambling the traffic.

> Today's city streets carry half a dozen different, contradictory types of traffic —pedestrians who want to stroll along; buses that want to go-stop-go; private

cars that want to go at an even rate without stopping and then find a place to park; other cars that want to pass the city altogether (but cannot); trucks, trolley cars, delivery boys on bikes, each with a different mission, each with a different rate of movement.

To try to funnel all these kinds of traffic through the same street at the same time is as absurd to Kahn as trying to funnel gas, hot water, cold water, sewage, and electric current through a single tube. This makes it impossible for the street to function effectively as a traffic artery. But it has an even more disastrous effect upon the buildings along either side, for no building can "work" satisfactorily at two different time-scales—one for pedestrians lazing along at 2 mph, the other for automobiles at 50 mph.

With its heavy wheeled traffic, narrow crowded sidewalks, solid walls and open ends, the typical American street acts like a simple conduit. A strong, linear current is set up which is hostile, both physically and psychologically, to the full development of urban life. It creates a riptide along the face of buildings where—to finish with hydraulic similes—there should be quiet water, coves, and bays. The very nature of social intercourse requires the cul-de-sac, the enclave, the shaded portico and sunny court—the zone between the full openness of the street and the full enclosure of the building.

The first step in reconstructing the street would obviously be to restore a healthy circulation between the city and the surrounding hinterland from which it draws its nourishment. And it should be apparent to any rational observer that this can only be accomplished by mass rapid transit: whatever the proper uses of the private automobile (and they are many and real) urban transport is clearly not one of them. It does not much matter what form this mass transit takes—subways, surface trains, aerial trams—technology makes the solution of this problem simple. Nor, in terms of the stakes involved, does it much matter what the necessary subsidies will amount to. The cost of the present urban chaos is quite literally incalculable.

When this fundamental task is accomplished, the reconstruction of the central city becomes possible. What precise lines this reconstruction should follow is still a matter of discussion among planners and architects. But there is general agreement that all surface transportation—public and private alike —would terminate at a ring of stations and storage garages (Kahn calls them "harbors") around the periphery of the central district. Subways, local buses, and taxis would handle local passenger traffic within the center, moving in channels strictly segregated from pedestrians. Trucks would have their own separate times and lanes of movement. This is the schematic substance of the famous Fort Worth plan of architect Victor Gruen. Although it now seems unlikely that the Texas city will ever enjoy the benefits of this plan, it has already become a classic. It visualized the conversion of the central city streets into landscaped pedestrial malls, with the existing gridiron pattern of intersecting conduits converted into a series of snug pedestrian-scaled cul-de-sacs. This pedestrian world was to be connected by a dense network of shuttle buses to a ring of bus terminals and parking facilities around the periphery. By its planned concentration of office buildings, stores, theaters, and public buildings of all sorts in the center, the Gruen plan sought to re-establish the walker's space as the nexus of the social, cultural, and commercial activities of the city.

The Gruen plan is perhaps the most mature American response to date to the crisis of the central city. It does not, of course, stand alone. As a result of Congressional legislation and appropriations for so-called urban renewal and redevelopment, we begin to have the means for this type of intervention in the urban crisis on a national scale. The means, but not yet the policy: for enough of these redevelopment projects are taking shape to make it clear that, though we are becoming aware of the need to act, we have a very unclear image of what should be done. Aside from the ineffable scent of profiteering and graft that surrounds some of the projects, most of them seem to be structured upon makeshift or improvised plans. Too often they appear as mere by-products of complex traffic arteries whose validity is open to question. Too many of them assume the form of luxury apartment towers standing in the midst of expensively landscaped deserts. And very few show any real grasp of the essential qualities of urban space.

Since few American architects and planners have ever had the opportunity to design projects of such dimensions before, a certain amount of initial fumbling was perhaps to be expected. But by now we should understand that one source of the exhilaration we experience in the great urban spaces of the world comes from the variety they always afford the senses. This variety is the expression of multiplicity and diversity of building type and tenancy. Thus, though neither could be called beautiful, both London's Trafalgar and New York's Times Square are almost always rewarding experiences to the pedestrian, at almost any time of day or night. On the other hand, a large single-use project like New York's Lincoln Center is not apt to yield the maximum of metropolitan excitement because its specialized use will lead to part-time, monochromatic activity. Traffic jams at curtain time will alternate with wasteland emptiness at others.

A second precious quality in successful urban space is its pedestrian scale. Most architecture is experienced (seen, heard, felt, smelled) along a plane five feet above the ground. That—and not an aerial vantage point—is the point of view from which urban spaces should be conceived. This does not mean that they need to be small—there is nothing domestic in the scale of Piazza San Marco in Venice or the Tuilleries in Paris—but rather that they should afford the pedestrian that sense of comprehensible organization, that delicious feeling of embrace and enclosure, which all the great urban spaces of the world provide.

A coherent policy toward the city, based upon a clear understanding of its cultural function, will also enable us better to regulate its relations with suburbs and hinterland. And one of the first objectives of such a policy would be to restore and preserve the special social and physical characteristics of each. It will not be enough to rehabilitate the center: the mindless squalor which today surrounds and isolates it must also be cleaned up. The endless semi-slums of Queens or South Chicago; the miles-long decay of Euclid Avenue in Cleveland; the obscene spoilation of the Jersey Meadows—all of these are symptoms of the same disease of urban sprawl which must be halted and then reversed.

If we are to preserve and extend the values we most cherish in our culture, then we must act to save their generator. The task will not be easy, cannot be quick, and certainly will not be "automatic." We must relinquish that childish American faith in *laissez-faire* which acts as though so delicate a mechanism as a city will repair itself, like those reptiles which are supposed to grow new tails to replace the dismembered ones. The task demands considered policy, planned and resolute action. The sheer magnitude of the issues involved permits nothing less.

CONCLUSION

Should anything be done to reverse the present direction of urban growth: Dare we tamper with the "natural" evolution of the city? If untouched, how far can a city sprawl?

The keen competition for space promoted a new family form in the city. The family's reduced size (see Chapter 10), a response to limited space, has been the subject of much dismay. The fertility of suburban families and the addition of "in-law" apartments to their homes gives some promise of a new kind of family organization with some characteristics of the old extended family. Certainly more conscious attention is being paid to family in the suburbs ("It's a terrible commute, but it's worth it for the kids") and to the community itself in a variety of pursuits from camellia clubs to fluoridation fights. Personality disorders resulting from the chaos of city life may be giving way to a newer neurosis based on the need to find a place and to fit in (see "The Westlake Ivy Controversy" in Chapter 22).

The ever-present dilemmas that man has known since time began are no more comfortable in the twentieth century. On the one hand, we have the problems of the city with a more or less stable population, and on the other hand, solid suburbia coupled to a procreative drive discomforting to contemplate.

The decentralization of the city's population and economic base across a sprawling, unplanned area loosely tied to the central city, but with little or no allegiance to it, is fearsome to ponder. As former city folk are joined by their country cousins in the suburbs, the spaces *between* central cities are filling up rapidly, forming a single urbanized area stretching unrelieved for distances of as much as 600 miles. Nearly 40 million Americans are now jammed into a "megalopolis" stretching from Boston, Massachusetts, to Washington, D.C.—20 per cent of our population living on 2 per cent of our land—a pattern that is being repeated to a lesser extent in certain other key areas of the United States. Whereas the older city exerts influence over, and may even dominate, the newer communities filling the open spaces, certain real and pressing problems resulting from the total urban growth are the responsibility of no political entity in particular. Smog, for instance, is no respecter of political boundaries or nonindustrial neighborhoods. The establishment of supermetropolitan jurisdictions is being studied and prescribed in certain areas of this country and Canada, but usually it is too late and too little in the more advanced cases. The chauvinistic attitudes expressed around the country over the surrendering of some local sovereignty also bode ill for early solutions.

There is a case to be made for the city, just as there is a case for the suburbs testified to by the migrant millions, and we still have a concrete need for the *real* country life, especially in view of the 220,000,000 Americans forecast by 1975. The question remains, where will the balance be struck between the rural-urban extremes? Or is it too presumptuous to hope for any definitive and final answer? Is the design merely one of moving from one expedient to another, and is megalopolis the design to which he must adjust? It is not only at this level that man seeks a place. His "quest for community" is conducted also on a grand scale; he looks for it at the national and even the supranational levels. Perhaps there is a relationship among the various types of community which will become clearer as we add to our knowledge of man in society. It might be that a better understanding of one will lead to a better understanding of another—from microcommunity to macrocommunity and vice-versa.

There is no alternative to a groping for expedients. New human situations do not lend themselves to solution by formula. We can, however, make a conscious effort to profit from past mistakes and successes. The ruthless bulldozing of orange groves in Southern California to make way for "G.I." homes has been superseded by the very practical dictate that people will pay more for a house with a few trees. Urban renewal schemes also are being modified constantly in the face of reality, and demolition sometimes yields to renovation. Happier, if not perfect, solutions are possible when a longer view in the affairs of man is taken. But we need a vantage point.

Notes

1. Origin of the terms used: *Megalopolis,* Jean Gottman; *Interurbia,* The J. Walter Thompson Company; and *Exurbia,* A. C. Spectorsky.
2. See Fred W. Cottrell, "Death by Dieselization," *American Sociological Review,* Vol. 16, No. 3, June 1951, pp. 358–365, for an explanation of what happens when the need for a city is abruptly removed.
3. Kingsley Davis, *Human Society,* New York, The Macmillan Company, 1954, p. 336.
4. Amos H. Hawley, *Human Ecology,* New York, Ronald Press, 1950, p. 288.
5. Robert E. Dickinson, *City, Religion, and Regionalism,* London, Kegan Paul, Trench, Trubner, 1947, Chapter 6.
6. Ernest W. Burgess, "The Growth of a City." See Robert E. Park, ed., *The City,* Chicago, University of Chicago Press, 1925, p. 55.

Selected Readings

Dube, S. C. *India's Changing Villages.* Ithaca: Cornell University, 1958.
Eglar, Z. *A Punjabi Village in Pakistan.* New York: Columbia University Press, 1960.
Goldschmidt, Walter. *As You Sow.* New York: Harcourt, Brace and Company, 1947.
Smith, T. C. *The Agrarian Origins of Modern Japan.* Stanford: Stanford University Press, 1959.
*Vidich, Arthur and Joseph Bensman. *Small Town in Mass Society.* New York: Anchor Books, 1961.
Vogt, Evon. *Modern Homesteaders.* Cambridge: Harvard University Press, 1955.
*Weber, Max. *The City.* New York: Collier Books, 1962.
West, James. *Plainville, U.S.A.* New York: Columbia University Press, 1945.

* Paperback edition.

Chapter 8

Social Stratification
in Urban Society

In studying the human group we noted four kinds of social status—ascribed, achieved, generic, and specific—and the relations among them. All societies distinguish among their members on the basis of status. When a society has organized itself for survival, it adds an element of rank, or reward, to status. This ranking by relative importance is called *social stratification.*

Social stratification may be likened to a ladder. The more important or significant the status the higher is its place up the ladder. The basis for judging the position of any single status is the society's attitude toward its characteristics. That a status will receive reward in accordance with its functional importance is probable, but not necessary. Status need be rewarded only to the degree that its importance is matched by difficulty of attainment.[1] Thus, even an important status may rank low if it is easy to attain. A status both important and not easily attainable is likely to rank high and people will seek it. A low-rated status not readily attainable, on the other hand, eventually may be excluded from the society altogether.

Four factors determine the development of a system of social stratification.[2] The first of these is the size of the society. In the smallest societies, which may number less than a hundred persons, the division of labor is based upon *ascribed* statuses. Age, sex, and kinship are the most important—and functional—statuses within such a society. It is difficult within this milieu to gain the prestige that will assure permanently high status in the eyes of others. Primitive society, in its determination to survive, establishes a system of social roles from which little deviance is tolerated. Traditional ways of behavior dominate the system because they work. Any new system might upset the balance of the web of life and lead to the extinction of the society. As a society increases in size, a more specialized division of labor takes place. The granting of social

148

status expands to include *achieved* status. An individual can develop a particular skill or talent not possessed by others, or by only a few, and perhaps be rewarded by a higher status. This is possible within a larger society because of the constant search for new efficiencies by which the population may be better served.

A second factor which determines the development of stratification is the degree of complexity of the economic system. This, of course, is closely related to the division of labor. Kurt Mayer points out in *Class and Society* that the absence of social stratification among the smallest societies does not result from any ideological commitment to equality. It is the consequence of the subsistence level at which such a society lives. There is so little to share that everyone possesses about the same amount of wealth. As the problem of survival is solved, as surpluses of wealth are created and accumulated, social stratification develops based on the relative accumulation of wealth.

A third factor in the development of stratification is social power. Social power may be defined simply as the ability to influence or control the behavior of others. It extends beyond the confines of individuals to embrace the array of community relations. In small societies primarily made up of kinship relations, social power does not exist.[3] Only in societies in which individuals can influence persons other than immediate relatives does this concept have meaning. In such societies the social status granted to those who possess power can become very complex, as we shall see in the last two parts of this book. Two elements that lend complexity to social power are the range and extent of individual power. Range of power refers to the number of different areas of social relations the individual can influence or control. Extent of power refers to the degree of influence or control that he can exercise in any one of these areas.

The final factor in the development of stratification is whether the status can be institutionalized. For social power to have real bearing on social stratification, the status must be reinforced and made permanent within the society. It must be institutionalized if the individual having power is to develop an ideology that will confer status. Institutionalization is also necessary if the status is to become part of the socialization process from generation to generation.

The history of mankind cities three major systems of social stratification: castes, estates, and classes. A caste system consists of a hierarchy of groups within the society. There is little or no movement—or mobility—from group to group. An individual born into a given caste tends to remain in that caste all of his life. Caste systems of social stratification, then, are based on an ascribed status and they vary from culture to culture. Probably the best known has been the caste system of the Hindus in India. The cultural basis of the Hindu caste system was threefold: (1) a hierarchal ordering of occupational statuses determined by (2) a religious dogma which, in turn, probably derived from (3) the cultural conquest by the Indo-Aryans of the darker skinned Dravidian peoples who originally inhabited the Indian subcontinent. A complex system of differentiation developed which was characterized by four major castes. These were the Brahmans, or priests; the Kshatryias, or warriors; the Vaisyas, or merchants and artisans; and the Sudras, or agricultural peasants. Outside of these four castes, and beneath them all, were the untouchables.[4]

Estates as a system of social stratification have been the product of feudal societies, most typically throughout medieval Europe. The European Estates system was predicated on a relatively closed hierarchical ordering of the population into such groupings as the monarch and his household, the lesser nobility and the priests, merchants and artisans, and free and bound peasants.[5] The Estates were kept separated by feudal law and by tradition. Some mobility was possible because of the right of the nobility to create titles and grant privileges. The clergy also found it necessary to recruit its members from the other Estates. In France, under the Bourbon monarchy, three Estates finally evolved. The First Estate was comprised of the clergy, and the Second Estate of the nobility. Together they represented about 5 per cent of the French population. The Third Estate included everyone else. Within each Estate there were informal distinctions made on the basis of family, title, and wealth. The unwieldiness of the system became apparent when, under Louis XVI, representative government based on the Estates system was attempted. But the Revolution of 1789 followed and the system as an effective form of social stratification vanished from the European scene.

Social class is the third form of social stratification. Classes result from the unequal distribution of wealth; hence, classes are related to the nature of the economic system.[6] Classes have neither legal status nor are they traditional in nature. The boundaries between them are vague and subject to redefinition. Classes are not hierarchical orderings of groups within the society, but are loose conglomerations of people who may not be aware of each other or of a common bond.[7] Classes are the product of those societies that have undergone industrialization and urbanization and within which the market has become a dominant force in shaping behavior.

SOCIAL STRATIFICATION IN THE URBAN COMMUNITY

The complexity of urban society arises from the division of labor within an industrial economy, the proliferation of social roles, the development of achieved rather than ascribed social status, and the specialization assumed by institutions other than the economy. Social stratification is therefore highly complex. Bearing in mind the definitions in the first portion of this chapter, let us turn now to an analysis of that complexity. There are three interrelated elements in social stratification in urban society: class, status, and power.

Class. Class is rooted in the economic pattern, referring, as we have said, to the unequal distribution of wealth. Occupation and income, therefore, become major determinants of social class. An immediate consequence of disparities in wealth is the differences that develop among the economic and social opportunities available to the individual. The clichés of our equalitarian-oriented society—that it "takes money to make money," or that "them that has, gets"—indicate that there are inequalities of wealth and opportunity. A capitalistic economy encourages rational social action by classes.[8] The necessity of the calculated pursuit of profit and increased economic opportunity are together the cause of such rational social action.

Class actions are related to rational economic activity, but it does not follow that man's behavior is determined by his class associations, as was maintained by Karl Marx. In the *Communist Manifesto*, for example, Marx wrote that the history of society was to be viewed as the history of class struggle. Not only did Marx imply that all social change was a reflection of changes in the nature of the forces of production, but also that the motivations of the individual were shaped by his position in the class structure. Such determinism is rejected here. Class is only one among other types of human association which influence individual behavior. Nor is it because rational behavior may exist in the economic system that traditional or effective social actions are eliminated everywhere else.

In the selection that follows, the late German sociologist, Karl Mannheim, explores the notions of class position, class, and class consciousness. He emphasized, as did Max Weber, the economic orientation of class but rejected the deterministic stand of Marx. The result is a valuable insight into one important aspect of human motivation.

*

. . . first we shall differentiate between *class position, class, and conscious class*. The first designates the location of the individuals and groups in the social order. Earlier we have pointed out that the term "social position" is more inclusive than "political position." Social location is a general term of reference to the continuing exposure of individuals to like influences or to the same opportunities, inducements, and restrictions. A common social habitat does not necessarily create like interests; for example, the common minority position of different ethnic groups in itself can be conceived without the involvement of group interests. The term "location" may even be widened to include such phenomena as generations and age groups. *Class position*, on the other hand, does imply a certain affinity of interests within a diversified society which selectively allocates power and distributes differential prerogative and economic opportunities.

To advance from the concept of position or location to the concept of class we must first familiarize ourselves with the positional character of behavior. We understand man primarily through his behavior and motivations, and these, in their turn, depend on his orientation in a given situation. We speak of a *positional behavior* if a person's conduct reveals his reaction to his location. The term *positional orientation* must not be construed deterministically, since a given position permits more than one type of reaction. At the same time a behavior is positional only if it is guided by the impulses which are latent in a location, as contrasted with a child or an insane person, neither of whom discerns his position or responds to it. A location has an objective and a subjective component. The objective character of a location can be defined without regard to the behavior of its occupants, for a position simply exists, no matter how or whether one responds to it. Although a position is actualized and becomes discernible only through the behavior of its holders, they may exist in it without responding to it in a predictable or typical manner.

The most important form of positional behavior is that which is solely guided by the economic interests of an individual as they are actualized primarily in the market. Now we may speak of a *class* if individuals act uniformly in accordance with their like interests and like position in the productive process. A *conscious class*, on the other hand, is constituted by the tendency of its members to act collectively in accordance with a conscious evaluation of their class position in relation to all other strata of society.

Class position, class, and conscious class constitute three levels of differ-

* From *Essays on the Sociology of Culture*, by Karl Mannheim. Oxford University Press, 1956. Reprinted by permission.

entiation. Their personnel need not, and usually do not, coincide. Class parties, unions, and pressure groups are often manifestations of the third stage—the conscious class. . . .

We do not maintain that human behavior is solely guided by economic interests, but we do submit that the structure of actions so motivated provides us with a useful model for sociological analysis; a fact well demonstrated by Max Weber. Although traditional conduct in itself is the opposite of rational behavior, it often preserves a previous core of rationality. Tradition may stem from past interests as much as from magic.

Quite often the layman may not identify the play of rational interests in irrationally motivated actions. The observance of religious precepts, in itself nonrational, often serves rational ends. Max Weber's familiar analysis of Puritan asceticism furnishes a good illustration. The primary motivation of this asceticism was unquestionably religious, yet it corresponded to a rational attitude towards economic values, demanded by an evolving commercial capitalism. In the long run man cannot act in complete disregard of his location and undo the social conditions of his existence; what matters, therefore, is what he does and not what he thinks he does. Actions may consistently attain a certain end without being motivated by it. Quite often an infinite series of minor, though unconscious, adaptations will ultimately redirect an originally dysfunctional type of behavior into rational channels.

Practically everybody has ambivalent motivations and more than one social habitat. Class position, therefore, is one of several locations and one of several motivations for action. . . .

These considerations must remain meaningless as long as one adheres to the dogmatic conception of class as the Marxist theory presents it. . . . Contrary to its positivistic intention, the Marxist philosophy follows the medieval type of conceptual realism whose ontology by-passes the individual. . . . It conceives class in the nature of a macro-anthropos and the individual merely as the tool of a collective leviathan. Marx' *class* appears to be as independent of the perceptions and reactions of the individual as the medieval universals. Once classes are so conceptualized they can easily be turned into verbalistic pigeonholes, and every individual is said to belong to one or another. Although the doctrine is not taught in this fashion, such a conclusion is hardly avoidable for those who think in the alternatives of class or nonclass. . . .

. . . Class as distinguished from class position cannot be thought of independently of the actions of individuals, but only as a group which homogeneously reacts to an identical economic position. Only his class motivations make an individual a member of a class. Once this is clear we are able to attach some significance to the varieties of motivations for political choices. Some persons are swayed by only one preponderant motivation, while others are subject to conflicting inducements. This is true . . . of anybody who belongs to a well-entrenched occupation to which outsiders have no easy access.

STATUS AND STYLE OF LIFE

The status element in urban stratification develops from the social interaction experienced among members of the same class. Such interaction occurs by virtue of shared economic interests. The result is an informal grouping of individuals and of families at the same level of status. Since they can afford approximately the same level of living, members of the same class tend to live near each other, enjoy the same kinds of recreation, dress alike—in short, create what Max Weber called a style of life.[9] In contrast to the rational social action related to class behavior, the activity of a status group is held together by the bonds of tradition and of sentiment which emerge spontaneously within it. The style of life of any status group is further reinforced by its use of urban space.[10]

Individuals who share the same style of life also tend to share in the use of urban spaces. Differentiated use of space, as we saw in Chapter 6, results from lack of intimacy with the urban community's entire space. People are drawn into those areas in which they can further their own life interests. Thus, the élite of an urban community will move in similar areas within their own community and, in our age of rapid transportation and communication, move within similar areas of other urban communities, domestic or foreign.[11] As Anselm Strauss said, "In any genuine sense, it can be said that the members of such a world live not only, say, in the Gold Coast area, but also elsewhere for part of the year—in a favorite resort, in a fine suburb, in Paris, or in all four places."[12]

The relationship between style of life and urban space was explored further by Strauss in the following selection. Strauss was careful to indicate that there was not only a spatial dimension to life styles in the city but also a dimension of time. Thus, the same street might exhibit one life style during the day and a quite different one at night.

*
Just as the downtown area, and even single streets, are differentiated by economic function, so we may regard them as differentiated by symbolic function. This statement has implications that are not immediately apparent. A convenient way to begin seeing these implications is to examine closely a single important downtown street. It will probably be used simultaneously

* Reprinted from *Images of the American City*, by Anselm Strauss, pp. 61–64. Copyright 1960 by The Fress Press, A Corporation. By permission of the publisher.

by several different kinds of populations, distinguishable by dress and posture. Other kinds of people will be wholly, or to a considerable extent, missing. (These may be found on other streets; for instance, the wealthier customers and strollers will be found [in New York City] on upper Fifth Avenue rather than below 42nd Street.) Just as several types of economic services can be found cheek by jowl on the same street, so may there be several symbolic functions performed by the same street. A restaurant there may serve expensive food; it may also serve leisure and a sense of luxury. Close by, another type of establishment may cater to another taste, an activity not entirely reducible to economic terms. The street may attract people who seek glamour, adventure, escape from a humdrum life, and who, though they may not spend a cent, feel wholly or partly satisfied by an evening on the street. The larger the downtown area, the more obviously districted will be the various economic and symbolic functions. A city as large as Chicago, for instance, has a separate hotel row, a separate élite shopping boulevard, a separate financial canyon; and on these streets may be seen different types of architecture, different types of clients and servicing agents, and different types of activities. During the evening some of the symbolic, if not indeed the economic, functions change on identical streets; that is, people are using different institutions, or using the same ones a little differently. The sociological question is always: "Who is found in such an area or on such a street, doing what, for what purposes, at any given hour?"

Over the years a downtown street can change wholly in economic and symbolic functions, as the center of town moves or as the city center grows larger and hence more differentiated. However, in American cities, some downtown streets seem to retain a remarkable affinity for the same kind of businesses, clients, visitors, and pleasure-seekers. Streets acquire and keep reputations. They evoke images in the minds of those who know these reputations; and presumably these images help attract and repel clients and visitors. From time to time, as the downtown district becomes more differentiated, functions break off from one street and become instituted in another. Thus, in Chicago, upper Michigan Avenue was opened with some fanfare during the present century, drawing away élite shops and shoppers from the more centrally located and famed State Street section. One can, if he is sufficiently imaginative, therefore, view the downtown area of any city as having different historical depths. . . .

To continue now with the complex symbolic functions of certain downtown streets, it is clearly observable that certain streets draw several different kinds of populations. The term "locale" shall refer to such a street. A street like Rush Street in Chicago, for example, is a locale where in the evening one may find—on the street and in the many restaurants and bars—a variety of customers, servicing agents, and visitors. Rush Street has its own atmosphere, as many people have observed, compounded of all these people and all these institutions. It is one of the glamour streets of Chicago. There one can see, if one has an eye for them, prostitutes, pimps, homosexuals, bisexuals, upper class men and women, university students, touts, artists, tourists, business men out for a good time with or without girlfriends, young men and women dating, people of various ethnic backgrounds, policemen, cabbies—the entire catalogue is much longer. Rush Street is a locale where people from many different urban worlds, with many styles of urbanity, pass each other, buy services from each other, talk to one another, and occasionally make friends with one another. Like animals using the same bit of land, people on Rush Street can interact almost subliminally, demanding nothing of each other, making no contracts with each other, merely passing each other or sitting near each other. But the interaction can also be contractual and exploitative, as when prostitutes find clients or pickpockets find marks. But most important, perhaps, there can occur at such locales a more sociable, more lasting kind of contact between peoples drawn from different worlds. It is at places like Rush Street that the orbits of many worlds intersect, so that persons may learn something of the ways of another world. In locales, as the orbits intersect, the physical segregation of these urban worlds is at a minimum.

Other streets in the city are inhabited and visited by persons drawn from just a few social worlds. Think, for instance, of the main street in a Polish area down whose length one can see only Polish people. The area may be visited occasionally by outsiders or patrolled by non-Polish policemen; but for the most part, especially at night, this is a street which quite literally belongs to the residents of the parish. (If anything, the side streets are even more insular.) Let us call such a street or area, where intersect only a minimum number of social worlds, a "location." At a location, the physical segregation of the people of a social world is maximized. Here they can openly indulge in ceremonial and ritual gestures, here they may speak a foreign language without shame. For it is here that an urban world is seen in the form of relatively public activities based on relatively widely shared symbols. It is here, too, that the outsider really knows that he is an outsider; and if he wishes to become an insider, he knows that he must learn the appropriate ways of this world. This kind of area, too, is characterized by quite exclusive, or semi-exclusive, spaces, as anyone who has entered a Polish tavern, to be eyed by the "regulars," knows. In the streets of such an area, the stranger is quickly spotted.

POWER

Power is closely related to both class and status. Those who have great wealth are able to control effectively, or at least influence, the economy. The rise and fall of stock-market prices, the decisions related to the rate of development of a business, the closing of a factory, and the relative confidence in the economy expressed by individuals of wealth—are all examples of social power. Individuals who have high social status, as distinct from status based on wealth alone, also can exercise power. Statesmen and scholars, celebrities and saints have been able to influence the course of events. In urban society the use of power is not, of course, the simple expression of an individual whim. Given the complexity of such a society, opposing or countervailing power may develop. From time to time, the need develops in both classes and status groups to express power in a formal and organized manner in order to ensure the level of life and the values of wealth and opportunity which they have established for themselves. Under such circumstances parties may develop as the means for expressing power.

Parties, as we typically think of them, signify some kind of group organization; they can, however, be individuals. Not only can one group seek to exercise power over other groups but also one individual can seek to exercise power over others. The following passage by Richard Schermerhorn introduces us to some of the implications of power structures. He first notes the four logical possibilities that exist in the exercise of power, and then indicates the kinds of resources that can be used to express power.

*
. . . the wider meaning of the term party should be emphasized since it can designate either an individual or a group. (Since some groups operate through institutions, here group is understood to include institutional arrangements as well.)

Because of this dual meaning of party, we are presented with four logical possibilities: (1) the behavior of an individual may dominate the behavior of another individual; (2) the behavior of an individual may dominate the behavior of a group; (3) the behavior of a group may dominate the behavior of an individual; (4) the behavior of a group may dominate the behavior of another group.

In the first case, if a boy won't eat until his mother turns on the television set, he has power over his mother. In the second case, if several members of a club decide to have a picnic but one person in the organization talks them out of it and into a swimming party instead, that individual has power over the club. In the third case, if the majority of a union votes to raise the annual dues and one of those who voted against the measure nevertheless pays the increased assessment, the union has power over that member. In the fourth and final case, if a real-estate lobby puts enough pressure on a state

* From *Society and Power*, by Richard A. Schermerhorn, pp. 15–18. Copyright 1961 by Random House, Inc. By permission.

legislature to defeat a bill for higher property taxes, the lobby has power over the legislature.

Some of these dominant influences may be operating simultaneously in a given case; they are often separable only in analysis. It is important to recognize that power may function in all four ways and thus transcend the purely interpersonal field of events. On the other hand, to say, as Robert Bierstedt does, that "the focus of power is in groups" and therefore in intergroup relations alone would eliminate power from interpersonal relations entirely and restrict it to the fourth possibility above. A broader connotation for the term would seem more reasonable.

Bierstedt is more persuasive when he declares that the source of power in human society is threefold: "(1) numbers of people, (2) social organization, and (3) resources," particularly where intergroup relations are concerned. In general, a group large in numbers with cohesive organization and adequate means will overcome the opposition of another group deficient in those characteristics. Nevertheless, unless what is meant by "resources" is clear, this concept could well restrict power to the intergroup field alone. Since Bierstedt has not spelled out the meaning of "resources" in detail, we must consider this point more fully.

Review of the evidence leads to the provisional conclusion that there are five types of resources that can be used to advance or to strengthen a power position: (1) military, police, or criminal power with its control over violence; (2) economic power with control over land, labor, wealth, or corporate production; (3) political power with control over legitimate and ultimate decision-making within a specified territory; (4) traditional or ideological power involving control over belief and value systems, religion, education, specialized knowledge, and propaganda; and (5) diversionary power with control over hedonic interests, recreation, and enjoyments. Even brief inspection of these five power resources makes it clear that they are available to individuals as well as to groups; it is equally obvious that all these resources are socially exercised.

Assuming that power is a dynamic process, we may then ask if it tends to repeat itself in easily identified ways. The answer is yes, though the patterns at times overlap. The power process frequently crystallizes into more or less stable configurations designated as centers or structures of power.

SOCIAL MOBILITY

Having reviewed the relations between class, status, and power, we can now turn to a fourth element of social stratification—social mobility. Social mobility may be defined as the possibility within a system of stratification for an individual to move up or down through the hierarchies of class, status, and power.[13]

Any society that has developed a system of social stratification will also experience social mobility. There are two reasons for this.[14] The first relates to the changing demands for performance. Those who possess power, and the high status accompanying it, may not have the ability to use it in a sound manner, or may use it in a fashion long outmoded. If talent from the lower strata of the society is excluded from the power system there develops the possibility of tension and challenge to those in leadership.[15] Mobility also will develop from changes in the supply of talent. No class or status group has a monopoly on intelligence or talent. These are scattered throughout the hierarchies of society. If a ruling clique intends to stay in power it must recruit from below, otherwise tensions and challenge to the system again may result.

Although social mobility occurs in any system of social stratification, it is widespread in societies that have undergone industrialization and urbanization.[16] A number of changes have taken place in the social organization of such societies enabling widespread social mobility.[17]

First, any change in the character of the social institutions of an industrial and urban society creates vacancies in the system of social stratification which must be filled. In the United States this has been exemplified by the changes that have taken place in the labor force. There has been a gradual increase in the proportion of so-called administrative or supervisory employees to production workers. In 1899 there were eight administrative employees for every 100 production workers. In 1957 the ratio was 30 to 100.[18] Essentially the same availability of vacancies among higher statuses can be expected as the society experiences shortages of engineers, doctors, teachers, ministers, and so on.

A second factor which contributes to social mobility is the nature of the birth rate. The families of men in the so-called higher-status occupations characteristically do not reproduce at a high enough rate to "replace" themselves. Society must reach down into the pools of intelligence and talent in the lower-status occupations. Added to this, most higher occupations are to be found in urban communities which have a lower birth rate than rural communities.[19] The need for labor in the urban community becomes an extra attraction to the rural population, many of whom already have been displaced by the mechanization of agriculture.

The third factor producing widespread social mobility is the changes in the statuses within the urban community. As industrialization continues to produce new efficiencies and modifies the nature of the division of labor some occupations become entirely obsolete while others, although continuing, lose prestige in the competition with newer occupations. The airplane pilot, for instance, has succeeded both the ship captain and the locomotive engineer in prestige.

The decline in the number of inherited statuses is the fourth factor relating to social mobility. The distinctions of feudal title in Europe have declined in significance. In America, even though we have not experienced real feudalism, the social prestige of inherited wealth has declined. This change is an aspect of the opening, within the society, of new avenues of social mobility. Perhaps the most important of these is higher education. Once only available to the wealthy, higher education is today within the reach of nearly everyone of ability. Public land grant colleges and free state and junior colleges have made access to higher education possible and, with it, access to occupations and styles of life determined by the acquired values and tastes of such an education.

The last factor contributing to widespread social mobility has been the removal of legal restrictions upon mobility. In Europe this was evidenced by the decline of the guild system (see Chapter 14) which controlled the economies of the urban communities in Europe in the Middle Ages and whose influence was felt sporadically into the nineteenth century. The decline, as well, of the estates system also removed the legal barriers of feudal law. In the United States the gradual movement toward the social emancipation of the Negro is indicative of this trend, particularly the declared unconstitutionality of the "Jim Crow" laws.

The forces producing social mobility are not yet fully understood. Nevertheless, it is obvious that the changes in the structure of the urban community do influence mobility patterns. In the following selection, Seymour Lipset and Reinhard Bendix consider the urbanization process as a source of motivation and aptitude for social mobility.

*

Evidence derived from a number of studies in different countries suggests that the related processes of urbanization and migration are major sources of social mobility. These data indicate that today, in some countries, migration from rural areas and smaller communities to metropolitan centers influences the placement of people in the occupational structure in the same way that large scale immigration once did. That is, at one time, in the United States and other immigrant-accepting countries, large numbers of immigrants entered the economic structure at its lowest level. The native-born, often children of immigrants themselves, were presumably able to

* From *Social Mobility in Industrial Societies*, by Seymour Lipset and Reinhard Bendix, pp. 204–213. By permission of the University of California Press.

secure the jobs which an expanding economy created on the next higher level. And though mass immigration into many countries has ended, high rates of internal migration now characterize their societies. In the United States, for example, such migration has the size of a major population movement. Between April, 1940, and April, 1947, 20.8 per cent of the total population changed their county of residence—a total of almost thirty million persons. In the relatively "normal" postwar year of 1953–1954, nearly ten million persons, or 6.4 per cent of the population, migrated across county lines. The Census of 1950 reports that in that year, thirty-five million persons, or 25.2 per cent of all United States residents, were living in states other than the one in which they were born.

Analysis of the Oakland study and of relevant materials from the University of Michigan's Survey Research Study of the 1952 elections shows the way in which this process operates. The Oakland data show, for example, that the larger a man's community of orientation (the community in which he spent his teens), the higher the status of the job he holds is likely to be. Of those who spent their formative years on farms, only 41 per cent achieved nonmanual positions; of those who spent them in small urban places, 53 per cent; and of those who grew up in large cities, 65 per cent.

The deviations from the above trend lie mainly in two largely non-bureaucratic or entrepreneurial groups, the self-employed and the professionals. In Oakland, the proportion of professionals of small-city origin is greater than the proportion from large cities, but nearly equal proportions of self-employed come from each type of community. As shall be shown later, the Research Center's national survey indicates that men of middle-class origin reared in small communities actually do as well or better than those reared in large cities: a finding particularly related to the fact that the male offspring of small-town middle-class families usually obtain a higher education than their large city compeers. It is probable that many natives of small communities who secure higher educations leave their home towns to go to the large cities, where greater opportunity exists. Thus, we find that size of community of orientation is most closely related to occupational position within the ranks of industry and large-scale organization. The smaller the community of orientation the less likely a lower-class individual is to be upwardly mobile within bureaucratic structures.

The inferences about the relationship between size of community of orientation and social mobility which have been drawn from our data may be tested directly by comparing the occupations of respondents with those of their fathers. It is clear . . . that working-class youth growing up in large cities are much more likely to reach high occupational status than those coming from smaller communities. This suggests anew that migration from rural areas and small cities to metropolitan areas serves to facilitate upward mobility by those native to urban life. It is important to note, however, that the advantage is concentrated in the sons of the working class. The data bearing on intragenerational mobility indicate a definite pattern. Those from smaller communities are more likely to fall from a nonmanual first job, and less likely to rise from a manual first job, than are those coming from larger communities. The factors which underlie these relationships are discussed below.

Table 1. Relationship Between Community of Orientation and Occupation, with Education Held Constant

| Occupational group of present job | Community of Orientation and Years of Education | | | | | | | | |
| | Farm | | | Under 250,000 | | | Over 250,000 | | |
	0–11	12	13+	0–11	12	13+	0–11	12	13+
Professional	2	2	35	0	10	35	2	3	20
Own business	13	11	12	12	12	10	16	15	7
Business executive and upper white collar	5	5	15	2	12	18	13	14	27
Lower white collar	7	24	15	17	22	10	15	30	22
Sales	9	7	3	6	8	5	5	11	7
Skilled	27	22	21	29	22	16	27	18	10
Semiskilled	22	20	0	22	14	4	18	7	7
Unskilled	14	9	0	13	2	2	5	2	0
Nonmanual	36	49	79	36	63	79	50	72	82
Manual	64	51	21	64	37	21	50	28	18
Number of respondents	157	55	34	108	51	57	185	151	97

[The accompanying table] . . . makes clear that, holding the level of achieved education constant, large-city natives are more likely to reach a high position within the bureaucracy of industry than are those from smaller communities. Nearly twice as many men from communities over 250,000 who have some higher education occupy high-status white-collar and executive positions as do educated men from small communities and farms (27 per cent, as against 18 and 15). The difference among those with less than high school education is even more striking: 13 per cent from large communities hold high bureaucratic positions, as against 2 per cent from small communities and 5 per cent from farms. Further evidence of the effect of urban environment on occupational success in business bureaucracies may be found in studies of the business elite. Warner and Abegglen note that men born in big cities are more likely to obtain positions at the top of the business world. The same result was obtained by Suzanne Keller, who found that although only 39.7 per cent of the population in 1890 lived in cities of 2,500 or more, the majority of the members of the business élite born about that time (65 per cent) were born in larger communities. Since both these studies selected their samples in such a way as to emphasize bureaucratic mobility, their findings support the hypothesis that urban residence during childhood facilitates bureaucratic careers.

Another interesting internal difference revealed in our study is the pattern for professionals (see accompanying table). More of the college-trained persons from smaller communities are professionals than those who originated in metropolitan centers. This finding is probably related to the fact, pointed out earlier, that many professionals who grow up in smaller communities migrate to big cities. Many from small communities who do well in the educational system have to leave their home towns to secure employment or remuneration commensurate with their training. Large cities attract two types of migrants from rural areas and smaller urban centers: a large majority who fill the lower rungs of the occupational ladder, and thus create a base upon which the dweller native to the metropolis may climb; and a minority of well-educated migrants who compete with the natives for positions at the top.

The effect of community size on occupational careers may be specified further by a consideration of data collected by the Survey Research Center of the University of Michigan in the course of their survey of a sample of the American population during the 1952 election. If we compare the rates of mobility in cities having more than 50,000 population with those of cities having less, the pattern suggested by the Oakland material is repeated; inhabitants of large cities have a higher rate of upward mobility, and a lower rate of downward movement, than those living in small ones.

The Survey Research Center also asked respondents to report the type of community in which they grew up: "Were you brought up mostly on a farm, mostly in a small town, or mostly in a big city?" Although there is undoubtedly a great deal of unreliability in the responses to this question, they do permit a further test of the relationship between size of community of orientation and rates of social mobility . . . Among men of working-class parentage, size of community of orientation is positively related to their opportunities for *upward* social mobility. Larger size of community of orientation is, however, related to *downward* mobility among those with a nonmanual family background. Although the differences are small, the data suggest that manual-workers' sons growing up in big cities have a better chance to move up than those reared in small towns, but that sons of middle-class families from small towns are less likely to fall in occupational status than those who grow up in large cities. The number of cases in the sample is unfortunately too small to permit any reliable comparison of the amount of social mobility related to both community of orientation and community of current residence. This four-variable breakdown suggests, however, that the mobility advantage held by the sons of manual workers raised in large cities as contrasted with those raised in small towns occurs only *within* large cities, since those who grew up in large cities but who now live in small cities or towns do very little better than those who grew up in small towns and still reside in small communities. Among current inhabitants of metropolitan areas whose fathers were manual workers, almost twice as many of those who also grew up in big cities have been upward mobile (38 per cent) as have those who grew up in small towns (22 per cent). There is no apparent sharp difference among the sons of nonmanuals when we classify their current jobs by communities of orientation and present residence.

The relationship between social origins and community of orientation may be further specified by studying the effect of educational attainments on occupational achievement. If the amount of education is held constant a pattern which emerged in the analysis of the Oakland materials is also suggested by the Center's national survey: that is, growing up in a big city constitutes a definite advantage for those who are handicapped educationally (less than four years of high school); but being reared in a large urban community is not a mobility asset for the better educated (high school graduation or more).

The analysis of the national survey data both reinforces and suggests some need to modify the conclusions based on the study of Oakland. The following patterns are suggested by the data cited above:

1. There is more upward and less downward mobility in large cities than in small towns.

2. The larger the community in which the son of a worker grew up, the better his chances for upward mobility, a relationship that does not hold for the sons of nonmanual fathers.

3. The positive effect of being reared in a large city on occupational opportunities is found among those with less than a high school education. Among those who have a high school education or better, size of community of orientation is not positively related to greater opportunity.

SOCIAL MOBILITY, LIFE STYLE, AND SOCIAL ROLE

Social mobility can integrate an individual's personality, provided he gains acceptance into the class and status group toward which he has been directing his behavior. The shift in status will also be positive if the individual experiences few, if any, discrepancies between conformity to the norms of the new class and any lingering loyalty to norms of the class he has left behind.

Yet social mobility is not invariably positive in its impact on the individual. The usual course of events in urban communities is for the individual to occupy a number of different social roles which convey statuses of various levels. Social mobility tends to accentuate the difference in these statuses. The result is a discrepancy of status.[20] In extreme cases of such discrepancy there may be a complete disorganization of the personality resulting from the inability of the individual to integrate the many things expected of him. This can result in a form of mental illness.[21]

As dramatic as the psychological consequences of mental illness may be, they are not the major response to social mobility. There is a more pervasive and subtle consequence. But let us go back a bit. In the chapter on group life we saw that when an individual behaved as others expected, he performed a social role. We noted also that the expectations imposed by society were more than any one person could meet. This gave rise to role strain and to means by which the individual might ameliorate that strain. One of the major forms of easing that strain was related to the individual's allocation of his time, energy, talent, and so forth. How much he allocated was defined by his commitment to the role and the rewards and punishments it carried. Implicit in the theory of role strain is the notion that the individual does not passively accept the norms of the situation, *but actively seeks to accommodate the situation to his own needs.* He may, in fact, seek actively to manipulate the situation in a manner most beneficial to the image others will have of him.

Now, any class, status group, or power group, or power relationship involves the playing of social roles. Social mobility is the acquisition of higher statuses in relation to those roles. In urban communities, therefore, social mobility is subject to that kind of behavior in which there is active manipulation of roles. This is done with the desire to create, or "give off," a favorable impression in order to be accepted into a particular class or status group.

The manipulation of roles is made possible in urban communities, first, by the anonymity of social relations. Because people seldom know one another beyond the confines of the specific situation in which they relate, it becomes almost necessary to take another person at his face value. What the person *says* he is, his manner of speech, and his over-all appearance become symbolic clues by which others may judge him.[22] "If he looks like a duck, walks like a duck, and talks like a duck, he must be a duck." A second factor encouraging manipulation of the situation in the urban setting is the division of space into orbits characteristic of particular styles of life. Thus, if an individual can acquire, however superficially, the outward appearance of a given life style and function within the known orbits related to it, he may be able to create the impression that he really belongs; George Bernard Shaw's Eliza Doolittle is a good example. A third factor which makes manipulation possible in urban communities is the brief duration of time within which any given relationship takes place. This simply means that few persons have the time really to know others in an intimate fashion. There is no time to peel off the façade of a social role and attempt to discover the "real person."

A brilliant analysis of manipulation of the situation and management of impressions has been written by Erving Goffman.[23] He indicates that, because of the lack of duration and the fragmentation of social relations in the urban community, those with whom an individual interacts will have to be satisfied with the impression they receive of him.[24] Therefore, the individual, in his own interests, will try to manipulate the situation. "He may wish . . . the others . . . to think highly of him, or to think that he thinks highly of them, or to perceive how in fact he feels toward them, or to obtain no clear-cut impression; he may wish to ensure sufficient harmony so that the interaction can be sustained, or to defraud, get rid of, confuse, mislead, antagonize, or insult them." [25]

The belief in his own impression that the individual fosters may range from complete sincerity to utter cynicism.[26] He may do so well in manipulating the situation that he is literally taken in by his own act. Or, he may be able to distinguish critically between the impression he is fostering and the reality of his concept of Self. In socially mobile situations the distinction is not easy to maintain. For example, the practical advantages of service organizations—from the Junior League to the hospital aid society—in promoting social mobility cannot be denied. At the same time the often humanitarian values in such groups constitute a powerful ideology in their own right.

It can never be assumed that the others in the situation would be any happier if they realized that manipulation was occurring. Indeed they may be happier never knowing. This is exemplified by the hypochondriac who receives prescriptions for sugar pills from the doctor, the debutante dancing with her relentlessly gay escort, or the college professor surrounded by eager graduate students.

The fostered impressions, especially those which have been institutionalized, are reinforced by what Goffman called the rhetoric of training.[27] It is that period of time during which the individual is socialized into both the "technical necessities" of the role and the mystical rituals and beliefs accompanying its style of life. The two, interacting upon each other, enable the individual to foster the impression that he is different from the ordinary folk in his society.

In the selection that follows E. McNamara gives us a humorous but subtly true insight into the role of the college teacher. Although Mc-Namara approached "teachermanship" from the viewpoint of ego satisfaction, there is little question that the manipulation of the college situation by the fledgling instructor was designed to ensure both his future in the college and his separation from his students.

*With the publications of *Gamesmanship, Lifemanship, Oneupmanship* and *Supermanship,* one might expect to see the subject of fruitful manipulation of one's environment for ego-gratification exhausted. Not so. For within the vast and multileveled field of life there are many areas untouched by the great work done by Potter and the pioneers of Madison Avenue. There are other worlds to conquer; some work of note may yet be done. (See pamphlet *On the Use of Neglected or Outdated Poets for Quotation on Dignified Occasions or to Cause Embarrassment.* Teachermanship studies monograph No. 1.) There is, for instance, the untouched field of teaching. The rising birth rate will ultimately lead to the anticipated and long dreaded over-expansion of students in the colleges. This, of course, will lead to a corresponding inflation in the faculties. What will result? Compartmentalization, loss of individualism.

The young instructor, especially, must become aware of this challenge. Lacking as yet in tenure, rank or publishing history, he must make his own existential way between his students and his department head, doing as much as possible to be *noticed,* yet as little real work as possible, so as to provide time for the solidification of his future (gaining of tenure, rank, salary, sabbaticals, when the boom is over and the unaware—those who did not face the challenge of teachermanship—will have fallen by the wayside). (See pamphlet *On the Use of Clichés to Promote Feeling in In-Group Solidarity.* Teachermanship studies monograph No. 8.) But I have amassed a small body of observations and have begun a controlled study. Here are five preliminary suggestions:

1. *Clothesmanship or OK Clothes.* This is of immediate importance. One's graduate school record, research, past experience mean *nothing* when contrasted with your initial impact on (*a*) your department head; (*b*) your classes; (*c*) ultimately, the dean. ("Who *is* that young man?") Tweeds, of course, are essential. Burlap would be more desirable, but a good basic impression can be attained by the thoughtful wearing of several moderately worn-out tweed jackets and flannel trousers and a maximum of two ties,

* From "Some Notes Towards the Establishment of Teachermanship," by E. McNarmara, *College English,* May 1961, pp. 579–580. Reprinted by permission of the National Council of Teachers of English and E. McNamara.

both either tweed or a very-muddy madder cloth. One should, above all, give the *feel* of tweed. One should somehow suggest that he is wearing tweed underwear, or even that his pyjamas are tweed. (All without actually saying so, of course. All must be conveyed by implication.)

2. *First Lecture.* There are two basic manoeuvres. One is the humorous, head-scratching, off-hand impromptu lecture. Rambling, witty, full of references to juxtaposed items (Bach and beer, Dylan Thomas and Elvis Presley) and ironic references to the administration, the heating plant and the local bars. The very next class, it goes without saying, is an essay test (unannounced, difficult, vague) on the purpose of the course.

The other basic manoeuvre is the direct opposite of the *off-hand upset.* It is the *basic bibliography ploy.* As the bell echoes die you enter, head slightly down, about a quire of mimeographed sheets clutched to your bosom in one hand, a briefcase in the other. Put both down. Unload the briefcase. A minimum of eight books is needed for effectiveness. (Important: Once having unloaded the books *do not refer to them at all for the balance of the period.*) The mimeographed sheets should consist of a course outline, at least sixteen pages, single-spaced. The text of this should not matter, since no one will read it. If necessary, use a bad stencil so that parts are illegible. The other mimeographed bundle will be a twenty-page bibliography which you will refer to slightingly and half-apologetically as "basic," or "elementary." This should have built-in errors (dates, accent marks) which you will *discover* as you thumb through it and the students will correct their own copies. It is well to have titles in languages other than English and French. German is good, but Swedish is better. Your opening lecture should be as incomprehensible as the course outline. Use phrases like, "Ultimately, our aim is quite simple . . ." and "The serious student will avail himself of . . ." Stare out of the window. Refer to obscure authorities, quote from Horace and then smile (or better, snicker. See my notes on the "snuffle-laugh" or "the library snigger"). The trauma inflicted by this opening lecture will last until mid-term.

3. *Transportation.* Bicycles of course are best. Some avant-garde practitioners are advocating the motorcycle or motor scooter. But for the novice, the *Basic Motor Gambit* should suffice. To begin with, any car will do. Imports are best, but an older, much-misused and dirty coupé of domestic make will do very well if the sub-ploy of the Rear Seat or Rear Ledge is used. Books or journals-translations of *American* poets into French, journals in such fields as "Cultural Dynamics" with articles such as "Evidence of Transvestitism in *Superman*," prominently displayed on the covers, *must seem carelessly thrown there.*

4. *OK Books.* Even as you are scrupulous about clothesmanship, so must you be about the magazines or/and books which you carry for display. Aristotle is always good. So are any publications of Grove Press or New Direc-

tions. *Scholarly journals must always be out of your field.* Cultivate a manner of carrying, so that the title may be withheld from view until interest is piqued. Note that interest, once aroused, may go so far as to look into the book or even to the borrowing of it. Hence, the sub-ploy of Margin-Marking must be used to ensure protection. *Margin marks must always seem enigmatic, thoughtful and should if possible refer to other books which are equally esoteric.* Thus, exclamation points, N.B., and the like are not as desirable as *Cf. Jung* or *Viz: Origen.*

5. *Paper Marking.* The basic aim, of course, is to mark the paper speedily, efficiently and if possible, without reading it. The primary ploy is the Incomplete Erasure of A Lower Grade. This usually forestalls any student objection. Cultivation of a vocabulary which indicates thoughtful effort on your part (words like "disappointing," "adequate," "wry," "crisp," "tendentious") should be worked at. Avoid such definite and positively connotative words as "good" and "bad."

These above, I suggest, are the basic gambits of teachermanship. Other innovations and changes may come along, but I feel certain that those mentioned here will remain classic. Already, research is going on beyond the frontiers: beards, whistling Bach in public places, progressive jazz, canes, vagaries of speech. (See monograph #2. *On the Use of Chiefly British Spelling to Suggest A Public School Background.*) But these are only variations on the classic principles educed here.

CONCLUSION

This chapter has dealt with four major aspects of social stratification: class, status, power, and social mobility. In the first part we reviewed the relation of the first three concepts, noting that when interaction within classes becomes frequent there emerges a style of life resting on the acquisition of status. Both classes and status groups may seek power within a community to ensure access to economic opportunity and to guard the prestige of the status group. Social mobility, the vertical movement of individuals throughout the stratification system of a community, is stimulated by the process of urbanization. Given the fragmentation and anonymity of urban life a manipulation of self impressions becomes possible to obtain access to a higher class or status.

Now that we have reviewed the general processes of community growth and development, and the nature of stratification within them, we can devote the remaining parts of the book to the study of specific institutions within communities.

Notes

1. Kingsley Davis, *Human Society*, New York: The Macmillan Company, 1949, p. 368.
2. A brief but forceful summary of these four points is to be found in Kurt B. Mayer, *Class and Society*, New York: Random House, 1955, rev. ed., pp. 4 ff.
3. *Ibid.*, p. 6.
4. E. A. H. Blunt, *The Caste System of Northern India*, London: Oxford University Press, 1931.
5. Mayer, *op. cit.*, p. 7.
6. That classes are rooted in the economic system is a contribution of Karl Marx and Friedrich Engels. See, *The Communist Manifesto*, New York: Crofts Classics, 1960. Although accepting the economic basis of class, later formulations of the concept went far beyond the determinism of Marx and Engels.
7. Mayer, *op. cit.*, p. 8.
8. Max Weber, *From Max Weber: Essays in Sociology*, ed. and trans. Hans Gerth and C. Wright Mills, New York: Oxford Galaxy Books, 1958, p. 279.
9. Weber, *op. cit.*, p. 187.
10. This is an ecological extension of the concept of life style. See Anselm Strauss, *Images of the American City*, New York: The Free Press, 1961, Chap. 4.
11. *Ibid.*, p. 66.
12. *Ibid.*, pp. 66–67.
13. Mayer, *op. cit.*, p. 27.
14. Seymour Lipset and Reinhard Bendix, *Social Mobility in Industrial Society*, Berkeley: University of California Press, 1959, pp. 2–3.
15. For a discussion of élite theories of rule see: Vilfredo Pareto, *Mind and Society*, ed. and trans. Arthur Livingston and Andrew Bongiorno, New York: Harcourt, Brace and Company, 1935, 4 vols.; Robert Michels, *Political Parties*, trans. Edan and Cedar Paul, New York: Collier Books, 1961; and Gaetano Mosca, *The Ruling Class*, trans. H. D. Kahn, New York: McGraw-Hill Book Company, 1939. For a recent addition see Seymour Lipset, *Political Man*, Garden City, New York: Doubleday and Company, 1960, Chapter 12.
16. Cf., Lipset and Bendix, *op. cit.*, p. 11.
17. Lipset and Bendix, *ibid.*, pp. 57–75. The following discussion is adapted from these pages.
18. *Ibid.*, p. 58.
19. See the discussion of differential fertility in Donald J. Bogue, *The Population of the United States*, Glencoe, Ill.: The Free Press, 1959, pp. 305 ff.
20. Lipset and Bendix, *op. cit.*, pp. 64 ff.
21. There are also structural consequences of social mobility that have significance to power and to voting behavior. These will be discussed in Chapter 21.
22. For an analysis of status symbols in relation to the anonymous relations in urban communities see William H. Form and Gregory P. Stone, "Urbanism, Anonymity, and Status Symbolism," *American Journal of Sociology*, Vol. LXII, March 1957, pp. 504–14.
23. Erving Goffman, *The Presentation of the Self in Everyday Life*. New York: Anchor Books, 1959.
24. *Ibid.*, p. 2.
25. *Ibid.*, p. 3.
26. *Ibid.*, pp. 16 ff.
27. *Ibid.*, p. 46.

Selected Readings

Bendix, Reinhard and Seymour Lipset, eds. *Class, Status, and Power*. Glencoe, Ill.: The Free Press, 1953.

Centers, Richard. *The Psychology of Social Classes*. Princeton: Princeton University Press, 1949.

Dahrendorf, Ralf. *Class and Class Conflict in Industrial Society*. Stanford: Stanford University Press, 1959.

*Dollard, John. *Caste and Class in a Southern Town*. New York: Anchor Books, 1959.

*Frazier, E. Franklin. *Black Bourgeoisie*. New York: Collier Books, 1962.

*Ganshof, F. L. *Feudalism*. Trans. P. M. Grierson. New York: Harper Torchbooks, 1961.

*Hollingshead, August. *Elmtown's Youth*. New York: John Wiley and Sons, 1949.

*Marx, Karl and Friedrich Engels. *The Communist Manifesto*. New York: Crofts Classics, 1960.

*Mayer, Kurt B. *Class and Society*. New York: Random House, 1955. Revised edition.

*Warner, W. Lloyd. *Social Class in America: The Evaluation of Status*. New York: Harper Torchbooks, 1961.

* Paperback edition.

Part Three
Institutions of Initial Socialization

The first parts of this book presented some conceptual tools for understanding human behavior and showed how the individual fitted into organized groups of various sorts. Among the considerations covered were two major factors—the growth of urbanization and the institutional theory of community life. In the next part we shall draw heavily on these as we study the institutions of initial socialization: the family, the church, and the school.

The family, church, and school are selected for study because they transmit to the child the behaviors, values, beliefs, and attitudes that form the culture of his society. To the extent that these institutions engage in socialization, they are among the first with which the child comes into contact. In this sense, they are viewed as institutions of *initial*, or primary, socialization. The socialization process, of course, continues beyond the period of childhood into adult roles. How adult socialization takes place is the subject of subsequent chapters.

Part Three contains four chapters. Chapter 9, based on the concepts related to change in community structure, is a study of the family, church, and schools in traditional societies. Not only are historical trends noted as these institutions undergo transition from the Colonial Period but also important reference is made to those islands of traditional society still existent in America. Chapter 10 surveys the family, church, and school in the urban setting. Utilizing the institutional theory of community, it traces the process of disintegration in urban communities and the ways in which the institutions of initial socialization contribute to that process. The specific function of socialization by the family, church, and school in the urban environment is explored in Chapter 11. Chapter 12 takes up certain selected social problems characteristic of the three institutions, stressing the interrelations between breakdown (disintegration) and disorder (disorganization). These are studied against the background of social stratification and secularization in American society.

Chapter 9

Family, Church, and School in a Traditional Setting

America's past continues to influence America's present. Rural domination of national politics, local control of schools, and belief in rugged individualism are all inheritances from a time gone by. Yet these persist today because of a fear that tradition and the society based on it are slipping away and are being replaced by something new and different— even something alien. This fear, which has pervaded American history, explains the frequent recurrence of reaction in politics, economics, and social attitudes.*

Tradition may be seen from several vantage points. It may be observed in the origins of American society. It may be found in the transformation of traditional elements into something else. It may reside as an enclave—or island—in urban America, or it may be viewed through the individual's own conception of a traditional society.

Specifically, we shall examine in this chapter the three institutions most basic to the preservation of American tradition—family, church, and school. The family, by continuing the species through reproduction and by raising the young, is the main force that confers social status on individuals. The family serves as a primary group in the process of socialization. Religion designates the place of the individual in the universe and assures him that he is relatively secure in an ordered, dependable world. Further, religion helps man to bridge the dark gaps between the known and the unknown. Modern education assists in the socialization of the child—in turning him into a social human being. In this important task, the school supplements the family's role. The more complex a culture becomes, the harder it is for the family to transmit the

* Chapter 21 contains a more detailed discussion of this phenomenon.

175

culture, and the education process, which becomes formalized, steps in to perform the job.

In the simplest traditional societies the functions of the church and school are carried on by the family. These functions remain informal. In America, however, the church was a going institution at the time of colonization, and the school emerged soon after.

COLONIAL AMERICA: THE FAMILY

The colonial experience in America was a struggle for survival. In response to the rigors of frontier life, the colonial family produced many offspring. Infant mortality was high. Machines and labor were scarce. The colonists met the problem with a large, tightly knit family of several generations, a more-or-less self-sufficient economic unit.

While the desire for freedom from religious oppression must not be understated, the single most important reason for the colonial venture—and subsequent immigration—was economic opportunity. Through the practice of *primogeniture*—the right of the eldest son to inherit the estate—and judicious selection of mates for marriage, an American aristocracy evolved although the frontier had a leveling effect. The aristocratic family was a model for the less successful family even though the "Tidewater aristocrat" often achieved his status through luck or scheming. Emulation led to equating the idea of private property, especially when acquired by the sweat of the brow, with familial stature. Property and family became a way of life.

The significance of keeping the large family intact as an economic unit is underscored by the number of marriages between widows and widowers. "Large families, even of twenty-six children of a single mother, are recorded, but infant mortality was very great. John Coleman and Judith Hobby had fourteen children, of whom five died at birth, and only four grew up and married. . . . Many mothers died at birth. An instance is given of a burying ground near Bath, Maine, in which there were the graves of ten married women, eight of whom had died between the ages of twenty-two and thirty, probably as a result of large families and overwork. Second marriages were the rule, though probably few were as sudden as that of the Sandemanian, Isaac Winslow, who proposed to Ben Davis's daughter on the eve of the day he buried his wife, and married her within a week." [1]

Divorce was uncommon. The Anglican Church refused to sanction it and the British government refused the right of colonial legislatures to grant divorces. Moreover, the law of supply and demand operated against the prevalence of divorce. There were rarely enough women to go around! On the moving frontier the shortage of women was often so acute that all romantic criteria for selecting mates were dropped in favor of the more practical dictates of child bearing. In addition, the physical strength of women was important, for draft animals were still in short supply and the rigors of frontier life demanded that all members of the family engage in manual labor.

The necessity of working together and the relative absence of entertainment, other than of their own creation, tended to mold the colonial family into a close and affectionate unit. It has been characteristic of the rural family in America to remain in close proximity even after separate households are established by the children. This is especially true of the male heir designated to carry on the family farm.[2]

The colonial family and later rural generations became the storehouse of much traditional thought and continuity. Day-to-day problems of survival forced these families to rely on their own ingenuity. They developed a suspicion and hostility to any form of outside aid, especially from governments beyond the local level.[*] The stoic and taciturn individual with the stern face, whom Grant Wood depicted in his oil painting "American Gothic," developed in a frequently unfriendly, often isolated environment. Long after hardship and remoteness had ended, this characteristic persisted. Even today the American version of traditional society endures amid a dwindling farm population.

COLONIAL AMERICA: THE CHURCH

The emphasis on property in the colonies, particularly in New England, was reinforced by the formal religious institutions. No institution will survive, it may be said, unless it adequately mirrors the values of a culture. The Puritan Church was no exception. Puritanism, with its teaching of self-discipline and self sacrifice, fitted neatly into the colonial setting. "That every man should have a calling and work hard on it was a first premise of Puritanism. . . . Even the man who has an income must work. Everyone has a talent for something, given of God, which he must improve. God has so contrived the world that men must seek the necessities of life in the earth or in the sea, but the objects of their search have been cunningly placed for the finding. . . . Men [should] devote themselves to making profits without succumbing to the tempta-

---

[*] Billions of dollars in government aid are spent through the farm program, but even many of those farmers who accept government loans resent the Federal government and are generally highly critical of the U.S. Department of Agriculture.

tions of profit. . . ." [3] An abundance of this world's treasure was considered a good indicator of the status of the owner in God's eyes, but, to soften the ethic for the less well-endowed, it was not the only factor in achieving a state of Grace.

The Puritan, or Congregational, Church also contained the doctrine of *predestination*, that is, all events are foreordained by God. The early American colonist, dependent as he was on the vagaries of nature, found it easy to accept this doctrine, both as an explanation for events and as a rationale for his own reactions. At the same time, and paradoxically, the American Puritan was not fatalistic but faced life with vigor and optimism.

The Puritan Church, as long as it adequately reflected the values and conditions of its membership, was able to maintain a kind of theocracy in New England. The position of the clergyman was pre-eminent in society. "The minister was truly the leader of his people. He comforted and reproved them, guided their spiritual footsteps, advised them in matters domestic and civil, and gave unity to their ecclesiastical life. He was the chief citizen of the town, reverenced by the old and regarded with something akin to awe by the young. When a stranger asked Parson Phillips of the South Church at Andover if he were 'the parson who serves here,' he received the reply, 'I am, Sir, the Parson who rules here.' " [4]

The theocracy, however, could not last forever. It had sown the seeds of its own demise at the outset with its idea of a covenant, or contract, with God. Each new settlement had its own covenant and its own ideas about the management of local affairs. With no clerical hierarchy to introduce a standard practice, democracy slowly seeped into New England—a democracy which spelled doom for the autocratic theologians and brought about a further curbing of Puritan dogma, allowing an outburst of new religious sects.

COLONIAL AMERICA: THE SCHOOL

The first assumption of responsibility by civil authorities for education began in the New England towns. "Education was a particular concern of the Puritans. Their movement was directed by university-trained divines, and embraced largely by middle-class merchants and landowning farmers, who enjoyed the benefits of education in Elizabethan England. Moreover, it was necessary for godliness that everyone learn to read the Bible." [5] The Massachusetts School Law of 1642 required that town officials compel parents to provide elementary instruction for their children. Although this law did not require that schools be established, it insisted that children be given instruction in the minimum essentials: reading, religion, and apprenticeship in a trade. By 1647 each town of 50 families was required to establish an elementary school and each town of 100 families to provide a Latin grammar school.

From the beginning, America exhibited more complexity than traditional societies generally. The family in Colonial America was already supplemented by formal institutions. However, while life had begun to be institutionalized, there was a high degree of integration and coordination among its components. As we trace the development of the family, the church, and the school in America, it will become clear that while there is increasing splitting apart of institutions in the urban setting, this does not necessarily follow in the rural areas.

INSTITUTIONS IN TRANSITION

Advancing technology in America has created a revolutionary effect in agriculture, a revolution that has continued to the present day, recently attaining the phase of automation. One major result of the agricultural revolution has been a sharp decrease in farm employment. This has given rise to a basic change in the rural family as members leave the farm to seek employment in urban industry. But this development is of relatively recent origin.

The family. The end of the Colonial Period ushered in a westward expansion that was to continue unabated for 100 years. Families began to move greater distances, carrying their traditions with them. Sons and daughters sometimes moved independently of parents—also carrying old traditions to new land. As New Englanders, New Yorkers, Virginians, and the rest gathered on the frontier, old patterns were modified. From the fusing of backgrounds came a new common tradition. Rural America became more homogeneous under frontier conditions.[6] Homogeneity, however, became militant, too, under various nativist movements, such as Know-Nothingism, Populism, and Progressivism—all aiming to protect traditional America against undesirable immigration, big business, or city ways. The pressure of technological advance proved irresistible. Although no longer the backbone of America, the farmer was still the repository of tradition, and he waged one of the longest rear-guard actions in history before yielding.[7]

The farm family remained large long after the need for large families had passed. Even today, though declining in size, farm families continue to have their former basic characteristics: "1. An attachment to the land that is deep and abiding; 2. A limited background of social participation; 3. A routine of life encompassing family members and adjusted to the demands of farming; 4. A well-defined attitude toward roles and statuses of family members, with the father as head and all others having a useful function; 5. An attitude of independence, except toward family members and close friends." [8]

The Church. In religion there was the Great Awakening, a movement that continues to the present day. The church of the frontier and the rural areas lost the reserve of the Puritans and also the Puritan intellectual flavor. "After ignorant and emotional people had tasted the strong drink of revivalism they cared no more for traditional worship . . ." [9] The calmer religions were still practiced but no longer did they enjoy religious hegemony. Sects multiplied (Chapter 20 contains a discussion of nativist movements). Religion remained very personal, perhaps more personal than the austere Puritanism, but the preacher never again achieved the status he held in the Puritan heyday. The farmer turned away from the minister and to the politician in temporal affairs, leaving the clergyman in charge of the spiritual realm. Yet the social gospel of the cities did not affect the rural church which continued its own pattern and retained much the same mores for generations.

The School. Local control of public education approached the status of religion in farm communities. Efforts to bring about change reflecting the changing culture were sometimes met with open hostility and finally accepted only grudgingly and belatedly. The little red school house, still to be found, is adequate for some purposes. Its defense is purely traditional, as has been the vigorous opposition to the consolidation of schools. But curricula have changed, especially to reflect advancement in agricultural technology. The idea persists that education must be purposeful and utilitarian—and that is part of the Puritan heritage.

RURAL YOUTH TODAY

Gradually, the margin of difference between rural and urban is being narrowed. The rise of the "factory farm," the diminishing size of the farm family, and the increasing acceptance of urban attitudes and values are all advanced as evidence of the growing similarity between the rural and the urban. What is happening to the rural adolescent in this merging of the world of the farm and the world of the city? The following article by Robert C. Bealer and Fern K. Willits presents the rural sociologists' analysis.

*In the past, the rural community in America was a fairly isolated little world populated by inhabitants who were similar in many respects. They evolved ways of living quite different from those of the city. The problems of existence were met in largely traditional terms.

But mass communication, improved transportation, and technology have increased the contacts between the once isolated rural settlements and the urban centers of population. The schools have moved to the towns as joint high schools replace the little red schoolhouse of the past. The "city slicker" and the "country hick" today read the same books, newspapers, and magazines, hear the same radio and television programs, and attend the same schools. Commercial and social intercourse go on at high rates. The rural community no longer exists as a geographically isolated unit, but this does not mean rural and urban are one.

In the contemporary context, the large urban center is believed to dominate life and radiate its cultural influence into outlying areas. Cities are generally viewed as the primary source of change, and rural areas are considered as the strongholds of traditionalism, although they, too, are undergoing rapid change. Rural-urban differences in values and attitudes are taken to be not simply dichotomous—all or nothing—as may have been appropriate fifty or even thirty years ago. Rather, it is believed there are gradations between the two, and one may speak of degrees of urbanity or of rurality. Thus, city residents are believed to be the least rural, and, hence, the least traditional. They are followed by small-town inhabitants; open country nonfarm dwellers are next; and farmers are believed to represent the popular characterization of rural most closely. This progression follows the presumed accessibility of these areas to metropolitan centers—a fact usually taken as causally significant. In any case, from a sociological perspective, differences in behavior between rural and urban or farm and nonfarm youth must be due to differences in social experiences which are fostered by the particular qualities of the locality in which the person resides.

Even today, the basic economic producing unit in agriculture is the family farm, and the scattered homestead pattern is the characteristic mode of settlement. Historically, this has limited the opportunities for contact with other people. While the rural person today is not geographically isolated, he still finds that he often must cover ten square miles of area to have the same number of contacts as one can make in a single city block. Furthermore, the children are often employed on the farm, and they can become a part of the working unit early in life. Greater family cohesiveness may result from this working together, and it seems likely that the parents would then represent a

* From "Rural Youth: A Case Study in the Rebelliousness of Adolescence," by Robert C. Bealer and Fern K. Willits, *The Annals*, Vol. 338, November 1961, pp. 64–68. Reprinted by permission of the authors and of the American Academy of Political and Social Sciences.

dominant positive point of reference for formulating the attitudes and values of farm youth. In contrast, the urban child is seldom engaged in family economic activity, nor does he need to exert great efforts to have social contacts with large numbers of other persons. As a result, the family is believed to be less of an influence on him. Compared with his city cousin, the farm youth is characteristically presented with fewer diverse points of view to challenge the position of his parents and, hence, would be less likely to rebel.

At the same time, although he probably attends a consolidated school with youth from urban areas, the rural child is still at a disadvantage in the degree to which he can participate in school and extracurricular activities, and it is in these situations that the unique behavior of adolescents would be most likely learned. Not only must the rural youth have access to some means of transportation so that he can get to town, but often he must be relieved of certain farm chores if he is to engage in the activities. We know that adolescents from farm homes participate less in school and community activities than do their less rural cousins. They, thus, may tend to have more limited association with their peers and less participation in and, hence, less probable acceptance of a rebellious youth subculture.

If the popular image of rural-urban differences is accurate, and if there is a rebellious, unified youth subculture, then rural adolescents should be less inclined to rebel than their urban peers. Furthermore, the degree of rebellion of farm youth should vary with the degree of participation in the youth subculture, a factor which is itself conditioned by where one lives. How true are these representations? This is a question of fact which, unfortunately, has been more often speculated upon than carefully examined by research techniques. However, such studies are not completely absent. They confirm some aspects and show certain others as startlingly lacking.

Although the adolescent is popularly characterized as rejecting traditional norms of conduct, empirical studies of rural youth have failed to support this notion. On the contrary, these young people tend to be critical of behavior which deviates from traditional rural values. Thus, a long-term study of nearly 8000 Pennsylvania youth, which we are conducting, shows that the rural adolescent is outspokenly traditional in regard to young persons drinking alcoholic beverages, smoking, loafing in town, and failing in school. That is, he is highly critical of these activities and, at least verbally, tends to reject them as proper modes of behavior, feeling that engagement in these matters should be strongly censured. He is somewhat less critical of card playing, staying out late, spending money unsupervised, and the use of cosmetics by adolescent girls. Only in regard to dancing and dating does the rural youth express a highly permissive and, hence, decidedly nontraditional position. On these two matters he feels that no condemnation is appropriate.

While rural youth do not, on the average, reject traditional attitudes concerning what constitutes proper and correct behavior, the relative rates of rejection tend to follow the degree of assumed participation in youth sub-culture. That is, youth in areas of low population density—rural areas—tend to be less rebellious in regard to societal norms than do their more urban cousins. Within the rural residence grouping, farm youth tend to be less permissive than youth from nonfarm homes. Town dwellers are more permissive than rural nonfarm residents. As has been previously suggested, farm youth may participate less in peer group activities. However, the distinction between farm and nonfarm residence in degree of rebelliousness does not appear to be only a reflection of this fact. If we are willing to accept that the degree of participation in school activities is also an indicator of involvement in the youth subculture, and if this factor is held constant, a remarkable thing occurs. Regardless of the degree of participation in school activities, consistent residence differences remain. Rural residents are more traditional than urban dwellers even when both are involved to the same degree in the youth subculture.

Even more interesting, the tendency to cling to traditional attitudes does not simply reflect the degree of physical isolation of the rural youth from the more rapidly changing and presumably more liberal urban centers. The opportunity for increased contact with other ways of life does not necessarily imply amalgamation of local cultures. Psychological and (or) social isolation may provide a separation as powerful as any geographical isolation of the past. Thus, it was found in our study that simple physical proximity to large metropolitan and smaller urban centers is not associated with lesser degrees of traditionalism, as would be expected under the idea of urban dominance. Farm youth residing within a few miles of large metropolises such as Pitts-burgh or Philadelphia do not present less traditional attitudes than farm youth residing great distances from these centers. Perhaps the rural dweller possesses an internalized concept of himself as happier, more God-fearing, and more American in his ways than the city person. Such an image, if wide-spread, could, even in the presence of interaction, promote a feeling of apart-ness from urban society and urban values.

The possible importance of this kind of isolation can be seen when one considers shifts in attitudes and values that have occurred. Traditional beliefs have changed over time. There is no question about this. Rural youth, in contrast to past years, have become less critical of deviation from tradi-tional norms of somber and staid conduct. But a more important feature is the degree to which change has occurred in relation to other parts of society. In this respect, the presence of a wide range of rural-urban contacts in highly industrialized and urbanized states, such as Pennsylvania, would lead most persons to expect that the rural and urban segments are becoming more similar and that the farm-nonfarm residence distinction is becoming pro-gressively less important in discussing variation in attitudes and behavior.

However, our study, for example, found that differences in the degree of traditionalism in attitude patterns between farm and nonfarm residents increased significantly between 1947 and 1960. Rather than rural young people becoming more alike, the results of this study show that the rural residence groupings have become gradually more differentiated. That is, although farm youth have changed their ideas, nonfarm adolescents have changed even faster. The relative gap has increased.

Why should this be? A conclusive answer is not available. The self-imposed isolation discussed above may be one aspect. The depopulation of most agricultural regions as a concomitant of the consolidation of farmsteads forced by the technological revolution in farming may be another factor. Those people who tend to be most urban or least traditional in their social outlook may be those most likely to leave the hinterland and move toward the cities. Research on this matter is inconclusive, but, if it is the case, the relative proportion of rural dwellers remaining on the farm who subscribe to traditional values and attitudes would tend to increase. If the resulting trend toward differentiation continues in the future, the residence variable may become increasingly important in discussing differences in degree of traditionalism within a youth subculture. To the extent that such distinctions can be found, they would tend to refute the notion of a homogeneous adolescent subculture as well as to cast some doubt on the omnipotence of the influence the city has on outlying areas.

Although the rural youth tends to express relatively traditional attitudes and values, parental norms need not coincide with these. It is the case, as one sociologist has put it, that there are "evaluative interest(s) in cultural patterns which we may call *acceptance* as distinguished from commitment." (Talcott Parsons, *The Social System*, Glencoe: The Free Press, 1951, p. 55.) Thus, as a Christian, one can accept the Sermon on the Mount without expecting literal conformity or commitment to it in everyday life. If traditional values are accepted in this sense but do not receive parental commitments, then, whether the adolescent accepts or rejects a traditional position may have little relationship to the degree of parent-youth conflict present. Conflict as used here does not refer only to open rebellion, but consists of simple disagreement between the norms of the youth and his parents.

The popular image of the closely knit farm family characterized by harmonious relationships between parents and children persists. The working together at common tasks is purported to lead to greater cohesiveness and toward elimination of parent-youth conflict. However, research has failed to substantiate this image. Most studies have found no association between place of residence and degree of conflict. Although a variety of instruments have been utilized to measure this factor, they generally present similar conclusions. In our study, for example, urban, rural nonfarm, and rural farm youths are equally likely to evaluate their parents' points of view —toward the behaviors used above in defining traditionalism—as "sensible," rather than as "too critical" or "not critical enough." Furthermore, this evaluation is the mode. For our study, this was as true in 1947 with one sample as in 1960 on the second group of students.

The fact, then, that farm youth tend to express more traditional attitudes than nonfarm adolescents does not result from higher rates of acceptance of parental viewpoints. Rather, it would seem to indicate the presence of differences between the residence groupings in the degree of traditionalism of parents. Since parental points of view are accepted at approximately the same rate by farm and nonfarm youths, and the former grouping tends to be more traditional than the latter, we can deduce that the farm parents present more critical or traditional positions than their nonfarm counterparts. Thus, the differential between farm and nonfarm youth in degree of traditionalism may reflect not adolescent rebellion but differences in the rate of adult rejection of these norms.

There is another, anomalous aspect to the rate of acceptance of parental views. In our study, although there is no difference between the proportion of farm and nonfarm adolescents who evaluate their parents as "sensible," there are significant differences when the adolescent's extent of participation in school activities is considered. But, as youths increased their involvement in school functions—and, presumably, in the subculture—the proportion of "sensible" answers for the family went up, not down, as would be expected if the subculture were rebellious and alien. This is true for both farm and nonfarm adolescents. In short, those who participate most in the youth subculture are also those who are least likely to reject parental norms. Therefore, it would seem more accurate to describe the subculture as accepting and conforming to parental norms of conduct rather than as rebellious in nature.

ENCLAVES

The modern American is often startled when he becomes aware of the several traditional enclaves that persist within, and yet apart from, the total culture. A number of groups fit this category. Certain religious sects, notably the Amish, and various ethnic groups that have gathered in their own ghettos, in Little Italy, in Chinatown, maintain a way of life in sharp contrast to the norm.[10] But perhaps the most remarkably intact enclave in America are the Spanish Americans of New Mexico—a near-classic example of a traditional society. The following excerpt from a work edited by Margaret Mead describes the major institutions in this enclave.

*
When the United States annexed the State of New Mexico in 1848, the non-Indian population consisted almost entirely of Spanish-speaking people. They were descendants of immigrants who had followed the Conquistadores from Mexico, and had settled in Indian territory in the borderlands along the Rio Grande. By the end of the seventeenth century, they had founded many communities such as those they had known in Mexico. They lived in villages centered around a chapel dedicated to a patron saint. Their cultural contacts were with Mexico. Many villagers tilled their own small plot of land, and also worked on the land of their *patrón*, often a wealthy relative, who had been given a large land-grant, and had assumed a position of responsibility toward the poorer villagers, the *peons*. Not until the middle of the nineteenth century, when New Mexico became part of the United States and the Santa Fe Trail was opened from Missouri, was there any shift in orientation northeastward to the United States. The original village *peon-patrón* pattern of Spanish American life was not greatly altered by the rancho-trader-army settlement patterns of the first "Anglo" migrants, the English-speaking. Americans. The Anglos came into the same territory but with such selectively different goals that the two cultures continued for a period with little intimate contact and with comparatively little friction or functional interrelation. Even in the latter part of the nineteenth century, Spanish Americans began to be drawn into the Anglo economy. In the twentieth century more and more Anglos have come into the region, until today they outnumber the Spanish Americans. Their dominance is more significant in terms of the human relations or technological matters. In place of the entrepreneurs and adventurers of early days are their settled descendants; in addition there are Anglo laborers, employees, carpenters, mechanics, government men, school-teachers, military personnel, members of all the professions. Characteristically, most of these have come with their families to make their homes, and hopefully their fortunes. The whole fabric of the American social system is represented. This has meant the growth of urban centers, of communications, of service trades, of industries, of wage-hour living, of railroads, highways and tourism, of schools, of research and scientific centers, of large military installations.

The shift of cultural emphasis in New Mexico has been rapid and recent. Potentialities for change in the lives of the Spanish Americans have suddenly been vastly increased. What then is the picture in Spanish American communities today? Are changes taking place? In what directions? To what advantage? At what cost? How is it that the Spanish American culture

* From *Cultural Patterns and Technical Change*, by Margaret Mead, New York: New American Library, 1955, pp. 151–162. Reprinted by permission of the United Nations Educational, Scientific, and Cultural Organization.

remains so clearly defined in spite of the impact of the Anglo-American way?

Here in New Mexico two peoples live and work side by side, yet each has a recognizable way of life of characteristic vitality. One is an enclave, the other the dominant culture group, the Anglos. The Spanish Americans are in daily contact with the dominant group, at work and at school, and in all political activity. Through sharp legalistic manipulation by members of the dominant group, the Spanish Americans have been deprived of much of their land. They are now suspicious of the dominant group; they fear its schemes for land improvement, its legal papers, the Anglos who ask questions for their records; yet they are in daily contact with this group, and are taking on many of its ways. And, historically and geographically, they form the fringe of another group, the people of Latin America, whose culture, language and religion they share.

The basic cultural fact of traditional Spanish American life is the village. To be Spanish American is to be of a village. There is no keen awareness of special national or cultural identity. Each village has its patron saint, who is a kind of companion-protector for the village as a whole and its individual members.

These villages which are the old Mexico of New Mexico do not stand out from the surrounding countryside. The sandy brown of old adobe and straw, the tan plastered walls, dark poles of the corral fences, merge with the prevailing natural colours. Beyond the squares of the fields and the lines of the irrigation ditches, lies the randomness of sagebrush and tumbleweed, wild flowers and grasses. Signs and billboards are absent, since these towns and villages are not for the chance stranger. They belong to people who depend on one another for their livelihoods and their diversions. To get news of local events, one must become acquainted with the villagers. No local newspaper tells which family has a new baby or has just lost a member; these are vital events but not vital statistics. To be Spanish American is to belong to a *familia*.

In the small household, the father is the central figure of authority and under the strongest obligations to support his wife and children. The elder brother (*hermano major*) is recognized apart from the other children and may have authority and obligations which are almost parental at times, explicitly so in the case of the death of the father. The pattern of the father's life keeps him away from the house a great deal of the time, tending to the farm, helping his relatives, working for wages. His leisure time is spent with other men around the plaza or in the bars. He may have to be away two or three months at a time herding, sawmilling, or on some other job. When not too far from home, he may have a son or nephew along with him, but relationships with his young children are distant and inconsistent. The father may be indulgent but he is also domineering.

The pattern of the dominant father is carried beyond the small household to the larger *familia*, and beyond that to the village, providing the structure for the *patrón* relationship. The Church structure uses the same concept of the father (*padre*) as leader, and where there is no resident priest, the *patrón* is apt to function as head of the local church.

The continuity of household life depends upon the mother, whose place is in the home as a matter of course, and whose function is to bear children and care for them. Women also care for small gardens and some domestic animals. They may go and help a neighbor or relative, but they do not work for wages outside the home. In case of the mother's death, a female relative may take over, usually an aunt or a grandmother; it is important that it be an adult, who will nurture the family. But an older sister may take on the care of the family, or even a brother in his teens.

There is a flow of neighborhood interaction; a woman will go to consult her mother on big and little matters. She accepts her maternal role, which is patterned after a continuing close relationship with her own mother. She may go with her husband to a local dance, or to town; but even on these occasions, children are along and she is not merely a wife; the mother role is ever present.

It is not too unusual to find some children of large families adopted by relatives who have none of their own. Every adult woman is expected to be a "mother" and adoptions bring the childless woman into harmony with the general pattern.

When parents have many children they know that they will not be lonely in their old age; their children will live near them, and they will have grand-children about them. As children give respect to their parents, grandparents command the respect of their grown children and have a somewhat in-dulgent relationship with their grandchildren. Age in itself is valued and honored. Children are not expected to go farther and faster than their parents, but to listen to their advice and learn from their experience, to consult the old people and heed their words. The truly aged are cared for by their children and other relatives. There is no traditional community system of welfare beyond the *familia*.

The Spanish American has two major links with the world beyond his village. Both of these are derived from the *familia* system. He is known through his relatives. The ties of brotherhood ensure his comfort and make him feel at home within the larger Spanish American society. His father, even more his *patrón*, is the link with the total community, Anglo and Spanish.

To be Spanish American is to be a brother. The basis of this system is again the *familia*. It relates to the solidarity which is set up over against the father-figure—originating in the unity of mother and children. By extension, it is "my group" against others who may dominate. But it includes the atmosphere of fraternity as much as of opposition. The way in which Spanish Americans perceive themselves as members of the same, or of different groups, defines the situations of cooperation or conflict within the system.

The primary group to which every Spanish American belongs is the family. The conflicts and hostilities which arise are interfamilial and particularly between unrelated families. Families may join in opposition to others on one issue, and oppose each other on another issue. Those held together by such interests may disagree over a proposed marriage. In opposition to the family principle, the women of the community make up one social grouping, the men another.

Church services, school meetings, political rallies and *fiestas* bring the whole village together. The church service is not, however, highly developed as a social occasion. It is an authority situation. When the service is over, the women go directly home. The men may stop to visit or to warm themselves at the fire in front of the church.

School meetings, political rallies, and *fiestas* are different. The Spanish American enters into such community activities without obligation, and without typcial Anglo restraint and self-consciousness. At a rally, the *patrón* is seeking favor more than dispensing it. He identifies himself with local interests: "All the time we are for the People and against the Public."

Fiesta is the occasion when the patron saint is honored and celebrated; it is traditionally a time of color and gaiety. The honor of the village is involved in honoring the patron saint. . . . At *fiesta* time, the saint is cherished, more than appealed to, less a *parent* and more a *brother*. Festivities are much in the spirit of baptismal or wedding celebrations when a new member is added to the family, but on a larger scale. Feasting and dancing go along with religious observation. The people are gay, and there may be some who are aggressive.

Fiesta demonstrates most clearly that the Church does not function simply as an external authority in Spanish American culture. The *Santos* are of the villages. They are both revered and beloved. Through them the sanctions of the Church as an institution are personalized and translated into the sanctions of the familiar community. And the relation to the saint is a personal one, imbuing daily life so naturally that only the observer notices that one aspect is religious, one secular. For example, a boy describing a basketball game blow by blow includes casually in his description the statement that he burned a candle for his side before the game began.

It is apparent that the family and the church are the paramount institutions for Spanish Americans. The school functions largely to teach sums. "All a man needs in school is arithmetic. If he can figure that is all a man needs in his work." [11] The cohesiveness of Spanish-American life is attributable to a strong emphasis on the hierarchy of authority, the opposite of the Puritan emphasis on covenants and contractual agreements.

*"In their [Spanish-American] communities younger relatives are subordinate to older kinsmen, females to males, and *peon* to *patrón*. The secular structure gears into the hierarchially arranged Catholic Church with its offices extending from the parish priest through the bishops, archbishops, cardinals, and on up to the Pope. Much the same kind of hierarchy is found in the sacred world of the Spanish-Americans, from the local images of the saints up to the Deity. Life flows secure in the traditional familial mold; the important thing is the present, with its immediate drama, color, and spontaneity. It is foolish to work too hard, and to worry about the future is even more ridiculous. About the mystery of the world neither curiosity nor knowledge extend much beyond a shrug of the shoulders and a '¿Quién sabe?' "

It is an understatement to say that education "for the children" while seemingly desired by Spanish-Americans, however vaguely, presents a real problem in motivating the student in terms of future benefits.

THE FUTURE OF TRADITIONAL SOCIETY IN AMERICA

Is there a traditional society in urban America?

The Puritans are gone although we can speak of the Puritan strain that persists in the broader American culture. A popular song of the First World War, "How Ya Gonna Keep 'Em Down on the Farm after They've Seen Paree?" contains more than a kernel of truth. Chinatown is more a tourist attraction today than a genuine enclave. The Spanish American's acceptance of electricity and the radio as desirable, and his rejection of running water as "unnatural," would seem to be another example of a rear-guard action destined to fail.

But elements of the traditional society persist in America. The three institutions we have examined—the family, the church, and the school— are essentially conservative in nature. These institutions, whether in farm communities, small towns, or cities, all share the responsibility for preserving a generalized tradition of individualism, family loyalty, private property, and Christianity. The less subject these institutions are to pressure from external forces the closer they will hew to a clearly defined tradition.

* From "A Study of Values," by Evon Vogt and John Roberts, *Scientific American*, July 1956, pp. 25–31, *passim*. Reprinted with permission. Copyright 1956 by Scientific American, Inc. All rights reserved.

The American farmer, living in semi-isolation and stressing local autonomy, is frequently alienated from the mainstream of American life. A fragment of traditional society may be found in the rural community. Homer Goodrich, a farmer all his life and a part-time columnist, sums up:

> Mentioning the good old time in B.A. [Before the Atom] must include the social life. Play parties were popular as many people still living can remember. "Old Dan Tucker" was swung around a lot but never got any older. These were distinguished by the absence of instrumental music and liquor which went with dances. Of course there were neighborhood parties and sometimes church affairs. Here in our kitchen of 12' × 27' there were countless parties. My father had them for his Sunday School class of young people.
>
> Then there were oyster suppers which began in a very peculiar way. They always started out as a rabbit hunt with men using clubs and dogs. These hunts usually took place when the ground was covered with snow and about 30 men and boys usually participated. The rabbits were skinned and sold, then the money used to buy oysters. In those days oysters all came in cans, but milk didn't. When I was a youngster, I thought the oysters grew in cans I guess. I never met one in a shell until years later. Believe it or not, those were the days. Some people might pity the poor oldtimers who had no movies, television, automobiles, airplanes, or atomic bombs. But I believe it is the people living today in this unsettled world who have the troubled times. I've had my 60 years in the best period of modern times. You can have the next. I have been privileged to have lived to see the change in two eras of our changing history. I prefer the flavor of the past.[12]

The people who have composed our traditional society were not especially endowed with virtue. They were ordinary men and women, in basic agreement as to the meaning of life and the rights and responsibilities of the individual. The values of the community shaped the character and conduct of the individual.[13] Right and wrong were predetermined by custom and tradition and the whole personality was shaped to the pattern of community life.

As late as the turn of the century, American society was still largely a collection of local units. As a result of the forces of progress, much of this has been changed. Despite the conservative influence of the family, the church, and the school there is little likelihood that this form of social existence will ever be restored. America is destined to be of urban character.

Notes

1. Charles M. Andrews, *Colonial Folkways*, New Haven: Yale University Press, 1919, p. 87.
2. See Catherine Drinker Bowen, *John Adams and the American Revolution*, Boston: Little, Brown and Company, 1950, for an explicit discussion of the operation of the family, inheritance, and aristocracy in Colonial America.
3. Perry Miller, *The New England Mind: From Colony to Province*, Cambridge: Harvard University Press, 1953, pp. 40–41.
4. Andrews, *op. cit.*, p. 166.
5. Samuel Eliot Morison and Henry Steele Commager, *The Growth of the American Republic*, Volume I, 5th Ed., New York: Oxford University Press, 1962, p. 63.
6. Max Lerner stresses the plurality of rural society in *America as a Civilization*, New York: Simon and Schuster, 1957, p. 145.
7. Now being conducted in Congress by the so-called Farm Bloc (See Chapter 22).
8. Ruth Shonle Cavan, *The American Family*, New York: Thomas Y. Crowell Company, 1953, p. 34.
9. *Ibid.*, p. 119.
10. See Oscar Handlin, *The Uprooted*, (Grosset's Universal Library Edition), New York: Little, Brown and Company, 1951, for a sympathetic history of the immigrant in America.
11. Margaret Mead, *Cultural Patterns and Technical Change*. New York: New American Library, 1955, p. 170.
12. *Columbus* (Kansas) *Advocate*, September 19, 1961.
13. David Riesman *et al*, *The Lonely Crowd* (Anchor Edition), New York: Doubleday and Company, Inc. 1955.

Selected Readings

Beardsley, R. K., John Hall, and Robert Ward. *Village Japan*. Chicago: University of Chicago Press, 1959.

Burgess, Ernest W., and Harvey Locke. *The Family*. New York: American Book Company, 1950.

Calhoun, Arthur. *A Social History of the American Family from Colonial Times to the Present*. New York: Barnes and Noble, 1945. 3 vols.

Cavan, Ruth. *The American Family*. New York: T. Y. Crowell, 1953.

Fox, Lorene. *The Rural Community and Its Schools*. New York: Columbia University Press, 1948.

Marriott, McKim. ed. *Village India*. Chicago: University of Chicago Press, 1955.

West, James. *Plainville, U.S.A.* New York: Columbia University Press, 1945.

Young, Pauline V. *Pilgrims of Russian Town*. Chicago: University of Chicago Press, 1932.

Chapter 10

Family, Church, and School in the Urban Setting

Urban life is in constant flux. Each human relationship in this setting is touched by the energetic quality of urban existence—and especially its institutions. In an urban society the rapid physical and social mobility, the highly varied population, and the vast technology requiring a change in the division of labor all indicate a form of social organization always subject to some upheaval.

Unlike traditional communities, institutional life in the urban environment is never stable. It does not have the bonds of kinship, family property, and ascribed social status. There is instead a constant evaluation of every phase of institutional activity; the time, the cost, and the efficiency of each activity is forever assessed. Nothing remains as it was. The search for profit, the greater production of economic and noneconomic goods and services, the rational use of space, and the development—in Max Weber's imagery [1]—of "machinelike, calculable law," demand new values continually. The sanctity of private property tumbles before the right of eminent domain. A hundred workers are replaced by a machine which does the job quicker and cheaper. The old neighborhood undergoes renewal and becomes commercialized.

In this atmosphere of flux, any change in one part of an institution produces changes in its other parts. This process of change is easily accomplished in the formalized, material aspects of the institution. It is never really difficult to change tangible things. Much more difficult is the problem of changing the nonmaterial, informalized parts of the institution, because it is harder to identify and shape attitudes, beliefs, and values than to put people into new jobs or move their places of residence.

For example, resistance to institutional change may be evident, and the change may be rejected. In another instance, people may give the impression of accepting change while actually resisting it. Some may even hide both resistance and rejection. This, of course, proves most diffi-

193

cult to discover because of the ability of some people to conceal their true feelings. One way to overcome resistance is to remove the old personnel from the institution—by dismissal or divorce—and replace them with individuals who are already committed to the change, or who can easily be trained to accept it. A second way, quite the opposite, is to disregard the resistance altogether. Both approaches create problems. In the former, the skills and experience of the old personnel are lost. In the latter, a cultural lag may develop, thus sharpening the difficulties provoked by change.

Not only do changes affect a particular institution; they may also create changes in other institutions and in related groups that are not institutionalized. George Homans has described such a series of changes in his analysis of a study of a community called Hilltown.[2]

Hilltown was a small community near a large metropolitan center. It had some industry, the usual small-town businesses, a school system of its own, a well-attended city council, and an assortment of business and social clubs. Eventually the industry disappeared. One mill burned down and was not rebuilt; another consolidated with a company outside of town, and a third shut down completely. The small business encountered competition from the more efficient establishments in the metropolitan center, and the decline in economic activity began to be felt in other phases of Hilltown life. Attendance dropped off at the business and social clubs. There was less interest and confidence in the city council in matters concerning the direction and destiny of the town because of the greater domination of Hilltown affairs by the metropolitan center and the state. This was intensified when the local high school closed, making it necessary for students to travel to the metropolitan high school. A core of the teaching force left town, the PTA ceased to exist, and the sense of community which many persons had felt in relation to their school diminished. In addition to these changes, a new population entered the community to occupy a new housing tract, even though most of these people worked in the metropolitan center. In the end, Hilltown became another satellite of the larger community.

Homans described the process of how a community disintegrates and loses its institutions or other forms of association. Whereas the institutions in traditional communities are relatively enduring, held together by old sentiments, reinforced bonds of close personal ties, and ascribed social status, institutions touched by urbanization are in a state of constant breakdown. New social forms emerge in the search for sound solutions to institutional problems. The existing systems fade. Institutional groups and the norms and values they prize become transitory at best. Individuals lose their attachment to one another. The informal groupings within institutions and the related associations beyond the confines of the institutions undergo decline, and individuals can no longer enjoy the informal ties that lift them above the formal roles and statuses imposed by the institution. As *Time* magazine reported early in 1963: "whether they wither away, become dormitories in suburbia, or merge with neighboring communities, the small towns of old are vanishing, and with them will vanish one dimension of the nation's life. The small town had its defects as a place to live in, and urban Americans . . . are likely to think of the small town only as narrow, ingrown, stunting. But for many, life there had its compensations— countryside within walking distance, acquaintances rather than hurrying strangers on the streets, and a serenity that city dwellers cannot even imagine." [3]

It is to be expected then that the institutions of family, church, and school form a different pattern in urban communities than in traditional societies. In urban areas, these institutions are separate. The family does not extend into every other institution with the interest, knowledgeability, and influence it had in the traditional setting. Instead the family has undergone a far-reaching modification of its place in society. The church, too, does not perform as it did in the traditional community. No longer small or based on the power and influence of a few families, with many of its functions now highly secularized, the church has become an institution which contributes to the energetic nature of urban life. The school faces two new problems: diversity and size. In order to meet the challenges of increased enrollments and the greater range of talent and interests in the student body, schools have developed courses of study, services, and staff specializations unheard of in communities of the past.

Let us turn now to a review of each of these institutions as they exist in urban America.

THE FAMILY

Urbanization has wrought many major changes in the nature of the family.[4] To begin with, the family has undergone a change in basic composition. In traditional societies families saw themselves as belonging to a single unit; they were outright kinship groups, or joint or extended families (that is, a number of families, related by blood or marriage who had lived in close association for generations). Urbanization and industrialization ended the need for the large family group. An industrialized economy does not lean on the family as a unit of production, nor does the limited space available in an urban community permit many families to live together as a unit. Thus, the typical family today consists of father, mother, and unmarried children: this is called the *nuclear family*.[5]

The changed composition of the family poses the question: who belongs to one's family? In a primitive society an individual can trace his relations through an infinitely complex system of kinship which reaches through the entire village or tribe. A villager in the Middle Ages would have related himself to his entire village. The American farmer, prior to the First World War, if asked to name his family, would have included his wife, children—married and single—his parents, his brothers and sisters and their families, a grandparent or two, and uncles, aunts, and cousins. In the urban scene, a distinction may now be made between *families of procreation* and *families of orientation*.

Families today begin as units of procreation—as nuclear families composed of father, mother, and unmarried children. The procreative force is the father and mother. To the children, however, this force is also a source of orientation. That is, the children adapt their behaviors, values, and attitudes to those of the parents; as yet, they are not themselves procreative. The distinction between procreation and orientation becomes clearer when one of the children, say a son, leaves home to marry and establish his own family. The son has thus established his own family of procreation, while his own parents become a family of orientation to him. He may seek the advice of his parents, but he need not follow it. He may move a great distance from the home of his parents. He may be employed in a form of work about which his father knows very little. As a result, when asked to name his family, the son will reply, himself, *his* wife, and *his* children. This is a far cry from the inclusiveness of the rural, traditional family, which has disappeared.

These two changes—composition and types of family—reflect a third important change in the nature of the family; its life cycle has become shorter than in traditional societies where close contact between successive generations tended to keep the family intact. This is particularly true when ownership of family property ensured stability of residence. The very nature of marriage and family life in urban society shortens the life cycle. In 1890 the median age at the time of first marriage was 26.1 years for husbands and 22 years for wives. In 1959 the comparable medians were 22.7 for husbands and 20.2 for wives.[7] The greatest number of births occur when the wife is between 20 and 24 years of age, although there is evidence to indicate that fertility reaches a peak at about age 19.[8] These data imply that the number of years from marriage and the birth of the first child to the time when the youngest child leaves home is fewer. Parents become middle-aged, "childless," married couples. Seldom is the youngest child living at home upon the retirement or death of a parent.

A fourth change in the family is the basis of its solidarity. Traditionally, the family has been the means of transferring property. As the farm declined as an important economic unit, however, and the division of labor of an industrial economy made it necessary for workers to leave home to earn a living, the family ceased to serve as a major source of solidarity. Farm land lost its significance as a form of property to leave to one's heirs. The houses of today are no longer to be regarded as permanent. They are to be consumed, much as one consumes an automobile. There is also the expectation that the children will eventually obtain homes of their own. With the transfer value of property greatly diminished, a new basis for family solidarity has been found in the marriage relationship. In traditional societies, marriage was of secondary importance to the handing down, or regulation, of property; marriage was regarded solely as the regulation of the society's sex patterns. In urban communities marriage, in contrast, is viewed as the basis of a sound family relationship. After the stereotypes of romantic love have faded, the bonds of sentiment formed through the exchange of affection create and sustain a marriage.[9] No matter how shaky some urban marriages may be, even leading to a number of divorces, the marital institution remains the source of family solidarity in the urban environment.

A final change in the family has affected its primary functions. Formerly, the family assumed the economic, recreational, religious, educational, and often, political functions of the society. The finer development of specialized institutions in urban society has sharply reduced the range of functions performed by the family. Some writers view this decline with alarm; they believe the family is becoming completely separated from society. It must be recognized, however, that families in traditional cultures performed their several functions because few, if any, institutions were capable of fulfilling them. In rural America, especially during the frontier era, the family undertook these functions to assure survival. The family was the economic unit because the farm was the first source of sustenance. It was the recreation center because there were no forms of commercial entertainment. It performed religious and educational functions because there were few churches and fewer schools. It was the political unit because the law was remote. The steady rise of effective institutions in urban areas has gradually relieved the family of these responsibilities. It has left the family with the unique task of bearing and rearing children, and transforming them into social beings. These have always been family functions, although somewhat obscured until recently by the nature of community organization, by the peculiar development of America as a frontier society, and by the periodic crises which have dotted American history.

As a dynamic system of social organization, urban society in America continues to change. One element of that change has been the rapid growth of communities at the edge of urban centers—fringe cities, suburbs, the rural-urban fringe. In the following article by E. Gartly Jaco and Ivan Belknap we observe the family, in the relatively new environment of the urban fringe, assuming characteristics and functions not seen in either the American rural or urban types. To the extent that the authors are correct, we find in the urban-fringe family another example of the unstable form which institutions assume in urban societies.

*
One modern school of family sociologists, represented chiefly by Zimmerman, considers the present urban American family an alarming instance of disintegration in the familial process. This disintegration is believed to have reached such extremes that the family can no longer adequately discharge vital functions such as reproduction and socialization. Writers of this school imply that American and Western civilization generally faces the dilemma of social collapse through failure of the family functions, or a return to some form of the large rural or semi-rural family system.

Another school considers the modern urban family to be making a reasonably satisfactory adjustment to population density, secondary relations, and diversity of urban institutions. Most demographers apparently agree that basic population trends have been in harmony with the assumptions of this latter school. Urban sociologists also have generally accepted the present urban "companionship," or small family as necessarily typical of urban communities. Burgess and Locke consider this type of family as one "which seeks to combine the values of both the old rural and the modern urban situations."

It is the purpose of this paper to point out certain trends that may be leading toward the emergence of a variant type of urban family which may

* From "The Family in the Urban Fringe," by E. Gartly Jaco and Ivan Belknap, *American Sociological Review*, Vol. 18, October 1953, pp. 551–557. Reprinted by permission of the authors and the American Sociological Association.

be able to maintain sufficient fertility and integration to satisfy the Zimmerman requisites and yet function adequately in the urban community. This variant type of urban family seems to be locating in the urban "fringe," as a product of changing ecological and demographic forces in metropolitan regions, and as a new functional adjustment of the family to the urban way of life. Because this family apparently represents primarily an adjustment to or a product of the peripheral metropolitan ecological area, it might be tentatively termed the "fringe family."

This new family form may be only temporarily connected, however, with the urban fringe. The new family type should not be construed as being permanently or intrinsically bound up with the "fringe." The "fringe family" label is offered only as a provisional, heuristic term which implies that this family form is initially a product of contemporary urban fringe development. This form may eventually spread to other ecological areas. Further research is needed, therefore, before a precise term pertaining to the social structure of this new family type can be given.

Satisfactory proof of the existence of such family form in significant numbers will require restudy of parts of current urban family sociology. In view of the present status of sociological data on the fringe, however, such proof will require considerable field research. Little attention has been paid by sociologists to any family form associated with the outskirts of the city. Also little systematic research has been done on the fringe as a social unit. At present, census and vital statistics data are inadequate for a thorough statistical analysis of the fringe; the former offering only data for 1950 on Standard Metropolitan Areas (these will not be useful for comparisons until 1960); and the vital statistics have no fringe definition at all. The census category of "rural nonfarm" is for the present about the only index of the fringe, but it includes many nonfringe components.

The following trends in American society do not prove conclusively the existence and operation of a fringe family. They do, however, indicate a very strong probability of the development of this form. Demographic, ecological, labor force, and stratification data justify the inference that such concerted forces *must* be affecting and sustained by the family system existing in such an area.

Demographic. Birth order is obviously an index of increasing or decreasing family size. The boom in first order of births during the war years has evidently not been sustained recently. However, an analysis of higher birth orders between 1942 and 1949 (comparative percentages computed by dividing the number of each birth order by total live births) reveals some noteworthy changes (Regional Summaries appear in Table 2.) Every state reporting has an increase in third order of births in 1949 over 1942. For fourth order of birth, 43 out of the 47 states reporting had equal or greater percentages for 1949 over 1942; the four states having less in 1949 were

Arkansas, New Mexico, Tennessee, and West Virginia, the latter having the greatest disparity of only one per cent. Apparently the fourth order of birth was the peak increase in 1949 over 1942, since only 17 states had equal or higher percentages of fifth orders in 1949. For the sixth order of birth, only nine states showed an increase in 1949. In sum, between 1942 and 1949, all states had higher third order of births in 1949, and 43 out of 47 for fourth order. Seventeen states showed a consistent gain in third through fifth orders in 1949 over 1942: Louisiana, Maryland, New Hampshire, Oregon, South Carolina, Texas, California, Connecticut, Idaho, Illinois, Michigan, Minnesota, New Jersey, New York, Ohio, Washington, and Wisconsin. The first six states were consistently higher in percentages from the third through the fifth birth orders. For the U.S. generally, Whelpton's cohort study substantiates our results in his 1925 cohort's experience.

Table 2. Percentages of 3rd, 4th, 5th, and 6th Birth Orders
In U.S. by Regions, 1942 and 1949

	Birth Order							
	Third		Fourth		Fifth		Sixth	
Region	1942	1949	1942	1949	1942	1949	1942	1949
New England	12.3	16.1	6.2	7.4	3.4	3.5	2.0	1.9
Middle Atlantic	12.0	15.1	5.9	6.6	3.2	3.1	1.9	1.6
East North Central	12.9	16.5	6.7	7.8	3.6	3.8	2.2	2.1
West North Central	13.7	16.8	7.6	8.4	4.5	4.3	2.8	2.4
South Atlantic	13.2	15.4	8.3	8.6	5.6	5.3	4.0	3.7
East South Central	13.3	14.8	9.0	8.9	6.3	5.9	4.7	4.2
West South Central	12.5	16.1	7.2	8.9	4.6	5.4	3.1	3.5
Mountain	14.4	17.2	8.3	9.1	5.2	4.9	3.3	2.9
Pacific	11.9	17.1	5.5	7.3	2.8	3.1	1.6	1.6

Kiser has pointed out the increase in fertility ratios since 1940 which are "proportionately heaviest among groups previously characterized by lowest fertility. Thus the percentage increases have been larger in the Northeast than in the South, larger among whites than nonwhites, larger among urban than rural-farm populations, and probably larger in the 'upper' than in the 'lower' socioeconomic classes."

Further data of a demographic order are suggested by Firey's finding of an excess of children under 10 years of age in the fringe of Flint, Michigan, in 1945. Scaff's study of a California suburb showed that the "commuting population adds young families and comparatively larger families to this community." Furthermore, "without question, the presence of the commuter group in the community introduces younger adults and children and helps to balance an age distribution that is otherwise heavily weighted by elderly people."

While the census area of rural nonfarm is not strictly identical to that of the urban fringe area, it does include the latter and offers a crude index of trends in the fringe. In 1949, for the first time, the number of children under 5 years of age per 1000 women was higher in the rural nonfarm area than in both urban and rural farm areas, showing a steadier and higher rise than for urban areas, while in 1949, the rural farm amount dropped. Further, the per cent distribution for 4 persons per household in 1950 was highest for rural nonfarm areas as compared to both urban and rural farm areas.

A recent study indicates an increase both in intra-urban and inter-urban migration to fringe areas. A sustained drop in rural-urban migration and in immigration points in the direction of even further growth for the fringe.

Thus, with a spurt in higher birth orders and excess numbers of young children associated with a jump in fringe in-migration, a trend toward increased family size in the fringe can be deducted.

Ecological. Perhaps the most significant single index of the increase in the fringe population is the comparative rates of growth between 1940 and 1950: central cities grew 13 per cent; the hinterland increased 5.7 per cent; but the outlying parts of central cities showed a jump of 34.7 per cent.

Home ownership is directly related to large families, both in urban and rural areas. Census figures show that home ownership has increased 53.9 per cent between 1940 and 1950, a change which may stimulate or be stimulated by larger families. The rate of home ownership in rural nonfarm areas from 1930 through 1950 has been closer to that of the rural farm than to that of the urban area.

An increase in the processes of concentration of population and decentralization of services is mentioned by Hauser and Blumenfield. Therefore, the growth of the urban fringe need not represent a deconcentration of urban population from central cities, but may indicate rather an expansion of urban population into broader territory. Many fringe areas exist apart from central city political boundaries only for a brief time until they become incorporated into the central city. However, the data accumulating on the ecology of the urban community do indicate a continuing increase in the distribution of the United States population into the fringe areas.

Labor Force. Whetten and Mitchell's study of a Connecticut suburb showed that "white-collar" workers predominated among occupational groups. However, movement to the fringe is not confined to the middle and upper economic levels. The spread of the concept of the guaranteed annual wage in American industry, taken with the increase in fringe population, indicates a drift to the fringe and to single-family dwellings by the so-called "blue-collar" workers. The bearing of the guaranteed wage on the possibility of home ownership in this latter group is clear enough. Moreover, by "living out" and "working in," as Liepmann puts it, the blue-collar worker may paradoxically increase his family stability as he increases his job mobility. By living in the fringe, that is, the worker ceases to be tied to a particular factory or combination residential-occupational area in the city. He is free to change his jobs without the disruption of a family stability caused by residential relocation.

With the increasing employment of women, single as well as married, many women who eventually marry and become mothers return to their early forms of work after their children reach a more independent age (Table 3). Increased employment of married women is conducive to fringe living. Being employed in an area distant from residence minimizes the conflict between the mother's familial and nonfamilial roles. It seems highly probable that the increase of employment of women in the higher age groups is partly an index of employment of fringe family mothers.

**Table 3. Percentage of Women in U.S. Labor Force,
by Marital and Familiar Status, 1949**

Status	Per Cent in Labor Force
All women in labor force	22.5
Women without children	28.7
With children under 6	10.0
With children some 6–11 only	24.7
With children some 12–17 only	31.3

Liepmann has pointed out that fringe families encourage and even require "secondary earners," particularly in lower economic groups. There are equally cogent reasons for the employment of higher status fringe mothers in view of the increasing costs of educating children, intensified by the inflation which has persisted since World War II. Lower age at marriage makes such employment of mothers consistent with a higher birth rate, while their superior education permits them to seek employment affording an economic surplus after they have paid for maids, kindergartens, and other maternal surrogates for the youngest children.

Social Stratification. Scaff holds that "education and membership in a profession become a badge of acceptance" in suburbs. Coupled with its matricentric orientation, social stratification in the fringe is probably more distinct and overt than is apparent in the central city, where the "élite" is composed of professionals and their wives or widows, while industrial workers occupy the lower social strata. If so, then social cleavages in the fringe may be disparate, and fixed along occupational lines.

Furthermore, if industrial workers make up the lower social strata and participate less in the suburban community, as Scaff's study indicates, then commuting by such a population may be viewed as "escape from status." That is, by "working in and living out," a worker may absent himself from his inferior social position during the working day. This would be especially true if the wife and older children are also employed. Indeed, such flexibility may make more tolerable the occupance of a lower social position in the fringe.

If one follows the clues suggested by current urban population and economic trends in the light of what is already known about the modern suburban family a number of inferences on the structure of the fringe family becomes possible. Some of the more important of these inferences involve the probable fringe family roles and the integration of this family at various stages of the institutional life cycle.

When the family selects the fringe for the sake of rearing children, this selection can be regarded as involving emphasis on the reproductive-socializing roles of father and mother. There is evidence that some movements to suburbs are carried out to improve the educational and recreational life of children. This improvement is a reciprocal affair, since in its very nature it involves not only a greater control over the children's environment but a strengthening of the significance of the parental roles and the associated roles of the siblings. This strengthening of the significance of the parental roles has already been examined for the mother by Mowrer, and by Burgess and Locke in their studies of the matricentric suburban family. With the increasing employment of mothers, the shorter work day and week, and the spread of relatively higher incomes among many employed classifications, the father will come to play a more prominent role in the family and the community than was possible either in the companionship or suburban matricentric family. In general it seems likely that all the family roles in the fringe family may be enhanced by proximity of members, and by mutual functional significance.

The Burgess viewpoint of family sociology, with certain qualifications, holds that the companionship family is more in line with other urban social institutions. In view of the powerful stress required by this form on the intrinsic husband-wife relationship rather than on the father-mother bond, the companionship family may represent less of an adaptation than a negation of the family's important functions. There is an implication in this position that as the family "gives in" and loses its historical functions, it becomes better adjusted to the urban environment. Hence the fringe type of family offers at least a compromise between familistic and companionship forms while maintaining at least an apparent emerging adaptation to the urban environment.

Implicit in the strengthening of the parental bonds in the fringe family is an increased control over the courtship process, and perhaps solidarity in the old age family roles. In the central city, anonymity and diversity of interaction minimizes parental control over children in the realm of courtship and dating. In the fringe, the courtship process can be confined in some degree to peer groups selected by parents in tacit agreement with other parents of like status. This represents a compromise between parental mate choice for the children, and the theoretical free choice implied in the dating pattern of the urban youth culture. This actuarial kind of control over the courtship process by fringe parents obviously gives greater continuity to the family process as experienced by both parents and children. This continuity, together with the heightened significance of the member relationships, may be one explanation of the greater number of children in the fringe.

Burgess and Locke list six long-time family-related trends which have been disrupted by the recent war and speculate about their continuation after the war. These are: (1) the declining birth rate; (2) the consequent smaller size of the family; (3) the increase in proportion of the married to those of marriageable age; (4) the decrease in the age at marriage; (5) the increase in the proportion of all women, and of married women gainfully employed; and (6) the decline in the historic functions of the family—economic, educational, recreational, religious, and protective. The apparent assumption is that, should these trends be only temporarily disrupted by the recent war, and should they continue as in the past, the companionship family will become institutionalized in the United States.

Trends pointed out in the preceding discussion, however, indicate that particularly for the rapidly increasing U.S. fringe area, a somewhat different picture is appearing: (1) sustained fertility through higher orders of birth; (2) a consequent increase in the size of the fringe family; (3) marriage rates for males higher in the rural nonfarm areas than in both urban and rural farm areas; (4) decrease in the age at marriage continuing; (5) employment of both single and married women increasing, particularly for the higher age groups and with mothers of children from 12 to 17 years of age; and (6) the historic functions of the family seemingly better retained in the fringe—the economic, with employment of mothers as secondary workers; the educational, in the selection of "better" schools for children; the recreational, in the encouragement of participation of children in selected peer groups and social sets; the religious, in belonging to and supporting the "right" churches, and the protective, in addition to the preceding, in providing the best care and rearing practices of medical and mental science.

There is some indication, therefore, that the interruption of the long-term trends listed above by Burgess and Locke may have become sustained in the fringe family. We can say definitely, at least, that this interruption has been associated with an enormous increase in the fringe population between 1940 and 1950, and that the concept of the fringe family may serve sociology as one useful research hypothesis for the analysis, in a relatively unexplored area, of the demographic, ecological, community structure and working force trends we have mentioned.

THE CHURCH

In the urban community there is no single institution that can be spoken of as *the* church. Here again there are several churches, and Thomas F. Hoult has suggested some typical characteristics that apply, more or less, to all of them.[11] Their congregations play the role of spectators more than participants. They are organized along the lines of a bureaucracy; they are staffed by professionally trained and salaried officials, with a ministry approaching religion in a business-like manner. Frequently the churches sponsor many subsidiary organizations, thus becoming centers for forms of congenial behavior.[12] Their buildings tend to become large and elaborate. Yet Hoult is the first to concede that his analysis is useful primarily as a point of departure.[13] There are many variations on this theme—from the cults and pentacostal sects to the wealthy, orthodox, and large centers of religious worship.

From the point of view of this chapter, variations in the structure of religious groups are to be expected. The question is: how do churches function in the urban setting in relation to the variations?

Religious membership in America is growing rapidly. In 1880, according to the National Council of Churches, 20 per cent of the population belonged to churches, whereas in 1956, 60 per cent of the population expressed religious affiliation.[14] A 1957 census report indicated that of those persons over 14 years of age, 96.4 per cent reported a church affiliation.[15] The data did not distinguish between affiliation and actual membership. Some 66 per cent reported themselves associated with a form of Protestantism, 25.7 per cent considered themselves Roman Catholic, and 3.2 per cent said they were Jewish.[16] The remainder either mentioned some other religious affiliation, did not reply, or expressed no religious ties.

Although most Protestants live in cities they also have the highest incidence of religious affiliation in small towns and in farm areas. Roman Catholics and Jews are almost entirely urban residents. Only 5.4 per cent of Roman Catholics and 0.2 per cent of Jews live on farms.[17] This may be a result of the fact that both these religious groups, having arrived in America in later stages of immigration than the Protestants, remained in the cities.[18] Religion in America is also highly diversified within the major denominations, among which are over 258 different sects.[19] Most divided are the various Protestant denominations, although the Roman Catholic and Jewish faiths also have their factions. In 1955 it was reported by the National Council of Churches that there were, for example, ten different sects among the Presbyterians, 22 among the Methodists, 27 among the Baptists, and 19 among the Lutherans.[20]

Given these facts, does religion function as a unifying force in the American urban scene? Much evidence has been presented to indicate that religion holds traditional societies together. But the very diversity of religious belief and organization in the urban setting presents another situation. As Robert K. Merton has noted,[21] when more than one religious denomination exists in a society there is a high probability that conflict will arise. This was certainly the case in Europe, although in America the conflict has not erupted as sharply. Competition might be a better word to use at this phase of our religious history. Among churches competition has developed for membership, for endowments, tax relief, building sites, and political and social influence, as well as for scriptural and ritualistic rights and prerogatives. Merton continues by indicating that a society achieves community of interest through commonly shared values and beliefs. But, he asks, what evidence is there to indicate that persons who claim no religious beliefs ". . . less often subscribe to certain common values and ends than those devoted to religious doctrines?" [22] Finally, Merton has questioned whether a common interest can be obtained if religious doctrines and beliefs do not coincide with nonreligious doctrines and beliefs. The situation becomes more challenging when different religious groups hold different views on the same subject—such as birth control—and, furthermore, when individuals who profess some religious affiliation are so able to compartmentalize their beliefs that they can believe two different things at the same time, without any apparent contradiction.

CHURCHES AND SECTS

To understand the diversity and the disintegrating effect of religion in urban communities let us turn to an analysis of the development of sects. The classic statement was made by the German sociologist Ernst Troeltsch.[23] A church, according to Troeltsch's characterization, is basically conservative. It attempts compromise with the social order and appeals to the middle and upper classes, and, finally, to the state. Because the church attempts to weave itself into the social order, it claims dominion over all. The church has a relatively permanent and continuous membership through the rite of baptism. The whole of life is viewed by the church as a preparation for a supernatural goal. An asceticism develops, but it is only another aspect of the preparation and is under the direction of the church.

The sect, on the other hand, which may include such apparently diverse associations as the monastic order of Roman Catholicism or the store-front congregations of the urban slum, rejects the compromises of the church. It becomes, instead, indifferent or hostile to the existing social order and to the state, or merely tolerates them. The sect does not attempt to incorporate itself into the general organization of society. Sects are generally lower-class movements which give themselves over rather fully to religious radicalism and direct, individualistic asceticism. Furthermore, sects are generally small in size of membership. Direct interaction does take place between the members, yet the membership lacks continuity and permanence because of its voluntary character.[24]

Within specifically Protestant Christianity there are four forms of sects.[25] The first type is the Conversionist sect, typically fundamentalist, looking upon the Bible as the only guide to salvation. Conversionist sects regard other sects, and the churches, as diluted by compromise. The redemption of sin through Christ is the test of admission to the sect. Such groups are often militantly evangelistic. The second type of sect is the Adventists who neither seek quick conversion nor rely on the emotionalism of the Conversionists. Adventists are essentially revolutionary: they look forward to the overthrow of the present world order and its replacement by a new kingdom based on the morality of Christ. The prophecies of the Old Testament are considered the proof for the coming revolution. A third type, the Introversionists, seeks the development of an inner spiritual self. The values of the sect are frequently viewed as incommunicable to others, and the membership assumes an élite quality. Introversionists withdraw from the world, disdaining evangelism. The Gnostics are the fourth type of sect. Gnostics emphasize the teaching of obscure doctrine. To them, traditional Christianity is considered outmoded and other sects and churches are viewed as backward or ignorant. Gnostic sects are not militantly evangelistic nor do they attempt to withdraw from the world. There is, rather, an application of Gnostic principles to everyday life for purposes of self-advancement.

How sects develop in the urban community is the subject of the following article by J. Milton Yinger. He relates urbanism, class, and social status to the emergence of sect development. He also develops some ideas about the consequences of such development which move beyond the immediate concerns of social organization to the psychological level of analysis.

*
[In] . . . the American scene, one can see many ways in which religious differences correspond to status differences. In the early years, status differences were correlated, to a degree, with geography, so that one could contrast the religious tendencies of the East with those of the frontier. [As H. Richard Neibuhr said:]

> The religion of the urban, commercial East tended to take on or to retain the typical features of all bourgeois or national religion—a polity corresponding to the order and character of class organized society, an intellectual conception of the content of faith, an ethics reflecting the needs and evaluations of a stable and commercial citizenry, a sober, ritualistic type of religious expression. The religion of the West, on the other hand, accepted or produced anew many of the characteristics of the faith of the disinherited, for the psychology of the frontier corresponds in many respects to the psychology of the revolutionary poor. This is especially true of the emotional character of religious experience, which seems to be required in the one case as in the other. The isolation of frontier life fostered craving for companionship, suppressed the gregarious tendency and so subjected the lonely settler to the temptations of crowd suggestions to an unusual degree.

This contrast combines the effects of many variables—degree of isolation, level of education, occupation, etc., as well as class—thus pointing to the need for avoiding an over-simplified view of the effects of class differences.

A number of studies in recent years have described the religious developments on our new "frontier"—the city—showing that many of the tendencies of the earlier days reappear. Although there are many sources of sectarian growth today, it is primarily among the recent migrants to the city, the urban "peasants," that sects are forming. And in these sects, the class element is clearly apparent. These groups differ widely from the denominations around them in theology, style of worship, ethical emphasis, and church organization. It is relevant to ask: What are some of the causes of the rise of these sects; how do they differ in religious behavior, and what are the consequences of their beliefs and practices?

When a lower-class person moves from a rural area into a city, to work in mill or factory, he is confronted with a number of difficult problems of adjustment. He is forced to accept an enormous change in his style of life—the rhythm of his work, the nature of his associations, his place in a neighborhood. He is likely to be almost wholly lacking in organized social contacts, because he enters the new society at its most poorly organized level. And his sense of isolation is increased by the way in which he is looked down upon by the established urban groups. This is the kind of problem with which religion might be expected to deal: You are not alone; you belong; your problems are not everlasting, or at least they have meaning in a transcenden-

* Reprinted from *Religion, Society, and the Individual*, pp. 166–173, by J. Milton Yinger. Copyright 1957 by The Macmillan Company. By permission of the publisher.

tal context. But the established churches of the city are poorly equipped to give these assurances to a lower class migrant from a rural area. For the most part they are fully accommodated to the middle and upper classes of the city—the forms of their services of worship, the content of the preaching, the programs and leadership of the various groups in the church are all adjusted to the urban members of long-standing. The lower-class sect movement, then, is in this situation an attempt to grapple with the problems faced by the migrant, a response to what Holt calls the "cultural shock" that comes from the shift to an urban life, an attempt to heal the distress caused by isolation and insecurity. It is not likely to be an economic protest, at least in any direct sense. The migrant may be better off financially in the city. He is almost certainly ill-equipped by earlier training to protest against his economic status. The established churches, in fact, are probably more liberal on economic issues than are the lower class sects. Far more than an economic protest, the urban sect demonstrates the widely different personality needs and modes of expression that one finds among status levels. The religious forms that have been accommodated to one status group are felt to be inadequate by another.

If the need for stable and secure social relations is one cause for the rise of the holiness and pentecostal sects, poverty itself is another. There was a rapid increase in such sects during the depression of the nineteen-thirties. Most of the churches with which the unemployed and the poverty-stricken had been associated—for many of them were members of established denominations—had little to say about this problem. They neither pressed for secular solutions or gave serious attention to a religious interpretation of the meaning of want. The small sects which sprang up among the poor, however, were diligently trying to give an interpretation of the economic distress of the members. Almost none of them, to be sure, gave—or give— any attention to the economic and political situation around them. The Winstanleys of our time seldom use religious terms; direct protests against secular institutions come from secular groups almost entirely, from labor unions, political movements, etc. As in Luther's Germany and pre-Cromwellian England, it is those with some hope of success who make direct protests—whether in religious or secular terms—against the ruling powers of their society. When these hopes are persistently frustrated, spiritual solutions are given more emphasis. So it is that among America's lower classes, those who are poorest off, those who have little chance to improve their lot by secular instruments, turn to religious interpretations of the meaning of poverty.

Closely related to isolation and poverty, is a third factor in the recent rise of sects in the United States: the need for an emotional expressiveness that is lacking in the dignified and ritualistic services of most of the churches. Clark calls the sects "refugees of the emotionally starved." The poor

". . . cannot afford, or do not have access to the recreations, associations, social functions, and cultural activities wherein the prosperous find outlets for their emotions." More than that, the *need* for emotional release may be greater among the lower classes, because of more frustrations and the monotony of many of their jobs. Liston Pope notes, with respect to a southern mill town, that life is monotonous and dull; production methods in the mills are largely mechanical; the worker has little opportunity for choice or control over the forces that influence his life. In the small religious group, the members can set their own schedule and determine their own modes of expression.

If these are indicative of the needs that foster the growth of class-differentiated sects in American society, we may now ask: How do the sects attempt to meet these needs? To those who feel isolated in the older churches, the new, small groups are their own, to lead, to organize as they like. (That the members may like very different things and compete for leadership is shown by the frequent splits that occur.) The sects are orthodox—according to their own standards—to the point of fanaticism. At first glance, this does not seem to be an adaptation to the problems of the religiously disinherited; but it becomes meaningful as a way of saying: we belong to a very highly selected and exclusive association. New members are admitted only after having given evidence of a religious experience and showing that they will abide by the group's norms. There is rigid enforcement of certain standards of behavior, a kind of modern asceticism that assures the members that they deserve to belong to the exclusive group and will share the rewards it promises. Pope indicates that the sects are very quick to expel members who violate their code (for such violations tear the fabric of their solutions to life's problems): "In 1938 one Free-Will Baptist Holiness Church in Gastonia received 33 new members and expelled 24 persons, of a total membership of 88. A Church of God with 143 members has expelled 30 in the last two years; another with 95 members has expelled 40; a third 101 members has expelled 20 in the last four years." For a person to be expelled from a church in our time is a rare occurrence. The exclusiveness and insistence upon "Puritan morality" of the sect is not simply ". . . elevating the manners they cannot well escape into moral virtues established by the will of God," as Clark describes it. It is, beyond that, the expression of the psychology of the sacrifice: We deserve religious success for our purity, for what we have given up. Anything or anybody who endangers that assurance must be cast out and repudiated.

Within the sect, the desires of the members for leadership, for status, for expression, for assurance that their difficult lot has some ultimate significance are dealt with. They can give free rein to their emotions and, as Clark says, "attribute the pleasant thrills thereof to a divine agency."

There is little direct challenge to the economic and political order within which they fare so poorly, although the "comfortable" people may be criticized for their "immorality." Most of the sects in American society today accept the basic secular institutions. Their members look for their reward in heaven or in some apocalyptic transformation of the world. According to the dominant theology, man is depraved. Only by the second-coming of Jesus will the world escape its ills. Other groups, such as the Jehovah's Witnesses, emphasize the withdrawal theme more strongly: Since this is a world of sin, we must not only be indifferent to it, but withdraw from it and refuse its commands over us. This is a somewhat less pessimistic response to the secular world, for it carries the implication—although often very obscurely— that some of the world's problems might be solved within a pure community of believers. But whether the acceptance or the avoidance theme is stronger —and both are almost always found—the sects deal with the economic problems of their members primarily by redefining them, not by offering ways in which they might be solved in terms of the "world's" definitions. Their solution of economic distress is a collective look to the future, beyond history. As Boison points out, this "solution" carries certain implications: It requires the coming to terms with God, as the doctrines of the sect interpret God; hence there is strong emphasis on confessions and the strict enforcement of rules. The realization that the sectarians have that their problems will not readily be solved precludes any "easy" religious solution. Their own experience has been so hard that they would not at all be convinced by easy formulas and doctrines.

Thus the sects strive to deal with the many needs of their members in terms that harmonize with their past training, their level of education, and their experiences in life. Pope (Liston Pope) summarizes this situation well when he writes:

> The sects substitute religious status for social status, a fact which may help to account for their emphasis on varying degrees of Grace. This emphasis, indeed, forms their most distinctive theological tenet. As over against the lack of religious differentiation within older denominations, the newer sects divide their members, and people in general, into several religious classifications: saved, sanctified, baptized with the Holy Ghost, baptized with water, recipient of the first, second, or third blessing and the like. What matters it, then, if a Methodist has more money but has never been baptized with the Holy Ghost? As over against segregation from the community, the newer sects affirm separation from the world; in the face of exclusion on educational, economic, and religious grounds, they affirm exclusion from their own fellowship of those who engage in mixed bathing, dancing, card playing, bobbing the hair, gambling, baseball, county fairs, drinking, and using tobacco. Because they have no jewelry to wear, they make refusal to wear jewelry, including wedding rings, a religious requirement. They transmute poverty into a symptom of Grace. Having no money, they redeem their economic status by rigid tithing of the small income they do possess, and thus far surpass members of churches of any other type or denomination in per capita contributions, despite the fact that they stand at the bottom of the economic scale.

The universal human skill of making virtue of necessity is nowhere put to more extensive use.

THE SCHOOL

It has been said that the school is truly a product of its community. In one degree or another it reaches out to touch almost every person and institution in the community. The children of the families in the community form its clientele. The adult population, many of whom continue as students in adult programs, pay taxes which help support the school. The school is conceived of by the community as a means of preparing children for the assumption of adult roles; the school, therefore, shares the initial socialization process with the family and church (see Chapter 11). The school of any particular community might be, from another viewpoint, the largest business in town. School budgets frequently total millions of dollars, the labor force for schools is one of the largest in any community, and schools are tremendous consumers of goods and services. They offer industrial and commercial curricula, and general and college preparatory curricula. Schools can also be the setting within which profound feelings of alienation emerge.

What are the consequences of such diversity? By substituting the word "education" for the word "religion" we can apply to the school the same question that Robert Merton asked of the church.

First, there is the tacit assumption that one primary function of education is the transmission of culture from one generation to the next. This is a way for ensuring the continuity of a culture. The basis of this assumption, as Merton noted of religion, might well derive from traditional societies—or from popular stereotypes patterned on the "little red school house" concept of education. In the diversified communities of urban society the assumption of a primarily transmissive function for education breaks down. Not only are there different types of schools devoted to special knowledges and skills, but there are also many different ideas held by persons about the kind of education their children should have. The school, in order to find some answer to its problems and criticisms, has tried to become all things to all men. This is especially so of the conception of the comprehensive high school. It is not our task to evaluate the educational worth of this development. What is important to note is that many children appear to be obtaining different kinds of education; and gone is continuity in the transmission of the culture.

Now, if we persist in viewing education as unifying the society, we are confronted with the difficulty of answering a question asked by Merton of religion: what evidence is there to indicate that the less well-educated or the uneducated accept the values and beliefs of the society any less than the well-educated? In addition, how do we explain that some of those who may be better educated are the most agnostic regarding the social order?

We must also ask whether education can unify, when certain of its assumptions do not coincide with the assumptions of family and church. This is seen in the history of American political institutions. The educational assumption about American political beliefs is that they must be questioned. In contrast, there is a strong opinion that to believe is enough.

Another aspect of schools contributing to their disintegrating effect is the trend toward loss of local control by the communities in which they are located. It is said that schools are products of their communities; but how much actual control do communities exercise? Although the situation varies from state to state, some generalizations can be drawn. The sources of school revenue, for example, have altered significantly. In the year 1929–1930, public schools in the United States received 0.4 per cent of their revenues from the federal government, 16.9 per cent from state government, 10.4 from county sources, and 72.3 per cent from local sources. In 1951–1952, revenue from the federal government had increased to 3.5 per cent and from state government to 38.6 per cent, while county and local sources had declined to 6.0 per cent and 51.8 per cent respectively.[26] The increase in state expenditures is the most significant and is related to capital outlay for building programs and salaries which, because of increased enrollments, local revenue cannot support.

With increased state expenditure has come an increase in state control. In contrast to the time when America was dominantly rural and county and local districts hired teachers according to their own standards, the states now accredit teachers according to legally prescribed courses of instruction and training. There are also state requirements for school curricula, ranging from the United States Constitution to driver education and first aid. States also approve textbooks and, in some cases, print their own for the elementary grades. Most important for the study of community institutions, states also prescribe the functions and powers of school administrators and school boards. Community schools retain only that power delegated by state legislatures. There are no sovereign powers below the level of states.

BUREAUCRATIC EDUCATION

The response that schools have made to the problems of size and diversity, and to the growing state control of the educational process, has been to tie together their organization and functions through bureaucratic means. Bureaucracy is a hierarchical system of formally prescribed roles and statuses with carefully calculated social distances between each; it is meant to persist over time regardless of who staffs any of the positions.[27] The formality and persistence of bureaucratic structure can be fully realized only if the system of law under which it operates is calculable and consistent.[28] The necessity of operating under law draws the bureaucracy—in this instance the school—away from the community which originated it, thus giving further impetus to the disintegration of urban institutions. The bureaucratization of the school also reduces the number of social situations in which individuals can relate to each other on an informal basis.

The specific effects of bureaucracy upon education are to be seen in the drive for standardization. A multiplication of administrative positions and of advisory committees has taken place to help ensure uniform educational goals and means of attaining them. Students are also affected by bureaucratization. They are "processed" by sorting machines. Their standardized examinations are electrically scored by clerks. The campus is now called "the plant," giving rise to the derisive phrase "the educational factory." In the essay that follows, Charles Page depicts a series of typical responses to the bureaucratization of education.

*
Whatever the effects on students, certain consequences of bureaucratization for teachers and administrators are becoming evident. These consequences include more or less typical modes of adaptation characteristic of any bureaucratic system. While it is by no means true that the behavior patterns of academic men are merely responses to their occupational environment, inspection of the collegiate realm suggests that the personalities of its inhabitants reflect, in some measure, the structural changes of the realm itself. Before presenting the specific types of adaptation, it must be stressed that the discussion no doubt omits some important modes of adjustment to the academic scene; that these "ideal-type" categories never square precisely with the facts of life; and that academic men, in their actual behavior, may tend to conform to one or more (or none) of the four following types.

* From Charles H. Page, "Bureaucracy in Higher Education," *The Journal of Higher Education*, Vol. V, January 1951, pp. 91–100. Reprinted by permission of the publisher.

The first type is the ritualist, the most frequently cited example of bureaucratic man. He is the occupant of a bureaucratic office, high or low in the hierarchy, whose official duties have become deeply ingrained habituations and whose attitudes toward the protocol of office are those of the "routineer." He has converted means into ends and has shifted matters of secular and instrumental concern to the realm of sacred values. He is the "master of red tape" beyond all others, the "bureaucratic virtuoso," in Weber's phrase.

The ritualist, we might assume, is to be found primarily among the occupants of administrative posts, and, of course, he does reside there. But a casual inspection of ourselves, the instructors, will reveal him here also. And more. For as bureaucracy spreads out into student life, it produces—or at least it brings into view—the student ritualists, some of whom become "big wheels" of formal campus activities (though not all "big wheels" are ritualists). In passing, it may be suggested, moreover, that, because of specific social and cultural conditions that cannot be treated here, more women than men—in administration, instructional staff, and student body —tend to conform to the routineer type. But this should not be taken as an invidious distinction. Men and women alike, in so far as their behavior and attitudes approach the ritualistic patterns, illustrate an understandable and inevitable form of social adaptation to the realities of bureaucratic structure.

Adaptation, in the case of the second type, the academic neurotic, is only partial and uneasy. The academic neurotic, generally, is confused by the apparent contradictions between professed norms and actual practice, frustrated by the "imposition" of bureaucracy's ways on his own being, and seemingly has little realistic understanding of the functional features of the system in which he operates. He is likely to shuttle between the formal and the informal structures, failing to recognize the vital functions served by both and unable to use effectively either aspect of the system for forwarding his own interests or for buttressing his own psychic comfort. He is, as we say, "all mixed up."

But the neurotic's confusion is rarely apparent to himself. On the contrary, he is often convinced, and voices his convictions frequently and in no uncertain terms, that he "knows what is going on"—in the president's office, in such-and-such committee, in this clique, in that department. And much of what "is going on," he may feel, is aimed at his own destruction. When this feeling is dominant, we see the clear case of the academic paranoid, the self-centered individual who detects in the life around him little beyond the diabolical machinations of his colleagues, all designed to undermine his own position. Extreme neuroticism of this type, in the individual instance, is not, of course, merely the product of bureaucracy. It may be the case, however, that the apparent increasing incidence of academic paranoia is related to the growing impersonality of academic life and the consequent social isolation of the individual (and, perhaps also, to the structurally induced increasing number of ritualists).

These features of the college environment usually do not disturb the third type, the academic robber baron. The robber baron, like the ritualist, is well adapted to his bureaucratic surroundings. But his adaptation takes a completely different form; for, rather than glorifying the routines of collegiate life, rather than making ends of means, he will, when it serves his own ends best, ignore bureaucratic propriety altogether. The ability to by-pass prescribed methods, to avoid consultations or procedures called for by the institution's formal code, to cut red tape, demands enormous skills, the courage of one's convictions, and an intense desire to further one's own ends. The robber baron manifests precisely these qualities, in much the same way that his prototype in another realm—say, a Carnegie or a Rockefeller—reveals these traits. If the academic robber baron is to escape disgrace and is to remain within the collegiate enterprise, he must possess a highly realistic knowledge of the academic world, must recognize the functionally strategic relationships in and between the formal and informal structures, and must display manipulative ability.

Robber barons need not be the villains of history; sometimes they are heroes. And this is the case of the academic robber baron as well. If their ends correspond with, or are congenial to, the professed goals of the institution itself, the robber baron may, in fact, become a collegiate saint. Just as we forgive and "canonize" our Carnegies and Russell Sages, once they have made good on the grand scale (i.e., have conformed to and confirmed the culturally approved value of material success) and once they have endowed posterity with socially useful edifices, so do we exalt our academic robber barons when they have conformed to and confirmed the highest values of education.

In the most extreme form of the fourth type, the academic rebel, the traditional values, the ends, of education are rejected, together with the entire apparatus of methods and of means. This educational revolutionist is not a nihilist or a pariah, however; for, although he rejects both the goals and the instruments of the ongoing system, at the same time he defines new ends and new means for their attainment. He may retain his position within the system, but, in this case, his subversive doctrines, however subtly expressed, lose their revolutionary force, for ultimately they are "toned down" and molded to fit the bureaucratic pattern. The rebel may, on the other hand, carry his doctrines into new educational ventures: he may build "experimental" schools, wherein, eventually, the forces of bureaucracy show themselves once more. In either case, it is worth observing, the original revolutionary views are necessarily changed to meet the structural demands of the organizational status quo.

The academic rebel, if he is to survive as a rebel, must, like the robber baron, comprehend the realities of his organization. More, he must compromise with them, in some measure. This is why most representatives of this type are academic reformers rather than revolutionists, who generally accept at least some of the professed ends of higher education and are satisfied to seek changes in the means. Most academic men, no doubt, at one time or another fall into this category. And most of them would agree, perhaps, that the academic reformer, if not the rebel, is a functionally essential and desirable element in the world of higher learning.

Typologies of this sort are dangerous devices in an essay of this kind, for the reader often misconstrues their chief purpose, i.e., to simplify the task of descriptive analysis. And even when this task is facilitated, the typology itself may, for certain problems, conceal more than it reveals. In the present instance, for example, it is very likely true that the most productive recruiting ground for the academic neurotic is among the "well-adapted" academic ritualists. If this be the case, it raises the whole question of ritualism as an effective mechanism of adaptation. Or, again, it is perhaps evident that the academic robber baron who becomes "canonized" into the academic saint is, in reality, or at least at one time was, the academic rebel. And if this be the case, it once more raises the problem of the nature of effective adaptation and, further, the vital question of the interrelationships between these various ideal types. These are important queries, and there are many others, of course, which a full-bodied study of the bureaucratization of higher learning would be forced to face.

Having reviewed the nature of family, church, and school in the urban setting, let us move on to how each relates to the process of socialization. In the next chapter we shall see how each of these institutions performs in the initial phases of socializing the child.

Notes

1. Max Weber, *General Economic History*, trans. F. Knight, New York: Collier Books, 1961, p. 252.
2. George Homans, *The Human Group*, New York: Harcourt, Brace and Company, 1950. See pp. 112 ff., especially.
3. "The Train Doesn't Stop Here Anymore," *Time*, Vol. LXXXI, No. 7, February 15, 1963, p. 28.
4. E. W. Burgess, "The Family in a Changing Society," *Cities and Society*, ed. Paul K. Hatt and A. J. Reiss, Glencoe, Ill.: The Free Press, 1957, Rev. Ed., p. 482.
5. George P. Murdock, *Social Structure*. The nuclear family, it must be noted, is nothing new in history. It has existed throughout history. It has been only recently, however, that the nuclear family has become the dominant form. The nuclear family is to be distinguished from a household. A household is an in-

218   Family, Church, School in Urban Setting

dividual or group occupying a dwelling unit. They may or may not be related, such as single persons, related persons, lodgers, foster children, employees sharing a unit, or any unrelated persons living together as partners. Cf., *1950 United States Census of the Population: U.S. Summary*, P-Cl, p. xiv.

6. Paul Glick, "The Family Life Cycle," *American Sociological Review*, Vol. 12, April 1947, pp. 164–74.
7. United States Department of Commerce, *Statistical Abstracts of the United States*, Table 69, p. 66.
8. Donald J. Bogue, *The Population of the United States*, Glencoe, Ill.: The Free Press, 1959, p. 321.
9. Hugo Beigel, "Romantic Love," *Sourcebook in Marriage and the Family*, ed. Marvin Sussman. New York: Houghton Mifflin Company, 1955, pp. 69–77.
10. Burgess, *op. cit.*, p. 483.
11. Thomas F. Hoult, *The Sociology of Religion*, New York: Dryden, 1958, pp. 152 ff.
12. Richard La Piere, *Collective Behavior*, New York: McGraw-Hill Book Company, 1938, Chapters VIII and IX.
13. Hoult, *op. cit.*, p. 154.
14. Cited in J. O. Hertzler, *American Social Institutions*, Boston: Allyn and Bacon, 1961, p. 491.
15. Bogue, *op. cit.*, p. 689.
16. *Ibid.*
17. *Ibid.*, p. 694.
18. Michael Argyle, *Religious Behavior*, Glencoe, Ill.: The Free Press, 1959, p. 135. See also Oscar Handlin, *The Uprooted*, New York: Universal Library, 1957.
19. Hertzler, *op. cit.*, p. 494.
20. *Ibid.*
21. Robert K. Merton, *Social Theory and Social Structure*, Glencoe, Ill.: The Free Press, 1957, rev., p. 29.
22. *Ibid.*
23. Ernst Troeltsch, *Social Teachings of the Christian Churches*, New York: Harper Torchbooks, 1960, 2 vols.
24. Troeltsch traced the church-sect dichotomy into the eighteenth century. In a succeeding volume, *Protestantism and Progress*, trans. W. Montgomery, Boston: Beacon Press, 1962, he continued to study the problem as it unfolded in a secular, capitalistic society.
25. Bryan R. Wilson, "An Analysis of Sect Development," *American Sociological Review*, Vol. 24, February 1959, pp. 5 ff.
26. Cited in H. Otto Dahlke, *Values in Culture and Classroom*, New York: Harper and Brothers, 1958, p. 33.
27. Cf., Robert K. Merton, "Bureaucratic Structure and Personality," *Social Forces*, Vol. XVIII, May 1940, pp. 561–568.
28. Max Weber, *From Max Weber: Essays in Sociology*, ed. and trans. H. H. Gerth and C. W. Mills, New York: Oxford Galaxy Books, pp. 216–221.

Selected Readings

Anshen, Ruth. *The Family: Its Function and Destiny*. New York: Harper and Brothers, 1959. Rev. Ed.
*Blau, Peter. *Bureaucracy in Modern Society*. New York: Random House, 1956.

Burgess, E. W., and Harvey J. Locke. *The Family.* New York: American Book Company, 1950.

*Clark, Burton R. *Educating the Expert Society.* San Francisco: Chandler Publishing Company, 1962.

*Nottingham, Elizabeth. *Religion and Society.* New York: Random House, 1960.

*Riesman, David. *Constraint and Variety in American Education.* New York: Anchor Books, 1959.

*Underwood, Kenneth. *Protestant and Catholic.* Boston: Beacon Press, 1962.

Weber, Max. *The Theory of Social and Economic Organization.* Trans. A. M. Henderson and T. Parsons. New York: Oxford University Press, 1947.

* Paperback edition.

Chapter 11

Formal Institutions of Socialization

The process that passes the heritage of a culture from one generation to the next, assuring the continuity of that culture, is called *socialization*. The more successfully this transfer is accomplished, the more easily individuals may be identified and accepted as members of society—as being "society broken." [1]

This chapter deals with the socialization of the child, the adolescent, and the young adult, for the human personality continues to develop and change through social interaction with others long after childhood has passed. "A freshman is socialized into the patterns of a college, an immigrant into the life of a new country, a recruit into the army, a new resident into a suburb, a medical student into a profession, a new patient into a hospital ward, and a bride into a marriage. . . . Socialization is a process that never ceases." [2]

Socialization transforms the raw biological materials inherited by the human being into the individual who lives in a society. Although we have yet to measure the full biological potentiality of man, many believe that what man can become is seldom, if ever, fully achieved. Thus, control over socialization is spotty at best. Differences exist between men of the same and different cultures because of the random nature of biological inheritance. Actually, the hereditary materials and their processing into the socialized individual differ in every instance. Hence, the possibilities for unique experiences and types of socializing agencies are numerous.

Yet society, through values, attitudes, and customs, does impose limits on individual differences. When an individual finds himself beyond these limits, whether through faulty biological inheritance or failure of the socialization process, the society takes steps to change him, or to isolate him from the group. The individual who habitually departs from acceptable norms of behavior cannot be tolerated, for the society, and the culture it seeks to preserve, considers the process of socialization a critical one.

THE FAMILY

With the first cry of the newborn, the family begins the long process of transforming the infant into a useful member of society. In a relative sense, as a culture advances, the family's role in the socialization process becomes one of interpreting and selecting the attitudes, values, and beliefs established by more specialized agencies.[3] Yet, due to the expansion of the culture, the period of preparation for life—"the period of infancy" —under the supervision of the family is lengthened appreciably.[4] No longer performing most of the functions of socialization, the family nevertheless remains a key agency in the process.

The American nuclear family is one of society's highly differentiated subsystems. Parents do not merely plan familial roles. They are also socializing agents. They fit family responsibilities with their roles in other phases of society. This is essential if they are to function effectively as socializing agents and as parents. The child is never socialized only with respect to his own family, but into social structures which permeate the family and extend beyond it.[5] How well the family performs as a socializing agency depends on how well it coincides with the society. The more that other social structures permeate the family, the greater is the likelihood that the family can select, interpret, evaluate, and transmit the culture satisfactorily to the child.

The following excerpt from *The Child and Society* by Frederick Elkin points up the role of the family in socialization.

* The family, as a socializing agent, necessarily transmits only segments of the wider culture to the child, the particular segments depending primarily on its social positions in the community. The family as a unit—and it is so viewed both by others and by the family members themselves—has many such positions, and accompanying each is a special cultural content and identification. To have a certain religious status means that the child learns particular prayers and rituals; it means also that he is identified with one particular group, distinct from others. To have a father who is a farmer or a doctor means that a given cultural content is passed on to the child; it also means a certain occupational identity. A similar situation exists for such statuses as race, social class, family name, nationality, and ethnic affiliation.

The parents, through their decisions, are partially responsible for the manner in which community and institutional forces impinge on the child. The parents decide where to live, where the family goes on vacation, whom the child may invite to the house, and often to which evening programs the TV set is tuned. Moreover, the family inevitably interprets this wider community to the child, passing judgment on institutions, neighbors, programs, and local group activities.

In any family, some of the behavior patterns that the child learns are characteristic of the larger culture, others are unique to the particular family. That the parents offer food and drink to guests is common to the culture; that they say "topsy" to mean bathroom is not; that the father goes to work is common; that he bakes cakes in his leisure time is not. Only when the child establishes relationships with other people and enlarges his outlook can he attain a relative perspective and learn the range of ways in which status behavior may be acceptably expressed.

Although the family, in some respects, should be viewed as a unit, it is in other respects more usefully conceived as a structure of complex interaction patterns. For each member there are different expectations of behavior and each, through his position and participation, has a unique role in socialization.

ROLE RELATIONSHIPS AND STATUSES

Each person's participations include many types of behavior, both in and out of the family. The mother prepares meals for the family, dresses the children, attends club meetings, writes Christmas cards, packs for holiday trips, gossips with neighboring housewives, and takes care of the child who is ill. The father serves drinks to guests, writes checks, washes the car, consoles the mother when she is upset, puts up curtain rods, attends business conventions, and takes part in numerous activities on his job. These various behaviors can be classified under particular status headings: the mother, depending on her activity and the perspective, is woman, wife, clubwoman, shopper, neighbor, church member, and daughter; the father is husband, host, office worker, handyman, lodge member, and home owner.

Each child too has his statuses. He may be son, eldest child, schoolboy, club member, pet owner, choir singer, member of a football team, and camper—each implying certain types of role behavior. The particular details vary with such characteristics as age, sex, health, capabilities, and family socioeconomic level.

Each status, we have observed, may be expressed in many different ways and with many different sentiments. Parents may be more or less expressive of their feelings, more or less authoritative, more or less protective. The mother, in dressing a young child, may demand or plead for his cooperation; the father in disciplining the child may be angry or businesslike. When the sentiments are typical of the larger culture group to which the family belongs, the child is more likely to take them for granted; when the sentiments are atypical, the child is apt to be conscious of his family's uniqueness.

The child learns values, sentiments, and status expectations through experiences with each member of the family. In a family with one child, there are three two-person relationships—father and mother, father and child, mother and child; in a family of five persons, there are ten two-person relationships; in a family of seven, twenty-one. The number of potential relationships in a family with three children, considering relationships between two persons and those between any one and combinations of two or more others, is sixty-five. This numerical factor, in itself, inevitably affects the particular character of emotional relations, cliques, and authority patterns. For example, in a family with one child—which serves as the model for the Oedipus complex—the emotional ties are likely to be concentrated, with resulting extreme jealousies. The presence of numerous brothers and sisters tends to obviate this particular problem, although at the same time it creates others.

In the family, as in any small group, patterns develop, and each individual comes to have a unique relationship with each other individual. The choice of topics of conversation, the manner of responding to requests, the reaction to a family member's stroke of good fortune, the type of humor—all vary depending on the particular relationship between the parties. The child's mother may berate him when he dirties his new clothes; his father may permit him to use the electric drill; his brother may initiate him into types of horseplay. If he tells a *risqué* story, his father reacts in one way, his mother in another, and his brother in still another. His father plays more roughly with him than he does with baby brother or the neighbor's son; his mother demands different tasks of him than of his sister. He observes as well the unique relationships of others. His mother discusses party dresses only with his sister, and his father wrangles about family finances only with his mother. It is through such experiences that the child becomes familiar with a range of emotional relationships and gains a knowledge of the status expectations of boy, girl, spouse, and children of different birth order.

The mechanisms of socialization are of special importance in the family. The child's first rewards and punishments, first image of himself, and first models of behavior are experienced in the family setting, and all help to develop a "personality base," subject to subsequent influences. The child's reaction to others is partially determined by his previous relationships with parents and siblings. And, as we have observed, personality type is closely related to the socialization process itself.

In the socialization of the child, members of his family use every technique and device that we have cited. They instruct, guide, respond to the child's actions, and bring him into their activities. Everyday behavior is especially important in showing the child the patterns and sentiments characteristic of his group. Dressing a child up when guests are expected suggests the importance of a family "front" and family solidarity. Attending a wedding suggests behavior and feelings suitable to the occasion. Casual remarks about carpenters or painters working in the house may suggest that his occupation is an unworthy vocation for a son.

The child, on his part, generally just "picks up" appropriate patterns and values. He observes, participates with others, plays at roles, and judges his own thoughts and behavior. Moreover, merely through emotional identification with his parents, be the occasion sad, happy, embarrassing, or annoying, he comes to know and experience many appropriate sentiments.

In their direct contact with the child, parents reward and punish. If the child behaves as they desire, he may be complimented, invited to participate, or given a prize; if he behaves otherwise, he may be slapped, shouted at, ignored, deprived of something he wishes, or accused of disappointing them. Parents thus indicate to the child that he cannot always behave as he pleases and that he should adhere to certain standards. Middle-class parents often suggest—explicitly or implicitly—that the child who suppresses or defers his immediate gratifications will be rewarded in the future. If he saves his money, he will earn enough to buy a bicycle; if he shares a toy with his brother, he will get a new one; if he obeys his parents, he will receive better Christmas presents.

In the earliest months of life, a child may conform to the wishes of his parents merely to gain their approval and avoid punishment. Once he develops a self (in the sense that George Mead used the term—see Chapter 3), and has the ability to view his own behavior, he can better understand the demands that are made of him and make more rapid strides in socialization. With a self, he becomes aware of his statuses and has guides for his behavior. His parents, for example, view him as a potential scholar. Internalizing their view of him, he too sees himself as a scholar, and he can now know the appropriate models and membership groups for this particular status. This same principle may be applied to delinquent behavior. The parents, for whatever reason, view the child as a "bad boy." Adopting the parents' image, the child sees himself as a "bad boy" and thereby plays the appropriate part and looks for appropriate models.

With self-awareness the child also becomes potentially more independent of his limited family perspective. Through contradictions within the family and contacts outside the home, he becomes more conscious of his family's and his own distinctive ways. Since the standards by which he judges himself may come to differ from those of his parents, he can justify more independent action. Further, he can take the position of outside groups, with other standards, and judge his own family. Thus, as the child makes use of his self, the significance to him of his parents' behavior changes considerably.

Considerations of socialization into sex roles should help to clarify the functions of the family. No adult role is more fundamental in any society. Many agencies share in teaching a child the expected behavior of his sex, but the family is pre-eminent.

The girl is to be socialized into the role of woman, the boy into the role of man. In our society, the most common pattern for the woman, following her schooling, is to take an appropriate job, marry, and perhaps continue to work until she has children. Her primary tasks then are to manage the home and care for the children. For the man, the job is more important; it remains the source of family income and the primary determinant of the family's socio-economic position.

Differences exist in expressive behavior, interests, and popular image. Men walk, talk, light matches, and cross their knees differently from women. Men are more concerned with sports and politics; women with fashions and beauty products. Men are considered to be more rugged and to speak more coarsely; women to be more sentimental and disposed to cry.

Leaving aside the influence of hereditary disposition—and there is no consensus on their relative significance—boys and girls come to learn their sex identities and expectations of behavior through differential observations, treatment, and emotional attachments. The significant others may be explicit and say, "Johnny is a boy and should behave like one." More often the definitions and treatments are unreflective and matter-of-course. The girl is (or, at least, was until recently) given pink, the boy blue; the girl a doll carriage and the boy a baseball glove. The boy is told to be brave, is complimented for throwing a ball well, may be locked out of the room when his mother is dressing, and kidded about being a Momma's boy. The girl is told to keep her dress down, is laughed at—or commended—for flirting, is admired for her curls, and teased for acting like a tomboy. The child, in innumerable instances of everyday life, has his behavior defined in sex-status terms and, in some way or another, is rewarded for appropriate behavior and ignored or punished for inappropriate behavior.

Of central importance, especially for an appropriate sex identity, are the models of behavior which significant others present to the child. Men and women behave differently before the child, and treat him differently. Women kiss him, dress him, prepare his meals, and use "feminine" expressions in talking to him. Men shake his hand, handle him more roughly, play ball with him, and take him fishing. The various individuals—and symbols held up for him to emulate are also sex identified—the boy is given a cowboy suit named after a western TV star or told to help around the house like the boy next door.

Learning a sex role is closely related to emotional attachments. An important problem for the boy is to emancipate himself from a dependency relationship with his mother and to identify or develop a "we" feeling with his father and other males. Since the boy in our society does not generally see his father at work, one significant dimension of the male model is often obscure. The story is told of the four-year-old boy playing "Daddy" who put on his hat and coat, said "Goodbye," and walked out of the front door, only to return a few minutes later because he didn't know what to do next. While employing his father as a sex status model, the boy must not become so closely identified that he wants to replace him in the immediate family— the danger of the Oedipus complex. The complementary problems of the young girl have their own variations.

Sex identity and role behavior are inseparable from the development of the self. Once the child learns his sex status, he can view his own behavior from the position of others and judge whether or not he is behaving properly. Thus the boy knows he shouldn't be interested in dolls, and the girl knows she may acceptably cringe at the sight of an earthworm. Moreover, the boy and girl can know which are appropriate models and which are not and can anticipate their future adult sex statuses with their respective rights and duties. Most children also so internalize these expectations that they can develop romantic and sexual attachments to members of the opposite sex. Confusion and uncertainty about self-image and sex identity can become a basis for homosexual tendencies.

In recent years, considerable discussion has concerned the changing patterns of sex roles and the ambiguity of sex models. Urbanization, technical specialization, changing birth rates, the extension of education, the growth of the mass media, and a generally rising standard of living have all affected the behavior of men and women and the patterns of socialization. Paid baby-sitters have replaced grandparents; children may never see many of their cousins; new appliances and service industries give the housewife more time for other activities; women train for professional careers and compete with men for available jobs; movie and TV stars quickly become widely known.

For the child, these changes and trends may present a confused picture. We need only note several female models that are currently esteemed in our society—the professional career woman, traditional housewife, glamour girl, "pal," and active clubwoman. The young girl not only becomes aware of such varied heroines, but is herself rewarded for correspondingly varied types of behavior—attractiveness to boys, ability in school, leadership qualities, cooking, all-around friendliness, and efficiency on the job. A similar situation exists for the boy. Among the popular models are sports and entertainment stars, the duty-abiding agent of the law, the successful business or professional man, the scientist; and he too is rewarded for such different types of behavior as scholastic achievement, popularity with girls, club leadership, success in sports, and dutiful aid to the family.

With so many sex status symbols, parents and other socializing agents may be inconsistent or uncertain in the paths of development they encourage and the models they resent. The child does not always know by which standards to judge himself and others. For some, the inconsistency of these images has undoubtedly made it difficult to develop harmonious and integrated heterosexual relationships. On the other hand, one should not assume that apparently logically contradictory roles are actually experienced as such. One study suggests that college girls are sophisticated enough to be aware of contradictory demands, yet experience no particular confusion in deciding how to behave in specific instances. They have, to their own satisfaction, worked out a *modus vivendi*. Perhaps at least some role confusion is a "normal" part of middle-class culture.

The child is not the only member of the family who undergoes transformation. A kind of "feedback" also takes place in the continuous socialization and resocialization of the adults. Parents interact with children and find their own personalities modified. This is particularly true where parents oversee their child's progress through school; the "New Mathematics," for example, which departs from the principles of mathematics taught to the fathers, has caused many an adult to learn new concepts of "matrices" along with his 12-year-old rather than check on the youth's mastery of what the father already knows.

THE SCHOOL

Socialization is an educative process. As cultures become more complex, specialized institutions, particularly the school, help transmit and preserve the culture for future generations. The school is charged with conserving tradition. Originally this was the limit of the school's authority. The *trivium* (grammar, logic, rhetoric) and *quadrivium* (arithmetic, geometry, astronomy, music) constituted the body of curricula in the Middle Ages. These elements of education, begun in the twelfth and thirteenth centuries in Europe, were transported to the New World by the Puritans. They lived on in this country as an important part of liberal education until the Industrial Revolution forced the practices of formal education into conflict with cultural change. This collision led to inevitable differences on substantive questions concerning the curriculum, and even over the very purpose of education.

At the same time that the school has performed its function of conserving tradition, it has—particularly in higher education—led society, through the student, to new and improved social concepts. If the conflict among professional educators over the proper role of the schools has waned, it has been replaced in some places by a conflict between home and school. Depending on his personality, the parent whose child is being taught the "New Mathematics" may either be helpful and encourage his child's learning, or he may resent modern concepts as an affront to his own upbringing and, as a result, confuse the child.

. . . Much of our thinking and many of our modes of interpretation have been revolutionized within the span of a generation or two. Utilizing the Comtean terminology, the shift has been from a theological to a scientific interpretation of life. The result of this sudden and relatively complete shift has been that large numbers of parents and elder kinsfolk still think in theological terms, whereas the children have acquired a scientific approach and mode of interpretation. Here is a significant cultural conflict coinciding with the difference between generations. Its seriousness varies from one part of the country to another, but seems to be more marked in the south and in parts of the west. In some cases, when families send their children to the Universities, often at considerable financial sacrifice, only to find them returning with this "new nonsense," the problem becomes particularly keen. At times, parents or children or both personalize the issue, and then the deeper loyalties of family life become involved.[6]

In the latter instance, such conflict can lead to what J. O. Hertzler has called *"desocialization"*—the reverse of socialization. Unless the socialization process operates efficiently, none of the systems that organize individual behavior is likely to be effective; in this event, disorganization may result.[7]

Just the same, our schools do succeed, although never perfectly, in playing their part in socialization, despite the problems confronting them. Formal education "does in a matter of days, months, or years what by the processes of slow, spontaneous, fumbling, trial-and-error acquisition or inexpert inculcation of social attitudes, rules, and ways would take several generations, and then because of their unsystematic nature, would leave vast gaps." [8]

In the following article Talcott Parsons examines the classroom, as distinguished from the total school, as a socializing agency and the role of the teacher in socialization.

THE ELEMENTARY SCHOOL

*
. . . [The school class] is an agency through which individual personalities are trained to be motivationally and technically adequate to the performance of adult roles. It is not the sole such agency; the family, informal

---

* From Talcott Parsons, "The School Class as a Social System," *Harvard Educational Review*, Fall 1959, pp. 297–318, *passim*. Reprinted by permission of the publisher.

"peer groups," churches, and sundry voluntary organizations all play a part, as does actual on-the-job training. But, in the period extending from entry into first grade until entry into the labor force or marriage . . . the school class may be regarded as the focal socializing agency.

The socialization function may be summed up as the development in individuals of the commitments and capacities which are essential prerequisites of their future role-performance. Commitments may be broken down in turn into two components: commitment to the implementation of the broad *values* of society, and commitment to the performance of a specific type of role within the *structure* of society. Thus a person in a relatively humble occupation may be a "solid citizen" in the sense of commitment to honest work in that occupation, without an intensive and sophisticated concern with the implementation of society's higher-level values. Capacities can also be broken down into two components, the first being competence or the skill to perform the tasks involved in the individual's roles, and the second being "role-responsibility" or the capacity to live up to other people's expectations of the interpersonal behavior appropriate to these roles. Thus a mechanic as well as a doctor needs to have not only the basic "skills of his trade," but also the ability to behave responsibly toward those people with whom he is brought into contact in his work.

While on the one hand, the school class my be regarded as a primary agency by which these different components and capacities are generated, on the other hand, it is, from the point of view of the society, an agency of "manpower" allocation. It is well known that in American society there is a very high, and probably increasing, correlation between one's status level in the society and one's level of educational attainment. Both social status and educational level are obviously related to the occupational status which is attained.

Entering the system of formal education is the child's first major step out of primary involvement in his family or orientation. Within the family certain foundations of his motivational system have been laid down. But the only characteristic fundamental to later roles which has clearly been "determined" and psychologically stamped in by that time is sex role. The post-oedipal child enters the system of formal education clearly categorized as boy or girl, but beyond that his *role* is not yet differentiated. The process of selection, by which persons will select and be selected for categories of roles, is yet to take place.

The school is the first socializing agency in the child's experience which institutionalizes a differentiation of status on nonbiological bases. Moreover, this is not an ascribed but an achieved status; it is the status "earned" by differential performance of the tasks set by the teacher, who is acting as an agent of the community's school system. Let us look at the structure of this situation.

In accord with the generally wide variability of American institutions, and of course the basically local control of school systems, there is considerable variability of school situations, but broadly they have a single relatively well-marked framework. Particularly in the primary part of the elementary grades, i.e., the first three grades, the basic pattern includes one main teacher for the class, who teaches all subjects and who is in charge of the class generally. Sometimes this early, and frequently in later grades, other teachers are brought in for a few special subjects, particularly gym, music, and art, but this does not alter the central position of the main teacher. This teacher is usually a woman. The class is with this one teacher for the school year, but usually no longer.

The class, then, is composed of about 25 age-peers of both sexes drawn from a relatively small geographical area—the neighborhood. Except for sex in certain respects, there is initially no formal basis for differentiation of status within the school class. The main structural differentiation develops gradually, on the single main axis indicated above as achievement. That the differentiation should occur on a single main axis is insured by four primary features of the situation. The first is the initial equalization of the "contestants" status by age and by "family background," the neighborhood being typically much more homogeneous than is the whole society. The second circumstance is the imposition of a common set of tasks which is, compared to most other task-areas, strikingly undifferentiated. The school situation is far more like a race in this respect than most role-performance situations. Third, there is the sharp polarization between the pupils in their initial equality and the *single* teacher who is an adult and "represents" the adult world. And fourth, there is a relatively systematic process of evaluation of the pupils' performances. From the point of view of a pupil, this evaluation, particularly (though not exclusively) in the form of report card marks, constitutes reward and/or punishment for past performance; from the viewpoint of the school system acting as an allocating agency, it is a basis of *selection* for future status in society. . . .

What, now, of the content of the "achievement" expected of elementary school children? Perhaps the best broad characterization which can be given is that it involves the types of performance which are, on the one hand, appropriate to the school situation and, on the other hand, are felt by adults to be important in themselves. This vague and somewhat circular characterization may,, as was mentioned earlier, be broken down into two main components. One of these is the more purely "cognitive" learning of information, skills, and frames of reference associated with empirical knowledge and technological mastery. The *written* language and the early phases of mathematical thinking are clearly vital; they involve cognitive skills at altogether new levels of generality and abstraction compared to those commanded by the preschool child. With these basic skills goes assimilation of much factual information about the world.

The second main component is what may broadly be called a "moral" one. In earlier generations of schooling this was known as "deportment." Somewhat more generally it might be called responsible citizenship in the school community. Such things as respect for the teacher, consideration and cooperativeness in relation to fellow-pupils, and good "work-habits" are the fundamentals, leading on to capacity for "leadership and initiative."

The striking fact about this achievement content is that in the elementary grades these two primary components are not clearly differentiated from each other. Rather, the pupil is evaluated in diffusely general terms; a *good* pupil is defined in terms of a fusion of the cognitive and the moral components, in which varying weight is given to one or the other. Broadly speaking, then, we may say that the "high achievers" of the elementary school are both the "bright" pupils, who catch on easily to their more strictly intellectual tasks, and the more "responsible" pupils, who "behave well" and on whom the teacher can "count" in her difficult problems of managing the class. One indication that this is the case is the fact that in elementary school the purely intellectual tasks are relatively easy for the pupil of high intellectual ability. In many such cases, it can be presumed that the primary challenge to the pupil is not to his intellectual, but to his "moral," capacities. On the whole, the progressive movement seems to have leaned in the direction of giving enhanced emphasis to this component, suggesting that of the two, it has tended to become the more problematical.

The essential point, then, seems to be that the elementary school, regarded in the light of its socialization function, is an agency which differentiates the school class broadly along a single continuum of achievement, the content of which is relative excellence in living up to the expectations imposed by the teacher as an agent of the adult society. The criteria of this achievement are, generally speaking, undifferentiated into the cognitive or technical component and the moral or "social" component. But with respect to its bearing on societal values, it is broadly a differentiation of *levels* of capacity to act in accord with these values. Though the relation is far from neatly uniform, this differentiation underlies the processes of selection for levels of status and role in the adult society.

Next, a few words should be said about the out-of-school context in which this process goes on. Besides the school class, there are clearly two primary social structures in which the child participates: the family and the child's informal "peer group."

The school age child, of course, continues to live in the parental household and to be highly dependent, emotionally as well as instrumentally, on his parents. But he is now spending several hours a day away from home, subject to a discipline and a reward system which are essentially independent of that administered by the parents. Moreover, the range of this independence gradually increases. As he grows older, he is permitted to range further territorially with neither parental nor school supervision, and to do an increasing range of things. He often gets an allowance for personal spending and begins to earn some money of his own. Generally, however, the emotional problem of dependence-independence continues to be a very salient one through this period, frequently with manifestations by the child of compulsive independence.

Concomitantly with this, the area for association with age-peers without detailed adult supervision expands. These associations are tied to the family, on the one hand, in that the home and yards of children who are neighbors and the adjacent streets serve as locations for their activities; and to the school, on the other hand, in that play periods and going to and from school provide occasions for informal association, even though organized extracurricular activities are introduced only later. Ways of bringing some of this activity under another sort of adult supervision are found in such organizations as the boy and girl scouts.

Two sociological characteristics of peer groups at this age are particularly striking. One is the fluidity of their boundaries, with individual children drifting into and out of associations. This element of "voluntary association" contrasts strikingly with the child's ascribed membership in the family and the school class, over which he has no control. The second characteristic is the peer group's sharp segregation by sex. To a striking degree this is enforced by the children themselves rather than by adults.

The psychological functions of peer association are suggested by these two characteristics. On the one hand, the peer group may be regarded as a field for the exercise of independence from adult control; hence it is not surprising that it is often a focus of behavior which goes beyond independence from adults to the range of adult-*disapproved* behavior; when this happens, it is the seed bed from which the extremists go over into delinquency. But another very important function is to provide the child a source of nonadult approval and acceptance. These depend on "technical" and "moral" criteria as diffuse as those required in the school situation. On the one hand, the peer group is a field for acquiring and displaying various types of "prowess"; for boys this is especially the physical prowess which may later ripen into athletic achievement. On the other hand, it is a matter of gaining acceptance from desirable peers as "belonging" in the group, which later ripens into the conception of the popular teen-ager, the "right guy." Thus the adult parents are augmented by age-peers as a source of rewards for performance and of security in acceptance.

The importance of the peer group for socialization in our type of society should be clear. The motivational foundations of character are inevitably first laid down through identification with parents, who are generation-superiors, and the generation difference is a type example of a hierarchical status difference. But an immense part of the individual's adult role performance will have to be in association with status-equals or near-equals. In this situation it is important to have a reorganization of the motivational structure so that the original dominance of the hierarchical axis is modified to strengthen the egalitarian components. The peer group plays a prominent part in this process.

Sex segregation of latency period peer groups may be regarded as a process of reinforcement of sex-role identification. Through intensive association with sex-peers and involvement in sex-typed activities, they strongly reinforce belongingness with other members of the same sex and contrast with the opposite sex. This is the more important because in the coeducational school a set of forces operates which specifically plays down sex-role differentiation.

It is notable that the latency period sex-role pattern, instead of institutionalizing relations to members of the opposite sex, is characterized by an avoidance of such relations, which only in adolescence gives way to dating. This avoidance is clearly associated with the process of reorganization of the erotic components of motivational structure. The pre-oedipal objects of erotic attachment were both intra-familial and generation-superior. In both respects there must be a fundamental shift by the time the child reaches adulthood. I would suggest that one of the main functions of the avoidance pattern is to help cope with the psychological difficulty of over-coming the earlier incestuous attachments, and hence to prepare the child for assuming an attachment to an age-mate of opposite sex later.

Seen in this perspective, the socialization function of the school class assumes a particular significance. The socialization functions of the family by this time are relatively residual, though their importance should not be underestimated. But the school remains adult-controlled and, moreover, induces basically the same kind of identification as was induced by the family in the child's pre-oedipal stage. This is to say that the learning of achievement-motivation is, psychologically speaking, a process of identification with the teacher, of doing well in school in order to please the teacher (often backed by the parents) in the same sense in which a pre-oedipal child learns new skills in order to please his mother.

In this connection I maintain that what is internalized through the process of identification is a reciprocal pattern of role-relationships. Unless there is a drastic failure of internalization altogether, not just one, but both sides of the interaction will be internalized. There will, however, be an emphasis on one or the other, so that some children will more nearly identify with the opposite role. Thus, in the pre-oedipal stage, the "independent" child has identified more with the parent, and the "dependent" one with the child-role vis-à-vis the parent.

In school the teacher is institutionally defined as superior to any pupil in knowledge of curriculum subject-matter and in responsibility as a good citizen of the school. In so far as the school class tends to be bifurcated (and of course the dichotomization is far from absolute), it will broadly be on the basis, on the one hand, of identification with the teacher, or acceptance of her role as a model; and, on the other hand, of identification with the pupil peer group.

These considerations suggest an interpretation of some features of the elementary teacher role in American society. The first major step in socialization, beyond that in the family, takes place in the elementary school, so it seems reasonable to expect that the teacher-figure should be characterized by a combination of similarities to and differences from parental figures. The teacher, then, is an adult, characterized by the generalized superiority, which a parent also has, of adult status relative to children. She is not, however, ascriptively related to her pupils, but is performing an occupational role—a role, however, in which the recipients of her services are tightly bound in solidarity to her and to each other. Furthermore, compared to a parent's, her responsibility to them is much more universalistic, this being reinforced, as we saw, by the size of the class; it is also much more oriented to performance rather than to solicitude for the emotional "needs" of the children. She is not entitled to suppress the distinction between high and low achievers, just because not being able to be included among the high group would be too hard on little Johnny—however much tendencies in this direction appear as deviant patterns. A mother, on the other hand, must give *first* priority to the needs of her child, regardless of his capacities to achieve.

It is also significant for the parallel of the elementary school class with the family that the teacher is normally a woman. As background it should be noted that in most European systems until recently, and often today in our private parochial and nonsectarian schools, the sexes have been segregated and each sex group has been taught by teachers of their own sex. Given coeducation, however, the woman teacher represents continuity with the role of the mother. Precisely the lack of differentiation in the elementary school "curriculum" between the components of subject-matter competence and social responsibility fits in with the greater diffuseness of the feminine role.

But at the same time, it is essential that the teacher is not a mother to her pupils, but must insist on universalistic norms and the differential reward of achievement. Above all she must be the agent of bringing about and legitimizing a differentiation of the school class on an achievement axis. This aspect of her role is furthered by the fact that in American society the feminine role is less confined to the familial context than in most other societies, but joins the masculine in occupational and associational concerns, though still with a greater relative emphasis on the family. Through identification with their teacher, children of both sexes learn that the category "woman" is not coextensive with "mother" (and future wife), but that the feminine role-personality is more complex than that.

The process of identification with the teacher which has been postulated here is furthered by the fact that in the elementary grades the child typically has one teacher, just as in the pre-oedipal period he had one parent, the mother, who was the focus of his object-relations. The continuity between the two phases is also favored by the fact that the teacher, like the mother, is a woman. But, if she acted only like a mother, there would be no genuine reorganization of the pupil's personality system. This reorganization is furthered by the features of the teacher role which differentiate it from the maternal. One further point is that while a child has one main teacher in each grade, he will usually have a new teacher when he progresses to the next higher grade. He is thus accustomed to the fact that teachers are, unlike mothers, "interchangeable" in a certain sense. The school year is long enough to form an important relationship to a particular teacher, but not long enough for a highly particularistic attachment to crystallize. More than in the parent-child relationship, in school the child must internalize his relation to the teacher's *role* rather than her particular personality; this is a major step in the internalization of universalistic patterns.

As we have noted, the general trend of American society has been toward a rapid upgrading in the educational status of the population. This means that, relative to past expectations, with each generation there is increased pressure to educational achievement, often associated with parents' occupational ambitions for their children. To a sociologist this is a more or less classical situation of anomic strain, and the youth-culture ideology which plays down intellectual interests and school performance seems to fit in this context. The orientation of the youth culture is, in the nature of the case, ambivalent, but for the reasons suggested, the anti-intellectual side of the ambivalence tends to be overtly stressed. One of the reasons for the dominance of the anti-school side of the ideology is that it provides a means of protest against adults, who are at the opposite pole in the socialization situation. In certain respects one would expect that the trend toward greater emphasis on independence, which we have associated with progressive education, would accentuate the strain in this area and hence the tendency to decry adult expectations. The whole problem should be subjected to a thorough analysis in the light of what we know about ideologies more generally.

The same general considerations are relevant to the much-discussed problem of juvenile delinquency. Both the general upgrading process and the pressure to enhanced independence should be expected to increase strain on the lower, most marginal groups. As the acceptable minimum of educational qualification rises, persons near and below the margin will tend to be pushed into an attitude of repudiation of these expectations. Truancy and delinquency are ways of expressing this repudiation. Thus the very *improvement* of educational standards in the society at large may well be a major factor in the failure of the educational process for a growing number at the lower end of the status and ability distribution. It should therefore not be too easily assumed that delinquency is a symptom of a *general* failure of the educational process.

THE SECONDARY SCHOOL

. . . The elementary school phase is concerned with the internalization in children of motivation to achievement, and the selection of persons on the basis of differential capacity for achievement. The focus is on the *level* of capacity. In the secondary school phase, on the other hand, the focus is on the differentiation of *qualitative types* of achievement. As in the elementary school, this differentiation cross-cuts sex role. I should also maintain that it cross-cuts the levels of achievement which have been differentiated out in the elementary phase.

In approaching the question of the types of capacity differentiated, it should be kept in mind that secondary school is the principal springboard from which lower-status persons will enter the labor force, whereas those achieving higher status will continue their formal education in college, and some of them beyond. Hence for the lower-status pupils the important line of differentiation should be the one which will lead into broadly different categories of jobs; for the higher-status pupils the differentiation will lead to broadly different roles in college.

My suggestion is that this differentiation separates those two components of achievement which we labelled "cognitive" and "moral" in discussing the elementary phase. Those relatively high in "cognitive" achievement will fit better in specific-function, more or less technical roles; those relatively high in "moral" achievement will tend toward diffuser, more "socially" or "humanly" oriented roles. In jobs not requiring college training, the one category may be thought of as comprising the more impersonal and technical occupations, such as "operatives," mechanics, or clerical workers; the other, as occupations where "human relations" are prominent, such as salesmen and agents of various sorts. At the college level, the differentiation certainly relates to concern, on the one hand, with the specifically intellectual curricular work of college and, on the other hand, with various types of diffuser responsibility in human relations, such as leadership roles in student government and extracurricular activities. Again, candidates for post-graduate professional training will probably be drawn mainly from the first of these two groups.

In the structure of the school, there appears to be a gradual transition from the earliest grades through high school, with the changes timed differently in different school systems. The structure emphasized in the first part of this discussion is most clearly marked in the first three "primary" grades. With progression to the higher grades, there is greater frequency of plural teachers, though very generally still a single main teacher. In the sixth grade and sometimes in the fifth, a man as main teacher, though uncommon, is by no means unheard of. With junior high school, however, the shift of pattern becomes more marked, and still more in senior high.

By that time the pupil has several different teachers of both sexes teaching him different subjects, which are more or less formally organized into different courses—college preparatory and others. Furthermore, with the choice of "elective" subjects, the members of the class in one subject no longer need be exactly the same as in another, so the pupil is much more systematically exposed to association with different people, both adults and age-peers, in different contexts. Moreover, the school he attends is likely to be substantially larger than was his elementary school, and to draw from a wider geographical area. Hence the child is exposed to a wider range of statuses than before, being thrown in with more age-peers whom he does not encounter in his neighborhood; it is less likely that his parents will know the parents of any given child with whom he associates. It is thus my impression that the transitions to junior high and senior high school are apt to mean a considerable reshuffling of friendships. Another conspicuous difference between the elementary and secondary levels is the great increase in high school of organized extracurricular activities. Now, for the first time, organized athletics become important, as do a variety of clubs and associations which are school-sponsored and supervised to varying degrees.

Two particularly important shifts in the patterning of youth culture occur in this period. One, of course, is the emergence of more positive cross-sex relationships outside the classroom, through dances, dating, and the like. The other is the much sharper prestige-stratification of informal peer groupings, with indeed an element of snobbery which often exceeds that of the adult community in which the school exists. Here it is important that though there is a broad correspondence between the prestige of friendship groups and the family status of their members, this, like the achievement order of the elementary school, is by no means a simple "mirroring" of the community stratification scale, for a considerable number of lower-status children get accepted into groups including members with higher family status than themselves. This stratified youth system operates as a genuine assortative mechanism; it does not simply reinforce ascribed status.

The prominence of this youth culture in the American secondary school is, in comparison with other societies, one of the hallmarks of the American educational system; it is much less prominent in most European systems. It may be said to constitute a kind of structural fusion between the school class and the peer-group structure of the elementary period. It seems clear that what I have called the "human relations" oriented contingent of the secondary school pupils are more active and prominent in extracurricular activities, and that this is one of the main foci of their differentiation from the more impersonally- and technically-oriented contingent. The personal qualities figuring most prominently in the human relations contingent can perhaps be summed up as the qualities that make for "popularity." I suggest that, from the point of view of the secondary school's selective function, the youth culture helps to differentiate between types of personalities which will, by and large, play different kinds of roles as adults.

The stratification of youth groups has, as noted, a selective function; it is a bridge between the achievement order and the adult stratification system of the community. But it also has another function. It is a focus of prestige which exists along side of, and is to a degree independent of, the achievement order focussing on school work as such. The attainment of prestige in the informal youth group is itself a form of valued achievement. Hence, among those individuals destined for higher status in society, one can discern two broad types: those whose school work is more or less outstanding and whose informal prestige is relatively satisfactory; and vice versa, those whose informal prestige is outstanding, and school performance satisfactory. Failing below certain minima in either respect would jeopardize the child's claim to belong in the upper group. It is an important point here that those clearly headed for college belong to peer groups which, while often depreciative of intensive concern with studies, also take for granted and reinforce a level of scholastic attainment which is necessary for admission to a good college. Pressure will be put on the individual who tends to fall below such a standard.

In discussing the elementary school level it will be remembered that we emphasized that the peer group served as an object of emotional dependency displaced from the family. In relation to the pressure for school achievement, therefore, it served at least partially as an expression of the lower-order motivational system *out* of which the child was in process of being socialized. On its own level, similar things can be said of the adolescent youth culture; it is in part an expression of regressive motivations. This is true of the emphasis on athletics despite its lack of relevance to adult roles, of the "homosexual" undertones of much intensive same-sex friendship, and of a certain "irresponsibility" in attitudes toward the opposite sex—e.g., the exploitative element in the attitudes of boys toward girls. This, however, is by no means the whole story. The youth culture is also a field for practicing the assumption of higher-order responsibilities, for conducting delicate human relations without immediate supervision and learning to accept the consequences. In this connection it is clearly of particular importance to the contingent we have spoken of as specializing in "human relations."

We can, perhaps, distinguish three different levels of crystallization of these youth-culture patterns. The middle one is that which may be considered age-appropriate without clear status-differentiation. The two key-notes here seem to be "being a good fellow" in the sense of general friendliness and being ready to take responsibility in informal social situations where some-thing needs to be done. Above this, we may speak of the higher level of "outstanding" popularity and qualities of "leadership" of the person who is turned to where unusual responsibilities are required. And below the mid-dle level are the youth patterns bordering on delinquency, withdrawal, and generally unacceptable behavior. Only this last level is clearly "regressive" relative to expectations of appropriate behavior for the age-grade. In judging these three levels, however, allowance should be made for a good many nuances. Most adolescents do a certain amount of experimenting with the borderline of the unacceptable patterns; that they should do so is to be ex-pected in view of the pressure toward independence from adults, and of the "collusion" which can be expected in reciprocal stimulation of age-peers. The question is whether this regressive behavior comes to be confirmed into a major pattern for the personality as a whole. Seen in this perspective, it seems legitimate to maintain that the middle and the higher patterns in-dicated are the major ones, and that only a minority of adolescents comes to be confirmed in a truly unacceptable pattern of living. This minority may well be a relatively constant proportion of the age cohort, but apart from situations of special social disorganization, the available evidence does not suggest that it has been a progressively growing one in recent years.

The patterning of cross-sex relations in the youth culture clearly fore-shadows future marriage and family formation. That it figures so promi-nently in school is related to the fact that in our society the element of ascrip-tion, including direct parental influence, in the choice of a marriage partner is strongly minimized. For the girl, it has the very important significance of reminding her that her adult status is going to be very much concerned with marriage and a family. This basic expectation for the girl stands in a certain tension to the school's curricular coeducation with its relative lack of differ-entiation by sex. But the extent to which the feminine role in American society continues to be anchored in marriage and the family should not be allowed to obscure the importance of coeducation. In the first place, the contribution of women in various extra-familial occupations and in com-munity affairs has been rapidly increasing, and certainly higher levels of edu-cation have served as a prerequisite to this contribution. At the same time, it is highly important that the woman's familial role should not be regarded as drastically segregated from the cultural concerns of the society as a whole. The educated woman has important functions *as wife and mother*, par-ticularly as an influence on her children in backing the schools and impress-ing on them the importance of education. It is, I think, broadly true that the immediate responsibility of women for family management has been increas-ing, though I am very skeptical of the alleged "abdication" of the American male. But precisely in the context of women's increased family responsibility, the influence of the mother both as agent of socialization and as role model is a crucial one. This influence should be evaluated in the light of the general upgrading process. It is very doubtful whether, apart from any other considerations, the motivational prerequisites of the general process could be sustained without sufficiently high education of the women who, as mothers, influence their children.

With the general cultural upgrading process in American society which has been going on for more than a century, the educational system has come to play an increasingly vital role. That this should be the case is, in my opinion, a consequence of the general trend to structural differentiation in the society. Relatively speaking, the school is a specialized agency. That it should increasingly have become the principal channel of selection as well as agency of socialization is in line with what one would expect in an increasingly differentiated as progressively more upgraded society. The legend of the "self-made man" has an element of nostalgic romanticism and is destined to become increasingly mythical, if by it is meant not just mobility from humble origins to high status, which does indeed continue to occur, but that the high status was attained through the "school of hard knocks" without the aid of formal education.

In addition to assimilating factual knowledge, the student achieves social control as he responds to the commands of parent, teacher, and peer. He is told where to sit, what to read, when to speak. Everywhere he is supervised, disciplined, and policed. These routine controls condition him for the rules that will apply in later life in the office, the factory, the church, or in other social situations.[9] Bossard sees the school as a work place where the child develops work behavior patterns. Moreover, the student is reimbursed for social control in a manner of speaking, from the public treasury which provides his educational facilities. He is also rewarded by his family which supplies his food, clothing, shelter, and other comforts.[10] In an important sense, socialization is measured by the individual's social control. If he can obey social norms, if he can blend his conduct with that of his fellows, regardless of his particular role in society, his behavior contributes to social order and he becomes an acceptable member of society.

THE CHURCH

In colonial Massachusetts the Puritan influence penetrated deeply into the lives of the faithful. Religion was practiced every day. Theology was tightly interwoven with politics, economics, and education. Under these circumstances the church as an institution could play an extremely important part in the socialization process.

An important factor in socialization is the necessity of intimate, frequent, and lasting contact between the agency of socialization and the individual being socialized. Whereas the Puritan Church (and certain latter-day denominations) had this kind of contact with the individual, the great bulk of churches in America today do not have the same close association with their parishioners. The separation of church and state, the secularization of education, the efficiency of business, have all contributed to the ineffectualness and compartmentalization of religion in America.

In spite of the decline in the temporal power of the church there has been a startling increase in church membership. An increase could be expected simply as a result of population growth, but the trebling of the percentage of church members—from 20 per cent of the population in 1880 to 60 per cent in 1956—is difficult to explain. "No responsible person maintains that the American people are three times as religious today as they were in 1880." [11]

Organized religion obviously still has a reason for existence. Even the predictions for its doomsday by dogmatists and secularists alike cannot render it expendable. The dogmatist broods over the watering down of church doctrine, and the secularist finds all the answers in science; but an institution growing at twice the rate of population increase must be filling a need. Many explanations for the resurgence of churches are advanced on the basis of the unsettled quality of modern life: the nuclear bomb, mass culture, or simply the high mobility of families and individuals. And "with the marked increase in marriage and birth rates, there has been a corresponding increase in young families with young children. Many of these depend not only on the schools but also on various church organizations and influences for a considerable amount of ethical instruction and social disciplining. Also, with the shrinking in size of home plants, the churches with their Sunday Schools, parties, athletics, and recreational activities provide various activities that relieve the pressure at home. The very fact of increasing memberships provides certain utilitarian and egotic advantages, such as the opportunity for making valuable economic, especially professional, contacts, with an implied commitment by the contactee because of a joint, even selected, membership; the opportunity to meet right and respectable people, and enjoyment of prestige, or at least the comforting thought, of doing the right thing." [12]

In addition to dealing with man's ultimate needs, the church also plays an important role in social areas, but this is a secular rather than a sacred role. The minister's interest in psychotherapy is a case in point.[13] The various social activities—summer camps, basketball teams, youth groups —all contribute to the socialization of the child, especially where the amount of contact is considerable; but this is secular socialization paralleling and augmenting the school. The injection of theological overtones into these activities is restrained; the church leadership usually settles for "moral" undertones lest too much "Christian fellowship" alienate the fun-seeking adolescent.

The parochial school is another matter. Maintained by the Roman Catholic Church and to a lesser extent by several Protestant denominations, these schools are generally staffed with members of religious teaching orders who are charged with keeping the faith. The impact of this type of religious instruction is difficult to assess; but if a child is drilled often enough in a religious dogma, and if the dogma is made a part of formal instruction and is reinforced at home, it is safe to assume that socialization is taking place. A trend toward an increased number of parochial schools on the elementary and secondary levels is evidence of an attempt on the part of certain denominations to coordinate the efforts of religious training in the home with those of the organized church.[14]

In either case, the religious or the moral lessons can produce conflict leading to "desocialization" if the practice in, say, the marketplace, is opposed to the teaching of the church. The "Sunday Christian" by his failure to demonstrate Christian ethics outside the confines of the church building is perhaps the greatest threat of all to organized religion as it attempts to instill ethical and moral behavior.

Churches in America do, in a variety of ways and in many degrees, contribute to the socialization of the child, making a particular contribution to social control. "They express the mores of society in terms of good and evil, purity and sin, salvation and damnation. One of the chief problems of a secular society is training young people with no church connections in the mores of the culture." [15] Will this continue to be true? An institution cannot function properly without a value system that remains intact. Religion is no exception. If the church is to meet its obligations as a functional agency it must not become the victim of dilettantism. "The radio program called 'This I believe,' . . . had—as someone said—plenty of 'believe' and quite a bit of 'I,' but not very much of 'this.' There was a great deal of 'faith' professed by the 'believers' who were often sublimely vague about just what it was they believed in. The program, a very popular one, was founded on a wide-spread attitude, the belief in believing, the faith in faith itself." [16]

As Walter Lippmann said many years ago: "When churches cease to paint the background of our lives, to nourish a *Weltanschauung*, strengthen man's ultimate purposes and reaffirm the deepest values of life, then the churches have ceased to meet the needs for which they exist." [17]

CONCLUSION

Socialization contains the antithetical forces of authority and equality. The authoritarian element is necessary to command obedience in desired patterns of behavior, especially when that behavior runs counter to biological urge. The young child cannot fully appreciate the necessity of all that is being inculcated, but some things must be accepted at face value. After all, at this point in the socialization process the child is absorbing the essentials of the culture—the folkways and mores—which by nature are largely constraining. "The official socializer—be he parent, educator, or master—is the representative of the greater authority of society." [18]

The equalitarian element arises out of a need for interaction among peers who possess no real power to coerce one another. As the child grows in years and escapes from the tyranny of adults, the nature of his respect for other people changes. Now he tends toward co-operation as the normal form of social balance. Insofar as individuals decide questions on an equal footing, the pressure they exercise upon each other becomes supplementary—or *collateral*. This collateral or equalitarian interaction is desired because a peer can pass on some of the more informal aspects of culture—symbolic shadings, fads, forbidden knowledge—which are sometimes unobtainable from persons in authority. Some of this knowledge is frowned on by society, yet it is a social necessity to the child, even if it is simply a pooling of ignorance. With all of the disadvantages of misinformation and inefficiency resulting from socialization by peers, the child acquires something that is very hard to achieve in an authoritarian setting, that is, an understanding of cooperation and the courage to stand up for his rights.[19] In other words, he may acquire in this way, the kind of enlightened, independent personality which is so necessary in a free society.

No single agency is capable of handling the entire task of "Americanizing" the child. The family must share the responsibility with the school, the church, peers, and other formal and informal institutions which directly and indirectly contribute to the transmission of our vast and diverse culture. The importance of this process cannot be overstated. Society exists only when its members have *accepted* its value system and are committed to those values. "A human person exists only insofar as he has taken 'society' into himself." [20]

Notes

1. J. O. Hertzler, *American Social Institutions,* Boston: Allyn and Bacon, Inc. 1961, p. 50.
2. Frederick Elkin, *The Child and Society,* New York: Random House, 1961, p. 101 ff.
3. James H. S. Bossard, *The Sociology of Child Development,* Rev. Ed., New York: Harper Brothers, 1954, p. 136.
4. *Ibid.*
5. Talcott Parsons and Robert F. Bales, *Family Socialization and Interaction Process,* Glencoe, Ill.: The Free Press, 1955, p. 35.
6. Bossard, *op. cit.,* pp. 520–521.
7. Hertzler, *op. cit.,* p. 50.
8. *Ibid.,* p. 372.
9. S. A. Queen, W. N. Chambers, and C. M. Winston, *The American Social System,* Boston: Houghton Mifflin Company, 1956, p. 71.
10. Bossard, *op. cit.,* p. 489.
11. Hertzler, *op. cit.,* pp. 491–492.
12. *Ibid.,* pp. 492–493.
13. See Louis Linn and Leo W. Schwarz, *Psychiatry and Religious Experience,* New York: Random House, 1958, pp. 3–22.
14. Rolfe Lanier Hunt, "Religion and Education," *Annals,* 332: November 1960, p. 89.
15. John Biesanz and Mavis Biesanz, *Modern Society,* New York: Prentice-Hall, Inc., 1953, p. 279.
16. William Lee Miller, "Religion and the American Way of Life," in *Religion and the Free Society,* New York: The Fund for the Republic, 1958, p. 6.
17. Walter Lippmann, *A Preface to Politics,* New York: Holt, 1917, pp. 181–182, as quoted in Hertzler, *op. cit.,* p. 502.
18. Kingsley Davis, *Human Society,* New York: The Macmillan Company, 1949, pp. 216–217.
19. *Ibid.,* pp. 217–218.
20. Parsons and Bales, *op. cit.,* p. 358.

Selected Readings

Abell, A. I. *The Urban Impact on American Protestantism, 1867–1900.* Cambridge: Harvard University Press, 1943.
Burgess, Ernest W., and Harvey Locke. *The Family.* New York: American Book Company, 1950.
Cavan, Ruth. *The American Family.* New York: T. Y. Crowell, 1953.

Dobriner, William. *The Suburban Community*. New York: G. P. Putnam's Sons, 1958.

Gordon, C. Wayne. *The Social System of the High School*. Glencoe, Ill.: The Free Press, 1957.

Lerner, Daniel. *The Passing of Traditional Society: Modernizing the Middle East*. Glencoe, Ill.: The Free Press, 1958.

Mead, Margaret. *The School in American Culture*. Cambridge: Harvard University Press, 1951.

Parsons, Talcott, *et al. Family, Socialization, and Interaction Process*. Glencoe, Ill.: The Free Press, 1955.

Schneider, Herbert. *Religion in 20th Century America*. Cambridge: Harvard University Press, 1952.

Young, Pauline V. *The Pilgrims of Russian Town*. Chicago: University of Chicago Press, 1932.

Chapter 12

Institutional Problems
of Initial Socialization

We have now seen the nature of institutions in urban communities, specifically the family, church, and school, and the ways in which they operate during the first phases of socialization. Another important approach to the study of American institutions is through their social problems. Marriage and family problems, population problems, challenges to the economic and political systems, racial tensions, housing, crime and delinquency, and alcoholism are forms of individual deviation which have attracted the attention of scholars. The study of social problems can be productive, for it gives both a picture of the reality of institutional life and an understanding of those factors contributing to the dynamism of life in urban communities.

The major obstacle to the study of social problems is the temptation to make evaluations. There has been a kind of romanticism in which the student of a particular problem laments the passing of a prior condition, viewing change as a grievous deviation. This attitude was apparent among social scientists, especially at the turn of the century. They believed that America—indeed, the whole of Western civilization—was moving toward a necessarily higher moral order, based on an assumption of equilibrium in the past, and that any change in the social order which threatened the attainment of that goal was undesirable.[1] Such an approach to social problems has led to some questionable conclusions. Divorce, crime and delinquency, alcoholism, and promiscuity are deplored not because they are behavior patterns that lead to the disintegration of the social order, but because they do not coincide with what *ought* to be.[2]

If we are to understand the nature of social problems within urban communities there must be an attempt to identify those factors that are related to disintegration. The institutional theory of the community is a helpful starting point. In that theory stated by George Homans,* a community begins to disintegrate when its major integrating institutions begin to be replaced by more efficient forms. In Hilltown this was exemplified by the decline of the economic system within the community and its replacement by newer efficiencies in the nearby urban center. Not only were other institutions within Hilltown affected by the decline of its economic system but so were the informal relationships within the community. The result to Hilltown, as a whole, was that the social system under which it had lived for so long was no longer able to control the behavior of individuals.[3]

When institutions and other forms of association can no longer control the behavior of their members, *social disorganization* has set in. Social disorganization is to be distinguished from social disintegration. The latter, as previously defined, refers to the loss of function by any institution within a community. Social disorganization, on the other hand, results from disintegration. Disorganization pertains to the internal collapse of norms and controls within a particular group. The school in Hilltown, for example, underwent disintegration as control over the school and student attendance was transferred to the urban center. The PTA, whose existence depended on the normal functioning of the schools in Hilltown, underwent disorganization when the system changed. The same process may recur in other communities whose institutions are undergoing change as a result of the appearance of new efficiencies.

This chapter is devoted to a description of the processes and effects of disintegration and disorganization upon the family, church, and school. Each of these institutions, as noted in Chapter 10, directly contributes to the disintegration of urban communities. The implications for social disorganization become clear if we know the group structure within institutions. Thus, if disintegration changes the values of an institution it may affect the relationships among the groups of the institution. A loss of control over group members may follow. In addition, the nature of disorganization may be understood through the values of competing institutions, especially when the values of one institution may conflict with those of another. The distintegration that results in such instances creates disorganization through the *anomie* arising among individuals caught in the conflict.[4] *Anomie* is the subjective feeling developed by individuals when they believe that goals cannot be attained through normal means.[5] Deviation may very well follow.

* See Chapter 10, p. 194.

In each of the following sections we shall see how the above processes operate in relation to the family, church, and school. The particular problems we have chosen to discuss are necessarily selective. No effort has been made to cover the full range of social problems.

FAMILY STABILITY

With the development of the specialized institutions characteristic of the urban community, the family realizes its own distinctive functions. These are the functions of giving and receiving affection, bearing and rearing children, and personality development. They represent the primary group qualities of family life. Yet, although primary in character, the family, too, is subject to social disorganization. It may lose control over its members through external factors in the urban environment and become a setting within which anomie appears.

The loss of family control over its members may result from the separateness and anonymity of urban life. Individuals in a family, according to the concept of community, tend to function within their own social orbits. Parents and children may have their own friends with no overlapping between these social spheres. There may also be a differing use of space within the community by the generations of the family. Husband and wife frequent certain homes, a night club or bowling alley, a concert hall or a corner bar. The older children of the family, of high school age, frequent the school grounds, a particular motion picture theatre, a drug store, the houses of certain friends. A smaller child may use his own and a neighbor's home, and some areas of the block on which he lives.

The separate nature of family social life is given further emphasis by the anonymity of the urban community. We must realize that the use of space is not necessarily related to the nearness of that space to one's house. There may be large areas of unused space between the residence and the place where social exchange occurs. Such distance lengthens the time during which the individual is anonymous.

What do the separateness—or segmentation—and anonymity of urban life mean to family solidarity? They mean that when any member of a family leaves the security and control of his residence, there goes with him the certainty that he will behave according to the norms that he has assimilated through the socialization process. The actual degree to which the norms have been assimilated is always unknown. Outside the immediate influence of the home the individual may be quite another person.

The development of anomie as a form of disorganization within the family is closely related to the segmentation and anonymity of urban life. Because the generations of a family tend to frequent different social worlds, using different spaces within the community, every possibility emerges that communication within the family may break down. To put it another way, the different social spheres and uses of space stimulate the development within the community of age and sex subcultures.[6]

Although found in nonurban families, the problem of communication within the urban family is intensified. There are matters that husbands and wives seldom, if ever, discuss with one another, but which they will discuss with someone else. There are many things that children will never say to their parents that they will tell one another. There are, of course, certain areas which families consider taboo to outsiders. Just what "things" fit into each category is not clear, but it is true that each member of the family may have one or more confidants. As Erving Goffman has pointed out, a confidant is someone who does not actually participate in a situation but to whom a participant will freely admit errors, bluffs, intrigues, and unspoken feelings.[7] Confidants are considered reliable because they are not participants. The fact that they exist in relation to family members is, itself, indicative of the failure of members, or their unwillingness, to recognize the formally prescribed roles and statuses within the family.

The programs, policies, values, and ends of other institutions may also contribute to a feeling of anomie. The expression by adolescents, "I don't know what to believe," reflects the lack of continuity and consistency between the value systems of urban institutions. The pull of conflicting loyalties on individuals is sometimes very great.

Still another source of family disorganization may be the discrepancy between expectation and individual resources to meet these expectations, resulting in role strain. In family roles the source of discrepancy may range from the structure of the family itself to the inner anxieties of the individual. One major source is the stereotyped role in which family members often perceive one another. Young husbands and wives, for example, in the first years of marriage, sometimes expect qualities that the partner is physically and psychologically unable to fulfill. The partner may attempt to play out the stereotype, however, to the end that inconsistent behavior, tension, and anxiety develop as a result of conflict between expectation and individual resource.[8]

SOCIAL CLASS AND FAMILY STABILITY

In the foregoing account of sources of family disorganization no attempt has been made to describe other symptoms of family disorganization, such as divorce, juvenile delinquency, or specific individual deviations which require special study. The primary question is: how often does disorganization appear in all families? We have discussed *the* family, as though all families in America experience the same pressures or, indeed, the same environment. From previous chapters we know that no such generalization is possible. One important way to distinguish between degrees of family disorganization is by the family's position in the class structure.

In the following article by August Hollingshead we shall see that class differences in family stability do exist—at least as far as limited evidence supports the generalization. It will be noted that Hollingshead divides the class structure into five categories: upper (with two subtypes), middle, lower-middle, the working class, and the lower class. This is but one scheme developed by American social scientists.[9] Each of the classes, possessing various degrees of access to economic opportunity, develops a particular style of life which finds its way into the families of that class.

*

Sociologists in recent years have become aware of the interdependence that exists between the family and status systems in American society, but no studies have been focused on the analysis of the problem of class differences in family stability. Consequently there is no comprehensive body of either quantitative or qualitative data that we may draw upon for a statement of similarities and differences in family stability and instability in the several classes found in our society. Official city, county, state, and national statistics on marriage and divorce do not recognize the existence of social classes, so these data are not appropriate for our purposes. In view of these limitations, this paper will merely outline some of the major differences in family stability revealed by studies of social stratification at the community level. However, before we turn to a discussion of the problem of family stability and the status structure, a few paragraphs of theoretical orientation are in order.

The nexus between the family and class systems arises from the fact that every individual is simultaneously a member of both systems. He is created in the family and placed in the class system whether he wills it or not. How-

* From August Hollingshead. "Class Differences in Family Stability," *Annals*, November 1950, pp. 39–46. Reprinted by permission of the American Academy of Political and Social Sciences and the author.

ever, the functions of the two systems are essentially different; the family is the procreative and primary training institution, whereas the class system functions as a ranking device. The two systems are interwoven at many points in ways that are too intricate for us to unravel here. It is sufficient for present purposes to point out that each individual's original position in the class system is ascribed to him on the basis of a combination of social and biological characteristics inherited from his family through genetic and social processes. This position may be modified, and in some cases changed sharply, during the course of the individual's life; but the point of origin in the status system for every individual is the family into which he is born.

The nuclear group of husband, wife, and dependent children constitutes the primary family and common household unit throughout our society. This group normally passes through a family cycle which begins with marriage and extends through the childbearing and child-rearing years and on into the old age of the parental pair. It is the maintenance of the family cycle from marriage to old age that we will take as our criterion of a stable family. Each marriage of a man and a woman brings into being a new family cycle. Upon the birth of their first child the nuclear pair becomes a family of procreation, but for the child this family of origin is his family of orientation. Thus, each individual who marries and rears children has a family of orientation and a family of procreation. He also has an ascribed status which he inherits from his family of orientation, and an achieved status which he acquires in the course of his life. His achieved status may be different from his ascribed status, but not necessarily, particularly from the viewpoint of class position; but his family of procreation, of necessity, is different from his family of orientation. In the case of a man, his achieved status normally becomes the status of his wife and of his children during their early years.

Each nuclear family is related to a number of other nuclear families by consanguineal and affinal ties. Also, each family in the kin group occupies a position in the status system. All nuclear families in a kin group may be in the same class or may be in different class positions from others. The latter situation is produced by mobility on the part of some individual families, while other families remain in the approximate status position ascribed to them by their family of orientation. This movement of the individual nuclear family in the status system, while it is approved, and often lauded as "the American way," has important effects on kin group relations.

With these considerations in mind, we turn to the discussion of class and family stability. We wish to warn the reader, however, that the statements presented in the following analysis are based on a few community studies in different parts of the Nation, and therefore the bases of the generalizations are fragmentary; heuristic observations are made in the hope that they will give readers new insight into these facets of our society.

Families in the upper class may be divided into two categories on the basis of the length of time they have occupied upper-class position: (1) *established* families, which have been in the upper class for two or more generations; and (2) *new* families, which have achieved their position through the success of the present adult generation.

Who one's ancestors were, and who one's relatives are, count for more in the established family group than what one has achieved in one's own lifetime. "Background" is stressed most heavily when it comes to the crucial question of whom a member may or may not marry, for marriage is the institution that determines membership in the family group. Indeed, one of the perennial problems of the established family is the control of the marriage choices of its young men. Young women can be controlled more easily than young men, because of the sheltered life they lead and their passive role in courtship. The passivity of the upper-class female, coupled with sex exploitation of females from lower social positions by upper-class males that sometimes leads to marriage, results in a considerable number of old maids in established upper-class families. Strong emphasis on family background is accompanied by the selection of marriage mates from within the old-family group in an exceptionally high percentage of cases, and if not from the old-family group, then from the new-family segment of the upper class. The degree of kinship solidarity, combined with intraclass marriages, found in this level results in a high order of stability in the upper class, in the extended kin group, and in the nuclear family within it.

The established upper-class family is basically an extended kin group, solidified by lineage and a heritage of common experience in a communal setting. A complicated network of consanguineal and affinal ties unites nuclear families of orientation and procreation into an in-group that rallies when its position is threatened by the behavior of one of its members, particularly where out-marriage is involved; this principle will be illustrated below. Each nuclear family usually maintains a separate household, but it does not conceive of itself as a unit apart from the larger kin group. The nuclear family is viewed as only a part of a broader kin group that includes the consanguineal descendants of a known ancestral pair, plus kin that have been brought into the group by marriage.

An important factor in the extended established family's ability to maintain its position through several generations is its economic security. Usually a number of different nuclear families within a kin group are supported, in part at least, by income from a family estate held in trust. Also, because of the practice of intramarriage it is not unusual for a family to be the beneficiary of two or more estates held in trust. For example, in an eastern community of some 80,000 population, one of these extended family groups is the beneficiary of a trust established a century ago that yields something over $300,000 annually, after taxes. This income is divided among 37 different nuclear families descended from the founder, 28 of whom live in the community; 23 of these families are beneficiaries of one other trust fund, and 14 receive income from two or more other trust funds. These different nuclear families regard themselves as parts of the Scott family; moreover, they are so regarded by other upper-class families, as well as by persons lower in the status system who know something of the details of the family history.

The Scott family has maintained its upper-class position locally for more than two centuries by a combination of property ownership, educational, legal, and political leadership, and control of marriages generation after generation. Its members are proud that it has never had a non-Protestant marriage in seven generations; only five divorces have been traced, but these are not mentioned; one desertion has been hinted, but not confirmed.

The tradition relative to Protestant intra-upper-class marriages had a severe test in recent years. A son in one family, who had spent four years in the armed services in the late war, asked a middle-class Catholic girl to marry him. The engagement was announced by the girl's family, to the consternation of the Scotts. The Scotts immediately brought pressure on the boy to "break off the affair." His mother "bristled" at the very idea of her son's marriage; his father "had a talk with him"; his 84-year-old paternal grandmother snorted, "A Scott marry a Flaherty, never!" A great-aunt remarked icily, "No Scott is dissolute enough to *have* to marry a Flaherty." After the first shock of indignation had passed, the young man was told he was welcome in "any Scott home" without that "Flaherty flip." A few weeks later his maternal grandfather told him he would be disinherited if he "demeaned" himself by marrying "that girl."

After several months of family and class pressure against the marriage, the young man "saw his error" and broke the engagement. A year later he married a family-approved "nice" girl from one of the other "old" families in the city. Today he is assistant cashier in his wife's family's bank, and his father is building him a fine suburban home.

Nancy Flaherty, when the storm broke over her engagement, quit her job as a secretary in an insurance office. A few weeks later she left home to seek a job in another city. After the engagement was broken she quit this job and went to New York City. Today she is unmarried, living alone, and working in New York.

This case illustrates a number of characteristics typical of the established upper-class family. It is stable, extended, tends to pull together when its position is threatened—in this instance by an out-marriage—exerts powerful controls on its members to ensure that their behavior conforms to family and class codes, and provides for its members economically by trust funds and appropriate positions.

The new upper-class family is characterized most decisively by phenomenal economic success during a short interval of time. Its meteoric rise in the economic system is normally the personal triumph of the money-maker. While its head is busy making a "million bucks," the family acquires the purchasable symbols associated with the wealthy American family: a large house, fine furniture, big automobiles, and expensive clothes. The new tycoon knows the power of money in the market place, and he often attempts to buy a high position in the status system. The new family is able to meet *the means test*, but not *the lineage test* of the established families. Consequently, it is generally systematically excluded from membership in the most prestigeful cliques and associations in the community. This is resented, especially by the wife and children; less often by the tycoon.

The new family is very unstable in comparison with the established family. It lacks the security of accepted position at the top of the local status system—a position that will come only through time; it cannot be purchased. The stabilizing influence exerted on the deviant individual by an extended family group, as well as friends, is absent. (Many upwardly mobile families break with their kin group as part of the price they pay for their mobility.) Then, too, the new family is composed of adults who are self-directing, full of initiative, believe in the freedom of the individual, and rely upon themselves rather than upon a kin group. The result is, speaking broadly, conspicuous expenditure, fast living insecurity, and family instability. Thus, we find divorces, broken homes, alcoholism, and other symptoms of disorganization in a large number of new families. Because new families are so conspicuous in their consumption and behavior they become, in the judgment of the general population, symbolic of upper-class actions and values, much to the detriment, and resentment, of established families.

The nuclear upper-middle-class family, composed of husband, wife, and two or three dependent children during the major years of the family cycle, is a very stable unit in comparison with the new upper-class family and the working-class family. Divorce is rare, desertion by the husband or wife is most infrequent, and premature death rates are low.

During the past half-century changes that have taken place in American society have created a demand for technically trained personnel in such large numbers that the old middle class could not provide enough recruits to fill the new positions. Concomitantly, our educational institutions expanded enormously to meet the need for professionally, scientifically, and administratively trained personnel. A vast area of opportunity opened for boys and girls in the lower-middle and working classes to move upward in the economic and status structures. Thus, the majority of upper-middle-class persons now above thirty-five years of age are upward mobile. Their mobility has been made possible by education, self-discipline, and opportunity in the professional and administrative channels of our economic system.

Geographic mobility has been a second concomitant in this process. The man or woman who is now in the upper-middle class more often than not left his home community as a young adult to attend college. After his formal schooling was completed he generally took a job in a different community from the one where he was trained, and often-times it was in a different one from his home town. If he began his adult work career with a national business firm, the chances are higher that he was transferred from one city to another as he moved up the job ladder.

Geographic movement is typical of an upward mobile family, even when it lives out the family cycle in its home community. In a large number of cases, when a mobile couple is newly married, both partners work. The couple often lives in an apartment or flat in a residential area that is not desirable as a permanent residence. As the husband achieves a higher economic status, the new family generally moves to a small single-family house, or a two-family one, farther from the center of the city, where there are yards and trees. Often about this time the wife quits work and the first of two or three children is born. A third or fouth move, some years later, into a six- to eight-room single-family house or a well landscaped lot in the better residential areas of the city or the suburbs normally completes the family's odyssey. While it is moving from house to house, many of its social contacts change as the husband passes through the successive stages of his business or professional career.

Even though there is a high prevalence of social and geographic mobility, and no extended kin group to bring pressure on the family, there is a negligible amount of instability. Self-discipline, the demands of the job, and the moral pressures exerted by friends and associates keep the nuclear family together. The principal family goals are success in business or a profession, a good college or university education for the children, and economic security for the parents in their old age. These goals are realized in the vast majority of cases, and the family is generally a happy, well-knit group.

The lower-middle-class family, like the upper middle, is a stable unit for the most part. In fact, there is no essential difference between these two levels of the status system in so far as family stability is concerned. In Elmtown 85 per cent of the upper-middle (class II) and 82 per cent of the lower-middle families (class III) were intact after fifteen and more years of marriage. Oren found in an industrial city in Connecticut that 93 per cent of the lower-middle families with adolescent children were unbroken after eighteen and more years of marriage.

Probably a higher proportion of lower-middle-class individuals have achieved their positions through their own efforts than is true of any other status level except the new family group in the upper class. The majority of lower-middle-class adults have come from a working-class background; many have an ethnic background of recent immigrant origin. Through ability, hard work, and an element of luck they have founded small businesses, operated by the family members, and a few employees, or acquired some technical training which has enabled them to obtain clerical, sales, and minor administrative posts in industry and government.

The major problems of the lower-middle-class family are connected with the security of its economic position and the education of its children. Parents generally have high educational aspirations for their children, but income limitations often compel them to compromise with less education than they desire, and possibly a different kind from what they would choose. Parents acutely see the need for a good formal education, and they make heavy sacrifices to give their children the educational training that will enable them to take over positions held by persons in the upper-middle class. By stressing education for the child, parents many times unwittingly create conflicts for themselves and their children, because the educational goals they set for the child train him in values that lead him away from his family. This process, while it does not have a direct bearing on the stability of the nuclear family, acts as a divisive factor that splits parents and children apart, as well as brothers and sisters who have received different amounts of education and follow different job channels.

The family cycle is broken prematurely in the working class about twice as frequently as it is in the middle classes. Community studies indicate that from one-fourth to one-third of working-class families are broken by divorce, desertion, and death of a marital partner, after a family of procreation has been started but before it is reared. This generalization does not include families broken before the birth of children or after they leave the parental home. In Elmtown I found that 33 per cent of the working-class families (class IV) had been broken after fifteen and more years of marriage; Oren reported that 29 per cent of his working-class families with adolescent children were broken ones. The norm and the ideal in the working class are a stable family, but broken homes occur with such frequency that most parents realize that they are, along with unemployment, a constant hazard.

Family instability is a product of the conditions under which most working-class families live. In the first place, they are completely dependent on the swings of the business cycle in our wage-price-profits system, for the working-class family is almost invariably supported by wages earned by the hour, the piece, the day, or the week. Ideally its wages are earned by the male head, but in a considerable proportion of families the wife too is employed as a wage earner outside the home. When a working-class wife takes a job it is for a substantial reason, usually necessity, rather than the desire for "a career."

The home is the center of family life, and the hope of most working-class families is a single-family dwelling with a yard; but from a fifth to one-half are forced to live in multiple dwelling units with inadequate space for family living. Added to this is the working-class *mos* that one is obligated to give shelter and care in a crisis to a husband's or wife's relatives or to a married child. Thus, in a considerable percentage of these families the home is shared with some relative. Then, too, resources are stringently limited, so when a family is faced with unemployment, illness, and death it must turn to someone for help. In such crises, a relative is called upon in most instances before some public agency. The relative normally has little to offer, but in most cases that little is shared with the family in need, even though grudgingly.

While crises draw family members together, they also act as divisive agents; for when a family has to share its limited living space and meager income with relatives, kin ties are soon strained, often to the breaking point. One family is not able to give aid to another on an extensive scale without impairing its own standard of living; possibly its own security may be jeopardized. In view of this risk, some persons do everything short of absolute refusal to aid a relative in distress; some even violate the "blood is thicker than water" *mos* and refuse to give help when it is required. This ordinarily results in the permanent destruction of kin ties, but it is justified by the belief that one's own family's needs come first.

Although the principle is stressed here that the working-class family lives very close to the limits of its economic resources at all times, and when a crisis comes its effects upon family stability are profound, we should not overlook the fact that moral, personal, and emotional factors contribute to family instability. It is possible that these factors are as important as the economic ones, but this and other observations made here need to be verified by field studies. Actually, while we know that the family at this level of the status structure is susceptible to instability, we have little knowledge derived from systematic research to tell us what cultural conditions are associated with unstable, in contrast to stable, families. A carefully planned series of studies of stable and unstable families with class level held constant is needed. Until this is done, we can only guess about the factors which condition stability and instability in family life.

Lower-class families exhibit the highest prevalence of instability of any class in the status structure. If we view the lower-class family in terms of a continuum, we find at one end stable families throughout the family cycle; at the other end, the nuclear family of a legally wedded husband and wife and dependent children has given way to a reciprocal companionate relationship between a man and a woman. This latter relationship, in most cases, is the result of their personal desire to live together; it is not legally sanctioned. A companionate family is often a complicated one. It may include the natural children of the couple, plus the woman's children from a previous legal or companionate relationship; also there may be dependent children of the man living with the woman. Normally, when the lower-class family is broken, as in the higher classes, the mother keeps the children.

However, the mother may desert her "man" for another man, and leave her children with him, her mother or sister, or a social agency. In the Deep South and Elmtown, from 50 to 60 per cent of lower-class family groups are broken once, and often more, by desertion, divorce, death, or separation, often due to imprisonment of the man, between marriage, legal or companionate, and its normal dissolution through the marriage of adult children and the death of aged parents.

Economic insecurity is but one of a number of factors that give rise to this amount of instability. Lower-class people are employed in the most menial, the poorest-paid, and the dirtiest jobs; these jobs also tend to be seasonal and cyclical, and of short duration. Moreover, from one-half to two-thirds of the wives are gainfully employed outside the home; in many cases they are the sole support of the family. However, the problem of economic insecurity does not account for amoral behavior that ranges from the flagrant violation of conventional sex mores to open rebellion against formal agencies of social control.

The very nature of our society may be responsible, in large part, for the number, the intensity, and the variety of social problems associated with the lower class. Such cultural values as individualism, wealth, position, and power must be considered in an analysis of social problems from the viewpoint of the class system. Ours is a competitive, acquisitive society where individuals successful in the competitive arena are admired by most other Americans; they achieve positions of prestige and of power desired by many and attained by few. Less successful individuals may struggle as hard but not be able to do more than hold the status in which they were born; their goal may be to avoid the sorry drift toward lower-class existence. Other individuals may fail in the struggle and sink to the bottom. To be sure, some were born there and failed to rise from the unenviable position they inherited at birth.

The interdependence between the family and status systems sketched here needs to be studied systematically before we can draw definitive generalizations that may be used as the basis for an action program to increase family stability. Isolated community studies indicate that there are functional linkages between the types as well as the amounts of family instability at different levels of the status structure. These indications ought to be analyzed by carefully designed research. If and when this is done, I believe we shall gain some valuable new insights into family and individual stability and instability.

THE CHURCH AND SECULARISM

Despite the large number of people who now claim religious affiliation there is a strong trend toward secularism in American life.[10] Secularization means that the bulk of one's life is determined by nontraditional, especially nonreligious, institutions. In Europe the secular trend was accompanied by some jarring conflicts beginning with the church-state struggles of the twelfth century, continuing through the Protestant Reformation, to the nineteenth-century arguments between church and state, exemplified by the clerical-anticlerical dispute in France. Secularization in America has seldom reached the proportions of the conflict in Europe because of the early separation of church and state. This fact, together with the growth of church membership between 1880 and 1950, leads to the question: how can we be said to be experiencing secularization at the same time that the churches are increasing in size?

An implicit assumption, frequently made explicit in times of crisis, is that we are a religious nation. The historical roots of this assumption are found in the colonial period: the English settlers were seeking religious freedom. Each war fought by America has been accompanied by the belief that God, creator of all men, was on our side. Our coins display the words "In God We Trust," Congress opens with prayer, court oaths end with the phrase "so help you God" as the witness places his hand upon the Bible, and the pledge of allegiance to the American flag contains the words "one nation, under God." This is hardly the record of a secular nation.

At the same time that we recognize the place of religion in American life we also discover a cynicism toward religion. Cynicism and secularism are not synonymous; rather, cynicism is a symptom of a secular trend. Cynicism can be recognized in the jokes about one-day-a-week Christians or Eastertime Christians. We also find it in the behavior of parents who insist that their children attend Sunday school but who themselves never enter the church. The notion that church is good in its place but that business is business further exemplifies the cynical attitude toward religion held by Americans.

In order to understand the contradiction, and it is a basic one, between religious growth and secularism let us review some of the factors that led to the secularization of American life. The processes of urbanization and industrialization, to be sure, are keys to understanding much of the secular trend. The efficiency of life caught up in these processes, the search for the new, and the market character of much institutional life have given momentum to secularization. Within urbanization and industrialization some other, more specific, factors can be noted.

One of these has been the long series of legal decisions supporting the separation of church and state.[11] Recently these decisions were reinforced by the 1962 United States Supreme Court ruling which reaffirmed the

First Amendment by declaring against a prayer approved by the New York State Regents for use in that state's public schools. Another factor contributing to secularization has been the automobile,[12] which has created a highly mobile population and made inroads on actual church attendance. The increase in Sunday entertainment, especially sporting events and television, has also added to the secularization of life. In urban fringe communities, many businesses now stay open on Sunday, creating further encroachment upon the Sabbath.

Changes in the nature and function of churches have contributed to the secular trend. Many charity services, formerly borne by religious groups, have been organized on a communitywide basis under quasi-governmental supervision. Churches have also become the setting within which social mobility is made possible through the establishment of club activities in the church; though based on religious motives, these activities easily become aids to the acquisition and maintenance of social honor.[13] Churches, through their close relationship with the social order, frequently reflect the style of life of their congregations.[14] This was to be seen in a community, such as Elmtown, studied by August Hollingshead, in which the Federated Church was considered the "society" church and the Faithful Holiness Tabernacle, located in a loft near the town canal, was at the bottom of the prestige scale.[15]

SECULARISM AND THE SCHOOL

Institutional competition, as a source of secularization, is seen in the rivalry between church and school. As already noted, there is little coordination among the institutions of a community. Religious goals and assumptions often do not coincide with those of nonreligious institutions. Because their staffs come from different traditions, such competition is probably inevitable. The basis of the competition, then, may be viewed as the questioning, by the leaders of one institution, of the motives, goals, and programs of the other.[16]

Many of the conflicts between church and school are reviewed in the following selection by Thomas F. Hoult. He discusses not only the general secularizing effects of formal education on attitudes but also the effects of a vulgarized conception of cultural relativity upon religious beliefs (see Chapter 5). The questions posed by Hoult's statements are important not only for the understanding of a particular institution but also for the social scientist. If objectivity and cultural relativism are used as major tools in the analysis of human behavior, because they free the scientist from conclusions about the data under observation, can the next step be taken if the spirit of science is to be maintained? Can the social scientist say that his methods are better and are capable of bringing man to a finer way of life? [17]

*
For better or for worse, formal education frequently leads people to con- clusions which undermine their spiritual convictions. William Graham Sumner, author of the sociological classic, *Folkways*, began his career as an Episcopalian minister. When he undertook his sociological studies, he said, he placed his religious beliefs "in a drawer." After finishing his new studies, he returned to the drawer to retrieve the beliefs which he thought he had only temporarily put aside. But when he opened the drawer, Sumner said, it was "empty." Sumner's experience epitomizes the effect which formal edu- cation can have on religious convictions.

Secular education is, of course, a potential threat to the beliefs of certain faiths. But even sectarian-controlled education can engender religious doubts when it deals with nonreligious subjects. For example, from 1896 until 1930, the schools of Zion City, Illinois, were controlled by the Catholic Apostolic Church, a fundamentalist group which believed that the world is flat because the Bible speaks of its "four corners." It is not difficult to imagine the religious doubts which must have arisen in the minds of Zion City pupils when they studied history and geography as required by state law.

In nineteenth-century Spain, Brenan relates, Church-controlled schools were fully aware of education's threat to religious orthodoxy:

> Until 1836 education had been almost entirely in the hands of the higher clergy and the religious orders. The Church at this time had not yet recovered from the shock that the French Revolution had given it and had a mortal dread of learning. Science, mathematics, agriculture and political economy were there- fore not taught, as they were considered dangerous subjects for any but trained theologians. The Jesuits frowned on history, which offered so many bad examples to the young and innocent. Almost the only subject that could be usefully studied at the universities was law. For though medicine was taught, it suffered from the suppression of that erroneous Lutheran notion upon the circulation of the blood, whilst if one touched on physics one had to remember that the Copernican system was still a *cosa de Inquisición*. In the elementary schools the children of the poor were deliberately not taught to read, but only to sew and to recite the Catechism. As the University of Cervera—the only university in Catalonia—declared in its famous address to Ferdinand VII: "Far be from us the dangerous novelty of thinking."

A number of empirical studies have shown the apparent effect of formal education on religious beliefs and practices. About thirty years ago, for example, Betts reported that ministry students expressed much more liberal attitudes than established ministers. This more liberal frame of mind was

* From Thomas Ford Hoult, *The Sociology of Religion*, pp. 320–325, copyright 1958, Holt, Rinehart, and Winston, Inc. By permission.

attributed to the generally higher educational level of the students as well as to the changing times. In this study, only 18 per cent of the students believed in physical resurrection, as compared with 62 per cent of the ministers polled; only 9 per cent of students, as compared with 60 per cent of the ministers, said they believed in the devil as an "actual person." A much more recent poll, sponsored by the *Catholic Digest* (Vol. 17, pp. 1–5, November 1952), showed that certain belief in God is lowest among college graduates and highest among grade-school graduates, with high-school graduates falling in between. Still another study, using established scales, measured the attitudes of Northwestern University students toward God and the church, as well as the influence of religious belief on conduct. Seniors and juniors, it was found, were consistently less religious than freshmen and sophomores. However, the special nature of students who drop out of college before graduating may have contributed to this result.

The increasing influence of education on Mormon life seems to be typical of education's effect on religious attitudes generally. In 1925, Nelson found, the size of Mormon families, in keeping with the Mormon condemnation of contraception, was unrelated to the educational level of Mormon parents. However, since 1925, as means of transportation and communication improved, the Mormons have been more and more integrated into the general American culture pattern—a pattern which includes the idea, current among the most educated, that large families impede the realization of certain status and security aspirations. Consequently, Mormon fertility rates (though still quite high) now vary by level of education, as do those of other Americans. In 1950, when Nelson studied a representative group of Mormon women forty-five years of age or older, he found that women with elementary-school education had 6.5 children; those with high-school education had 4.8 children; and those with college education, 4.2 children. The differences, though small, are statistically significant and not due to chance variations.

In another part of the world, Ryan found that level of education was the determining factor in the attitudes of Hinayana Buddhist priests toward birth control. Among the priests interviewed, all the educated accepted birth control; but the priests whose faith had not been "watered down" by education declared that birth control violated fundamental Buddhist tenets. In the United States, Sturges discovered that, with one exception in the case of private prayer, five basic types of devotions are practiced less often by college students than by adult members (many of whom never attended college) of the same religion. A study at the University of Hawaii disclosed that the students there tended to break away from the faith of their families and join more liberal groups. In South Carolina, a study of one thousand students at five colleges revealed that only 2.2 per cent of the students believed that their parents' attitudes toward religion were absolutely correct. Almost 13

per cent of the students asserted that their parents were "narrow" in their
religious beliefs, and 15 per cent said "old-fashioned."

Two basic aspects of secular education tend to undermine traditional
religious beliefs: the stress on the idea that reliable conclusions can be
drawn only on the basis of empirical proof or logical analysis, and the
philosophy of cultural relativism. Both of these philosophies have become so
widely accepted in the West that many religious organizations have difficulty
maintaining adherence to their traditional views—in accordance with the
factors summed up in the principle of sociocultural compatibility. . . .
Traditional religious convictions, founded ultimately on faith, obviously
cannot be maintained as easily among those who are conditioned to demand
proof in the scientific sense. As Hollingshead wrote of the youth of Elmtown:

> It is difficult for the serious student to reconcile the contradictions between
> what he learns in the religious compartment of his culture with what he is
> taught in school. His doubts on religious questions are increased particularly
> when representatives of the church deny facts taught in school without providing
> any proof beyond assertions that what they believe is "true" and the "facts" of
> science are "untrue," or when in a shamefaced manner they turn from the
> question the child asked to some other topic.

Cultural relativism, which arises from the legitimate desire of educators to
increase the objectivity of students toward themselves and their world, views
each culture in terms of its own customs, history, and values. More often
than not, however, cultural relativism leads to moral relativism, which claims
that each of the many moral, ethical, and religious systems has its validity.
This point of view implies that religious believers who claim to have a corner
on truth are simply manifesting ethnocentrism or bigotry. Thus, moral relativism hardly encourages people to maintain their adherence to a particular
faith. But relativism not only undermines established religious values. It is
sometimes suggested as a substitute for traditional religious values.

The philosophy of relativism, as Frank Hartung has made clear, is not
nearly so free of value judgments as its proponents sometimes claim. The
very fact that relativism is promoted as a "better" point of view because it
is "objective" and not "burdened with value judgment" is an indication that
it is *itself* a value judgment. Indeed, enthusiastic relativists manifest many
of the characteristics of confirmed religionists going through the cult or even
the sect stage of institutionalization. Already dominating a number of secular
schools and professional (mostly social science) organizations, relativists look
with scorn at the alleged inadequacy of other points of view. Asserting that
only when their values triumph can there be real peace among men, they
hope to see other viewpoints superseded by their own.

In a sense, then, the effects of formal education on religious values and
loyalties constitute a full circle. First, usually unintentionally, the historical

and contemporary facts brought out in the educational process cause many people to question the basis of religious values. Next, secular education stresses objectivity and the need to understand the values of all groups. This is "cultural relativity," the extension of which, moral relativism, teaches that all moral ideas have equal validity if viewed in terms of their own history. Finally, relativism, often promoted as a "better" value scheme, takes on many of the attributes of the "narrow" religions whose values it questions, and becomes itself a substitute "religion." The circle is then complete: educational policies which begin by undermining religion end by contributing to the creation of what is, for all practical purposes, a new point of view that is essentially religious in nature.

THE SCHOOL AND SOCIAL STRATIFICATION

As urbanization has developed, the school, like the family, has assumed specialized functions in the socialization process. Free public education has emerged fully only within the last 100 years, and secondary education only since the second decade of this century. Before the 1860's public education was limited by the nature of community life, and by the fact that many schools, especially colleges and universities, were private. With the passage of compulsory school laws from 1852 to 1918, with the Michigan Supreme Court decision of 1874 granting the use of tax revenue for secondary education, and with the passage by Congress of the Morrill Land Grant Act of 1862 which made possible public state universities, public tax-supported education became a legal reality.

The number of students attending school has been steadily higher with gradual increases in elementary school enrollment and a near-revolution in secondary school enrollment. In 1951–52, 85 per cent of all children between 5 and 17 years of age were in school.[18] The figure is all the more startling when it is realized that the population between ages 5–17 in 1951–52 was close in number to the *total* population of the United States in 1869–70. [19]

The basic philosophy of American public education is equality. The tradition of equality has been part of the American scene since the early Republic, and education is regarded as one means by which to realize equality of opportunity. The second basis of the equalitarian belief in American education stems from a more practical consideration—taxation. Local taxes, especially those on property, support the schools, and since the public pays the taxes, the taxpayer is able to ensure an equal educational opportunity for his children.

Yet the equalitarian belief regarding public education is not a reality. Many inequalities, individual abilities aside, do exist.

First—and most dramatically emphasized since the United States Supreme Court decision of 1954 which ruled against segregated schools —there has been racial inequality in education.[20] In 1940, the median school years completed for all male nonwhites in the United States was 5.4 years and for nonwhite females 6.1 years.[21] In the same year in thirteen Southern states and the District of Columbia there were 37.7 Negro pupils per teacher as against 29.2 white pupils per teacher; the per-pupil expenditure for teachers' salaries was $13.35 for Negroes and $35.86 for whites; and the average school year was 156.3 days for Negroes and 170.8 days for whites.[22] By 1950 the median years of school completed for nonwhite males had risen only to 6.5 years and for nonwhite females to 7.4 years. The comparable median for white males in 1940 was 8.7 years and for white females 8.8 years. By 1950 the median years of schooling completed by whites was 9.3 years for males and 10.0 years for females.[23]

Inequality of education also exists in relation to residence. In 1950 the median years of school completed by urban residents was 10.0 years, by rural nonfarm residents 8.9 years, and by rural farm residents 8.4 years.[24] Some racial overlapping necessarily affects the residential data. The 1950 United States Census reported only two dominantly rural geographic regions: the South Atlantic region—the Carolinas, Georgia, and Florida —and the East South Central region—Kentucky, Tennessee, Alabama, and Mississippi. The South, in general, has the largest farm population in the United States.

A more subtle form of inequality results from class and style of life. Although class does not appear to influence informal patterns of inter-action at the elementary school level,[25] there is evidence to indicate that it does assume an important function in the high school.[26] The 1925 study of Middletown by the Lynds indicated that the style of life of the parents—clothing, money, clubs, and leadership positions—were set into motion during the high school years.[27] The Lynds' later study of the same community during the Depression indicated that the pace of social life in the high school had not declined. Although officially banned by law, sororities and fraternities continued in the high school under the guise of social clubs, thus meeting the social ambitions of the parents.[28]

More direct implications of the influence of social class on the school are to be found in the studies of the Illinois community known variously as Jonesville or Elmtown. With regard to extracurricular activities in the high school, there was a close connection between participation and social class. All the upper and upper-middle class students participated in school activities, but only 27 per cent of the students from the lower classes.[29] During one school year, no boys and only one girl from the lower class attended any school dances, none of the lower-class students belonged to any of the music groups in the school, and none was elected to any student body office.[30]

The effects of the system of cliques, activities, and other types of social association based on class and life style constitute the informal system of the school. Even though school authorities, officially, may not take notice of the influences of the informal system they are, nevertheless, affected by it. In the Jonesville study it was found, for example, that class structure was related to school attendance. All of the upper and upper-middle class children were in attendance. Only 11.3 per cent of the lower class attended the high school.[31] There also appeared to be a class bias in the curriculum of the high school. The curriculum consisted of three courses of study: College Preparatory, General, and Commercial. Students from the upper and upper-middle classes numbered 64.3 per cent in the College Preparatory course, whereas 51.4 per cent was in the General and 21.2 per cent in the Commercial. The two lower classes were similar: 8.7 per cent were in the College Preparatory course, 58.5 per cent in the General, and 32.8 per cent in the Commercial.[32]

If the formal structure of the school, especially its bureaucratic organization, can be called rational then the informal organization is irrational. As Otto Dahlke pointed out, the informal order is a consequence of the studied insults, snubs, and slurs which the ingroups heap upon the outgroups.[33] To the extent that the formal organization of the school accepts certain informal standards based on class and life style within it, the school not only perpetuates the informal system but also contributes to the disintegration of the urban community and to the disorganization of its groups and individuals. In such cases the school often spins off those who do not conform to middle-class values, despite its equalitarian nature.

The result is that the institution of the public school has been stereotyped around middle-class values and ends. Most teachers are middle class, most of the extracurricular activities of the school are directed toward middle-class ends, such as leadership, and most of the curriculum is scaled to a narrowly conceived range of mental abilities related to middle-class ends. This is indicated further in the performance tests that examine mental skills, in the emphasis on verbal skills, and in the grouping of students. All these factors of the middle-class stereotype of the school are brought out in the following selection by Allison Davis. The passage, taken from a larger work which examined class bias in mental testing, questions the stereotype and seeks to lay a foundation for a more realistic development of public education.

*
The present intelligence tests offer one of many instances, to be found in the public schools, of the arbitrary restriction of the goals of the pupils' learning to a very narrow range of activities. The people who devise and teach the curricula of the public schools are nearly all middle class. More than 95 per cent of the teachers in the communities in New England, the deep South, and the Midwest to which I have referred previously in this paper, are middle class. Like any particular culture, that of the middle class emphasizes a rather narrow range of mental abilities and problems.

The culture of the school, therefore, selects only mental problems which are highly valued in middle-class life, and which appear to provide adaptive training for those who wish to learn the skills and values of the adult culture. If we wish to train a wide range of mental activities in the pupil, however, we need to ask ourselves at least the following questions:

1. Does the public school emphasize a range of mental problems and skills which is too narrow to develop most of the abilities necessary for attainment even in middle-class culture itself?

2. Does the public school select a range of mental problems and skills which is so narrow that the school fails to develop much of the mental potential of lower-class pupils?

These questions are posed here as the most important of the hypotheses for intensive research which have been suggested to us by our findings on socialization and on mental problem-solving. In the remainder of this paper, these problems will be examined briefly, in an exploratory way.

From his middle-class culture, learned from his parents, teachers, and friends, both the teacher and the professor of education have learned to regard certain mental interests and skills, certain moral values, as the "best," or "most cultured," or "most intelligent." Granted that, for this society, the basic *moral* values of middle-class people may be the most adaptive for survival, it does not follow that present-day middle-class academic skills and goals are most effective in developing the intellectual, imaginative, and problem-solving activities of human beings.

The school culture itself is a narrow selection of a few highly traditional activities and skills, arbitrarily taken from middle-class culture as a broader whole. To cite a case, the skills most highly valued by middle-class people are verbal comprehension and fluency. It is probable, however, that these

* Reprinted by permission of the publishers from Allison Davis. *Social Class Influences Upon Learning*, pp. 88–100. Cambridge, Mass.: Harvard University Press. Copyright 1948 by The President and Fellows of Harvard College.

skills do not require very high-level mental ability for those who live in either upper-middle-class or upper-class culture. Verbal tasks probably lie somewhere about at the mid-point of the difficulty-range of intellectual skills. Many types of invention, of creativeness, of analytical organization, and indeed of symbolic manipulation are certainly more rare and more valuable to mankind than is skill in standard English, or standard French, or standard German. Moreover, as pointed out previously in this paper, the intelligence necessary to acquire skill in the English language ranks only moderately high as compared with the complex mental activity required to learn any one of several American Indian "primitive" languages!

Just as we have been taught by our narrow academic culture both to stereotype our intelligence-test problems, and to accord the highest educational value to linguistic training, so also we have been led by scholastic culture to overrate reading as a means of developing mental processes. Reading is made the basis of the child's mental training in the first school years. Upon this basis he is usually segregated into one of the classroom's or the school's homogeneous "ability-groups." Through his early classroom experiences in learning to read, and through the accompanying prestige or stigma he meets in the classroom, the child's basic concept of his mental adequacy is learned.

Does reading deserve this high place in the first three or four years of schooling? My observations and interviews in nearly five hundred classrooms during the last four years lead me to doubt that reading helps the young child learn to solve the more basic types of mental problems. In our schools, reading consists chiefly of learning to recognize written symbols, to pronounce them, and to paraphrase them. These trainings are carried on in the classroom day in and day out, year after year, and receive greatest emphasis from the teacher. Yet it seems clear to me that they stimulate only a very narrow range of thought-processess.

The hypotheses to be tested by research upon reading include first those having to do with concept-formation. Does his reading in school help the young child to learn most of his words and most of his concepts? Does not the school practice in reading concern itself chiefly with the learning of symbols and the ordering of symbols? If this is true, does this undue emphasis upon symbols result from the fact that other types of experience in the classroom are too limited to develop most areas of concept-formation and reasoning?

The second group of hypotheses concerns the experiences symbolized by the written signs which the child learns to read in school. We have only to look at the books used in the first three or four grades to recognize that the experiences symbolized are far more simple than those which the child has already met in his daily life. In the first grade, he learns to read "I see the boy" long after he has learned to speak and to think in complex-compound sentences, or to outwit his father or mother in family arguments, or to solve some problems in intelligence tests which his parents cannot solve! The same child who has to spend months learning to recognize those types of verbal symbols which give children most trouble—the symbols for abstract experiences, pronouns, and verbal auxiliaries—has already been speaking and understanding these same words in conversation for years!

Now it is well and necessary for a six-year-old to learn to read the written symbols, "I see a cat" or "Mary went to Grandmother's house." He must learn to recognize the written symbols sooner or later. But scientists and teachers must not therefore conclude that this task should be the prime endeavor of his first years in school. He is in school primarily to learn how to think, to develop his reason, his insight, his invention, his imagination.

The academic function of the school is to help the child learn how to solve a wide range of mental problems. Of how much value is reading in helping the young child learn to solve mental problems? In the simple stories which he reads and paraphrases, all the problems except those of vocabulary, word recognition, and syntax are solved for him by the writer. He learns a new and important concept only once in a blue moon from his primer; even then, he learns it chiefly by memory and by simple association. In other words, there is little chance for the child to learn to recognize, to define, and to analyze problems in any exploratory or empirical way in reading; in his primer, he simply learns to decode someone's thoughts about a cat, or a grandmother, or a circus, or a trip to the country.

One must recognize, therefore, that the experiences symbolized in the child's books usually do not interest him. The stories seem foolish to lower-class children because the experiences appear unreal, the words strange. To the middle-class child, the drive of seeking his parents' and teacher's approval is usually strong enough to keep him trying, but not strong enough to make him *like* reading. Since the stories are written chiefly to teach certain words, and are organized, therefore, around the repetition of these words, they make little sense as a view of reality to the middle-class child, either.

Thus reading fails to give pupils any great skill in solving problems (1) because it limits its problems largely to purely verbal ones, and (2) because its problems are felt by the pupil to have little importance in his life outside the school.

The basic criticism of the school's great emphasis upon reading, therefore, is this: Reading teaches too little skill in problem-solving (either of a rational, empirical, or inventive kind) to justify the first place it holds in the curriculum. Learning the skill of decoding written communication is important, but not so important for the development of mental ability as the pupil's analysis of his own experience, and his drawing of correct inferences from this analysis. How often does one observe curriculum activities which guide this kind of learning?

The likelihood that the school will be able to discover units of discussion and study which will develop a wider range of mental problem-solving activities in pupils is greatly reduced, furthermore, by the practice of so-called homogeneous grouping. Nearly all such segregation of pupils into "fast" and "slow" groups is based upon their reading scores or intelligence-test scores. These scores in turn, as well as ratings by teachers, are strongly related to the social-class culture of the pupil. The result of this circular process of evaluating mental ability and achievement is that homogeneous grouping strengthens the social-class discrimination within the school, and maintains the narrow academic stereotyping of the curriculum.

Homogeneous grouping really sets up different social and cultural groups within the school, and thus establishes different learning environments. Most middle-class pupils are placed in the "faster" groups, while most lower-class pupils are placed in the "slower" groups. Because selection is based upon reading scores and/or intelligence-test scores, many abilities and problem-solving activities are not considered. The result is that most of the middle-class group, and most of the lower-class group lose something. Segregated from each other, unable therefore either to stimulate or to imitate each other, each group fails to learn well those problem-solving activities and insights in which the other group excels. Both groups lose more than they gain.

This field needs sound experimental research, in which the following safeguards must be taken: (1) The factor of homogeneous or heterogeneous grouping as an aid to learning must be measured apart from either the factor of the techniques of the teacher or the factor of the personality of the teacher. Thus, teachers in each experimental group must use the same method, have the same type of personality, and be equally driven to succeed. (2) Under no circumstances should teachers' or administrators' ratings of the relative "success" of these two methods of grouping be accepted as of any use in measuring the results. Most teachers prefer homogeneous grouping, because by rotation of classes each teacher receives a chance to teach a "fast" and "successful" group, and thus gets both a sense of achievement and the approval of the principal. Likewise, the middle-class work-habits of the "fast" group tend to prejudice the teachers in their favor. (3) The mental problems used in the experiment should include some from daily experiences common to all socio-economic groups; the problems should not be limited to the routine scholastic exercises used on achievement tests. (4) The results should be measured objectively, and orally, so that reading will not be a factor in every test of attainment taken by each experimental group, but only in the specific test of reading.

All our findings point to the same conclusion: The greatest need of education is for intensive research to discover the best curricula for developing children's basic mental activities; such activities, that is, as the analysis and organization of observed experiences, the drawing of inferences, the development of inventiveness. The present curricula are stereotyped and arbitrary selections from a narrow area of middle-class culture. Academic culture is one of the most conservative and ritualized aspects of human culture. Its formalization, its lack of functional connection with the daily problems of life, has given a bloodless, fossilized character to the classroom which all of us recognize. For over a generation, no basically new types of mental problems have been added to intelligence tests. For untold generations, we have been unable to think of anything to put into the curriculum which will be more helpful in guiding the basic mental development of children than vocabulary-building, reading, spelling, and routine arithmetical memorizing. Even as we read this, many of us will think it absurd to suppose that reading and arithmetic are not the best activities for teaching children to solve mental problems.

Let us ask ourselves this simple question, however, What proportion of the *basic mental problems* met by children (and by adults for that matter) in their daily life can be solved by having a large standard vocabulary, or skill in reading, or skill in arithmetical processes? Do these trainings teach a human being correct habits of making inferences or of gaining insight about most of the difficult mental problems which he faces? Does one observe in more than one out of twenty public-school classrooms any activities which help children to learn how to reason, to analyze, to invent; or does one observe instead activities of memorizing, of learning symbols, of reading or listening to predigested solutions by other people, and of paraphrasing ("telling the meaning") of other people's words? Most observers would find the latter.

Indeed, the most important inference to be made from the studies briefly reported in this paper, dealing with the socialization and mental activities of children, is that most of our efforts to revise the curricula of the public schools have been superficial. To make the schools a place where children may learn to analyze facts, to reason from them, to develop insight and inventiveness, we need far more than a systematic method for teaching words or numbers. Those attempts, moreover, which start with sweeping generalizations about reality, or community experiences, and other such goals all start at the wrong end of the learning sequence.

We need to start with simple situations, drawn from the daily life of the pupil. As yet, we do not know what these situations are. We do not know how to use them to guide the drawing of inferences, the processes of reasoning. All we know is that they must be very explicit and short sequences of acts, so that the learner may actually infer the relationship between specific events. The situations must also be chosen from the common life of all the pupils, so that the problems will motivate all social classes. Finally, these curriculum-experiences must be intensive, not vague and general; they must be at the molecular level of analysis, so that the child may carry a problem through all the detailed steps to the solution. Yet they will be simple and realistic problems.

Those who revise the curriculum in this intensive way will change the whole course of human education in our society.

In this chapter we have reviewed the nature of social disorganization in the three institutions of primary socialization. Each institution, through community disintegration, experiences a collapse of group solidarity, of loss of control over its members, and of *anomie*. In two cases disorganization was related to social class and, in the third, to secularization. In all cases, these were merely indicative of the possible range of problems encountered by these three institutions. In all cases, too, disorganization as experienced by the family, church, and school, though not directly caused in every instance by urbanization, is accelerated by the ever-changing environment of the urban community.

Notes

1. See E. A. Ross, *Social Control*, New York: The Macmillan Company, 1901; Charles Cooley, *Social Organization, Two Major Works of Charles H. Cooley*, Glencoe, Ill.: The Free Press, 1956, and Cooley's *The Social Process*, New York: Scribner's Sons, 1918. Overtones of sociological romanticism can be found in a recent work such as that by David Riesman and his associates. See, *The Lonely Crowd*, New York: Anchor Books, 1950.
2. Cf., Don Martindale, "Social Disorganization: The Conflict of Normative and Empirical Approaches," *Modern Sociological Theory in Continuity and Change*, ed. Howard Becker and Alvin Boskoff, New York: Dryden Press, 1957, p. 359.
3. George Homans, *The Human Group*, New York: Harcourt, Brace and Company, 1950, pp. 336 ff. For a statement of the applicability of Homans' work to the study of social disorganization see Martindale, *op. cit.*, pp. 362 f.
4. Cf., Melvin Seeman, "On the Meaning of Alienation," *American Sociological Review*, vol. 24, December 1959, pp. 787 ff. For the classic statement of *anomie* see Emile Durkheim, *The Division of Labor in Society*, ed. G. Simpson, Glencoe, Ill.: The Free Press, 1947, pp. 353 ff. For a theory of individual adaptations to *anomie* see Robert K. Merton, *Social Theory and Social Structure*, Glencoe, Ill.: The Free Press, 1957, rev., pp. 139 ff.
5. Seeman, *op. cit.*, p. 788.
6. For definitions of various types of subcultures see Richard T. La Piere, *A Theory of Social Control*, New York: McGraw-Hill Book Company, 1954, pp. 34 ff. See also James S. Colemen, *The Adolescent Society*, New York: The Free Press of Glencoe, 1961.
7. *The Presentation of the Self in Everyday Life*, New York: Anchor Books, 1959, p. 159.
8. *Ibid.*, Chapter VI. See, also, Karen Horney, *Neurosis and Human Growth*, New York: W. W. Norton, 1950.
9. Hollingshead's system is similar to that of W. Lloyd Warner. See Warner, *Social Class in America*, New York: Harper Torchbooks, 1961.

10. For a survey of the many problem areas in religion see *The Annals of the American Academy of Political and Social Sciences*, vol. 332, November, 1960.
11. Cf. Robert and Helen Lynd, *Middletown in Transition*, New York: Harcourt, Brace and Company, 1937, pp. 416–417.
12. *Ibid.*, p. 307.
13. Cf., C. Wayne Gordon and Nicholas Babchuk "A Typology of Voluntary Associations," *American Sociological Review*, Vol. 24, February 1959, pp. 24–25.
14. Walter Goldschmidt, "Class Denominationalism in Rural California Churches," *American Journal of Sociology*, Vol. 49, January 1944, pp. 348–355; and Thomas Ford Hoult, "Economic Class Consciousness in American Protestantism," *American Sociological Review*, Vol. 15, February 1950, pp. 97–100.
15. August Hollingshead, *Elmtown's Youth*. New York: John Wiley and Sons, 1949, p. 68.
16. *Ibid.*, p. 153.
17. Cf., Robert Lynd, *Knowledge for What?*, Princeton, Princeton University Press, 1939; and George Lundberg, *Can Science Save Us?*, New York: Longmans, Green, 1947.
18. H. Otto Dahlke, *Values in Culture and Classroom*, New York: Harper and Brothers, 1958, p. 25.
19. *Ibid.*
20. Although the data are now outdated, a clear discussion of segregation in education may be found in Arnold Rose, *The Negro in American Life*, New York: Harper and Brothers, 1948, pp. 116 ff.
21. Dahlke, *op. cit.*, Table 4, p. 31.
22. Rose, *op. cit.*, p. 117.
23. Dahlke, *op. cit.*, Table 4.
24. *Ibid.*
25. *Ibid.*, pp. 328–330.
26. Other factors such as color, nationality, and religion also influence interactional patterns in the high school. *Ibid.*, pp. 336 ff.
27. *Middletown*, New York: Harcourt, Brace and Company. 1929, pp. 211 ff.
28. *Middletown in Transition*, p. 171.
29. Hollingshead, *Elmtown's Youth*, p. 201.
30. *Ibid.*, pp. 198 ff.
31. W. Lloyd Warner and Associates, *Democracy in Jonesville*, New York: Harper and Brothers, 1949, Table 14, p. 206.
32. *Ibid.*, p. 208.
33. Dahlke, *op. cit.*, pp. 349–351.

Selected Readings

Berg, Irwin, and B. M. Bass, eds. *Conformity and Deviation*, New York: Harper and Bros., 1961.
Blanshard, Paul. *American Freedom and Catholic Power*. Boston: Beacon Press, 1949.
*Dollard, John. *Caste and Class in a Southern Town*. New York: Anchor Book, 1959.
Locke, Harvey. *Predicting Adjustment in Marriage*, New York: Henry Holt, 1951.
Merton, Robert K., and Robert Nisbet. *Contemporary Social Problems*. New York; Harcourt, Brace and Company, 1961.

*McGee, Reece. *Social Disorganization in America*. San Francisco: Chandler Publishing Company, 1961.

Thayer, V. T. *The Attack Upon the American Secular School*. Boston: Beacon Press, 1951.

Warner, W. Lloyd, *et al*. *Who Shall Be Educated?* New York: Harper and Bros., 1944.

Young, Michael and Peter Willmott. *Family and Kinship in East London*. Glencoe, Ill.: The Fress Press, 1957.

* Paperback edition.

Part Four
Institutions of Transition

In Part Three we surveyed the key agencies that socialize the child. As the child leaves home, both literally and figuratively, and passes to maturity, he moves through one or more of several possible institutions that aid his transition from child to man. This passage is not easy in America. The period of transition is protracted and the definition of adulthood is vague in all but the legal sense.

Among the transitional agencies awaiting the adolescent are the first job, early marriage, college, and the military establishment. These institutions, of course, perform other functions, but their role in the continuing socialization process needs explanation because its significance is often obscured by the more central services of these institutions.

If the child may be thought of as a passive recipient of the forces in his environment, and the adult as actively engaged in continuous relationships with the institutions of his society, then the period between— the transitional period—is one of learning to shift from receiving to giving. From the confusion of adolescence where this change begins, the individual enters an even more confusing period between adolescence and manhood. The term of confinement is uncertain, and the way out is beyond the power of the individual to determine. His status as an adult depends on the acceptance by others of his new role.

A further complication affecting this transition is the increasing complexity of socialization as an individual matures. The personality structure is fixed early in life and personality develops in a cumulative manner. Therefore, successive experiences must be tested against the growing body of culture assimilated by the individual. In a society such as ours the chances for conflict and the resistance to its settlement increase as the individual grows older.

An institution has its own ends to serve. The kinds of behavior it seeks to obtain may or may not harmonize with the basic personality of the recipient of socialization or with other institutions. There is always some role strain created by the various behaviors which institutions demand of individuals, but it is possible to reach a point beyond which the threat to the nature of the personality and the integrity of the institution becomes serious. If the institutional roles of enough members of society become incompatible, social disorganization follows. In a period of rapid technological advance and cultural lag there is constant danger of this occurring. Attention must then be given to finding means for tightening institutional structures and making the institutional system compatible.

Rather than disorganization, however, it is the cohesiveness of American society which is remarkable. In the face of tremendous strains we have maintained political, economic, and social stability. Primary responsibility for this achievement rests with the effectiveness of the socialization process all along the line. Yet particularly notable is the fact that there is so little alienation of future adult members of society from the culture in the critical transitional period between adolescence and manhood. By and large the efforts of the business manager, the spouse, the college teacher, and the military cadre to initiate the adolescent into the particular institution have been successful because the requirements of the institution are compatible enough with the individual's background to prevent disorder. Institutions, through interlocking memberships and intertwined interests, must support each other and establish common standards in what William Graham Sumner has called the "strain of consistency."

This part consists of a single chapter which is concerned with the role played by the military establishment in the transitional stage of socialization.

Chapter 13

The Military
as an Institution of Transition

Taken together, the armed forces of America form an institution primarily concerned with national security. A corollary function, which has grown in importance with the military establishment itself, is the transformation of civilian to soldier. For millions of young people, military service offers these possibilities: a substitute for the security of the home, and an opportunity to experiment in a relatively controlled and impersonal adult environment with independence and maturity. Through reinforcing the adolescent's groping toward maturity by requiring responsibility, as well as granting him freedom, the military institution acts as a transitional agency of socialization.

Despite the development of modern weapons that reduce the need for large numbers while demanding greater skills and training, the likelihood is that the size of troops to man conventional weapons will not diminish appreciably in the near future.[1] Young people will continue to plan a part of their youth around the demands of the nation as presented in the foreword of a booklet used for counseling high school students:

> Whether our great nation be in a state of crisis or
> whether it be at peace with the world, young people
> should make carefully formulated plans for themselves.
> One cannot make plans for himself isolated from his
> fellowmen, or from his country or the world. Therefore
> when young people plan constructively for a worthwhile
> life, they not only plan for themselves but for our
> nation as well.[2]

Over 20 years of compulsory military service has left its mark on the American people. "Overt opposition to the system, even political criticism of its injustices, is virtually absent." [3]

Approximately one million teen-agers are currently in the armed forces,[4] and perhaps another million on active duty have just passed the teen

277

years. Almost 20 million servicemen have been returned to civilian life since 1945. Did the experience change them? Will it change those still to be called? This chapter tries to piece together bits of research and opinion to explain the process and result of military socialization.

RECRUITMENT

Quotas of men are assigned to recruiting offices and selective service boards depending on manpower needs and local recruiting success. Impressment, the bogey of the War of 1812, is no longer a recruiting technique, yet the quotas must be filled. The military draft was introduced in the United States during the Civil War but with moderate success. The New York "Draft Riots" of 1863 indicated that this method of recruiting was looked upon with as much distaste as impressment. Two World Wars, however, and the Korean Police Action have brought a degree of acceptance of compulsory military service.

The demands of an advancing war technology have created a major shift in recruitment techniques. Although Selective Service continues to function in many locales, the specialized armed services now employ great effort in appealing to men with the greatest potential of existing skills. Emphasis is also placed on specific career interest, as the technical complexity of many military occupations makes high turnover of personnel costly and inefficient. In slick, eye-catching brochures, there is even talk of a "new Army." Addressing the parent, one of these says. "It's the kind of Army *you* never knew. . . ." [5]

In keeping with today's practical approach to living, the armed forces make a special appeal to the recruit in terms of long-range benefits. "Step into a future . . . skilled by top training." [6] Or in the case of assignments not readily transferable to civilian life, there is still the older appeal: "You're a man of the world as a combat soldier!" [7] But the main emphasis of the military establishment is not directed toward staffing for combat, but rather for supporting roles.[8] Today's army, under certain conditions, will guarantee in writing that the recruit will receive training in the Army Graduate Specialists' Program, in one of 107 technical courses, and that most of them "are related to comparable jobs in civilian life." [9] Moreover, "most employers give preference to young men who have completed their military obligation." [10] The army's interest in training civilian technicians is, of course, merely a means to an end; by offering inducements for longer enlistments and benefits for re-enlistment, the Army hopes to retain a high percentage of these technicians as career soldiers.

Recruiting teams appear at high school and college campuses with increasing regularity to acquaint students with their programs. Special visits to the home by recruiting officers are often arranged. The high school graduate has an especially difficult decision to make if he is college bound. Should he ask for educational deferment and risk immediate draft with no option should he fall below certain academic standards, or should he enlist now to take advantage of enlistment options but risk not getting into the college of his choice? The high school graduate with no further educational plans faces a similar decision; in his case his military (draft) status may be very important to his employment. Marriage plans are also influenced by impending military service—especially since a recent change in Selective Service exempts married men.

Military programs offered to college students tend to be more attractive because the college student is the potential officer candidate. Despite the greater lures offered the college student, a Cornell University study found that most of them are not impressed and tend to be essentially negative toward their military service obligations. "The present generation of college men faces, along with other young men, the prospect of being called upon to serve in this country's armed forces. Such a compulsory service during peacetime is a new development in the military policy of the United States. It will call for readjustment of the normal transition from teen-ager to young adult, involving an interruption of vocational plans and requiring the acceptance of a period of personal sacrifice." [11] It should be pointed out again, however, that despite the inconvenience and the actual hardship frequently involved in military service, the young American seems to accept it in a dutiful way— "without complaint but without enthusiasm." [12]

THE MILITARY EXPERIENCE: BASIC TRAINING
FOR THE ENLISTED MAN

Military service demands that the inductee effect a sudden and sharp break with civilian life. He is severed, literally and symbolically, from his past, literally by the fact that basic military training takes place in complete isolation from the civilian world, and symbolically by the GI haircut, the extensive inoculation program, and the general introduction to the rigid caste system of the Army. Active duty is deliberately planned to be a dramatically different world to the inductee, based on the assumption that a quick and decisive break with civilian life is the most effective means of facilitating socialization into the military community.[13]

The military establishment, although a different kind of life, takes special pains in the assimilation of new members. "Not only must the

new recruit . . . learn a complex of technical skills. He is also expected
to master an elaborate code of social behavior and professional honor,
since membership in the military means participation in an organizational community which regulates behavior both on and off the 'job.' " [14]
The inductee's basic reluctance to do so may stem in part from the
female-dominated contemporary American family. "These 'matriarchal'
tendencies, to the extent that they exist, extend maternal concern and
care toward over-protection. The psychodynamics of its results are complex, but among the most important effects is the inflation of the
growing child's ego, to the extent that he may always be reluctant to
surrender it to any group or interest not for his own direct personal
benefit, or be placed in a subordinate position. This is directly pertinent
to the egocentric orientation of the American. It further clarifies the
relatively low value placed on status, power, authority, and discipline.
They are not only dominated by self-value, but the coercion through
love in the mother-dominated family does not prepare the individual for
strict obedience or leave him with an attitude of over-exaggeration of
authority's power." [15] It is probably American self-interest that eventually causes the individual to subordinate certain values when the state
requires him to serve a term in the service. Thus, a paradoxical situation
is reconciled and an effective military establishment is possible.

The success of adjustment to military life depends on the basic personality of the recruit, his predisposition to military service, and his
comparison of military with civilian experiences. "Since the martial
values are largely feudal virtues, and since Army resentments are conditioned by the expectations with which the soldier starts and his sense of
his worth as an individual, it is the better educated men from urban and
industrial areas for whom the Army experience becomes an ordeal." [16]
On the other hand, many men "find a home in the Army." In the words
of the noted comedian, Buddy Hackett: "I thought my ma was a good
cook until I got drafted!" The often quoted term of derision among
servicemen during the Second World War, "You never had it so good,"
contains considerable truth, especially for recruits of deprived origin.
"(The) soldier who fared best in Army life was likely to be a boy with
little education, coming from a farm or a small town." [17]

The recruit whose talents are solely in the intellectual field has a
difficult time adjusting to the heavy masculine roles of basic training.
The cadre's insistence on toughness, ruggedness, and stamina may be too
demanding on the recruit and his only recourse may be to what David
Schneider calls the "sick role" which is an attempt at exemption from
the masculine demands of army life.[18] Initially he receives sympathy,

but if his attitude persists, he is soon left out of the group and finally isolated. The threat of isolation, more implicit than explicit, usually is sufficient to cause the "sick role" to be relinquished, perhaps through some form of overcompensation, such as driving oneself at high psychological cost to master masculine performance. Self-interest moves him.

The importance of self-interest is recognized by the cadres in the services today and is capitalized on in the assimilation process. "At the most personal level the recruit faces a loss of privacy and exposure to a pervasive set of controls (and) the training cadres—officers and enlisted men—must establish their competence and their interest in their men, for they cannot rely merely on their ultimate military authority and sanctions." [19] The Air Force has studied its assimilation problems [20] and found that perceptions of the Air Force and self-perception change during training. In the beginning the men look to their cadres almost exclusively for the "rules of the game." But as the game proceeds, as the fledglings begin to think of themselves as airmen, they make up unofficial "rules," and seek shortcuts. The more alert soon discover some things that are never checked, even though checking is officially required, and there are other things that do not have to be done, so long as the appearance of doing them is maintained. To the trainees it sometimes seems as though the Air Force *expects* them to indulge in certain "patterned evasions," and that the men who discover the shortcuts need not feel any guilt.

Shortcuts are learned primarily from peers, rather than superiors; thus, as in civilian life, an important part of socialization is informal. The men who are most sensitive to suggestion and opportunity are able to separate the requirements likely to be tested, and so avoid the displeasures of authority in the form of crackdowns. Others, who appear to have more rigid personalities, never seem to be able to master the situation. They are unable to sense subtle differences between situations and are more likely to incur the displeasure of both the Air Force and their peers. If these men do not soon conform, their psychological isolation leads to social isolation, causing them to be weeded out as misfits through transfer, reassignment, or, in gross cases, discharge from the service.[21]

The enlisted man is the inferior in the military caste system. In most instances he is under the complete domination of his superiors. "In this uncomfortable position he has only two means for protecting himself: (1) his peer group, the efficacy of which depends in large part upon specific and external factors over which he has no control; and (2) his knowledge of, and consequent ability to predict and adapt to, the behavior of his superiors." [22]

This section should make it clear that the typical recruit, often removed from the protective and familiar environment of family and friends for the first time, must face a hostile world and learn to cope with it.

Military socialization is usually successful, although the reason is not always clear. The chance to "become a man" in an impersonal environment may be a powerful motivator. Note that for many young men this is the first opportunity to act as an equal among older men, where actions speak louder than age. The challenge from the Marine drill instructor to "Do it better than I can" arouses a combination of fear, hatred, and admiration and is certainly a large part of the Marine Corps' success in turning out an identifiable product.

**THE MILITARY EXPERIENCE: BASIC TRAINING
FOR THE CAREER OFFICER**

In the cold war the preponderance of billets for commissioned officers are filled by career soldiers. The professional soldier receives indoctrination similar to the citizen-soldier, but because of his superior position and cadre role, the career officer's training is more extensive and intense. The military academy offers the social scientist much promise for study of institutionalized behavior. The Coast Guard Academy at New London, Connecticut, is the locale of the following study by S. M. Dornbusch. Some useful insights into military socialization may be gained from it.

*
The function of a military academy is to make officers out of civilians or enlisted men. The objective is accomplished by a two-fold process of transmitting technical knowledge and of instilling in the candidates an outlook considered appropriate for members of the profession. This paper is concerned with the latter of these processes, the assimilating function of the military academy. Assimilation is viewed as "a process of interpenetration and fusion in which persons and groups acquire the memories, sentiments, and attitudes of other persons and groups, and, by sharing their experience and history, are incorporated with them in a common cultural life. . . . The unity thus achieved is not necessarily or even normally like-mindedness; it is rather a unity of experience and of orientation, out of which may develop a

* S. M. Dornbusch, "The Military Academy as an Assimilating Institution," *Social Forces*, 33:4, May 1955, pp. 316–321. Reprinted by permission of the University of North Carolina Press.

community of purpose and action."

Data for this study consist almost entirely of retrospective material, based on ten months spent as a cadet at the United States Coast Guard Academy. The selective nature of memory obviously may introduce serious deficiencies in the present formulation. Unfortunately, it is unlikely that more objective evidence on life within the Academy will be forthcoming. Cadets cannot keep diaries, are formally forbidden to utter a word of criticism of the Academy to an outsider, and are informally limited in the matters which are to be discussed in letters or conversations. The lack of objective data is regrettable, but the process of assimilation is present here in an extreme form. Insight into this process can better be developed by the study of such an explicit, overt case of assimilation.

The Coast Guard Academy, like West Point and Annapolis, provides four years of training for a career as a regular officer. Unlike the other service academies, however, its cadet corps is small, seldom exceeding 350 cadets. This disparity in size probably produces comparable differences in the methods of informal social control. Therefore, all the findings reported here may not be applicable to the other academies. It is believed, however, that many of the mechanisms through which this military academy fulfills its assimilating function will be found in a wide variety of social institutions.

The new cadet, or "swab," is the lowest of the low. The assignment of low status is useful in producing a correspondingly high evaluation of successfully completing the steps in an Academy career and requires that there be a loss of identity in terms of pre-existing statuses. This clean break with the past must be achieved in a relatively short period. For two months, therefore, the swab is not allowed to leave the base or to engage in social intercourse with noncadets. This complete isolation helps to produce a unified group of swabs, rather than a heterogeneous collection of persons of high and low status. Uniforms are issued on the first day, and discussions of wealth and family background are taboo. Although the pay of the cadet is very low, he is not permitted to receive money from home. The role of the cadet must supersede other roles the individual has been accustomed to play. There are few clues left which will reveal social status in the outside world.

It is clear that the existence of minority-group status on the part of some cadets would tend to break down this desired equality. The sole minority group present was the Jews, who, with a few exceptions, had been informally excluded before 1944. At that time 18 Jews were admitted in a class of 162. Their status as Jews made them objects of scrutiny by the upper classmen, so that their violations of rules were more often noted. Except for this "spotlight," however, the Jews reported no discrimination against them—they, too, were treated as swabs.

There are two organized structures of rules which regulate the cadet's behavior. The first of these is the body of regulations of the Academy, considered by the public to be the primary source of control. These regulations are similar to the code of ethics of any profession. They serve in part as propaganda to influence outsiders. An additional function is to provide negative sanctions which are applied to violations of the second set of expectations, the informal rules. Offenses against the informal rules are merely labeled as breaches of the formal code, and the appropriate punishment according to the regulations is then imposed. This punitive system conceals the existence of the informal set of controls.

The informal traditions of the Academy are more functionally related to the existing set of circumstances than are the regulations, for although these traditions are fairly rigid, they are more easily forgotten or changed than are the formal regulations. Unlike other informal codes, the Academy code of traditions is in part written, appearing in the manual for entering cadets.

In case of conflict between the regulations and tradition, the regulations are superseded. For example, it is against the regulations to have candy in one's room. A first classman orders a swab to bring him candy. Caught en route by an officer, the swab offers no excuse and is given 15 demerits. First classmen are then informally told by the classmate involved that they are to withhold demerits for this swab until he has been excused for offenses totaling 15 demerits. Experience at an Academy teaches future officers that regulations are not considered of paramount importance when they conflict with informal codes—a principle noted by other observers.

Sometimes situations arise in which the application of either form of control is circumvented by the commanding officer. The following case is an example. Cadets cannot drink, cannot smoke in public, can never go above the first floor in a hotel. It would seem quite clear, therefore, that the possessor of a venereal disease would be summarily dismissed. Cadets at the Academy believed that two upper-class cadets had contracted a venereal disease, were cured, and given no punishment. One of the cadets was an outstanding athlete, brilliant student, and popular classmate. Cadets were told that a direct appeal by the commanding officer to the Commandant of the Coast Guard resulted in the decision to hush up the entire affair, with the second cadet getting the same treatment as his more popular colleague. The event indicated the possibility of individualization of treatment when rules are violated by officers.

The control system operated through the class hierarchy. The first class, consisting of cadets in their third or fourth year at the Academy, are only nominally under the control of the officers of the Academy. Only one or two officers attempt to check on the activities of the first classmen, who are able to break most of the minor regulations with impunity. The first class is given almost complete control over the rest of the cadet corps. Informally, certain leading cadets are even called in to advise the officers on important disciplinary matters. There are one or two classes between the first classmen and the swabs, depending on the existence of a three- or four-year course. These middle classes haze the swabs. Hazing is forbidden by the regulations, but the practice is a hallowed tradition of the Academy. The first class demands that this hazing take place, and, since they have the power to give demerits, all members of the middle classes are compelled to haze the new cadets.

As a consequence of undergoing this very unpleasant experience together, the swab class develops remarkable unity. For example, if a cadet cannot answer an oral question addressed to him by his teacher, no other member of his class will answer. All reply, "I can't say, sir," leaving the teacher without a clue to the state of knowledge of this student compared to the rest of the class. This group cohesion persists throughout the Academy period, with first classmen refusing to give demerits to their classmates unless an officer directly orders them to do so.

The honor system, demanding that offenses by classmates be reported, is not part of the Coast Guard Academy tradition. It seems probable that the honor system, if enforced, would tend to break down the social solidarity which the hazing develops within each class.

The basis for interclass solidarity, the development of group feeling on the part of the entire cadet corps, is not so obvious. It occurs through informal contacts between the upper classmen and swabs, a type of fraternization which occurs despite the fact it traditionally is discouraged. The men who haze the swab and order him hazed live in the same wing of the dormitory that he does. Coming from an outside world which disapproves of authoritarian punishment and aggressiveness, they are ashamed of their behavior. They are eager to convince the swab that they are good fellows. They visit his room to explain why they are being so harsh this week or to tell of a mistake he is making. Close friendships sometimes arise through such behavior. These friendships must be concealed. One first classman often ordered his room cleaned by the writer as a "punishment," then settled down for an uninterrupted chat. Such informal contacts serve to unite the classes and spread a "we-feeling" through the Academy.

In addition, the knowledge of common interests and a common destiny serves as a unifying force that binds together all Academy graduates. This is expressed in the identification of the interest of the individual with the interest of the Coast Guard. A large appropriation or an increase in the size of the Coast Guard will speed the rate of promotion for all, whether ensign or captain. A winning football team at the Academy may familiarize more civilians with the name of their common alma mater. Good publicity for the Coast Guard raises the status of the Coast Guard officer.

The Coast Guard regulars are united in their disdain for the reserves. There are few reserve officers during peacetime, but in wartime the reserve officers soon outnumber the regulars. The reserves do not achieve the higher ranks, but they are a threat to the cadets and recent graduates of the Academy. The reserves receive in a few months the rank that the regulars reach only after four grueling years. The Academy men therefore protectively stigmatize the reserves as incompetents. If a cadet falters on the parade ground, he is told, "You're marching like a reserve." Swabs are told to square their shoulders while on liberty, "or else how will people know you are not a reserve?" Myths spring up—stories of reserve commanders who must call on regular ensigns for advice. The net effect is reassurance that although the interlopers may have the same rank, they do not have equal status.

Another out-group is constituted by the enlisted men, who are considered to be of inferior ability and eager for leadership. Segregation of cadets and enlisted men enables this view to be propagated. Moreover, such segregation helps to keep associations within higher status social groups. There is only one leak in this insulating dike. The pharmacist mates at sick bay have direct contact with the cadets, and are the only enlisted personnel whom cadets meet on an equal basis. The pharmacist mates take pleasure in reviling the Academy, labeling it "the p——k factory." Some of the cadets without military experience are puzzled by such an attitude, which is inconsistent with their acquired respect for the Academy.

The military services provide an excellent example of a bureaucratic structure. The emphasis is upon the office with its sets of rights and duties, rather than on the man. It is a system of rules with little regard for the individual case. The method of promotion within the Coast Guard perfectly illustrates this bureaucratic character. Unlike the Army or Navy, promotions in the Coast Guard up to the rank of lieutenant-commander do not even depend on the evaluation of superior officers. Promotion comes solely according to seniority, which is based on class standing at the Academy. The 50th man in the 1947 class will be lieutenant-commander before the 51st man, and the latter will be promoted before the 1st man in the 1948 class.

The hazing system contributes directly to acceptance of the bureaucratic structure of the Coast Guard, for the system is always viewed by its participants as not involving the personal character of the swab or upper classman. One is not being hazed because the upper classman is a sadist, but because one is at the time in a junior status. Those who haze do not pretend to be superior to those who are being hazed. Since some of those who haze you will also try to teach you how to stay out of trouble, it becomes impossible to attribute evil characteristics to those who injure you. The swab knows he will have his turn at hazing others. At most, individual idiosyncrasies will just affect the type of hazing done.

This emphasis on the relativity of status is explicitly made on the traditional Gizmo Day, on which the swabs and their hazers reverse roles. The swabs-for-a-day take their licking without flinching and do not seek revenge later, for they are aware that they are under the surveillance of the first classmen. After the saturnalia, the swabs are increasingly conscious of their inability to blame particular persons for their troubles.

Upper classmen show the same resentment against the stringent restrictions upon their lives, and the manner in which they express themselves indicates a feeling of being ruled by impersonal forces. They say, "You can't buck the System." As one writer puts it, "The best attitude the new cadet can have is one of unquestioning acceptance of tradition and custom."

There is a complete absence of charismatic veneration of the Coast Guard heroes of the past and present. Stirring events are recalled, not as examples of the genius of a particular leader, but as part of the history of the great organization which they will serve. A captain is a cadet thirty years older and wiser. Such views prepare these men for their roles in the bureaucracy.

A bureaucratic structure requires a stable set of mutual expectations among the occupants of offices. The Academy develops this ability to view the behavior of others in terms of a pre-ordained set of standards. In addition to preparing the cadet for later service as an officer, the predictability of the behavior of his fellows enables the cadet to achieve a high degree of internal stability. Although he engages in a continual bustle of activity, he always knows his place in the system and the degree to which he is fulfilling the expectations of his role.

Sharing common symbols and objects, the cadets interact with an ease of communication seldom found in everyday life. The cadet is told what is right and wrong, and, if he disagrees, there are few opportunities to translate mental reservations into action. The "generalized other" speaks with a unitary voice which is uncommon in modern societies. To illustrate, an upper classman ordered a swab to pick up some pieces of paper on the floor of a washroom. The latter refused and walked away. There were no repercussions. The swab knew that, if he refused, the upper classman would be startled by the choice of such an unconventional way of getting expelled from the Academy. Wondering what was happening, the upper classman would re-define his own behavior, seeing it as an attack on the high status of the cadet. Picking up litter in a washroom is "dirty work," fit only for enlisted men. The swab was sure that the upper classman shared this common universe of discourse and never considered the possibility that he would not agree on the definition of the situation.

Interaction with classmates can proceed on a level of confidence that only intimate friends achieve in the outside world. These men are in a union of sympathy, sharing the same troubles, never confiding secrets to upper classmen, never criticizing one another to outsiders. Each is close to only a few but is friendly with most of the men in his class.

When interacting with an upper classman in private, a different orientation is useful. The swab does not guess the reason why he is being addressed, but instead assumes a formal air of deference. If the upper classman says, "Aw cut it out," the swab relaxes. In this manner the role of the upper classman is explicitly denoted in each situation.

In addition to providing predictability of the behavior of others, the Academy provides a second set of satisfactions in the self-process. An increase in the cadet's self-esteem develops in conjunction with identification in his new role. Told that they are members of an elite group respected by the community, most cadets begin to feel at ease in a superordinate role. One may be a low-ranking cadet, but cadets as a group have high status. When cadets visit home for the first time, there is a conflict between the lofty role that they wish to play and the role to which their parents are accustomed. Upon return to the Academy, much conversation is concerned with the way things at home have changed.

This feeling of superiority helps to develop self-confidence in those cadets who previously had a low evaluation of themselves. It directly enters into relationships with girls, with whom many boys lack self-confidence. It soon becomes apparent that any cadet can get a date whenever he wishes, and he even begins to feel that he is a good "catch." The cadet's conception of himself is directly influenced by this new way of viewing the behavior of himself and others. As one cadet put it, "I used to be shy. Now I'm reserved."

A desire for vertical social mobility on the part of many cadets serves as one means of legitimizing the traditional practices of the Academy. The cadets are told that they will be members of the social elite during the later stages of their career. The obstacles that they meet at the Academy are then viewed as the usual barriers to social mobility in the United States, a challenge to be surmounted.

Various practices at the Academy reinforce the cadets' feeling that they are learning how to enter the upper classes. There is a strong emphasis on etiquette, from calling cards to table manners. The Tactics Officer has been known to give long lectures on such topics as the manner of drinking soup from an almost empty bowl. The cadet must submit for approval the name of the girl he intends to take to the monthly formal dance. Girls attending the upper-class college in the vicinity are automatically acceptable, but some cadets claim that their dates have been rejected because they are in a low status occupation such as waitress.

Another Academy tradition actively, though informally, encourages contact with higher status girls. After the swabs have been completely isolated for two months, they are invited to a dance at which all the girls are relatives or friends of Coast Guard officers. A week later the girls at the nearby college have a dance for the swabs. The next week end finds the swab compelled to invite an acceptable girl to a formal reception. He must necessarily choose from the only girls in the area whom he knows, those that he met during the recent hours of social intercourse.

In addition to the social mobility theme which views the rigors of Academy life as obstacles to upward mobility, there is a more open method of justifying traditionally legitimated ways of doing things. The phrase, "separating the men from the boys" is used to meet objections to practices which seem inefficient or foolish. Traditional standards are thus redefined as further tests of ability to take punishment. Harsh practices are defended as methods by which the insincere, incompetent, or undisciplined cadets are weeded out. Cadets who rebel and resign are merely showing lack of character.

Almost all cadets accept to some extent this traditional view of resignations as admissions of defeat. Of the 162 entering cadets in 1944, only 52 graduated in 1948. Most of the 110 resignations were entirely voluntary without pressure from the Academy authorities. Most of these resignations came at a time when the hazing was comparatively moderate. Cadets who wish to resign do not leave at a time when the hazing might be considered the cause of their departure. One cadet's history illustrates this desire to have the resignation appear completely voluntary. Asked to resign because of his lack of physical coordination, he spent an entire year building up his physique, returned to the Academy, finished his swab year, and then joyously quit. "It took me three years, but I showed them."

Every cadet who voluntarily resigns is a threat to the morale of the cadet corps, since he has rejected the values of the Academy. Although cadets have enlisted for seven years and could theoretically be forced to remain at the Academy, the usual procedure is to isolate them from the swabs and rush acceptance of their resignation. During the period before the acceptance is final, the cadets who have resigned are freed from the usual duties of their classmates, which action effectively isolates them from cadets who might be affected by their contagious disenchantment.

Everett C. Hughes has developed the concept of "reality shock," the sudden realization of the disparity between the way a job is envisaged before beginning work and the actual work situation. In the course of its 75-year history the Coast Guard Academy has wittingly or unwittingly developed certain measures to lessen reality shock in the new ensign. The first classmen, soon to be officers, are aided in lessening the conflict between the internalized rules of the Academy world and the standards for officer conduct.

On a formal level the first classmen are often reminded that they are about to experience a relative decline in status. On their first ship they will be given the most disagreeable duties. The first classmen accept this and joke about how their attitudes will change under a harsh captain. On a more concrete level, first classmen are given week-end leaves during the last six months of their stay at the Academy. These leaves allow them to escape from the restrictive atmosphere of the nearby area. It is believed wise to let them engage in orgiastic behavior while still cadets, rather than suddenly release all controls upon graduation.

Rumors at the Academy also help to prepare the cadets for their jobs as officers. Several of the instructors at the Academy were supposed to have been transferred from sea duty because of their incompetence. Such tales protect the cadets from developing a romantic conception of the qualities of Coast Guard officers, as well as providing a graphic illustration of how securely the bureaucratic structure protects officers from their own derelictions. In addition, many stories were told about a junior officer whose career at the Academy had been singularly brilliant. He had completely failed in his handling of enlisted men because he had carried over the high standards of the Academy. The cadets were thus oriented to a different conception of discipline when dealing with enlisted personnel.

The United States Coast Guard Academy performs an assimilating function. It isolates cadets from the outside world, helps them to identify themselves with a new role, and thus changes their self-conception. The manner in which the institution inculcates a bureaucratic spirit and prevents reality shock is also considered in this analysis.

The present investigation is admittedly fragmentary. Much of the most relevant material is simply not available. It is also clear that one cannot assume that this analysis applies completely to any other military academy. However, as an extreme example of an assimilating institution, there is considerable material which can be related to other institutions in a comparative framework.

Because so much socialization has already taken place by the time the cadet enters a military academy, the educational experience at the academy cannot obliterate the individual personality and so produce a "perfect" graduate who will be just like all his classmates.[23] A deep and lasting impression is made, however, standards of behavior are set, and like-mindedness about military honor and the sense of fraternity which prevail among military men is instilled.[24]

THE CITIZEN SOLDIER AND THE CAREER SOLDIER COMPARED

The officer candidate must be able to obey, interpret, and use both formal and informal aspects of military life to survive successfully in his altered environment. The main difference between socialization of the citizen soldier and the professional soldier is that the former can compartmentalize his military education (he knows the term of his enlistment), whereas the career man must make his training a permanent and integral part of his personality. "The professional officer enters a career in which a single authority regulates all his life opportunities. Indeed, the officer candidate finds that the full life cycle of his daily existence comes under the control of this single authority, for military life is institutional life. Beyond the technical skills that he acquires, the academies must prepare him for the particular style of life of military existence and indoctrinate him in the importance of heroic leadership. They must seek to waken regional ties and develop a sense of broader national identity." [25]

THE RETURN TO CIVILIAN LIFE

The problem of readjustment to civilian life for the honorably discharged serviceman is not the subject of much concern today, but in
1945 there was dismay over the more than 15 million veterans who were
about to be returned to civilian life. The magnitude of demobilization
after the Second World War—practically an entire generation of Americans—had never before been experienced. Following the Civil War and
the First World War, the nation suffered serious veterans' readjustment
problems, but there was no trouble following the Second World War.

A number of factors operated to alleviate veteran resentment and dissatisfaction after the Second World War: postwar prosperity, readjustment allowances, job security, on-the-job training, and vocational rehabilitation. The famous "GI Bill," or Public Law 346 of the 78th Congress, has enriched the veteran and the country immeasurably with training and educational benefits. Public Law 550 for Korean veterans and
Public Law 346 provided for the training of a total of three and one-half
million men and women.[26]

When the young serviceman is discharged he may return to a civilian
status for which he is no longer suited. If he returns home and the
family expects him to assume an adolescent role, the relationship will be
strained. If he returns to school he may find his contemporaries "too
young." If he takes a job he may not be given the same authority and
responsibility he carried in the service. In other words, the exserviceman
finds himself cast in roles that are not mature or demanding. This situation is resolved by capitulation on one side or the other: either he is
recognized as being mature and competent and he achieves his real
status, or he returns to an earlier stage of life and accepts that status. In
most cases the young veteran achieves adult standing. But in this technological age, the young adult is expected to have attained more training
and education than in previous generations; thus, while he is accorded
nominal adult status, the young veteran often finds himself still in an
undefined state between adolescence and full manhood.

CONCLUSION

Even in wartime the military experience is artificial to the citizen-
soldier; peacetime conscription is still more artificial. "Since the potential selectee tends to evaluate the threat to national security as one
involving total war, he finds it difficult to believe that his limited personal contribution is of any relevance. Those who have served in the cold
war army, while they may understand the relevance of basic training,

report to their civilian contacts that after basic training most of their military experience seemed without point." [27] The citizen-soldier resists rigid militarism, thus only *partial socialization* occurs.[28] The traditional American antimilitaristic posture appears to be in little danger of reversal.

But, if old-style "spit and polish" militarism, in and of itself, is no threat to the American heritage, does the possibility exist that millions of servicemen will become so imbued with socialized institutions—the military establishment, for example—that the free enterprise system will be replaced by a welfare state? [29] It is probably more accurate to cite military training for assistance in developing individual ability to adapt to the requirements of bureaucratic organization which characterize civilian institutions, particularly the large corporation.[30]

Is the exserviceman better for his military training? Is he more mature and thus better able to make important life decisions? Some men benefit more from military training than others because of their ability to profit from experience, but most are changed perhaps for the better because of certain qualities inherent in military life: self-denial, discipline, teamwork, and physical conditioning. These are desirable qualities, given the complexity of modern life, both in and out of the military establishment, as has been pointed out in the recent past by proponents of universal military training. Moreover, under the impact of automation, the number of new employment opportunities has begun to lag behind the rate of growth in the labor forces. The military establishment provides a sop for unemployment as well as training which makes the veteran in many instances more employable than he was before his military experience.

In the final analysis, the armed forces of America have become expedients for continuing socialization, and important props under the nation's economy. As with the hasty structures erected in 1946 to house veterans on college campuses across the country, "temporary" has a way of becoming "permanent." The largest "peacetime" military establishment in our history, as a typical bureaucracy, will tend to perpetuate itself and protect the benefits of its hierarchy. Social scientists must find the means to study the military more vigorously and thoroughly than has so far been possible.

The military has been treated as an important agency of socialization during the critical period of transition from adolescent to man. The remainder of the book will be devoted to the adult milieu with frequent references to the socialization theme, as the process continues in diminishing degree throughout life.

Notes

1. See Morris Janowitz, *Sociology and the Military Establishment*, New York: Russell Sage Foundation, 1959. Professor Janowitz sees a decline in the importance of the citizen-soldier and an increasing reliance on a highly mobile professional military establishment (p. 22).
2. *Your Life Plans and the Armed Forces*, Washington: American Council on Education, 1955, p. v.
3. Janowitz, *op. cit.*, p. 49.
4. "Not all teen-agers participate in the teen-age culture. Those who are in the civilian labor force (4,419,000 in January 1961), who are in the armed services (about 904,000), or who are married (about 1,206,000 in 1959)—something like 6½ million all told (out of 19,000,000 in 1959)—are chronologically, but not necessarily culturally, teen-agers. They are neophytes in the adult culture of our society. They may share some aspects of teen-age culture, but for the most part, they are expected to perform adult roles in adult dress. Teen-age culture is essentially the culture of a leisure class." Jessie Bernard, "Teen-Age Culture: An Overview," *The Annals of the American Academy*, 338, Nov. 1961, p. 2.
5. ME62–125B; U.S. Government Printing Office, 1962, p. 2.
6. O–430415, U.S. Goevrnment Printing Office, 1957 (Revised).
7. ME62R–119B, U.S. Government Printing Office, 1962, pp. 28–29. You can qualify as a combat soldier if you can "truly" answer yes to the following questions: "Am I man enough to take a new direction and give up the old routine? Will I really enjoy the chance of adventure in far-away places? Am I in tough physical condition—able to take a rugged, outdoor life? Am I able to think for myself in a tight spot? Am I a good team player, when teamwork counts most? Do I have mechanical aptitude? Am I better than average in character and responsibility?" *Ibid.* p. 5.
8. In 1954 less than 30 per cent of Army personnel could be classified as "military type" (combat soldiers) while over 70 per cent were classified as holding "civilian type" occupations. (Janowitz, *op. cit.*, p. 32.)
9. ME62R–103B, U.S. Government Printing Office, 1961, p. 13.
10. *Ibid.*, p. 45.
11. Edward Suchman, Robin M. Williams, Jr., and Rose K. Goldsen, "Student Reaction to Impending Military Service," *American Sociological Review*, Vol. 18, June 1953, 293–304.
12. Philip E. Jacob, *Changing Values in College*, New York: Harper & Brothers, 1957, as quoted in Leonard Freedman and Cornelius P. Cotter, (eds.), *Issues of the Sixties*, San Francisco: Wadsworth, 1961, p. 245.
13. Janowitz, *op. cit.*, p. 55.
14. *Ibid.*, p. 44.
15. The military elements are: "a hierarchy of offices with parallel status and overtones of 'caste'; impersonalized authority and rigid discipline—exercised and maintained through these offices; power; orderliness and calculability; hardness-virility; group solidarity in the primary sense." George D. Spindler, "American Character as Revealed by the Military," *Psychiatry*, Vol. 11, 275–281, 1948, as quoted in Yehudi A. Cohen, *Social Structure and Personality*, New York: Holt, Rinehart and Winston, 1961, pp. 232–233.
16. Max Lerner, *America as a Civilization*, New York: Simon and Schuster, 1957, pp. 914–915.
17. *Ibid.*, p. 914. But Samuel Stouffer, *et al.*, in *The American Soldier*, Vol. I, maintain that "evidence seems to show that a stable home background (authori-

tarian?), a healthy childhood, good work habits in school, and association with other boys and girls, including participation in sports, were assets for the young civilian who put on the uniform and tried to adjust to Army life." P. 144.

18. David M. Schneider, "The Social Dynamics of Physical Disability in Army Basic Training," *Psychiatry*, Vol. X (1947), 323–333, as quoted in Clyde Kluckhohn and Henry A. Murray, eds., *Personality in Nature, Society, and Culture*, New York: Alfred A. Knopf, 1953, p. 397. Janowitz also comments on masculinity: "The type of personality which seeks excessively to 'prove' his masculinity in the military environment is represented by the 'neurotic' recruit whose military behavior under stress is most likely to be highly unsatisfactory" (*op. cit.*, p. 47).

19. Janowitz, *op. cit.*, p. 55.

20. This discussion is based on a study by Mortimer A. Sullivan, Jr., Stuart A. Queen, and Ralph C. Patrick, Jr., "Participant Observation as Employed in the Study of a Military Training Program," *American Sociological Review*, 23:6, December 1958, 660–667.

21. Schneider, *loc. cit.*

22. Reece McGee, *Social Disorganization in America*, San Francisco: Chandler Publishing Company, 1962, p. 126.

23. Morris Janowitz, *The Professional Soldier*, Glencoe, Ill.: The Free Press, 1960, p. 127. The cadet must learn to conform. Those incapable of doing so drop out. Through a process of "natural selection" those who are left to graduate are more "like-minded." "According to one (U.S. Military) academy psychiatrist, the cadet is a more dependent personality than is the average college man." P. 136.

24. *Ibid.*, p. 127.

25. Bradford Morse, "The Veteran and His Education," *Higher Education*, Vol. XVI, March 1960, pp. 3–6, 16–19. "In engineering nearly a half million veterans have received training; in physical and natural sciences, 134,000; in teacher education programs, 371,000; in medical and related sciences, 209,000—77,000 in professional medical courses." P. 17.

26. Janowitz, *Sociology and the Military Establishment*, p. 49.

27. Frederick Elkin, *The Child and Society*, New York: Random House, 1960, pp. 103–104.

28. Several high ranking military officers recently have perceived this and caused some public concern when they launched an indoctrination program tailored along ultraconservative economic lines. See Chapter 22.

29. See Chapter 23 for a brief analysis of the effect of military expenditures on the economy and the dangers of a new kind of militarism.

30. See Chapter 17 for a discussion of bureaucratic roles in the corporation.

Selected Readings

Ekrich, Arthur. *The Civilian and the Military*. New York: Oxford University Press, 1956.

Human Behavior in Military Society. American Journal of Sociology. Vol. 51, March 1946, pp. 359–508. Special Issue.

Huntington, Samuel. *The Soldier and the State*. Cambridge: Harvard University Press, 1957.

Mandelbaum, David. *Soldier Groups and Negro Soldiers*. Berkeley: University of California Press, 1952.

Mills, C. Wright. *The Power Elite*. New York: Oxford University Press, 1956.

Shea, Nancy. *The Army Wife*. New York: Harper and Bros., 1954.

Stouffer, Samuel, *et al. The American Soldier: Adjustment during Army Life*. Princeton: Princeton University Press, 1959.

Part Five
Economic Institutions

The maintenance of society is the function of several institutions, including the familial, the welfare, and the economic. Because the material aspects of existence take precedence over the nonmaterial, it is of critical importance to understand the nature of economic institutions.

In the chapters that follow, the nature of economics will be explored, the historical development of capitalism will be traced, the ideologies of American capitalism will be analyzed, the socialization of economic roles will be demonstrated, and some of the crucial problems facing contemporary American economic institutions will be exposed.

Economic activity is the one aspect of social life in which all adults must engage. It is an activity that usually demands the bulk of our alert hours. Other activities can be shunted aside, but there can be little interruption of our efforts to sustain ourselves. For the adult all other activities are subordinate to the economic.

The overriding importance of the economic function—the satisfaction of human needs and wants—makes it subject, paradoxically, to both intensive and extensive organization, and at the same time to sudden and widespread disorganization. As J. O. Hertzler has said, "No other department of life presents more occasions for disorder and aggression. It is a realm in which the strong, the brutal, and the inhuman would be the 'haves,' and the more gentle and decent, the 'have nots.' There cannot be any cooperation (even of two persons), any division of labor, any utilization of experienced principles of cause and effect or technological procedures without organization by means of informal and formal rules and established physical and social forms and procedures. In brief, economic life must be and is institutionalized."

Like other institutions the economic exist within a broader framework and are subject to influence by those other institutions, and in turn, modify them. The relationship of religion and government, social class and education, and so forth, to economics—in short, the interplay of culture and behavior—will be discussed in the following pages.

Chapter 14

Economics *Qua* Economics

In the simplest cultures, man produces and consumes only to subsist: he provides his own food, clothing, and shelter, and nothing more. For him, the choice among the surrounding resources is extremely narrow. But as the culture grows more complex, the use of resources increases, and man works harder to satisfy his desires, which now go beyond necessities for subsistence to the more complicated area of psychological and social wants. These new wants, unlike the need for sustaining oneself, are learned from watching other persons. Economists believe these wants can be expanded limitlessly, or more properly, limited only by individual ability and by the time available for using what the culture produces. It is the function of an economic system, in other words, to satisfy human wants.

How well a man, a tribe, or a nation satisfies wants above the mere level of subsistence is referred to as the *standard of living*. The standard of living may very well vary from one individual, tribe, or nation to the next. It is in this respect that the United States is often contrasted with, say, India, or with an emergent nation of Africa.

At the basis of economic thought are the resources on which people depend. They are not always plentiful, and very few simple cultures enjoy freedom from a major economic problem—a shortage of *resources*. Rare indeed is the island paradise in which climate, soil, and sea are so bountiful that man need expend no energy on food, clothing, and shelter. And certainly no complex culture will ever reach this ideal state because of the ever-increasing growth of new psychological and social wants.

Each culture determines and defines its own resources. But since a resource is considered a *scarce* commodity, an economic problem arises over its division or *allocation* among all possible users and for all conceivable uses. A resource must also be *impersonally transferable* from one use, user, time, or place to another. Custom, law, and way of life affect the scarcity and transferability of resources. Cattle, for example, are regarded as a resource to be used for economic advantage in the

297

United States, but not in India where the thought of harming a *spiritual symbol* is repugnant to the devout Hindu.

Few resources satisfy human wants directly; they must be combined or converted into a new resource capable of fulfilling some want. Thus, iron ore is turned into steel, and steel into an automobile or refrigerator. By processing the natural resource into something that can be used, man manipulates his environment to create *economic value*. Specifically, this is the economic concept of *added value:* man changes a resource into what people want. The more they want it, the greater—to use a term favored by economists—the *demand*. The greater the demand, the more valuable the resource becomes, and the more it is worth. Man may further increase the value of resources in demand by making them scarce —that is, by limiting what economists call their *supply*. However, re- sources must be made available to those who want them at the time and place they are wanted. Thus, the original resource acquires something new—the *basic utilities* of form and accessibility.

The existence of resources in a form in which they are wanted stimu- lates economic activity in the *market*. This is a term given to the setting in which people obtain resources in exchange for payment or other resources. In the market there are tendencies to limit supply in order to keep values high. But the high value of scarce goods—that is, resources— induces owners or manufacturers to supply them to the market, which reduces their scarcity and lowers their value. As the supply of the valu- able goods grows more plentiful, the goods lose worth. An economic system is thus dynamic, which is discouraging to those who want to reduce scarcity but not their profits.

Perfect allocation of resources—having the proper amount of the proper resource at the proper place at the proper time—occurs when value is added without shifting the resources from one use, time, or place, to another. Misallocation in any branch of economic activity— that is, too much of one resource, too little of another—always means that value is lost. There is also a loss in value when a resource is not used to its fullest capacity. Of course, all economic systems misallocate re- sources in varying degrees. In judging how effectively an economic system performs we should consider how nearly the standard of perfect alloca- tion is reached.

It is clear that there must be a conflict between unlimited wants and limited resources. Because of this conflict, the consumer must choose among his economic objectives, and among the means for attaining them. Five goals may be cited as the objectives of a sound economic system: efficiency (optimum allocation of resources); progress (improvement of means for attaining ends); stability (steady growth without great fluctuations of price and productivity); equality (distribution of the fruits of production in some ideal manner); and freedom (a range of choice for consumer, producer, and worker). As a science, however, economics is concerned with means, not goals.

THE CLASSICAL VIEW

Yet Western economic thought is based on an idea of how the economy *ought* to work, and how it would work if organized on the "classical" scheme. That scheme assumes a number of small economic units, each separately striving for its own gain. The result is that, in theory, the whole group achieves a high and stable level of efficiency in the use of economic resources. The following excerpt from a study by the California State Department of Education illustrates the "orthodox," or conservative, or classical, view of economics.

*
Economics is the social science that analyzes the data, issues, and public policies connected with the production, distribution, and consumption of wealth and income. It is a seamless web of reasoning that begins with the facts of scarcity and unlimited wants and proceeds through specialized production, interdependence, exchange, markets, price, costs, and public policy. Emphasized are economic stability and growth, the allocation of resources to their most important uses, an equitable distribution of income, and, in our economy, a wide range of economic freedom for workers to choose their jobs, consumers to choose goods, and investors and entrepreneurs to own property and choose their investments.

All problems that may properly be termed "economic" must be considered within the framework of this process of reasoning whether they originate in capitalist, socialist, fascist, or communist countries. Economic theory has been defined as "a method rather than a doctrine, an apparatus of the mind, a technique of thinking which helps its possessor to draw correct conclusions." The study of economics is thus important to the individual and society for both the knowledge gained and the thinking processes acquired. Valid information about our economy and the ability to use it effectively are indispensable to effective citizenship on many of the most pressing public issues of the day.

Consideration of specialized areas in economics must be firmly rooted in this process of reasoning. Important areas in economics include the fields of

* "Generalizations from Economics," *Report of the State Central Committee on Social Studies,* Sacramento, California State Department of Education, November 1959.

money and banking, business cycles, public finance and taxation, industrial organization and public policies toward business, labor-management rela-- tions, accounting, finance, statistics, consumer economics, international trade and finance, economic growth, and comparative economic systems.

ECONOMIC ENDS AND MEANS

Economic welfare is a goal in most, if not all, modern economic societies. It is believed to be beneficial for people to have more economic goods rather than less, that poverty *per se* is not a desirable state of affairs. Many economists believe not only that economic welfare is one of the important qualities of a good society but also that economic progress makes the other qualities of that society easier to attain, that the creative arts—such as painting, music, and literature—are more apt to flourish in a highly productive economy than in a poverty-stricken one.

Productive resources are scarce and human wants unlimited. Inasmuch as man cannot satisfy all of his desires for material goods, he has to make choices. The essence of "economy" lies in making wise choices in economic matters, such as between saving and spending, the object of expenditure, the kind of investment, and the choice of job. The "real cost" of any end product is thus the alternatives sacrificed in producing it. This is known in economics as the "opportunity cost principle."

THE GROSS NATIONAL PRODUCT—A MEASUREMENT OF ECONOMIC ACHIEVEMENT

The size of the Gross National Product (consisting of the total value of all economic goods—products and services—produced annually) depends upon many conditions. Included are (*a*) the extent and richness of natural resources; (*b*) the number, quality, and motivation of the working population; (*c*) the amount and nature of the capital goods (factories, houses, bridges, roads, machines, and tools of all kinds) created through saving and investment; (*d*) the effectiveness of investors and entrepreneurs in organizing and energizing productive activity; (*e*) the existence of a large free-trade area in which the free flow of goods permits each locality to specialize in the production of those goods in which it has the greatest relative advantage and to obtain other goods by trade, which in economics is known as the "principle of comparative advantage"; and (*f*) the presence of economic and political institutions which are conducive to, and encourage, creative and productive effort on the part of all human beings. To preserve these several conditions upon which high productivity (and consequently our high plane of living) rests, conservation must be practiced.

The size of both the GNP and population greatly influences economic welfare. Economic welfare depends upon the race between population growth and resource exhaustion on the one hand, and the improvement in techniques of production and expansion of capital goods, on the other. The economic optimum would be that size population relative to other resources that would produce the largest output per man-hour of labor, other things being equal. As population grows relative to other resources (land and capital goods) beyond this point of diminishing returns, output per worker declines. in the absence of improvements in technology. This principle is known in economics as the "law of diminishing return."

The full use of productive facilities directly influences economic welfare. Fluctuations tend to be more severe in industrially-advanced nations than in primitive ones. In the industrially-advanced societies specialization and complexity are vastly greater, shifts in demand and changes in techniques are more frequent, a large proportion of resources are devoted to the production of durable consumer and producer goods, and the possibility and likelihood of substantial changes in the volume of investment expenditures are greater in the face of the people's desire to save a fairly stable part of their incomes.

Government can contribute to the maintenance of high-level production and employment, rapid economic growth and progress, and a stable dollar, by proper use of governmental authority which necessitates appropriate monetary, fiscal, and debt-management policies.

High per capita income is due to high productivity of labor. The total income of a society is its total output of goods. It follows that, if American labor is ten times as productive as foreign labor, American wages can be ten times as high as abroad without interfering with the ability of American industry to sell its products in world markets. High wages thus rest on high productivity, not a tariff.

THE COMPOSITION OF INCOME—THE ALLOCATION OF RESOURCES

Basic in economic organization is the task of devising a means of securing effective cooperation among the specialized producers in the system. The economic system must determine how much of each commodity and service to produce and how each unit of each resource is to be allocated to its most important use.

In a competitive, private-enterprise system, prices indicate the relative value of goods and services. Price, on the one hand, reflects the willingness of buyers to buy and sellers to sell, and, on the other hand, influences the actions of both consumers and producers. A relatively high price tends to restrict current consumption and to stimulate production of a larger supply in the future, whereas a relatively low price does the reverse. Raising or lowering a competitive price by artificial means, whether by private monopoly or by governmental authority, is likely to aggravate the very situation such action is designed to alleviate, unless accompanied by the power to affect directly future demand or supply in an appropriate manner.

A market price system works best when both buyers and sellers are highly competitive, well informed, and able and disposed to act on their information (competition-knowledge-mobility). It follows that the free enterprise system is supported and strengthened by government action designed to keep markets free (anti-trust policy), buyers and sellers informed (prohibition of false advertising and laws against misrepresentation) and mobile. At the very minimum, government must maintain order and justice, protect property, enforce contracts and provide a money system in order for free enterprise to flourish.

In some fields of economic activity, because of special economic conditions (public utilities), the government has been authorized to regulate the prices charged (to insure that they are fair and not unjustly discriminatory) and the quality of service rendered by a private producer (electric power, gas, telephone) or to undertake public ownership and operation (water, post office).

There are many ways to organize economic activity. Most national economies in the world today, though differing in fundamental respects, make considerable use of the price system for the purpose of rationing goods, providing incentives to call forth productive services, and allocating resources to their best uses. A free society provides opportunity and incentives for the individual to hazard what he owns in an effort to make a profit.

THE DISTRIBUTION OF INCOME

In a competitive system, the prices paid for productive services also serve to divide the total output of goods among those responsible for their production. Thus, the wages of workers, the dividends of investors, and the rents of landlords all provide the money incomes which determine the size of each individual's claim to actual goods and services.

In a competitive market, each productive agent tends to receive as income a sum equal to the value of his productive contribution to society. The greater the demand of the public for the particular service or product and the smaller the supply, the larger the income. Those possessing the greatest skills demanded by the public tend to receive the highest income. Inequality in the distribution of income thus arises from unequal payments for human services as well as the unequal ownership of property. At the same time, the opportunity for a larger income provides the incentive to develop one's abilities to the utmost, to save and acquire property, and to use resources most efficiently and productively.

Imperfections in competition create important public problems. Monopoly power whether on the side of buyers or sellers, management or labor, or private groups sometimes supported by government is usually exercised with resulting distortion in the allocation of resources and distribution of income.

The way to increase the plane of living of all the people is to increase productivity. Historically, this has been the source of the tremendous economic achievement in the United States. Industrial output per man-hour has increased six-fold since about 1850. Half of this gain has been taken in shorter hours (and more leisure) and half in more goods. Thus, the average length of the work week has been cut in half, and at the same time, real income per capita has tripled. The grinding poverty in which a large part of the world's population live today is due to the sheer unproductivity of human labor, not to a deficiency in purchasing power or an imperfection in the distribution of income.

The economic problem is an inevitable feature of human life. Since the resources of the world are scarce and do not satisfy all wants, the study of economics, both theoretical and applied, becomes a necessary inclusion in the basic education of all people. The individual makes economic decisions throughout his life, and through voting and other types of community participation, helps to decide problems involving the economic welfare of all people.

Western classical economic thought is founded, as just illustrated, on a neat, logical system of laws. Adam Smith, around whom the "classical school" was organized, said that everything turned out for the best if the economic system was not tampered with by government or powerful private groups—as if an "invisible hand" guided the economic process. Man tampered with this system of fixed laws at his own peril. By permitting people to buy and sell according to individual preferences, a country could achieve complete harmony in production and demand.

Classical economics tends to ignore reality by emphasizing the study of laws and models. And while laws and models do touch actual conditions at points, the disparities between law and reality have sometimes been so great that belief in the law has approached dogma. Moreover, according to J. K. Galbraith, "at the higher levels economics divorces itself fully from practical questions . . . [and] much of it . . . may with good conscience be ignored." [1]

ECONOMIC REVISIONISTS

But some economists persist in examining the real world and thereby modifying, at least, the classical model. A little over 30 years ago the idea of *imperfect* competition was advanced by Edward Chamberlin and Joan Robinson. This theory attacked the assumption at the very heart of classical economics: that a market economy always achieved greatest efficiency and stability under conditions of *perfect* or pure competition. Imperfect competition contends that some markets, notably industrial markets, are neither purely competitive nor purely monopolistic, but contain elements of both. Today *oligopoly*, the presence of several large competitors, results in imperfect or monopolistic competition and is generally accepted as a fact of economic life in industrial society.

A few years after the Chamberlin-Robinson modification, an economic theory so threatening to the classical model in the minds of orthodox economists as to be termed revolutionary was introduced by John Maynard Keynes. The "Keynesian Revolution," denying the "invisible hand" of Adam Smith, held that the capitalist system could not automatically run itself and maintain full employment. At times something had to be done to make it work, and that "something" was soon to be called "pump priming"—with government agencies "priming the pump."

There was no connection between these two recent theories. The former dealt with particular markets, the latter with the total market economy and money system; but each departed from classical doctrine and each was a major event altering the course of modern economic thought. Today both theories are considered to be amendments to the classical model, as classical doctrine exhibits a remarkable flexibility in adapting to new situations.

The continuing process of amendment is brought up to date in the following article by Ben W. Lewis entitled "Recent Developments in Economics." In addition to discussing the increasing importance of the mathematical approach, Professor Lewis calls attention to the contributions that other social science disciplines can make to the understanding of economic phenomena.

*

The movements in economics that got underway in the thirties gained impetus from World War II and picked up momentum in the years that have followed. The war brought economists in droves again to Washington and to government posts throughout the country, and again the call was for the use of positive economics in the making of public decisions. The allocation of strategic materials, the pricing and rationing of goods at all market levels, the pricing of labor services, the direction of labor effort and of investment, the export and import of commodities—all of these tasks and more which, under what we somewhat fancifully refer to as "normal" conditions, we entrust largely to the processes of the market, were made the subject of conscious public determination and action. This was positive economics on a grand scale, and the whole complex afforded a magnificent model for the testing of economic hypotheses across the board. Conditions

* Ben W. Lewis, "Recent Developments in Economics," *Liberal Education*, May 1961, pp. 265–277. Reprinted by permission of the Association of American Colleges.

did not permit the testing to be carried out with scientific precision, of course, but economists learned much and were impelled to learn more. You can learn quite a lot about a railroad—or an economy—by trying to run one.

Marked advances were made during the years immediately preceding World War II in our understanding of the great problems of macroeconomics. Since the war the advances have continued, but it is evident from the post-war experience of our economy and its economists with inflation, unemployment, development, and growth that the end of the assignment still lies ahead. We have been confronted by a persistent rise in the general level of prices and at the same time have been nagged by unemployment. Our normal interest, stemming from simple considerations of human welfare, in the factors and processes favorable to long-run improvement in the performance of our own and other economies has been recharged by international political developments. Economics is at work in all of these areas, at levels both of theory and policy, and with all of the hypotheses, instruments and procedures it can command.

Monetary theory, in partial eclipse for a number of years, is presently enjoying a considerable revival. The venerable Quantity Theory of Money, accepted in some form by most economists before the Great Depression, suffered severe reverses with the coming of Keynes, and was virtually swept from the stage. The earlier interest in the price level or purchasing power of money was superseded by a growing concern over income theory and the behavior of real output and employment. . . . Since the war, however, the quantity of money has managed a comeback as an important variable, and at the moment is sharing the stage, in a strong supporting role, with income theory, and fiscal policy. At least two major works in this area have appeared since Keynes, and new syntheses of income and monetary theory are being developed. These are considerably more complex than either of the older and simpler quantity or income theories, and involve a significant modification of both. They embrace the money supply, the demand for money balances, propensities to consume and save, the marginal efficiency of capital, and monetary institutions. Not the least of the forces influencing the nature, direction and extent of the present resurgence of activity in this field are the great flood of statistical material and the development of new and refined statistical methods. These have resulted in greatly expanded empirical and econometric research.

An interesting interplay between theory and policies in the monetary field occurred during and for a short period following World War II. Wartime experience demonstrated clearly that, even if monetary policy could not end a slump, it could, if directed to the purpose, prevent interest rates from rising despite an unprecedented volume of government borrowing and a consequently unprecedented government debt. This was an enticing discovery to those who found low interest rates desirable—including the Secretary of the Treasury—and monetary policy continued to be devoted to this end even though it tended to conflict with the anti-inflation efforts of other agencies of the government, until an (uneasy) accord was reached in 1951. Only then was monetary policy again directed toward stabilization of the price level. The debate again got underway as to the efficacy of monetary policy as a stabilization tool and as to its proper role in relation to fiscal policy in this capacity.

Controversy within the profession is far from stilled on the relative culpability of cost-push and demand-pull as generators of inflation, and on the relative merits of, and exact assignments to be given to, monetary, debt management and fiscal measures, and to a lesser extent, direct controls, as instruments for its containment. There is lack of agreement as well over the precise shape and composition of each of these sets of instruments, and over the degree and extent to which each should be employed and the precise timing of its employment.

Much the same kind of general observations can be made on the progress of economics in laying open and treating the endemic problem of unemployment. Involuntary idleness, swelling and receding but always present, is the course of a market economy, both for those directly affected and for the rest of society. We have never been free from unemployment; and since the war, and even now when our economy is performing at record or near-record levels of over-all productivity, we are painfully aware that too large a percentage of those who want to work can find no work to do. Economists are chipping away at the hard facts of this problem with analytical tools that have been markedly refined and sharpened in recent years. There is much agreeement on the identity, nature and operation of, and the relationship between, important variables, and a considerable degree of precision and certainty is slowly taking the place of guesses and estimates.

Here as in the case of inflation there still are many unknowns that need to be known, and there will always be unknowns that are unknowable. The operating units with which economics deal are free, independent human beings. Expectations, which play a major part in determining the level of economic activity, can never be captured and secured as surely as events. Both inflation and employment are played upon by other than economic forces, and in some measure at least, their treatment involves society in a choice between incompatible goals: it is by no means certain that society can have all that it would like in the way of full employment save at the cost of more than it wants of inflation, just as its pursuit of technological advance can be prosecuted fully only at the cost of increased insecurity. All of this is simply to point out that really substantial development in economics is not the equivalent of an end to all economic problems.

Controveries over the diagnoses and the most efficacious prescriptions for the treatment of the mass problems of our economy—inflation, unemployment, growth—as is the nature of controversies, are open for all to see and hear. And, since they are manifestations of the process by which understanding is reached, they are not particularly to be deplored. But what is possibly less evident (and also encouraging), is that the areas of agreement are increasing in size and number. Irreconcilable conflicts over particular theories and policies are giving way noticeably to efforts to devise formulae which will join and so enlist the positive qualities of erstwhile alternative findings and proposals in combined attacks upon the problems which plague us. Not the least important of the propositions on which substantial agreement is in prospect is that the problems of aggregative economics are amenable to purposeful action by an intelligent and informed society. But much remains to be done; the imperative demand upon our theory for greater and greater precision has still to be met. It seems altogether doubtful that economists or economist-coached public officials will ever achieve in the world of affairs the proficiency enjoyed by our introductory students in the classroom in controlling the intricate mechanisms of the economy.

It is tempting to treat the work of economists since World War II in the area of economic growth and development as the counterpart in scope and significance of their activities in the area of income and employment which were touched off by the Great Depression. Certainly there is a similarity in the fact that the increased scientific interest in growth and development is a direct product of the times—in this case the national drive to build up and hold the underdeveloped countries of the world within our sphere of influence, and the national concern over the outcome of our productivity race with the Soviet Union. "Growthmanship" is a national preoccupation, and economists are among those most preoccupied.

Courses in economic growth and development are now standard offerings for both undergraduates and graduates in our departments of economics, and college and university institutes and programs on growth and development, often specially endowed or supported by special grants, are proliferating at a rate matched only by the rate at which articles and textbooks on the subject are pouring from the presses. The already sizable collection of country studies prepared by independent scholars and by teams of experts on the basis of on-the-spot investigation is growing steadily. Foreign students come to us by the hundred to learn the mysteries and acquire the touch. American economists by the dozen, under arrangements with governments (our own and foreign), universities, and foundations are shuttling back and forth between their home stations and the campuses and the development and planning boards of underdeveloped countries, as lecturers and technical advisers. "Become an Economist and See the World" is today a meaningful and alluring slogan. The movement is reminiscent of the mass migration from campuses to Washington in the flush days of the New Deal.

Despite the external similarities, however, it is not yet clear that the current excitement in the area of growth and development is on all fours with the income-employment ferment of the thirties, as measured by its effects to date on systematic theory or on systematic public policy for either underdeveloped or well-developed countries. Much useful analysis, model building and critical debate is taking place, and an impressive array of special growth and development concepts, with a matching vocabulary, continues to emerge. An assortment of theories has been advanced to explain how growth begins and is sustained. There is more than a semblance of agreement on the range of forces and variables that have played a significant part in the past and that probably should be taken into account in constructing development policies and programs to be carried out in the future. There is much less agreement, however, on emphases and phasing. In seeking to learn from the past, it is not always easy (or even possible) to distinguish between causation and coincidence, or to ascertain with certainty the actual direction of causation. The rival claims of chickens and eggs for primacy have nowhere been more baffling than in the area of development and growth.

It is in the study of economic development and growth that the need for the more recently devised methods and techniques of economic analysis (about which more will be said later in this paper) is felt most keenly, and where they have been employed most extensively, and with a good deal of operational usefulness. Input-output analysis, linear programming and operations research are examples. But more, and more than economics alone can furnish, is required.

One of the most striking qualities of the process by which different economies seem to grow to higher and higher levels of sustainable *per capita* productivity and income is diversity—differences in speed and course, and in the substance and shadings of the total context in which the process occurs. Fruitful study of the many-sided phenomenon of growth calls for skill in the gathering, ordering, and interpretation of facts, and for the time-tested tools and ways of thinking of the economist—his concern with order, with scarcity and allocation, priority and opportunity cost, productivity, capital formation, income determination, trade, and the like. But the attack on the mysteries of growth, particularly on the forces at work in the early stages of growth in underdeveloped countries, calls also for the contributions of disciplines other than economics. Penetrating and imaginative economic investigation and analysis need to be reinforced by understanding of such factors as motivation, creativity, cultures, taboos, "know-how," organization, social and political institutions, and a host of others. Fortunately, all of this is coming to be recognized, and increasingly the insights and skills of the psychologist, the sociologist, the political scientist, the anthropologist and the historian, together with those of the administrator, the engineer, and the man of business and finance, are being linked to and integrated with those of the economist.

Admittedly, growth and development theory and policy have not yet "arrived." At the levels of both theory and policy formulation, and with reference to the growth problems present in countries at all stages of economic development, differences are wide and sharp. These differences narrow into crevices, however, in comparison to the chasms that frequently separate development programs as formulated, recommended and "accepted," from programs as put into effect. Virtually every underdeveloped country has achieved or is in the process of achieving (or is having thrust upon it) an impressive "Development Plan"—sometimes in several volumes, with appendices. The "plan" may be followed in practice more or less closely or it may be ignored. In any case, sooner or later, development in greater or lesser degree may occur. One prediction, however, seems safe: an underdeveloped country which exposes itself to, and participates seriously in, the exercise of development planning (even though its planning reflects the present unsettled state of development theory) will be the gainer—possibly from a resulting "plan"; most certainly from the *process* of planning, from the experience of facing up squarely to the task of economizing.

There is, to be sure, just a touch of showmanship in some of the current development effort—possibly no more than is required to put development theory to work. The main sweep, however, is clearly sound; its sources, directions, procedures, and techniques are in the best scientific tradition, and it is making headway. And economists (and airlines) are having a wonderful time.

The classical theory of international trade, also severely shaken by the Keynesians, is currently being subjected to further competitive pressure from new theories of economic growth. Essentially, what was involved in the earlier coup was the replacement of the traditional processes of the specie-flow-price mechanism, as an automatic equilibrator of the balances of payments between nations, by income changes, and the attendant multiplier. The gold standard broke down, first in theory (along with the quantity theory of money), and then in practice, when governments refused to permit their internal economies to be ruled by international flows of gold; and the way was cleared for new doctrine and new control devices.

Currently, we are witnessing a most startling, almost incredible phenomenon—probing, critical, damaging questions being directed at the venerable Law of Comparative Advantage, whose standing in the community of economic theory has, until very recently, placed it almost above questioning. True, the law has been brought in for questioning before, but its inquisitors have not succeeded in impairing its reputation. In practice, of course, the law has been disregarded fully as much as it has been observed; on no issue of economic policy have economic scholars over the years been less effective in influencing "practical" policy makers than on the removal of barriers to specialization and trade.

Growth theory has now come forward to challenge anew the theoretical impeccability of the Law of Comparative Advantage. The chief criticism of comparative advantage is that it "is essentially a static concept which ignores a variety of dynamic elements." [2] The issue is important to persons charged with the formulation of development policy governing the allocation of investment funds and scarce resources in underdeveloped countries. "The classical analysis focuses on long-run tendencies and equilibrium conditions, while modern theories of growth [based on assumptions quite different from those underlying the doctrine of comparative advantage] are concerned with the interaction among producing and consuming units in a dynamic system." It is suggested that to modify comparative advantage to take account of dynamic considerations would be to "rob the original doctrine of much of its practical value." What is needed, and what is being sought, is a resolution of the two approaches sufficiently specific to be useful in guiding actual allocation decisions. It is by no means clear at this stage that the search will be successful—that any reconciliation will eventuate in principles that can, without modification in individual cases by "other considerations," be employed to dictate development programs.

Great stimulus was given by the war and its aftermath to intensive and imaginative inductive studies of firms, industries, and markets. We know vastly more, and we are adding daily to our knowledge and understanding, of the theory and practice of pricing, of market strategies, and of investment and output determination, and hence of the real nature of incentives, motives, markets, and competition as forces for the ordering of our economy and the achievement of the economic goals to which we aspire. This has direct significance for policy in such fields as antitrust, and also for the rate and service activities of our public regulatory agencies.

Comparable studies and investigations are underway in the economics of labor. Wage negotiations under collective bargaining do not constitute an exact science, but it goes without saying that wages have a tremendous impact upon the economy and all of its participants, and that the formulation of wage standards related functionally to other significant, interrelated economic variables and to declared economic goals is essential if the institution of collective bargaining is to persist as a feature of our free society. The study of wages, in all of their aspects and effects—upon particular and general prices, output, and employment—and involving empirical and statistical research and testing as well as model building and theoretical analysis, is making a large claim upon the interest and time of labor economists today. . . .

Possibly the most striking of recent developments is the spate of new methods and tools of economic analysis, and the new language which is being employed in the study and presentation of economics. Mathematics has always been used in economics, but until recently the language of economics was predominantly verbal (as it still is in the introductory courses). Today, however, the benighted economist whose mathematical training stopped with long division finds it quite impossible to read beyond the dedication in advanced treatises, and it is scarcely worth his while to take the wrapper off the current issues of the learned journals. It has become necessary for economics to employ a language that can deal precisely and with logical consistency with the masses of significant economic variables and relationships of which it has become increasingly aware, and which it now takes carefully into account as it moves ahead. Mathematics, to those who understand it and appreciate its possibilities, is such a language. It can, however, be a deceptive language: it can convey the appearance of an exactness which does not, and very possibly cannot, exist; and it has a remarkable capacity to lure the susceptible into mistaking intellectual gymnastics for fruiftul research. Nonetheless, the most sceptical nonmathematicians concede that the careful and skillful use of mathematics can extend—and is in fact extending—the frontiers of economics.

The mathematical approach is being supplemented by the *simulation* technique in the construction and use of theories or models for explaining or prescribing economic behavior. Simulation is described as "a technique for building theories that reproduce part or all of the output of a behaving system. The system can be an aggregate of behaving units, an entire economy, or a particular unit, a human decision-maker. The output can be one aggregated element, e.g., that interest rate which clears the money market, or the whole host of thoughts, associations, and actions employed by a man while he solves a specified problem." [3] The process of simulation involves constructing a theory, or model, of a system that prescribes the system's processes. These processes can refer to macro as well as micro elements and the prescriptive detail reflects the researcher's knowledge of and interest in particular parts of the system. By carrying out the processes postulated in the theory, a hypothetical stream of behavior is generated that can be compared with the stream of behavior of the original system." [4] One writer believes that "The advent of computers in general and the techniques of simulation in particular open up possibilities for the growth of a new scientific institutional economics." [5]

There has been continued growth in the sheer mass of useful economic statistics, and their refinement and adaptation both to inductive research and to the testing of hypotheses have more than kept pace with the growing volume. Increased statistics are opening new doors for theory, and in turn theory is demanding more statistics. The collection, preparation, analysis, and application of statistics have snowballed in the past quarter-century, and out of the marriage of statistical analysis and mathematical economics has emerged a thriving "econometrics"—a "type of economic analysis in which the general theoretical approach—often formulated in explicitly mathematical terms—is combined—frequently through the medium of intricate statistical procedures—with empirical measurement of *economic phenomena.*" [6]

"By carrying out the different stages of research [the theoretical development and the testing of hypotheses, and even, to some extent, the exploration of the problem] in closer conjunction with each other, a considerably greater degree of economic design can be employed in the research, and the resulting analysis will benefit by greater consistency and integration than would have been possible otherwise." [7]

A considerable volume of decision-oriented economic analysis is going on today under the broad and impressive canopy of *Operations Research*—which has been characterized by a recent expositor as an approach or method or point of view, the essence of which is "that a phenomenon is understood when and only when it has been expressed as a formal, really mechanistic, quantitative model, and that, furthermore, all the phenomena within the purview of science . . . can be so expressed with sufficient persistence and ingenuity." A corollary of this point of view is a "preference for symbolic, as opposed to verbal, modes of expression and reasoning." Operations research, we are told, is "all research [undertaken] in this spirit intended to help solve practical, immediate problems in the fields of business, governmental or military administration or the like." [8] Operations analysts are for the most part engineers, mathematicians, statisticians, and natural scientists by training, but several well-known operations research programs are pointed directly toward economic problem situations, and others have important implications for, and may find direct use in helping to resolve economic issues.

Linear Programming seeks to order the combination of scarce resources available to a business firm and to allocate their use as between the firm's activities so that the objectives of the firm will be achieved in the maximum possible degree—to plot the best course of resource use. It is applicable to a wide variety of "maximizing" situations facing the management of a firm—situations in which conventional micro-economic theory has always assumed that management, because this is the only "rational" way to behave, proceeds deftly, surely, and swiftly to optimum choices as between a multitude of competing alternatives. Economic theory knows this assumption to be unreal, but it has not worried too much about the precise nature and extent of its departure from reality. Linear programming, together with research generally in this area, promises to bring greater rationality and higher quality to management decision-making, and in the process to bring a larger measure of reality to economic theory. Micro-economic theory, for example, would be materially enriched by an improved understanding of how price and output decisions are actually made.

Input-Output analysis is allied to linear programming but is concerned with inter-industry relationships and the study of *general* economic equilibrium, as distinct from processes within a firm. It undertakes to calculate the demands which various sectors of the economy place upon other sectors in order to carry out a given program of production, and to reach an harmonious pattern of output levels for the several sectors regarded as a whole.[9] Such analysis is proving useful in the prosecution of development programs, as well as in other situations where public mobilization and allocation of economic resources on a broad front are called for.

Still another promising theoretical development is *Organization Theory*, which recognizes that the individual makes economic (and other) decisions not alone as an individual but within the framework of organizations in which he assumes roles as he carries out the many aspects of his economic life. Organizations, themselves molded by individuals, powerfully affect individuals in their economic activities. The content, shape, and limits of organization theory are still fluid, but it is tending to serve as a focal point for game theory, decision theory, information and communication theory, group theory and motivational theory; and model building, mathematics, and simulation have all found their way into its methodolgy. Hopefully, the pursuit of knowledge along these lines and in this context will enhance our understanding of the activities of individuals as producers and consumers, and of firms, markets and, indeed, of whole economies. . . .

"Economics has been moving steadily into new areas where the power of the classical equilibrium model has never been demonstrated, and where its adequacy must be considered anew. Labor economics is such an area, oligopoly or imperfect competition theory another, decision-making under uncertainty a third, and the theory of economic development a fourth. In all of these areas the complexity and instability of his environment becomes a central feature of the choices that economic man faces. To explain his behavior in the face of this complexity, the theory must describe him as something more than a featureless, adaptive organism; it must incorporate at least some description of the processes and mechanisms through which the adaptation takes place." [10]

Here surely is the crowning scene, the ultimate: tight-fisted, profit-eyed, indispensable "Economic Man" himself, for nearly two centuries the hardiest character in economics, in the clinic for observation, the prognosis unfavorable. . . .

Economists are making [a] . . . move toward spreading economic understanding, by giving active, organized support to improved teaching of economics in the *schools*. The case for economics in the schools is as broad and firmly based as the case for democracy itself. Increasingly, the public problems with which citizens are required to cope are *economic* public problems, and our democratic society will not survive beyond the day when our citizens fail to discharge the political-economic responsibilities which democracy places upon them. Our citizens, for the most part, do not go to college, and the only contact which most of them have with formal economic reasoning is in courses in economics, social studies, and American history in the schools. Economics in the schools today is in an unhappy state; just how unhappy is indicated by the fact that the staid, almost immovable American Economic Association has been sufficiently shocked to undertake an active program, in cooperation with educators, to do what it can to repair a situation which its own earlier neglect helped to create.

CONCLUSION

The California study quoted earlier in this chapter was an outgrowth of the concern of the A.E.A. noted by Professor Lewis. It should be recognized that in the study the general classical assumptions remain: that man seeks gain in an area of relatively free choice, that he competes with others in a somewhat rational way, and that the study of economics is one of relations of limited resources to unlimited desires. The fact that most economists believe this to be the most desirable way of organizing economic life has resulted in a tendency to return to the study of the way men ought to act. John Stuart Mill, one of the early classical revisionists, wrote in his *Principles of Political Economy* in 1848 (the same year another pair of revisionists, Marx and Engels, published their *Communist Manifesto*) that the distribution of wealth "is a matter of human institution solely." It "depends on the laws and customs of society. The rules by which it is determined are what the opinions and feeling of the ruling portion of the community make them, and are very different in differing ages and countries; and might be still more different, if mankind so chose." [11] It may be premature to speak of economic laws.

Thus, we turn from economic abstractions to the effects of economic decisions on the lives of people, how those decisions are made, and some of the paradoxes of our economic system. But a word of warning by J. K. Galbraith should be heeded: "I would not excuse anyone from mastering the basic ideas and terminology of economics." [12]

Notes

1. John Kenneth Galbraith, "The Language of Economics," *Fortune*, December 1962, pp. 169, 171.
2. The quotations in this paragraph are taken from, and the discussion is based on, the manuscript of a survey article, "Comparative Advantage and Development Policy," by H. B. Chenery, scheduled for publication in the March 1961 issue of the *American Economic Review*.

3. G. P. E. Clarkson and H. A. Simon, "Simulation of Individual and Group Behavior," *American Economic Review*, December 1960, p. 920.
4. *Ibid.*
5. Martin Shubik, "Simulation of the Industry and the Firm," *American Economic Review*, December 1960, p. 917.
6. W. Leontief, in *A Survey of Contemporary Economics*, Vol. I, H. S. Ellis, editor, 1948, p. 388.
7. Richard Ruggles, in *A Survey of Contemporary Economics*, Vol. II, B. F. Haley, editor, 1952, p. 423. Mention might be made specifically of econometric research directed to the study of the whole economy by employing a dynamic mathematical model. See the review article, C. F. Christ, "Aggregate Econometric Models," *American Economic Review*, June 1956, p. 385.
8. Robert Dorfman, "Operations Research," *American Economic Review*, September 1960, pp. 577, 578.
9. Robert Dorfman, "Mathematical or 'Linear' Programming," *American Economic Review*, December 1953, pp. 797, 824.
10. H. A. Simon, "Theories of Decision-Making in Economics and Behavioral Science," *American Economic Review*, June 1959, pp. 255–256.
11. George Soule, *Ideas of the Great Economists*, Mentor Edition, New York: The New American Library, 1952, p. 90.
12. Galbraith, *op. cit.*, p. 171.

Selected Readings

*Heilbroner, Robert L., *The Making of Economic Society*, Englewood Cliffs, N. J., Prentice-Hall, Inc., 1962.
*Heilbroner, *The Worldly Philosophers*, New York, Simon and Schuster, 1953.
McCracken, Harlan L., *Keynesian Economics in the Stream of Economic Thought*, Baton Rouge, Louisiana State University, 1961.
Slichter, Sumner H., "The Passing of Keynesian Economics," *The Atlantic Monthly*, November 1959.
*Soule, George, *The Ideas of the Great Economists*, Mentor Edition, New York, The New American Library, 1952.

* Paperback edition.

Chapter 15

Historical Backgrounds
of Our Economic Institutions

Modern economic structure is rooted in the manorial system of the Middle Ages of Western Europe. Feudalism was the reigning political organization, and the manorial system its economic arm. The manor "imposed itself upon the whole life of its inhabitants" as the principal social and economic institution of the period.[1] Vast estates were controlled by nobles and higher clergy while their vassals tilled the land. This was an agrarian economy. The manor functioned as a relatively self-sufficient economic unit, although there was some exchange of commerce between manors, and between the manor and embryo towns.

In the manorial system "there were no loose, disorderly ends; everything was knotted into a firm relationship with every other thing." [2] The lord of the manor provided farm lands and protection for his vassals who, in turn, supplied the manor with food and other necessities. Clearly defined relationships and a sense of security on both sides, derived from this mutual-service society, perpetuated this system in some parts of Europe for 1000 years, roughly from A.D. 500 to 1500, and vestiges of the manor continued as late as the nineteenth century in Russia.

The manor also functioned as a business institution to barter for salt and other items not found or produced on the premises. But, as trade increased, the barter system was gradually replaced by a monetary system. In order to obtain money for his transactions the lord of the manor accepted and then demanded money in place of service from his vassals. The peasant was forced to change his generations-old practices, for the shift to the use of money had begun. The pressure on the peasant to produce surpluses to pay his money to his lord was solved by the needs of the bourgeoisie—the merchants and artisans—of the new towns. Incapable of provisioning themselves, these merchants and artisans depended on the peasantry for their daily bread.[3]

The growing substitution of money payments for labor services accelerated the breakdown of the manorial system. "This process depended necessarily upon an increased quantity of buying and selling, which, in turn, depended upon markets and other agencies facilitating sales." [4] The town with its regular markets and special fairs met these requirements and so hastened the end of feudalism. Economic, political, religious, and social organization were dramatically influenced by the revival of the cities. Capitalism emerged and the *bourgeoisie* demanded a political voice; the Church reversed its attitude toward profit and interest; and rigid social stratification became more flexible as serfs purchased their freedom. In short, Europe in the twelfth century was poised on the brink of a Commercial Revolution. The development of the town economy and early capitalism served as the springboard to the modern period.

THE RISE OF CITIES AND ECONOMIC ACTIVITY

The early medieval period in Western Europe was characterized by the absence of large and prosperous cities, which left the Church as the primary source of exchange between communities and offered virtually no opportunity for economic expansion. However, as the barbarian invasions decreased and the struggle for power between church and state lost momentum, an increasing orderliness of society developed outside the manorial system; trade and industry—the economic activities which create and support cities—became stabilized, and expanded.

In Italy, Spain, and southern France, a number of ancient Roman *municipia*, which had escaped destruction by the barbarians, preserved the remnants of an earlier culture to form the basis for the rise of cities. A favorable location frequently contributed to the rapid growth of a little village: seaports with good harbors, a river's edge with a bridge or ford, or a confluence of streams and old established trade routes. More often towns developed around a castle where the common people could find protection and employment. Artisans and merchants were attracted to monasteries for much the same reason.

The eleventh century brought an increase in population, of which the majority would have been glad to remain peasants bound to the soil. But the manors could use only so many. The surplus serfs were set "free," and like the unemployed of today, the "out-of-work" gravitated to the towns.[5] Underlying the Crusades movement, and the migrations of country populations to towns, was simply a "demand for more commodities to feed more mouths and clothe more bodies." [6] As trade expanded, the wealth of the merchant and artisan increased, and there was greater employment for labor. The growing distinction between wealth and servitude provided the necessary impetus for the great emancipation of cities which was to continue for more than 200 years. Thus, in the late Middle Ages, a renaissance of town life followed the rebirth of commerce and industry. During this period, from the middle of the tenth to the fourteenth century, virtually all the towns of Europe were revived. So intense was this renaissance that, "besides those countries in which urban life had always lingered on, such as Italy and the south of France, almost the whole of the West became covered with cities. The reappearance and extension of this urban life, which had been so shattered during the early Middle Ages, was closely connected with the formation and progress of the industrial and commercial classes." [7]

The emancipation of a town was occasionally accomplished by force of arms, but more often it was to the economic advantage of the manorial lord to grant a measure of freedom to the towns in his charge. This freedom ranged from release from required services to complete autonomy. No matter how attained, these rights were always set forth in a formal, written document, the charter.

The movement toward independence for the towns was not confined to any one country or area but spread almost simultaneously throughout Germany, Italy, England, Flanders, and France. Each country worked out its town structure according to its own circumstances and national characteristics. The result was the formation of the *stadt* in Germany, the *city* in Italy, the *borough* in England, and the *commune* in France.[8]

The *communes* of France illustrate best the variety of forms assumed by the new units. In the north of France the *commune jurée* was most prevalent: "all members bound themselves together by a mutual oath, which was the essential feature, the most important bond of unity, and a method of safeguarding their mutual rights." The *commune* frequently had the status of a vassal and, as such, swore an oath to the overlord; some *communes* occupied very independent positions, even to the point of having vassals of their own, while others were more limited in scope, but all were largely self-governing and able to act as a legal person. The *consulates* in the south of France knew greater independence than any other type of *commune:* indeed, Marseilles was practically a republic for a time. In the *consulate* the assembly of inhabitants played a greater role; and even the nobility, who were excluded from the government of the *commune jurée,* shared a large portion of authority. The *cité* was a special form of military *commune.* In central France the *ville de bourgeoisie* or *commune surveillée,* which possessed certain characteristics of the *commune* without the real political power, predominated. "A privileged community rather than a free *commune*," a *commune jurée* could very readily be transformed into a *commune surveillée*. And finally there were the specially created rural towns: the military *bastides* in the south; the *villes-neuves* of economic character in the north; and those towns created primarily by churches and monasteries, the *sauvetés*.[9]

The *commune* was the last remnant of the feudal system—a *bourgeois* group which either forced its way or was accepted willingly into the sphere of nobility. In fact, the *commune* took the place of the noble, controlling the town, yet carrying out the ordinary duties of a vassal although having vassals itself, and having its own court of justice.[10] It was simply a phase of economic development—neither a break with the past nor a revolution against feudal ideas—consistent with the period of feudalism in which it arose.

To the merchants who lived in the little feudal villages, and who formed the progressive element, must be given credit for the emancipation of towns: "the servitude in which the merchant and artisan lived became incompatible with the exigencies of their economic expansion. It was for this reason that the merchants, who between 1004 and 1080 were beginning to be called burgesses (*burgenses*) because of their habitual residence in the suburbs and new quarters of the fortified towns (*burgs*), sought in voluntary association the means of defense, which the feudal authorities could not provide them." [11]

Because the population of the new urban areas primarily formed a commercial society, there was a shift of social ideas. This shift resulted in the strongest practical criticism of the prevailing clerical theories of property and money-making. The reappearance of money changed the whole medieval outlook toward property. The eleventh-century mind saw wealth as the service a landholder could command. As money replaced the manorial system as the foundation of state organization, elaborate royal exchequers were organized throughout Europe and the idea of service *per se* diminished. For the first time in many centuries the land was thought of in terms of money equivalents, as an entity in itself, as a source of wealth, to be owned directly and absolutely, not simply in terms of conditional services.[12]

Underlying all forms of medieval *commune* there appeared a universal, continuous, and realistic policy pursued by urban states—a policy governed entirely by economic interests; its aim was to develop the power of production. Regardless of its system of government, the urban community in every case was motivated by the same ends that inspired the struggles for emancipation. The city had to insure the expansion of economic privilege, the power and prestige of the municipal state, and to this end once again had to challenge the prevailing feudal powers. "In order to better preserve them [municipal freedoms], it even resigned itself to renounce its exclusiveness and to form fraternities and leagues with other towns, such as those which were organized among the Lombard and Tuscan cities, the sixty-two cities of the Rhineland, the sixty-seven Flemish cities, the thirty-two cities of Leon and Galicia, and the maritime cities of Catabria, whose action safeguarded the liberties and economic prosperity of vast regions." [13]

Communal power reached its peak in the twelfth century, followed by a gradual decline as privileges began to be substituted for rights, and the ambition for freedom succumbed to the stronger ambition for trade. The Hanseatic League of almost 100 towns flourished briefly in the fourteenth and early fifteenth centuries, but it, too, succumbed. The individual town was far too weak to stave off the constantly increasing power of a government tending toward centralization. Many of the weaker associations were eliminated by financial difficulties; internal dissension wrecked the *commune*—the upper classes refusing to share power with the poorer members—and weakened the urban centers against external foes.

Many theories have been advanced for the origin of towns, but economic progress is the only cause that can be isolated as universal and underlying all the different immediate reasons, and all the complex forms of individual communal development. The city was responsible for the death of feudalism but, unable to provide an alternative form of stability, so essential for trade, it was compelled to support a new form of political organization. This form, the national state, fell prey to monarchial ambitions: "Royal support insidiously paved the way for royal predominance." [14]

The loss of the city's political autonomy should not be confused with a decline in importance of the urban movement. New forms of economic activity and new types of economic organization were constantly evolving in the towns and cities. "They were places not merely in which new commodities were traded and whence new markets and sources of supply were explored and conquered but in which appeared the first signs of new class relations based on alterations in the social division of labor." [15]

Town charters often contained codes regulating the sale and quality of all merchandise, but since high quality in a product cannot be regulated without involving the integrity of the maker, the civic authorities encouraged the organization of voluntary associations called craft guilds. The artisans welcomed these associations as a means of protecting themselves from competition. The town fathers were interested in protecting the consumer from fraud and in imposing the Catholic morality of a *justum pretium* (just price), while the guild members sought professional monopoly. To obtain honesty and quality the authorities sacrificed the principle of *justum pretium*.[16] With the consumer at the mercy of the guilds the expression became *caveat emptor* (let the buyer beware).

Within the guild a member sought the kind of protection he had known under the manorial lord: protection from foreign competition as well as protection from his fellow members. This subordination of the individual for the protection of all had, as its counterpart, the destruction of initiative. "No one was permitted to harm others by methods which enabled him to produce more quickly and more cheaply than they. Technical progress took on the appearance of disloyalty. The ideal was stable conditions in a stable industry." [17]

As long as the master craftsman abided by the strict regulations of the guild he could not rise above his fellow members and they all remained *petits bourgeois*. This system stressed security to the extent that it may be described as "noncapitalistic." [18] But eventually the craft guild was torn with internal dissension, as the more creative and productive members sought higher compensation for their ability and were forced either to capture the guild or evade it in some way. These members were becoming capitalists, interested in finding a more efficient means of employing investment capital.

THE EMERGENCE OF CAPITALISM

The fair was another contributor to the demise of the craft guild and its economic restrictions. The fair was an agency for trade extending far beyond the range of goods normally found in a town market. Caught up in a spirit of gaiety and excitement, coupled with religious overtones, the guild regulations against outside competition were often swept aside. The fair provided a meeting ground for merchants, wholesalers, money changers, bankers, and consumers who often traveled great distances to attend. Large transactions and poor travel facilities necessitated the use of new negotiable instruments such as bills of exchange, letters of credit, and promissory notes. Thus, the advance of credit and the expansion of trade were facilitated by the fair. By the time that unhappy artisans precipitated the decline of fairs in the fourteenth century, capitalism had arrived fully on the scene. The exclusiveness and privilege embodied in the craft guilds were through. The capitalist required complete freedom of movement.

The Italians were the first great capitalists. The following essay by H. R. Trevor-Roper illustrates their flexibility, ingenuity, and vitality.

*
We Europeans are parochial in our historical outlook. We recognise antiquity and our modern civilisation—for both are European ages: but the intervening period of Asiatic domination we dismiss as the Dark Ages. Now that the Dark Age of Asia is receding, the greatness of Europe, so long taken for granted, begins again to require explanation. How was it that that ruined and forgotten peninsula, whose civilisation once seemed to have passed away for ever, recovered power and wealth and culture to dominate the world again?

Partly, no doubt, thanks to the Church. Christianity, that Asiatic religion, profoundly modified by its adoption among the barbarians of Europe, provided, from the eleventh century, such slogans of war and conquest as Marxism, a European religion, similarly modified, now supplies to the natives of Asia. The crusades were Europe's protest against the dominance of Asia, Pope Gregory VII our Mao Tse-tung. And yet crusades alone are not enough. Fanaticism we have always with us: it only succeeds when it can also finance itself at a profit, and thereby tame and rationalize its own spirit. The revival of Europe was not achieved by Peter the Hermit, that Frankish *marabout*, but by the merchants of those Italian cities, last links with antiquity and the East, who, by financing and exploiting the crusades, led trade and civilization back to the West.

What a debt we owe to those few survivors of antique capitalism! Europe around them was almost entirely rural; trade had shrunk to the peddling of pilgrims; the techniques of large-scale commerce, denounced by the furious Fathers of the Church, had been largely forgotten; and in the Rome of Gregory the Great, capital of the Christian world, there had been, it seems, but a single banker. But in Venice, Bari and Amalfi—outposts of Byzantium and the East—the old techniques were preserved or rediscovered: the Venetians, financing and insuring their voyages by a system of partnership, settled at Constantinople and Alexandria and monopolized the trade of the Empire; and when the brief splendor of Amalfi and Bari was snuffed out, the fishermen of Genoa and Pisa inherited their commerce. By the time the

* From "The Medieval Italian Capitalists," from *Men and Events*, pp. 18–23, by H. R. Trevor-Roper. Copyright 1957 by W. A. Evill and A. D. Peters. Reprinted with permission of Harper and Row, Publishers, Inc.

Papacy was ready to proclaim the crusades, these three capitalist cities were equipped to finance, transport, and supply them. They earned their reward: their quarters and capitulations in captured towns throughout the Mediterranean—even in Constantinople itself—gave them the trade of the whole sea; they became bankers to the Popes who directed the campaigns, to the impoverished noblemen who fought in them. The Syrian seafarers retreated before them; the Jews declined into local usurers; and by tapping African gold in the Barbary ports they refreshed, indirectly, the economy of the whole continent. Behind them, in Piedmont and Tuscany, capital was accumulated, the wool industry organized, and banking begun: and industry and banking in turn raised up two inland cities—Milan and Florence—to rival the sea ports of Venice and Genoa as capitals of the mercantile world.

Throughout the Middle Ages these four cities held their position. In the great trade-boom which followed the crusades, when the Mongolian peace opened all Asia to their agents, they eclipsed all their rivals and solemnized their ascendancy by minting their own coins in the gold which they had reintroduced to Europe. In each of them, in the thirteenth century, the mercantile classes rose to political power; in each of them the form of that power was different. . . .

Venice, the earliest of all, retained throughout its original character. It was the city not of industry, nor of international finance (its only industry was the state-owned naval arsenal, its only borrower the city government), but of commercial capitalism and Eastern trade. Further, Venice was not merely (like Genoa) an oligarchy of great merchants: it was a mercantile state, whose machinery of government served not the interests of the merchants, but the commerce of the state. The 200 great merchant families might organize themselves around their empires in the Levant; but policy, appointments, war, the rules of commerce itself were strictly determined by the state. There were no private fleets, no private monopolies, but a state fleet, state monopolies, a whole economy directed by the state. In no Italian republic was the power and intervention of the state as firm as in the classic whig republic, in which alone, in a long history, the aristocracy was not split by faction or attenuated by exile—which alone gave to Europe not only wealth and culture, but a new political ideal: the "Venetian aristocracy."

What a contrast with Genoa! Genoa too was a purely commercial state, without industry. There too the government was controlled by great capitalist families. But there was no state. Government was the prey of faction: families with great private monopolies, great private fleets, struggled to control it. Having cornered the alum of Phocaea, Benedetto Zaccaria, in the thirteenth century, became admiral of Genoa and used his own fleet, headed by his flagship Divizia—"Wealth"—not only to crush the rival commerce of Pisa, but also, by capturing a personal empire, to monopolize every process in his cornered goods; and when the impecunious city wished to send a naval expedition against Monaco, it could only finance it by converting the sailors into a company to capture Chios on a profit-making basis. This cutthroat individualism, this religion of private wealth, enabled the Genoese to perfect many commercial techniques—portulan maps, bookkeeping by double entry, professional insurance; it denied them civic prosperity. Even when the creditors of state amalgamated themselves into a state bank, the Casa di S. Giorgio, the bank did not serve, it exploited the state: it became the means whereby a few rich families managed the treasury, the colonies, and trade in the interest of their private monopolies. And meanwhile the defeated families fled abroad or sold their skill to foreign powers—like that Genoese bank-agent who, having learned his employers' philosophy that gold is the key of earth and heaven, transferred his service to Spain and discovered America for the new masters of his city.

Those who suppose that the spirit of capitalism is hostile to art should clutch at the solitary instance of Genoa to support their fantasies: alone among Italian communes it was exempt from the Renaissance. But what of Venice, what of Siena, what of the Flemish towns, what of the greatest capitalist city of Italy—Florence? Tuscany came late to world commerce: Florence was a banking and industrial city long before it possessed a seaport, and the vast financial power of its great family companies was based first on a highly organized cloth industry, then on a fortunate alliance with Rome. In the thirteenth century a group of exiled Florentine citizens financed the papal conquest of Sicily and thereby their own return to power in Florence; and thereafter "the Guelf alliance" of Pope, King of Sicily, and Florentine bankers remained a constant in politics. At the end of the century, when the crash of the Bonsignori, "the Rothschilds of the thirteenth century" ruined the great banking houses of Siena, the Florentine companies were supreme. In Italy they organized a multiplicity of business, in food and clothing, metals and spices, relics, *objets d'art*, and slaves; they had branches in Italy and abroad; they accepted deposits and advanced loans; they handled the revenues of Popes and kings; they established mints and insurance companies, postal and intelligence services—until in the end their vast fortunes depended on credit and their credit on the politics of their royal clients. A political scare in 1342 caused a rush on the banks that ruined the lesser companies; and even the three great survivors—the Bardi, the Peruzzi, the Acciaiuoli—"the columns of Christendom"—crashed four years later with the failure of their greatest client, Edward III of England. Nevertheless, the system was reorganized and continued: its leaders controlled government and policy and finance in their own interest; they seemed immune—except from proletarian rising or *coups d'état* by ambitious individuals among themselves. In the end it was the latter that prevailed: the greatest financial dynasty of Florence—the Medici—became the Grand Dukes of Tuscany.

Meanwhile what of the Church, whose alliance, whose war-slogans, whose financial needs had so favored the communes? Christianity was a pacifist religion, and its original anticapitalist doctrines had been reformulated with an added emphasis for a society of rural barbarians. The pacifism indeed had been rejected in the eleventh century; what of the anticapitalism, now that the Church and its allies were alike great capitalist organizations? Little by little the orthodox faced their dilemma. Sometimes there were spectacular *crises de conscience*. So a Sienese financier in 1360 abandoned his office and, magnifying the name of Jesus through the villages of Tuscany, founded the mendicant order of the Gesuati. Others compromised less painfully by vicarious sacrifice: the Florentine millionaires gave largely to the poor, commissioned Giotto and Orcagna to glorify holy Poverty in paint, and arranged for their own burial by the mendicant orders which they had enriched. But this delicate equilibrium could not last for ever. Already at the end of the fourteenth century a mendicant friar was preaching that wealth was an estate pleasing to God (he soon became a rich cardinal); a few years later a Sienese saint would affirm the legitimacy of usury, the utility of high finance; and a Florentine bishop would argue that wealth, however acquired, was intrinsically good. A century later, when the Genoese plutocracy hovered on the edge of heresy, a Jesuit reclaimed them by his famous sermons on the rate of interest.

. . . Venice long dominated the trade of the East, a model of government to other merchant states; Tuscany, with its new port of Leghorn, became a great commercial power; and the century of Spanish predominance has been called, in the history of finance, "the century of the Genoese." And if Genoa and Florence had lost their civic independence, their exiled citizens, like Europeans today, carried their talents abroad. The Genoese bankers became grandees of Spain, the Florentines peers of France. Even in England the family of an exiled Genoese financier propped up, by a quadruple marriage, the Protectoral house of Cromwell, and a member of the expatriate Florentine family of Dante's Beatrice designed, for Queen Elizabeth, the fortifications of Berwick-on-Tweed.

THE COMMERCIAL REVOLUTION

The highly profitable trade begun with the East, as a result of the Crusades, was monopolized by the Italian city-states until the Age of Discovery signaled the end of Venetian dominance. With the discovery of new trade routes and new "indies," the Spanish, Portuguese, English, French, and Dutch began to expand their own horizons.

The transformation of European populations from rural to urban, and of political structures from feudal to nation states, begun several centuries earlier, was accelerated by the tremendous increase in commerce. The period 1400 and 1700 is called the Commercial Revolution, one of many labels attached to this seminal phase in history. The Renaissance, The Reformation, The Age of Discovery, The Age of Absolutism, and The Age of Mercantilism are other terms emphasizing various aspects of the period.

The expansion of trade, the "opening" of Europe, and the Church reforms all made possible the emergence of a new concept of state embodied in the absolute person of the monarch who, with the aid of capitalism and in the void left by decline in Church authority, pulled together the fragments of feudalism to form the nation, under strong central control. The capitalist supported this consolidation of power because his national and international economic interests could not be protected otherwise. The discoveries of new trade routes and new lands were financed jointly by kings and capitalists. Armies and navies were necessary to protect the new trade and colonies. National strength bought with tax monies derived from commerce brought prestige to the king. Protection of commerce benefited the investors. Internal quarrels of the Church permitted heretical scientific discoveries to be applied in the interest of the state and commerce; the invention of movable type made possible the mass printing of books and laid the groundwork for technical as well as humanistic advance. Universities secured endowments from wealthy merchants; the Protestant Reformation made possible the religious sanction and elevation of the profit motive; the king, mutually aided by capitalist and clerical factions, was able to consolidate his nation, and especially his own position as a "divine right."

By attempting to persuade the king to enact legislation which would discriminate against foreign competition, businessmen sought the same kind of protection and privilege previously found in the craft guilds. Duties and prohibitions of the medieval period were reactivated to become approved devices of national commercial policy. Maintaining the power of the national state—that is, to finance the men and weapons of war—required vast sums of metallic money. Any transaction that brought gold and silver into the country was viewed as desirable; and the encouragement of manufacturing called *bullionism*, because it commanded the largest amount of gold and silver, was seen as the patriotic duty of all citizens.

The system developing from the joining of economic and political interests was called *mercantilism*. The theory of mercantilism was simply to achieve a perpetual "favorable balance of trade" or an excess of exports over imports, which would provide the revenues desired by king and capitalist alike. The founding of the American Colonies by England was one example of an attempt to apply mercantile theory. The Colonies were established for the express purpose of providing cheap raw materials for British manufacture, and markets for surplus British production. The Acts of Trade and Navigation, a contributing cause of the American Revolution, were a collection of several generations of mercantilist regulations. That mercantilism failed in the New World was typical of the poverty of the theory; but if mercantilism failed as a grand scheme, it was highly successful in a limited sense, for it placed the power of the state behind capitalism and so hastened the transition from a feudal to a capitalistic economy. Large scale ventures required more capital investment and sharing of the risk than a single individual or partnership could bear. Deriving its name from the practice of accumulating sufficient funds by assessing each shareholder, the joint-stock company emerged for large ventures. As a further means of assuming risk, shares in these companies were gradually made divisible into salable units and, finally, the concept of paid-up shares developed, no longer subject to assessment. Hence, the idea of limited liability has become one of the distinctive features of modern corporate practice.

Mercantilism can be seen as a voluntary system of a totalitarian nature with all the resources of a nation turned to national enrichment. In the beginning, merchants beseeched the government for legislation useful in promoting their own profits. When, by the eighteenth century, they were a good deal stronger they sought means of shaking off government *controls* which were now seen as oppressive. This was accomplished by operating outside the regulations or by capturing the government.

The growing demand for consumer goods encouraged business expansion, and a new industrial practice replaced the guild system. The new practice was the domestic system. A merchant capitalist, or entrepreneur, bought raw materials and distributed them to artisans to be processed in their own homes for specified wages. The finished product belonged to the entrepreneur, who disposed of it in the market. This system was thoroughly capitalistic. Industrial policies and practices were dictated by the owners of capital; hence, a clear differentiation arose between making goods and making money.

The following excerpt sums up the effect of the Commercial Revolution on the habits of individuals and nations.

* The discovery of the Atlantic routes marked or caused a revolution in this respect; a revolution that took some centuries to produce its full effect. Commerce began to assume not merely a new scale, but a new character; it did not merely employ larger vessels and greater capital, it shipped popular cargoes. When the Dutch and the English first competed in the East, the Spice Islands were counted the chief prize; by the end of the eighteenth century the Spice Islands and India had changed places, and it was doubted whether the cost of keeping those islands was repaid by their profits. For commerce had begun to provide for the many; to depend on popular consumption; to enter into the daily life of the ordinary man. India and America sent new delicacies to England, and in the course of a century, owing to a number of causes—the growth of commercial capital, the development of the arts and machinery of trade, the improvement of transport, changes of habits and manner of life—those delicacies were brought within reach of the poorer classes and passed into general consumption. Tea, sugar, and tobacco took the place of pepper, spices, and cloves, as the chief articles of commerce.

Tea, when first imported by the East India Company, was a highly priced luxury, but by the middle of the eighteenth century it was a popular drink. A writer complained as early as 1742 that "the meanest families" in the Lowlands of Scotland had given up beer for tea. Cobbett, and Hanway, the philanthropist, agreed that tea drinking was robbing the English people both of their health and their beauty. "Your very chambermaids," wrote Hanway "have lost their bloom by sipping Tea." By 1828 the yearly consumption of tea in these islands had reached 36,000,000 lbs. Sugar grew rapidly in favor. In the Middle Ages the Englishman sweetened his food with honey. Until the seventeenth century sugar was a rich man's luxury; at the beginning of the eighteenth century England imported 20,000,000 lbs., and by 1782, 160,000,000 lbs. Rice was another novelty brought from America. In a cookery book printed in 1734 there is not a single recipe for the preparation of rice; in another printed at the end of the century there are twenty-two.

Thus ships were now sailing across the Atlantic, or rounding the Cape of Good Hope, bringing cargoes destined, not for palace or cathedral, but for the alley and the cottage; Capitalist commerce was providing for the wants of the peasant and the workman, as well as for the taste of noble or cardinal, rich merchant or prosperous lawyer. Owing to new resources, new products, new materials, new habits, expansion of wealth and the development of finance, commerce increased rapidly in volume and scale, and this change in degree was accompanied or followed by a change in kind. The day when more profit was to be made by carrying tea for the poor from India than by

* J. L. and Barbara Hammond, *The Rise of Modern Industry*, London: Methuen & Co. Ltd., 1951, pp. 21–23. By permission of the publishers.

carrying pepper for the rich from Java marked an important stage in the progress of the world to the modern system.

The commercial revolution of the fifteenth and sixteenth centuries was an essential preliminary to the industrial revolution of the eighteenth and nineteenth centuries. For capitalist manufacture on the modern scale was only possible when capital could be applied to the production of goods that were consumed by the mass of the people, and it was the use of capital for this purpose that gave the Industrial Revolution its sweeping character. As pepper gives way to tea, so silk gives way to cotton. The relations of Europe and the world outside are reversed: Europe that had drawn on Asia for manufactures takes the lead in production. The conditions arise that make possible so strange a spectacle as that of a Lancashire town using a raw material, not grown on English soil, to produce goods that are exported for popular consumption to India or China. England has learnt how to make greater fortunes from clothing the poor in the simple fabrics of Manchester than had ever been made from clothing the rich in the gorgeous fantasies of Babylon or Damascus.

. . . The wants of the ordinary man were supplied in the early Middle Ages, as in the days of Greece and Rome, either by himself and his family or by his neighbors; in the next stage these wants were supplied by special persons plying a craft, in a village or small town, organized sometimes in guilds; in the third stage the provision of those needs became the business of individual or group production and large-scale merchanting; in the fourth it became the business of large scale production. At that point the world passes to the industrial age: to an age in which commerce and finance are no longer aspects, growing in importance, yet still aspects of its life, but the basis on which a society depends. The English people were the first to develop this system, to enjoy its wealth, to suffer its evils, to struggle with its problems, and to build on this foundation an imposing place and power in the world.

THE INDUSTRIAL REVOLUTION

As stated by the Hammonds, the English were the first people to pass into the industrial age which brought the substitution of machines for the tools of craftsmen, machine labor for human labor, and new kinds of power for manpower. England had entered "the years of coal, iron, and steam." [19]

The Industrial Revolution has been viewed alternately as a "smoking hell" by historians of a pessimistic turn, and as a remarkable period of enterprise and achievement by optimists.[20] In the following excerpt, Karl de Schweinitz, Jr. presents a brief and balanced analysis of what must be considered a crucial phase in Western cultural evolution:

* In the years from 1760 to 1840 Great Britain developed the characteristics of industrial society: the factory system and wage labor; high urban population concentrations; a systematic internal transportation network; capital intensive methods of production. So profound were these developments that the period traditionally is called the Industrial Revolution. In only little more than two generations the Feudal and mercantilistic organization of economic activity was replaced by sef-regulating markets. A new way of life arose which was both cause and effect of the industrial age. Great Britain in 1840 was significantly different from Great Britain in 1760.

In the eighteenth century, the increased demand for goods arising from the expansion of world markets revealed a series of bottlenecks which restricted the productive capacity of the British economy. These bottlenecks stimulated people, close enough to the production processes to be aware of their technological inadequacies, to experiment with new methods of production. Entrepreneurship flourished and, in consequence, as the eighteenth century unfolded, one bottleneck after another was broken. The internal transportation system, which early in the century was almost inoperative, was improved by the construction of canals and turnpikes. The open field system was destroyed by the enclosures in the last half of the century. The disaster facing the iron industry because of the disappearance of the forest was averted by the perfection of the coking process. In the textile industry a series of mechanical inventions made the factory system a more economical form of organization than the domestic system, and, when Watt perfected the steam engine, it became possible for factories to be located in urban areas. Watt's steam engine also facilitated the drainage of the coal mines, giving an impetus to the production of coal.

By the turn of the nineteenth century the British economy was rapidly approaching the railway age. The shackles of mercantilism had been perceptibly loosened and, if there were still abundant traces of the older forms of economic organization, the future nonetheless lay with industrial capitalism. The metamorphosis and expansion of the textile industry and the increasing utilization of steam by British firms created a greater market for the products of the metallurgical industry, the development of which eventually made possible the construction of railways.

The entrepreneurs who pioneered the new industrial techniques did not have ready access to a supply of capital. In the middle of the eighteenth century, investment in industrial enterprise, with its commitments to fixed assets, had not yet become common. Furthermore, the joint-stock company was not yet the common form of organization in industrial enterprise. It was not possible, then, to reach the saving public by selling shares.

* Karl de Schweinitz, Jr., "Economic Growth, Coercion, and Freedom," *World Politics*, ix:2, January 1957, pp. 171–179 *passim*.

Confronted by these difficulties . . . entrepreneurs could most expeditiously finance industrial growth through retained earnings, a process facilitated by the rise of prices relative to wages—in other words, by a widening of the inequality of income.

The atrophy of the guilds and the delayed growth of the trade unions were symptomatic of the hiatus, so successfully exploited by industrial capitalism, between the old world of corporate responsibility and the new world of individual responsibility.

As the tempo of the Industrial Revolution picked up during the nineteenth century, the ranks of the proletariat increased. Although ostensibly aided by the repeal of the Combination Acts of 1824, the trade unions still were not able to achieve permanent organization. Not only was the government willing to persecute union members when successful organizational action seemed imminent, but the instability of income in industrial capitalism inhibited the building-up of the financial strength of the unions.

The absence of political democracy and of an independent union movement compelled the worker to accept the verdict of the market with respect to the distribution of income. Industrial capitalism thus developed amidst institutions which prevented the investment surplus from being dissipated in additional consumption.

. . . As the Industrial Revolution developed beyond a certain critical stage—perhaps the fourth decade of the 19th century—elements in the objective environment started to lower perceptibly the coercive potential of economic growth. The national product had risen enough to allow the real income of many workers to increase without reducing the investment surplus. At the end of the Industrial Revolution, many workers had raised their standard of consumption and some had increased their level of saving as well. Economic growth contained within itself the means of ameliorating its coercive impact.

Furthermore, while it destroyed many handicrafts, the Industrial Revolution proliferated the number of skilled and semi-skilled industrial occupations on which the economy depended. There were, then, employment opportunities created that tended to increase the degree of upward social mobility, at least within the broad aggregate we have called the working classes. Rather than increasing the homogeneity of the class structure, as Marx would have us believe, the Industrial Revolution increased its heterogeneity. Some workers thereby acquired a special stake in the system. Finally, the labor force became further removed from the mercantilist world, the further the nineteenth century advanced. A new generation of workers whose links with that world were weak and who were more accustomed than their fathers to the ways of the industrial world formed the core of the labor force. Being more completely a part of one way of life, the workers were more likely to become habituated to the values it represented.

T. S. Ashton has written corroboratively:

> In 1802 George Chalmers remarked that the laborious classes were "too wealthy to covet the pittance of the soldier, or too independent to court the dangers of the sailor." There were, true enough, many vagrants and paupers, but, even before the new Poor Law came in, the hordes of the "indigent and distressed" had probably shrunk. Hours of labour were long, and holidays few; there is a mass of evidence that employment in factories was harmful to the health and morals of the young . . . But against all this must be set the lessening of strain on those who worked in the heavy trades, and the decline in the number of crippled and deformed people that followed the introduction of power in places like Sheffield. There must be set, also, the reduction of sweating of women and young children, the rise in family earnings, the greater regularity of pay, and the gain in welfare that came as industrial work was taken out of the home.[21]

Indeed, economic growth contained within itself the means of softening its coercive impact, and successful capitalism produced the seeds of a vital trade union movement. Just as industrialists needed predictability of markets for long-term profits, industrial workers needed stable employment to produce the surplus wages to support union organization.

Yet all of this was accomplished without the destruction of society, despite the strains imposed on society by the push and pull of rapid economic development. "This was the Victorian lesson, and one very well worth learning . . . ; the achievement of social peace." [22]

After the Industrial Revolution "the essential distinction in earlier times between enterprise and avarice was lost, and the idea of efficiency assumed the role of one of the highest moral virtues." [23] The revolution provided an important base for consolidating and extending its teachings in the so-called Age of Moguls and the later "managerial revolution."

Favored by a timely combination of political maturity, growing supplies of land, labor, and capital, technological discovery and invention, a revolution in agriculture, and extensive coal deposits, Britain was the first nation to derive great economic and political power from industrialization. Although late on the industrial scene, most of Europe, the United States, and Japan closed the gap in short order. By the end of the nineteenth century Germany and America had successfully challenged British leadership in heavy industry, but all nations benefited immeasurably from the pioneering, trial-and-error progress of British industrialism.

America's particular contributions to the industrial progress of the world have been the invention of interchangeable parts—formerly called the "American System" in Europe—standardization, assembly-line techniques, and mass production. These resulted in the greater specialization of labor and simplification of the work process. The importance of these and other changes in the relationship of labor to production will be examined in Chapter 17.

CONCLUSION

As historic changes take place in the economic institutions, certain patterns of behavior are repeated. The desire of man to find security, first in informal, then formal voluntary associations has been illustrated in the manorial system, the town, the guild, the nation; and, as we shall see, in trade unions, cartels, corporations, trusts, market sharing, and professional associations.[24] These associations represent, in each case, the consolidation and institutionalization of some revolutionary change wrought by individuals who broke the bonds of existing economic, political, or social circumstances. *Laissez faire*—that is, letting people do what they choose without interference—and private enterprise, the ideological successors to mercantilism, are often spoken of as synonymous with individualism, and perhaps this was true in the beginning. But as individuals attain their goals, they tend to block the road to others. There is now something to be guarded, and like-minded individuals form protective associations. As they rationalize their actions, the revolution begins to fade and becomes tradition, complete with its own myths and regulations.

The true *spirit* of capitalism is incompatible with tradition. The pioneer capitalist is interested in the idea of profit rather than in money itself. He enjoys the game; he is not seeking security. His associations tend to be short-lived and are terminated when they become static, stagnant, and unchallenging. From the Italian capitalist to the contemporary "discounter," [25] the pattern appears to remain the same. The *forward* movement of Western economies has been piloted by these "rugged individualists," not by the great merchants or industrialists or financiers *as such*. The "lone wolf" capitalist is absorbed with risk for the sheer sake of risk—with the process of venture—which is the spirit of capitalism as distinguished from the consolidation and conservation of capital.

But there is more to capitalism than a capricious spirit. There is the *substance* of capitalism, the power developed out of man's labor and acquisitiveness when these are orderly and efficient. This power can bring physical security to the majority; but security is fleeting and must be retrieved constantly through the vitality of the capitalistic system. The drift toward conservatism and institutionalization makes it necessary for the spirit of capitalism to inject new blood into the system in the form of new business and production techniques, new products, new markets, and new capital. The remaining chapters in Part Five explore the scope of American capitalism.

Notes

1. Henri Pirenne, *Economic and Social History of Medieval Europe*, New York: Harcourt, Brace and Company, 1937, pp. 63–64.
2. Oscar Handlin, *The Uprooted* (Grosset's Universal Library Edition), New York: Grosset and Dunlap, 1951, p. 9.
3. Pirenne, *op. cit.*, p. 79.
4. E. A. J. Johnson and Herman E. Krooss, *The American Economy*, Englewood Cliffs: Prentice-Hall, Inc., 1960, p. 25.
5. Summerfield Baldwin, *Business in the Middle Ages*, New York: Henry Holt and Company, 1937, p. 49.
6. *Ibid.*, p. 40.
7. P. Boissonnade, *Life and Work in Medieval Europe*, New York: Alfred A. Knopf, 1927, p. 191. The early Middle Ages, dating approximately from A.D. 500 to 1000, have sometimes been called the Dark Ages because of the barbarian intrusions. However, the latter term is seldom used by modern historians. The late Middle Ages span the period from the eleventh century to the Renaissance.
8. Eleanor C. Lodge, "The Communal Movement, Especially in France," in *The Cambridge Medieval History*, Vol. V., J. R. Tanner, C. W. Previté-Orton, and Z. N. Brooke (eds.), New York: The Macmillan Company, 1929, p. 624.
9. *Ibid.*, pp. 626–629.
10. V. Langlois, "Evolution in the Direction of Monarchy," in *Medieval France*, Arthur Tilley (ed.), Cambridge: The Harvard University Press, 1922, p. 67.
11. Boissonnade, *op. cit.*, pp. 192–193.
12. E. F. Jacob, "The Growth of Autonomy," in *Encyclopaedia of the Social Sciences*, Vol. I., Edwin R. A. Seligman (ed.), New York: The Macmillan Company, 1930, pp. 75–76.
13. Boissonnade, *op. cit.*, pp. 200–201.
14. Lodge, *op. cit.*, p. 625.
15. Bert F. Hoselitz, *Sociological Aspects of Economic Growth*, Glencoe, Ill.: The Free Press, 1960, p. 170.
16. Pirenne, *op. cit.*, pp. 182–183.
17. *Ibid.*, pp. 185–186.
18. *Ibid.*, p. 187.
19. W. Woodruff, "Capitalism and the Historians," *Journal of Economic History*, XVI:1, March 1956, p. 2.
20. *Ibid.*, p. 1.
21. T. S. Ashton, *The Industrial Revolution*, London: Oxford University Press, 1948, p. 160.
22. Woodruff, *op. cit.*, p. 8.

23. *Ibid.*, p. 14.
24. Johnson and Krooss see the essence of the craft guild living on in such groups as the American Medical Association. *Op. cit.*, p. 38.
25. See the discussion of Eugene Kerkauf and his discount operation, E. J. Korvette, Inc., in Chapter XVIII.

Selected Readings

Ashton, T. S. *The Industrial Revolution*. London: Oxford University Press, 1948.
*Drucker, Peter. *The Concept of the Corporation*. Boston: Beacon Press, 1961.
*Hammond, J. L. and B. *The Bleak Age*. Baltimore: Penguin Books, 1947.
Heckscher, Eli. *Mercantilism*. New York: The Macmillan Company, 1955. 2 vols.
*Nowell, Charles. *Great Discoveries and the First Colonial Empires*. Ithaca: Cornell University Press, 1961.
*Polanyi, Karl. *The Great Transformation*. Boston: Beacon Press, 1959.
*Sievers, Allen. *Revolution, Evolution, and the Economic Order*. Englewood Cliffs: Spectrum Books, 1962.
*Sombart, Werner. *The Jews and Modern Capitalism*. New York: Collier Books, 1961.
*Toynbee, Arnold. *The Industrial Revolution*. Boston: Beacon Press, 1960.
*Weber, Max. *General Economic History*. New York: Collier Books, 1961.

* Paperback edition.

Chapter 16

The Ideologies
of American Capitalism

The great changes described in Chapter 15—the decline of the guild system, the rise of new means of organizing labor, the commercial and industrial revolutions—brought into being a new economic system. That system was modern industrial capitalism.

THE NATURE OF INDUSTRIAL CAPITALISM

Industrial capitalism, as Max Weber classified it, has six major factors by which its existence may be presupposed.[1] The first is an accounting system for a rational calculation of profit. All phases of investment, services, and costs, including those of the investor, are taken into account.[2] A second factor is the development of a free market in which there are no arbitrary limitations on consumption, such as restrictions of class. The third factor is the development of a scheme of production of goods and services through the application of technology. This makes possible a more exact calculation of time, cost, and efficiency. Calculable law is the fourth factor. Such law removes arbitrary power of decision among rulers which, if allowed to exist, would limit the applicability of the above processes. The fifth factor is the presence of a free labor pool. This is a necessary condition, for workingmen must sell their labor in order to subsist; hence, the costs of labor in production can be anticipated by the producer. The commercialization of life is the final factor by which the existence of industrial capitalism can be presumed. Commercialization refers to the sharing of ownership by converting the tools and facilities of production into negotiable paper, such as stocks and bonds, thus giving rise to speculation.

Modern industrial capitalism rose in the seventeenth and eighteenth centuries, although capitalism existed in an early form in the Italian city-states of the late Middle Ages. Capitalistic enterprise also existed in the ancient urban civilizations of Babylonia and the Near East.[3]

Weber has pointed out, however, that non-Western forms of capitalism, and those capitalistic enterprises that existed in the West prior to the seventeenth century, were not in every respect similar to industrial capitalism. He called them forms of political capitalism,[4] not interested in a rational calculation of profit, but in profits derived from the preparation and conduct of war, conquest, and the economic opportunities created by political administration. Thus, industrial capitalism is a unique development among economic systems.

Industrial capitalism had its first upsurge in England, and shortly after, in the United States. In both countries, the rise of industrial capitalism was accompanied by the emergence of the middle class, persons who owned and operated their own property. This was the class to be named the *bourgeoisie* by Karl Marx. Ownership of a business or factory was based on personal investment, family wealth, or capital belonging to friends. In the early factory system it was not unusual to find the principal owner working in a supervisory capacity within the plant.

The growth of the middle class in both England and America was not without difficulty. The middle class in England met with increasing opposition from the hereditary aristocracy, especially as the new class infringed on economic opportunity which the aristocracy had previously enjoyed under the various forms of political capitalism. In America, before the Revolutionary War, class domination of the colonial economy took the form of imperial decrees from the British mercantile system, as Britain enjoyed the economic benefits of political rule. Under the mercantile system domestic American manufacturing was strictly limited, and trade in exports and imports restricted to Britain. Under the Articles of Confederation after the Revolution, economic chaos prevailed as each state was empowered to tax imports, coin its own money, and act as an autonomous legal power.

England and America gradually enacted reforms which freed the middle classes from tradition, and from unsound economic practices. A series of reform bills in England, beginning in 1832, changed the system of parliamentary seating to give industrial areas representation in Parliament for the first time. Before the Reform Bill of 1832, for example, two representatives were sent to Parliament from the deserted site of Old Sarum, but the large industrial city of Manchester had not one.[5] In America, the Constitution, which established a centralized government, created a favorable climate for business: no longer could any state levy taxes on goods transported between states, or coin its own money; and no state could refuse to honor the legal actions of another.[6]

As the rapidly growing industrial middle class accumulated the economic and political power basic to a new institution, it also developed the need for an acceptable explanation of middle-class existence. In other words, an institutionalized middle class needed an ideology. Having an ideology satisfies members of the class by justifying their role in it; the explanation for the class becomes logical, and members accept the class and their roles in it as normal and natural.

The remaining sections of this chapter review the changing ideologies within the industrial capitalistic system which more than explain the operation of the system. They functioned, first, to justify the break with traditional forms of production, labor, and authority, and second, to justify the assumption of authority by a particular class. There have been three phases in the development of ideologies within industrial capitalism: the development of an entrepreneurial ideology, followed by the ideology of the robber barons or moguls, and last, the ideology of modern management.

THE ENTREPRENEURIAL IDEOLOGY

During the late eighteenth century, in England and in America, the industrial middle class developed an entrepreneurial ideology.[7] This was the ideology that sought to justify the middle-class break with political capitalism, to explain its growing political and economic eminence, and to rationalize its authority over the working class.

The document that systematically stated the entrepreneurial ideology of the early industrial middle class was Adam Smith's *An Inquiry into the Nature and Causes of the Wealth of Nations*. Smith's work, to be sure, was not the only one to expound the early ideology. Ministers, pamphleteers, and the industrialists, themselves, contributed to its formulation.[8] Many statements were more lucid and shorter than Smith's but few presented more detailed insight and grasp of broad vistas of knowledge. *The Wealth of Nations* appeared, interestingly enough, in 1776, and was an immediate success. There were five editions of the book before Smith's death.

The Wealth of Nations began with the question: how can a nation increase its wealth? Smith did not believe that the mercantile system, by which government regulated commerce, was the answer. He believed that mercantilism disturbed the functioning of certain natural processes. The most important natural process was the division of labor. A man had to be free in order to pursue his natural talents. Idleness, carelessness, and slothfulness developed when men were bound to tasks for which they were not naturally gifted. As a man did what he could do best, thus pursuing his own self-interests, there would be an increase in his skill, a saving of time, and an increase in production. This led, in turn, to further efficiency as the worker, his mind fixed on a specific operation, discovered an easier and shorter way of completing it. A natural expansion of the technological base of production would then follow, leading to a more rational calculation of profits to the benefit of all.

What are the implications of Smith's theories? Clearly, he stated that government should not interfere with the *market*. He was also quite clear in his view that all men should do what suited them best. This belief was, of course, in direct conflict with the traditional concepts of labor still existing in England and elsewhere as a vestige of the feudal system. Indeed, the first reactions to Smith were based on the notion that to create a free labor market would lead to chaos. But Smith had an answer. As each man did what he was naturally endowed for, and as each applied himself with concentration to those skills, a natural harmony of relationships would result. Each individual would eventually find his own strand in the web of life.

The division of labor, according to Smith, was limited by the extent of the market, just as was the amount of any item that could be produced. In rural areas a particular specialization might have little or no marketability; of necessity, therefore, the individual had to perform other tasks in order to live. In a city it was usually easier to apply one's skills. Smith noted with optimism that it would not be long until the diversified market of the city would be carried to the rural areas, thus alleviating all problems.

What, in Smith's thinking, justified the control of the economic system by the middle class? He did not give a direct answer to this question, for his thinking was not directed to any one class. Smith indicated that the natural effort of every individual to better his own condition was such a powerful force that it could overcome all obstacles and carry the individual and the society to wealth and prosperity. This was all the justification the middle class needed, for it then pointed to its own prosperity as a triumph of individual initiative; and to the working class as people without drive—idle, careless, and slothful. Success was a triumph of virtue.

Further justification of the position of the industrial middle class came from Thomas R. Malthus, whose famous *Essay on Population*, published in 1798, did much to comfort the conscience of the wealthy.[9]

Malthus based his thesis on the idea that population increased, according to a law of nature, faster than the means of subsistence. The only way to check population increase was to stop vice and misery, or to instill strict moral codes and delay marriage. No census had ever been taken in England, but Malthus believed that the poor had the highest birth rate, and that their wretched condition was their own creation. Self-discipline and adherence to strict morality was their only hope. Aid from the wealthy was of no benefit for it would only increase the birth rate of the lower classes. The wealthy could only set a moral example by encouraging thrift, cleanliness, and prudence. If the poor continued to suffer, despite all efforts to educate them, the fault would be their own.

We find in Smith and Malthus the attempts to interpret economic and other social phenomena by appealing to natural law and to moral rightness stemming from those laws. Certainly there was nothing new in this, as Cicero, a senator of ancient Rome, indicated in his dialogue, *The Laws*. The difference appears when we understand that, in the ideology of the early entrepreneurs, natural law ceased to be a philosophical concept, and became, instead, a fact. As the nineteenth century unfolded, new "facts" were added to the ideology.

SOCIAL DARWINISM IN AMERICA: THE ENTREPRENEUR AS MOGUL

The initial phase of industrial capitalism passed quickly into a second phase as the nineteenth century progressed. The rapid growth of technology, the trend toward increased centralization of the means of production, and the rapid expansion of markets led, as we saw in the last chapter, to the formation of corporations. The rise of the corporation as a means of raising capital was a new experience in nineteenth-century America. In 1800, there were some two-score corporations in England and France, but, by that same year, 300 corporations had been chartered in the United States.[10] The corporation was used widely as a means of raising capital in America where there were comparatively few persons of great wealth but many businesses—especially those on a large scale, such as transport—that needed great sums of capital. The corporation was an excellent method for obtaining small sums of investment capital from a large number of investors.[11]

With the emergence of the corporation as the principal vehicle of business, three major trends developed. One was the beginning of a distinction between ownership and management. No longer did one individual attempt to understand intimately the nature of the production process or the many purposes of the product. These matters could best be left to a small but competent managerial group. The second trend was the increasing fluidity of ownership. Property was in the form of transferable and negotiable paper such as stocks and bonds; ownership could change hands in a matter of minutes. This, of course, stimulated speculation which led, in turn, to the third trend of the nineteenth century—corporate development, or the concentration of ownership. With no personal income taxes, little or no governmental regulation of investment procedures, and with industrialization not yet fully developed, those who gained control of key forms of production and distribution could, financially speaking, conquer a nation.

The result was a new breed of entrepreneur known variously as titan, robber baron, mogul. Men such as Jay Gould, J. Pierpont Morgan, the Rockefellers, William Vanderbilt, Andrew Carnegie, Jay Cooke, James Fisk, Collis Huntington, and Leland Stanford became the leaders of America's new industrial enterprise. In the main, these were men born to humble circumstances. Gould and John D. Rockefeller were sons of farmers, Huntington was a peddler, and Cooke worked as a clerk on the frontier.[12] They created the image of the self-made man, exemplified the optimism of America, and became symbols of individualism.

The moguls achieved their eminence, literally, by any method that brought desired results.[13] Few hesitated to bribe congressmen, to ruin competitors by any means available from dynamiting to kidnapping, or to manipulate stock transactions.[14] A railroad controversy between Fisk and Morgan was settled by mounting two steam engines at opposite ends of track and running them into each other.[15] Commodore Vanderbilt, in heaping revenge on some of his associates who had tried to ruin him, asked, "What do I care about the law? Hain't I got the power?" [16] In one of the most famous cases of bilking investors, Henry Rogers and William Rockefeller borrowed money to cover their purchase of the Anaconda Copper Company from Marcus Daly for $39 million. Rockefeller and Rogers then created a dummy copper company, sold $75 million in stock through the New York Stock Exchange, retired the loan for $39 million and pocketed $36 million in personal profit, together with the Anaconda properties.[17]

In many of these transactions the moguls, America's staunchest defenders of free enterprise, sought government assistance. The Morrill Tariff of 1861 reversed the downward trend of American tariffs and established the policy of high protective tariffs.[18] The tariff not only meant protection for domestic industries but also provided a means of financing the Civil War other than by taxes, and, incidentally, favored the expansion of industrial capitalism. Although repudiated in the following election, the McKinley Tariff of 1890 increased the rate almost 50 per cent.[19] The moguls also profited from government land grants, especially to the railroads.

The great financial empires soon brought cries of monopoly. Adam Smith had already pointed out the dangers of monopoly by stating that monopolistic practices destroyed competition, the self-regulating mechanism of the market. Monopoly would also increase prices and deprive the monopolistic enterprise of any opportunity in new areas of manufacturing which could prove beneficial to the monopoly and to the society at large.

Urban, middle-class professionals and small businessmen had the greatest fear of monopoly. Professionals, especially those in law and university teaching, feared the potential control of monopolies over their occupations. Small businessmen could not compete with the production and distribution facilities of the large corporations. These two economic groups were joined by the consumer who faced the prospect of manipulated prices. The fears of these groups expressed themselves in federal legislation. The Sherman Antitrust Act was passed in 1890 with the hope that it would reconstitute the natural competition of the market. Although greeted with much enthusiasm, the Act was not really enforced until the time of Theodore Roosevelt, and then without much effect on the continuing consolidation of business.[20]

The moguls could not ignore the public concern over monopolistic enterprise. The middle class was a politically significant segment of the population, and the potential power of that class could be unleashed against big business. Government, to be courted when needed for economic assistance, could not be permitted to interfere with the trend of business. A new ideology was needed. To say that success was a hallmark of the virtuous was no longer sufficient. A more vigorous ideology, one in keeping with the men who lived by it, was necessary.

The new entrepreneurial ideology blended the older virtues necessary for success, the concept of the struggle for existence, and the teachings of Darwinian evolution.[21] Success and riches were now considered to be an indication of progress and the reward of those who survived the struggle for existence in the economic arena.[22] Poverty was the hopeless existence of those who lost. The evils which permeated economic—and political—life were the realities of civilization, inevitable by-products of the struggle for existence.[23] Ostentation, ambition, and the love of wealth might have evil effects on some, but were, on the whole, considered good for the society.

The great power wielded by the moguls was considered to be a natural consequence of the survival of the fittest. As F. O. Willey wrote in 1896, "the power to originate and conduct great industrial enterprises and accumulate great fortunes . . . always has been and always will be the inheritance of the few." [24] At the same time the workers were considered lacking courage and intelligence, incapable of assuming responsibility. "He was born a salaried man," wrote N. C. Fowler in his book, *The Boy, How To Help Him Succeed,* "and a salaried man he had better remain." [25]

Great wealth and authority over the workingman were thus granted ideological justification in a "social biology," based on the biological theories of Darwin.

Nowhere was the entrepreneurial ideology of late nineteenth-century America more clearly stated than in the writings of Andrew Carnegie. Carnegie was a boy when his father emigrated from Scotland to the United States. As a youth he learned telegraphy and worked for the Pennsylvania Railroad. He rose to division manager at 24. Carnegie invested his money in various companies and, in 1864, entered the iron business. In 1873 he built his first steel plant. Carnegie retired in 1901 with a fortune estimated to be $500 million. Upon his retirement he devoted himself to philanthropy, established a series of libraries, the Carnegie Institute of Technology, and the Carnegie Foundation, as well as presenting large sums of money to various universities. He also turned his interests to writing and published five books. One of his earliest essays entitled "Wealth" (written in 1899) is reproduced below.

Carnegie's article is an explanation of the great discrepancies of wealth between the rich and poor, and how this situation is to be reconciled in a democratic society whose value system is focused on equality. Carnegie began by dismissing as communistic or anarchistic any questioning of inequities that might exist under the system of industrial capitalism. The natural laws of society were not to be questioned. From that position he moved into the clichés of his time: the movement into industrial and urban society extracted its toll from the people; although many people suffered, the fittest survived; the fittest were those who had great wealth; men of great wealth were trustees of the greatest good for society. Today Carnegie's essay may sound like a reborn paternalism from the early eighteenth century. In his day there were many who saw Utopia in his words.

*

The problem of our age is the proper administration of wealth, so that the ties of brotherhood may still bind together the rich and poor in harmonious relationship. The conditions of human life have not only been changed, but revolutionized, within the past few hundred years. In former days there was little difference between the dwelling, dress, food, and environment of the chief and those of his retainers. The Indians are today where civilized man then was. When visiting the Sioux, I was led to the wigwam of the chief. It was just like the others in external appearance, and even within the difference was trifling between it and those of the poorest of his braves. The contrast between the palace of the millionaire and the cottage of the laborer with us today measures the change which has come with civilization.

This change, however, is not to be deplored, but welcomed as highly beneficial. It is well, nay, essential for the progress of the race, that the houses of some should be homes for all that is highest and best in literature and the arts, and for all the refinements of civilization, rather than that none should be so. Much better this great irregularity than universal squalor. Without wealth there can be no Maecenas. The "good old times" were not good old times. Neither master nor servant was as well situated then as today. A relapse to old conditions would be disastrous to both—not the least so to him who serves—and would sweep away civilization with it. But whether the change be for good or ill, it is upon us, beyond our power to alter, and therefore to be accepted and made the best of. It is a waste of time to criticize the inevitable.

It is easy to see how the change has come. One illustration will serve for almost every phase of the cause. In the manufacture of products we have the whole story. It applies to all combinations of human industry, as stimulated and enlarged by the inventions of this scientific age. Formerly articles were manufactured at the domestic hearth or in small shops which formed part of the household. The master and his apprentices worked side by side, the latter living with the master, and therefore subject to the same conditions. When these apprentices rose to be masters, there was little or no change in their mode of life, and they, in turn, educated in the same routine succeeding apprentices. There was, substantially, social equality, and even political equality, for those engaged in industrial pursuits had then little or no political voice in the State.

But the inevitable result of such a mode of manufacture was crude articles

* From Andrew Carnegie, "Wealth," North American Review, Vol. 148, June 1889, pp. 653–664.

at high prices. Today the world obtains commodities of excellent quality at prices which even the generation preceding this would have deemed incredible. In the commercial world similar causes have produced similar results, and the race is benefited thereby. The poor enjoy what the rich could not before afford. What were the luxuries have become the necessaries of life. The laborer has now more comforts than the farmer had a few generations ago. The farmer has more luxuries than the landlord had, and is more richly clad and better housed. The landlord has books and pictures rarer, and appointments more artistic, than the king could then obtain.

The price we pay for this salutary change is, no doubt, great. We assemble thousands of operatives in the factory, in the mine, and the counting-house, of whom the employer can know little or nothing, and to whom the employer is little better than a myth. All intercourse between them is at an end. Rigid Castes are formed and, as usual, mutual ignorance breeds mutual distrust. Each Caste is without sympathy for the other, and ready to credit anything disparaging in regard to it. Under the law of competition, the employer of thousands is forced into the strictest economies, among which the rates paid to labor figure prominently, and often there is friction between the employer and the employed, between capital and labor, between rich and poor. Human society loses homogeneity.

The price which society pays for the law of competition, like the price it pays for cheap comforts and luxuries, is also great; but the advantages of this law are also greater still, for it is to this law that we owe our wonderful material development, which brings improved conditions in its train. But, whether the law be benign or not, we must say of it, as we say of the change in the conditions of men to which we have referred: It is here; we cannot evade it; no substitutes for it have been found; and while the law may be sometimes hard for the individual, it is best for the race, because it insures the survival of the fittest in every department. We accept and welcome, therefore, as conditions to which we must accommodate ourselves, great inequality of environment, the concentration of business, industrial and commercial, in the hands of a few, and the law of competition between these, as being not only beneficial, but essential for the future progress of the race. Having accepted these, it follows that there must be great scope for the exercise of special ability in the merchant and in the manufacturer who has to conduct affairs upon a great scale. That this talent for organization and management is rare among men is proved by the fact that it invariably secures for its possessor enormous rewards, no matter where or under what laws or conditions. The experienced in affairs always rate the MAN whose services can be obtained as a partner as not only the first consideration, but such as to render the question of his capital scarcely worth considering, for such men soon create capital; while, without the special talent required, capital soon takes wings. Such men become interested in firms or corporations using millions; and estimating only simple interest to be made upon the capital invested, it is inevitable that their income must exceed their expenditures, and that they must accumulate wealth. Nor is there any middle ground which such men can occupy, because the great manufacturing or commercial concern which does not earn at least interest upon its capital soon becomes bankrupt. It must either go forward or fall behind: to stand still is impossible. It is a condition essential for its successful operation that it should be thus far profitable, and even that, in addition to interest on capital, it should make profit. It is a law, as certain as any of the others named, that men possessed of this peculiar talent for affairs, under the free play of economic forces, must, of necessity, soon be in receipt of more revenue than can be judiciously expended upon themselves; and this law is as beneficial for the race as the others.

Objections to the foundations upon which society is based are not in order, because the condition of the race is better with these than it has been with any others which have been tried. Of the effect of any new substitutes proposed we cannot be sure. The Socialist or Anarchist who seeks to overturn present conditions is to be regarded as attacking the foundation upon which civilization itself rests, for civilization took its start from the day that the capable, industrious workman said to his incompetent and lazy fellow, "If thou dost not sow, thou shalt not reap," and thus ended primitive Communism by separating the drones from the bees. One who studies this subject will soon be brought face to face with the conclusion that upon the sacredness of property civilization itself depends—the right of the laborer to his hundred dollars in the savings bank, and equally the legal right of the millionaire to his millions. To those who propose to substitute Communism for this intense Individualism the answer, therefore, is: The race has tried that. All progress from that barbarous day to the present time has resulted from its displacement. Not evil, but good, has come to the race from the accumulation of wealth by those who have the ability and energy that produces it. But even if we admit for a moment that it might be better for the race to discard its present foundation, Individualism—that it is a nobler ideal that man should labor, not for himself alone, but in and for a brotherhood of his fellows, and share with them all in common, realizing Swedenborg's idea of Heaven, where, as he says, the angels derive their happiness, not from laboring for self, but for each other—even admit all this, and a sufficient answer is: This is not evolution, but revolution. It necessitates the changing of human nature itself—a work of aeons, even if it were good to change it, which we cannot know. It is not practicable in our day or in our age. Even if desirable theoretically, it belongs to another and long-succeeding sociological stratum. Our duty is with what is practicable now; with the next step possible in our day and generation. It is criminal to waste our energies in endeavoring to uproot, when all we can profitably or possibly accomplish is to bend the universal tree of humanity a little in the direction most favorable to the production of good fruit under existing circumstances. We might as well urge the destruction of the highest existing type of man because he failed to reach our ideal as to favor the destruction of Individualism, Private Property, the Law of Accumulation of Wealth, and the Law of Competition; for these are the highest results of human experience, the soil in which society so far has produced the best fruit. Unequally or unjustly, perhaps, as these laws sometimes operate, and imperfect as they appear to the Idealist, they are, nevertheless, like the highest type of man, the best and most valuable of all that humanity has yet accomplished.

We start, then, with a condition of affairs under which the best interests of the race are promoted, but which inevitably gives wealth to the few. Thus far, accepting conditions as they exist, the situation can be surveyed and pronounced good. The question then arises—and, if the foregoing be correct, it is the only question with which we have to deal—What is the proper mode of administering wealth after the laws upon which civilization is founded have thrown it into the hands of the few? And it is of this great question that I believe I offer the true solution. It will be understood that *fortunes* are here spoken of, not moderate sums saved by many years of effort, the returns from which are required for the comfortable maintenance and education of families. This is not *wealth*, but only *competence*, which it should be the aim of all to acquire.

There are but three modes in which surplus wealth can be disposed of. It can be left to the families of the decedents; or it can be bequeathed for public purposes; or, finally, it can be administered during their lives by its possessors. Under the first and second modes most of the wealth of the world that has reached the few has hitherto been applied. Let us in turn consider each of these modes. The first is the most injudicious. In monarchical countries, the estates and the greatest portion of the wealth are left to the first son, that the vanity of the parent may be gratified by the thought that his name and title are to descend to succeeding generations unimpaired. The condition of this class in Europe today teaches the futility of such hopes or ambitions. The successors have become impoverished through their follies or from the fall in the value of land. Even in Great Britain the strict law of entail has been found inadequate to maintain the status of an hereditary class. Its soil is rapidly passing into the hands of the stranger. Under republican institutions the division of property among the children is much fairer, but the question which forces itself upon thoughtful men in all lands is: Why should men leave great fortunes to their children? If this is done from affection, is it not misguided affection? Observation teaches that, generally speaking, it is not well for the children that they should be so burdened. Neither is it well for the state. Beyond providing for the wife and daughters moderate sources of income, and very moderate allowances indeed, if any, for the sons, men may well hesitate, for it is no longer questionable that great sums bequeathed oftener work more for the injury than for the good of the recipients. Wise men will soon conclude that, for the best interests of the members of their families and of the state, such bequests are an improper use of their means.

It is not suggested that men who have failed to educate their sons to earn a livelihood shall cast them adrift in poverty. If any man has seen fit to rear his sons with a view to their living idle lives, or, what is highly commendable, has instilled in them the sentiment that they are in a position to labor for public ends without reference to pecuniary considerations, then, of course, the duty of the parent is to see that such are provided for *in moderation*. There are instances of millionaires' sons unspoiled by wealth, who, being rich, still perform great services in the community. Such are the very salt of the earth, as valuable as, unfortunately, they are rare; still it is not the exception, but the rule, that men must regard, and, looking at the usual result of enormous sums conferred upon legatees, the thoughtful man must shortly say, "I would as soon leave to my son a curse as the almighty dollar," and admit to himself that it is not the welfare of the children, but family pride, which inspires these enormous legacies.

As to the second mode, that of leaving wealth at death for public uses, it may be said that this is only a means for the disposal of wealth, provided a man is content to wait until he is dead before it becomes of much good in the world. Knowledge of the results of legacies bequeathed is not calculated to inspire the brightest hopes of much posthumous good being accomplished. The cases are not few in which the real object sought by the testator is not attained, nor are they few in which his real wishes are thwarted. In many cases the bequests are so used as to become only monuments of his folly. It is well to remember that it requires the exercise of not less ability than that which acquired the wealth to use it so as to be really beneficial to the community. Besides this, it may fairly be said that no man is to be extolled for doing what he cannot help doing, nor is he to be thanked by the community to which he only leaves wealth at death. Men who leave vast sums in this way may fairly be thought men who would not have left it at all, had they been able to take it with them. The memories of such cannot be held in grateful remembrance, for there is no grace in their gifts. It is not to be wondered at that such bequests seem so generally to lack the blessing.

The growing disposition to tax more and more heavily large estates left at death is a cheering indication of the growth of a salutary change in public opinion. The State of Pennsylvania now takes—subject to some exceptions—one-tenth of the property left by its citizens. The budget presented in the British Parliament the other day proposes to increase the death-duties; and, most significant of all, the new tax is to be a graduated one. Of all forms of taxation, this seems the wisest. Men who continue hoarding great sums all their lives, the proper use of which for public ends would work good to the community, should be made to feel that the community, in the form of the state, cannot thus be deprived of its proper share. By taxing estates heavily at death the state marks its condemnation of the selfish millionaire's unworthy life.

It is desirable that nations should go much further in this direction. Indeed, it is difficult to set bounds to the share of a rich man's estate which should go at his death to the public through the agency of the state, and by all means such taxes should be graduated, beginning at nothing upon moderate sums to dependents, and increasing rapidly as the amounts swell, until of the millionaire's hoard, as of Shylock's at least

"_____The other half

Comes to the privy coffer of the state."

This policy would work powerfully to induce the rich man to attend to the administration of wealth during his life, which is the end that society should always have in view, as being that by far most fruitful for the people. Nor need it be feared that this policy would sap the root of enterprise and render men less anxious to accumulate, for to the class whose ambition it is to leave great fortunes and be talked about after their death, it will attract even more attention, and, indeed, be a somewhat nobler ambition to have enormous sums paid over to the state from their fortunes.

There remains, then, only one mode of using great fortunes; but in this we have the true antidote for the temporary unequal distribution of wealth, the reconciliation of the rich and the poor—a reign of harmony—another ideal, differing, indeed, from that of the Communist in requiring only the further evolution of existing conditions, not the total overthrow of our civilization. It is founded upon the present most intense individualism, and the race is prepared to put it in practice by degrees whenever it pleases. Under its sway we shall have an ideal state, in which the surplus wealth of the few will become, in the best sense, the property of the many, because administered for the common good, and this wealth, passing through the hands of the few, can be made a much more potent force for the elevation of our race than if it had been distributed in small sums to the people themselves. Even the poorest can be made to see this, and to agree that great sums gathered by some of their fellow-citizens and spent for public purposes, from which the masses reap the principal benefit, are more valuable to them than if scattered among them through the course of many years in trifling amounts.

If we consider what results flow from the Cooper Institute, for instance, to the best portion of the race in New York not possessed of means, and compare these with those which would have arisen for the good of the masses from an equal sum distributed by Mr. Cooper in his lifetime in the form of wages, which is the highest form of distribution, being for work done and not for charity, we can form some estimate of the possibilities for the improvement of the race which lie embedded in the present law of the accumulation of wealth. Much of this sum, if distributed in small quantities among the people, would have been wasted in the indulgence of appetite, some of it in excess, and it may be doubted whether even the part put to the best use, that of adding to the comforts of the home, would have yielded results for the race, as a race, at all comparable to those which are flowing and are to flow from the Cooper Institute from generation to generation. Let the advocate of violent or radical change ponder well this thought.

We might even go so far as to take another instance, that of Mr. Tilden's bequest of five millions of dollars for a free library in the city of New York, but in referring to this one cannot help saying involuntarily, How much better if Mr. Tilden had devoted the last years of his own life to the proper administration of this immense sum; in which case neither legal contest nor any other cause of delay could have interfered with his aims. But let us assume that Mr. Tilden's millions finally became the means of giving to this city a noble public library, where the treasures of the world contained in books will be open to all forever, without money and without price. Considering the good of that part of the race which congregates in and around Manhattan Island, would its permanent benefit have been better promoted had these millions been allowed to circulate in small sums through the hands of the masses? Even the most strenuous advocate of Communism must entertain a doubt upon this subject. Most of those who think will probably entertain no doubt whatever.

Poor and restricted are our opportunities in this life; narrow our horizon; our best work most imperfect; but rich men should be thankful for one inestimable boon. They have it in their power during their lives to busy themselves in organizing benefactions from which the masses of their fellows will derive lasting advantage, and thus dignify their own lives. The highest life is probably to be reached, not by such imitation of the life of Christ as Count Tolstoï gives us, but, while animated by Christ's spirit, by recognizing the changed conditions of this age, and adopting modes of expressing this spirit suitable to the changed conditions under which we live; still laboring for the good of our fellows, which was the essence of his life and teaching, but laboring in a different manner.

This, then, is held to be the duty of the man of Wealth: First, to set an example of modest, unostentatious living, shunning display or extravagance; to provide moderately for the legitimate wants of those dependent upon him; and after doing so to consider all surplus revenues which come to him simply as trust funds, which he is called upon to administer, and strictly bound as a matter of duty to administer in the manner which, in his judgment, is best calculated to produce the most beneficial results for the community—the man of wealth thus becoming the mere agent and trustee for his poorer brethren, bringing to their service his superior wisdom, experience, and ability to administer, doing for them better than they would or could do for themselves. . . .

THE IDEOLOGIES OF MANAGEMENT

Although the bases for change were evident during his lifetime, Carnegie did not live to see the revolution that was to come in the nature of corporate ownership and authority. The revolution had its beginnings in the continued growth of industrialization, and the subsequent diversification of industry, brought about by the involvement of America in two World Wars, by an expanding population, by urbanization of the frontier, by exploitation of natural resources, and by the continued development of technology. The power of the moguls was also checked by legislative action, particularly the Clayton Antitrust Act of 1914, which curbed the establishment of interlocking boards of directors, forbade one corporation to buy the stock of another if this maneuver decreased competition, and forbade manufacturers to have "tie in" agreements with dealers, by which the dealer would not handle the products of a competitor.[26] The result was a decline in the personal control of corporate enterprises and the manipulation of large fortunes. "These units have been supplanted in even greater measure," wrote Adolph Berle and Gardiner Means, "by great aggregations in which tens and even hundreds of thousands of workers and property worth hundreds of millions of dollars, belonging to tens or even hundreds of thousands of individuals, are combined through the corporate mechanism into a single producing organization under unified control and management." [27]

Unlike the earlier periods of speculative finance, rigid state and federal controls now regulate stock transactions; the Anaconda Copper deal referred to earlier is virtually impossible today. This signifies that ownership is now depersonalized.[28] Indeed, present-day ownership is so fluid and divided that the corporation assumes an independent existence.[29]

Ownership has become depersonalized, then, without bringing chaos to industrial life—primarily because of the tremendous extension of managerial control. In 1899 there were eight administrative employees for every 100 production workers. In 1957, the ratio had increased to 30:100, resulting in the bureaucratic organization of modern industrial capitalism—probably its most outstanding contemporary feature. Bureaucracy functions in fixed and official areas of responsibility, with duties carried out by persons qualified to serve in such capacities.[30] Bureaucratic management has the specific function of coordinating the specialized tasks of the modern industrial plant, of developing meaningful and continuous communication among departments, and of transmitting policy decisions from one level to another.

Because of the size and complexity of modern industrial organization, the entrepreneurial ideologies of the last century have had little direct appeal to the modern manager who finds it difficult to imagine the self-made man in a bureaucracy. The new image of success is centered about a bureaucratic career. "[T]he corporation," stated A. P. Sloan, "[is] a pyramid of opportunities from the bottom toward the top with thousands of chances for advancement." [31] Sloan's statement contains remnants of the old virtues and the initiative of the entrepreneurial ideologies in addition to the personal qualities necessary for advancement in the atmosphere of bureaucratic anonymity. Such characteristics as sincerity, earnestness, good grooming, and optimism have become the conventional appeals of bureaucratic promotion. It is no wonder that aids to self-help, from the New Thought movement of the early decades of this century to Dale Carnegie and Norman Vincent Peale, have enjoyed great popularity. With such guides readily available the possibilities for manipulating bureaucratic roles are made manifest.[32] All of these elements of change have formed the basis of the ideology of management by which the bureaucrats of modern industrial capitalism explain their assumption of power and authority over the workers.

A significant contribution was made to the ideology of management by Frederick W. Taylor, who evolved the concept of "scientific management." [33] This was a concept based on the analysis of every task in the line of production, in an effort to discover the best way to achieve the end of production. Once discovered, absolute conformity to the job analysis had to be maintained. In order to obtain the greatest efficiency from job analysis there also had to be a scientific selection of workers to get the right man into the right job. In this manner, efficiency of production would increase in the most logical way, resulting in benefits for both employers and employees.

Taylor's ideas were, in one sense, an extension of Adam Smith. Taylor believed that the concentration of effort by a worker on that task for which he was best suited would lead to prosperity for all. But in another sense, unlike Smith, Taylor did not believe that the worker could realize his potentialities himself. He had to be trained by management, a rejection of the natural process of self-interest.

Scientific management also sought to remove arbitrariness from managerial rule. Not caprice, but scientific analysis of production tasks was to be the guiding principle. Although this notion was a threat to some and forestalled complete acceptance of Taylor's ideas, it was in keeping with the orderly processes needed to make a large bureaucracy function smoothly. Taylor believed that by removing arbitrary decision-making from management a spirit of cooperation would result between employers and employees.

The cooperation anticipated by Taylor wrought some important changes that were to contribute to the ideology of management. First, the notion that only the fittest survive declined. By the 1930's an awareness of workers as "human beings" had become widespread in management. To treat workers otherwise was considered the source of low morale, confusion, and poor workmanship.[34] Second, the belief in cooperation evolved into the ideological principle of teamwork. As members of the team, management had to see to it that the workers were happy in their work, that they looked to the corporation, rather than to the unions, for the means of satisfying their needs, and that incentives of increased status in the bureaucratic pyramid were held out as the reward for being a good member of the team. The notion of teamwork, in turn, created a third change that has contributed significantly to the ideology of management. This is the human relations approach to management-worker relations.[35] No longer is the worker to be driven; he is to be motivated. The manager is to get along with his employees by showing sincere interest and by establishing close interpersonal contact with them.[36] The human relations ideology, in short, is a method of obtaining direct control over the worker by cutting through the secondary group atmosphere of the corporation and establishing primary group relationships.

In the following selection we find the diverse features of the ideology of management brought together by David Lilienthal, former director of the Tennessee Valley Authority. He notes that there has been a great amount of self-consciousness about our material abundance and about the size of our corporate structure. A constant criticism, he believes, is that big business and materialism have been responsible for the decline of individualism. Rather than continuing such criticism, he makes a positive statement regarding both material abundance and bigness. He goes on to indicate that, because of the human-relations approach of modern management and increased technology, there will be an increase in individuality. Lilienthal's statement is a farewell to the era of the *bourgeoisie,* the entrepreneur. At the same time it is a statement that carries forward into the epoch of bigness an inheritance, first from the eighteenth century, that man can guide his own destiny, and second, an apology for that bigness, reminiscent of Andrew Carnegie.

*
One of the major reservations about Bigness, and the society upon which, in a physical sense, it is built, is that it has a blighting effect upon the individual. This objection ranges from the effect of Big Business upon the ability of an individual to begin a business of his own and prosper in it, to the more philosophical but none the less real objection that Bigness tends to destroy the sense of importance, and the freedom to be oneself which are integral to individualism as a tenet of democratic faith.

I recently noted a newspaper advertisement which began:

AN OPEN LETTER

For more than 20 years, it has been my ambition to operate a business of my own, in which I make the decisions, assume all responsibility, and take all the blame.

This announcement of the opening of a new business—in this case a restaurant and cocktail lounge—strikes a very familiar American note and one of central relevance in considering the harmful effects of Bigness upon the individual's independence.

To want to set up in business for himself, to be his "own boss," is as much a part of the American tradition as razzing the umpire, or the Sunday-afternoon nap. The tradition is far from dead: there are over ten million men and women who are their "own bosses," or "active proprietors" in the terminology of the census; these figures do not include farming, which is, of course, the largest independent business group of all.

But there are millions of people who can never expect to set out in business for themselves, or be in a position "to make all the decisions," in the sense of the open letter of the proud new proprietor of Rennie's Old Castle Inn. Bigness is indeed making us more nearly a nation of employees; in some cases several hundred thousand individuals working for the same employer.

As it affects the lives and aspirations of our young men and women particularly it is undeniable that this represents what a thoughtful friend of mine has described as "a great break with tradition." Upon graduation from a university, in the twenties, he and some of his friends were recruited for employment with one of our largest and best Big Businesses of a generation ago (as it is still today).

We were dismayed (he writes me), at the vista of mediocre aspiration and of compartmentalized lives. The course of a big business career was predictable and foreclosed. It was also, as the personnel department pointed out, secure. The appeal of graduated salary raises and retirement on a pension was held out as the big lure. But in my high school days the appeal had been to ambition, a good deal was said about achievement and independence.

Have we lost something very precious, since for so many millions "working for yourself" is no longer a possible course? I think we have indeed lost something of great value.

How great is this loss? In the first place, to be realistic, one should remember that it is not everyone by any manner of means who really wants "to make the decisions, assume all responsibility, and take all the blame."

Beyond that, we must keep reminding ourselves of how many small jobs and businesses—of a kind that never existed before—the era of Bigness has brought with it. Today the manufacture of automobiles is obviously not a good place for a man to start to be his own boss. But the automobile has certainly spawned tens of thousands of independent or semi-independent one-man businesses; they can be seen along every highway of this highly mobile land—not only filling stations, small repair shops, vegetable stands and the like, but hundreds of one-building factories that manufacture parts and components of the intricate machinery of a motorcar.

But there are far more important considerations even than these. I refer to the great strides being made in big industry, by management and by labor organizations, to enable individual workers to find a new kind of personal and individual satisfaction in their jobs, that replaces and perhaps in some ways sharpens the old-time satisfactions of independence in the days of small self-owned enterprise.

In the past quarter of a century there has probably been more realistic effort in industry devoted to a better understanding of the worker *as an individual*, and his relations to other individuals, than ever before in history.

In point of fact, the individual human being has become the very center of management's and labor's concern in some of our more progressive huge business undertakings. What is it that gives workers their chief satisfaction? What are the chief causes of their dissatisfaction on the job? How can the relations between men, working together, be improved? How can men find in their work and associations in large organizations and with huge machines the quality of satisfaction and joy which craftsmen of old found in theirs? In their creative effort to demonstrate that "the proper study of mankind is man," modern management and unions are laying the foundation of a new individualism.

Largely because of the productivity of Bigness most of man's independence need no longer come from his job directly. Now machines and better management together with a new social opinion and the consequences of labor organizations' efforts have provided workers, in Big Business particularly, with a spectacular increase in leisure, and consequently a proportionate increase in independence. The total percentage of a man's week *which is his own* has markedly increased.

When the hours of labor are cut from sixty a week to forty—and we can afford this chiefly because of the new productivity of large-scale industry—we have thereby added twenty hours to each man's independence every week. In those added hours he is his "own boss," not in the sense of the man who owns his own business, but potentially in an even more meaningful sense.

It is plain that larger units of human organization are the order of the future. As I write, the radio announces that three men have crossed and recrossed the Atlantic within the hours of daylight. More significant even than this physical contraction are the tidal currents that move us irresistibly toward closer contact and greater cohesion among once disparate peoples, and thereby to larger and larger economic and political units of people, in short, toward Bigness.

What then of the individual, in this trend toward Bigness? There is a general assumption that the bigger the organization the smaller the individual, the less freedom to be himself. My own observation casts doubt upon this proposition. My impression is that the large unit *potentially* provides an opportunity for the flourishing of individuality as great, perhaps even greater than the small unit toward which our backward glances are cast with such an undisguised sense of loss.

Dr. Margaret Mead, the noted anthropologist, is one of a handful of scholars who have closely studied small and simple societies at first hand. Her testimony was impressive, therefore, when at a recent International Symposium on Anthropology, the press reported her as saying that " 'oneness' of the world in the future did not mean that individuality would suffer. She said all the evidence showed that large and complex societies gave much more play to the individual than small groups could afford to give."

We are living in a society in which, for the first time in history, almost all its benefits—physical and nonmaterial—are enjoyed not only by a few at the top but by everyone, all up and down the line. As a measure of the increased value attached to the worth of *all* individuals, this is a profound ethical and spiritual advance. Individualism has reached a new high point in this machine civilization of ours.

The ancient world of Greece and Rome created great art and literature; but this was produced for a limited aristocracy and in a society based upon human slavery. The magnificent castles and cathedrals of the Middle Ages came out of a society of half-starved serfs. The Industrial Revolution of the eighteenth century brought to a few great wealth and political power; but the machine was master for most of the population, and they derived from it only an urban life uglier than the pastoral poverty that afflicted the peasants before them.

Today one finds the physical benefits of our society distributed widely, to almost everyone, with scant regard to status, class, or origin of the individual. Much the same is true of such benefits as education, police protection, recreation, health measures, etc., and of such precious nonmaterial benefits as the ability (as well as the right) of the individual in this country to move freely from place to place, or from job to job.

In any judgment upon the place of the individual in our new industrial society of Bigness, such factors as these revolutionary advances must be neither overlooked nor obscured.

The effect of Bigness upon the soul, in short whether it makes for better human beings, is of course a most subtle and complex subject. My qualifications to discuss it with authority are negligible, and I shall touch only its outer dimensions here.

There are those who feel that modern science, technology and machines have not made human beings better. They tend to discount the virtues of physical improvement—housing, sanitation, mobility, refrigeration, communication and so on—which technology and machines have brought the individual.

To those who take this general view, machines and Bigness are virtually one and the same evil. Machines mean Bigness, and both are of doubtful value.

I encountered this emotion in the Tennessee Valley. When electricity was beginning to find its way into farm homes, or even towns where it had never before been known, there were objections that hill farmers' lives would not be helped but harmed by these conveniences. Such views, however, I never heard from the farmers and their wives of that valley. I noticed that the skeptics of machinery lived in towns and cities, where they had themselves long been surrounded by these mechanical aids.

I have visited the hinterlands of Central America, India, Pakistan, Japan, Siam, Egypt. There I saw primitive living, unaffected by modern machinery or technology; this did much to confirm my feeling that machines and their development provide the greatest opportunity in the whole history of mankind to improve the lot of the individual human being.

The continued contraction of the area in which men's backs do the hard, exhausting drudgery of this country is directly related to Bigness. It is size only that can produce the machinery in quantity and at low enough prices to make this epochal transformation a reality in our time. It has taken Bigness to make these things commonplace in millions of homes instead of confining them to the homes of a few people of means.

Wherever human beings live in utter and hopeless poverty, wherever they must do work that is exhausting and bestial and unfit for human beings (and this is the rule rather than the exception in many parts of the world today), wherever individuals live in abject insecurity and fear of hunger and exposure and disease, the spirit of such individuals is degraded, the dignity of man and the integrity of his individuality as a human being is violated. Hence, it seems to me, wherever Bigness and the machine have alleviated or eliminated such degradation of the human spirit, the inner life of man has, to this degree at least, been enriched and nourished.

There was an old dream: the independent man in his own little shop or business. It *was* a good dream.

There is a new dream: a world of great machines, with man in control, devising and making use of these inanimate creatures to build a new kind of independence, a new awareness of beauty, a new spirit of brotherliness.

The brain of man conceived these fabulous machines, and the intellect of man can master them to further the highest purposes of human freedom and culture.

Bigness can become an expression of the heroic size of man himself as he comes to a new-found greatness. . . .

CHALLENGES TO THE MANAGERIAL IDEOLOGY

The notion that bigness is a result of teamwork among executives, managers, and workers plus the ideology of human relations are the ingredients of modern industrial and corporate bureaucracy. However, as Reinhard Bendix has noted, two contrary principles influence corporate operation.[37]

First, the size and complexity of industrial and corporate bureaucracy make it necessary to standardize jobs and the regulations which govern them. The effect of this, in contrast to Lilienthal's assessment, is not to increase individualism. It is a concerted effort to reduce it. The need to be able to coordinate and anticipate the behavior of the parts of the enterprise thus becomes paramount.

The second and directly opposite principle is that as the size and complexity of organization increase it becomes *actually* an impossibility to have effective control over all subordinate decisions; therefore, as the bureaucracy increases in size, the possibility of decisions being made independently increases. This is probably the side of managerial operations to which Lilienthal was referring. The human relations ideology, as Bendix indicated, is invoked at this point to emphasize teamwork in decision-making and to ensure the "right" use of discretion.[38]

The problem of the conflicting pressures to which these contrary principles give rise will be discussed at the end of the next chapter.

The effectiveness of the ideology of managerial power is being constantly affected by challenges from outside the managerial hierarchy. The first challenge is from socialism. As J. K. Galbraith has pointed out, the tone of businessmen, since the depression of the 1930's, has been a fear reaction.[39] Such clichés as "creeping socialism," "police state," and "communist blueprint (or timetable)" have echoed in the speeches of corporation presidents, management associations, real estate associations, and the United States Chamber of Commerce.

Such fear is a response not so much to the threat of the Soviet Union as a military power which possesses a competing economic ideology, as a response to the actions of the government of the United States. Changes in the corporate tax structure, government intercession in business operations—as the exertion of Presidential power in 1962 to compel some steel corporations to lower prices—public welfare programs, farm programs, and the income tax, have been called socialistic.

The fear of socialism contains, however, some contradictory elements. Whereas the ideology of bigness implies a certain vigor and natural evolvement out of the era of the moguls, the fear of socialism implies that capitalism is a fragile system indeed. This can be explained in part as a residue of Adam Smith's "invisible hand" with which nothing must interfere. But such fear must also be explained in relation to the transitions within the economy itself: changes from a sectional to a national, even an international, economy, which is often subject to forces beyond the control of the domestic system; the very size and complexity of the corporate system, which is a constant strain to supervise; and the separation of ownership from management.

These changes indicate a growing loss of free decision-making by the capitalistic system as a whole as it must respond to pressures imposed upon it by competing systems. They also indicate a lack of effective control by the managerial bureaucracy over significant segments of the economy. It is not surprising, as we shall see in a succeeding chapter, that the fear of socialism finds expression in ultraconservative political organizations.

Probably the greatest contradiction in the fear of bureaucratic management is the interdependency of business and government which has emerged in the last century. In the efforts of the managerial ideology to halt the inroads of "socialism" there have been frequent appeals to increase the powers of congressional investigating committees. The pleas by business for the maintenance of favorable government economic practices, such as government contracts and oil depletion allowances, and the annual battles that rage over the Reciprocal Trade Act testify to the need for a government economic program. In short, the business community decides when it wants government intervention in the economic system. At the ideological level such intervention is roundly condemned, but at the practical or operational level it is an accepted and often welcomed fact.

A second major challenge to the managerial ideology by forces outside of the managerial bureaucracy is to be found in labor unions.[40] The importance of labor unions in this respect is not that the worker feels any greater loyalty to the union than he does to the company that employs him. It has been reported that workers are capable of expressing equal loyalty to both, even though the two may be in conflict.[41] What is important is that unions provide for the development of tactics through which to deviate from the managerial ideology. Slow-downs, questions about the quality of work, and, ultimately, the strike are cases in point. Unions also provide a setting outside of the job in which the managerial ideology can be discounted or entirely dismissed.[42] Such opportunities are offered through union meetings and the formal appeals in union literature, and through those informal relationships among workers that unions may be able to foster through social activities.

A third area of challenge to the ideology of management is to be found in consumers. The growth, strength, and efficiency of bigness, exemplified in Lilienthal's essay, is supposed to bring with it the good life. More goods, inexpensively made, serviceable, and durable, have been important aspects of management's appeal to the consumers. This side of the managerial ideology, frequently ignored, is one of its most important facets, for the consumer is ultimately the judge of the efficiency of the business system. The final question of the managerial ideology is no longer "can it be produced?" but "will it sell?"

A problem arises when the interpretation of the good life held by management differs from the interpretation of the good life held by consumers. In the last few years consumers have made increasing demands for business to recognize the consumer's interpretation of quality and service.[43] There is indication that the consumer, even more than the labor union member, is in a position to discount and dismiss managerial appeals.

Consumers can also influence management's interpretation of its own ideology. Such influence stems from the way in which consumers use their purchasing income. All consumers must meet certain needs—food, clothing, shelter, and certain services. Because there is, more often than not, a choice to be made by consumers among the suppliers of their needs, what they spend on needs becomes a measure of the quality, service, and durability of goods and services. This principle is even more true of the income used for discretionary spending. If Sylvia Porter is correct that there is a trend by consumers toward selecting goods and services of higher quality and aesthetic appeal, then consumers influence the producers of the goods and services by the uses to which they put their discretionary income.

The final problem of any ideology is the extent to which those from whom loyalty is expected remain loyal. This brings us to an analysis of the socialization of economic roles which shall be discussed in the next chapter.

Notes

1. *General Economic History*, New York: Collier Books, 1961, Chapters 22–24.
2. Max Weber, *From Max Weber: Essays in Sociology*, ed. and trans. H. H. Gerth and C. W. Mills, New York: Oxford Galaxy Books, 1958, p. 68.
3. Max Weber, *The Protestant Ethic and the Spirit of Capitalism*, trans. T. Parsons, New York: Scribner's, 1958, p. 19.
4. *The Theory of Social and Economic Organization*, trans. and ed. H. H. Henderson and T. Parsons, Glencoe, Ill.: The Free Press, 1947, pp. 278 ff. See also, *From Max Weber: Essays in Sociology*, pp. 66–68.
5. E. M. Hulme, *A History of the British People*, New York: Century Company, 1924, p. 526.
6. Thomas Cochran, *Basic History of American Business*, Princeton: D. Van Nostrand, 1959, p. 38.
7. Rinehard Bendix, *Work and Authority in Industry*, New York: John Wiley and Sons, Inc., 1957, p. 2.
8. *Ibid.*, Chapter 2, *passim.*
9. Cf., *Ibid.*, pp. 78 ff.
10. Cochran, *op. cit.*, p. 40.
11. *Ibid.*, p. 41.
12. Harold Faulkner, *American Political and Social History*, New York: Appleton-Century-Crofts, 1957 (7th ed.), p. 512.
13. For a curious plea for revision of the history of the era see, Edward C. Kirkland, "The Robber Barons Revisited," *American Historical Review*, Vol. LXVI, October 1960, pp. 68–73.
14. Faulkner, *op. cit.*, p. 513.
15. Robert Heilbroner, *The Worldly Philosophers*, New York: Simon and Schuster, 1953, p. 201.
16. Quoted in *ibid.*, p. 201.
17. *Ibid.*, pp. 202–203.
18. Faulkner, *op. cit.*, p. 482.
19. *Ibid.*, p. 607.
20. *Ibid.*, p. 604.
21. Bendix, *op. cit.*, p. 256.

22. *Ibid.*
23. *Ibid.*
24. Quoted in *ibid.*, p. 259.
25. Quoted in *ibid.*
26. Faulkner, *op. cit.*, p. 751. Another act which also curbed the power of the moguls was the ratification in 1913 of the Sixteenth Amendment to the Constitution, making possible tax on personal income.
27. *The Modern Corporation and Private Property*, New York: The Macmillan Company, 1932, pp. 2–3.
28. From Walter Rathenau as cited in *ibid.*, p. 352.
29. *Ibid.*
30. Weber, *From Max Weber: Essays in Sociology*, p. 196.
31. Quoted in Bendix, *op. cit.*, p. 307.
32. See Chapter XVI.
33. Bendix, *op. cit.*, pp. 274–281.
34. *Ibid.* Bendix goes on to note that the older conceptions of wage incentives and initiative and creativity were not completely dropped, but remained latent in the newer ideology. *Ibid.*, p. 295.
35. *Ibid.*, pp. 308–340. This section of Bendix's work contains a detailed analysis of the impact of the work of Elton Mayo upon the ideology of management.
36. *Ibid.*, p. 321. The human relations approach has been one of the initiating factors in the development of industrial psychology.
37. Bendix, *op. cit.*, p. 336.
38. *Ibid.* Bendix also indicates that too much teamwork threatens to eliminate discretionary decision-making altogether. It is perhaps for this reason that it is at subordinate levels of bureaucratic organization that ritualists are to be found. See Peter M. Blau, *Bureaucracy in Modern Society*, New York: Random House, 1956, pp. 85 ff. Bureaucratic ritualism thus becomes a means of maintaining what few crumbs of discretionary decision-making they possess. Teamwork and individualism in decision-making have been combined in the technique known as "brain-storming."
39. J. K. Galbraith, *American Capitalism*, Boston: Houghton-Mifflin, 1962, pp. 2 ff.
40. Bendix, *op. cit.*, p. 338.
41. *Ibid.*, p. 339.
42. *Ibid.*
43. Sylvia Porter, "The Consumers Want Quality," *San Francisco Chronicle*, January 8, 1963, p. 54.

Selected Readings

*Hofstadter, Richard. *Social Darwinism in American Thought*. Boston: Beacon Press, 1955, rev. ed.
*Hofstadter, Richard. *The Age of Reform*. New York: Alfred Knopf, 1955.
Mayo, Elton, *The Social Problems of an Industrial Civilization*. Boston: Harvard Graduate School of Business Administration, 1945.
McClosky, Robert. *American Conservatism in the Age of Enterprise*. Cambridge: Harvard University Press, 1951.
*Moore, Wilbert. *Economy and Society*. New York: Random House, 1955.

*Sombart, Werner. *The Jews and Modern Capitalism.* New York: Collier Books, 1962.
*Soule, George. *The Ideas of the Great Economists.* New York: Mentor Books, 1952.
*Tawney, Robert. *Religion and the Rise of Capitalism.* New York: Mentor Books, 1947.
*Weber, Max. *The Protestant Ethic and the Spirit of Capitalism.* Trans. T. Parsons. New York: Scribner's, 1958.

* Paperback edition.

Chapter 17

The Socialization
of Economic Roles

Another important aspect of modern economic life is the socialization of the economic role. These are the ways in which the individual acquires the principles of his occupational role and thus becomes a part of the economic institution. Occupational roles are one type of social role, and may be defined as the behavior expected in a given occupation.[1]

The standards of behavior for an occupational role are set by the formal and informal organizations within the occupation. On the one hand, there are the behaviors approved by the official, often bureaucratic, system containing the occupation. These behaviors include a "qualitative expectation," or a level of performance, and a "quantitative expectation," or production. They also include the number of hours and days to be spent performing the role, the channels for communicating with superiors and subordinates, and the ethics of each. There are, on the other hand, the behaviors sanctioned by the unofficial system, which arise from the informal groupings within the economic institution. Frequently, the expectations of the latter system supplement the expectations of the former by cutting across involved bureaucratic rigmarole, resulting in continuous, although nonbureaucratic, production.[2] But the expectations of the two systems may often be antagonistic. Under these circumstances, the individual can experience conflict from having to play two contradictory roles in two different social systems, each with its own standards and values.

The diversity and complexity of the modern economic system make it likely that the behaviors expected in an occupational role will operate with greatest intensity "on the job." Most individuals in society do not know enough about, or even care about, such specialized tasks as "heel seat scourer" or "gore stapler" (both occupations relate to shoe production) to be concerned with the expectations of occupations. There are, by contrast, other occupations which do carry expectations beyond the work site. This is especially true of the professions. Doctors, lawyers, ministers, and teachers have difficulty throwing off, even if they should desire, the mantle of their professions.

The principal reason for the differing degrees of expectations between shoemakers and doctors is that an occupational role carries with it an achieved social status. There are, to be sure, sex and age factors often related to occupational roles, but no individual is in a particular occupation because of an ascribed characteristic alone. Some occupations involve a greater amount of achievement than others; this, in itself, becomes the basis of a differentiation of social status. As one study has indicated, highly specialized training and a great amount of public responsibility confer high occupational status, whereas unskilled, low paid, "dirty" jobs, involving little or no public responsibility are considered to be of low status.[3] Some occupations, in addition, are specific in their status, whereas others are generic. Most clerical occupations and most occupations related to industrial production have specific statuses. Professional occupations have meaning and significance to the entire community and are, therefore, generic in status.

The expectations related to occupational roles are frequently stereotyped. For this reason individual differences between members of a given occupation are often blotted out in favor of an over-all idea regarding the ideal member. Stereotyping can be observed quite clearly in relation to the professions. The ingredients of a professional stereotype include such elements as dedication, faithful application of knowledge, sound judgment, and fairness toward those who seek the services of the professional. Yet, contradictory forces may operate in the fulfillment of the professional role. The minister may be quite cynical, the doctor may possess incomplete knowledge, the teacher may not inspire his students, and the lawyer may rely on emotional appeals rather than legal skill. But insofar as the stereotype of the occupational role has been adopted, the professional may be able to manipulate an impression of conformity to it. As Erving Goffman has noted, the others may not want the truth and may be satisfied with the illusion created by the individual.[4]

The actual means by which individuals are socialized into occupational roles vary considerably. Such factors as sex, occupation of parent, parental expectations, and the expectations of other adults are important. The influence of peers, social class, the occupational choices within one's community, educational level, and previous work experience are also important factors. A host of individual psychological considerations ranging from aptitude and intelligence to the degree of identification with others whom the individual considers significant in his life further influence the formation of attitudes that determine an occupational choice.

Once an occupation is selected still other factors operate to shape behavior and attitudes toward work. The training period required in most professions is a time during which, as noted in Chapter 8, the spiritual values of the occupation are socialized into the individual. Many corporations have training programs in which the potential bureaucrat learns the accepted posture of the junior executive. For workmen there may also be training programs and "break-in" periods during which the new employee is acquainted with the norms of the task. Once an individual begins to practice his occupation, whether it be doctor, lawyer, barber, stenographer, or assembly-line worker, he is aware of the influence of other workers who have already made their own interpretations of the formal system of expectations. Thus, the initiation of the worker into the informal system comprises a significant aspect of socialization.

In the sections that follow, the socialization of three different types of occupational roles are studied. The first is the socialization into the medical profession as illustrated by the medical student. The second is the socialization of bureaucratic roles in industrial management. The last section involves worker roles in industry, exemplified by an automobile factory. These three examples are only a few of the many different kinds of occupational roles that could have been studied.[5] They do cover, however, a typical range of occupations.

THE SOCIALIZATION OF THE PROFESSIONAL:
THE MEDICAL STUDENT

When we think of the professions, such occupations as doctor, lawyer, minister, and college professor come immediately to mind. The professions involve a long period of training, carried out under the control of the profession and frequently sanctioned by state governments.[6] Not only are the skill and knowledge necessary to satisfy the requirements of the profession learned, but so are the attitudes, controls, and self-feeling that create professional solidarity.[7] It is generally assumed that when an individual enters a profession he intends to stay for life.[8] He is so committed not only because of the time and expense of training but also because of the enduring interpersonal contacts with other members of the profession; the satisfactions of having created a career of one's own; and the oft-joked-about but intangible rewards related to the service nature of many professions. "The profession," as Everett C. Hughes has said, "claims and aims to become a moral unit." [9]

Professional occupations, certainly those mentioned, are generally segregated from the ethics, practices, and relationships of the market economy. There is seldom competitive bidding for the price of services, although variations in fees do occur. A client or patient seeks a service, not an object, from someone in the professions. The professional, conversely, seldom treats the client or patient as a customer.

Nowhere are these factors more apparent than in the medical profession, especially in the role of the doctor. The occupational role of doctor is well-defined: to understand and alleviate sickness.[10] In our American society we have become more dependent on the profession of medicine to cure our ills than ever before in history.[11] Because he possesses exclusive information, holds a license to practice, and has been granted a mandate,[12] the doctor has a high generic status in our contemporary society.

The acquisition of that status, together with the specific skills and knowledge necessary to meet the requirements of being a doctor, is the function of the medical school. Typically the first-year medical student is filled with enthusiasm and ideals. He believes that the study of medicine is wonderful and that he will spend a lifetime aiding mankind.[13] The first-year student also believes in a given body of factual knowledge which, once mastered, will make him a good doctor.[14] Much of his idealism stems from the attitudes about medicine implicit in the culture. It also may result from an enthusiasm about medicine carried over from the age at which the career decision was made. Natalie Rogoff noted that the younger the age at which the decision to study medicine was made, the greater the commitment.[15]

Actual study in medical school creates disillusionment forcing the student to set aside for a time his idealism.[16] He finds that classes in the first two years are similar to those experienced in college. He finds there is more medical knowledge than he can possibly master in the time given him. The disillusionment is reinforced when he learns that he will not be attending many patients.[17]

During the last two years of medical school the student enters clinical study at which time he comes into contact with patients in the medical school hospital. Ideally he expects to aid suffering humanity. In reality, as he attends the cases to which he has been assigned and assists in surgery, he is bombarded with endless technical questions by the faculty.

His patients become a series of problems in medicine. Many of the tasks which the student is required to perform, such as pathology reports and endless charts of unchanging facts on terminal patients, are considered by students to be irrelevant to actual medical practice.[18] As the period of training nears an end, however, and the pressure of "getting through" eases off, there is a reassertion of the original idealism of the first-year student. The graduating senior begins to plan for the type of medical career that will bring his idealization to reality.

The four years of medical school accomplish more than the transmission of certain skills. They actively change the individual's self-image from that of student to doctor. The forces that influence this change are analyzed by Mary Jean Huntington in the following selection. The particular phase of training, the formal and informal interaction with other students, the doctors and nurses, and the patients are among the forces directing the change in self-image.

*
Interest in some of the processes through which medical students come to regard themselves as doctors stems in part from consideration of the importance of a fully developed professional self-image in later medical practice. Presumably, the physicians who consistently feel and think like doctors are able to carry out the doctor's role more effectively than those who have not fully incorporated such a self-image. Thinking of themselves as doctors may help practitioners maintain confidence in their capacity to deal with difficult medical tasks. This, in turn, probably reduces the amount of personal strain they might otherwise experience in conforming to the exacting obligations of their professional role.

If defining themselves as physicians enables practitioners to perform their work more easily, it is useful to investigate how a professional self-image first develops. This paper will discuss some of the first phases in the gradual transformation of young neophytes, who define themselves as students, into physicians able to identify themselves fully with their professional role.

It is of course evident to all that students typically think of themselves primarily as students at the beginning of their medical training and come progressively to think of themselves as doctors as they advance through medical school. Students at three medical schools were asked: "In the most recent dealings you have had with patients, how have you tended to think of yourself, primarily as a doctor rather than as a student, or primarily as a student rather than as a doctor?" A substantial minority of students in the

* Mary Jean Huntington, "The Development of a Professional Self-Image" reprinted by permission of the publishers from Robert K. Merton, George Reader, and Patricia Kendall, editors, The Student Physician, pp. 179–187, Cambridge, Mass.: Harvard University Press, copyright 1957 by the Commonwealth Fund.

first two years of training, approximately 30 per cent, reported that they felt primarily like doctors; by the end of the third year, 59 per cent indicated that they felt more like doctors, and just prior to graduation, this proportion had increased to 83 per cent. These figures are shown in Table 4.

**Table 4. Self-Images in Dealing With Patients,
according to Class in Medical School**

Class in medical school	Percentage of students who thought of themselves "primarily as doctors"	No. of students *
End of 1st year	31	(162)
End of 2nd year	30	(159)
End of 3rd year	59	(752)
End of 4th year	83	(759)

* Percentages are based on the aggregation of two classes of first-year students, and two classes of second-year students at Western Reserve University School of Medicine, and on eight combined classes of third-year and of fourth-year students at Western Reserve, University of Pennsylvania School of Medicine, and Cornell University Medical College—all of whom were asked the question stated above.

The central fact of this progression of self-images scarcely requires explanation. But these figures also exhibit a collateral pattern which is not self evident: an appreciable number of students report that they felt more like physicians than students while still in their early years of training. What, then, accounts for this fact that some students and not others see themselves primarily as doctors as early as the end of their first years of medical school?

In the course of their first-year studies, medical students have sustained contact with persons holding other statuses within the medical school and, occasionally, in the teaching hospital: other students, faculty members, nurses, and patients. The relationships students have with persons in each of these statuses are by no means identical. Patients, for example, obviously differ from faculty members in their images and expectations of medical students. And, in turn, these expectations diverge from those of classmates or of nurses. Such a complex of role relationships which persons have by virtue of occupying a particular status has been described as their *role set*.

Because they find themselves in situations calling for widely disparate attitudes and behavior, students *at any one stage in their training* tend to think of themselves now as students, now as physicians, as they work in diverse social contexts.

The first-year student who thought of himself as a doctor while in contact with his instructors or classmates is clearly the rare exception. The tendency is somewhat more common in relation to nurses, and most marked in connection with patients. The second column in Table 5 suggests one explanation of the "unstable" self-image held by students at a single point in their medical training, for there is a consonance between the status that students believe others in their role set assign them and the status to which students assign themselves. This tendency for individuals to live up to the role expectations of those with whom they are interacting and to come to perceive themselves in accordance with these expectations has long been recognized but little investigated. The evidence in Table 5 and other material to be presented below lend support to this proposition.

Table 5. Self-Images and Attributed Images of First-Year Students in Diverse Role Relationships

In their dealings with:	Percentage who thought of themselves as doctors	Percentage who thought others defined them as doctors *
Faculty	2	2
Classmates	3	0
Nurses	12	8
Patients	31	75
No. of students	(162)	(162)

* Percentages are based on the aggregation of two classes of first-year students at Western Reserve University School of Medicine. The percentages in column 2 are based on answers to the following question: "In your recent dealings with (patients, classmates, instructors, nurses), how have they thought of you, by and large, primarily as a doctor rather than as a student, or primarily as a student rather than as a doctor?"

Fully aware that they are just beginning their medical training, first-year students when interacting with classmates think of each other primarily as students. This is reflected in their self-definitions. When students interact with instructors, furthermore, the disparity between their own competence, experience, and status, and those of faculty members is apparent in both.

The data concerning nurses and patients require a word of explanation about the special circumstances of the first-year student at Western Reserve School of Medicine. Every student is provided with the opportunity of having patient contacts early in his first year. Each is assigned a family to follow during his first year and preferably through all four years of medical school. This serves to introduce students to the patient-physician relationship, and allows them to act in a role approximating that of physician, although it of course involves only limited responsibility in helping a family cope with health problems that might arise. In the assigned families, the wife is pregnant, but there is no serious or long-standing history of medical, emotional, or social pathology. Students are expected to *observe* their patients during the course of pregnancy, the delivery, and the early growth and development of the child. These continued observations in the hospital and in the home of the family provide students with early clinical experience which is correlated with didactic instruction by clinical preceptors.

When students see their assigned patients in the hospital, they are acting out some limited aspects of the role of physician while nurses are acting in their professional role as a member of the medical team. Nurses tend, in such a situation, to expect of students the behavior appropriate to physicians. In conforming to these expectations, so far as their medical student status allows, first-year students—about 12 per cent of them—begin to think of themselves more as doctors than as students.

It is vis-à-vis patients, more than with any other status in their role set, that medical students even as early as the end of their first year of training tend to see themselves as physicians. Some 31 per cent of the students reported this self-image. However limited the medical knowledge of first-year students, and they are usually aware that it is severely limited, it is, in general, considerably greater than that of the patients with whom they have contact. Moreover, the fact that students partly serve in the capacity of physician leads some patients to assign them the status of doctor. To the extent that patients define students as doctors and expect them to conform to the behavior appropriate to that role, students are likely to act as if they were doctors.

Thirty-nine per cent of the 117 first-year students who thought that their patients regarded them primarily as doctors also thought of themselves primarily as doctors, whereas only 6 per cent of the 35 first-year students who thought that their patients regarded them primarily as students thought of themselves as doctors.

Self-images appear, then, to be in part "reflections" of the expectations of others. As students are defined by their parents, so do they tend to define themselves. But we are on less than firm footing with this inference, because it is not based on reports from patients. The data might be interpreted in quite another way: as students define themselves so do *they think* patients define them. Other data in hand permit a rough test of this second interpretation. The same students had been asked a year earlier, before they had actually entered medical school, whether they *expected* to think of themselves primarily as students or as doctors when they came to work with patients. This information provides a clue to the initial "definition of the situation" with which students began their dealings with patients.

These initial states of mind do not appear to have colored students' impressions of the image which patients have of them. Of those who expected to play the role of doctor, 78 per cent felt, a year later, that they had been so defined by patients; of those who expected to play the role of student, almost exactly the same proportion, 77 per cent, felt that they had been defined, contrary to their own expectations, as doctors.

At the same time, self-confirming tendencies do appear when anticipated and actual *self*-images are compared. The majority—51 per cent—of the 41 students who had expected that they would feel more like doctors reported at the end of the year that they so defined themselves, compared with only 24 per cent of the 111 students who had anticipated that they would feel more like students than doctors.

First-year medical students tend to maintain their expected self-conceptions; however, as we saw earlier, they are not immune to the cues furnished by the limited contacts they have with patients. When these two factors are considered simultaneously, it appears that the majority of students maintain their expected self-image throughout the first year. This was somewhat more marked if they felt that patients also perceived them in this role rather than in another role. Specifically, 78 per cent of the 58 students whose expected self-image corresponded to the image they felt patients had of them maintained the same self-image from the beginning to the end of the first year, whereas only 64 per cent of the 94 students whose expected self-image differed from the image they felt patients had of them maintained the same self-image throughout the year.

There is the further question of elements in the student's relationships with patients which promote the formation of one or another self-image. As was indicated earlier, at Western Reserve occasions arise even as early as the first year of medical school, where students put into effect some peripheral skills of the medical role. It is these types of occasions that will be considered.

In addition to observing patients during the course of pregnancy and the delivery and subsequent development of the child, students are expected to develop a sense of responsibility for the continuing care of their patients; if the mother or other family member needs medical attention at any time, the student is reached directly by the family and is expected to make the necessary arrangements for the patient to get appropriate medical care. The students do not of course practice medicine. They have only limited medical responsibility when dealing with patients, and their performance is closely supervised.

Since each student has only one family to follow, this allows for fairly wide variation in the objective experience students meet. By tracing the developing self-images of those who report different types of experiences with their families, we can begin to detect what it is in their first contacts with patients that facilitates a sense of growing doctorhood among some students.

Merely having a family assigned to them is hardly likely to help students feel like doctors—unless occasions arise in which they are called upon to exercise the obligations of their new role as quasi-physician. Aside from providing students with the opportunity to observe the medically interesting processes of pregnancy and birth and development of a child, certain families will not present distinct problems that require the further services of students. When this is the case, students may have little chance to establish ongoing relationships with their patients, and consequently, to perform their assigned role.

From all this we can understand why students who reported that no medical problems arose in their families were not as likely to think of themselves primarily as doctors as those whose families presented medical problems during the course of the year. This should be seen in perspective. After all, these are first- and second-year students and this overarching fact keeps the great majority of them from adopting an image of themselves as physicians. Nevertheless, differences in the run of experience with patients do appear to affect the formation of such self-images. Thirty per cent of the 129 first- and second-year students whose families had definite medical problems came to see themselves primarily as doctors, in comparison with a bare 5 per cent of the 22 students whose families did not present medical problems.

The opportunity to establish a quasi-physician-patient relationship and to test out one's ability in this role is not enough to lead most students to think of themselves primarily as doctors rather than students. The amount of difficulty they experience in handling patients further affects the formation of the self-image. For some students, the requirements of the assigned task may outrun their still very limited capacities in both the technical and the interpersonal spheres. Such experiences will probably impede their developing a sense of doctorhood. But where the task and their abilities seem to the students to be matched, they are likely to feel they have handled the situation well—not very differently from the way a doctor would. Even in the first year, fully 45 per cent of the 29 students who reported having had no difficulty in handling patients indicated that they felt more like doctors than students; this compares with 29 per cent of the 91 who had little difficulty and 25 per cent of the 32 who had a fair or considerable amount of difficulty in handling patients. (The question read: "From your own experience, how much difficulty would you say you have in handling patients?")

As students move through medical school, they of course tend to develop an image of themselves as doctors rather than as merely students, especially in their clinical years when they have substantial contact with patients. We find that at each phase of their training, students' self-images tend to vary as they interact with faculty members, classmates, nurses, and patients, i.e., with persons in their role set who have varying expectations of them.

The relationships of students with patients were chosen for more detailed analysis of some of the factors facilitating the formation of a professional self-image in this social context. The professional relations of preclinical students at Western Reserve with families assigned to them provide a suitable set of materials, allowing us to isolate processes operating in student-patient relationships which are not readily distinguishable when students come to have wider experience with numerous patients. In accord with the hypothesis that individuals tend to develop a self-image which reflects the images others have of them, it was found that students who noted that their patients assigned them to the role of physician were more likely than other students to begin to think of themselves as doctors.

It was further found that, within this context, the requirements of the patient also affected the development of a professional self-image by the student. The opportunity to act in the role of quasi-physician facilitated the sense of growing doctorhood; specifically, those students whose families presented medical problems were more likely than others to think of themselves primarily as doctors rather than students. Furthermore, students who felt they handled the problems of their assigned families without difficulty showed a greater tendency to develop this professional self-image, even as early as the end of their first year.

Further inquiry is being directed to additional factors entering into the early development of the professional self-image. It will then be in order to find out how these self-images, developed early in the training period, affect the pace and character of students' subsequent learning in medical school.

THE SOCIALIZATION OF MANAGERIAL ROLES

The role of a manager in a modern corporation is a bureaucratic role. The old time entrepreneur has practically disappeared from the business world to be replaced by the full-time bureaucrat. Let us review some of the salient features of industrial or corporate bureaucracy.[19]

Bureaucratic roles are specialized and involve the recruitment of persons possessing specific qualities for a specific job. The elaboration of these qualities usually entails a training period in which the prospective manager is introduced to the operations of the particular corporation. The training period, however, also involves socialization into the values of the bureaucratic system.[20] The task of executive management is to coordinate a large number of bureaucratic specializations into a predictable system of behavior. The roles within a bureaucratic system then become formal and routine. Routinization and formalization permit the system to continue operation regardless of personnel turnover, or conflict and rivalry among individuals. Corporate bureaucracy is also a hierarchical system of statuses with certain amounts of authority delegated to each. Specific control exists over a limited area for which each individual bureaucrat is judged to be competent: the bureaucrat, under these circumstances, is not in any sense a final authority. There is, instead, a pyramid of authority above him.

Bureaucratic management is a full-time, semiprofessional, career. A long period of training is required, usually in engineering or business administration, followed frequently by a second period of indoctrination by the corporation, after which the individual enters the pyramid through which he fully expects to advance.[21] Communication within the bureaucracy is indirect, thus creating a secondary group atmosphere between the levels of the hierarchy.[22] An individual on a lower level may be known to another at a higher level only by name and reputation. Although the human-relations aspect of the ideology of management refers to direct contact between persons, the difficulty of carrying out direct contact to the fullest intent results in the creation of intermediate functionaries who represent management at successive levels.

There are two broad categories of management: the executive and the specialist.[23] Executives are " . . . persons in responsible and continuous control of the organization as an operating unit and in position to formulate general objectives of the organization." [24] The executive is not the most skilled workman nor need he possess an intimate knowledge of functions at other levels of management; but he is considered to be the best coordinator.[25] The executive, by wise recruitment, by establishing channels of communication, by obtaining a high level of performance from employees at all levels, and through the establishment of policies and procedures, must secure loyalty to the organization and to the hierarchy of authority.[26]

No single definition encompasses the second category of manager. Junior executives—often called middle management—technicians, and supervisors, constitute a heterogeneous collection of skills, talents, and duties. It is the task of executive management to coordinate these into a meaningful series of relationships. Middle management is an intermediate core of managers who transmit executive decisions to the supervisors. Because executive decisions are often stated in generalities it is the particular duty of middle management to clarify these statements.[27] Technicians are concerned with the production process. Engineers, statisticians, accountants, personnel officers; those who represent the corporation—lawyers, advertising agents, and market analysts; and those involved in industrial research are considered technicians. Supervisors, especially foremen, are concerned with the direct supervision of workers.

As in the case of professional roles, the socialization into bureaucratic corporation management begins early in life. Young people, though not generally participating directly in the bureaucracy, are frequently the object of bureaucratic procedures. This is seen in education, especially at the college level (see Chapter 10).[28]

Corporate bureaucracy expects a large-scale commitment from the individual, and to this end many corporations now conduct management schools. The Vick Chemical Company established a famous management school in the early 1930's.[29] The emphasis of the school was on applied merchandising with no attention given to managerial training, as such, nor to human relations. In the following selection, William H. Whyte, Jr., describes the program of the General Electric Corporation. The General Electric program preceded the Vick program, and actually set an example for the current trend of management training. The General Electric program is extremely formal, including faculties, graduating classes, and alumni, and covers not only training in the specifics of bureaucratic roles, but also political orientation. It is a program which attempts to involve as much of the personality as possible, so that the managerial role becomes paramount and, therefore, predictable.[30]

*

The most immediately apparent thing about the General Electric program is the fact that it *is* a school. While the plants serve as part of the campus, the company maintains a full-time staff of 250 instructors and an educational plant complete to such details as company-published textbooks, examinations, classrooms, and alumni publications. In direct operating costs alone the company spends over five million dollars annually—a budget larger than many a medium-sized college.

The program is highly centralized. To keep this plant running, GE's corps of recruiters each year delivers between 1000 and 1500 college graduates, mostly engineers, to the company's Schenectady headquarters. There the trainees enter what is for them a continuation of college life. Like fraternity brothers, they live together in boarding houses and attend classes in groups. For afterhours recreation, they have the privileges of the Edison Club where, along with other GE employees with college degrees, they can meet after classes to play golf, bridge, and enjoy a planned series of parties and dances. (GE employees who haven't gone to college are eligible to join if they have achieved a supervisory rating.)

The curriculum is arranged in much the same manner as a university's. The trainee enters under one of several courses, such as engineering and

* From William H. Whyte, Jr., *The Organization Man*, pp. 120–125. Copyright 1956 by William H. Whyte, Jr. Reprinted by permission of Simon and Schuster, Inc.

accounting. All these courses will have much in common, however, for the trainee's first eighteen months are regarded as the basic part of his training. At the end of this time he will then go on to a "major." If he has been in the manufacturing training course, for example, he can elect as a major factory operations, manufacturing engineering, production and purchasing, or plant engineering.

The work the trainee does during this training is not, like Vick's applied merchandising, considered an end in itself. From time to time the trainee will work at specific jobs, but these jobs, while not mere make-work, are outside the regular cost-accounted operations of the company. The company considers them vehicles for training, and it rotates students from one to another on a regular schedule.

The most noteworthy feature of the General Electric approach is the emphasis on the "professional" manager. As in all training programs, the bulk of the instruction is on specifics. Unlike most, however, there is considerable study in subjects that cut across every kind of job. Trainees study personnel philosophy, labor relations, law, and, most important, the managerial viewpoint. [Among other things, the trainees take HOBSO. This is the course in How Our Business System Operates, originally developed by Du Pont to inoculate blue-collar employees against creeping socialism. Though GE has no reason to fear its trainees are ideologically unsound, it explains that the course will help them "detect any bad guidance they receive from union and political leaders, and even from educational and spiritual leaders."]

Only a minority of the trainees will ever become managers; in ten years 1500 to 2000 executive slots will open up, and this means that most of the thousands of young men trained during this time will never get further than middle management. Nevertheless, it is those future executive slots that the company is thinking of, and it makes its concern plain to the trainee. On the report card form for trainees, there is a space for an evaluation as to whether the trainee is suited "for individual contribution" or whether, instead, he is suited "to manage the work of others." The company tells the trainees that it is perfectly all right for them to aim at "individual contribution," which is to say, a specialty. It would be a dull trainee, however, who did not pause before consigning himself to such a role. In one of GE's textbooks there is a picture of a man looking at two ladders. One leads up to a specialty, the other to general managing. The question before the young man, the textbook states, is: "Will I specialize in a particular field?—or "Will I become broad-gauge, capable of effort in many fields?"

Who wants to be narrow-gauge? Trainees do not have to read too strenuously between the lines to see that one should aim to manage; as a matter of fact, they are predisposed to read a good bit more between the lines than many of their elders would like them to. Which brings us to an important point. In gauging the impact of the curriculum on the young man, his predispositions are as important as the weighting of the courses. Elders at General Electric can demonstrate that the actual amount of time devoted to the abstract arts of management is far less than the time devoted to specific skills. But the managerial part is what the trainees want to hear— and they want to hear it so much that one hour's exposure to the managerial view can be as four or five hours of something else in proportion to its effect on impressionable minds. Trainees are interested, to be sure, in how turbines are made, in the techniques of the accounting department and such, but they do not want to be *too* interested. It would make them unbalanced.

They regard specific work very much as many educators view "subject matter" courses: narrowing. As trainees play back the lesson, they see a distinction, sometimes a downright antithesis, between the qualities of the broad-gauge executive and the qualities that one must have to do a superlative piece of concrete work. Not work itself but the managing of other people's work is the skill that they aspire to. As they describe it, the manager is a man in charge of people getting along together, and his *expertise* is relatively independent of who or what is being managed. Or why.

Not surprisingly, the part of the curriculum for which they have the greatest affinity is the human-relations instruction. They are particularly enthusiastic about the "Effective Presentation" course worked up by the sales-training department. They can hardly be blamed. "YOU CAN ALWAYS GET ANYBODY TO DO WHAT YOU WISH," the textbook proclaims. To this end the students spend four months eagerly studying a battery of communication techniques and psychological principles which General Electric tells them will help them to be good managers. (Sample principle: "Never say anything controversial.")

There is nothing novel about teaching people how to manipulate other people, and GE's scientific psychological techniques bear a strong resemblance to the how-to-be-a-success precepts standard in the U.S. for decades. What is different about them is their justification. They are not presented on the grounds that they will help make people do what you want them to do so that you can make more money. GE trainees see it in much more eleemosynary terms. They do like the part about selling yourself to others so you can get ahead, for they think a lot about this. But they don't abide the thought of enemies on the other side of the counter; they see the manipulative skills as something that in the long run will make other people *happy*. When in years to come the trainees are charged with the destiny of subordinates—a possibility most take remarkably much for granted—they will be able to achieve a stable, well-adjusted work group. They won't drive subordinates, they explain. They will motivate them.

Trainees are also predisposed to emphasis on cooperation rather than competition, and this they get too. The emphasis is built into the structure of the school. For one thing, the student is given a high measure of security from the beginning, and while there may be promotion of the fittest there can be survival for all. There are exceptions, but one must be a very odd ball to be one. For the first two years the trainee is part of a system in which his salary raises will be automatic, and while later on he will be more on his own there will be no planned elimination as there was at Vick, nor an up-or-out policy such as the Navy's.

To get ahead, of course, one must compete—but not too much, and certainly not too obviously. While overt ambition is a bad posture for the ambitious anywhere, the GE system has especial sanctions for the rate-buster. The trainee is, first of all, a member of a group, and the group is entrusted to a surprising degree with the resolution of his future. How well, the company wants to know, does he fit in? His fellow trainees provide the answer, and in the "case study" group discussions the eager beaver or the deviant is quickly exposed. And brought to heel. Trainees speak frequently of the way close fraternity life atmosphere is valuable in ironing out some trainees' aberrant tendencies. It may be tough on him, they concede, but better now than later. In a few years the trainee will be released from this close association and the social character that he has perfected will be a fundamental necessity; he will be moving from one company branch to another, and he must be able to fit into the same kind of integrated social system.

The company officially recognizes the disciplining of the group. In its periodic rating of the man, the company frequently calls on his comrades to participate in the rating. If a man is liked especially well not only by his superiors but by his peers, he may be given the job of guiding about eight or ten of his fellow trainees. He is now a "sign-up," and if he keeps on maturing he may become a "head-of-tests," the seven "sign-ups" reporting to him. Since the opinions of one's peers are so integral to advancement, this system virtually insures that the overzealous or the "knocker" type of man will not get ahead—or, at the very least, that he will successfully remold himself to the managerial image.

The fact that the trainee must spend so much time thinking of what other people think of him does not oppress him. Quite the opposite, the constant surveillance is one of the things the average trainee talks about most enthusiastically. The rating system is highly standardized, he explains; it is the product of *many* people rather than one, and this denominator of judgments frees him from the harshness or caprice that might result from the traditional boss-employee relationship. He is also freed from being ignored; the system insures that other people must be thinking about him quite as much as he is thinking about them, and for this reason he won't get pigeonholed. At General Electric, as one trainee remarked, not only can't you get lost, you can't even hide.

Needless to say, ambition still pulses, and I am not trying to suggest that the General Electric man is any less set on the main chance than my Vick comrades. It is quite obvious, nevertheless, that he must pursue the main chance in a much more delicate fashion. To get ahead, he must cooperate with the others—but cooperate *better* than they do.

The rules of the game do permit a few lapses, but these lapses, characteristically, are the display of personality. Somewhere along the line the trainees must get themselves hired into a regular job, and to do this they must attract the attention of superiors. There is a tacit understanding among trainees that it is perfectly all right to make a bald play to get on a first name-basis with superiors that might do one some good. "As soon as you know your way around a new department you start telephoning," one trainee explains, tapping the intercommunication telephone directory. "Believe me, this little green book here is a man's best friend." The company encourages superiors to encourage this kind of contact. "I or anybody else," another trainee says, "can walk into a manager's office just as easily as we can each other's. By ten o'clock of the day I hit the New York office I was calling everybody by his first name."

THE SOCIALIZATION OF INDUSTRIAL WORKER ROLES

Managerial ideologies do not operate exclusively within the sphere of the managerial bureaucracy. They are also directed toward the workers or, in managerial terminology, the operatives. There are two reasons for this. First, workers ultimately implement policy. There is, then, concern for making workers feel they are part of a team (see the essay by David Lilienthal in Chapter 16). Second, workers, in the form of organized labor, represent a challenge to managerial authority, presenting problems for both management and workers in relation to degrees of commitment in their respective roles. Before we discuss the implications of these issues, we must first understand the nature of the worker in the industrial hierarchy.

Industrial workers are an even more heterogeneous collection of skills and talents than is specialized management. Some generalities, however, are possible. The industrial worker functions at a low level of skill and a nonexistent level of creativity. Most industrial tasks are learned in a short period of time—a few hours or one or two days, at the most. This is possible through the division of labor within industrial plants, especially in assembly-line types of industry, where practically anyone can be put in any job, and replaced with no problems. No creativity is involved in industrial work at the operative level; individual initiative has been removed from the production process in order to calculate productive capacity more rationally. This means that industrial work tasks are routine, concentrated, and supervised.[31]

Industrial workers often operate under two sets of expectations: those of the formal bureaucratic system and those of the informal system created by fellow workers. This duality of expectations operates, of course, at both the professional and managerial levels. Doctors may set up certain hospital procedures and then, under the stress of emergencies, proceed to circumvent every one of them. Management is capable of the same action. In fact, it has been noted in corporate bureaucracies that certain policies and procedures are established in full expectation that they will be circumvented. But the duality of expectations of the industrial worker are of a different order. Doctors create both the formal and informal expectations for doctors. Managers create both the formal and informal expectations for managers. Workers do not create the system of formal expectations under which they operate. These are handed down by management.

The expectations made of workers by the formal system are based on the position of the workers in the pyramidal structure of the corporation. Workers are expected to cooperate with managerial decisions and policies; they are expected to be devoted to the assigned limited technical duty. Such narrowly defined interests, furthermore, are ideally motivated by the rewards and advancement proffered by management.[32]

When, as noted in other contexts, persons interact frequently in a formally prescribed pattern, certain sentiments of liking will emerge among them to encourage interaction above and beyond the formal system.[33] Thus, informal worker groups appear within the formal work situation. The informal system develops its own pattern of social roles, social status, controls, and rewards. There may be informal worker groups that—to use production norms as a major index of behavior—have high production ratios.[34] But informal work groups may also work against formal expectations, and produce less than is expected of them.[35]

The prevalence of high informal production standards depends on a group structure in which individual needs for recognition and security are not extreme, and in which the members are motivated to maintain mutually satisfying relationships and the informal norms.[36] Many newer forms of technology, however, have increased the physical distance between work stations, increased the noise level, and decreased opportunities for informal worker contact.[37] Such circumstances make it difficult to create, on either the formal or informal level, a group interested in increasing its productivity.[38]

Managerial norms are often inimical to the personal interests of the individual worker because of the high productivity expected and the price paid by the worker in terms of fatigue and tension. Informal groupings, as noted, may be difficult to maintain. It is not surprising to find that a typical worker reaction to such circumstances is alienation.

Alienation may take the form of powerlessness. This refers to the expectation held by the individual "that his own behavior cannot determine the occurrence of the outcomes, or reinforcements, he seeks." [39] Powerlessness is illustrated by the fact that the worker is the lowest man in the hierarchy of corporate organization. He has little access, except through a bureaucratically organized union, to management. Management itself may appear hostile, aloof, and imposing. What the worker does, and how and when he does it are decisions over which he has no control. These are decisions made by management.

A second form of alienation that the worker may experience is normlessness or *anomie*. As we have seen, this is the expectation held by the individual "that socially unapproved behaviors are required to achieve given goals." [40] For the worker this means that self-satisfaction and freedom from fatigue and tension cannot be achieved by adhering to the norms established by management. Norms established by the informal group, even though they may be in opposition to those of the formal system, are those to which the worker conforms. It is only in such behavior that he can find fulfillment of his individual psychological and social needs for interaction, security, and recognition.

A third form of alienation is self-estrangement. This is defined as "the degree of dependence of the given behavior upon anticipated future rewards . . . that lie outside of the activity itself." [41] This simply means that the specific type of work to which most industrial workers are assigned is degrading, lacks any self-involvement in an intellectual and creative sense, and is foreign to the interests and capacities of the individual. The Real Self, as Karen Horney called it, is submerged beneath the routine and formality of assembly-line production.

All of these aspects of alienation are illustrated in the following argumentative article by Harvey Swados. He describes in an impressionistic manner the responses of workers to automobile assembly-line production. Swados challenges the belief that the worker, oriented to middle-class consumption patterns, is happy because he now can participate in the acquisition of material wealth. This essay can easily be dismissed as a romantic search for a psychological reality that somehow has been crushed by corporate business in one immense, crass, materialistic

gesture. Yet, to dismiss the essay on such grounds is to say that alienation of the worker does not exist.

*

"From where we sit in the company," says one of the best personnel men in
the country, "we have to look at only the aspects of work that cut across all
sorts of jobs—administration and human relations. Now these are aspects of
work, abstractions, but it's easy for personnel people to get so hipped on their
importance that they look on the specific tasks of making things and selling
them as secondary. . . ." (*The Organization Man*, by William H. Whyte, Jr.)

The personnel man who made this remark to Mr. Whyte differed from
his brothers only in that he had a moment of insight. Actually, "the specific
tasks of making things" are now not only regarded by his white-collar fellows as "secondary," but as irrelevant to the vaguer but more "challenging"
tasks of the man at the desk. This is true not just of the personnel man,
who places workers, replaces them, displaces them—in brief, manipulates
them. The union leader also, who represents workers and sometimes manipulates them, seems increasingly to regard what his workers do as merely
subsidiary to the job he himself is doing in the larger community. This job
may be building the Red Cross or the Community Chest, or it may sometimes be—as the Senate hearings suggest—participating in such communal
endeavors as gambling, prostitution, and improving the breed. In any case,
the impression is left that the problems of the workers in the background
(or underground) have been stabilized, if not permanently solved.

With the personnel man and the union leader, both of whom presumably
see the worker from day to day, growing so far away from him, it is hardly
to be wondered at that the middle class in general, and articulate middle-
class intellectuals in particular, see the worker vaguely, as through a cloud.
One gets the impression that when they do consider him, they operate
from one of two unspoken assumptions: (1) the worker has died out like
the passenger pigeon, or is dying out, or becoming accultured, like the
Navajo; (2) if he *is* still around, he is just like the rest of us—fat, satisfied,
smug, a little restless, but hardly distinguishable from his fellow TV-viewers
of the middle class.

Lest it be thought that (1) is somewhat exaggerated, I hasten to quote
from a recently published article apparently dedicated to the laudable task
of urging slothful middle-class intellectuals to wake up and live: "The old-
style sweatshop crippled mainly the working people. Now there are no
workers left in America; we are almost all middle class as to income and
expectations." I do not believe the writer meant to state—although he comes
perilously close to it—that nobody works any more. If I understand him

* From "The Myth of the Happy Worker," A *Radical's America*, by Harvey
Swados. Copyright 1957, by Harvey Swados. Reprinted by permission of Little,
Brown and Company—Atlantic Monthly Press.

correctly, he is referring to the fact that the worker's rise in real income over the last decade, plus the diffusion of middle-class tastes and values throughout a large part of the underlying population, have made it increasingly difficult to tell blue-collar from white-coller worker without a program. In short, if the worker earns like the middle class, votes like the middle class, dresses like the middle class, dreams like the middle class, then he ceases to exist as a worker.

But there is one thing that the worker doesn't do like the middle class: he works like a worker. The steel-mill puddler does not yet sort memos, the coal miner does not yet sit in conferences, the cotton millhand does not yet sip martinis from his lunchbox. The worker's attitude toward his work is generally compounded of hatred, shame, and resignation.

Before I spell out what I think this means, I should like first to examine some of the implications of the widely held belief that "we are almost all middle-class as to income and expectations." I am neither economist, sociologist, nor politician, and I hold in my hand no doctored statistics to be haggled over. I am by profession a writer who has had occasion to work in factories at various times during the thirties, forties, and fifties. The following observations are simply impressions based on my last period of factory servitude, in 1956.

The average automobile worker gets a little better than two dollars an hour. As such he is one of the best-paid factory workers in the country. After twenty years of militant struggle led by the union that I believe to be still the finest and most democratic labor organization in the United States, he is earning less than the starting salaries offered to inexperienced and often semi-literate college graduates without dependents. After compulsory deductions for taxes, social security, old-age insurance, and union dues, and optional deductions for hospitalization and assorted charities, his pay check for forty hours of work is going to be closer to seventy than to eighty dollars a week. Does this make him middle class as to income? Does it rate with the weekly take of a dentist, an accountant, a salesman, a draftsman, a journalist? Surely it would be more to the point to ask how a family man can get by in the fifties on that kind of income. I know how he does it, and I should think the answers would be a little disconcerting to those who wax glib on the satisfactory status of the "formerly" underprivileged.

For one thing, he works a lot longer than forty hours a week—when he can. Since no automobile company is as yet in a position to guarantee its workers anything like fifty weeks of steady forty-hour paychecks, the auto worker knows he has to make it while he can. During peak production periods he therefore puts in nine, ten, eleven, and often twelve hours a day on the assembly line for weeks on end. And that's not all. If he had dependents, as like as not he also holds down a "spare-time" job. I have worked on the line with men who doubled as mechanics, repairmen, salesmen, con-tractors, builders, farmers, cab-drivers, lumberyard workers, countermen. I would guess that there are many more of these than show up in the official statistics: often a man will work for less if he can be paid under the counter with tax-free dollars.

Nor is that all. The factory worker with dependents cannot carry the debt load he now shoulders—the middle-class debt load, if you like, of nagging payments on car, washer, dryer, TV, clothing, house itself—with-out family help. Even if he puts in fifty, sixty, or seventy hours a week at one or two jobs, he has to count on his wife's paycheck, or his son's, his daughter's, his brother-in-law's; or on his mother's social security, or his father's veteran's pension. The working-class family today is not typically held together by the male wage earner, but by multiple wage earners often of several generations who club together to get the things they want and need—or are pressured into believing they must have. It is at best a pre-carious arrangement; as for its toll on the physical organism and the psyche, that is a question perhaps worthy of further investigation by those who currently pronounce themselves bored with Utopia Unlimited in the Fat Fifties.

But what of the worker's middle-class expectations? I had been under the impression that this was the rock on which Socialist agitation had foundered for generations: it proved useless to tell the proletarian that he had a world to win when he was reasonably certain that with a few breaks he could have his own gas station. If these expectations have changed at all in recent years, they would seem to have narrowed rather than expanded, leaving a psychological increment of resignation rather than of unbounded optimism (except among the very young—and even among them the optimism focuses more often on better-paying opportunities elsewhere in the labor market than on illusory hopes of swift status advancement). The worker's expectations are for better pay, more humane working conditions, more job security. As long as he feels that he is going to achieve them through an extension of existing conditions, for that long he is going to continue to be a middle-class conservative in temper. But only for that long.

I suspect that what middle-class writers mean by the worker's middle-class expectations are his cravings for commodities—his determination to have not only fin-tailed cars and single-unit washer-dryers, but butterfly chairs in the rumpus room, African masks on the wall, and power boats in the garage. Before the middle-class intellectuals condemn these expectations too harshly, let them consider, first, who has been utilizing every known technique of suasion and propaganda to convert luxuries into necessities, and second, at what cost these new necessities are acquired by the American working-class family.

Now I should like to return to the second image of the American worker:

satisfied, doped by TV, essentially middle class in outlook. This is an image bred not of communication with workers (except as mediated by hired interviewers sent "into the field" like anthropologists or entomologists), but of contempt for people, based perhaps on self-contempt and on a feeling among intellectuals that the worker has let them down. In order to see this clearly, we have to place it against the intellectual's changing attitudes toward the worker since the thirties.

At the time of the organization of the C.I.O., the middle-class intellectual saw the proletarian as society's figure of virtue—heroic, magnanimous, bearing in his loins the seeds of a better future; he would have found ludicrous the suggestion that a sit-down striker might harbor anti-Semitic feelings. After Pearl Harbor, the glamorization of the worker was taken over as a function of government. Then, however, he was no longer the builder of the future good society; instead he was second only to the fighting man as the vital winner of the war. Many intellectuals, as government employees, found themselves helping to create this new portrait of the worker as patriot.

But in the decade following the war, intellectuals have discovered that workers are no longer either building socialism or forging the tools of victory. All they are doing is making the things that other people buy. That, and participating in the great commodity scramble. The disillusionment, it would seem, is almost too terrible to bear. Word has gotten around among the highbrows that the worker is not heroic or idealistic; public-opinion polls prove that he wants barbecue pits more than foreign aid and air-conditioning more than desegregation, that he doesn't particularly want to go on strike, that he is reluctant to form a Labor Party, that he votes for Stevenson and often even for Eisenhower and Nixon—that he is, in short, animated by the same aspirations as drive the middle class onward and upward in suburbia.

There is of course a certain admixture of self-delusion in the middle-class attitude that workers are now the same as everybody else. For me it was expressed most precisely last year in the dismay and sympathy with which middle-class friends greeted the news that I had gone back to work in a factory. If workers are now full-fledged members of the middle class, why the dismay? What difference whether one sits in an office or stands in a shop? The answer is so obvious that one feels shame at laboring the point. But I have news for my friends among the intellectuals. The answer is obvious to workers, too.

They know that there is a difference between working with your back and working with your behind. (I do not make the distinction between hand-work and brain-work, since we are all learning that white-collar work is becoming less and less brain-work.) They know that they work harder than the middle class for less money. Nor is it simply a question of status, that magic word so dear to the hearts of the sociologues, the new anatomizers of the American corpus. It is not simply status-hunger that makes a man hate work which pays *less* than other work he knows about, if *more* than any other work he has been trained for (the only reason my fellow-workers stayed on the assembly line, they told me again and again). It is not simply status-hunger that makes a man hate work that is mindless, endless, stupefying, sweaty, filthy, noisy, exhausting, insecure in its prospects, and practically without hope of advancement.

The plain truth is that factory work is degrading. It is degrading to any man who ever dreams of doing something worthwhile with his life; and it is about time we faced the fact. The more a man is exposed to middle-class values, the more sophisticated he becomes and the more production-line work is degrading to him. The immigrant who slaved in the poorly lighted, foul, vermin-ridden sweatshop found his work less degrading than the native-born high school graduate who reads "Judge Parker," "Rex Morgan, M.D.," and "Judd Saxon, Business Executive," in the funnies, and works in a fluorescent factory with ticker-tape production-control machines. For the immigrant laborer, even the one who did not dream of socialism, his long hours were going to buy him freedom. For the factory worker of the fifties, his long hours are going to buy him commodities . . . and maybe reduce a few of his debts.

Almost without exception, the men with whom I worked on the assembly line last year felt like trapped animals. Depending on their age and personal circumstances, they were either resigned to their fate, furiously angry at *themselves* for what they were doing, or desperately hunting other work that would pay as well and in addition offer some variety, some prospect of change and betterment. They were sick of being pushed around by harried foremen (themselves more pitied than hated), sick of working like blinkered donkeys, sick of being dependent for their livelihood on a maniacal production-merchandising set-up, sick of working in a place where there was no spot to relax during the twelve-minute rest period. (Some day—let us hope—we will marvel that production was still so worshiped in the fifties that new factories could be built with every splendid facility for the storage and movement of essential parts, but with no place for a resting worker to sit down for a moment but on a fire plug, the edge of a packing case, or the sputum- and oil-stained stairway of a toilet.)

The older men stay put and wait for their vacations. But since the assembly line demands young blood (you will have a hard time getting hired if you are over thirty-five), the factory in which I worked was aswarm with new faces every day; labor turnover was so fantastic and absenteeism so rampant, with the young men knocking off a day or two every week to hunt up other jobs, that the company was forced to overhire in order to have sufficient workers on hand at the starting siren.

To those who will object—fortified by their readings in C. Wright Mills and A. C. Spectorsky—that the white-collar commuter, too, dislikes his work, accepts it only because it buys his family commodities, and is constantly on the prowl for other work, I can only reply that for me at any rate this is proof not of the disappearance of the working-class but of the proletarianization of the middle class. Perhaps it is not taking place quite in the way that Marx envisaged it, but the alienation of the white-collar man (like that of the laborer) from both his tools and whatever he produces, the slavery that chains the exurbanite to the commuting timetable (as the worker is still chained to the time-clock), the anxiety that sends the white-collar man home with his briefcase for an evening's overtime), the displacement of the white-collar slum from the wrong side of the tracks to the suburbs (just as the working-class slum is moved from old-law tenements to skyscraper barracks) —all these mean to me that the white-collar man is entering (though his arms may be loaded with commodities) the grey world of the working man.

Three quotations from men with whom I worked may help to bring my view into focus:

Before starting work: "Come on, suckers, they say the Foundation wants to give away *more* than half a billion this year. Let's do and die for the old Foundation."

During rest period: "Ever stop to think how we crawl here bumper to bumper, and crawl home bumper to bumper, and we've got to turn out more every minute to keep our jobs, when there isn't even any room for them on the highways?"

At quitting time (this from older foremen, whose job is not only to keep things moving, but by extension to serve as company spokesmen): "You're smart to get out of here. . . . I curse the day I ever started, now I'm stuck: any man with brains that stays here ought to have his head examined. This is no place for an intelligent human being."

Such is the attitude toward the work. And toward the product? On the one hand it is admired and desired as a symbol of freedom, almost a substitute for freedom, not because the worker participated in making it, but because our whole culture is dedicated to the proposition that the automobile is both necessary and beautiful. On the other hand it is hated and despised— so much that if your new car smells bad it may be due to a banana peel crammed down its gullet and sealed up thereafter, so much so that if your dealer can't locate the rattle in your new car you might ask him to open the welds on one of those tail fins and vacuum out the nuts and bolts thrown in by workers sabotaging their own product.

Sooner or later, if we want a decent society—by which I do not mean a society glutted with commodities or one maintained in precarious equilibrium by over-buying and forced premature obsolescence—we are going to have to come face to face with the problem of work. Apparently the Russians have committed themselves to the replenishment of their labor force through automatic recruitment of those intellectually incapable of keeping up with severe scholastic requirements in the public educational system. Apparently we, too, are heading in the same direction: although our economy is not directed, and although college education is as yet far from free, we seem to be operating in this capitalist economy on the totalitarian assumption that we can funnel the underprivileged, undereducated, or just plain underequipped, into the factory, where we can proceed to forget about them once we have posted the minimum fair labor standards on the factory wall.

If this is what we want, let's be honest enough to say so. If we conclude that there is nothing noble about repetitive work, but that it is nevertheless good enough for the lower orders, let's say that, too, so we will at least know where we stand. But if we cling to the belief that other men are our brothers, not just Egyptians, or Israelis, or Hungarians, but *all* men, including millions of Americans who grind their lives away on an insane treadmill, then we will have to start thinking about how their work and their lives can be made meaningful. That is what I assume the Hungarians, both workers and intellectuals, have been thinking about. Since no one has been ordering us what to think, since no one has been forbidding our intellectuals to fraternize with our workers, shouldn't it be a little easier for us to admit, first, that our problems exist, then to state them, and then to see if we can resolve them?

SOCIALIZATION AND IDEOLOGICAL STRAIN

The socialization of economic roles involves not only the induction of the individual into the skills and abilities of the occupation but also, to re-emphasize a point, the adoption of the role's ideologies. This is not accomplished with ease; in fact, quite the opposite may be true. Much time, talent, and money is spent reiterating the "spiritual values" of an economic role. More often than not, these efforts are directed toward those *already* pursuing the occupation. The expounding of occupational ideologies may be looked on, then, as efforts to maintain the loyalties of those who are already assumed to be loyal.

Why can it not be assumed that, once induction into an occupational role has been completed, socialization is also completed? A number of factors, operating within any occupational situation, enable the members to discount or even dismiss the official occupational ideologies.

One of these factors is the complex nature of the division of labor. Within many occupations there will be a diversity of skills, interests, and abilities. Medicine may be considered a single unified profession from a layman's viewpoint. But within the profession is a series of specializations, based on the nature of medical practice. Within management there is the distinction between executives, middle management, and specialists. Workers are, of course, the most specialized category in the labor force. To the extent that each specialization is the basis for interaction at a formal level, it can be theoretically expected that interaction will also take place at an informal level. This leads to the development of interpersonal norms, sentiments, and statuses which, in turn, may lead to group interpretations of the occupational ideology. Such interpretations may reinforce the ideologies or may direct behavior away from them. The direction taken and the factors leading in that direction are not important here. The point is that an alternative course to the ideology is possible.

A second factor which makes it possible to discount or dismiss an occupational ideology is the fact that total commitment to the ideology is never guaranteed. Professions speak of "100% professional conduct," and corporations boast of the "company man," but there is a distinction to be made between overt behavior, and covert attitudes. The ideal situation from the point of view of management would be if overt behavior were a direct reflection of covert attitudes. But this can never be assumed. Indeed, outward conformity to the ideology may be only a front, as Erving Goffman has noted (see Chapter 8), which can cover a wide range of attitudes.

The third factor is the presence of competing ideologies. Management must compete with labor, and vice versa, and management and the professions must compete with those economic and political ideologies that would create change in their own occupations. The presence of competing ideologies does not necessarily mean that an individual, who is thereby able to discount or dismiss the ideology of his occupation, will "go over" to the other side. This would mean that the individual gives up the rights and prerogatives of his own occupation—a sacrifice not many are willing to make. There are, instead, more subtle ways in which disaffection with an ideology can take place under the pressure of competing ideologies. Erving Goffman has described them under the colorful terminology of "defrocked priests" and "renegades." [42] The defrocked priests of an occupation are those who expose, often in the press, the secrets of the occupation. Doctors have told of fee-splitting arrangements with colleagues; businessmen have exposed planned obsolescence and price-fixing arrangements; and workers have revealed union blackmail and terrorism. The renegade is one who, feeling keenly outside pressures, assumes a moral stand regarding the expectations of his occupation. He feels that those in the occupation are, as Goffman noted, false to the ideals of the occupation.[43] The assumption of both types is that if reform were to take place in the occupation, the pressures caused by the competing ideologies would cease.

These factors make it clear that loyalty to an occupational ideology cannot be assumed. On-the-job supervision cannot guarantee it. It is not surprising to find, therefore, that many occupations devote much time expounding their ideologies away from the place of work. This has become one of the major functions of those voluntary associations related to various occupations. The American Medical Association, the National Association of Manufacturers, and the A.F.L.-C.I.O. are typical. It is organizations such as these which seek further to formalize the socialization process.

Frequently overlooked by the members of an occupation is the fact that such voluntary associations may develop their own interpretations of the occupational ideology. These associations frequently become ends in themselves for the membership, and—especially, for the leadership. Thus, an interpretation which emphasizes the perpetuation of the association is created, couched in the appeal that the organization speaks for the "responsible members" of the occupation. Such a statement wards off criticism from those members of the occupation who do not believe in the goals of the association and perpetuates a "right" and "wrong" distinction in the minds of the public.

The emergence of voluntary associations, representing occupational interests and ideologies, can have an unanticipated but very important consequence. The feeling may be generated among the membership that the bureaucracy of the association has time and talent to devote full attention to the problems of the occupation; that the bureaucracy is the source of wisdom and expertness. Regulation of the membership then shifts from control by the members to control by the bureaucratic hierarchy. Thus, a new element of authority is introduced into the occupation, an element which has a place and an existence quite apart from the actual job. The problem now facing the association bureaucracy becomes one of convincing its membership that the organization functions in the best interests of the occupation. To the degree that the bureaucracy establishes this belief in the minds of the membership, it reinforces the socialization of the particular ideology, be it professional, managerial, or labor.

Notes

1. Robert W. White, *Lives in Progress*, New York: Dryden Press, 1952, p. 125.
2. Professor Rinehard Bendix once mentioned an interesting case of what he called "organizational sabotage" in a German factory during the Second World War. The regular workers were inducted into the armed forces and were replaced in the factory by prisoners from a nearby concentration camp. In all their behavior every official rule and procedure was followed to the letter. The consequence was a slow-down in production.
3. C. C. North and Paul K. Hatt, "Jobs and Occupations: A Popular Evaluation," *Opinion News*, Vol. K, September 1, 1947, pp. 3–13.
4. *The Presentation of the Self in Everyday Life*, New York: Anchor Books, 1959, Chapter 1, *et passim*.
5. Cf., Everett C. Hughes, *Men and Their Work*, Glencoe, Ill.: The Free Press, 1958, pp. 33–34.
6. *Ibid.*, p. 33.
7. *Ibid.*
8. White, *op. cit.*, p. 126.
9. Hughes, *op. cit.*, p. 33.
10. *Ibid.*, p. 126.
11. *Ibid.*, pp. 117, *et passim*.
12. For a full discussion of the distinctions between license and mandate and their meaning to professions and near-professions see Hughes, *op. cit.*, pp. 78–87.
13. Howard S. Becker and Blanche Geer, "The Fate of Idealism in the Medical School," *American Sociological Review*, Vol. 23, February 1958, p. 51.
14. *Ibid.*
15. Natalie Rogoff, "The Decision to Study Medicine," *The Student Physician*, ed. Robert K. Merton, *et al.* Cambridge: Harvard University Press, 1957, pp. 109–129.
16. Becker and Greer, *op. cit.*, pp. 51 ff.
17. *Ibid.*, pp. 53 ff.
18. *Ibid.*, p. 54.
19. The following discussion is summarized from Wilbert E. Moore, *Industrial Relations and the Social Order*, New York: The Macmillan Company, 1950, pp. 105–114. For a case study of the functions of bureaucracy see Alvin Gouldner, *Patterns of Industrial Bureaucracy*, Glencoe, Ill.: The Free Press, 1954.
20. Managerial training and on-job rituals often are reinforced by life in what has come to be known as the "executive" or "package" suburb. See Seymour Freedgood, "Life in Bloomfield Hills," *Fortune*, Vol. LXIV, July 1961, pp. 145–149; and "Life in Buckhead," *Fortune*, Vol. LXIV, September 1961, pp. 109–114.
21. For a study of administrative succession see Oscar Grusky, "Corporate Size, Bureaucratization, and Managerial Succession," *American Journal of Sociology*, Vol. LXVII, November 1961, pp. 261–269.
22. Cf., Robert K. Merton, *Social Theory and Social Structure* (Rev. Ed.), Glencoe, Ill.: The Free Press, 1957, pp. 202 ff.
23. Moore, *op. cit.*, Chapters VII and VIII.
24. *Ibid.*, p. 124. Original in italics.
25. *Ibid.*
26. *Ibid.*, pp. 126 ff. For a full discussion see Chester I. Bernard, *The Functions of the Executive*, Cambridge: Harvard University Press, 1938.

27. Moore, *op. cit.*, p. 149.
28. The registration process at the beginning of each semester illustrates this point quite clearly. How many generations of students have suffered the frustration of losing their place in line because the yellow card was not on top of the pile in their hand!
29. William H. Whyte, Jr., *The Organization Man*, New York: Simon and Schuster, 1956, pp. 112 ff.
30. The very predictability of bureaucratic behavior creates an unanticipated consequence and an eventual bureaucratic dysfunction. The managerial skills which are learned as absolutes at one point become obsolete at another. Recalling Veblen, this is what Roebrt Merton has referred to as trained incapacity. Merton, *op. cit.*, p. 154.
31. See W. V. Faunce, E. Hardin, and E. H. Jacobson, "Automation and the Employee," *The Annals of the American Academy of Political and Social Science*, Vol. 340, March 1962, pp. 63 ff.
32. Moore, *op. cit.*, p. 331.
33. George C. Homans, *The Human Group*, New York: Harcourt Brace and Company, 1950, p. 112.
34. Cf., S. E. Seashore, *Group Cohesiveness in the Informal Work Group*, Ann Arbor: University of Michigan Press, 1954.
35. Cf., F. J. Roethlisberger and W. J. Dickson, *Management and the Worker*, Cambridge: Harvard University Press, 1939, p. 522.
36. A. Zaleznik, C. R. Christiansen, and F. J. Roethlisberger, *The Motivation, Productivity, and Satisfaction of Workers*, Boston: Harvard Graduate School of Business Administration, 1958, p. 41.
37. Faunce, *et al.*, *op. cit.*, p. 63.
38. Zaleznik, *et al.*, *op. cit.*, p. 41.
39. Melvin Seeman, "On the Meaning of Alienation," *American Sociological Review*, Vol. 24, December 1959, p. 784.
40. *Ibid.*, p. 788.
41. *Ibid.*, p. 790.
42. *The Presentation of the Self in Everyday Life*, New York: Anchor Books, 1959, pp. 164–165.
43. *Ibid.*

Selected Readings

*Blau, Peter. *Bureaucracy in Modern Society*. New York: Random House, 1956.
Caplow, Theodore. *The Sociology of Work*. Minneapolis: University of Minnesota Press, 1954.
Fortune Editors. *The Executive Life*. Garden City, New York: Doubleday and Company, 1956.
Lazarsfeld, Paul F. and Wagner Thielens. *The Academic Mind*. Glencoe, Ill.: The Free Press, 1958.
Merton, Robert K. *et al.*, eds. *Reader in Bureaucracy*. Glencoe, Ill.: The Free Press, 1952.
*Mills, C. Wright. *White Collar*. New York: Oxford Galaxy Books, 1951.
*Naegele, Kaspar D. *Health, Illness, and Society*. New York: Random House, 1962.
*Riesman, David, and associates. *The Lonely Crowd*. New York: Anchor Books, 1953.

Warner, W. Lloyd and Norman Martin, eds. *Industrial Man.* New York: Harper and Bros., 1959.

Whyte, William Foote. *Men at Work.* Homewood, Ill.: Dorsey-Irwin, 1961.

Zaleznik, A. *Worker Satisfaction and Development.* Boston: Harvard Graduate School of Business Administration, 1956.

* Paperback edition.

Chapter 18

Crises of Contemporary
Economic Institutions

Participation by all segments of society in America's wealth has brought
the nation to a stage in economic development that might be called
"people's capitalism." The innovation of the department store and the
mail-order house in the last quarter of the nineteenth century pointed
the direction we were to travel in evolving the highest standard of living
in the world. A number of problems, however, beset this form of
capitalism. Business cycles, government interference, taxation, labor
disputes, planned obsolescence, consumer sovereignty, and new forms of
competition are some of the factors that create pitfalls for the economy.

The kind of mass society that has grown up in America, supported
by science and technology and organized primarily by private enterprise,
has come to rely heavily on the corporation as the specific instrument
for handling the many details of large-scale business organization. In
addition to its economic functions, the corporation is also a social system
affecting the lives of employees, stockholders, and consumers as its
influence spreads and interacts with other forms of business organization
and with other institutions. Given the characteristics of the corporation
—separation of ownership and management, bureaucratic structure,
tendency toward concentration—will the corporation, as a social institution, fail as it matures? Does increasing bureaucracy and professionalism
in management lead to social remoteness as relationships within the
corporation become more impersonal? Does concentration through expansion and merger contribute a physical quality to social remoteness as
frequent transfers make "corporate hoboes" of middle management?
Will this ultimate solution to economic organization create social disorganization? Or has the corporation become a way of life with its own
integrity apart from the broader culture?

The government—primarily the federal government, but also at the
state and local levels—participates actively in the economy as a regulator,

396

arbiter, producer, and consumer. Public controversy arises over the extent of government involvement in the economy; some believe that government has gone too far, others that it has not gone far enough. Emotions run high in discussions of minimum wage laws, tariffs, deficit spending, and taxes.

Our position in world affairs and the continuing threat to national security have forced greater responsibility on the federal government; in order to maintain our position, the government has felt it necessary to intervene more often and in more areas of the economy than during the great industrial expansion of the late nineteenth century or the booming twenties. Marked economic growth occurred under those periods of *laissez-faire* which have come to be considered prerequisite to economic progress in some quarters; and any government action is viewed with alarm as a threat to American capitalism. As seen in Chapter 16, *laissez-faire* as a pure doctrine never existed and the argument really centers around the *degree* of government involvement.

The consumer does not exist apart from the total economy, although he has often been treated as though he existed merely to serve the needs of production. Henry Ford's comment, "They can have any color they want as long as it's black," illustrates one aspect of an older attitude toward the consumer. But Ford's cult of efficiency ran into the new consumer with his independent and capricious exercise of discretionary spending power. The increasing ability of the consumer to employ discretion in his purchases has wreaked havoc on curves of production. The consumer stands today as the most powerful force in the American economy; *caveat emptor* has become *caveat venditor*—let the seller beware. Moreover, it has been primarily as a result of the efforts of organized labor to redistribute the wealth of America that the consumer occupies his crucial position in the economy.

Capitalism, business practices, government, labor, and consumption have changed over the years. Many problems besetting the American economic system stem from the failure of various sectors in the economy to recognize these changes. Old arguments, reinforced by tradition, carry the conviction and force of romanticism. The major stumbling blocks to economic growth are internal, created by those members of society who would rather cling to tradition than adjust to the present, and by those who "overcompensate."

This is not to say that there is nothing valuable in the past. On the contrary, we should know the past as well as the present in order to preserve that which stands the test of the present. Private property, competition, and individual initiative have all survived, but with modification. Changing institutions are the signs of life in our economy. To remain viable an economy must be dynamic; and while no one wants the economy to die, sooner or later everyone is disturbed by change. In Chapter 22 we shall discuss the problem of extreme resistance to change as neo-Puritanism. The remaining part of this chapter is an examination of the problems resulting from change in three basic elements of our business economy: production, distribution, and consumption.

PRODUCTION

Big business has the inherent problems of all large-scale organization, and a few unique to itself. With two hundred of the largest corporations directly influencing three-quarters of American business life, the scope of bigness in business and industry is more than sufficient to be, *ipso facto*, a primary source of economic change. As business organizations become large, they tend to become more bureaucratic, which contributes to further growth. As in any large-scale organization, the business bureaucracy can foster empire-building, become top-heavy with managerial "fat," and stagnate. Too many functionaries, unable to communicate with one another, lead to inefficiency and loss of profit, and ultimately to failure, merger, or both. The remaining businesses redivide the market and become still larger. This is an aspect of the trend toward concentration in industry noted by many economists.

When big business is conducted in an efficient manner it may be successful in dominating the market—only to find it has run afoul the antitrust regulations. In the corporate search for security, management must somehow find the area of safety between failure and too much success. "Tutored by its attorneys, barbered and cosmeticized by Madison Avenue, nourished, even sanctified by war and cold war, and enthroned by public opinion which sees only 'goodness' in bigness that is well-mannered and well-behaved, the giant corporation exhibits the supreme confidence and assurance that bespeak stature, status, and a clear conscience." [1]

Proof of stature, if not clear conscience, is the recent price-fixing litigation involving some of the largest electrical manufacturers in the United States. The litigation was instigated by the Tennessee Valley Authority's displeasure at receiving many identical sealed bids on equipment that was to be built to specifications. The Justice Department and a Congressional investigating committee uncovered evidence that 29 corporations had "conspired to fix prices, rig bids, and divide markets on electrical equipment valued at $1,750,000,000 annually." ² Judge J. Cullen Ganey, who heard the case, said, "This is a shocking indictment of a vast section of our economy, for what is really at stake here is the survival of the kind of economy under which this country has grown great, the free enterprise system." ³ He saw many of the involved individuals "torn between conscience and approved corporate policy . . . the company man, the conformist, who goes along with his superiors and finds balm for his conscience in additional comforts and the security of his place in the corporate set-up." ⁴ In this case the men singled out for prosecution, mostly from middle management, had failed to stay in the gray area of safety and were considered expendable by the corporations: "Security of his place in the corporate set-up" had vanished for those who had not played the game well enough.

Despite the fact that these corporations were adjudged to have conspired on everything from two-dollar insulators to multimillion-dollar turbine generators and had persisted in their conspiracies for as long as eight years,⁵ few Americans apparently felt the conspirators were in any sense "guilty" of violating the sacred precepts of free enterprise. Yet, they had agreed not to compete. Moreover, the reasons for which the electrical equipment manufacturers agreed to "cooperate" are still there and are not likely to soon disappear: "Chronic over-capacity continues to exert a strong downward pressure on prices. Corporation pressure is stronger than ever on executives, who must struggle to fulfill the conflicting demands of bigger gross sales on the one hand and more profits per dollar of net sales on the other." ⁶ But to compete on a real price basis would prove disastrous for the big companies whose size requires predictability of markets for production runs, if they are to take advantage of their size. Besides, employment hinges on the confidence that management has in its market potential.

Is this a moral question? The following article by David T. Bazelon suggests that capitalism has changed so much, and the character of property ownership has been so altered, as to make meaningless moral arguments based on the old litany of free enterprise.

*
 We seem, as a nation, to be committed equally to increasing production and deceiving ourselves about our productive system. The realities of the American economy are massive and dominant in our way of life; and they are extraordinarily dynamic and original in their evolving nature. But the

rhetoric we employ to describe this core activity of ours is overwhelmingly obscurantist: reality and image are hardly within hailing distance. To put it simply, we suffer from an astonishing amount of downright mythical thinking about money and property and basic economic organization. While we all know that America manufactures as much as all the rest of the world, the words, images, and ideological structures we use to represent to ourselves what we are and what we do tend to be a quarter, a half, or even a full century old. Old, irrelevant, and misleading.

This stricture applies to liberals and socialists as well as to N.A.M. [National Association of Manufacturers] publicists and their businessmen backers. Indeed, to be fair, one should credit many of the centrally placed executives and managers with a distinctly superior though unshared comprehension of our economic system. As for the rest of us, we seem to have been too busy enjoying its beneficence to have bothered to examine its realities. It is about time we began.

The falsification of economic reality, buttressed by the laziness (or something) of the educated, is becoming a highly organized, even essential, instrument of policy—and that is always dangerous, politically, morally, and intellectually. To obscure, as a matter of policy, the existence and nature of the dominant power in a society is to undermine the basic creative sources of social life. This falsification presents America in the classic image of free enterprise and private-property capitalism; its consequence is to conceal the incontestable fact that we are dominated by great faceless corporations "owned" by no one and run by self-designated "managers."

There is a great deal of talk on Madison Avenue these days about the "corporate image," which means giving a humanized face to these impersonal structures. And the New York Stock Exchange publicists are pushing hard the idea of a "People's Capitalism," which has as much to do with capitalism proper as "People's Democracy" has to do with democracy proper. The purpose of these maneuvers is to plug some of the more gaping holes in the traditional web of justifications which, before the New Deal, was deemed sufficient in itself.

What is being simultaneously justified and obscured is the revolutionary emergence of a new American property system—and the fact that the men in control of it, the managers, occupy unexampled positions of power and privilege which are not based on entrepreneurial accumulation or private ownership, to which they were "elected" only by their peers, and for which they have been answerable only to history.

The managers of corporate industrial wealth and the big-money funds—along with their expert advisers—are the ones who are creating the new system; they run it, and they also best understand it. They know everything worth knowing in a practical way about money, property, and basic economic organization—because that's what they manage. They milk the pre-tax dollar and thread their way through government regulation on behalf of all sizable funds or forms of wealth. They are personally intimate with the intricacies of the fragmentation of property ownership and the alienation of capital because their very existence derives from those crucial changes in our property system.

What are some of the things the managers "know" that the rest have not gotten around to learning? We had better—because of their elaborate nature —avoid the subjects of the tax-torn dollar and other government regulation. But we might take a straight look at property as such. And here the invitation to understanding reads: *Nothing is very private in a mass society, including property.*

Advanced or even adequate thinking about property by the people who manage it requires what might be called a nonpossessory or nonowning frame of mind. As any good manager knows, ownership is irrelevant—the main thing is control. And frequently control is created or ensured by means of *giving up* ownership or by having certain others own the property. Management control of big corporations, for instance, is based on a dispersal of stock ownership among as large a public as possible: A.T.&T. has 1,600,000 stockholders, no one of whom owns more than one-thirtieth of one per cent. The Ford family retained control over Henry Ford's creation only by giving its stock in the company to a foundation; if it had held on to ownership, it would have lost control. Sears, Roebuck is controlled by company stock held in the company's pension trust: here the management consolidated its position by "giving away" huge sums of money. Managers manage, they don't own.

In a modern law school, some of the best all-round fun is had in arriving at a definition of property. The faculty considers it a first essential for the development of legal technique to tease the apprentice lawyers out of their ordinary received notions.

First off, the basic image of property—land and things—is pooh-poohed; then the search for a definition is carried through contract rights, choses in action (unrealized rights, including claims in court), and other intangibles. The class then thinks it has the answer: property is rights—called property rights or, in the short form, property. This is the point at which the modern professor enjoys himself most, and to confound the class completely he pulls out a case in which a property right is recognized and enforced by a court for the first time—a good one is the early radio broadcasting case in which a court first held that the right to broadcast a description of a baseball game "belonged" to the baseball club, could be disposed of by it, and could not be pirated by a party lacking contractual privilege from the "owner." Then the *coup de grâce*: Did the court enforce the club owner's right because it was a property right, or was it a property right because the court enforced it? A smile settles on the professor's face, and the pot of gold is indicated: property is a right of use or disposition which will be enforced by a court. On that day we are men; and the legal elite is then prepared to go out, tautology in hand, and grow rich defending and creating such rights.

But a whisper of doubt remains as older tautologies assert themselves: land is land, to own is to own, and all property, like land, is supposed to be owned. Yes, but less frequently nowadays by any one person. Take land, for example: the bank holds a first mortgage on the suburban home, the contractor has a material man's lien, various governmental authorities hold tax liens, the niece of the guy who sold it to you is suing you because her uncle didn't have the right to convey it, and you hocked your equity in order to post bond for your brother-in-law. Who owns the house? Why everybody who has an enforceable right to its use or disposition; and all the possible rights in and to the home, the whole bundle, add up to *the* ownership of it. In our crowded, mobile society there has occurred a very extensive fragmentation of property ownership.

Some things are too big to own. If the suburban home is too much for me, and a car is too much for an industrial worker, then General Motors is too much for a du Pont, and Standard Oil of New Jersey is too much for a Rockefeller. The use of the word "ownership" in referring to an agglomeration of industrial capacity like General Motors is, to put it kindly, overripe. And the simple designation of our system as one based on "private" property is not merely overripe, it is a calculated deceit. The managers know that the ownership of General Motors is irrelevant, but their spokesmen spend millions attempting to convince us that General Motors—and all publicly held American corporations—are owned by, you guessed it, the people-public. When they say "owned," they mean for us to "feel" the word in the utterly primitive sense. As Keith Funston of the New York Stock Exchange remarked to a group of advertising men, this "is a very humanizing bit of news."

One can face the question "Who owns General Motors?" if one will face the answer—"Nobody." But that is inconceivable, you say. Our training in property thinking (or lack of it) induces a certain horror in contemplating anything so big and so valuable walking around unowned! We abhor the vacuum of nonownership. But how *could* GM be "owned"? The total assets of this corporation amount to nearly $7 billion and the market value of its common stock is in excess of $13 billion. There are more than 750,000 stockholders. A control block of stock, usually put at between twenty and fifty-one per cent, affords a means of translating ownership into control; but this is a feature of the aggregate, not of individual shares—and the courts so recognize it. When du Pont disposes of the major part of its holdings in the company, there will not be anything like a control block in the GM situation.

The notion that GM (or any one of the great majority of our public corporations) is "owned" proceeds from the time-honored assumption that to own stock is to own the corporation. If we examine this old-fashioned "self-evident" truth empirically, we note that what the public stockholder actually has is three double-edged rights: (1) he can sell his stock at a profit or at a loss; (2) he can receive or fail to receive a variable dividend; and (3) he can vote "Yes" or "No" on certain issues affecting control of the corporation and the disposition of its properties. The first two items indicate that he owns a negotiable instrument of a certain character—consisting of an "iffy" return on capital and a lottery ticket on market appreciation. Let us look more closely at the third item, the only one of the three that even looks like ownership of the corporation itself. What does the stockholder's vote mean? To skip over several stages of a dull argument, it means that the voter can effect changes of control over "his" property, the corporation, or it means approximately nothing. Can he do this? The answer is "No," not unless an ambitious, well-heeled syndicate mounts a campaign to do so, and thus gives *him* the opportunity to support *them*. This does not happen at all often.

A mite of ownership, indeed. Especially when one considers that the essential difference between the incumbent and contending control groups is apt to be that the one has been at that particular trough for a period of time and the other has not. Moreover, in the absence of blatant mismanagement or special business reverses, it is next to impossible to unseat an in-group that is on the alert and well advised by experts. Unlike a campaign for political office, the "ins" have at their disposal not only the corporate patronage but also the corporate treasury; and the voting apathy of the citizen is a form of frenzied activity compared to that of the lottery-ticket holder. As a recent writer so felicitously put it, "The modern proxy contest is at best a device for tempering autocracy by invasion." Following the New York Central and Montgomery Ward fights, in theory the SEC put the final kibosh on the matter by promulgating proxy-fight regulations which ensure that only nice people fighting a good clean fight may now do battle in the arena of what is charmingly called "corporate democracy."

The fundamental meaning of private property is private control over the property one owns, and all the stockholder owns is a share of stock. The corporation is not private property—only the share of stock is.

Twenty-seven years after the publication of A. A. Berle and Gardiner C. Means's *The Modern Corporation and Private Property*, the crucial lessons of that landmark work have not been generally assimilated even among the educated. The processes there described have in the meantime undergone an extensive development. These were adumbrated by Mr. Berle in a brilliant little essay written for the Fund for the Republic a couple of years ago, in which he states flatly that the American corporate system now represents "the highest concentration of economic power in recorded history." The ever-present factual ground of his thinking, which simply cannot be repeated often enough, is that 150 corporations hold sway over fifty per cent of American manufacturing, based on asset values. On the same basis, "about two-thirds of the economically productive assets of the United States, excluding agriculture, are owned by a group of not more than 500 corporations."

The liberal view since the Progressive era has been that big corporations mean big capitalists. The point that has to be gotten into the liberal skull is that the manager is not a capitalist at all: he is a new fish.

The day of classic capitalism based on private property is gone. This is not a matter of ideology, it is a simple question of observable fact.

In comprehending the demise of the private-property system, it may be helpful to think of property as being of two kinds—"thing-property" and "rights-property." The former would be the plants, machines, railroads, buildings, etc., most of which are organized in great corporate units. The latter would be pieces of paper, like stock certificates and bonds, representing certain direct entitlements relating to such property. Now we have to complicate the picture a little by indicating a third, hybrid form of property— liquid capital organized in huge blocks, mediating between corporate thing-property and personal rights-property. An example would be the $13 billion or so in mutual funds (growing at the rate of $100 million a month). The point here is that a mutual fund would be capable of exercising ownership control over thing-property, but no one could exercise ownership control over a big mutual fund. The same would hold true of many banks, insurance companies, and pension trusts.

Now, as a consequence of the dispersion decreed by the estate and income tax laws, and the raw fact that corporations and big-money funds get bigger and bigger, there is observable *an increasing fragmentation of rights-property and an increasing concentration and accumulation of thing-property (and hybrid-property)*. Rights-property remains private, but it is just paper—somewhat like money, except that it earns and changes in value. Most thing-property is not private, because it is not owned by private persons and, as we shall see, it does not exist, in the last analysis, for private purposes.

It is beyond the scope of this essay to indicate the concentration of rights-property, but a few facts may help to suggest the truth of the situation. The Stock Exchange propagandists tell us, and we should believe them, that there are more than ten million American stockholders. They tell us nothing, however, about the concentration of holdings. Now besides the fact everybody knows that Nelson Rockefeller owns more stock than most gas-station attendants, we do have some 1957 Federal Reserve Board figures to help us out. At that time, the board reported that there were 56.1 million spending units in the United States, and that 11 per cent of these owned some publicly held stock. Only three per cent, however, held investments valued at more than $10,000, and no more than eight per cent of the units had an annual income of $10,000 or more. Which bears out what everyone knows anyway, that the distribution of the ownership of income paper is something like the distribution of income itself, only more so; and there is almost none of this paper at and below the median level of income (except insurance, life-and-death savings, etc.), where the imperatives of consumption are absolute.

The psychology (if not the fact) of private-property ownership goes very deep; as Mr. Berle has suggested, we are "the most violently private-property-minded country in the world." There was a profound truth in Jefferson's image of a democracy as a society of small property holders—even if in our day it is so impractical as to be tragic. If a man plants himself firmly upon the rock of his property ownership, he has an independence, and a sense of secure equality with other individuals similarly situated, which indeed does make him, as Jefferson believed, the truly anointed member of a democratic community. Now on what rock does the highly paid corporate executive stand, with his expense account, his stock options, his pension plan, deferred compensation, and death benefits? He stands on the "rock" of his acceptability to his board of directors and other superiors in a bureaucratic hierarchy. No rock at all; so he buries himself in work, in the immediate present of power and privileged consumption.

We should not confuse standard of living with accumulation. The thirty thousand corporate executives earning $50,000 or more a year (as reported by Fortune a few years ago), and indeed all the managers, have excellent and even magnificent standards of living. Mr. J. A. Livingston, a perceptive financial writer for the Philadelphia Bulletin, thinks that the "tax-sheltered managerial élite" is "an over-privileged class in a democratic society." But they are workers and spenders, not accumulators. They don't build family financial empires any longer—the estate and income-tax laws, and the corporate bureaucratic organization of wealth, have seen to that. Somebody could doubtless still build a temporary empire by merchandising a frozen daiquiri that can be drunk under water. But such events no longer characterize the system.

Free enterprise, motored by that hallowed value, individual initiative, and based on private property for real, has become a minority sector of the economy; still noisy, exhilarating, and important, but no longer the big show. Also, it is quite significant that two of the more substantial success stories of recent times—Reynolds Metals and Kaiser Aluminum—each involves government beneficence as well as individual initiative.

Perhaps this point that the important managers are mostly not important accumulators can best be made by recalling what the old days were like—before the Pecora investigation and New Deal securities legislation, for instance. Describing the business system in the heyday of American capitalist accumulation, in The Theory of Business Enterprise, Thorstein Veblen devotes several choice pages to the "accumulation of wealth" by corporate executives. His point was that the corporation men made their fortunes by trading in the stock of the corporations they managed. To this end, their purpose was served by a "discrepancy . . . between the actual and the putative earning-capacity of the corporation's capital." So the directorate gave out "partial information, as well as misinformation" to create such discrepancies. If this was not sufficient, some actual mismanagement could be indulged, if desired, to depress the stock. In those days—what the liberal muckrakers called the "robber baron" period—great fortunes could be and were accumulated.

And today? Apart from taxes, Section 16(b) of the Securities Exchange Act of 1934 imposes an absolute liability in favor of the corporation with respect to any insider's short-swing profits in such transactions (which are a matter of public record). Where statutes are not sufficient, the revolution in the corporate common law effected by the brilliant practitioners of minority-stockholder litigation ensures that the managers remain housebroken, as they have been for some decades. This does not imply that insider information is not valuable today; one should not under-emphasize the extent to which the corporate world has learned to live with restricting legislation and litigation; but the fact remains that control of a corporation is not the paved highway to an accumulation of great wealth which it once was. Now it is, by and large, just a very good job, in terms of both power and material welfare. But the power is based on position, not ownership; and the material advantages are standard-of-living advantages—nothing really important in the way of accumulation. (Not more than enough to support one wife and a lazy son or two after one's death.) . . .

What are the aims of the big corporations that dominate our national life? They are bureaucracies, so they have, at least in the first instance, the purposes of any bureaucratic structure: (1) to maintain itself, (2) to grow bigger, and (3) incidentally to accomplish the function that justifies its existence. The profit motive of corporations—their basic vestigial connection with capitalism proper—subserves all three of these bureaucratic purposes, but especially the second. Corporations are, after all, mainly a means of accumulating and maintaining wealth in an organized form: they are the only remaining legal form of a perpetuity, apart from the sovereign state itself. But there is no perpetuity in the ownership or the control of corporations.

The difference between an economic organization like General Motors or A.T.&T. and a $10-million or even a $50-million corporation is not the simple additive one of size. At some point a change in quantity becomes a change in quality, and a new property form is created. Moreover, a smaller corporation may drag along or fail, and only a limited number of people are hurt; but the giants cannot be allowed to fail, and indeed they cannot be allowed for long to function at much below their optimum capacity. National production and the fate of a people would be decisively affected.

Little corporations get bigger—by accumulation, by merger, and simply because we have an expanding economy. At a certain point they transcend their original nature and then two crucial economic events occur simultaneously: there has been a new addition of $X million to the sphere of quasi-public or unprivate property and a subtraction of the same amount from the private-property, free-enterprise sector. Note these facts: between 1949 and 1954, the number of mergers tripled. In recent years, two-thirds of all mergers have been of small companies into larger ones with assets of over $10 million. In this sense, as well as more obvious ones, the quasi-public giants are destroying free enterprise and private property. The tax law, as well as many other economic factors, has contributed to the formation of mergers. The tax-free reorganization sections of the Tax Code, which allow for the nonrecognition of gain or loss in certain major corporate transactions including mergers, provides positive encouragement to the growth of bigness.

Also, bigness is bigger than any balance sheet will reveal—since many smaller companies are organized in constellations around the giants. There are undoubtedly a number of auto-parts manufacturers and other suppliers that might just as well constitute themselves as divisions of General Motors, for all the make-believe independence their freedom entails. (Some giants have purposefully organized their industries in this way as a defense against the anti-trust laws, as well as a means of keeping the unions in line.)

The problem of bigness has been with us since the building of the railroads a century ago, and of course it was a great political issue in the trust-busting era around the turn of the century. From that day till this, the liberal view has been to prevent or disperse the concentration of economic power, rather than to accept it and control it. This has been the impulse behind a considerable amount of fundamental legislation—the Sherman and Clayton Acts, the Robinson-Patman Act, resale price maintenance, the setting up of the Federal Trade Commission, etc. Whatever else may be said of this great effort to preserve capitalism in its classic image, it must at least be pointed out that it has failed. It may have slowed down or in some cases deflected the basic trend, and it certainly made a lot of lawyers rich; but after fifty years of this sort of thing our economy is more than ever dominated by big corporations. If the program is justified as a form of public subsidy to free enterprise in the form of small business, similar to our approach to the farmers, then it is perhaps acceptable. But as a comprehensive program or theory, it is mostly irrelevant to U.S. society.

This liberal attitude is based as solidly on the atavistic myths—of free enterprise and private property—as any N.A.M. speech is. Each group is working a different side of a street that runs through a ghost town.

Marx and Veblen among others were quite right after all in one fundamental insight; industrialism was bound eventually to burst out of the strait
jacket of early capitalist forms of property—if not into socialism, then into
"Americanism." An industrial system, as distinct from an ideology or way of
doing business, has a dynamic of its own, which is just simply to be itself,
to produce efficiently. As long as a society can afford not to produce—is able
to deny the industrial dynamic—it can join any property system and any
economic ideology it may whimsically desire with the actual system of industry. But when production becomes imperative, any form of property and
any ideological element may be required to give way. Give way in fact, of
course, not necessarily in name. Which accounts for many of the misnamed
facts in our industrial picture.

The end of capitalism in America as a recognizable entity results from
three major historical events—the Great Depression, the Second World
War, and this endless cold war involving continuous competition in production with the Soviet Union. Many good Democrats feel that the New Deal
saved capitalism, but that is putting things wrong end up: corporate concentration saved (and imperceptibly transcended) capitalism, while the New
Deal merely saved the corporations, by making it possible for them to produce again. That remains one of the primary functions of our Federal
government—to keep saving the corporations. It is unnecessary to refer in
detail to the numerous means the government has used to bolster purchasing
power, or to help organize corporations among themselves. To indicate the
scope of the latter, Mr. Berle asserts that "Roughly two-thirds of American
industry and much of American finance is controlled by a formal or informal
Federal industrial plan."

Not only do corporations regulate themselves through government agencies and similar devices, but it is a fact—to be obscured only by conventional
thinking—that the very existence of an A.T.&T. or a GM or an RCA is in
itself a form of economic planning on a national industrial scale: True, such
planning has no broad or socially debated purpose, and is subject to no
exterior responsibility other than the brute verdict of events—but still it *is*
that rationalized economic planning so dear to the hearts of older socialists.
(It seems an amusing irony that the creepiest part of creeping socialism
should be its daily augmentation by the corporate managers.)

So, among other things, the imperatives of production result in an accelerated corporate rationalization of the economy. Let us state these
imperatives seriatim, so as to recognize their overwhelming force:

Thou shalt not allow another Great Depression.

Thou shalt produce fully and efficiently.

Thou shalt compete globally with the Soviet Union—a competition whose
key terms are not merely tons of steel and numbers of automobiles but the
purposeful organization of production and the rate of industrial growth.

Finally, thou shalt raise and spread the American standard of living.

Almost everything unique about our system results from the action of these imperatives. Since they cannot be expected to diminish, it is fair to assume that we will continue to change in the direction already marked out. We may all see the day again (as with the NRA) when the president of, say, General Motors insists on more "socialist" control over industry. After all, what's good for the country may also be good for General Motors—at least for the *people* of General Motors, if not for the Thing Itself.

So that's our unnamed property system, still woodenly or deceitfully miscalled "private." But is all this a word game? No. The issue is, first, to recognize the existence of this crucial power now held by corporate and other managers, and then to request them to justify it to us. Power must be legitimated, otherwise any talk of law itself, much less democratic citizenship, becomes absurdly irrelevant. There are two somewhat contradictory "legitimations" of corporate power current today, one obscurely explicit and the other largely implied: (1) it doesn't exist, and (2) it "works."

The claim that it doesn't exist derives entirely from the word "private": corporations are private property, and thus are assimilated to an older system of justifications. This view leads one to the truly remarkable proposition that the personality of a young executive (and that of his fiancée) is *not* private, but the multibillion-dollar telephone system *is!*

The legitimation of corporate power because it "works" amounts to what is probably the lowest level of ideology yet reached by man in his brief but painful rise from the prelingual slime. To coin a lawyer-like phrase, it is unanswerable, contemptible, and irrelevant—and is to be understood as meaning nothing more than *You got yours, Jack.* As long as Jack accepts the statement, it is indeed unanswerable—and we are well on our way to accepting unlegitimated power at the very center of our civilization. The worst effect of the lack of legitimation is, as C. Wright Mills screamingly asserts, that ideology and then ideas and finally mind itself become irrelevant to national life. And this is profoundly frightening.

Incentive among individuals in America is not dead, but it has a new objective. When society was simple, a man sweated and saved to accumulate wealth for the benefit of his children. His goal was to create an estate, a collection of valuable assets, to be passed on to his heirs. All this has changed. Now, as a general rule, people are more interested in providing for themselves to enjoy a comfortable retirement. Assured of a wage that always guarantees subsistence, but that may not enable putting very much aside, the average individual looks to his retirement program for satisfaction of his ultimate wants. Thus, incentive becomes motivated by one's own security, not by the needs of the next generation.

Encouraging the individual to have this new incentive is the impersonal nature of industrial life. Ownership is far removed from control of the organization which employs him. He is a cipher to the owners of business and industry; he has no personality in their eyes. Nor do the many stockholders fare any better. They are remote from the management of the enterprise and "hang on" in the hope of retiring on their capital and dividends or interest payments. Rather than take an active part in the affairs of the company, they continually vote confidence in the existing board of directors and management who are usually complete strangers to them.

Both employees and stockholders are appeased by handsome "annual reports" prepared by management. These reports seldom contain any disquieting information. They rarely state that management has faltered; on the contrary, they emphasize the positive so that those who rely on the company to achieve their incentives are not jolted. There is nothing sinister in optimistic reports, but they do point up the fact that employees and stockholders, lacking firsthand knowledge of the operation, must depend on such reports to foresee their future. In this sense, the modern stockholder "owns" the company the same way that an employee "owns" his job.

To put this another way, security is more important than risk. Annuities—that is, retirement payments—are a better measure of achievement than profits. From the rank-and-file employee in mine, factory, or office, through management, to ownership, there is a yearning to get rid of wage, salary, interest, or profit risks. But this massive concern for security and elimination of risk, which has been called "the rationalization of life," impedes economic development and, more than any other single factor, probably accounts for the slowing American rate of growth.[7]

The corporation provides the leadership for this cautious, conservative attitude. It has stunted incentive by controlling competition. While the surroundings are contemporary, the corporate actors, instead of being vice-presidents, production managers, and blue-collar workers, could equally be master craftsmen, journeymen, and apprentices of the craft guilds; for like the guilds, the corporation seeks to protect itself from encroachment, from daring rivals. It is not surprising that the giant corporation, with far more to protect than the guilds, should attempt to justify its method of operation and limiting of incentive. Those who condemn and prosecute it for market sharing are intellectually dishonest in the conventional moral sense, for market sharing fits the spirit of the times. "Competition today is captive of bigness; . . . competition is more controlled than controlling; . . . its temper is lessened; its tautness gone slack." [8]

Actually there are other forms of competition besides *pure*—or price—competition. *Nonprice* competition, for example, consists of promotional efforts to distinguish the features of one product from another—no mean task when products tend to be very similar. *Innovative* competition takes place when a new product competes with an old—for example, manmade fibers as against natural fibers. The rate of new product ideas has been higher since the Second World War than ever in history. Only by diversifying have many old line concerns been able to continue operation in the face of such competition. And dissimilar products also compete when the consumer has a choice in his purchases. For example, producers of durable goods, such as automobiles, have found that they must now compete with recreational services, such as foreign travel, for the consumer's dollar.

Today's types of competition have brought a new alphabetical term into common business usage: R & D—research and development. New production techniques for reducing costs, ideas for improvement of products, and the development of completely new products, occur daily in business as a result of research and development. Pure competition may be the economist's model of progress, but its lack has not particularly handicapped the forward motion of technology.

The export of products is another matter. Here manufacturers must frequently compete in the world market on a price basis without any kind of help. As the older industrialized nations become revitalized, we shall need their markets more than they need ours. The European Common Market has already begun to push us hard in some product areas. Our leadership in productivity and technological and managerial expertness, barely 30 years old, is partially the result of the weaknesses and misfortunes of others rather than our strengths. "In 1946 all of the 13,000 refrigerators and 1,000 washing machines sold in Brazil were imported from the United States. By 1956 Brazilian sales of these two appliances had risen to 150,000 and 40,000 respectively—but not a single refrigerator or a washing machine was imported from the United States!" [9] In order to maintain our own standard of living and high requirements for national defense, we must earn enough foreign exchange by selling our goods abroad to pay for vitally necessary imports. The government may be called on for assistance if industry cannot handle foreign price competition of its own accord—"any ideological element may be required to give way."

DISTRIBUTION

The discussion so far has centered on the producer in our economy. Production is tangible and therefore readily measurable; but the role of marketing, or distribution, has been grossly misunderstood and misappraised. The value of a product itself—or *form* utility—derived from mining, milling, and manufacturing, is easy to appreciate. The values of *time, place,* and *possession,* being intangible, are more difficult to understand. But having goods *when* they are wanted, *where* they are wanted, and facilitating *transfer* of possession and ownership, has become the key to American economic growth.

For many years after the onset of the Industrial Revolution, the accent in *economizing* [10] was on manufacturing. This was summed up as a *Production Economy.* As the problems of production were solved it became apparent that mass production, to be efficient, required mass consumption. At the turn of this century we entered a *Marketing Economy* where the stress was on the *distribution* of goods and services.

We assume that our retail outlets, supermarkets, department stores, all will have what we want. Yet it has been estimated that on an average we live 1000 miles from the sources of food products, and perhaps twice as far from nonfood items we commonly purchase and consume. This vast and constant feat of supplying our wants requires the combined efforts of middlemen engaged in the transporting, storing, promoting, and selling of practically all the items we consume. Taking risks is an important part of the marketing process, as failure to present merchandise at the *right place,* at the *right time,* in the *right amount,* or at the *right price* can cause a considerable loss to the middleman.

The coordinating agency of production, distribution, and consumption, is distribution. In the marketplace buyer and seller meet. The success of marketing determines the size of the economy. Although only an intermediary function, marketing plays the leading role in business primarily because it is the most difficult area remaining to be conquered. We can produce endless amounts of goods but have not yet mastered the technique of disposing of them.

The growing power and sophistication of the consumer has created a shift in corporate thinking about form utility. The increasing importance of the consumer has brought about the development of a *total marketing concept:* the report of consumer preferences through the distributor to the producer, and the *teaming* of distributor and producer to decide, on the basis of evidence, what the consumer wants and what he is most likely to buy. In other words, *the right merchandise.*

The courtship of the consumer has also necessitated discovering why he buys. The term which encompasses all efforts to find out, through behavioral science techniques, consumer behavior in the market is *motivation research.* These qualitative methods, supplementing the more orthodox quantitative market research—or nose counting—are employed in the hope of finding the *real* reason why people buy. Although the promoters of this relatively new field have exaggerated claims about the useful insights to be drawn from the limited research conducted, and professional critics of advertising have helped to sell the idea that motivation research firms work miracles, the advertising agencies which conduct or contract for this research will not contradict the critics, since their stock in trade is the persuasion, if not the outright manipulation, of consumers.[11]

The area of business and industry most subject to criticism, then, is the sales promotion phase of distribution, particularly advertising and personal selling—although packaging costs are sometimes as high as advertising. Because it is intangible and subject to exaggeration, sales promotion is viewed by many critics, including classical economists, at best, as unessential and, at worst, as evil exploitation. Essential or not, sales promotion costs are high. Roughly, half of what the ultimate consumer spends for his merchandise goes for manufacturing costs; the other half goes to the middleman engaged in marketing activities. Approximately a quarter of every consumer dollar pays for advertising, packaging, personal selling, and other promotional activities.

If buying will take place without the persuasion of sales promotion and without materially reducing over-all consumption, then we are paying too much for the goods we buy. There are times when this is substantially the case. Before the Industrial Revolution, the supply of consumer goods was extremely limited and the few products available were sought eagerly by the affluent few. Very little merchandise was manufactured in advance of sales. Today speculative production is the rule and buyers must be sought, except in the rare instance of a *seller's market,* as during and after the Second World War.

But in a *buyer's market,* which is most characteristic of modern America, the consumer must be cajoled into a buying mood. Harry R.

Tosdal calls this "economic leadership" and builds a strong case in the following excerpt for the necessity of such leadership.

* The aggregate objectives of those who sell are economically and socially desirable because in their totality the achievement constitutes high and rising living standards for all the people. The aggregate objective in a high-level economy characterized by consumer freedom of choice is attained only by billions of consumer buying actions. These are based upon individual decisions, individual choices. In short, to rephrase Thomas Nixon Carver's statement about prices when he said, "There are no such things as general prices, only millions of individual prices in individual transactions," so there are no such things as general sales or general buying action, only billions of individual sales or individual purchases. If the results of these buying actions lead to higher standards of living and the methods of leadership to bring about these purchases are consistent with social welfare, we can conclude that the objectives, both in aggregate and individually, are socially desirable.

The economic and social desirability of high and rising standards of living for the whole population of a country has been asserted and defended above. Some have objected that the success of our economy in raising levels of living will in the not far distant future bring us to the point of "saturation." One must disagree for a variety of reasons. Professor George Katona of the University of Michigan, a penetrating student of consumer demand, writes to this point in a recent editorial:

> The notion of "saturation" of the market is based on old-fashioned psychological assumptions which in turn rest on the analogy of biological drives; for example, if an animal is hungry, it is motivated to search for food; after it has eaten, the motive disappears or becomes weak. The saturation concept has resulted in dire predictions about the future of the U.S. economy. Some people point to the large proportion of U.S. families that already possess major goods, such as refrigerators (over 80%) or automobiles (about 70%), and they argue that in the future sales will be limited largely to replacement needs.
>
> But social motives are different from biological ones. Levels of aspiration—in sports, for school grades, for position, for income and for goods—most commonly rise with achievement. A beginner in golf, for instance, may strive hard to achieve a score of 100. When he has achieved his goal, he invariably raises his sights. We give up aspirations when we have failed, not when we have succeeded.
>
> In the economic field a family that has saved enough to buy a home usually sets out on a new objective, such as college education for the children; fulfillment of one aim leads to striving for another. Indeed, in a recent survey it was found that this applied to goods already owned; families with a refrigerator in good operating condition often were preparing to buy a larger one or one with shelves on the door and a better freezing compartment.

* From Harry R. Tosdal, *Selling in Our Economy*, pp. 319–328. Copyright 1957. Reprinted by permission of Richard D. Irwin, Inc.

We translate our needs into demand when we are optimistic, confident and secure. We are saturated, on the other hand, when we are pessimistic, insecure, and especially when our past endeavors have been unsuccessful.

It is conceivable that we may arrive at the point where having achieved generally the quantitative and qualitative standards of consumptive desire, we shall choose more leisure to attain greater progress in areas other than material advancement and thus eventually reach a plateau of production of goods and services. But the world generally is far from any such point so that we may accept the need for high and rising standards of living as a working hypothesis that will serve for an unforeseeably long period.

There are those who, of course, take the aristocratic point of view that high and rising standards of living are for the "classes"—not for the "masses"—a viewpoint implicit in Ortega y Gasset's *Revolt of the Masses*. It reflects the attitude of those who believe that culture should be and must be the possession of the few, a philosophy that is being disproved. There are others who assert that the good life can best be attained by limiting desire and consumption to subsistence, and few comforts. Emphasis is to be placed on nonmaterial activities, on education, literature and the arts, religion, avocation, recreation. But all of these hold exceptional views, and throughout the world there is a desire for higher standards of living, which constitutes a powerful social and political force for good or evil. For that desire may lead to political and social upheavals of types that can bring only disaster unless conditions are basically favorable to increasing production and productivity of the population.

The objectives of selling and the methods used to intensify desire are consistent with public welfare despite the fact that the motives of most sellers are concerned with the sellers' welfare. The buying action that results is usually an element in the complex of buying activities that bring high and rising levels of living into being.

The results of selling in terms of high and rapidly rising standards of living mean that whatever the factors involved, multitudes of purchases have been made. The influences of education, habit, example have all been operative, and the bulk of sales has probably been helped by one or several of these. Consumption habits, even though not grouped into stratified patterns, require effort to change. As research has shown, many consumers cling to a standard of living once attained and change with reluctance. Social pressures and the desire to emulate friends and neighbors play an important part. Education brings children and youth into contact with aspects of better living standards and affect later desires for housing, furnishings, food, and dress.

Powerful as all these influences are, it must be remembered that some of them owe their origin and characteristics to previous selling effort. The neighbors may have bought the refrigerator or the television set when influenced to buy by a salesman or advertisement. If satisfied, the buyer began to tell others about it. As several in a group had purchased a television set, the pressure on nontelevision owners to buy increased. Meanwhile, regularly, persistently, selling effort continued, so that later buyers were induced to purchase both by social pressure and selling effort, past and current alike.

Education is likely to follow rather than to lead the procession of those who seek to influence the consumer to buy. Education may develop levels of aspiration for standards of living. It may or may not furnish help to attain those standards. It tends not to push specific products, at least not until products are established and much selling has been done.

The persuasive effort of sellers appears to be enormously more potent than the effort of consumer groups, government consumer advisory services, or educational institutions in the development of buying action for those goods and services which fall in the classification of postponable, caprice, or discretionary. More people are engaged in influencing purchase, more effort is expended and the motivation to sell is greater and more direct. While no statistical records are available for measure, it appears that selling effort is so important a form of economic leadership in terms of employment, cost, and achievement that neither laymen nor economist should be indifferent to it.

The results that have been achieved and for which selling should receive its full share of credit have been attained because through selling a chain reaction is started that energizes the whole economic system. In brief, selling:

In making a sale and obtaining immediate buying action, plus establishing a better basis for making future sales:

Justifies and permits production, usually in advance of sale;

Enables improvements in production methods to be adopted and processes improved so as to increase productivity of labor and capital investment;

Enables research to be carried on to find new end products and better methods of making them;

Enables enterprise to introduce new products and recover costs and obtain profit within time intervals necessary for existence and growth;

Reduces the time required for production so that buyers have more time to enjoy results of labor;

Enables new enterprise to start and secure income needed to survive and prosper.

It is obvious that a high and rising standard of living means high and increasing production of goods and services. For Santa Claus politics to the contrary notwithstanding, standards of living for all the people depend upon the production of goods and services and not upon political promises or redistribution of the earned production of the few. Unless there is an increasing production of goods and services, there can be redistribution only of what has been produced. Generally higher standards of living cannot thus be developed or sustained. To bring about that high production of goods and services requires large-scale production on the supply side and the application of pertinent technology.

Since it is evident that a higher standard of living for the people requires that goods be distributed to them, we must recognize that in a money economy with consumer freedom of choice, in a society in which allotment by government is not the rule, those who aspire to consume must purchase and must have purchasing power with which to acquire those goods in exchange. By and large, therefore, beyond the necessities of life provided under relief, pensions, and limited plans for social care, those purchasers who desire to participate in the high standard of living must acquire purchasing power with which to make that desire effective.

In our society, men ordinarily must work for what they get in the way of income. Although fraud, luck, inheritance, and stealing may furnish purchasing power to some people, most of us expect to have to work for a living. Our effectiveness and usefulness in that work is at least a rough measure of the kind of living standards that we enjoy individually. Both the amount of work we do, the character of that work, and the intelligence with which we apply ourselves to work will depend upon whether the incentive is sufficient to induce us to put forth our best efforts. For a large proportion of our people, the principal incentive is the paycheck, because that represents the means of acquiring the things that are considered desirable.

People work to get the things they want. If they do not want things that require money, they will not work to get money. The general truth of this statement and its limitations are attested by many types of war and postwar experience; further proof has been developed by psychological, sociological, and anthropological investigation. At any rate, there are many facts in all these fields which warrant the hypothesis that human beings will not work for those things that make up a high standard of living unless they want those things enough to overcome whatever disutility work possesses for them. Historical evidence supports the statement that standards of living in many parts of the world have remained at the same low levels for centuries. Innovation was frowned upon and social stratification apparently froze living standards. One could point out that even during World War II, the production of essential war materials in the Philippines, for instance of oils and fats, as well as production of other types of products elsewhere, proceeded very slowly whenever the workers found they could not buy things with the money they were given in return for the work. Again, it has been asserted that absenteeism in England was prevalent because under the austerity regime workers could not buy the things they wanted for the pay they received. These are little more than straws in the wind; but I think we must recognize the importance of the factor of wants and demands, not only in determining the types of goods to be produced, but also in motivation to produce. The intensity of desire has a direct bearing on the amounts and types of work that will be done in order to secure such goods and therefore, in part, in order to produce the goods necessary for a high living standard.

In our existing economy, goods must be produced in large quantities, distributed over larger or smaller areas to eventual retail buyers. Consumers' knowledge, both of the goods which are or might be available and of their own future desires at the time that the goods are manufactured, is extremely limited. The producer must, therefore, produce in advance of his detailed knowledge of consumer desires and consumer wants. He often produces for a market of which he knows nothing directly, selling his goods to those middle-men who have come into existence in order to help with the function of distributing goods in small quantities to fit the consumer needs.

It has been shown that established producers must dispose of their goods at remunerative prices if goods are to continue to be made. Prospective buyers must be induced to buy in quanities that permit eventual profitable opera-tion of the enterprise. Such inducement to buy, such persuasion as may be utilized to get prospective buyers to purchase, may be subject to abuse. But by and large, such persuasion is consistent with public interest and is, in fact, essential to the maintenance of free enterprise, to the development of new and better products and services, and indirectly, therefore, to the growth of employment. Eventually, even technological progress depends upon success-ful sale of industry's production. . . .

In short, selling effort is the energizer of our economic machine. Its power may be misapplied, but its necessity in influencing our people to want higher and rising standards of living cannot be denied. Selling effort is necessary to make people both desire and achieve a higher level of living. Selling is neces-sary that firms which introduce unfamiliar products may live and old firms may continue to exist and perform their services for the public. The develop-ment and functioning of the production structure necessary for a high standard of living has depended and will continue to depend upon the energizing influence of selling effort, whether that effort be in the form of advertising or personal selling, or in the manifold minor aspects of marketing persuasion.

The need for improved effectiveness in all phases of marketing effort is admitted; and the challenge to business to bring about improvement is furnished by free competition. The alternative of detailed government plan-ning and allotment assumes a degree of understanding and wisdom, a managerial and administrative capacity of a magnitude that mankind has not produced. And no society has yet matched the free-enterprise system of the United States in its provision of higher standards of living for all the people. But we must not forget that while free enterprise connotes freedom to fail as well as freedom to succeed, the urge to succeed furnishes the motive power for producing and distributing the commodities and services required for the standards and planes of living to which we aspire. And only with the contribution of adequate selling leadership can the people in a free enterprise economy achieve both high material levels of living and an unparalleled opportunity for the development of the other areas of the good life.

The competition desired by Professor Tosdal is probably more common among retailers than at any other level of business. That price competition exists there, as it does not in manufacturing, is largely due to the relatively slight amount of concentration in retailing. The 1954 Census of Business showed 1,721,650 retail establishments, as compared with 252,318 wholesalers, and 317,000 manufacturers.[12] Notwithstanding the great grocery and department store chains, all types of chains of four or more stores accounted for only 24 per cent of all retail business in 1954; and the total mail-order-house business was only 0.9 per cent of total retail sales that year.[13]

In sharp contrast to manufacturing, where entry is often difficult or impossible, virtually all types of retail stores are still being successfully started. The exception is the department store, which has seen practically no new major entries in the field, aside from branches and mergers, since the turn of this century. The position of the department store with its emphasis on customer services continued virtually unchallenged for over 50 years. Secure in their position, department stores rarely emphasized price and developed orthodox, genteel business practices—until the advent of the discount store.

Reminiscent of early commercial capitalists, the discounters threw convention aside and overnight brought about a minor revolution in buying habits. With a capital $4,000 in 1948, Eugene Ferkauf—who will serve as our example—increased the net worth of his company, E. J. Korvette, Inc., to $40 million in 1962, with annual sales of discounted merchandise of $230 million.[14] Repeating the development of the supermarket, the typical discount house opened in the low-rent districts, often in old warehouses, with few fixtures, and none of the amenities of orthodox retailing. Discount houses were a self-service operation, and few old-line merchants believed that customers would be willing, for example, to haul television sets to their cars in sufficient quantities to warrant concern. But they were wrong, and soon the discount house and the department store were in direct competition for the mass market. Some department stores held their ground, others retreated, and still others mounted a counterattack on the discounter's own terms.

Combining showmanship with cut prices, the discount house rescued retailing from a sluggish condition. But more important for competition, price cutting ran afoul the fair trade laws, aimed at restricting competition in order to stabilize the price level. This legal price fixing had been on the books since the depression and was actually protection for the inefficient retailer. Hence, the determination of merchants like Ferkauf to circumvent and test these legal restrictions on the free operation of the economy can be viewed as not only in the best interests of the consumer, but of the retail industry as well.

Retailing, wholesaling, and transportation are "middlemen" activities which cost money, but the expensive aspect of distribution is sales promotion. The high-pressure salesman and product packaging, both costing billions of dollars annually, receive a fair measure of criticism, but special venom is reserved for advertising and its primary symbol—Madison Avenue. This vast manipulative power, as popularized in Vance Packard's *Hidden Persuaders*, forces the consumer to buy *what he does not want*—and, the critics would add, what he has no *legitimate* need for.[15] Were this an accurate appraisal of the role of advertising, "Madison Avenue economic leadership" would, simply through the control of the volume of advertising expenditures, also control the economy. So far this has not been the case, but the stock in trade of the advertising man is persuasion. Would he deny that he lacks power to persuade? He would not; by remaining silent he tacitly admits to being a great persuader and thereby reinforces what Martin Mayer considered to be a false appraisal: "The frivolity of our customary approach to advertising stems from two American folk myths. Although they contradict each other, most people manage to believe in both: (1) They are confident that, personally, they are seldom if ever influenced by advertising; and (2) they believe that advertising is immensely powerful in molding the actions of the community." [16]

The truth is, of course, that advertising is immensely successful in selling some products, a dismal failure in others, and of middle value in helping to sell most. The businessman, like the critic and the consumer, is suspicious of advertising. He dislikes the difficulty of assessing the efficacy of his sales promotion program; although he intuitively senses that advertising helps, he really cannot be sure it is pulling its own weight. John Wanamaker, the great American merchant, summed up this quandary many years ago when he said, "I know that at least half the money I spend on advertising is wasted, but I can never tell which half." The role of advertising is to link human desires with production and so create mass markets. Advertising has the same relationship to distribution as the assembly line has to production. Currently the behavioral sciences are being tapped as a possible source of insight into the enigmatic behavior of the consumer.

Despite the innovations of discounters, improvement in the transportation and handling of goods, and vast expansion of consumer credit, marketing has not kept pace with production: automation in industry is not being matched by automation in distribution. To cope with this problem, the marketing executive is making a rapid advance to top positions in industry over the production or finance executive. As our economic system evolves, problems of distribution will become more important and more critical, both from the standpoint of consumer satisfaction and from the standpoint of effective functioning of the economy.

CONSUMPTION

Today's consumer poses the chief problem for the forces of production because he does not abide by fixed rules of consumption. His whimsy is the major uncontrollable factor, the unknown quantity that causes distribution to lag behind production.

For several generations after the beginning of the Industrial Revolution the consumer behaved more or less in accordance with the concept of economic man. But once past the level of subsistence, the older concept of man as a calculating, rational being crumbled under the impact of unleashed desires which are still neither fully understood nor appreciated. Although price remains a powerful sales tool, it fails often enough to indicate that the consumer frequently shuns a lower price in favor of some other kind of satisfaction. The first clue to a change in consumer behavior was the failure, in 1927, of the old black Model T. Henry Ford had so refined production techniques, arriving at the zenith of efficiency through the assembly line and standardization, that none of his competitors could touch his price. The durable "flivver" was selling for about $350. Objectively, there was no more economical, private, self-propelled vehicle. But the capricious consumer rejected the Model T in favor of the era of automatic devices, high styling, bright colors, and planned obsolescence.

What makes the consumer do as he does? Consumer behavior is difficult to predict because of the general increase in affluence and economic improvement of the mass of society. Augmented through the mass media and coupled with formal education, enhanced consumer sophistication has created the so-called Consumer Movement, a body conceivably comprised of 180 million parts.

As the consumer's income rises he spends proportionately less on food and utilities, roughly as much as before on shelter and clothing, and proportionately more on all other categories, including savings. In other words, he has acquired an increasing ability to exercise choice, or discretion, in his purchases over and above the relatively fixed expenses for food and utilities. This is a slight modernization of "Engel's Laws." [17] In 1941 the typical average income was $1,458, of which $1,107 was spent for basic living costs, $2 for federal income tax, and $439 for discretionary spending. By 1958 this average income had climbed to $5,235, basic costs for the same standard of living had increased to $2,005, the federal government took $415 in taxes, and the family increased its discretionary income to $2,815. Even after adjusting the 1958 dollar to 1941, the average family still had $1,407.50 in discretionary income as contrasted with $439 in 1941.[18]

Has he spent this discretionary income wisely? There appears to be an essential conservatism in the consumer. "Consumers desire and expect only *slightly* more than they have. Even though aspirations rise with accomplishments, consumers do not easily lose sight of reality." [19] Moreover, the consumer constantly needs *new* stimulation. The same news about increasing production, sales, and profits ceases to be news. "If nothing really new happens they tend to wonder and to become cautious." [20] Thus, product innovation, whether in a completely different product or merely a significant styling change, is necessary to keep the consumer interested in the market.

We can begin to formulate a new general law of consumption with corollaries:

The Law: The more money or purchasing power a family has, the less the percentage spent on necessities.

First Corollary: The less a family *has* to use its income for necessities, the more it has for saving and *un*necessities;

Second Corollary: the more a family spends for *un*necessities, the more those *un*necessities become necessities;

Third Corollary: therefore, shopping goods, largely *un*necessities, tend to move into the convenience goods category as *average* income increases;

Fourth Corollary: items subject to impulse buying tend to increase in their unit price and broaden in scope;

Fifth Corollary: the increase in the unit price and scope of impulse buying tends to induce retailers and manufacturers, because of potential profit, to broaden their offerings;

Sixth Corollary: this broadening often leads to the addition of "foreign" lines resulting in *mixed retailing*—or scrambled selling—and business mergers;

Seventh Corollary: the demand for more convenient handling of shopping goods and impulse items by consumer and merchant alike results in a packaging revolution;

Eighth Corollary: the packaging revolution coupled with the education to self-service makes it possible for items heretofore considered to be too expensive, too unattractive, too inconvenient, or too specialized, to be sold to different kinds of purchasers in different kinds of settings;

Ninth Corollary: all these things affect not only marketing, but production as well, as markets continue to reflect the change in the affluence and attitudes of the ultimate consumer; advertising, packaging, and product design must be made appealing to a shifting target.

Other effects wrought by the changing status of the consumer are probably to be discovered. And while it is possible to speak of the consumer as an average or a mass, the consumer remains an individual, motivated by a bewildering variety of forces. Pierre Martineau has made some interesting observations about the effect of social class on consumer attitudes, using W. Lloyd Warner's criteria for social class in metropolitan Chicago.[21] For example, because their perceptions of life differ, the various classes patronize different stores, buy different brands of products—even though the price is more or less the same—have different spending-saving attitudes, and tend to put their savings into different places. Different backgrounds cause individuals to read different meanings into the same store or bank architecture, package design, and "bird-in-the-hand" appeals by sellers. "Each human is motivated by various compulsive forces within him—certain biological urges and certain acquired wants—to realize numerous goals. But the yardstick for evaluating the worth of these goals [is] supplied by group pressures. Other people have to validate our choices. The things we buy and do that offer the most satisfaction are those which are also valued by our friends, our groups, our class. Very rarely do our actions, our attitudes, or our purchases run counter to the approved tastes of those around us. The penalty for nonconformity is literally ostracism. An imposing list of studies points out that those who do not accept group standards have few friends, little influence, and much anxiety." [22]

Although the consumer, by some standards of criteria, is not rational, neither is he as capricious as some critics have asserted. The consumer can afford to be impulsive in certain purchases, generally pertaining to small self-indulgence items. As affluence increases, the unit price of impulse items also tends to rise; shopping goods once requiring careful consideration become subject to impulse buying when the consumer has increased discretion. "Though not rational and not fully logical, [the consumer] is conservative and sane. The much maligned, often misunderstood, and unorganized consumer is a stabilizing force in our economy." [23]

Neither "economic man" nor "all *id*," today's consumer always desires and is occasionally capable of carefully reasoned action. Even when he behaves irrationally and knows it, he wishes to sound and appear responsible. He needs to justify his buying decisions with "good" reasons, which are not the same as "empirically valid" reasons. The astute seller is aware of this and tries to provide the consumer with a "good" reason to buy. Not too long ago the automobile industry stressed safety in its products: padded dashboards, safety rims, redesigned steering wheels. It was soon discovered that these "rational" features made the buyer uncomfortable; they reminded him of the grim statistics of highway deaths. Other reasons for buying were sought, which would not suggest so vividly the dangers of motoring—comfort, economy, resale value. These reasons may not have always been as scientifically sound but they were certainly less reminiscent of danger.

An ordinary product like a cake mix can present a problem in motivation. "Negative feelings that housewives have about food mixes include the following: they feel guilty about using them; they feel their use indicates poor housekeeping; they feel mixes are synthetic; they feel a threat to their use of cooking and baking as a source of praise; they feel mixes are unnatural and the easy way out." [24] The early cake mixes were too "easy." The housewife had merely to add a liquid and bake. So much consumer resistance was encountered that the powdered egg was removed and today the housewife adds *her own fresh eggs*; the mix sells phenomenally. Somehow creativity has been restored—at least in the mind of the consumer.

But has the consumer spent well? The answer, of course, depends on one's criteria. We can say that we are depleting our natural resources too rapidly for socially undesirable ends. On the other hand, it can be pointed out that this is the free choice of society, to buy or not to buy. Who is to say that society is to be denied this freedom of choice—who should have a right to tell a person what his private gratifications *ought* to be?

CONCLUSION

The return of vigorous competition to any kind in business is not an unmixed blessing. The consumer may find it satisfying to watch a price war, but like all wars this one has its casualties. Less efficient operators are forced out and their employees along with them. Automated factories and self-service stores, requiring fewer hands than the older forms of production and distribution, cannot absorb the displaced worker. Moreover, price wars and non-price competition, carried to the ultimate, can only result in monopoly. Is it any wonder that businessmen have scouted every conceivable way to compete that would not be ruinous to them? Trading stamps, free balloons, loss leaders, trade-ins, free coffee, are typical of the promotional devices employed to keep business alive.

The new entrant in any field of business has the opportunity, perhaps the duty, to break with tradition and cut his own pattern, but eventually his technique becomes confining, too—more so because it is of his own making. Korvette, the discounter, has moved to Fifth Avenue. Does he now have something to protect, and will he, too, devote his attention to preserving his new position in the economy?

In manufacturing there are success stories to parallel Ferkauf's: the new electronics ventures, the Hiller helicopter, ballpoint pens, all the new production ideas that succeed.[25] But they, too, become less competitive with prosperity. Instead of offering trading stamps, the manufacturer may employ planned obsolescence [26] to encourage repeat sales. The growing weakness of planned obsolescence can be demonstrated objectively in the rapid depletion of our natural resources, and the success of the Volkswagen; we pay for our "free" trading stamps in the retailer's markup, and most of the competitive edge gained by early trading stamp merchants has long since been lost. The "bandwagon" effect eventually palls on the consumer. Planned obsolescence and loss leaders [27] are two devices employed by businessmen in the attempt to foster innovation in a rational way. Such attempts, however carefully contrived, sooner or later lose their novelty, prove too costly, and must be scrapped.

The *object* of all productive activity is to supply human wants. The object of all business is to give consumers the goods and services *they* demand. Profit is the *incentive*, not the object, of business. The failure to distinguish between the two has led to certain abuses by businessmen and misunderstanding by the public at large. Criticism and reform can follow swiftly. In America this has been minimal, contrasted with Western Europe; we still have no direct government control over business policies and no central planning of business investment.[28]

Violent claims to the contrary notwithstanding, there has not been much actual disturbance in the top wealth-holders in America. The richest 1 per cent of Americans now possess approximately 28 per cent of the entire personal wealth, almost the identical amount held by this group on the eve of the New Deal.[29] And 32 million Americans still do not share in the Affluent Society. By American standards they are "ill-clothed, ill-housed, and ill-fed." In a nation that consumes half the world's production with only 6 per cent of the world's population, these citizens are underprivileged, in the sense that their capacity to consume is limited.[30]

As Americans become more aware of the activities of business and of the nature of ownership and control, they may react to the distinction between free enterprise as a creed, and the workings of the economy as an actuality, in a way that will lead to greater central control by the government. "[The] constant change in the use of 'discretionary income' gives the economy its unique dynamism and precludes almost by defini-tion attempts to control it from a central watchtower." [31] Still, the un-conscious wisdom of consumers as a "countervailing power" [32] against Big Business and Big Labor may be lost; the loss would be tragic because the more decision-makers there are, the less the likelihood of excessive reactions. A recent case in the Soviet Union illustrates the danger of central planning unresponsive to private need. The State Distribution Trust decided there were too many toothbrushes and diverted production to artificial flowers and plastic toys, only to discover belatedly that it had grossly misallocated production.[33] With the growth of consumer power and sophistication has come greater economic stability, but the balance is delicate. The consumer will not fail to be impressed by the antics of those who scoff at the law, as exemplified by the electrical industry, or the ensconced labor leader, or the panoramic spectacle of industrial giants so great that "What's good for General Motors is good for Amer-ica" becomes literally true. He will see "far-flung bureaucratic enterprises operating in acceptable efficiency in response to a mélange of partially identified motives and incentives—with each enterprise held in dubious ownership by thousands on thousands of persons passively quiet in their shadowy remoteness, and with each enterprise apparently quite capable, under responsible direction, of coordination with others in bureaucratic operation on an even wider scale." [34] It might occur to the consumer as citizen—unaware of his "countervailing power"—that government could free him from the "coercion of compassionless markets . . . [and] the whims of corporate conscience," [35] thereby running the risk of substituting one kind of coldblooded bureaucracy for another.

However, we are not talking about "robber barons" who manifest the short and selfish view of social responsibility. The consumer "votes" his confidence in the businessman when he buys, the political representative votes his confidence in legislation, and labor and farm groups must also be considered. In short, American business, semipublic in structure and operation, depends for its very existence on the good will of all its constituents. "Only the deliberately dishonest and the ignorant in business today would favor short-run views and indifference to the social consequences of business behavior." [36]

The politician, the intellectual, and the businessman have, in turn, been the three leadership categories most subject to scapegoating in American history. They have often deserved part of the blame for ills of the time. Currently, the businessman holds an enviable position in society; he is enjoying his moment of esteem. But because of his leadership position in society and his command of economic power, he is sometimes tempted to step over into other areas. For the businessman as a businessman to pontificate on politics, religion, or morals is to invite not only rejection by society but censure as well. To place his position and power behind extremist movements in the belief that he can reverse cultural change which he views as harmful is to beg the question and perhaps accelerate that change. Such behavior is either deliberately dishonest, or ignorant.

If the American economy is to prosper, and is to continue in its characteristic dynamism, the businessman must rededicate himself to the objectives that have built this economy:

• "The ingenious production of goods and services of high quality at the lowest possible prices.

• Prospecting for and exploiting new frontiers of economic opportunity.

• Helping to provide and support (but not dictating to) the community's institutions of learning and artistic refinement.

• Guarding jealously the individual's civil liberties, which the business leader's prestige and means—and self-interest—admirably suit him to defend." [37]

Notes

1. Ben W. Lewis, "Open Season on Bigness," *Harvard Business Review*, Vol. 37, May–June 1959, p. 110.
2. Richard Austin Smith, "The Incredible Electrical Conspiracy," *Fortune*, April 1961, p. 133.
3. *Ibid.*
4. *Ibid.*
5. *Ibid.*
6. Smith, *op. cit.*, May 1961, p. 222.
7. An absorbing discussion of the need for achievement and economic growth can be found in David C. McClelland's *The Achieving Society*, Princeton: D. Van Nostrand Company, Inc., 1961.
8. Lewis, *op. cit.*, p. 110. The electrical companies' "not guilty" plea is another matter.
9. Peter F. Drucker, "Realities of Our World Position," *Harvard Business Review*, Vol. 37, May–June 1959, pp. 42–43.
10. To bring about the constant and continuing use of natural and human resources as men in society want them to be used.
11. See Vance Packard's *The Hidden Persuaders*, New York: Pocketbooks, Inc., 1958, for an example of myth building. Also see Martin Mayer's *Madison Avenue, USA*, New York: Harper & Brothers, 1958, as an example of myth exploding. And also see various accounts of the Ford Motor Company's "Edsel" fiasco as an example of how confusing the total marketing concept can be for the producer. The article by Perrin Stryker called "Motivation Research," *Fortune*, June 1956, pp. 144–147, 222–232, is still one of the soundest analyses available.
12. E. Jerome McCarthy, *Basic Marketing*, Homewood: Richard D. Irwin, Inc., 1960, p. 354.
13. *Ibid.*, pp. 368–369.
14. From *Time*, Vol. LXXX, July 6, 1962, pp. 57–61 (cover story).
15. "(The consumer) . . . is subjected to the forces of advertising and emulation by which production creates its own demand." John Kenneth Galbraith, *The Affluent Society*, Boston: Houghton Mifflin Company, 1958, p. 260. Most economists, true to their simplified models, still tend to ignore or discount the influence of sales promotion on the economy.
16. Martin Mayer, "What Is Advertising Good For?" *Harper's*, February 1958, p. 25.
17. First published in 1857, Ernst Engel, a German statistician, postulated four laws applying to the manner in which working-class families spent their income as they *move* from one income level to another:
    1. As a family's income increases, a smaller percentage is spent on food.
    2. As a family's income increases, approximately the same percentage is spent on clothing.
    3. As a family's income increases, approximately the same percentage is spent on rent, fuel, and other household operations.
    4. As a family's income increases, an increasing percentage is spent on all other items.
    From T. N. Beckman, H. H. Maynard, and W. R. Davidson, *Principles of Marketing*, 6th ed., New York: The Ronald Press Company, 1957, pp. 92–94.
18. Stuart Henderson Britt, *The Spenders*, New York: McGraw-Hill Book Company, Inc., 1960, pp. 74–75.

19. George Katona, *The Powerful Consumer*, New York: McGraw-Hill Book Company, Inc., 1960, p. 238.
20. *Ibid.*
21. Pierre Martineau, *Motivation in Advertising*, New York: McGraw-Hill Book Company, Inc., 1957, pp. 163–172 *et passim.*
22. *Ibid.*
23. Martineau, *op. cit.*, p. 242.
24. George Horsley Smith, *Motivation Research in Advertising and Marketing*, New York: McGraw-Hill Book Company, Inc., 1954, p. 222.
25. There is now even a frozen daiquiri mix being marketed, but its underwater characteristics are not known.
26. The term "planned obsolescence" is used here to refer primarily to styling changes. The other aspect, built-in failure, is so negligible as to be unimportant to the discussion. But if the myth of built-in failure becomes strong enough— "they just don't build them like they used to"—and there is even a little evidence to substantiate it, then whole industries might suffer ruin.
27. A loss leader is a retail item that is usually well known, widely used, and branded, which is offered at a substantial price reduction to lure customer traffic to the store. The hope is that while picking out the loss leader, the customer also will buy regularly priced merchandise.
28. Katona, *op. cit.*, p. 243.
29. Robert J. Lampman, *The Share of Top-Wealth Holders in National Wealth, 1922–1956*, Princeton: Princeton University Press, 1962.
30. See, for example, Robert Theobald, "Poverty in the Affluent Society," *Challenge*, Vol. 11, January 1963, pp. 22–24.
31. John Chamberlain, "History of American Business," *Fortune*, May 1962, p. 256.
32. This useful term was first introduced by John Kenneth Galbraith in *American Capitalism*, Boston: Houghton Mifflin Company, 1952. Galbraith specifically denied any such power to the masses of unorganized consumers. This was the contribution of George Katona, *op. cit.*, p. 243.
33. *Time*, July 13, 1962, p. 36. *Time* added editorially: "The obvious solution to the shortage is ideologically sound but unsanitary: communize privately held toothbrushes."
34. Lewis, *op. cit.*, p. 113.
35. *Ibid.*
36. Maurice Baum, "The Case for Business Civilization," *Harvard Business Reivew*, Vol. 38, November–December 1960, p. 64.
37. Lawrence G. Lavengood, "Ameircan Business and the Piety of Profits," *Harvard Business Review*, Vol. 37, November–December 1959, p. 55.

Selected Readings

*Editors of Fortune. *America in the Sixties*. New York: Harper Torchbooks, 1961.
*Galbraith, John Kenneth. *The Great Crash: 1929*. Boston: Houghton Mifflin, 1961.
Katona, George and Eva Mueller. *Consumer Expectations: 1953–1956*. Ann Arbor: University of Michigan Press, 1957.
Kuznets, Simon. *Economic Change: Selected Essays in Business Cycles, National Income, and Economic Growth*. New York: W. W. Norton, 1953.
Potter, David M., *People of Plenty*, Chicago: University of Chicago Press, 1954.
Schumpeter, Joseph. *Capitalism, Socialism, and Democracy*. New York: Harper and Bros., 1950. 3rd ed.

Weiss, E. B. *Mass Marketing to the "400" Mass Retailers*. New York: Printer's Ink, 1950.

Whyte, William H. *Is Anyobdy Listening?* New York: Simon and Schuster, 1952.

* Paperback edition.

Part Six
Political Institutions

Political institutions are established among men to regularize and control their relationship to the end that peace, order, and stability prevail and the culture endures. This formalization of control becomes necessary when informal controls (customs) cannot cope with the demands of an increasingly complex social organization. Government becomes "the epitome of societal organization."

The complete history of the origin and development of political institutions lies beyond the scope of this book, but by confining our concerns to the American political tradition, practical origins and their development are discernible.

Part Six consists of five chapters and draws heavily upon the concepts developed in previous chapters. For example, in Chapter 19 there is the close relationship between the development of capitalism and the growth of representative institutions. Voting behavior, discussed in Chapter 21, bears a striking resemblance to some aspects of consumer behavior, and "status politics," described in Chapter 22, is as much an expression of social mobility as is neighborhood, house type, and membership in voluntary organizations.

Chapter 19 is devoted to the European origins of American political institutions with special emphasis on our feudal and English antecedents. The conflict of ideologies and their reconciliation is the particular substance of Chapter 20. In Chapter 21 the central concern of political science—power—is examined, along with the socialization of political beliefs. The varied nature of American society and the resultant pluralism could possibly lead to an exaggerated nationalism in the "Quest for Community" described in Chapter 22. Finally, in Chapter 23 the continuing growth and existence of a large military establishment is examined as a dominant factor in the public sector of our economy and as an important element in political and geopolitical decision-making.

Chapter 19

Historical Backgrounds
of Political Institutions

As a group is formed, a need to administer its affairs is immediately apparent. Be it family, church, school, business, or state, some ruling force is required to arbitrate and settle disputes, promote internal cohesion, maintain effective operation, and preserve order. In the state, this function is performed by government.

Government is that part of the state which directs the affairs of the whole institution. A state maintains integrity through its government. The government exercises administrative power through its officials—those individuals elected or appointed to office—or through those who seize control of government machinery. Because the state, the largest group created by man, coincides with society, and because its government protects all subordinate groups, government is the "epitome of societal regulation." [1]

The imperatives of government, called laws, derive from the mores of society as a result of external threats to society's existence. Thus, government is concerned with social control in the broad sense, leaving the details of social behavior, the folkways, to subordinate groups. In a totalitarian state—a state suffering a real or imagined threat from external forces—the subordinate groups have very few opportunities to control their own social conduct. That is, in a totalitarian state national and individual culture patterns are uniform and conform to a single standard; all details of group and individual behavior are directed toward the benefit of the state as determined and ordered by the government.

The citizen is an involuntary member of the state. He must obey the laws of the land or suffer penalties for disobedience. Even when the state is not totalitarian, government overrides all other institutions concerned with the public interest, provided it has been entrusted with the power to do so.

Power is the ability to achieve results through concerted action. It flows from widespread support among members of the society. Power signifies a political relationship between a group and its leaders and underlies the processes by which the affairs of an organized group are managed. To be sustained, power must assume a form that all accept as rightful and valid. When based on respect and esteem, power assumes the weight of *authority*. Confronted with power the citizen may choose to support or oppose, but confronted with authority he must obey. When society feels that the order demanded by its government is just, that order will endure until the governed weaken their support, and the authority of the government to enforce order diminishes.

The authority vested in the government is based in the long run on a reciprocal relationship between the state and its administrators. This relationship is called *politics*, the science of organizing, regulating, and administering the state. Politics is a dynamic process of deciding between alternatives in fundamental issues. Leslie Lipson has isolated five basic issues which must be satisfactorily resolved through political means:

> The First Issue is the choice between equality or inequality.
> The Second Issue is the choice between a pluralist or monistic state.
> The Third Issue is the choice between freedom or dictatorship.
> The Fourth Issue is the choice between a dispersion of powers or their unification.
> The Fifth Issue is the choice between a multitude of states or a universal state.[2]

In practice there are usually more than two possibilities within each issue, but basically these five are the issues that confront men who establish governments.

Because politics is a dynamic process issues are constantly being tested, examined, and reappraised. "The history of politics, described in one sentence, consists in trying out alternative solutions for the basic issues in altered combinations." [3]

THE EVOLUTION OF POLITICAL THOUGHT

As an old democracy America possesses an enduring order built on satisfactory solutions of the great political issues. It is simple to ascribe wisdom and virtue to the system without acknowledging political evolution beyond the genius of the Founding Fathers. Yet neither the American political system, nor any other for that matter, sprang full blossomed on the world scene at any one point in history, or from any one set of circumstances, or from any one spirit or source.

In his preface to *The Evolution of Political Thought*, C. Northcote Parkinson cautions against assuming the supremacy, finality, and single causation of any political form.

*
[An implicit fallacy in books devoted to the history of political thought] is the idea that political thought is confined to authors and denied to everyone else. By this reasoning we must learn the ideas of Plato and Laski and can safely ignore those of Pericles and Churchill. This is surely to give an absurd weight to the accident of authorship. The idea expressed verbally or in action may be at least as novel and potent as the idea expressed with pen and ink. Closely connected with this fallacy is the idea that political theory has its origin in ancient Greece. The classically-educated historian has rarely thought it necessary to go either further back or further afield. He may have been misled by the derivation of the words in use; and yet the absurdity of this would seem obvious enough. To deny that there were politics before the Greeks invented the word is no more reasonable than to assume that the Greeks were uncivilized until the Romans had taught them Latin.

If it is wrong to conclude that all political theory began with Plato, it is at least equally wrong to suppose that all political thinking has been done in Europe and America. Of nearly every basic political concept it is true to say that the Greeks had a word for it and often the word that is still in use. That is not to say, however, that there is no Chinese word with a similar meaning. Still less need we assume that the Chinese and Indians have had no ideas of their own. There are books purporting to summarize the history of political thought of which it can truly be said that they do nothing of the kind. Candid at least are the book titles in which "Western" political thought is specified and more candid still those which define their even narrower scope "From Bacon to Halifax." But while there is reason to commend the honesty of those who profess to do no more than they have done, there is less to be said for their originality and courage. Too many have followed each other along the same well-trodden track. Too few have seen that a history of political thought must be world-wide if it is not to be fallacious.

Another impression which the reader may gain from reading the current books on political thought is that the development of political institutions has progressed steadily from the days of Lycurgus or Solon down to the present day; the ultimate achievement being British Parliamentary Democracy or else perhaps the American Way of Life. There are here two separate fallacies involved. The first lies in the assumption that all history illustrates a story of betterment or progress with ourselves as the final product. The

* From C. Northcote Parkinson, *The Evolution of Political Thought*, pp. 7–15. Boston: Houghton Mifflin Company. Copyright 1958 by C. Northcote Parkinson. By permission.

second lies in the assumption that such progress as there has been is a Western achievement in which no oriental can claim even the smallest share. History records no such monopoly and no such unbroken progression. What the historian does find, however, is a recurrence of the belief that perfection has been reached and that a given constitution (like that of the United States) represents finality. There is, in fact, no historical reason for supposing that our present systems of governance are other than quite temporary expedients. To demonstrate, therefore, that all progress leads upward to these pinnacles of wisdom is peculiarly needless. In such an attempt one ignores half the work that has already been done and all the work that is still to do.

The belief that the present or else some other recommended constitution can represent finality is as old or older than Plato. It runs through many of the texts which the student is required to read. It forms even now the basis for heated discussions as to what form of rule is best. It is essentially pre-Darwinian, however, as a mode of thought. No believer in evolution would expect to find that sort of finality. He would rather regard society as a growing tree than as a building nearing its completion. He would hope to trace a pattern of growth and decay. He would question, on principle, whether any society could be static. He would see in finality nothing more nor less than death. In practice, however, it is easier for the student of today to appreciate how institutions have evolved than to grasp that their evolution must and should continue. Even when the likelihood of further development is recognized, it is usually seen as a perfecting of what exists; as the process, for example, by which representative democracy can be made more representative still. But history shows us no previous example of institutions thus perfected. It reveals rather a sequence in which one form of rule replaces another, each in turn achieving not perfection but decay. The fallacy of the Utopians is to suppose that finality can and should be attained. To the believer in evolution nothing could seem less probable.

One other error implied in the existing textbooks is that the published works of political theorists have had a vast influence on actual events. The student is all too apt to visualize each leader as one likely to refer to a book before deciding upon a policy. But Robespierre no more slept with *Le Contrat Social* under his pillow than did Louis XVI refer to the *Leviathan*. No actual politician is greatly influenced by a book of political theory, although many have been influenced by a book of religion. The politician who reads at all will have read not only the text which the historian thinks significant but forty-nine other forgotten works of which the historian has never even heard. And if one book appears to have been his favorite it will be because the author recommends what he, the ruler, has already decided to do; or what indeed he has already done. Historically, the book comes afterward to defend the deed. This is not to say that the book is always *written* after the revolution it seems to justify. It may be written beforehand, gaining its wide circulation only after the event. The books, by contrast, which supported the losing cause have been forgotten, overlooked, destroyed—or else never published. There is thus a natural selection among books, giving to some the popularity and survival which rewards what is relevant to the mood of an age, and ensuring for others the oblivion reserved for all that seems eccentric and out of tune. In ancient China (as in modern China) the books out of accord with the party line were deliberately burnt. In England or America the books thus out of step will remain unpublished for lack of expected sales. It is not books which influence political events. It is the events which decide which book is to be pulped and which made compulsory reading in the schools.

The significance then of the political theorist is not that he guided the ruler but that he provided the ruler with a rational explanation of what he, the ruler, had already done. His works to that extent throw light upon the age in which he lived—or at any rate upon the age in which his works were widely read. But to interpret policy throughout the ages in terms of its literary justification is open to certain objections, of which the chief is that politics are far older than political theory. To begin the story where it is usually made to begin (in Athens of the 5th century B.C.) is to omit the essential background to all human affairs—the background studied by the anthropologist. It would be untrue to say that all authors on the history of political theory have ignored this background. It is with reference to it, however, that they prove least convincing. They are apt to perpetuate by quotation the mistakes made (perhaps unavoidably) by the earlier political thinkers. These philosophers were apt to picture a happy community of primitive men suddenly deciding to organize themselves and elect a ruler.

"I assume" writes Rousseau (Social Contract, J. J. Rousseau), "that men have reached a point at which the obstacles that endanger their preservation in the state of nature overcome by their resistance the forces which each individual can exert with a view to maintaining himself in that state. Then this primitive condition can no longer subsist, and the human race would perish unless it changed its mode of existence. . . .

"[The problem is] to find a form of association which may defend and protect with the whole force of the community the person and property of every associate, and by means of which, each, coalescing with all, may nevertheless obey only himself and remain as free as before. [To this problem the Social Contract furnishes the solution.]

"The clauses of this contract are so determined . . . that, although they have never perhaps been formally enunciated, they are everywhere the same, everywhere tacitly admitted and recognized."

There might be no great harm in reading this piece of eighteenth century rhetoric provided that the antidote were to follow. The student who is advised to read drivel should at least be warned that it is drivel he is being asked to read. Wild guesses about primitive man are needless, for primitive man has survived for our study. And even the slightest acquaintance with the aborigines of Australia, Malaya, or Borneo will convince the student that no human beings have ever come together with an open mind to discuss the basis of their social organization. Nor is there any reason to suppose that our primitive ancestors in Europe or indeed in ancient Britain were in this respect very different from the peoples whose culture has remained primitive. There has never been a clean page upon which to write a constitution. Man had, from the start, physical, biological, and mental characteristics; and many of these he still retains. It is by these inherited characteristics, dating back for thousands of years, that his political institutions have been influenced. Books which fail to make this clear are as misleading as they are tedious, as dangerous as they are wrong.

It is no wonder that the social anthropologist turns with disgust from works of political theory. In a recent and important work on the political structure of African tribes, the editors explain how unhelpful they found these works to be.

> We have not found that the theories of political philosophers have helped us to understand the societies we have studied and we consider them of little scientific value; for their conclusions are seldom formulated in terms of observed behavior or capable of being tested by this criterion. Political philosophy has chiefly concerned itself with how men *ought* to live and what form of government they *ought* to have, rather than with what *are* their political habits and institutions.
>
> In so far as political philosophers have attempted to understand existing institutions instead of trying to justify or undermine them, they have done so in terms of popular psychology or of history. They have generally had recourse to hypotheses about earlier stages of human society presumed to be devoid of political institutions. . . . (*African Political Systems*. M. Fortes and E. E. Evans-Pritchard. Oxford, 1940. 4th Impression, 1950.)

The editors, in this instance, find some excuse for the political theorist in that "little anthropological research has been conducted into primitive political systems" and even less effort made to correlate what little has been done. While it is thus true to say that the subject remains largely unexplored, it is also manifest (even from such knowledge as there is) that the theories of "original contract" are baseless suppositions. The anthropologist may not be ready to explain how political institutions first came into being but he is at least prepared to describe theories as "unscientific" which are supported neither by evidence nor probability.

. . . . As the Greeks perceived, there are, broadly speaking, three alternatives in government; rule by one, rule by a few, and rule by many. Rule by one person can take the form of Monarchy, Despotism, or Dictatorship. Monarchy is the rule by a King or Queen, depending upon religion, descent, election, or established custom. Despotism is the rule by a King or Queen, established and maintained by force or cunning. Dictatorship is rule by a person who is neither King nor Queen whose authority derives from a particular emergency and whose office is widely regarded as a temporary expedient. Rule by a few can take the form of Feudalism, Aristocracy, or Oligarchy. Feudalism is rule by nobles, each with control of some province or locality and many almost independent of any centralized authority. Aristocracy is rule by persons enjoying a special and often inherited respect, acting mainly through a central government under their own control. (Theocracy, or rule by a priesthood, is one form of Aristocracy.) Oligarchy is rule by a few persons with no special claim to respect other than for their wealth, ability, or vigor. (Bureaucracy, or rule by officials, is one form of Oligarchy.) Rule by many can take the form of Democracy, Representative Democracy, or Anarchy. Democracy is rule by all or by a majority of the voters, by direct expression of their will. Representative Democracy is rule by all or a majority of the voters but through elected representatives. Anarchy, if it can be termed a form of rule, means the refusal of a large number to be ruled at all.

Although the basic forms of government are only three, it would obviously be wrong to expect any government to conform exactly to any one of them. In practice, forms of rule are often mixed. Thus, a pure monarchy or despotism is difficult to maintain for long except over a relatively small area. A single ruler soon needs help and, in seeking it, becomes a little less absolute. Despotism or even Dictatorship may become monarchy by virtue of time and habit. A Democracy may still retain elements of earlier forms of rule. When, therefore, a State is here described as, say, an Aristocracy, it must be taken to mean the preponderance of Aristocratic rule, not the exclusion of any other form.

If we owe some of our terminology to Plato, it is from both Plato and Aristotle that we take the idea of sequence. As a scientist and the son of a physician, Aristotle perceived that forms of rule decay and so give place to others. He did not prescribe a single type of constitution as best for every State. The laws toward which he was feeling his way were not *The Laws* of Plato but the laws of change. With his aid we can readily perceive at least a tendency for Monarchy to turn into Aristocracy or Feudalism, for Aristocracy to become Democracy (perhaps via Oligarchy), for Democracy to turn into chaos, and for order to be restored by a Despotism or Dictatorship. When the Dictatorship gives place to Monarchy the wheel has turned full circle and the process may begin again. It would, of course, be a gross exaggeration to represent this tendency as an invariable rule. The sequence is subject to many variations and exceptions. It can be disrupted as a result of war. And different lands within the same civilization develop at different speeds so that, existing side by side, they represent different stages of the same sequence. Thus a historian of the remote future might remark that the countries of Europe mostly passed from Democracy to Dictatorship during the first half of the Twentieth Century. This would be true, broadly speaking, but he would have to note certain exceptions and explain that the various transitions were not simultaneous and that the countries affected were not necessarily adjacent to each other. We today can generalize about the past in much the same way, again noting the exceptions. And one factor which we can observe as regulating the speed of change is the area and physical nature of the country to be governed. It is almost impossible to govern a vast and diverse area except by loyally upholding a more or less divine Monarch. While the sequence of the forms of rule may be roughly followed, the tendency is to hurry through the forms that are obviously unworkable and return with relief to the form which offers most stability. It is perhaps this factor more than any other which prevents much valid generalization about any given period. If the Athenians were democrats when the Persians were not, it was basically because they had a different problem to solve.

. . . . During the life of a given civilization the lands affected by it may undergo different forms of rule, and perhaps in a more or less logical sequence, but the civilization has a life cycle of its own and one perhaps uninfluenced by political ideas. The rise and fall of civilizations might best be studied in terms of climate, food supply, soil-erosion, reproduction, and disease. As compared with factors such as these, the forms of rule are a superficial matter. It is true that certain forms of government are often associated with a civilization's early development. It would be far more difficult and controversial to show what type of government prevailed at its zenith or during its decay. There is, to begin with, a difficulty in agreeing as to when the zenith was reached and almost as great a difficulty in fixing a period for a civilization's end.

Man has passed through many ages in the period of recorded history: through the tribal stage to the Greco-Roman civilization, through political relapse with the barbarian invasions, through feudalism and development of the national state as we know it.

The many ideological strains that constitute our political heritage can be traced through the development of Western civilization. The economic aspects of the break-up of the medieval social order have already been examined. The close ties between economic and political institutions are apparent at each stage of development of governmental forms. Religion and other social institutions have also contributed their influence to the formation of the democratic state.

The most useful explanation of our political evolution entails a re-examination of the medieval epoch, this time from the political standpoint. The state in the Middle Ages was held together by the moral authority of the Church. The Reformation and the Renaissance had a secularizing effect on the state, which underwent further modification in the nineteenth century under the impact of the Industrial Revolution and the French Revolution. Out of these and other forces rose the democratic and the totalitarian states of today.

THE MEDIEVAL STATE

The roots of feudalism go very deep. It is possible to isolate Roman and Germanic customs that contributed substantially to feudal institutions. For instance, the Roman estates called *latifundia* became the feudal manor. During the troubled times of the invasions and Roman decline, small landowners turned their properties over to large holders of the *latifundia* in return for protection, entering into contractual relationships composed of *patrocinium* (personal dependence) and *precarium* (financial dependence) which became fused with German *comitatus* (personal fealty). When, under the Mayors of the Palace, *precarium*, and *comitatus* coalesced, full-fledged feudalism was the result.[4] Indeed, the fact of feudalism was long past before historians discovered that a great epoch had been created. The "ism" came so naturally, without revolution, that those involved were unaware of making history or setting precedents.

The early Carolingians, especially Charlemagne, arrested the social disintegration that resulted from the Germanic invasions and united their tribes and peoples under something like a central government. Had all external dangers been removed during and after Charlemagne's reign, there seems to be no doubt that feudalism would not have developed. Feudalism was a necessity: a protection against enemies, both human and economic.

The political necessity of feudalism was caused primarily by the financial structure: without currency and with an almost totally agrarian economy, the only economic reality was land and the produce of land.[5] With little means or incentive to trade ideas and products with other political units, there followed the self-centered development of feudalism. It is doubtful, in view of the continuing invasions, whether Charlemagne's vast Empire could have remained intact, even had he been followed by strong and able rulers.

The old Germanic custom of equal inheritance sufficed to rend the Empire among three greedy heirs; thus, the arrangements at Verdun between Lothair, Charles, and Louis, Charlemagne's grandsons, were to foreshadow the future map of Western Europe. In the East Frankish kingdom of Louis were the Teutonic-speaking peoples, the forerunners of modern Germany. France was to evolve from the descendants of Romanized Gauls speaking Romance languages who composed the West Frankish kingdom of Charles. Lothair's kingdom, lying between, never became one national state because of its lack of cohesion, but was instead destined to be a plum sought by stronger neighbors.

Faced with darker days than those of the barbarian invasions, Western Europe in the ninth and tenth centuries was forced to organize, locally, for its own protection. In the fertile soil of necessity feudalism took root, flourished, and saved Western Europe from complete dissolution. Feudalism, then, is the term representing that period between the dismemberment of the Carolingian Empire and the growth of national states. It is a broad term encompassing the peculiar, dynamic institutions of the time.

France was the first area on the continent to know the fury of invading Vikings, and French nobles were quick to increase their political power at the expense of the monarchy. This was done by building castles for the protection of the local folk who, once protected, became the Count's "men." When it was discovered that the castle could be used not only against an invader but also to flaunt royal authority, noble turned upon smaller noble forcing acceptance of his rule, with the result that France, at the beginning of the tenth century, comprised many distinct territorial divisions. "The castle . . . is the crystallization of developed feudalism. It emphasizes the fact that the suzerainty of the lord is a local fact, based on the possession of land." [6]

Germany, on the other hand, did not fall victim to the Vikings for some years, and her peoples were not subjected to vassalage to the same extent as the French. The relatively free status of the German freemen, an extensive, if not homogeneous, class, is a distinguishing factor between Germany and France. With a strong sense of their own inherent rights, these freemen resisted inroads against their liberty.

Reaction to the stress of invasion was quite different in Germany. Instead of many small territorial units as in France, the Viking invaders of Germany were faced by five great duchies. Able to extract a large grant of land in Normandy, the invaders did not fare so well in the east.

In both France and Germany military leaders came to the fore and assumed control of their weaker countrymen. In the tenth and eleventh centuries when the West Franks were breaking up into a series of local states, the East Franks seemed to attain increasing solidarity. While strong kings were on the throne in the east, their dukes were made to toe the mark; but as the kingship disintegrated through land tenures, the nobility increased in power to the point where Germany, like France of an earlier day, splintered into a group of feudal states.[7]

Conrad I, elected to the throne in 911, had no Carolingian blood and so could not benefit from the veneration of that house. He was the first German king to be openly opposed by the nobles. This action further disorganized central authority and contributed to the establishment of hereditary dukedoms, which tended to raise this nobility to a level with the monarchy.

After the Normans established their foothold in France, the French monarchy deteriorated rapidly until Hugh Capet, Mayor of the Palace, assumed the crown in 987. The importance of this event lies not only in the establishment of the Capetian line, which terminated with Louis XVI on the guillotine in 1793, but also in the fact that Hugh's estates, the centrally located *Ile de France*, were to serve as the nucleus of a reconstructed monarchy. Germany was without such a royal domain.[8]

With Hugh Capet the long process of uniting France began. Using every known means, honest and dishonest, the Capetians proceeded to unite into their own hands all the separate sovereignties spun off by the force of feudalism until they held them all—they were the creators of modern France. In Normandy, for reasons not clearly understood, feudal institutions were more uniform than in the other principalities. "Throughout Normandy . . . the substitution of feudal tenure for other forms of land-holding seems to have been remarkably complete, and the definition of feudal service in precise quotas of knights to have been especially early." Without the duke's authority, no one could build a castle, coin money, regulate sea trade, or hold trials in more serious cases—formal warfare was a monopoly of the duke.[9]

The other duchies varied widely in their use of feudal institutions in the eleventh century. None possessed a really centralized administration; and Burgundy, without ducal control, was in a state of chaos, as were the other duchies where the theoretical ruler had lost power. It must be remembered that, weak as it appears, the concentrated authority of French dukes greatly exceeded that exercised by the German feudal nobility.

The establishment of the principle of primogeniture in France by the Capetians was one of the chief factors in the doom of feudalism, although the shadow was destined to live on. Primogeniture, together with the Capetian practice of reacquiring land through *escheat and forfeiture*, prevented the further dissipation of crown lands.

By the eleventh century France as yet was not functioning as a unified state. The heads of the splinter states enjoyed the substance of regal power. Indeed, "the conception of the kingly divine right and of the king as suzerain governing with his barons existed together and remained irreconcilable." [10]

The Ottonian Italian policy, which resulted in the revival of the imperial title, prevented the German kings from attacking the matter of centralization with the same vigor as the Capetians. Although the Germans were strong rulers, they failed to keep their powerful feudal lords in check.

At some point in the eleventh or twelfth century the feudal scale between France and Germany stood at balance; but as France approached unity, Germany receded.

Early in the eleventh century, Germany experienced the stirrings of economic recovery; money began to circulate as towns assumed importance. Complete recovery would depend on a strong monarch, but this was not to be.

The changing social picture brought to the fore a new and distinctive class, the *ministeriales*. These men, of servile birth, tended to degrade the nobility by their upward penetration into the privileged plane. The lack of close feudal ties in Germany forced the nobility to rely on the *ministeriales* for administrative duties. In return for their service, the *ministeriales* were rewarded as vassals, although they could not claim the same privileges as the nobles. By the twelfth century, establishment of the *ministeriales* class was complete when the performance of military service, the supreme dignity of the noble, was accorded them. The status in fact, though not in law, became hereditary. The growth of this new class to a position of importance accounted for a remarkable difference between German and French feudalism. France, by maintaining a relatively pure aristocracy, was able to rid herself of those Carolingian institutions common to both France and Germany, while Germany fostered and embellished them.

As a law of succession, France made the fiefs inheritable. Germany had no such law and succession remained an act of grace on the part of the king. The ancient Germanic law of equal inheritance remained strong in some quarters, while the principle of primogeniture, although practiced, was never established. [11]

In France, the Church did not become completely feudalized. The secular clergy succumbed to the trend, but the sacred clergy in the abbeys and monasteries, though exposed to secular methods, were much more disciplined. They were forced to defend clerical estates in the customary manner, but avoided becoming vassals themselves. Cluny is the perfect example of this type, claiming autonomy and paying allegiance only to the papacy.[12]

In Germany the Cluniac influence gave strength to the papacy in the person of Hildebrand who, as Pope Gregory VII, touched off the investiture controversy—a conflict between the Church and lay princes over who should install the king. Up to this time, the German kings had been strong enough to allay the spread of feudalism, but the combination of Church and Saxon rebellion threw all Germany into confusion and anarchy. "What the ninth century had done for France, transforming French society into a feudal society, was accomplished in Germany by the civil wars during the reign of Henry IV." [13]

The regal authority was so diminished that the German feudal institutions were altered radically, as was the texture of society. Those freemen who were strong became noble, bound to higher lords by ties of vassalage and homage, while those freemen who were not strong became weaker and went down to serfdom under the stress.[14]

Like French feudalism in the reign of the last Carolingians and first Capetians, the German feudal system now suffered the separation of vassal from lord. Germany now felt the tug of the centrifugal force which was to reduce her, in territory and politically, "to a rope of sand," and the kingship to a position of "magnificent insignificance." [15]

German feudalism precluded the development of a uniform system of law. "This is exactly opposite to the tendency in France where the growth of the crown gradually reduced, and even effaced, the law of the provincial dynasts, and the établissements and ordonnances of the French kings became more and more the law of the realm." Feudal Germany, by drifting away from homogeneity, succeeded in erasing all trace of general law—not only the ancient Germanic codes, but also the Carolingian principles became obsolete. The law tended toward particularism—that is, it became more and more localized. Each political unit had its own laws; "the will of petty dynasts commingled with the debris of the past." [16]

While Germany was in process of dissolution, France under Philip II, called Augustus, established the principle that the feudal hierarchy culminated in the king who was vassal to none.[17] Louis IX (St. Louis),

Philip's grandson, founded an appellate royal court at Paris which followed the principles of Roman law. Money, becoming more prevalent, had to be coined by the crown to be legal tender throughout the kingdom; money issued by feudal lords was acceptable only within their own domains.

Feudalism as a political force in France practically disappeared with the Hundred Years' War, although the nobles retained their social rank and privilege until the French Revolution. The rise of cities and the financial support of the new middle class enabled the kings to throw off the last vestiges of feudal pressures. By the close of the Middle Ages, France had become an absolute monarchy.[18]

Germany followed an opposite course. Early France had been a multitude of small holdings; Germany was now a horde of little states, each clinging to its own custom. "The later history of German feudalism is an appallingly complicated subject." The institutions of feudalism flourished here long after they had died out in the west.[19]

Heinrich Mitteis maintained that there was nothing essentially centrifugal in feudalism itself, but that it acted only on the German Empire and not on the German principalities. On the contrary, these principalities paralleled, on a smaller scale, the constitutional development in the west. Out of these principalities, rather than the Empire, rose the modern German state.[20]

In Germany, feudalism became politically sovereign, but less a constitutional system than a dissolution of all centralized public power. In France, on the other hand, the increasing power of the Crown gradually deprived the feudal lords of power and authority, reducing them to a social caste.

Feudalism performed a necessary task, succeeding where Rome had failed against the Germans, and as the later Carolingians had not against the invaders of their day. Feudalism organized local resistance to free Western Europe of the barbarian menace. But where it had utility during the stormy ninth and tenth centuries, feudalism later became a system of exploitation of the weak by the strong—of the majority by the minority. As a military system of offense and defense feudalism proved adequate; but as a political system it fell short. While feudalism did not maintain order effectively, it did contain certain features of extreme importance to future generations. The feudal class, although aristocratic, harbored within its own confines political ideas that were "essentially democratic." [21] And within the walls of the new towns developed another important element in political evolution, the town charter which spelled out the rights and obligations of citizenship and the relation of town to ruler. An old German proverb says: to breathe town air makes a man free.

In addition to these factors was St. Thomas Aquinas' revival of the Aristotelian concept of government based on man's social nature and the organization of government based on the superior wisdom and morality of the ruler for the benefit of the ruled. In Aquinas' *Summa Theologica*, written about A.D. 1250, the natural law doctrine of the Stoic philosophers became integrated into the Christian teaching of divine order. It was supplemented by a just regard for the sound legal vigor of the Roman jurists and joined with the Aristotelian emphasis on norms. Out of this fusion came the concept of *constitutionalism*, the weakening of monarchy through election and the tempering of royal power by extending popular participation in government.[22]

THE ENGLISH BASIS OF THE AMERICAN SYSTEM

Under feudalism individuals were born into a certain status and were subordinate to the group; the group rather than the individual was responsible for crime. Whole communities were accountable for the behavior of a single wrongdoer; the group rather than the individual held the land. But during the fifteenth and sixteenth centuries a change took place. Europe was advancing toward concepts of the state as we know it, in which individuals were free—able to contract for themselves; able to determine their own destinies; responsible individually for misdeeds; able to own land outright. And as Parkinson points out: "Once the individual becomes the unit, divorced from his clan or village, he is immeasurably weakened in his relationship with the state. And the state is correspondingly strengthened as group loyalties disappear." [23]

Thus, as society becomes urbanized—as primary relationships are exchanged for secondary associations—the groundwork is laid for nationalism, whether democratic or tyrannical. "If you met an Englishman in the street in the fourteenth century and asked him what his country did for him and what he owed to her, he might well be nonplussed. No one did anything for him, but he certainly owed a week's service annually to the baron, and eggs to the abbey, and so on. Two centuries later he would have known the answer, for by that time political authority had crystallized in the nation." [24]

In Chapter 15 the development of the strong national state was discussed—paralleling the expansion of trade, as emergent national economies smashed local trade barriers, and the feudal system itself. Between the last half of the fifteenth century and the end of the Napoleonic Wars (1815), the modern national state took form. Loyalty and obedience were transferred from the local ruler to the monarch, or national ruler. In Chapter 22 the transfer of loyalty from the individual national leader to the nation—the phenomenon of *nationalism*—will be examined as it exists in America.

The king who ruled the new national state was absolute monarch. Since his word was law, the king himself was above the law. This was the "Divine Right of Kings." If the monarch was capricious in his regard for the interests of his citizens, deeming his interests *their* interests (*"L'état, c'est moi"*), dissatisfaction with his rule was likely to follow. The burden of taxes and the disruption of commerce by incessant warfare created a powerful opposition to the monarch in the entrepreneurial class. This class became largely alienated from the monarchy, the institution that it had done so much to create. Supported in many instances by the *bourgeoisie*, the free thinkers and the discontented political and religious groups began to press for reform.

Reform began early in England and continued steadily and in advance of other European nations. The thirteenth century was very fruitful, politically, in England. Many contributions by the English to the development of representative government, as well as our filial relationship, make English political evolution important to us. Most of our governmental concepts are derived from the English tradition.

Magna Carta was wrested from King John by his disenchanted barons on the field at Runnymede in 1215. As a document primarily designed to restore the old feudal privileges, Magna Carta may be thought of as reactionary, as feudalism gave way to a new order. But certain clauses were so worded as to provide the basis for future liberty, by establishing the general principle that the king was *subordinate* to the law. At various times suppressed, altered, and modified, Magna Carta has survived as one of the main foundations of the British common law.

No man has ever ruled alone. Even the most absolute of monarchs must turn to others for advice. In England, the advisors of the medieval kings were called the *Curia Regis* or Great Council. Composed of the upper nobility and higher clergy, it was essentially this group who won Magna Carta from King John. Through force of arms and control of the purse—that is, the exchequer—first accomplished at Runnymede, the *Curia Regis* expanded its influence in the legislative, executive, and judicial areas, and gradually evolved into the House of Lords.

The British Parliament, perhaps the greatest contribution to representative government in recorded history, was the product of a power struggle, first between king and baron, and then between the king—united with the upper nobility—and the commoner. Simon de Montfort, a baronial opponent of the temporarily deposed King Henry III, unwittingly established a precedent by calling not only the upper nobility to a *parlement*, or "a talking," but also the knights and burgesses of the towns. This occurred in 1265, seven years after the barons had established another precedent, the *regular* calling of a parliament.

The knights and burgesses who had served on "sworn inquests," juries of commoners appointed by the crown to help attend to local affairs, constituted the group that evolved into the House of Commons. Needing popular, but not legal, support to levy taxes, Edward I in 1295 formalized the practice of summoning commoners to sit in Parliament in the "Model Parliament."

The first Parliament was a unicameral legislature which by the nature of the social relationships of the estates discouraged debate; vassals were reluctant to contradict their lords, and parish priests acceded to bishops. In 1331, the Parliament became bicameral, but many generations were to pass before the new House of Commons became supreme. King and noble still possessed sufficient military prowess to keep the struggle for political power among themselves. The War of the Roses (1455–1485), a dynastic struggle between the Houses of Lancaster and York, not only brought to a close the feudal era in England, but, together with the Black Death, so decimated the nobility that the importance of the monarchy was vastly enhanced under the Tudors (1485–1603). Greater importance was given to lesser individuals, as ascribed status—acquiring position by birth—gave way to achievement in the void left by the demise of the upper nobility.

The Tudors introduced a century of strong, autocratic, and absolute rule in England. By using their power to maintain law, order, and national prosperity, they were able to retain their position despite the precedent for more popular rule. The Stuart House (1603–1714) was not as skillful in governing. The Stuarts did not hold with representative assembly, and Parliament, which had at least convened under the Tudors, now began to seek recognition. The latent precedents of Magna Carta and the Model Parliament became the clarion call for reform, and in 1642 civil war broke. This was the first middle-class revolution—the Puritan Revolution. Charles I was overthrown and beheaded. Charles II was called to the throne following an Interregnum under Cromwell. Charles' brother and successor, James II, was deposed in the bloodless Glorious Revolution (1688–1689) and Parliament emerged as the dominant force in British government. Other measures strengthening the British constitution followed quickly, measures which were to provide America with certain fundamental concepts of constitutional liberty: the Bill of Rights (1689) provided that the king could not suspend laws or maintain a standing army without the consent of Parliament; the consent of Parliament had to be given to all taxes levied in England; debate and elections were to be free; frequent sessions of Parliament were to be called; individuals had the right of petition and protection from excessive bail. The Act of Settlement (1700–1701) provided that Parliament could dispose of succession to the Crown and that judges should hold office for life, or tenure of good behavior.

In the long struggle between Crown and Parliament factions were created around the adversaries. One important change in English politics was the crystallization of these factions into political parties. The first formal political party in the modern sense was the Whig Party. The Whigs stood for the supremacy of Parliament and the interests of the middle class. Opposing the Whigs was the Tory Party which, although against a Catholic king, stood for a strong monarchy and the interests of the landed aristocracy. Political parties in England and America still follow organizational and tactical patterns established in the seventeenth century.

CONCLUSION

The level of political reform that swept away absolutism in England —and later in France—could not have been reached without a sound basis in reason, and without apologists. Hobbes' *Leviathan* (1651), an argument in favor of absolute monarchy, was written *after* the Puritan Revolution. The *Leviathan* contradicted the *fact* of Parliamentary government and limited powers, and, as a result, no Hobbesian school arose in British and American political thought, although Hobbes has markedly influenced various countries with traditions of absolute, despotic government.[25] On the other hand the writings of Locke in *Two Treatises on Government* (1690) were contemporary with and supported the political facts in England; they formed the bases for later attacks on absolutism, prominent among them being the American Colonies' rejection of Parliamentary absolutism. More than an apologia, the *Two Treatises* drew a sharp distinction between the state and society, viewing the latter as the more enduring and important. And because it was derived from society, government could be dissolved by society when specified ends and purposes were no longer being met—the doctrine of *popular sovereignty*. Locke's idea of *social contract* was a relationship that existed between subjects and subjects, not between subjects and sovereign. The latter is a *fiduciary trust* in which the people are both trustor and beneficiary, and the government is trustee. "In the theory of divine right, only the ruler has rights; in the theory of contract, both the people and the government have rights; in Locke's conception of *government as trust, only the people have rights*." [26] And, as William Ebenstein further indicated, "Every piece of significant political writing is a fragment of the autobiography of its age; yet it becomes great only if in addition to its vital connection with the period from which it springs, it possesses a universal appeal because of its general human interest." [27]

Three-quarters of a century later in France, Jean Jacques Rousseau was to modify the writings of Locke in his own *Social Contract* (1762). To achieve equality, he projected the idea of individual liberty as the end of government. The former could not exist without the latter. Rousseau's government *is* the people who are sovereign and cannot divest themselves of the *inalienable* and *indivisible*. Where Locke had discounted economic inequality in the quest for liberty and viewed property as liberating its owner rather than enslaving others, Rousseau recognized property as a form of private domination to be kept under control by the public interest of the community, the omniscient *General Will*. Thus, the minority is protected through the wisdom of the majority.

The extreme formulation of Rousseau—that *man can be forced to be free*, that his freedom is not necessarily what a man thinks, but what the General Will says it is—was used later by Hegel and the modern worshipers of the state, and has made Rousseau the father of nationalism.[28] Napoleon carried the Rousseau-inspired French Revolution to virtually all of Western and Central Europe where imposed governmental reforms "forced men to be free" for a time. Rousseau did not live to see whether the General Will really was omniscient beyond the Swiss cantons he had observed and admired, but his message has been a powerful inspiration for men who feel enchained.

The reconciliation of dictatorship and freedom, the third of Lipson's issues, is the greatest problem confronting a democracy. A balance between the extremes of regimentation and anarchy has been maintained in England and America without resort to violence, except in the Puritan Revolution, the American Revolution, and the Civil War, for a total of 500 years. Perhaps the Lockean recognition of the right to rebel, which is at the base of our two systems of government, is our source of stability. "Whatever the social or economic system that may exist at a particular time—be it a pioneering frontier country or an old established society, vigorous, self-confident capitalism or mature, skeptical industrialism, welfare New Dealism or experimental democratic socialism—the right to rebel remains the great, perhaps the greatest, tradition in British and American politics. Rebelliousness, too, can paradoxically grow into tradition: the tradition of the dignity of man and of his unbreakable spirit." [30]

The real genius of our political system rests in the resilience of Americans under the impact of a changing world. We have been able to accommodate to rapidly changing conditions while maintaining a dynamic resolution of the Great Issues. This is the fact that overshadows the deeds of great men in American history, no matter how great the man or how great the deed. The remaining chapters in Part Six are devoted to an analysis of the means by which we have achieved our political stability and some of the overriding problems that must be resolved if we are to preserve our record.

Notes

1. J. O. Hertzler, *American Social Institutions*, Boston: Allyn and Bacon, Inc., 1961, p. 394.
2. Leslie Lipson, *The Great Issues of Politics*, New York: Prentice-Hall, Inc., 1954, p. 94.
3. *Ibid.*, p. 95.
4. G. G. Coulton, *Medieval Panorama*, New York: The Macmillan Company, 1938, pp. 51–52.
5. *Ibid.*, pp. 46–47.
6. Joan Evans, *Life in Mediaeval France*, Oxford: Oxford University Press, 1925, p. 42.
7. Carl Stephenson, *Mediaeval Feudalism*, Ithaca: Cornell University Press, 1942, pp. 92–93.
8. *Ibid.*
9. *Ibid.*, pp. 84–85.
10. C. Petit-Dutaillis, *The Feudal Monarchy in France and England*, E. D. Hunt, trans., London: Routledge & Kegan Paul, Ltd., 1949, p. 326.
11. James Westfall Thompson, *Feudal Germany*, Chicago: The University of Chicago Press, 1923, pp. 310–311, 323–326 *passim*.
12. Arthur Tilley, *Medieval France*, Cambridge: The University Press, 1922, pp. 45–46.
13. G. Barraclough, *The Origins of Modern Germany*, Oxford: Basil Blackford, 1949, p. 136.
14. Thompson, *op. cit.*, pp. 299–302.
15. *Ibid.*, p. 321.

16. *Ibid.*, p. 318–319.
17. Petit-Dutaillis, *op. cit.*, p. 201.
18. Stephenson, *op. cit.*, p. 101.
19. *Ibid.*, pp. 101–102.
20. Heinrich Mitteis, "Feudalism and the German Constitution," in *Mediaeval Germany: 911–1250*, G. Barraclough, trans., Oxford: Basil Blackwell, 1948, pp. 266–267.
21. Sidney Painter, *Mediaeval Society*, Ithaca: Cornell University Press, 1951, p. 100.
22. Heinz Eulau, "Political Science," in *A Reader's Guide to the Social Sciences*, Bert F. Hoseltitz, ed., Glencoe: The Fress Press, 1959, p. 96, and William Ebenstein, *Great Political Thinkers* (Second Edition), New York: Rinehart & Company, Inc., 1956, pp. 216, 219.
23. C. Northcote Parkinson, *op. cit.*, p. 171.
24. J. D. Mabbott, *The State and the Citizen*, London: Hutchinson's University Library, 1947, p. 11.
25. Ebenstein, *op. cit.*, p. 341.
26. *Ibid.*, pp. 366–367.
27. *Ibid.*, p. 365.
28. Ebenstein, *op. cit.*, pp. 417–418.
30. Ebenstein, *op. cit.*, p. 371.

Selected Readings

*Becker, Carl. *The Heavenly City of the Eighteenth Century Philosophers*. New Haven: Yale University Press, 1959.

*Blankston, George. *The Economic Basis of Politics*. New York: Random House, 1960.

*Brinton, Crane. *English Political Thought in the 19th Century*. New York: Harper Torchbooks, 1962.

Gough, J. W. *The Social Contract*. Oxford: The Clarendon Press, 1957.

Lindsay, A. D. *The Modern Democratic State*. New York: Oxford University Press, 1947. Vol. I.

McIlwain, C. H. *The Growth of Political Thought in the West*. New York: The Macmillan Company, 1932.

*Painter, Sidney. *Medieval Society*. Ithaca: Cornell University Press, 1962.

Palmer, R. R. *The Age of the Democratic Revolution*. Princeton: Princeton University Press, 1959. Vol. I.

Strauss, Leo. *Natural Right and History*. Chicago: University of Chicago Press, 1953.

*Talmon, J. L. *Origins of Totalitarian Democracy*. New York: Praeger, 1961.

* Paperback edition.

Chapter 20

The Ideologies of
American Democracy

More than one hundred years elapsed between the discovery of the New
World and the appearance of permanent English colonies on the eastern
seaboard of North America. During these years the Spanish colonized
the hemisphere extensively. By the time the Pilgrims celebrated their
first Thanksgiving in New England, the Spanish Conquistadores had
created an empire in America that was the envy of Europe. Great universities founded by the Spaniards in Mexico City and Lima by the
middle of the sixteenth century give some indication of the extent of the
Spanish civilization, and an elaborate bureaucracy was in existence well
before 1600 to administer the annual transportation of $30 million in
precious metals to Spain.

The brilliant outcome of the Spanish conquest from both the spiritual
and material points of view (*Fé y oro*—faith and gold) was the prod to
Elizabethan England. The growth of naval and maritime power under
the Tudors, and the Stuarts' suppression of the struggles with Spain
and Scotland, freed English manpower and capital for more useful pursuits. With the establishment of the colony of Virginia in 1607, England began to push Spain out of North America.

The English colonists settled in the New World primarily for economic reasons. Even the religious dissenters came to acquire land and
the prestige associated with ownership of land. Other factors, of course,
gave impetus to emigration. The doctrine of mercantilism, prevalent in
England at that time, certainly encouraged colonization, and governmental support for colonial schemes was easy to obtain.

The colonies also served other purposes. They were viewed as suitable
grounds for the disposal of undesirable political heretics and convicted
felons. A few perhaps emigrated in search of adventure—the French
coureurs de bois, for example. English statesmen and writers, advancing

arguments for colonization, stressed its role in weakening Spain, the need for an outlet for England's "surplus" population, the colonial part in helping England become economically self-sufficient, and the opportunity to convert American Indians to the Church of England.

The original stock of most colonies was English, and the fundamental ideas remained English despite a considerable influx of Scots-Irish and Germans from the Palatinate of the Rhine. Very few colonists came to America with the idea of abandoning the social structure they had known. Even those with the primary intent of acquiring cheap land did not seek to establish an egalitarian society based on independent land ownership. Rather, they thought in terms of establishing a society very much like the one they had known in the Old World; but each colonist hoped to find for *himself* a better position in American society than he had had in England. Although most emigrants left England and other countries because they had not fit in some way, they did not lose contact with Europe. Neither did they proclaim independence from European ideas and customs.

As stressed by those urging colonization the religious motive clearly played a part in the founding of the New England colonies, Maryland, and the Quaker group (New Jersey, Pennsylvania, and Delaware). Most of the colonies had legally established, tax-supported churches—the Puritan (Congregational) Church in New England, and the Anglican (Episcopal) Church in New York and the South. In some colonies there were even religious qualifications for holding office and voting. The power of the Puritan clergy over temporal affairs in the colonial period was discussed in Chapter 9.

THE PURITAN STRAIN

Of all the ideologies contributing to the formation of American democracy, the most difficult to assess is Puritanism. It may be, as Ralph Barton Perry said, "We are still drawing upon the reserves of spiritual vigor which they accumulated." [1] Puritanism may have been responsible for modern capitalism, the Industrial Revolution, the American devotion to constitutionalism, self-reliance, and sobriety. On the other hand, it may have been the *reaction* to Puritanism that had the greater impact on the shaping of American life. [2]

The fact is that the further we are removed in time, the more difficult it is to understand the Puritan mind; but because of its importance, we dare not dismiss Puritanism in the effort to understand and appreciate our heritage. New England Puritans thought of themselves as being led by Divine Providence to a New Canaan where they were to create a new society which would be a model for the whole world: the church incarnate—the City of God. God's Will was revealed in the scriptures where man could find and understand it by means of the infallible dialectic of which the Puritan preachers were masters. An equally infallible technique for making truth known was rhetoric, also a part of Puritan professional skill.

The theological technician in the pulpit, in order to maintain his position as teacher of rulers as well as ruled, had to make his lessons intelligible, relevant, and useful to all. The history of Puritan doctrine is, therefore, the history of the transformations of that doctrine to cope with the unprecedented and constantly changing conditions of life in the New World. The idea of the Covenant of Grace softened the harsh principles of Calvinism; [3] and, in the sphere of social and political relations, this concept bore importance in providing ideological justification for limiting secular authority.

The Puritans were bold reasoners. They could always fall back on revelation, but they felt they had done God a service when they defended truth by their own wit without making use of His word. They made a concerted effort to prove that the moral regulations of an ideal Christian commonwealth should coincide with rational and humane ideas; and in this argument, as in their political theory, they bequeathed an important heritage to eighteenth-century America: that the law of God is, in effect, a specific enactment of the general law of nature, and all civil regulations ought likewise to be derived from universal rules.

The Puritan clergy were under great compulsion to clear God of the charge of arbitrary government. They sought to place the burden of success or failure on men. The doctrine of the Covenant of Grace had to relate intimately to the social history of their time, to the point of view they were defending in the political and economic struggles, and to the alliance of Puritanism and the common law. When these theologians are viewed historically, they seem to have served the cause of their political party more than their creed; and since their party dominated the scene in New England, their theology was of lasting importance to the political and social order.

Puritan theology was essentially part of a widespread tendency in European thought to change social relationships from status to contract. These changes reflected the revolution in society, but not the direction of the revolt. When English Puritans turned to the theory of contract, it was only in part to protect their rights against absolutism. The theory also justified the subordination of individuals to the state, once the ideals of the state had been rightly conceived and the power of enforcement placed in the correct hands. In New England the constitutional aspect of the theory could be subordinated to the religious aspect with its deliberate aims of authoritarianism and intolerance.

Soon after migrating to Massachusetts and Connecticut, the colonists found they not only had fled illegal demands. They also had given their consent to the quest for a form of civil government which they were not to determine themselves but were bound to accept. Differences in position and wealth within the social hierarchy were ordained by God. But these decrees, like His decrees in physics and in conversion, were thoroughly reasonable and just, and accomplished naturally.

The Puritan leaders were pressed to justify their high-handed actions. They had to secure the aims of faith by proving that men had consented rationally to them in a covenant. The tenets of faith were thus shown to be one with reason. They could not foresee how short the time would be until the findings of reason would suffice without faith, until the deductions of logic would provide political wisdom, and politicians no longer would be obliged to heed the requirements of theology.

The vitality of the early theologians in adapting Puritanism to the times faded as their successors in the late seventeenth century failed to supply the spiritual and political needs of an ever-changing community which was already beginning to heed the cry of the Great Awakening. The alliance of Puritanism with political particularism and oligarchy made it unacceptable to men who were becoming economically independent and attracted to the new Enlightenment. Moreover, the growing separation of church and state was exemplified in the Act of Toleration passed by Parliament in 1688. Socially, there was a rising resentment in the colonies on the part of religious dissenters who were not only déclassés but also forced to pay taxes in support of the established churches. Although disestablishment did not come in Massachusetts until after 1800, the Puritan Theocracy finally died with the vacating of the old Massachusetts Bay Charter by the Crown in 1684.

But Puritanism, if dead as a political and religious force, was to linger as a moral spirit: democracy has derived much from the covenant, the congregation, and the town meeting. Alan Simpson sums up the Puritan contribution:

*

Let us return to the Puritan's impact on politics. Among his virtues I would list:

1. *His contribution to our system of limited government.* The original Puritans had a genuine basis for their distrust of arbitrary power in addition to their experience of arbitrary government. They thought that man was too sinful to be trusted with too much power. They were likely to make an exception of the saint, but, once saints were prevented from ruling, they had kept their conviction that nobody else should be trusted. The Puritan tradition, with its everlasting insistence that only God is worthy of worship, is one insurance among Anglo-Saxon people that the state has no claim to worship. Fortunately, there are many other securities, but no one will under-value the stubbornness of this one. They have defended, in season and out of season, the right to preach, to criticize, and to judge. . . .

2. *His contribution to self-government—to the development of initiative and self-reliance in the body of the community.* The Puritan pilgrimage has been a perpetual pilgrimage in self-help. The significance of the dissenting chapel as a training ground for working-class leadership in English history has often been emphasized, and much the same services have been performed by the free church tradition in America. Nor should we forget, in the nineteenth century as in the seventeenth, the direct transfer from church affairs to political affairs of certain techniques of action. The political meeting of the nineteenth century owes an obvious, if not wholly healthy, debt to the camp meeting of the revivalist preacher.

3. *His contribution to education.* The most anti-intellectual Puritan has been obliged to master at least one book—and that a great one. The most intellectual Puritans, in their desire to promote saving knowledge, have thrown up academy after academy, college after college, until their influence has been writ large over the history of education in England and America.

4. *His contribution to morality.* The Puritan code has its repellent fea-tures, but it is no bad thing to have habits of honesty, sobriety, responsibility, and hard work impressed on a community. It seems probable that the acquisitive energy of the nineteenth century would have created far more havoc than it did without the restraining influence of this evangelical spirit.

Finally, there is the contribution which Puritanism within the religous tradition of Anglo-Saxon peoples, has made to "the class peace." Almost the worst thing that can happen to the politics of a modern society is to have them polarized around social classes. Any force which works across these divisions, and either conceals or cements them, has a permanent claim on our gratitude.

As the limitations of Puritanism have been sufficiently stressed in these

* Reprinted from *Puritanism in Old and New England* by *Alan Simpson.* Copyright 1955 by the University of Chicago Press. By permission.

essays, I shall quote only one passage which seems to sum them up. I might have chosen for censure the *cri de coeur* of the nonconformist conscience in nineteenth-century English politics as it appears in the protest of the famous preacher Hugh Price Hughes: "What is morally wrong can never be politically right." Instead, I shall take a passage from an American sermon called "Puritan Principles and the Modern World," which was delivered in 1897:

> Puritanism stands for reality; for character; for clean living as a condition of public service; for recognition of responsibility to God; for the supremacy of the spirit. When Oliver Cromwell entered Parliament in 1653, and said, pointing to one member, "There sits a taker of bribes"; to another, "There sits a man whose religion is a farce"; to another, using the hardest name possible, which I soften, "There sits a man whose personal conduct is impure and foul"; and then in the name of Almighty God broke up the Parliament, he was the impersonation of Puritanism; and for one, I wish he would rise from his grave and in the same spirit enter some of our halls of legislation, both state and national.

That passage, with its conviction that righteousness ought to prevail, with its tendency to make the Puritan's own moral character a test of political fitness, and with its pressure to turn politics, which ought to be the art of reconciliation, into a moral crusade, reminds us of the darkest blot on his political record.

THE CONFLICT BETWEEN DEMOCRACY AND PROPERTY

Very early in American history a schism was created between the owners of property and those without it. The democracy that did exist was reserved for the "elect" of the communion of "saints"—the congregation of the Puritan Church. New members were admitted only by satisfying the elders that they were of the elect. The most satisfactory way to demonstrate election was the possession of worldly goods, a simple test of Grace. Threatened with exclusion from political, social, and religious leadership, indigent colonials moved to the Piedmont and Transmontane interior. There land was plentiful and free, religion more flexible, and social stigma nonexistent. Aside from their displeasure over religious taxation, the dissenters paid little heed to tidewater politics. It was only when the land they had labored over but never owned was either sold to speculators or taxed by legislatures in which they had no representation that the schism between the two factions assumed severe proportions. "The eastern belt of settlement, controlling the assemblies, managed to keep the frontier underrepresented; and by rigging the tax pattern, by forcing the frontiersmen to travel long distances to get justice, and by buying frontier products cheap and selling imported goods dear, the Easterners built up a sectional antagonism that broke out, later, in movements like the Paxton Boys, the Regulators, and Shays's Rebellion. If the government of George III had not diverted America's attention to other things, there might have been a civil war within the colonies instead of a war for independence from Britain." 4

The movement toward separation from England received support from those who stood to gain from independence. Not the least of the early political firebrands were debtors who sought relief or outright repudiation of their obligations to government, merchant, or both. It was only in the late stages of the pre-Revolutionary period that the middle class threw its weight behind the cause. The radicals were rewarded for their perseverance and strength with the weak government of the Articles of Confederation, epitomizing the radical notion, "that government governs best which governs least."

Many creditors were not satisfied with this wisdom and on the state level moved to recapture the quality of government they had known as colonials. By establishing high property qualifications for voting, the conservative Massachusetts Constitution of 1780 vested control of the government once again in the hands of businessmen in the eastern part of the state, rather than in the western farmers. The conservative financial policy of the state legislature, which called for high property taxes to pay off the state war debt at par, favored the owners of securities, who often purchased them at depreciated prices as speculative investments.

Farm prices were low. The western Massachusetts yeoman found it difficult to pay his debts, and foreclosures were common in the early 1780's. The combination of economic and political grievances led to an agrarian protest movement under the leadership of the ex-Revolutionary War officer, Daniel Shays. The basic demands of the eighteenth-century farmers contained elements that have been common in American history: reform of the tax system, scaling down of the public debt, liberalization of the state constitution, and the issuance of paper money to boost prices and make it easier to pay debts. A radical minority advocated the breakup of large landed estates to be sold to small farmers, and the proceeds used to reduce the public debt. The protests culminated in 1786 in open rebellion against the authority of the state. Western farmers, turning on the courts, forcibly prevented foreclosures by intimidating court officers. Shays's insurrectionary band was quickly suppressed, but by the Massachusetts militia, financed by contributions from Boston merchants.

To conservatives everywhere, the inability of the Confederation government to deal with an uprising such as this was a threat to their

security and to peace and tranquility. To farmers and other Americans of
radical view, on the other hand, the rebellion was a good omen. Jefferson, in Paris, was still convinced of the rightness of the Lockean principle of the right of the people to revolt when they found conditions
oppressive. "The tree of liberty," he argued, must be periodically
"watered with the blood of tyrants and patriots." The conservative sentiment that resulted in the Constitution of 1789 is summed up in the following address by a Brown University senior in 1786.

*
  It is allowed by all good Politicians that no form of government was ever
better calculated to preserve the rights of mankind and make the subjects
happy than that of Great Britain.
  It joins the two extreams of Monarchy and Democracy and forms that
Glorious ballance of Power which checks Usurpation and Tyranny in the
throne and equally checks the Power in the hands of the people: which
when left without restraint: like a Conflagration consumes the body from
whence it originates.
  As for the right of Taxation Claimed by the British Parliament even admitting of it to take place with all force yet when Great Britain should have
found by experience how much it impeded the Growth and population of
these Colonies, and of Consequence injured the Interest and happiness of
the whole nation it is unreasonable to think 'tis folly to suppose that this
pretended right would have been long in force.
  It has been found by experience; it appears evident from the nature of
governments that Republics can never flourish or answer the end of Society;
but only in Countries of Small extent—
  This vast Continent is too widely extended to form a Republican government;
  It is too unwieldly and unconnected to form a strict Union of Consequence its political Countenance must be weak and sickly Buisiness can
never be transacted with despatch, or in Season; and it is next to impossible
to accomplish and matters relating to the whole Secrecy and expedition so
necessary in war are impractible. The Enemy will know our designs before we
can carry them into execution; and while we are making the necessary
preparation, it will either anticipate the blow or be prepaired for the attack.
We have heard much said in favour of the Glorious Liberty we have obtained by independence.
  But let us stop a moment and count the Cost of this boasted aquisition—

* Robert E. Moody, ed., "Oratorical Afterthoughts on American Independence,"
New England Quarterly, VIII (September 1935), pp. 415–417, as quoted in Ray
Allen Billington, et al., eds. *The Making of American Democracy* (Vol. I) New
York: Holt, Rinehart and Winston, 1962.

England before the American Revolution stood in the same Relationship to us as a Parent does to his child.

She was honourable amoung the nations; and like the Lionness in the forest her voice protected her young where ever it went.

Her Arm she extended over these Colonies and when our savage enemies invaded us She sent her veteran troops Commanded by some of the greatest Generals Europe ever boasted; who United with Americas Sons drove our enemies from our borders; and with their blood: bought us the victory! These were the most flourishing most happy days America ever saw.

But that fatal hour in which the Sword of Civil war was drawn: this pleasing Scene was changed—Consternation and distress sat on every Countenance; Fifty thousand souls fell victims to this Cruel war. Our Towns and lands were laid waste.

Our Fathers, Brothers, and Children in thousands fell around us; and our Breavest youth in the gay morn of Life armed at the rising hopes and pleasing prospects of future Glory were Cut off by untimely Death. Where ere we turned our Eyes we saw the breathless Corse; The Din of war Lamentation and sorrow Continually sounded in our Ears: and the virgin Distress echoed in the evning gales. To these we must now subjoin the flood of Luxury and vice introduced by this unnatural war: vices which have Corrupted our former honest simple manners, and will soon fix us down in abject Slavery; and ripen us for heavens severest Judgment. Add to these immence debt foreign and domestic; into which thus we are plunged; The Interest of which thus early in the morn of Independency is (*blank*) per Annum. Here then is a Sacrifice of Life Virtue and property; to gain what? An imaginary Liberty! Are we more free than we use ot be? We enjoyed formerly all the Liberty Consistent with good government. What has since been aded is but Licentiousness.

Let us next view our present Situation of affairs. From a stagnation of business during the war we have run into an excess of Trade and thereby (strip) ourselves of nearly all our Circulating medium.—

America is in debts for millions more than She has money to pay; while her Commerce (which is almost the only way of surplying a Country situated like ours, with money and is the strongest bond of Union between Nations) is decreased in proportion to the scarcity of money.

Thus we are without money, Trade, and parmenent Alliances—Our repeated Attempts to surply the Defficiency of money by a paper Currency have destroyed our national Faith at home and abroad: and ruined thousands of our worthy Citizens—

The large extent of each State together with their Different manners and Customs fills them with Jealousies and animosities towards each other and prevent their vesting Congress as a head with that Power which is absolutely necessary in all governments But little regarde is paid to our Laws:

Our public pentioners are more numerous now than ever they were under the British Administration.

Our agriculture and manufactures are neglected while we revel in all the Luxuries of foreign Countries.

THE CONSTITUTION AND THE IDEOLOGY OF MATERIALISM

There have been two great "single cause" theories of American history. Both attracted schools around them immediately and aroused scholarly hostility. One is the economic determinism of Charles A. Beard, in collateral descent with Marxism; the other is Frederick Jackson Turner's frontier thesis, which will be discussed presently.

Somewhat iconoclastic, Beard's *An Economic Interpretation of the Constitution*, though not creating a revolution in historiography, does stand as a milestone in the writing and teaching of American history and cannot be ignored. From an analysis of the interests of the Founding Fathers, Beard drew the following conclusions:

*
The movement for the Constitution of the United States was originated and carried through principally by four groups of personalty interests which had been adversely affected under the Articles of Confederation: money, public securities, manufactures, and trade and shipping.

The first firm steps toward the formation of the Constitution were taken by a small and active group of men immediately interested through their personal possessions in the outcome of their labors.

No popular vote was taken directly or indirectly on the proposition to call the Convention which drafted the Constitution.

A large propertyless mass was, under the prevailing suffrage qualifications, excluded at the outset from participation (through representatives) in the work of framing the Constitution.

The members of the Philadelphia Convention which drafted the Constitution were, with a few exceptions, immediately, directly, and personally interested in, and derived economic advantages from, the establishment of the new system.

The Constitution was essentially an economic document based upon the concept that the fundamental private rights of property are anterior to government and morally beyond the reach of popular majorities.

The major portion of the members of the Convention are on record as recognizing the claim of property to a special and defensive position in the Constitution.

* Reprinted from *An Economic Interpretation of the Constitution*, pp. 324–325, by Charles A. Beard. Copyright 1913 by The Macmillan Company, renewed 1941 by Charles A. Beard. By permission.

In the ratification of the Constitution, about three-fourths of the adult males failed to vote on the question, having abstained from the elections at which delegates to the state conventions were chosen, either on account of their indifference or their disfranchisement by property qualifications.

The Constitution was ratified by a vote of probably not more than one-sixth of the adult males.

It is questionable whether a majority of the voters participating in the elections for the state conventions in New York, Massachusetts, New Hampshire, Virginia, and South Carolina, actually approved the ratification of the Constitution.

The leaders who supported the Constitution in the ratifying conventions represented the same economic groups as the members of the Philadelphia Convention; and in a large number of instances they were also directly and personally interested in the outcome of their efforts.

In the ratification, it became manifest that the line of cleavage for and against the Constitution was between substantial personalty interests on the one hand and the small farming and debtor interests on the other.

The Constitution was not created by "the whole people" as the jurists have said; neither was it created by "the states" as Southern nullifiers long contended; but it was the work of a consolidated group whose interests knew no state boundaries and were truly national in their scope.

Written in 1913, *An Economic Interpretation of the Constitution* is still drawing fire from critics. One recent counter to Beard made the following point-by-point rejoinder.

*
Perhaps we can never be completely objective in history, but certainly we can be more objective than Beard was in this book. Naturally the historian must always be aware of the biases, the subjectivity, the pitfalls that confront him, but this does not mean that he should not make an effort to overcome these obstacles. Whether Beard had his thesis before he had his evidence, as some have said, is a question that each reader must answer for himself. Certain it is that the evidence does not justify the thesis.

So instead of the Beard interpretation that the Constitution was put over undemocratically in an undemocratic society by personal property, the following fourteen paragraphs are offered as a possible interpretation of the Constitution and as suggestions for future research on that document.

1. The movement for the Constitution was originated and carried through by men who had long been important in both economic and political affairs in their respective states. Some of them owned personalty, more of them owned realty, and if their property was adversely affected by conditions under

---

* Reprinted from *Charles Beard and the Constitution*, pp. 195–200, by Robert E. Brown. Copyright 1956, Princeton University Press. By permission.

the Articles of Confederation, so also was the property of the bulk of the people in the country, middle-class farmers as well as town artisans.

2. The movement for the Constitution, like most important movements, was undoubtedly started by a small group of men. They were probably interested personally in the outcome of their labors, but the benefits which they expected were not confined to personal property or, for that matter, strictly to things economic. And if their own interests would be enhanced by a new government, similar interests of other men, whether argicultural or commercial, would also be enhanced.

3. Naturally there was no popular vote on the calling of the convention which drafted the Constitution. Election of delegates by state legislatures was the constitutional method under the Articles of Confederation, and had been the method long established in this country. Delegates to the Albany Congress, the Stamp Act Congress, the First Continental Congress, the Second Continental Congress, and subsequent congresses under the Articles were all elected by state legislatures, not by the people. Even the Articles of Confederation had been sanctioned by state legislatures, not by popular vote. This is not to say that the Constitutional Convention should not have been elected directly by the people, but only that such a procedure would have been unusual at the time. Some of the opponents of the Constitution later stressed, without avail, the fact that the Convention had not been directly elected. But at the time the Convention met, the people in general seemed to be about as much concerned over the fact that they had not elected the delegates as the people of this country are now concerned over the fact that they do not elect our delegates to the United Nations.

4. Present evidence seems to indicate that there were no "propertyless masses" who were excluded from the suffrage at the time. Most men were middle-class farmers who owned realty and were qualified voters, and, as the men in the Convention said, mechanics had always voted in the cities. Until credible evidence proves otherwise, we can assume that state legislatures were fairly representative at the time. We cannot condone the fact that a few men were probably disfranchised by prevailing property qualifications, but it makes a great deal of difference to an interpretation of the Constitution whether the disfranchised comprised ninety-five per cent of the adult men or only five per cent. Figures which give percentages of voters in terms of the entire population are misleading, since less than twenty per cent of the people were adult men. And finally, the voting qualifications favored realty, not personalty.

5. If the members of the Convention were directly interested in the outcome of their work and expected to derive benefits from the establishment of the new system, so also did most of the people of the country. We have many statements to the effect that the people in general expected substantial benefits from the labors of the Convention.

6. The Constitution was not just an economic document, although economic factors were undoubtedly important. Since most of the people were middle-class and had private property, practically everybody was interested in the protection of property. A constitution which did not protect property would have been rejected without any question, for the American people had fought the Revolution for the preservation of life, liberty, and property. Many people believed that the Constitution did not go far enough to protect property, and they wrote these views into the amendments to the Constitution. But property was not the only concern of those who wrote and ratified the Constitution, and we would be doing a grave injustice to the political sagacity of the Founding Fathers if we assumed that property or personal gain was their only motive.

7. Naturally the delegates recognized that the protection of property was important under government, but they also recognized that personal rights were equally important. In fact, persons and property were usually bracketed together as the chief objects of government protection.

8. If three-fourths of the adult males failed to vote on the election of delegates to ratifying conventions, this fact signified indifference, not disfranchisement. We must not confuse those who could *not* vote with those who *could* vote but failed to exercise their right. Many men at the time bewailed the fact that only a small portion of the voters ever exercised their prerogative. But this in itself should stand as evidence that the conflict over the Constitution was not very bitter, for if these people had felt strongly one way or the other, more of them would have voted.

Even if we deny the evidence which I have presented and insist that American society was undemocratic in 1787, we must still accept the fact that the men who wrote the Constitution believed that they were writing it for a democratic society. They did not hide behind an iron curtain of secrecy and devise the kind of conservative government that they wanted without regard to the views and interests of "the people." More than anything else, they were aware that "the people" would have to ratify what they proposed, and that therefore any government which would be acceptable to the people must of necessity incorporate much of what was customary at the time. The men at Philadelphia were practical politicians, not political theorists. They recognized the multitude of different ideas and interests that had to be reconciled and compromised before a constitution would be acceptable. They were far too practical, and represented far too many clashing interests themselves, to fashion a government weighted in favor of personalty or to believe that the people would adopt such a government.

9. If the Constitution was ratified by a vote of only one-sixth of the adult men, that again demonstrates indifference and not disfranchisement. Of the one-fourth of the adult males who voted, nearly two-thirds favored the Constitution. Present evidence does not permit us to say what the popular vote

was except as it was measured by the votes of the ratifying conventions.

10. Until we know what the popular vote was, we cannot say that it is questionable whether a majority of the voters in several states favored the Constitution. Too many delegates were sent uninstructed. Neither can we count the towns which did not send delegates on the side of those opposed to the Constitution. Both items would signify indifference rather than sharp conflict over ratification.

11. The ratifying conventions were elected for the specific purpose of adopting or rejecting the Constitution. The people in general had anywhere from several weeks to several months to decide the question. If they did not like the new government, or if they did not know whether they liked it, they could have voted no and there would have been no Constitution. Naturally the leaders in the ratifying conventions represented the same interests as the members of the Constitutional Convention—mainly realty and some personalty. But they also represented their constituents in these same interests, especially realty.

12. If the conflict over ratification had been between substantial personalty interests on the one hand and small farmers and debtors on the other, there would not have been a constitution. The small farmers comprised such an overwhelming percentage of the voters that they could have rejected the new government without any trouble. Farmers and debtors are not synonymous terms and should not be confused as such. A town-by-town or county-by-county record of the vote would show clearly how the farmers voted.

13. The Constitution was created about as much by the whole people as any government could be which embraced a large area and depended on representation rather than on direct participation. It was also created in part by the states, for as the Records show, there was strong state sentiment at the time which had to be appeased by compromise. And it was created by compromising a whole host of interests throughout the country, without which compromises it could never have been adopted.

14. If the intellectual historians are correct, we cannot explain the Constitution without considering the psychological factors also. Men are motivated by what they believe as well as by what they have. Sometimes their actions can be explained on the basis of what they hope to have or hope that their children will have. Madison understood this fact when he said that the universal hope of acquiring property tended to dispose people to look favorably upon property. It is even possible that some men support a given economic system when they themselves have nothing to gain by it. So we would want to know what the people in 1787 thought of their class status. Did workers and small farmers believe that they were lower-class, or did they, as many workers do now, consider themselves middle-class? Were the common people trying to eliminate the Washingtons, Adamses, Hamiltons, and Pinckneys, or were they trying to join them?

As did Beard's fourteen conclusions, these fourteen suggestions really add up to two major propositions: the Constitution was adopted in a society which was fundamentally democratic, not undemocratic; and it was adopted by a people who were primarily middle-class property owners, especially farmers who owned realty, not just by the owners of personalty. At present these points seem to be justified by the evidence, but if better evidence in the future disproves or modifies them, we must accept that evidence and change our interpretation accordingly.

After this critical analysis, we should at least not begin future research on this period of American history with the illusion that the Beard thesis of the Constitution is valid. If historians insist on accepting the Beard thesis in spite of this analysis, however, they must do so with the full knowledge that their acceptance is founded on "an act of faith," not an analysis of historical method, and that they are indulging in a "noble dream," not history.

Sometime after he had written the *Economic Interpretation*, Beard attempted to justify and qualify his position.

*

. . . . It has been lightly assumed by superficial critics, if not readers of the volume, that I have "accused the members of the Convention of working merely for their own pockets." The falsity of this charge can be seen by reference to page 73 of the original text still standing. There I say clearly: "The only point considered here is: Did they (the members) represent distinct groups whose economic interests they understood and felt in concrete, definite form through their own personal experience with identical property rights, or were they working merely under the guidance of abstract principles of political science?"

It has also been lightly assumed that this volume pretends to show that the form of government established and powers conferred were "determined" in every detail by the conflict of economic interests. Such pretension was never in my mind; nor do I think that it is explicit or implicit in the pages which follow. I have never been able to discover all-pervading determinism in history. . . .

Nevertheless, whoever leaves economic pressures out of history or out of the discussion of public questions is in mortal peril of substituting mythology for reality and confusing issues instead of clarifying them. It was largely by recognizing the power of economic interests in the field of politics and making skillful use of them that the Fathers of the American Constitution placed themselves among the great practicing statesmen of all ages and gave instructions to succeeding generations in the art of government. By the

* Reprinted with permission of the publishers from *An Economic Interpretation of the Constitution*, pp. xxi–xvii, by Charles A. Beard. Copyright 1913 by The Macmillan Company, renewed 1941 by Charles A. Beard.

assiduous study of their works and by displaying their courage and their insight into the economic interests underlying all constitutional formalities, men and women of our generation may guarantee the perpetuity of government under law, as distinguished from the arbitrament of force. It is for us, recipients of their heritage, to inquire constantly and persistently, when theories of national power or states' rights are propounded: "What interests are behind them and to whose advantage will changes or the maintenance of old forms accrue?" By refusing to do this we become victims of history—clay in the hands of its makers.

THE COMMON MAN AND THE IDEOLOGY OF IDEALISM

If the material bias of economic determinism is distasteful, another powerful strain running through American history is the romantic notion of rugged individualism, forged into democracy by the moving frontier. This paragraph in the report of the Superintendent of the Census of 1890 caused Frederick Jackson Turner to formulate a new theory for the shaping of the American character:

Up to and including 1880 the country had a frontier of settlement, but at the present the unsettled area has been so broken into by isolated bodies of settlement that there can hardly be said to be a frontier line. In the discussion of its extent, its westward movement, etc., it can not, therefore, any longer have a place in the census reports.[5]

For three centuries Americans had always been able to look westward to virgin land. "Go West" was a safety valve for the fast growing country. But the passing of the free land and the cessation of an imaginary idea of opportunity in the West helped to build a realistic civilization on the ashes of a romantic one.

Richard Hofstadter sums up the Turner thesis in the following article, which has as its main purpose the synthesizing of the more important arguments and findings of Turner's critics.

*

Turner wrote his memorable essay, "The Significance of the Frontier in American History," during that period of growing tension between the Eastern and Western United States which culminated in the Bryan campaign of 1896. An expression of rising Western self-consciousness, Turner's thesis was meant to challenge the dominant academic school of Eastern historians then led by his former teacher, Herbert Baxter Adams. The members of this school concerned themselves chiefly with the development of American

* Reprinted from Richard Hofstadter, "Turner and the Frontier Myth," *The American Scholar*, Vol. 18, No. 4, Autumn 1949, pp. 433–443. Copyright 1949 by The United Chapters of Phi Beta Kappa. By permission of the publishers.

political institutions. Their controlling assumption was that American democracy and local self-government had come, by way of England, from remote Anglo-Saxon political institutions like the Witanagemot, which could be traced back to the forests of Germany. Under the sway of Darwinian evolutionism, they followed the genetic method with the passion of zealots and doctrinaires; they attributed to political institutions a kind of self-contained and self-determining cycle of growth comparable to that of a living organism.

Like the Easterners, Turner was an evolutionist concerned primarily with political forms. But in contrast to the Adams school, with its reliance upon racial heredity and self-determined growth, Turner looked for the influence of environment. In his opinion, the Adams school was paying far too much attention to the European "germs" of American institutions, and far too little to the American soil in which these "germs" had grown. It was not the self-unfolding of important institutions, but rather the events that took place on native grounds, that decided the course of American development. The unique and distinguishing elements of American history could be found on the American scene in the shape of the frontier and free land. "The existence of an area of free land, its continuous recession, and the advance of American settlement westward explain American development."

American evolution, Turner believed, had been a repeated return to primitive conditions on a continually receding frontier line, a constant repetition of development from simple conditions to a complex society. From this perennial rebirth and fluidity of American life, and from its continual re-exposure to the simplicity of primitive society, had come the forces dominant in the American character. And as the frontier advanced, society moved steadily away from European influences, grew steadily on distinctive American lines. To study this advance and the men who had been fashioned by it was "to study the really American part of our history. . . ."

But the strength of Turner's thesis, which had an influence extending far beyond the historical profession, rested upon the appeal of the frontier to the American imagination. Some of its initial impetus no doubt came from the Western agrarian revolt of the nineties; before long, however, it lost its vague Populist edge and became identified with a complacent nationalist romanticism, as congenial to the Eastern mind as to the Western. The notion of an aggressive pioneering national spirit nurtured by repeated exposure to primitive conditions became a means to national self-glorification. Appealing to the common desire to root native history in native soil, the Turner thesis sanctioned the tendency to shrink from comparative reference to the experience of other peoples. It also satisfied the desire, common in the age of Progressivism and muckraking, to have a "materialist" interpretation of history that did not risk the ideological pitfalls of the class struggle idea. Happily it was vague enough to be used in different, often opposite ways. Conservatives could point to the value of the hardihood and rugged individualism allegedly derived from the frontier heritage. Those who wanted to justify a "progressive" departure could answer that the frontier period, after all, *was* over. As late as 1932, in his memorable Commonwealth Club address, Franklin D. Roosevelt utilized the Turnerían inheritance as the historical rationale of the New Deal: "Our last frontier has long since been reached, and there is practically no more free land. . . . There is no safety valve in the form of a Western prairie to which those thrown out of work by the Eastern machines can go for a new start. . . ."

The initial plausibility of the Turner thesis lies in the patent fact that no nation could spend more than a century developing an immense continental empire without being deeply affected by it. Few critics question the great importance of the inland empire, or that Turner originally performed a service for historical writing by directing attention to it. Many accept Turner's emphasis on the frontier as one of several valid but limited perspectives on American history. But it has been forcefully denied that the frontier deserves any special pre-eminence among several major factors in "explaining" American development. The question has also been raised (and frequently answered in the negative) whether Turner analyzed the frontier process itself clearly or correctly. . . .

As a form of geographical determinism, the frontier interpretation is vulnerable on still another ground. If the frontier alone was a self-sufficient source of democracy and individualism, whatever the institutions and ideas the frontiersmen brought with them, frontiers elsewhere ought to have had a similar effect. The early frontier of seignorial French Canada, the South American frontier, and the Siberian frontier should have fostered democracy and individualism. The frontier should have forged the same kind of democracy when planters came to Mississippi as when yeomen farmers came to Illinois. Turner's dictum, "American democracy came out of the American forest," proved to be a questionable improvement upon the notion of his predecessors that it came out of the German forest. Plainly the whole complex of institutions, habits and ideas that men brought to the frontier was left out of his formula, and it was these things, not bare geography, that had been decisive. Turner's analysis, as George Warren Pierson aptly put it, hung too much on real estate, not enough on a state of mind. . . .

Both great periods of the upsurge of democracy in nineteenth-century America, the Jeffersonian and the Jacksonian, are far more intelligible in terms of social classes than of the East or the West, if only because both had so much strength in Eastern and urban areas. Jeffersonianism, which was strong among seaboard slaveholders and in many of the towns, is somewhat more comprehensible as a movement of agrarians against capitalists, than as a movement of the frontier against the East. The age of Jackson has been held up more than any other as an example of the democratic spirit of the frontier in action. Yet Arthur M. Schlesinger, Jr.'s recent study of that era does not employ the frontier thesis, and it is highly successful in asserting the crucial role of Eastern Jacksonians. With the exception of a few scattered local areas, many of which were in the West, Jackson swept the country when he was elected in 1828, and Jacksonian democracy can best be understood as a nationwide movement, supported by parts of the planting, farming, laboring, and entrepreneurial classes.

It may be conceded to the Turnerians that the West occasionally gave democratic ideas an especially favorable area for operation—but it should be conceded in return that these ideas were generated in the Eastern United States and in Western civilization as a whole. By and large, Western settlers appear to have been more imitative than original in their political institutions. The case for the West as a special source of individualism is similarly mixed. It is possible to point to a fairly strong stream of Western demands for governmental interferences of one kind or another from the days of internal improvements to the age of railroad regulation, parity, and price supports.

One of the most criticized aspects of Turner's conception of American history, the so-called safety-valve thesis, maintains that the availability of free land as a refuge for the oppressed and discontented has alleviated American social conflicts, minimized industrial strife, and contributed to the backwardness of the American labor movement. As Turner expressed it, the American worker was never compelled to accept inferior wages because he could "with a slight effort" reach free country and set up in farming. "Whenever social conditions tended to crystallize in the East, whenever capital tended to impede the freedom of the mass, there was this gate of escape to the free conditions of the frontier," where "free lands promoted individualism, economic equality, freedom to rise, democracy."

The expression "free land" is itself misleading. Land was relatively cheap in the United States during the nineteenth century, but the difference between free land and cheap land was crucial. Up to 1820 the basic price of land was $2.00 an acre, and for years afterward it was $1.25. Slight as it may seem, this represented a large sum to the Eastern worker, whose wage was generally about $1.00 a day. Economic historians have estimated that during the 1850's, $1000 represented a fairly typical cost for setting up a farm on virgin prairie land, or buying an established one; and the cost of transporting a worker's family from, say, Massachusetts or New York to Illinois or Iowa was a serious additional burden. Farming, moreover, is no enterprise for an amateur, nor one at which he has a good chance of success. The value of "free land" in alleviating distress has been challenged by several writers who have pointed out that periods of depression were the very periods when it was most difficult for the Eastern worker to move. Scattered instances of working-class migration to the West can be pointed to, but detailed studies of the origins of migrants have failed to substantiate the Turner thesis. . . .

In spite of these criticisms, something has been salvaged from the safety-valve thesis. Although the West was not filled up by workers moving in time of depression, the evidence indicates that it was filled up by farmers moving in times of prosperity. In this way the presence of available land is generally conceded to have played an important part in relieving *rural* discontent— the dominant form of discontent in nineteenth-century America. And it presumably had a roundabout effect on the urban situation. In Europe the city was the characteristic haven of the surplus farm population. Insofar as the comparable surplus population of the United States took another choice —migration further West—instead of swelling the ranks of the urban working class, there may have been an indirect operation of the safety valve. Its magnitude and importance are uncertain.

But the safety valve principle also operated in reverse, and it is a signal weakness of the Turner version that it concentrates attention on much the less significant of two population movements. The dominant tide of migration from 1860 to 1900 was not from East to West, but from the farm to the city. In forty years the farm population grew by about nine million, while the nonfarm population grew by almost thirty-six million. It was the cities that received not only the bulk of the immigration from abroad, but also the bulk of the surplus farm population. This flow of the farm surplus to the cities may have been intermittent, broken and partially reversed during depression periods, but its net size is undeniable. Fred A. Shannon has estimated that "at least twenty farmers moved to town for each industrial laborer who moved to the land, and ten sons of farmers went to the city for each one who became the owner of a new farm anywhere in the nation." It is possible that the acuteness of the agrarian unrest of the 1890's can be traced in some part to the fact that the pace of city growth had slackened off, and that this safety valve for the farmers was beginning to fail. At any rate, to follow the Turnerian emphasis upon "free land" as a primary outlet, and to ignore the migration to the cities, is to perpetuate a major distortion of American history.

Finally, Turner acknowledged but failed to see the full importance for his thesis of the fact that the United States not only had a frontier but was a frontier—a major outlet for the countries of Western Europe during the nineteenth century. From 1820 to 1929, the total European emigration to the United States was more than 37,500,000—a number only a million short of the entire population of the United States in 1870. In one decade alone, 1901–1910, 8,795,000 people came from Europe. If Europe shared to such a major extent in this safety-valve economy, its uniqueness for American development must be considerably modified. The mingling of peoples that took place in the United States must be placed alongside the presence of "free land" in explaining American development; the closure of the American gates after the First World War becomes an historical event of broader significance than the disappearance of the frontier line in 1890. And the facts of immigration probably provide a better key to the character of the American labor movement than any speculation about the effects of "free land" upon workers who could not reach it.

But Turner's ideas are far from extinct. In the ten years following Hofstadter's summation, a research team headed by Merle Curti of the University of Wisconsin visited a one-time frontier community to "try to apply objective tests to the Turner thesis about democracy, and to use these methods as well as traditional ones in a study at the grass roots of the frontier history of a Wisconsin county." [6] The following is an excerpt from Professor Curti's "conclusion."

*
It is important in considering the meaning of our findings to keep two things clearly in mind. First, we have not tried to test *the Turner thesis*, but rather our interpretation of Turner's theory that the ready accessibility of free or almost free land promoted economic equality and that this was followed by political equality. Second, we have not claimed that Trempealeau County was a typical frontier. There were, as Turner insisted, many kinds of frontiers, and frontier experiences were complex and varied. . . .

We are thus brought back finally, in interpreting our data on economic standing and economic change in the farm population, to our theory that the kind and amount of change and advance we found in early Trempealeau would be likely to occur only under conditions offering very unusual stimulus and opportunity. We do not think, nor as a matter of fact did Turner think, that only a Western frontier could provide such conditions. We suggested in our chapter on the fortunes of new farmers that similar conditions might also be found in an area undergoing very rapid democratic industrialization or in one where a depression was followed by a period of full employment and the release of new energies and talents among the people. In our county, however, that stimulus and that opportunity were largely provided, we believe, by frontier conditions.

It is difficult to say just how frontier experiences modified personalities that had been in greater or lesser degree shaped by the cultures of older parts of the United States and of the Old World. Young children who lived their formative years in the county during the frontier period might be expected to have developed personalities reflecting both the culture of parents

* Reprinted from *The Making of an American Community*, pp. 442, 446–448, by Merle Curti with the permission of the publishers, Stanford University Press. © 1959 by the Board of Trustees of the Leland Stanford Junior University.

and the actualities of the making of new communities. We cannot speak on this matter with benefit of quantitative findings, interviews, or projective tests, but we can still safely make certain points. The detailed and voluminous diaries of Alex Arnold, who came to Galesville as a youth, show that in his case the problem incidental to living in a new community sharpened certain traits and developed certain potentialities.

We can also report that the biographical and autobiographical material assembled by Judge Anderson, an immigrant who in his later years interviewed scores of still-living pioneers, gives some support to a thesis frequently presented in his newspaper by Samuel Luce. Editor Luce was not only an informed and sensitive spokesman for Trempealeau County, but he had wide and intimate knowledge of its people. With Judge Anderson, Luce believed that frontier experiences brought out or accentuated certain traits or potentialities in men, women, and children whose personalities obviously owed much to older cultures. These men again and again noted, and often gave specific examples to back up their observation, that frontier experiences in Trempealeau promoted self-confidence, optimism, resourcefulness, perseverance, a quickening of "mental faculties," and, especially, neighborly cooperation, as well as individual initiative and sense of responsibility. We also may assume that this belief itself, frequently expressed in the newspapers, at old settlers' reunions, and on other ceremonial occasions, in some measure influenced behavior. For the belief must have tended to set up certain expectations of behavior in personal and social situations and tended to strengthen certain motives—notably those now referred to by some social scientists as affiliation and achievement motives.

While interrelationships between cultural heritage, frontier experience, and personality and values cannot be measured exactly, we can be assured of the great importance of the governmental blueprints that were at hand from the first. These blueprints provided rules and regulations for establishing representative county government, for making new towns as population increased, and for widespread male participation in decision-making at the town-meeting level. State government also provided judicial arrangements for handling personal and cultural conflicts. All of these imported institutions provided a frame within which democracy was to be tested.

These institutions were subject to special strains inherent in the situations characteristic of the frontier experience in Trempealeau. One of the most important sources of strain was the dynamic nature of the population and of its distribution. The rapid development of the central and northern parts of the county raised the question of the relative roles in important decisions affecting the whole county of the newer northern majority and the older southern towns wishing to prolong their initial possession of the county seat. In somewhat the same way, the make-up of the Republican conventions was constantly being contested: at one time the smaller towns were overrepresented, at other times underrepresented. But out of sustained public discussion, voting and voting again, decisions were made, and remade, in accordance with the democratic principle of majority rule and consideration of minority interests.

A word here needs to be said about the demonstrated capacity of the Norwegian Americans, who formed the great majority in the new town of Pigeon, to come quickly and efficiently to terms with the democratic apparatus of the town meeting imported from New England to this frontier.

In one important respect the situation inherent in the Trempealeau frontier experience retarded for a time, at least in certain ways, the realization of the ideal of educational equality of opportunity: the children of American and British stock on the whole enjoyed greater opportunity than others to obtain such knowledge and skills as the public schools offered. With the development of better roads, the establishment of teachers' institutes, greater tax assets, and general acculturation, the disparity of the more pronounced frontier period lessened.

Believing that democracy means, among other things, multiple leadership, we asked what impact the frontier situations had on opportunity for leadership. It was clear that experience in leadership in older communities, amount of property on hand when migration to the county took place, and personal qualities all played an important part in leadership. But it is apparent that situations characteristic of the frontier also played a role. In the period before 1860 it was somewhat easier for young men to establish positions of leadership, in relation to the total population, than in the 1860's and especially in the 1870's. At all times, economic status counted; but the point to be made here is that, as our quantitative evidence shows, all sectors of the gainfully employed population were improving their status, both in the flourishing 1860's and even on the whole during the hard times of the 1870's, and all sectors furnished leaders. Further, while in the early period those born in non-English-speaking countries did not attain positions of leadership in proportion to the place their compatriots held in the total population, in the 1870's this situation was changing.

In sum, our study, both in its quantitative and qualitative aspects, lends support to what we believe are the main implications of Turner's thesis about the frontier and democracy, so far as Trempealeau County is concerned. It is indeed true that several important qualifications must be made—that for instance by some tests there was more democracy, as we defined it, in the 1870's than in the 1850's and early 1860's. But such qualifications are balanced by our findings which indicate that Turner's poetical vision of free land and of relatively equal opportunity was for a great many people being realized in Trempealeau County. The story of the making of this American community is a story of progress toward democracy.

THE PRAGMATIC RECONCILIATION

From Horace Greeley's dictum "go West" to novels, movies, and television, the appeal of the old West would indicate a broad basis for the popularity enjoyed by the Turner school. Turner's emphasis on individualism *and* democracy is the more appealing of the alternatives between the materialism of Beard and the idealism of Turner. Yet there can be no doubt that the mundane matter of acquisitiveness has been an important force in our development. Both theses are interesting and do much to explain that elusive abstraction known as the American Spirit. However, both contain the basic limitation of any attempt to reduce a complex truth to a simplified falsehood.

One is romantic and the other is cynically realistic. Each has its clarifying value, and neither can be completely set aside as an explanation for the course of American civilization. Actually the two theories can be reconciled readily if it is accepted that they really are the dominating motives of American life. If true, the tensions generated by these two forces could account for the vitality of America.

The reconciliation, if any, has come through William James's *pragmatism*,[7] the peculiarly American philosophy which says reality is that which works for us, and truth is that which we want to believe. Faced with the practical fact of declining membership, the Puritans *created* the Covenant of Grace; and when that proved insufficient they created the Half-Way Covenant.[8] The "ideals" of Calvinism were compromised for "practical" reasons. The Founding Fathers, in an effort to gain broad acceptance for the Constitution, employed the label "federal" to allay the fears of the bulk of Americans about strong central government—another compromise with principle. Pragmatism was in the air: American conquerors of the wilderness judged program and action by consequences.

Pragmatism evolved in response to Social Darwinism during the Age of Reform, the period of Populism, the Muckrakers, and Progressivism. It simply gave intellectual respectability to an approach as old as humanity itself, an approach which appears wherever formative civilizations have material problems to overcome. A philosophy of action with little credence in absolutism—except human dignity and freedom—pragmatism fitted well with the dualism of American life. Torn between the ideal and the material, pragmatism refuses to choose. Operating through compromise, it seeks to preserve as much as possible of the ideal while attaining the practical ends of society.

Compromise as a concept is unpalatable to many people, even when they share its fruits. Compromise is frequently mistaken for *anomie*. Although American political and economic progress and stability have come largely as a result of reconciling opposing forces, some individuals yearn for an immutable truth. The unyielding truth seeker has often been a potent force in America, sometimes for progress, sometimes for reaction, sometimes for both; the abolitionist was a case point. In Chapter 22 the right wing in America will be examined.

The American genius has listened alternately to two voices: the spiritual and the opportune. During some periods of our history one has sounded more loudly than the other, but at no period has the voice of either been completely silent. Our destiny has been shaped by these twin concepts. Throughout our rise to power and greatness there has been present the uneasy combination of spiritual conviction and material opportunism.

Man cannot live by bread alone—nor by moral abstractions. In the United States, a steady balance of both has been maintained.

Notes

1. Ralph Barton Perry, *Puritanism and Democracy*, New York: The Vanguard Press, 1944, p. 268.
2. Thomas Jefferson Wertenbaker, *The Puritan Oligarchy*, New York: Charles Scribner's Sons, 1947.
3. "The God of John Calvin was both absolute and arbitrary. After Adam's fall the human race was destined to eternal damnation, but through the merits and intercession of Christ, God consented to save a certain predetermined number from hell. He selected these by methods known only to Himself, with complete arbitrariness so far as men might discern. But the God of New England, though absolute, was not arbitrary. So far as His dealings with men were concerned, He had voluntarily placed Himself under a code: the Covenant of Grace. This, as interpreted by our theologians, meant that God's redeeming Grace was bestowed on any person who sincerely and completely believed in God, and surrendered himself to God. Such a one, no matter how grievously he had sinned, could join the Covenant, and lay hold on Grace." Samuel Eliot Morison, *The Intellectual Life of Colonial New England*, New York: New York University Press, 1956, p. 160.
4. Samuel Eliot Morison and Henry Steele Commager, *The Growth of the American Republic*, Vol. I, 5th Ed., New York: Oxford University Press, 1962, p. 105.
5. As quoted in Morison and Commager, *op. cit.*, Vol. II, p. 157.
6. Merle Curti, *The Making of an American Community*, Stanford: Stanford University Press, 1959, p. 1.
7. William James, *Pragmatism*, New York: Longmans Green, 1907.
8. A system by which children of adults who were not communicants could be baptized if their parents made a mere profession of faith.

Selected Readings

*Adler, Selig. *The Isolationist Impulse.* New York: Collier Books, 1961.
*Beard, Charles. *The Supreme Court and the Constitution.* Englewood Cliffs, N. J.: Spectrum Books, 1962.
*Becker, Carl. *The Declaration of Independence.* New York: Vintage Books, 1960.
*Bryce, James. *The American Commonwealth.* New York: Capricorn Books, 1960. 2 Vols.
Commager, Henry Steele. *The American Mind.* New Haven: Yale University Press, 1950.
Weldon, T. D. *States and Morals.* New York: McGraw-Hill Book Company, 1947.
*Wilson, Woodrow. *The New Freedom.* Englewood Cliffs, N. J.: Spectrum Books, 1961.
*Wriston, Henry M., ed., *Goals for Americans.* Englewood Cliffs, N. J.: Spectrum Books, 1960.

* Paperback edition.

Chapter 21

Power and Ideology

Political ideologies often refer to an ideal social condition. Power, in contrast, reflects an existing social condition. In this chapter, we shall examine power in American society. First we shall review some of the characteristics of power and who wields it in society. Then we shall discuss the socialization of political beliefs and how they are expressed in voting at the polls.

As noted in Chapter 8, power is the ability of an individual or a group to achieve a goal, even in the face of opposition from others.[1] In this sense, power is the capacity of one group or individual to influence or restrain the actions of others in order to promote its own objective. In America power is plural and fluid.[2] It is possessed by many different groups. It has shifted from one region to another and has fluctuated among the classes.[3] In the period of the early Republic, for example, the New England and Middle Atlantic aristocracy wielded great power. Later, in the Jacksonian era the center of power shifted to the common man and to the newer regions of the Southern frontier and the Ohio Valley.

Because of its pluralistic nature, a number of different kinds of power can be expressed in communal action. The kind of power selected depends on the group expressing the power and the values it seeks or wishes to maintain.[4] Power, therefore, is related to groups of values. Harold Lasswell and Abraham Kaplan distinguish among eight types of values: power, respect, rectitude, affection, well-being, wealth, skill, and enlightenment.[5] These values may be cultivated independently; nevertheless, they tend to be interrelated. Moreover, each type of value produces a corresponding form of power. For example, power as a value gives rise to political power; the pursuit of wealth creates a compound form of economic and political power—ecopolitical power; and skill results in expertness.[6]

Each type of value is pursued or supported by its form of power. The wish to seek those offices that permit control of others is expressed through political power. The pursuit of wealth requires the combined form of ecopolitical power because access to wealth and maintaining it entails not only business ability but also the exercise of political influence. Skills are protected by expertness; that is, by creating the impression that they are special and difficult to acquire. Forms of power, just like values, may interrelate, as illustrated by the member of a management group who advances by playing company politics rather than by skill alone. Or this may be seen in the individual who desires political office in order to carry on his financial activities behind the cloak of official capacity.

Power is never equally distributed. "There is no power where power is equal." [7] Power may be distributed in two directions: vertical or horizontal. The vertical distribution of power is absolute. It was characteristic of medieval and early modern societies. During the Middle Ages, the feudal lord commanded the fealty of his vassals. In the sixteenth and seventeenth centuries, under the ideology of the divine right of kings, the monarch ruled absolutely. When Louis XIV said, "L'état c'est moi" ("I am the state"), he uttered a political reality. In our own times vertical distribution of power has been exemplified by rulers who attained power through mass appeals.[8] The fascist dictators, Adolf Hitler in Germany and Benito Mussolini in Italy, were examples of recent rulers who sought complete power. Horizontal distribution of power, on the other hand, signifies a broad sharing of power throughout society. Some may have more power than others, since a horizontal distribution does not imply equality, but no one has absolute power. As we shall see, vertical power structures typify totalitarian or dictatorial forms of rule, whereas horizontal power structures tend to be characteristic of democracy.

Power is checked by those who are subject to it. This is called countervailing power.[9] If those subjected to power believe that the group in power is exercising it well, they do not contest the power and stability prevails. If, however, those subjected to power feel that it is not being used wisely, and that their interests can be best served by some other relationship, they will seek actively to gain the power.

Countervailing power applies to both democratic and absolute societies. In democratic societies the desire for a greater share of power among groups within the population may be the basis for changing a power relationship. In America, for example, this has resulted in the formation of the National Association for the Advancement of Colored People and the ensuing struggle to abolish Jim Crow laws and obtain equal voting rights for the Negro.[10] In absolute societies, the desire is often to *displace* the group in power and remove the basis of its right to power.[11] Given the nature of absolute rule, there are seldom any legal channels through which these goals can be attained. Revolution is frequently the result. These were the circumstances behind the democratic revolutions in England, America, and France. Certainly these were the circumstances leading the Russian Revolution of 1917. They also apply to the perennial revolutionary spirit of the Latin American states. The Russian and Latin American lessons underscore the problem of displacing one power group with another: absolutism frequently begets absolutism.

THE LOCATION OF POWER

Let us shift attention from the nature of power to its location, first in the local community and then in the nation-state. In both we shall place special stress on American political parties.

It is a truism of political science that those who are named to official positions of power within a local community, such as a municipal government, may not be those who actually possess power. This idea has existed in the folklore of American politics for a very long time. Such phrases as "the smoke-filled room," and "those who pull the strings of city government," or "the phantom government," have been symbols of behind-the-scenes power. Within recent years the social sciences have begun to study the location of power in local communities and have discovered a variety of patterns.[12]

A local community may choose to surrender its power to groups outside of the community. In the study of a rural village by Arthur Vidich and Joseph Bensman it was found that the village board did not accept the political power granted to it but, instead, adapted its actions to larger units of power, such as the state government, which taxed, subsidized, and provided facilities of various kinds to the village.[13] The village board eventually became incapable of solving any local problem unless outside sources of aid were available. [14]

A variation on this theme is found when a particular form of power withdraws from the community because of social changes occurring in the entire society. This was the case of Cibola, a community studied by Robert O. Schulze.[15] Schulze was concerned primarily with eco-political power. He found that before 1900 the economically dominant individuals in Cibola were residents of the community. All economic units were locally owned, and persons considered to be economically dominant were actually associated with the local economic system.[16] Since the turn of the century, especially since 1930, the economy of Cibola has been drawn into that of the nearby urban center. Business mergers, absentee owners, the establishment by outside corporations of branches within the community, and the decline of interlocking local ownership and directorship resulted in the withdrawal of the economically dominant from Cibola's political life. A shift in power relationships took place. The direction of the civic and political life of Cibola has now passed to a cluster of owners of small businesses and a group of professionals, of whom few can be classified as economically dominant within the community. The corporations which are absentee-owned have maintained a hands-off policy of Cibola's political life.[17]

Community power may also be located in a number of countervailing groups cutting across a variety of values. These groups are, therefore, only loosely integrated, or not integrated at all. Two non-American examples illustrate this point. Loose integration of community power appears to be characteristic of Tijuana, Mexico.[18] The power relationships of business leaders, government officials, and labor leaders constantly fluctuate. The full integration of these groups is reduced by the exclusion of politics and labor from the style of life of the businessmen, and by the control of many communal functions by forces outside of Tijuana in other parts of Mexico and in the United States. A similar finding was presented in a study of Windsor, Ontario.[19] In Windsor, however, the power groups are not even loosely integrated. Big business—Ford and Chrysler—the Roman Catholic Church, the unions, and the local small business group form four cohesive but distinct power structures within the city. As a result, power seems to be shared—at least it was reported to be difficult to tell which group was most influential.

These studies demonstrate the pluralistic nature of community power, but emphasize only political or ecopolitical power. When the other values, respect, rectitude, well-being, affection, skill, and enlightenment, are taken into account, the kinds of power noted by Lasswell and Kaplan are manifest. The appearance of the latter increases the number of groups that will pursue or maintain these values. The result is that the pluralistic nature of community power is extended beyond political and ecopolitical forms.

Now consider power in the nation-state. The concept of the nation is ambiguous. Some definitions treat as nations those territorial units having a common language, religion, and tradition, but this fails before examples of a nation such as Switzerland which contains three language groups and three sets of traditions, and is divided into Protestant and Catholic religions. The United States and the Soviet Union are also examples of heterogeneous nations. According to Max Weber, if the concept of nation means anything, it refers to a community of sentiment.[20] Sentiment, in this sense, means that the citizens have similar political hopes and aspirations.[21] A State, in contrast, is that system which successfully claims "the monopoly on the legitimate use of force within a given territory." [22] It makes no difference whether the State is organized along the lines of a theocracy, monarchy, dictatorship, or democracy. The principle is always the same: the State claims authority over all forms of human association within its jurisdiction.[23]

The history of Western civilization experienced first the rise of the State, then the emergence of the nation.[24] Frequently the State has been the unit of society to which many institutions attach themselves. We saw evidence of this in the study of early economic institutions in America which floundered badly until the Constitution guaranteed a more rational ordering of economic relationships. A State becomes a nation when its people exhibit common political aspirations and share common social experiences, such as wars and economic crises. If, in its formation, active cooperation from all citizens toward the realization of shared goals is expected, a democratic State is likely to emerge.[25] If, in contrast, expectations of a passive nature are made of the role of citizen and a distinction is made—based on some ideology, such as race—between rulers and ruled a nationalism results which, in turn, breeds despotism.[26]

The rise of the State tends to make political other forms of power.[27] This occurs because, given the monopolistic nature of the State, minor power groups can implant their values on the population only by gaining political power. An industrial clique, for example, may wish to gain and hold wealth. It possesses a definite philosophy of the best way to do this, but seldom is such a clique autonomous enough to exercise its philosophy without first gaining a measure of political power. This has been a common occurrence in America. Southern cotton growers, during the Jacksonian era, wanted to establish a free-trade system with Europe. The only way they could exercise their philosophy was to attempt control of Congress in order to control tariffs. Today, the American Medical Association—at first glance a nonpolitical organization—has fought compulsory health insurance laws and medical care for the aged programs in order to protect a particular philosophy of the economics of medical practice. Even values of skill, such as aesthetic values, can be politicized. During the Great Depression of the 1930's many artists banded together in various associations. The American Artists' Union, the American Artists' Congress, and the United American Artists were examples. One of the major objectives of these organizations was government subsidization of their members' art work.

The State is the ultimate embodiment of power. As such, it asserts authority through laws, decrees, judicial decisions, and where necessary, through force. The State, however, as the foregoing examples imply, is only one center of power among countervailing centers, potential or real.

In absolutist States the existence of centers of countervailing power is potential. The State seeks to absorb such centers into its own power structure or systematically destroys and replaces them with organizations of its own. This was characteristic of the Nazi rise to power in Germany. On March 23, 1933, the German parliament, or Reichstag, passed Hitler's infamous Enabling Act which stipulated that the power of legislation—including taxation and foreign treaties—was removed from the Reichstag and given to the Cabinet, which was Hitler. Any laws passed by the Cabinet could deviate from the Constitution.[28] One by one, the political parties of the German Republic were dissolved, leaving the Nazis in complete power.

In democratic States the plurality of power is real. The existence of many organizations, typically called pressure groups and political parties, function as countervailing forces to the autonomy of the State.

Pressure groups are organized to pursue in a peaceful fashion the special interests of their members. In America, the Farm Bloc, the American Medical Association, the National Education Association, and the unions have been among the most persistent and powerful pressure groups. Although pressure groups may favor one political party over another, they characteristically cut across party lines to gain wider appeal for their programs. Pressure groups frequently influence the platforms of the major political parties by lobbying at the national conventions. They also influence candidates by threatening support of the opposition and by campaigns to direct public opinion.[29] The American Medical Association, for example, in 1948, hired a public relations firm at $100,000 a year to assist in its fight against compulsory health insurance. Over 55 million pieces of AMA literature were distributed and 65,000 posters displayed in doctors' offices.[30]

Pressure groups illustrate the principles of countervailing power in the

American scene, but the two major political parties also exemplify the concept. Observers of the American party system are often puzzled by the fact that there are only two parties of any consequence, in contrast to the multiparty system of many European nations. Neither the Republican nor Democratic party has philosophies that can be construed as being in opposition to one another. Indeed, the philosophies within each party range from ultraconservative to ultraliberal. There is often a lack of unanimity between the wings of each party. Conservative Republicans and conservative Democrats may agree on an issue of federal aid to education but split on a tariff question. Liberal Republicans and liberal Democrats have voted together on issues of civil rights, but oppose one another on questions of budget. American parties span not only a geographic continent but also a continent of interests. The parties have become channels to express the desires of class and status groups of all kinds. But each party, regardless of the internal diversity of interests has one commanding goal: the acquisition of political office and the exercise of related powers. Thus, according to the ideal, can the interests of the party best be served. What is not foreseen is the contradiction inherent in the system. The broad range of interests within each party makes it impossible for all views to be represented, and the party in power tends to assume the political ideals and program of the person in office. The presidency is the ultimate example.

One of the shrewdest observers of the American scene was the English political scientist and leader of the intellectual wing of the British Labor Party, Harold Laski. His essay which follows reveals many of the characteristics of the American party system. He indicated the conservative and liberal forces within both the Republican and Democratic parties, and illustrated the pluralistic nature of party interest. Laski also pointed out a challenge to the American party system: the choice, in a world of insecurity, between rejecting democracy and turning to a rule of ecopolitical interests, and recognizing the obligations of a democratic nation in an interdependent world.

*
Few things are more curious to the foreign observer than the character of political parties in the United States. In one sense they are only national in extent at election times; in another, they are far more effectively local organizations which cohere about persons rather than about ideas. They hardly represent even interests in the sense that one can distinguish be-

* From *American Democracy*, pp. 78–82, by Harold J. Laski. Copyright 1948 by The Viking Press, Inc. Reprinted by permission.

tween the purposes they serve. It is, indeed, difficult to find criteria by which to lay down permanent ideas which are Republican in contrast to permanent ideas which are Democratic. It is, of course, true that the attitude of the Democrats to the Negro problem differs from the attitude of the Republicans; but that is an attitude which derives rather from geographical distribution than from any basis in ideological approach. On all other matters, each party overlaps the other in all matters of doctrine. On the whole, the Republicans derive their main strength from industrial, and the Democrats from agrarian, interests; but Maine and Vermont are both overwhelmingly Republican and, at the same time, overwhelmingly agrarian. On the whole, again, the main incidence of finance-capitalism is probably Republican rather than Democratic. Yet, from time to time, the Democrats have attracted to their support some of the wealthiest members of the financial aristocracy. It would not be an easy thing to distinguish, except from the angle of electoral history, the platforms of either party. And the change in the personnel of each can be made, as it seems, without undue effort. For Mr. Henry A. Wallace, the son of a Republican Secretary of Agriculture, was first the holder of that position in the cabinet of Franklin Roosevelt and later his vice-president; while Mr. Wendell Willkie, the Republican candidate of 1940, was a warm supporter of Mr. Roosevelt in 1932. Mr. Harold Ickes, the Secretary of the Interior in Mr. Roosevelt's cabinet after 1933, was a Progressive Republican in 1912, and an ardent enthusiast for the elder Roosevelt in that famous campaign.

This kind of confusion is the natural outcome of the party system in America. For no party has a permanent leader; the president, while he is in office, has a transcendent influence upon the party which has nominated him, and it is usual for ex-presidents, and even ex-presidential candidates, to play an important role in their party—yet it is never quite clear what the role will be. Ex-Governor Landon of Kansas and ex-President Hoover are content to be "regular" Republicans who support whatever the National Convention of their party has decided; but it is far from clear whether Mr. Willkie would have been content with that kind of regularity. Former Senator Burton Wheeler has been the Progressive candidate for the vice-presidency; but there are few Republicans who have spent more energies in fighting President Roosevelt. In a formal sense, too, men like former Representative Dies of Texas, or Senator Byrd of Virginia, are members of the Democratic party; but it would have been impossible for President Roosevelt to place any reliance upon their support of the kind that he could place upon the late Senator Robinson of Arkansas, or Senator Wagner of New York. An American political party has far less continuity of principle than an English political party; it is rather a group of supporters gathered round a temporary leader who imposes upon them what influence he can. The unity of the two major parties arises less from the principles they apply to the issues before them than from the quality of the personality in the leader each chooses for the time being. And if the leader, on defeat, is replaced by another leader, as Mr. Willkie in 1940 was replaced by Mr. Dewey in 1944, the whole incidence of party emphasis may change because the outlook of the leader has changed.

The fact is that political parties in the United States, because they are the parties of a continent, are rarely unified in a European sense of the term. They are much more like a bloc of interests than a system of principles. They are, as it were, a sum of numbers added together the different integers of which may never be the same in any two presidential years. The machine in each state may have the same composition over a long period; but that does not mean that it defines the national objective in the same way or that it will appeal to the electors by the same methods. It has only one unchanging aim, the attainment of office and, therewith, the power that office confers. Within either of the major parties, there may be every shade of opinion from far to the Left to the extreme Right. Senator Norris of Nebraska was for most of his career a member of the Republican party; but it would have been very difficult to discover any principle of action that he held in common with either Senator Lodge or Senator Mark Hanna, who were also Republicans. The opinions of Senator "Cotton Ed" Smith or Senator George had nothing in common with those of Senator Cutting or Senator Black; but all of them were members of the Democratic party. The truth is that a continent so vast makes almost all parties a federation of interests between which such a compromise can be arrived at as is judged likely to be compatible either with keeping or with attaining political office.

The life of the party has the character that might be expected from the immense variety in the life of the American nation. And in each part of the continent the party adjusts itself to the historical and economic conditions of the area in which it is operating. Neither Republican nor Democrat would venture to forget the significance of the Scandinavian settlements in Minnesota either in choosing its candidates or in expounding its programme. Nor would either attack the Roman Catholic Church or Eire in New York or Massachusetts, as neither would attack Fundamentalism in Kentucky or Tennessee. Each has to consider a mass of special interests, sometimes racial, sometimes religious, sometimes economic, which it is rarely easy to arrange in a single pattern. That is why a presidential election will flank a nominee from one section of the country by a nominee from another section. That is why, also, it is difficult to know whether an outstanding personality is more helpful or more harmful to the fortunes of a party than a candidate who is likely to arouse the minimum of resentment. It is, of course, true that for practically half a century the Democrats had to bear the burden of the defeat of the South in the Civil War; there is a real sense in which it is true to say that it took the First World War to purge the Republican party of the conviction that Appomattox conferred upon it a title to the permanent government of the nation so that a Democratic victory might be regarded as inherently unnatural. That a man as honest and upright as Andrew D. White, the first president of Cornell University, could force himself to vote for James G. Blaine in 1884, even while he was aware that Blaine was both corrupt and untruthful is an interesting relic of that conviction. What really restored the balance was the realization that the outcome of merely "waving the bloody shirt" was to sacrifice agriculture and the West to industry and eastern finance. The critical date was the rejection by the Republicans of Theodore Roosevelt as their candidate in 1912. For that was an announcement that, under the color of a great mass of patriotic rhetoric, the Republican party was content to be merely the instrument of Big Business. The assumed radicalism of Theodore Roosevelt was, in fact, far more a matter of striking postures than of actual deeds. But the fact that he was regarded as dangerous by that senatorial oligarchy which hardly concealed the maneuvers of Wall Street, and State Street deprived the Republican party of a pretension to a national outlook which a little more skill would have enabled it to exploit for many more years.

What is now clear about the character of political parties on the federal plane is that the Second World War will compel them to make an adjustment that is likely to be far deeper than either is now ready to concede. The New Deal has already thrown a number of ancient traditions into the melting pot, of which not the least important is that whatever the lip-service paid to "rugged individualism," however deep the formal protest against the growth of federal power, both parties know that American democracy will find it hard to survive a second great depression of the scale of 1929. That means that it is highly unlikely that the main foundations of the New Deal can be undone without the loss not merely of that trade-union vote which is being increasingly organized, but the loss, also, of millions of votes of men and women who know that it is in the power of the federal government to prevent mass unemployment. And to this knowledge there must be added the expectation of many millions of Americans, which no party dare evade attempting to fulfill, that they will be suitably rewarded for the part they have played—and it is a great part—in achieving victory over the enemy in the Second World War.

On a superficial view, it is striking not merely that so little headway has been made by socialism or communism in the United States, but, even more, that the trade-unions should have rested content with the working of a party system which has offered them so little of the power they have been able to achieve on the European continent. All efforts so far at the creation of a mass-voting third party have failed dismally. The Socialist party of the United States has decreased in strength since 1933. The American Communist party has never even seemed to be more than a branch of the Soviet

Foreign Office *in partibus infidelium*. The party of the elder La Follette, which polled some four million votes in the presidential election of 1924, was rather the expiring convulsions of the old Progressive movement than the birth of a really new force; and though Farmer-Labor parties have had brief epochs of success in North Dakota and Minnesota, their victories have been rather an episode than a creation. There was a long epoch of municipal social-ism in Milwaukee, though it hardly went as far as the normal governmental commitments of Manchester or of Glasgow; and a reformist Socialist mayor has long been elected to office by the voters of Bridgeport, Connecticut. Dis-tinguished philosophers, like John Dewey, have, from time to time, spon-sored national committees, like the Committee of Forty-Eight, which they fondly hoped might become something more than a pale flicker of transient dissatisfaction with the two historic parties. But, so far, no movement has had the strength or the drive of that Progressive movement which Theodore Roosevelt proposed should march out to Armageddon in the name of the Lord; and no one, looking back at the Progressive movement, can see in it anything more than a means of enabling the older parties to take account of issues they were seeking to evade. The striking thing of the past dozen years is that, using an instrument which had little relation to the ends he encompassed, President Franklin Roosevelt brought into being a positive federal state in America even though he was never seeking deliberately to serve a social philosophy of which that state was the expression. The most brilliant empiricist American politics has ever known was driven on by large and impersonal forces which he rarely stayed to examine.

It is tolerably certain, I think, that when the Democratic party nomi-nated Franklin Roosevelt in 1932, it had not the remotest conception of the consequences of its decision; and it is not less certain that he himself had little more than a vague sense that the state power should be used to help the underprivileged. Yet his election marks an epoch in the history of the United States of which the impact on political parties is certain to be as deep as that of the Civil War. It is one of those rare cases in which the sweep of events carries its main figure an immense distance beyond the point he had intended to go. And the outcome of this journey is pretty certain to be that the America of the next generation will either have to adapt its party structure to a far more positive democracy than any it has so far known, and that whether Republicans or Democrats be in power; or else it will move rapidly to some American form of corporate state which will prove incompatible with the traditions of political democracy in the United States. It is important to remember that those traditions go very deep in American history, and it will not be easy to abandon them without what may prove, if the attempt be made, as decisive an event as the Russian Revolution.

For the factor that is going to alter the whole basis of the party system in America is the twofold coincidence that the conclusion of its pioneering age is accompanied by its need to accept the responsibilities of leadership in an interdependent world. Whatever the rhetoric beneath which American parties go forward to the work of adapting the United States to its new tasks, it is, I think, certain that it will become altogether a society which tries to fulfill the democratic ideal or a society which tries wholly to deny it. It can no more survive as a plutodemocracy than it could, before the Civil War, survive half slave and half free. It is unnecessary to deny that in both the major American parties there are forces, not without considerable influence, which will do all they can to arrest, if not to prevent, the fulfillment of democracy—forces that are, in their ultimate nature, economic, but which receive expression now as religious reaction, now as racial prejudice, now as gangsterism and racketeering on a scale large enough, as in places like Jersey City, to corrupt the administration and the courts of law. But it is significant that an America which sought to preserve the power of plutodemocracy would have to make the grave choice between a profound diminution in its standard of living and an embarkation on a policy of economic imperialism which would in the end almost certainly unite against America forces which her citizens could not hope to overcome. And it is probable that before it was well advanced in either of these directions the whole basis of its party system would be challenged successfully. In the party evolution of the United States in the next generation there will, no doubt, be reaction as well as advance. But it is hardly possible, on the evidence, not to feel that the impersonal forces of the world are shaping American destiny in a democratic direction which no party can deny and yet survive. Here is the real promise of American life.

THE SOCIALIZATION OF POLITICAL BELIEFS

Laski emphasized the location and expression of power, especially political power. Both result from the total political behavior, or lack of it, of the individuals within the society.[31] Political behavior, broadly speaking, has two sources. The first is the institutional pattern of the society. In America, the wide range of institutionalized political groupings in which an individual may involve himself becomes an important factor in shaping the direction of political behavior. The politics of the businessmen's association, the local PTA, the school board, the town council, and so on, through a myriad of activities, exemplify the ways in which varying degrees of political involvement can be expressed and varying kinds of personal interests can be represented. The pluralistic nature of the two major political parties reinforces this activity at higher levels of involvement. At a still higher level the legal basis of pluralistic activity is expressed in the Constitution through the distinction between federal and state government powers, representation in Congress, and the First Amendment which restricts government interference in speech, press, assembly, and petition.

The second source of political behavior is the psychological composition of the individual. This involves the study of the socialization of those feelings, motivations, and attitudes that compose his political beliefs. The socialization process, as we have seen, does not operate separately from institutional influences. Institutionalized political groups may instill in the individual certain attitudes common to a particular group. Seldom, however, do individuals wait until they are able to participate in such groups to form their political beliefs. Formation begins early in life.

The early socialization of political beliefs begins in the home. The social basis includes the class and life style of the family within its community. The family provides a way of life, as we saw in Chapter 8, characterized by tradition, influence, prestige, and property relations—which it seeks to enhance or maintain. The class position of the family offers certain opportunities within the economic system. Each of these may be expressed in attitudes and beliefs about the political behavior necessary to maintain or raise the position of the family. Specific government programs of taxation, subsidization of local industry, labor decisions, welfare legislation, and public services, such as roads, schools, and water, are typical of the kinds of activities in which a family may find restriction or enhancement of its opportunities.

In America, one of the more specific ways in which political attitude is expressed is through party preference. This, too, is related to the family. One study of 4500 high-school students in five Midwestern states indicated a very high relationship between the political affiliation of parents and the preferences of their children.[32] Another study of opinion formation in the 1948 presidential election indicated that individuals make the same political choices as their fathers.[33] These, and other studies of voting, have led to the conclusion that there is a consistency of political belief within families. Such consistency is at once a result of identification by the child with the parents and of self-insulation. The child in American society ordinarily does not possess information about the political process and is isolated from it by the interests of his peers and the legal restrictions of age. It is not surprising, therefore, that he would assume the political beliefs of the parent. If the older child does become interested in politics and discovers beliefs antagonistic to those he acquired from his parents, he may insulate himself against parental views as a means of minimizing conflicts and disagreements within the family.[34]

The above discussion assumes that normal relations exist within the family. A variety of circumstances may arise to negate that assumption. Divorce, or the rejection of parents by the child, may impair the usual transmission of the political beliefs of the parents.[35] This does not mean that every difference in political belief between parents and children is attributable to family difficulties, but that a breakdown in the pattern of role relationships can have an influence on the political beliefs of the child.

In the following article Robert E. Lane explores the question of sons against their fathers and the political implications of this interaction.

*

Loosely speaking, there are three ways in which a father lays the foundations for his son's political beliefs. He may do this, first, through indoctrination, both overt and covert as a model for imitation, so that the son picks up the loyalties, beliefs, and values of the old man. Second, he places the child in a social context, giving him an ethnicity, class position, and community or regional environment. And, he helps to shape political beliefs by his personal relations with his son and by the way he molds the personality which must sustain and develop a social orientation. The combination of these three processes produces the "Mendelian law" of politics: the inheritance of political loyalties and beliefs. But while imitation and common social stakes tend to enforce this law, the socialization process may work to repeal it. It is the socialization process, the way in which fathers and sons get along with each other, that we examine in this paper.

Some perspective is gained by noting a number of possible models of the way fathers through their rearing practices may affect their sons' social outlook. The German model of the stern father who emphasizes masculine "hardness" and "fitness" in the son, and who monopolizes the opportunity for conversation at the dinner table, is one that has been explored at length. The Japanese father, partially deified like his ancestors, strictly attentive to protocol and detail in the home, is another. The Russian father image— the gruff, indulgent, somewhat undisciplined but spontaneous and warm individual—is a third. And the American father is said to be more of a brother than a father, joined with his son under the same female yoke, uninspired but certainly not frightening. Here is an image to compare with others and, as with the other models, its caricaturistic exaggeration nevertheless represents an identifiable likeness.

* From Robert E. Lane, "Fathers and Sons: Foundations of Political Belief," *American Sociological Review*, Vol. 24, August 1959, pp. 502–511. Reprinted by permission of the author and the American Sociological Association.

The father-son relationship may be explored with the help of data on the lives and politics of fifteen men interviewed recently at considerable length. These men represent a random sample drawn from the voting list of 220 citizens living in a moderate income housing development in an Eastern industrial city. Out of fifteen asked, fifteen (prompted by a modest stipend) agreed to be interviewed, even though these interviews ranged from ten to fifteen hours, administered in from four to seven installments. The characteristics of the sample are as follows:

> They were all white, married, fathers, urban, and Eastern.
> Their incomes ranged from 2400 to 6300 dollars (with one exception: his income was about 10,000 dollars in 1957).
> Ten had working class occupations such as painter, plumber, policeman, railroad fireman, and machine operator. Five had white collar occupations such as salesman, bookkeeper, and supply clerk.
> Their ages ranged from 25 to 54 years—most of them were in their thirties.
> Twelve were Catholic, two Protestant, and one was Jewish.
> All are native-born; their nationality backgrounds include: six Italian, five Irish, one Polish, one Swedish, one Russian (Jewish), and one Yankee.
> All were employed at the time of the interviews.
> Three concluded their schooling after grammar school and eight after some high school; two finished high school, one had some college training, and one went to graduate school.

The interviews were taped, with the permission of the interviewees, and transcribed for analysis. There was an agenda of topics and questions but the interviews were not closely structured, being conducted with probes and follow-up questions in a conversational style. The topics included: (1) current social questions, such as foreign policy, unions, taxes, and desegregation; (2) political parties; (3) political leaders and leadership; (4) social groups and group memberships; (5) ideological orientation toward "democracy," "freedom," "equality," and "government;" (6) personal values and philosophies of life; (7) personality dimensions—partially explored through standard tests; (8) life histories, including attitudes toward parents, brothers and sisters, school, and so forth.

In addition to the interviews, a group of tests were administered on anxiety, authoritarianism, *anomie*, information, and certain social attitudes.

The characteristics of the sample, as in any study, affect the relationships discovered. It should be stressed that this is a sample of men who, by and large, are well adjusted to society: they are married and have children, hold steady jobs, they are voters. This probably implies that any warping of personality which may have taken place in childhood was marginal. We are, then, dealing with the relationships of childhood experiences and political expression in a moderately "normal" group. We are not involved with the extremes of personality damage, or the bottom rung of the social ladder, or a highly socially alienated group. Unlike the studies of American Communists or of nativist agitators, this paper is concerned with middle and normal America, with more or less adjusted people. This is an important point because our findings differ in certain respects from those of other studies, but they do not necessarily conflict with them.

The influence of the son's rebellious attitudes toward his father has often been said to be important in explaining radical movements, particularly "youth movements." The son's basic position is one of growing from complete dependence to independence. During the later stages of this growth he and his father each must make a rather drastic adjustment to the changing relationship called forth by the son's maturation. Under certain circumstances the son may rebel against the family and particularly against the father. Is this the typical American pattern—as Erikson denies? Unlike German youth, he argues, American youngsters do not rebel, although willing and able to do so, because the paternal discipline is not something to rebel against.

We explored the question of rebellion, particularly in its political aspects, with our fifteen men and found that there was indeed very little evidence of the kind of relationship that Erikson describes in the German situation. Apparently, only rarely did a family-shattering clash of wills occur when the son thought himself old enough to behave as a man. The father-son opposition took relatively minor forms: the question of what hour to come in at night, the use of the family car, the son's conduct in school. Concerning the political expression of such rebellious feelings, there were strong indications that this subject remained on the periphery of the men's world of experience.

Although the major evidence comes from the biographical material, answers to a question on youthful rebellion or radicalism are revealing. Rapuano, an auto parts supply man with a rather undisciplined tendency to vent his aggression on social targets (communists and doctors), responds in bewilderment and finally denies any such tendency. O'Hara, an oiler in a large factory and one of the more class-conscious interviewees, is confused and takes the question to mean rebellion against his brothers and sisters. Woodside, a policeman who rejected his father with venom, responds to an inquiry about his own youthful rebellion or radicalism:

> I do remember through the depression that my folks mentioned that it seems as though more could have been done—that the parties should have made more means of work so that the poverty wouldn't be existing so much around you— and, not only around you—but with you yourself.

He turns the question of his own rebellion and radicalism into a family matter: the family was more or less disgruntled. Only one man, better educated than others, speaks of his own moderate radicalism in a way which could be interpreted as a search for independence from or opposition to his parents.

There are several reasons why political expression of youthful defiance failed to come off. One is the low salience of politics for the parents. Few of the men could remember many political discussions in the home and some were uncertain whether their parents were Democrats or Republicans. If the old man cared so little about politics, there was little reason to challenge him in this area. Another reason is that when there is a need to assert independence there are ways of doing it which come closer to the paternal (and generally American) value scheme. One of these is to quit school. Four or five men sought independence and the economic foundations for a life no longer dependent on paternal pleasure by leaving school shortly before they were ready to graduate—thus striking directly at the interests of parents determined to see their children "get ahead in the world." Of course this act had compensations for parents in need of money, but there seems to have been more of a genuine conflict of wills in this area than in any other. Quitting school, in some ways, is the American youth's equivalent of his European opposite of conservative parentage joining a socialist or fascist party.

Two reasons then for the apolitical quality of youthful revolt are the low salience of politics in the American home and the opportunity for rebellion in other ways. A third reason may be—to use a hyperbole—the relatively low salience of the father in the American scheme. We asked our men, "Who made the important decisions in your parents' household?" One replied that they were jointly made, two that their fathers made the important decisions, and twelve testified that mother was boss. The statement of Ruggiero, a maintenance engineer and supply man from a remarkably happy home, typifies the most frequent point of view:

> "Which of your parents would you say was the boss in your family?"—I'd say my mother. My father was easy-going in the house. . . . We found that mother ran the house exactly the way she wanted to. She took care of the money, too. Paid all the bills. She still does.

Now it may be that from a child's perspective that Mother is usually boss. But the near unanimity on this point is convincing, all the more so because the accompanying comments generally show no overlord in the background. Even in this immigrant and second generation population Mom had taken over. Why, then, rebel against Father?

There is a fourth reason for the generally low rate of political rebellion. In the American home a child is given considerable latitude. "Permissiveness" is the term used currently to express this idea and although the term and idea are in bad odor among some critics, it is clear that the prevailing standards of child care even twenty years ago allowed a degree of freedom in school, neighborhood, and home not generally prevalent in Europe or Asia. To a large extent, the boy is on his own. This is Erikson's point, but we can illustrate it in detail. Thus Farrel, a man from a working class background whose schooling included graduate study, reports on his tendency to political radicalism in his youth: "I think there must also be the adolescent revolt aspect, which was never acute with me. . . . There was, as far as I was concerned, no necessity for it to be acute. I didn't feel hemmed in by my parents." Rapuano talks of his "reckless" youth in which he ran free with other boys, and some of the men speak of their parents' preoccupations that gave them opportunity to live a "free life." Many of the boys had earned money for their own as well as their families' use by selling papers, working in grocery stores, or cleaning up the school. Nor was this freedom attributable to parental indifference. When Rapuano was struck by a school teacher, his mother (not his father) visited the school to beat the teacher with a stick. A free child assured of supportive parental assistance when in need does not need to rebel.

A minority of four or five of these children, however, had suffered under controls which seem strict by most American standards.

VOTING BEHAVIOR

Voting is probably the most tangible expression of political behavior. Ideally it is a reflection of the rational decision-making of the voter. A careful weighing of issues and candidates, a gathering of information, and informed conversation are supposed to precede the trip to the polls. Organizations, such as the League of Women Voters, are devoted to the creation of an informed electorate. But the facts of voting as practiced by many people reveal a highly irrational activity.

Homogeneity of political attitudes gives rise to homogeneity in voting. This is one source of irrationality at the polls. Studies, such as those carried out in Elmira, New York,[36] and in Erie County, Ohio,[37] indicate that husbands and wives, friends and coworkers, tend to vote alike. People who share the same position in the class system and profess the same religion also tend to vote the same way. Homogeneity of voting extends beyond the confines of the family. Henry W. Riecken has suggested that an explanation for such homogeneity can be obtained by inverting the now-familiar hypothesis of George Homans.[38] Instead of indicating that sentiments of liking will emerge from social interaction, Riecken suggests, with respect to voting, it would be proper to say that people want to be liked; therefore, they attempt to bring their political preferences in line with those of the groups with which they associate. When an individual strays from the standard path attempts will be made to reindoctrinate him. If these fail, he will be rejected by the group.[39]

Another source of irrationality in voting is the personal factors relating to candidates which influence preference. In a study of a campaign for the office of mayor in Boston, Murray Levin found that the election was not decided so much on the basis of campaign issues as upon visceral reactions.[40] Negative reactions included such images as "something about his eyes," "tough looking," "talked funny," "little Napoleon." Positive reactions included "good to his family," "a nice quiet manner," and "a clean fighter." Such images may also function at the national level: Thomas Dewey's mustache, Truman's use of language, Eisenhower's fatherly look.[41] Such visceral reactions do not occur separately from the issues, but the candidate's image is of importance to the voting public.

Voters may exhibit attitudes, in addition, which reveal a disenchantment with the whole process of voting. These may be a reflection of the *perceived* power structure of a given community. In the Levin study of Boston politics many voters felt that both candidates were dishonest, would deal with racketeers, and double-talked the voter. They felt that voting was of no use because everything had been "fixed" beforehand.[42] At the national party level, although there are some who would extol the lack of differences,[43] the voter often does not perceive any difference between candidates or political philosophies. He does not, therefore, deem his vote important. Such disenchantment with the voting process can be termed political alienation.[44]

Political alienation may take any of four forms.[45] Powerlessness, the first form, is the expectation held by the voter that any political action on his part will not influence the outcomes or the benefits he seeks. This results from the belief, real or imagined, that a political élite actually dominates the system.

Meaninglessness is the second form of political alienation. This results from the voter's confusion regarding what he ought to believe. The voter may feel that there is no real difference between candidates or that sufficient information is not available by which a rational decision can be made. This may be compounded at the local community level, as Levin noted,[46] because municipal government is built around services, and elections emphasize personalities rather than issues or programs. Adequate and accurate information about candidates is difficult to obtain. The result is a bewildered voter, relying, of necessity, on his visceral reactions.

Normlessness, or *anomie*, is a third form of political alienation. This is the expectation on the part of the voter that desired goals can be achieved only outside of the accepted system. *Anomie* is then closely related to the voter's feelings of powerlessness. As Levin pointed out,[47] individuals will resort to corrupt practice if they feel that this is the only means to solve their political problems.

Self-estrangement is the fourth form of political alienation. It is the feeling that no satisfaction can be derived from participation as a citizen in political activity. This form of alienation helps explain those who participate in political activity for personal gain, rather than from civic pride or responsibility. Self-estrangement also helps explain the politically apathetic who spurn all political activity in favor of other forms of community endeavor, or retreat from any responsibility whatsoever.

In the following selection Levin relates the aforementioned forms of political alienation to such considerations as class, age, and religious affiliation. He then discusses the ways in which alienation is expressed and its relevance for democratic theory.

*

Four aspects of political alienation—powerlessness, meaninglessness, the lowering of norms, and estrangement—have been distinguished. The extent to which a particular individual is affected by any one of these forms can be related to such variables as social class, age, and religion.

Separation of a population according to income tends to include separation according to education and occupation as well. Data on income were obtained in this survey and will be used as a gross measure of social-class difference. The majority of the Boston electorate, who are elementary or high-school graduates, employed in blue-collar or white-collar jobs, and in the lower-income group might be expected to feel alienated primarily in the sense of powerlessness. It is this group which is in fact furthest removed from the seats of political power. They have relatively little contact with the city as compared to home owners and businessmen, and when they do have contact, they lack the economic means to participate in the "business" of politics. Collins' major campaign appeal was directed to those who feel powerless. His campaign slogan was "Stop Power Politics," and he presented himself as leading a battle against the politicians. Powers' prolific use of political endorsements did not hinder the image Collins was creating. The data collected in our survey show that the lower-income groups switched from Powers to Collins in larger proportions than did the middle- or upper-income groups. This implies that feelings of powerlessness were greater in the lower-income groups.

In contrast to the lower-income groups, the upper-income groups, who have more economic power, might be expected to experience political alienation in the forms of meaninglessness, lowering of norms, and estrangement more than in the form of powerlessness. Upper-income groups have more

* From Murray Levin, *The Alienated Voter*, pp. 64–75. Copyright 1960, Holt, Rinehart, and Winston, Inc. By permission.

education, which tends to develop more rigorous standards of clarity of information on which to base decisions. The data show that this group had greater interest in political programs and expressed fewer "gut reactions" than did lower-income groups. With higher standards of clarity there is likely to be stronger feelings of political meaninglessness.

The upper-income groups include businessmen and property owners who necessarily have more contact with the city because they may require licenses of various kinds, tax abatements, and building inspection certificates. Since they have economic power, they are in a position to purchase special political consideration. Those who do this will experience political alienation in the form of lowering of political norms.

Upper-income groups include some individuals with a sense of community responsibility. Because of the disjunction of their political values and the political structure, they are likely to be active in nonpolitical civic activities such as charities or service organizations.

Age is another variable related to political alienation. Older persons, who have lived in Boston for many years and have observed the political structure over a long time, might be expected to show greater feelings of alienation. This age group had the largest proportion of individuals who thought that the man they supported would be no better than his opponent. Having observed more elections, they seem to feel more strongly that the effect of their vote makes little difference in the long run.

Religion is another sociocultural variable to be considered. Since Boston is a strongly Catholic city, it might be expected that Protestants and Jews, having less political power, would have stronger feelings of political alienation. In support of this are the facts that a smaller percentage of Protestants and Jews voted than did Catholics and that a greater proportion voted for Collins, whose campaign was largely an appeal to the politically alienated.

Feelings of political alienation may be expressed through rational activism, withdrawal, projection, or identification with a charismatic leader. These are conscious or unconscious mechanisms by which an individual may handle the uncomfortable feelings of political alienation. Some forms of alienation lead to specific mechanisms, for example, feelings of estrangement inevitably lead to withdrawal because gratification is found only in nonpolitical activity. Other forms may result in one or more of several mechanisms, for example, feelings of powerlessness may lead to political activism or to projection and identification with a charismatic leader.

Rational activism is political action based on a realistic evaluation of the political situation, the object of which is to promote a political structure consonant with political values. The frustration arising from political alienation can be a spur to rational activism; feelings of powerlessness can lead to increased political activity. Feelings of meaninglessness can lead to demands for more information rather than withdrawal or "blind" voting.

And guilt, resulting from normlessness, can result in activity directed toward raising political standards. Mature individuals, who are those able to tolerate frustration and to act on their beliefs, are those most likely to handle their feelings of political alienation through rational activism. This activity may occur within existing political institutions or it may be directed toward the creation of a new set of political institutions. Rational activism is more likely to be the response to feelings of political alienation when individuals believe that their activity has a reasonable chance of bringing about a change.

Political withdrawal is the removal of an individual's interest and activity from politics. This may occur as a result of a conscious rational decision based on a realistic estimate of the political situation or as an affective, unconscious response. In the latter case the anger and resentment of political alienation may be internalized within the individual rather than expressed outwardly. This mechanism is more likely to occur when the individual feels that any political effort on his part has little chance of producing an effect.

Although an individual may have withdrawn from political interests, he is not likely to escape entirely from politics. Municipal problems of education, traffic, and taxes may affect him personally, or he may note the recurrent exposure of corruption in newspapers. Consequently additional mechanisms of expression of political alienation are likely to be used. There may be projection, identification with a charismatic leader, or rational activism.

Feelings of anger and resentment which arise from political alienation may be projected on to some other individual or group. This group is seen as participating in a hostile conspiracy. Political leaders may use this mechanism because it establishes a sense of identity between them and the voters to whom they are appealing.

The conspiratorial theory is particularly appealing to individuals who have feelings of powerlessness and normlessness because it accounts for the absence of power and the lowering of values in a simple and easily understood fashion. The individual who projects sees himself as powerless because sinister forces have successfully conspired to destroy the traditional political rules in such a way that he is excluded from exercising his rights. Hofstadter has observed that:

> this kind of thinking frequently occurs when political and social antagonisms are sharp. Certain audiences are especially susceptible to it—particularly, those who have obtained a low level of education, whose access to information is poor, and who are so completely shut out from access to the centers of power that they feel deprived of self-defense and subjected to unlimited manipulation by those who wield power.

Another mechanism for dealing with feelings of political alienation is identification with a charismatic leader. This is the attempt of an individual to feel powerful by incorporating within himself the attitudes, beliefs, and actions held by a leader whom he perceives as powerful. "Charismatic" refers to an extraordinary quality of a person regardless of whether this quality is actual, alleged, or presumed. In taking over the attributes of a charismatic leader, the individual may enter into activity he would otherwise abhor. German *bourgeoisie* who identified with Hitler approved of and took part in behavior their consciences would otherwise not allow them to do.

Rational activism is behavior based on logical reasoning and an undistorted perception of political realities. Withdrawal may be a rational response in some situations and an irrational, affective response in other circumstances. The mechanisms of projection resulting in conspiratorial thinking and identification with a charismatic leader are irrational, affective responses. They are also regressive, in that they are more characteristic of a child's than of an adult's handling of a problem.

When feelings of political alienation are widespread, individuals will adopt one or more of the mechanisms we have described to handle the frustration and anxiety associated with them. The political behavior of each individual will be affected by the particular mechanism or mechanisms he selects.

We have described the forms of political alienation and the mechanisms by which they may be expressed. When political alienation is widespread, it may be a major factor in determining the outcome of an election. The astute politician is aware of this; consequently his strategy takes these factors into account.

The election we have analyzed took place in a community where feelings of political alienation, frustration, and disillusionment with the political process are widespread. When this situation exists, the voting behavior of the electorate is less predictable than otherwise, since a decision is likely to arise from negative rather than from positive convictions and may change on the basis of minor issues, fleeting incidents, or "gut reactions."

The analysis of the statements of the individuals we interviewed shows that they hold an image of the political structure which is similar to that developed by modern political science. They perceive the hierarchical arrangements of power and influence, and they relate various power groupings to each other. They are aware of the uses and abuses of political office; and they know that their role is not the one that the grammar-school version of democratic theory taught them. They have, however, greatly exaggerated their lack of power and, perhaps, the extent of corruption. The election, after all, resulted in the downfall of the group associated with one candidate and the elevation to power of another group which probably did not believe it had a serious chance of winning. All the money that was given to the group which lost the election and all the promises that may have been made to the contributors have been to no avail, for the personnel now in power are different. The antagonisms built up during the campaign may mean that the "outs" are really out of City Hall in the near future.

The election upset was to a large extent a response to feelings of political alienation. Senator Powers followed the time-honored rules of campaigning. He spent large amounts of money on advertising which portrayed him as a devoted public servant and friend of the people, shook as many hands as possible, attended numerous house parties, recounted his experience, contributed to charities of all faiths, was photographed with prominent religious leaders, attacked his opponent, and emphasized the support of municipal, state, and national politicians; but although he had 54 per cent more votes than Collins in the primary, he failed to win. This has shaken politicians' faith in the traditional vote-getting techniques.

Although there are many reasons why Powers lost, it is clear that one of the most important was the fact that he presented himself as a powerful professional politician—a serious mistake in a community where a considerable amount of political alienation exists. The alienated are not positively disposed toward those whom they identify as powerful. Under these circumstances, the candidate must re-evaluate old methods, reformulate his strategy, and experiment with new techniques. A number of countervailing strategies are available to him.

The candidate may create a strong sense of identity with the electorate by presenting himself as the underdog in a struggle against a power élite. Whether he does this or not, he certainly should not emphasize a background of power or the massive support of other political figures who may also be associated with "the powerful." Since an elaborate campaign is viewed as collusion with "the powerful," the candidate must avoid the appearance of an opulent campaign.

Of course, a candidate may appeal to regressive mechanisms of projection and identification with a charismatic leader. Collins successfully appealed to those who tend to think in conspiratorial terms (a form of projection) via his slogan, "Stop power politics, elect a hands-free mayor," and such techniques as his essay contest on a definition of "power politics." The electorate, however, did not view him as a charismatic leader.

The professional politicians may court popular esteem by throwing the support of "the organization" behind a "clean" amateur; that is, some well-known citizen who has not had contact with the politician and therefore does not share their stigma. The stigma which is attached to "the politician" by the alienated is not likely to rub off on such an individual, at least during the beginning of the campaign. The difficulty with this procedure, from the point of view of "the organization," is that such a candidate may be unreliable.

Theories concerning the causes of alienation refer to almost every conceivable "malady" of modern civilization from the decline of religion to the effects of mass production. Students of politics who have dealt with political apathy and indifference customarily point out that the size of modern states and the technical nature of so many political questions tend to dwarf the individual voter and make him politically inept. Many scholars who have analyzed the structure and distribution of power in modern political parties indicate that the need for specialization and division of labor requires a hard core of active leaders who determine policy with the passive approval of the membership. Others point out that the remoteness of political events and the barriers to the flow of accurate political information prevent the voters from developing an accurate picture of political realities which makes it difficult for them to make what they consider to be meaningful choices. All of these factors tend to reduce, if not annihilate, the political power of the individual voter which leaves him bewildered, apathetic, and alienated.

Prominent among these explanations of the causes of political alienation is Kornhauser's theory of "mass society." Kornhauser defines mass society as a

> situation in which the aggregate of individuals are related to one another only by way of their relation to a common authority, especially the state. That is, individuals are not directly related to one another in a variety of independent groups. A population in this condition is not insulated in any way from the ruling group, nor yet from elements within itself.

He argues that the absence of autonomous groups through which individuals may unite to forward their political interest by bringing pressure to bear on the élite leaves the population in an atomized situation which leads to feelings of alienation.

In such a situation the alienated are disposed "to engage in extreme behavior to excape from these tensions." When an independent group life is absent, individuals are ready for mobilization by élites for membership in mass movements which provide opportunities for expressing resentment. Kornhauser indicates that the alienated are likely to pressure élites through direct and immediate action for satisfactions which were previously supplied through membership in a plurality of independent and proximate groups. Mass action, that is, action which is not mediated through independent groups, "tends to be irrational and unrestrained, since there are few points at which it may be checked by personal experience and the experience of others." Direct mass action tends to be undemocratic because it is not restrained by institutions which are designed to insure majority rule and minority rights. Thus Kornhauser sees mass society as producing the atomized and alienated man who tends to search for new and direct modes of political action.

Although most scholars who have advanced these theories point out that democratic theory as it was developed in the seventeenth and eighteenth centuries is archaic, the elementary and secondary schools continue to teach and the students continue to believe that it is eminently workable. The latter tend to place the blame for political apathy and frustration on the improper functioning of democratic institutions, particularly corruption. This permits them to identify political alienation as a temporary aberration which will disappear when city hall is cleaned up. The fact is that city hall is sometimes cleaned up and the average voter continues to feel that he is the political outsider. This is partly because he continues to believe in the classical theory of democracy which leads him to expect more from the political system than is possible.

Since feelings of political alienation arise from the disjunction of political values and structure, we must examine both. We choose to examine liberal democratic values and structure, although an analysis of political alienation in terms of nonliberal values and structure is possible.

The Lockian version of democratic theory which dominates American political thought holds that government should be based on the rule of majority. According to this view the masses play the active role by framing and answering political questions while elected officials act as passive agents executing their will. The theory presupposes the ability of the majority to change the government through peaceful constitutional procedures, or, as a last resort, through revolution. The state in Lockian theory is a neutral agency settling disputes according to objective principles of reason and justice.

The roles which the democratic citizen should play according to this scheme are numerous. He is supposed to be interested in political affairs, have a capacity for discussion, and expose himself to, and rationally evaluate, information which may or may not be congenial to his political taste. The democratic citizen is also expected to act on the basis of principles (natural law) which are self-evident and which refer not only to his personal interest but also to the common good.

Those who accept this theory expect that they will be powerful, that is, have the power to select, influence, and remove officials. They also expect that they will have enough information to make what they consider to be a rational choice between meaningful alternatives. Finally, they expect that they will be able to do this through existing institutions without violating their standards of political ethics. Thus, democratic man assumes that he has the right to feel politically powerful, meaningful, and moral.

Democratic man not only expects that he will be able to play these roles but he also expects rational, legitimate, and honest behavior by public officials. He expects, in other words, regularity of public performance, order, and due process of law for all. In a political system where many individuals believe that corruption is widespread and political power is concentrated and abused, the expectations of the citizens with respect to order and due process of law are not met, and they come to believe that they are foreigners (aliens) in the political structure. In other words, for them the political structure, as structure, as regular performance, has ceased. This causes them to feel politically alienated.

In effect, democratic theory is one of the sources of political alienation. Feelings of political alienation will arise when the political role that an individual expects to play and believes is rightfully his cannot be realized. These feelings may result from the fact that the role assignments are unrealistic, that is, they demand more than can be fulfilled or promise more than can realistically be implemented. The fact that they cannot be realized does not mean that they will not be desired. If the roles are, in fact, possible, feelings of alienation may arise from the fact that the political structure prevents the playing of the roles. Thus political roles may be utopian or realistic, while political structures may lead to the fulfillment or denial of those roles which are possible. If the roles are utopian, no political structure can lead to their realization.

Feelings of alienation will arise in individuals who accept the classical democratic theory because it demands more of the individual citizen than he can realistically fulfill and promises more than can be delivered. Most citizens do not and cannot play an active role or display the sustained interest in politics required of them by the theory. The majority do not engage in true discussion, are not well informed or motivated, and do not vote on the basis of principles. Indeed, the principles of right reason and justice, which are supposed to be self-evident and to supply a framework for political action, are precisely what appear to be so much in dispute. The theory also fails to account for the necessary roles of leadership and exaggerates the active role of the masses. Those who do lead are therefore regarded as potential usurpers of what rightfully belongs to the electorate. The theory also leads its followers to believe that the bargaining and compromising, which is so essential to democratic politics, is necessarily evil. In short, the roles as defined by eighteenth-century democratic theory are too demanding and the political structure designed to implement them cannot be what it is supposed to be. This does not mean that democracy is impossible or that its normative value system should be abandoned as incompatible with the nature of man. It does mean that the classical theory of democracy must be revised to fit the realities of modern politics. We accept the view of Berelson that "the classical political philosophers were right in the direction of their assessment of the virtues of the citizen. But they demanded those virtues in too extreme and doctrinal a form." If individuals continue to believe in the classical view, they will feel politically alienated.

In this chapter we have discussed the forms of power and their relationship to values, the location of power in the local community and the nation-state, the socialization of political beliefs, and their expression in the voting process. This chapter ends on the note of political alienation which is particularly relevant for the subjects of the following chapters: American nationalism and the military in the national scene. The politically alienated form the core of the disenchanted in a mass society. They are ripe for the appeals of demagogues who seek an undemocratic political and social order. As the cold war continues can the American state realize its goals as a democratic nation now that it is supporting for the first time in history a large and permanent military establishment? We shall explore the impact of these two considerations in the succeeding two chapters.

Notes

1. Max Weber, *From Max Weber: Essays in Sociology*, trans. and ed. H. H. Gerth and C. W. Mills, New York: Oxford Galaxy Books, 1958, p. 180. See, also Chapter 8, herein.
2. Max Lerner, *America as a Civilization*, New York: Simon and Schuster, 1957, p. 398. The pluralistic view of power is a contrast to the thesis advanced by C. Wright Mills, *The Power Elite*, New York: Oxford University Press, 1956. It was the contention of Mills that power, in response to cold-war pressures, has become concentrated in a triumvirate of power composed of government, the military, and big business. See also Robert A. Dahl, "A Critique of the Ruling Elite Model," *American Political Science Review*, Vol. LII, June 1958, pp. 463–469.
3. Lerner, *loc. cit.*
4. Harold D. Lasswell and Abraham Kaplan, *Power and Society, A Framework for Political Inquiry*, New Haven: Yale University Press, 1950, Chapter V, *et passim*.
5. *Ibid.*, p. 97.
6. *Ibid.*
7. Robert MacIver and Charles H. Page, *Society*, New York: Rinehart, 1949, p. 67.
8. Cf., Philip Selznick, "Institutional Vulnerability in Mass Society," *American Journal of Sociology*, Vol. LVI, January 1951, pp. 320–31; and William Kornhauser, *The Politics of Mass Society*, Glencoe, Ill.: The Free Press, 1959.
9. For an application of the concept to the economic sphere see, John Kenneth Galbraith, *American Capitalism*, Boston: Houghton-Mifflin, 1962, pp. 111 ff. See, also, Chapter 17 herein.
10. Cf., Richard A. Schermerhorn, *Society and Power*, New York: Random House, 1961, pp. 72–76.
11. *Ibid.*, p. 81.
12. This notion of community power follows from the pluralism noted above. One of the major exponents of the opposite view of an élite structure at the community level is Floyd Hunter, *Community Power Structure*, Chapel Hill: University of North Carolina Press, 1953. Hunter's study appears to contain some methodological difficulties that have engendered a good deal of critical comment. See the following representative articles: Nelson W. Polsby, "Three Problems in the Analysis of Community Power," *American Sociological Review*, Vol. 24, December 1959, pp. 796–803; Raymond Wolfinger, "Reputation and

Power and Ideology

Reality in the Study of Community Power," *American Sociological Review*, Vol. 25, October 1960, pp. 636–644; and Lawrence J. R. Herson, "In the Footsteps of Community Power," *American Political Science Review*, Vol. LV, December 1961, pp. 817–830.

13. *Small Town in Mass Society*, Princeton: Princeton University Press, 1958, pp. 98 ff.

14. *Ibid.*, p. 100.

15. "The Role of Economic Dominants in Community Power Structure," *American Sociological Review*, Vol. 23, February 1958, pp. 3–9.

16. *Ibid.*, p. 6.

17. *Ibid.*, p. 7.

18. Orrin Klapp and L. V. Padgett, "Power Structure and Decision-Making in a Mexican Border City," *American Journal of Sociology*, Vol. LXV, January 1960, pp. 400–406.

19. C. W. M. Hart, "Industrial Relations Research and Industry," *Canadian Journal of Economics and Political Science*, Vol. 15, February 1959, pp. 53–73, as cited in Schermerhorn, *op. cit.*, p. 96.

20. Weber, *op. cit.*, p. 176.

21. *Ibid.* See also A. D. Lindsay, *The Modern Democratic State*, New York: Oxford University Press, 1947, p. 151.

22. Weber, *op. cit.*, p. 78. Original in italics.

23. From Walter Lippmann as quoted in Robert Nisbet, *The Quest for Community*, New York: Oxford University Press, 1963, pp. 102–103.

24. Lindsay, *op. cit.*, *passim.*

25. *Ibid.*, p. 151.

26. *Ibid.*

27. Schermerhorn, *op. cit.*, p. 43.

28. William L. Shirer, *The Rise and Fall of the Third Reich*, New York: Simon and Schuster, 1960, p. 198.

29. Don Martindale, *American Society*, Princeton: D. Van Nostrand and Company, 1960, p. 408.

30. Cited in *ibid.*

31. Theoretically the smallest unit of political power is the individual. Because this phenomenon is so little discussed in this way, the authors have sought to explain it in terms of what they call a Torg (T). The name is derived from that of a colleague, Lenard Grote, who became the first mayor of the community in which he lives. Thus, with Ma representing majority (over 21 years of age), and I representing interest, the Torg can be expressed as $T = MaI$. But the individual does not function in a political vacuum. The following factors must be taken into account: political affiliation (A); local community or grass-roots political activity ($a\rho$); community apathy (a). The functioning of these factors in relation to each other may be thought of as a Torgolplex (TT). That these, however, will function in an expression of positive political activity is only a low power probability ($\propto$) caused by unknown factors such as lack of information, faulty perceptions, and the like. A Torgolplex, therefore, may be expressed as follows:

$$TT = \left[\frac{(MaI)^{\ a\rho}}{a} \right]$$

Thus, individual power (Torg) is expressed in relation to political affiliation, and is nurtured by political activity at the grassroots level. Apathy may function to minimize or enhance such interest and activity. Unknown factors operate upon the entire complex, making its positive expression problematic.

32. Cited in H. H. Remmers, "The Early Socialization of Attitudes," *American Voting Behavior*, ed. Eugene Burdick and A. J. Brodbeck, Glencoe, Ill.: The Free Press, 1959, pp. 58–60.
33. Bernard Berelson, Paul Lazarsfeld, and William McPhee, *Voting*, Chicago: University of Chicago Press, 1954, pp. 331–335, *et passim*.
34. Remmers, *op. cit.*, p. 61.
35. Cf., Eleanor MacCoby, "Youth and Political Change," *Public Opinion Quarterly*, Vol. XVII, January 1954, pp. 23–29.
36. Berelson, *op. cit.*
37. Paul F. Lazarsfeld, Bernard Berelson, and Hazel Baudet, *The People's Choice*, New York: Columbia University Press, 1948, 2nd. Ed.
38. Riecken, in Burdick and Brodbeck, *op. cit.*, pp. 163–164.
39. That this type of political behavior is possible has been suggested in the context of other studies. See: Erving Goffman, *The Presentation of the Self in Everyday Life*, New York: Anchor Books, 1959; William H. Whyte, Jr., *The Organization Man*, New York: Simon and Schuster, 1956; and David Riesman and associates, *The Lonely Crowd*, New York: Anchor Books, 1956.
40. Murray Levin, *The Alienated Voter*, New York: Holt, Rinehart, and Winston, 1960, pp. 43 ff.
41. Cited in Franz Alexander, "Emotional Factors in Voting Behavior," in Burdick and Brodbeck, *op. cit.*, p. 302.
42. Levin, *op. cit.*, p. 59.
43. Cf., John Hicks, *The American Tradition*, Boston: Houghton Mifflin, 1955, pp. 12–13.
44. Cf., J. E. Horton and W. E. Thompson, "Powerlessness and Political Negativism," *American Journal of Sociological Review*, Vol. LXVII, March 1962, pp. 485–493.
45. Levin, *op. cit.*, pp. 61 ff. See also, Melvin Seeman, "On the Meaning of Alienation," *American Sociological Review*, Vol. 24, December 1959, pp. 783–791.
46. Levin, *op. cit.*, p. 63.
47. *Ibid.*, p. 64.

Selected Readings

*Baker, Gordon. *Rural vs. Urban Political Power*. New York: Random House, 1960.

*Blankston, George I. *The Economic Basis of Politics*. New York: Random House, 1960.

Hyman, Herbert. *Political Socialization*. Glencoe, Ill.: The Free Press, 1959.

Key, V. O. *Politics, Parties, and Pressure Groups*. New York: Thomas Y. Crowell, 1958.

Kornhauser, Arthur, ed., *Problems of Power in American Democracy*. Detroit: Wayne State University, 1957.

Lipset, Seymour Martin. *Political Man*. Garden City, N.Y.: Doubleday and Company, 1960.

*Lubell, Samuel. *The Future of American Politics*. New York: Anchor Books, 1956.

MacIver, Robert. *The Web of Government*. New York: The Macmillan Company, 1947.

Neumann, Franz. *The Democratic and Authoritarian State*. Glencoe, Ill.: The Free Press, 1957.

* Paperback edition.

Chapter 22

The American Nation-State:
The Quest for Community

The history of power relationships in America resembles that of other countries of Western civilization: the establishment of the State was followed by the development of the nation. The substance of this chapter consists of the factors that led to the founding of the State and the nation in America, followed by a consideration of some of the conflicting issues facing the American nation-state. It will conclude with a discussion of the interrelations of some selected American institutions with the State.

THE AMERICAN NATION-STATE

When the thirteen colonies revolted against English rule they were not welded together by a national spirit. Theirs was a revolution against the excesses of British monarchy as experienced by each colony. The elements that are generally conceded to characterize a nation were not present. There was no uniform communication. The various colonial charters, although based largely upon representative government, were sufficiently different to give the colonies separate political backgrounds. By the 1770's, economic differences that were to cause the sectionalism of the early 1800's were asserting themselves. The colonies were also a heterogeneous mixture of English, French, Dutch, and German. There was, in addition, an absence of a community of feeling about a common political future, which is the hallmark of a nation. The Revolutionary War was actually the first commonly shared experience of the colonists.[1] Even so, there were many who did not favor the war, with the result that many colonists returned to England as soon as possible or emigrated to Canada.

That the State developed first is not surprising. The victory of the Revolution brought the establishment of government under the Articles of Confederation. Economic chaos resulted, and the growing political autonomy of each state gave the impression of thirteen disunited political entities clinging grimly to the Atlantic seaboard. It was the subsequent ratification of the Constitution which brought order out of the chaos. A central government was established bringing cohesion to the economy, and the political autonomy of the states diminished. A wise afterthought to the Constitution was the Bill of Rights, important not because it guaranteed certain rights to individuals, but because of the restrictions it imposed upon State authority. An interesting aspect of the Bill of Rights is that these rights are safeguarded for individuals by the power of the State.

This particular power of the State has developed not only through specific legislative action but also through the interpretive and review powers of the Supreme Court. Nowhere in the Constitution do these powers appear. They were established largely through two cases which the court considered. The first was the case of Marbury vs. Madison. In his opinion in this case, Chief Justice John Marshall wrote the guiding principle for the court thereafter. All laws, federal or state, which violated the spirit of the Constitution were invalid. Furthermore, all courts and government departments were bound by the Constitution. Thus, the principle of the supremacy of the Constitution was established.[2] For the individual this means that it is of more importance that he is a citizen of the United States, than a citizen of any one of the states. This principle was again expressed in the 1954 case of Brown vs. Board of Education in Topeka, in which segregation of school facilities on the basis of race was declared unconstitutional. In 1819 the case of McCulloch vs. Maryland provided the basis of the broad interpretive powers of the Supreme Court, which had been a source of conflict since Alexander Hamilton first sought to establish that very principle. Once established, the principle of broad interpretation of the Constitution freed the Congress from the necessity of continuous, specific legislation to bring the Constitution up to date. That many state supreme courts have adhered to a rigid interpretation of their respective constitutions has resulted in frequent legislative log-jams in state capitals.

The State—that is, the federal government—has grown consistently from the period in which the Constitution was ratified to the present day. This is reflected in expenditures by the United States government. From 1789 to 1800 the average yearly expenditure by the State was $5,776,000.[3] Between 1841 and 1850 annual expenditures averaged some $34 million. From 1896 to 1900 the government spent a yearly average of $457,451,000. In 1963 the expenditures of the federal government approached the $100 billion mark. Increased expenditures are a consequence of a number of diverse factors: territorial expansion; increased population; greater involvement in world affairs, and the concomitant development of a permanent armament industry and military establishment; as well as increased services by the government resulting in an expansion in federal bureaucracy.

The growth of the State has created a trend toward centralization of functions under the State. The State, as we shall see in the later sections of this chapter, has effectively entered the economy. The large size of the federal budget, federal loans, government-owned transportation facilities, and state subsidization of private industries are indicative of the place of government in the economy. In local communities, the federal government subsidizes municipal governments for such functions as community planning. The federal government is involved also in welfare, land reclamation, public utilities, and education. But the engagement by the federal government in these and other functions is not a usurpation of the rights of the states. In the greater number of examples, extragovernmental functions of the State are derived from the expressed or implied powers granted by the Constitution. Among the specified powers of Congress are taxation, roads, military affairs, foreign affairs, interstate commerce, and the granting of copyrights and patents. A final power given to Congress is flexible: to make all laws necessary to carry out the powers of Congress and the powers vested by the Constitution in the government or any of its departments or officers. This final power provided the implied means by which the powers of the law-making, the judiciary, and, especially, the executive branches of government could be expanded.

With the State as a legitimization of force firmly established under the Constitution, what factors contributed to the evolution of that body of sentiment which led to the formation of the nation as a form of community? [4] These can be classified under two broad categories: common social experiences and commonly shared crises.

Two common social experiences which helped to create the sentiments leading to the formation of the American nation were the frontier and immigration.[5] Neither of these was experienced personally by every American.

The frontier did exist, nonetheless, for over a century, nurtured by the ideology of Manifest Destiny. In passing years, it rapidly became one of the most romanticized and idealized American experiences—a myth more real than the fact. In a nation of few traditions and little history, the frontier provided the folk heroes out of which a community of belief could emerge. In this sense, the frontier provided an example of a created tradition in which the population could vicariously participate.

Immigration provided another basis for the growth of the American nation. Over 35 million people came to the United States as immigrants after 1820. Individualism, resourcefulness, and adaptability were as much a part of their experience as they were on the frontier. An additional aspect of the immigration experience was assimilation. Many first generation immigrants, to be sure, sought to reconstruct the way of life of the fatherland in Little Italy, Deutschland, Russiantown, the Ghetto, and Chinatown. But by the second generation a drift away from the behaviors and values of the Old World was evident as the younger people found new opportunities and values in American society.

The above experiences might have gone for naught had not an interdependence of national life been created. Without the railroads, coaches, canals, and finally airlines, without the telegraph, radio, and finally television, the diffusion of people across the space of a continent and the dissemination of American culture would have been immeasurably more difficult.

Those crises that threatened to undermine the American people were most contributory to the establishment of the American nation. One of the most dramatic of these was the Civil War. The war had many roots, of course; but one major cause was the challenge to the federal government by the states-rights, sectionalist, Southern states. The slaughter of the war itself and the bitter period of Reconstruction also threatened the nation. Out of the strife emerged a unity as sectional differences were gradually minimized, and new crises threatened the nation. America became involved in two world wars.

America entered the First World War late, and fought for only 19 months. Yet, almost five million men were mobilized and the industries of the nation were quickly diverted to war production. It was the first foreign war to cut deeply across the whole of the nation. The period following the First World War brought an isolationist reaction. This, together with rampant nationalism in Europe, led to successive victories for fascism. The result was the rise to power of Mussolini and Hitler. The Second World War was a year-and-a-half old when America entered. This time some ten million men were mobilized to fight on two fronts, Europe and the Pacific. Instead of 19 months, America was in conflict from December, 1941, to August, 1945. The length of the war, the depth of the involvement, and the alternatives to losing, made the Second World War the culminating experience in the formation of the American nation.

Not only war but also economic crises helped to shape the American nation. The greatest of these was the Depression of the 1930's.[6] The Depression followed the crash of the stock market in October, 1929. Confidence in the capitalistic system faltered. Investment fell off sharply. By 1933 there were 12,830,000 unemployed.[7] Belief spread that revolution would take place, but revolution did not occur. Instead people switched their votes to the Democratic Party and Franklin Roosevelt. Political order was sustained.

The growth of the American nation-state as a form of community has been the long-term result of those social forces that have decreased the relevance of traditional forms of association.[8] Small town and city, church, school, and family are no longer adequate to blend the diversities of a pluralistic society.

The growth of the nation-state has brought renewed emphasis to the belief in nationalism. Nationalism is composed of a set of circumstances and beliefs that may vary considerably.[9] It may be founded partly on myth which becomes reality for its adherents. The myth often evokes the belief in a common history, which can be invented, and a glorious future for the nation as a world power. Such an appeal may lead the population beyond the ties that bind them together as a community, into despotism. This can be termed *integral* nationalism. At this point, patriotic zeal becomes transformed into fanaticism, and national consciousness acquires a racial flavor. The Nazi ideology in Germany from the early 1920's through the Second World War illustrated these characteristics. Although America exhibits nationalistic tendencies, the very pluralism of the society thus far has prevailed against the development of despotism. The form of nationalism that has grown in America is best characterized as *liberal* nationalism, emphasizing the rights of individuals within the nation and the right of self-determination of all peoples.

In the following sections of this chapter some selected areas of conflict are discussed to illustrate the nature of the choice between an atomistic society, which ends in a totalitarian State, and a pluralistic society, which maintains a democratic ideology.

THE WELFARE STATE

In the late nineteenth century a series of events resulting from the industrialization and urbanization of America brought to an end the doctrine of *laissez faire,* in which the government ostensibly refrained from interference or intervention in economic and social affairs. Agrarian discontent led to the Interstate Commerce Act of 1887. As a result, the burden of regulation of business was shifted from state and local levels, which could not affect public carriers and banking beyond their own political boundaries, to the federal government. This shift, reflecting the changing nature and scope of American business and agriculture, signaled the beginnings of a more positive and intimate government attitude toward the welfare of the citizenry.

Whether it is accurate to speak of America as a Welfare State is subject to debate: If the term means complete cradle-to-grave care, no state in the world is a Welfare State; if it means any amount of social legislation, all modern states are Welfare States; and if it means only *certain* kinds of social legislation such as free public education, free medical care in whole or in part, or social security measures, most modern states are Welfare States. In any case, it is a fact that the federal government, as well as state and local governments, has heightened the degree of its participation in social welfare, and business welfare, ever since Populist —agrarian—pressure was first applied before the turn of the century. All levels of government now touch our daily lives. They reach into intimate areas at one time reserved for the individual, the family, the church, or the employer.

Such an "invasion of privacy," although resented by many citizens, is in reality an attempt to answer the unprecedented problems confronting urbanized, industrialized, bureaucratized societies. Life has become so complex that the old solutions fail to apply and may even aggravate the conditions they are trying to alleviate. Answers become outmoded very fast in the pace of our contemporary existence. The "farm problem," as an example, has created a new breed of administrator who, by the nature of the times and work, is forced "to live in the short-term, to become [master] of the short-term solution." [10] But short-term soon becomes long-run in a bureaucratic structure; one of the most valid criticisms of the Welfare State is the tendency of new measures to be piled atop the old, without superseding the old. The result is that new legislation frequently works at cross-purposes with old legislation, thus creating a situation rife with confusion, inequity, and expense.[11]

This is the price for continuing the essential democracy of our system of government. Few of us are willing to pay the greater price, in terms of civil liberties, to achieve the theoretical efficiency of either *laissez faire* or totalitarianism. However, some would "solve" our problems by returning to government as it existed, say, before the Civil War. Others, equally enthusiastic about the merits of their solution, see us better off under greater government control. Those who identify with the former position exhibit "classic" nineteenth-century liberal characteristics, whereas those who embrace the latter are cast in the twentieth-century liberal mold. Both positions have been tried and found wanting.

The New Deal of Franklin Delano Roosevelt, faced with the deepest and most widespread depression in American economic history, stands as the high-water mark of welfare legislation in America. In a desperate effort to stem the tide of business failure, bank closing, and joblessness, the "first one-hundred days" of the New Deal produced a welter of swiftly written and rapidly considered measures, aimed more at restoring a hopeful attitude of mind than actually correcting the economic failure. "But above all try something," was Roosevelt's motto in his first administration.

The United States did not succumb to ideologies of the right or the left during the unsettled 1930's, testifying to the successful restoration of hope by the New Deal. Yet that some nine million were still unemployed in 1940 was mute evidence of the failure of the New Deal economic programs. It should be remembered, however, that the second Roosevelt Administration was much more conservative than the first; and it is possible that the President's loss of interest in rewriting the National Industrial Recovery Act, declared unconstitutional in 1935, and in pushing the "pump-priming" Public Works Administration—in short, his own growing conservatism—was responsible, in part, for the failure of the economic aspect of his programs. The advent of the war economy in 1941 dispelled the last of the Great Depression.[12]

The New Deal has different meaning for different people. To some, because it saved their homes, it symbolized humanitarianism. To some, because it attempted a number of liberal reforms, it symbolized the closest approach to the true spirit of democracy. To some, because labor was encouraged to organize and become more powerful, it symbolized the dignity of the common man. But to some it symbolized socialism and the loss of American principles. Hardly a social issue is raised today, from local welfare and urban renewal to federal aid to education and medical aid for the aged, that does not find proponents invoking the spirit of FDR, and opponents inveighing against "another New Deal giveaway." "Few serious minds believe any longer that one can set down 'blue-prints' and through 'social engineering' bring about a new utopia of social harmony. At the same time, the older 'counterbeliefs' have lost their intellectual force as well. Few 'classic' liberals insist that the State should play no role in the economy, and few serious conservatives, at least in England and on the Continent, believe that the Welfare State is 'the road to serfdom.' " [13]

FREEDOM, LOYALTY, AND DISSENT

If young people, and intellectuals, for differing reasons, are bored with the old arguments, others are not. There is an issue interrelated with the Welfare State that yet stirs ideological controversy, and that is in the area of civil liberties.

Despite essential agreement among liberals and conservatives over the desirability of decentralized political and economic power, the fact remains that the tendency toward concentration continues. In certain respects we all benefit from bigness. David Lilienthal in *Big Business* and J. K. Galbraith in *American Capitalism* defend bigness in business as a force for good provided there is, to use Galbraith's term, a "countervailing power" to offset the evils of concentration. Big government is one of the countervailing powers.[14] There is an almost innate fear of bigness in government, sometimes born of ignorance, sometimes derived from intimate experience. Circumstances rather than individuals have conspired to force the federal government to gather the elements of power into a great bureaucratic structure.

Although not absolute, the federal government's power has increased steadily, and at the expense of the state, the locality, and the individual. Every transfer of power reopens the states' rights controversy. The doctrine of states' rights, the idea that the state government is sovereign in certain reserved areas, was first tested in the Constitutional Convention and has been steadily advanced in a variety of forms. States' rights is generally manifested as sectionalism: New England merchants vs. the "Warhawks" in 1812, agrarian South vs. industrial North culminating in the Civil War, "Free Silver" West vs. "Hard Money" East in the Bryan era. Sectionalism today is found in the farm bloc, a loose association of states whose economies are based primarily on agriculture. Lacking numerical and financial strength, these states have managed to maintain a disproportionate amount of political bargaining power by re-electing representatives to Congress and controlling congressional committee chairmanships through the seniority system.[15] But states' rights has also provided a platform in recent years for another curious combination of anachronisms, definable as neo-Puritanism and neo-Know-Nothingism, which transcendentally demand "less government and more responsibility."

In the years since 1945, years of rapid change and anxiety, the nation has seen a bewildering increase of sectlike reform groups come and go. Every period in our history has been characterized by an outburst of protest groups, but the postwar period is unusual because of the presence of financially strong and highly vocal groups of dissent, in a period marked by increasing prosperity.

During the Great Depression balance was struck between protest from the left and the right. People had a range of choice from communism through fascism. But the cold war era has given birth almost exclusively to rightwing groups. Formerly the protest was against Jews, Negroes, Catholics, Capitalists, the New Deal, Communism, Fascism, Hoover Republicans, labor unions, and so on. Today, although occasionally one hears of the "NAACP-Jewish-Communist-Papal Plot," the ultraright reformists soft-pedal charges against minority groups to concentrate on the threat of internal communist subversion.

The absence of any important protest from the left is indicative of the essential conservatism of America and its political parties. Both Democrats and Republicans are parallel coalitions of the relatively narrow range of political preferences traditionally expressed by the bulk of Americans. To apply the term conservative to the extreme right is to make the expression meaningless and confusing. The terms reaction or pseudoconservatism are more accurate since these groups desire to "roll back" certain kinds of legislation. A conservative seeks to preserve and perfect that which exists; a reactionary would return to some point in history—usually highly romanticized—which he deems more desirable.

The numerical, and particularly the financial, strength of such organizations as the John Birch Society, the Christian Anti-Communism Crusade, Freedom Forum, "We, the People!," the Conservative Society of America, the National Indignation Convention, and the All-American Society, have caused some alarm in observers and politicians, particularly among the latter when they are not seeking re-election. Senator Stephen M. Young of Ohio has said: "I believe the radical right today is an even deadlier threat to our democratic convictions than are the American adherents to Communism. Although the danger from internal Communism has been lessening, the radicals of the right . . . are trying to destroy the civil liberties and institutions which are the foundations of freedom." [16]

Chauvinism, a common denominator of the far right, is not new in America, but the stress placed on internal purification has long been dormant; hence, the labels neo-Puritan and neo-Know-Nothing which reflect strong elements of fundamentalist Christianity and nativism.

The idea of right thinking is the chief panacea offered by Robert Welch in his *Blue Book of the John Birch Society*: "The man who is to me the most profound of all Americans, Ralph Waldo Emerson, once said that every mind must make its choice between truth and repose." [17] But where Emerson and the Transcendentalists were not interested in carrying the rest of America with them by force, the Birch Society and similar organizations militantly insist on the "rightness" of their programs.[18] "We are going to cut through the red tape and parliamentary briar patches and road blocks of confused purpose with direct authority at every turn. The men who join the John Birch Society during the next few months or years are going to be doing so primarily because they believe in me [Robert Welch] and what I am doing and are willing to accept my leadership anyway. And we are going to use that loyalty, like every other resource, to the fullest possible advantage that we can. Whenever and wherever, either through infiltration by the enemy or honest differences of opinion, that loyalty ceases to be sufficient to keep some fragment in line, we are not going to be in the position of having the Society's work weakened by raging debates. We are not going to have factions developing on the two-sides-to-every-question theme." [19]

These programs, in sharp contrast to the kinds of specific programs advanced by Communists, Socialists, Technocrats, the Townsend Plan, the German-American Bund, and others in the 1930's, are vague and have as targets will-o'-the-wisp "they's." [20] The difference between the two types is accounted for by the kind of politics involved: the difference between interest or class politics and status politics. Writing at the end of the McCarthy Era in 1954, Richard Hofstadter distinguished between the two and accounted for the rightist phenomenon.

*
In a country where physical needs have been, by the scale of the world's living standards, on the whole well met, the luxury of questing after status has assumed an unusually prominent place in our civic consciousness. Political life is not simply an arena in which the conflicting interests of various social groups in concrete material gains are fought out; it is also an arena

* Richard Hofstadter, "The Pseudo-Conservative Revolt," in *The New American Right*, pp. 43–52, by Daniel Bell, New York: 1955. Copyright 1955 by Criterion Books, Inc. Reprinted by permission of the publisher.

into which status aspirations and frustrations are, as the psychologists would say, projected. It is at this point that the issues of politics, or the pretended issues of politics, become interwoven with and dependent upon the personal problems of individuals. We have, at all times, two kinds of processes going on in inextricable connection with each other: *interest politics*, the clash of material aims and needs among various groups and blocs; and *status politics*, the clash of various projective rationalizations arising from status aspirations and other personal motives. In times of depression and economic discontent—and by and large in times of acute national emergency—politics is more clearly a matter of interests, although of course status considerations are still present. In times of prosperity and general well-being on the material plane, status considerations among the masses can become much more influential in our politics. The two periods in our recent history in which status politics has been particularly prominent, the present era and the 1920's, have both been periods of prosperity. . . .

Paradoxically the intense status concerns of present-day politics are shared by two types of persons who arrive at them, in a sense, from opposite directions. The first are found among same types of old-family, Anglo-Saxon Protestants, and the second are found among many types of immigrant families, most notably among the Germans and Irish, who are very frequently Catholic. The Anglo-Saxons are most disposed toward pseudo-conservatism when they are losing caste, the immigrants when they are gaining.

Consider first the old-family Americans. These people, whose stocks were once far more unequivocally dominant in America than they are today, feel that their ancestors made and settled and fought for this country. They have a certain inherited sense of proprietorship in it. Since America has always accorded a certain special deference to old families—so many of our families are *new*—these people have considerable claims to status by descent, which they celebrate by membership in such organizations as the D.A.R. and the S.A.R. But large numbers of them are actually losing their other claims to status. For there are among them a considerable number of the shabby genteel, of those who for one reason or another have lost their old objective positions in the life of business and politics and the professions, and who therefore cling with exceptional desperation to such remnants of their prestige as they can muster from their ancestors. These people, although very often quite well-to-do, feel that they have been pushed out of their rightful place in American life, even out of their neighborhoods. Most of them have been traditional Republicans by family inheritance, and they have felt themselves edged aside by the immigrants, the trade unions, and the urban machines in the past thirty years. When the immigrants were weak, these native elements used to indulge themselves in ethnic and religious snobberies at their expense. Now the immigrant groups have developed ample means, political and economic, of self-defense, and the second and third generations have become considerably more capable of looking out for themselves. Some of the old-family Americans have turned to find new objects for their resentment among liberals, left-wingers, intellectuals and the like—for in true pseudo-conservative fashion they relish weak victims and shrink from asserting themselves against the strong.

New-family Americans have had their own peculiar status problem. From 1881 to 1900 over 8,800,000 immigrants came here, during the next twenty years another 14,500,000. These immigrants, together with their descendants, constitute such a large portion of the population that Margaret Mead, in a stimulating analysis of our national character, has persuasively urged that the characteristic American outlook is now a third-generation point of view. In their search for new lives and new nationality, these immigrants have suffered much, and they have been rebuffed and made to feel inferior by the "native stock," commonly being excluded from the better occupations and even from what has bitterly been called "first-class citizenship." Insecurity over social status has thus been mixed with insecurity over one's very identity and sense of belonging. Achieving a better type of job or a better social status and becoming "more American" have become practically synonymous, and the passions that ordinarily attach to social position have been vastly heightened by being associated with the need to belong.

The problems raised by the tasks of keeping the family together, disciplining children for the American race for success, trying to conform to unfamiliar standards, protecting economic and social status won at the cost of much sacrifice, holding the respect of children who grow American more rapidly than their parents, have thrown heavy burdens on the internal relationships of many new American families. Both new and old American families have been troubled by the changes of the past thirty years—the new because of their striving for middle-class respectability and American identity, the old because of their efforts to maintain an inherited social position and to realize under increasingly unfavorable social conditions imperatives of character and personal conduct deriving from nineteenth-century, Yankee-Protestant-rural backgrounds. The relations between generations, being cast in no stable mold, have been disordered, and the status anxieties of parents have been inflicted upon children. Often parents entertain status aspirations that they are unable to gratify, or that they can gratify only at exceptional psychic cost. Their children are expected to relieve their frustrations and redeem their lives. They become objects to be manipulated to that end. An extraordinarily high level of achievement is expected of them, and along with it a tremendous effort to conform and be respectable. From the standpoint of the children these expectations often appear in the form of an exorbitantly demanding authority that one dare not question or defy. Resistance and hostility, finding no moderate outlet in give-and-take, have to be suppressed, and reappear in the form of an internal destructive rage.

An enormous hostility to authority, which cannot be admitted to consciousness, calls forth a massive over compensation which is manifest in the form of extravagant submissiveness to strong power. Among those found by Adorno and his colleagues to have strong ethnic prejudices and pseudo-conservative tendencies, there is high proportion of persons who have been unable to develop the capacity to criticize justly and in moderation the failings of parents and who are profoundly intolerant of the ambiguities of thought and feeling that one is so likely to find in real-life situations. For pseudo-conservatism is among other things a disorder in relation to authority, characterized by an inability to find other modes for human relationship than those of more or less complete domination or submission. The pseudo-conservative always imagines himself to be dominated and imposed upon because he feels that he is not dominant, and knows of no other way of interpreting his position. He imagines that his own government and his own leadership are engaged in a more or less continuous conspiracy against him because he has come to think of authority only as something that aims to manipulate and deprive him. It is for this reason, among others, that he enjoys seeing outstanding generals, distinguished secretaries of state, and prominent scholars browbeaten and humiliated.

Status problems take on a special importance in American life because a very large part of the population suffers from one of the most troublesome of all status questions: unable to enjoy the simple luxury of assuming their own nationality as a natural event, they are tormented by a nagging doubt as to whether they are really and truly and fully American. Since their forebears voluntarily left one country and embraced another, they cannot, as people do elsewhere, think of nationality as something that comes with birth; for them it is a matter of *choice*, and an object of striving. This is one reason why problems of "loyalty" arouse such an emotional response in many Americans and why it is so hard in the American climate of opinion to make any clear distinction between the problem of national security and the question of personal loyalty. Of course there is no real reason to doubt the loyalty to America of the immigrants and their descendants, or their willingness to serve the country as fully as if their ancestors had lived here for three centuries. None the less, they have been thrown on the defensive by those who have in the past cast doubts upon the fullness of their Americanism. . . .

The primary value of patriotic societies and anti-subversive ideologies to their exponents can be found here. They provide additional and continued reassurance both to those who are of old American ancestry and have other status grievances and to those who are of recent American ancestry and therefore feel in need of reassurance about their nationality. Veterans' organizations offer the same satisfaction—what better evidence can there be of the genuineness of nationality and of *earned* citizenship than military service under the flag of one's country? Of course such organizations, once they exist, are liable to exploitation by vested interests that can use them as pressure groups on behalf of particular measures and interests. (Veterans' groups, since they lobby for the concrete interests of veterans, have a double role in this respect.) But the cement that holds them together is the status motivation and the desire for an identity.

Sociological studies have shown that there is a close relation between social mobility and ethnic prejudice. Persons moving downward, and even upward under many circumstances, in the social scale tend to show greater prejudice against such ethnic minorities as the Jews and Negroes than commonly prevails in the social strata they have left or are entering. While the existing studies in this field have been focused upon prejudice rather than the kind of hyper-patriotism and hyper-conformism that I am most concerned with, I believe that the typical prejudiced person and the typical pseudo-conservative dissenter are usually the same person, that the mechanisms at work in both complexes are quite the same, and that it is merely the expediencies and the strategy of the situation today that cause groups that once stressed racial discrimination to find other scapegoats. Both the displaced old-American type and the new ethnic elements that are so desperately eager for reassurance of their fundamental Americanism can conveniently converge upon liberals, critics, and nonconformists of various sorts, as well as Communists and suspected Communists. To proclaim themselves vigilant in the pursuit of those who are even so much as accused of "disloyalty" to the United States is a way not only of reasserting but of advertising their own loyalty—and one of the chief characteristics of American superpatriotism is its constant inner urge toward self-advertisement. One notable quality in this new wave of conformism is that its advocates are much happier to have as their objects of hatred the Anglo-Saxon, Eastern, Ivy League intellectual gentlemen than they are with such bedraggled souls as, say, the Rosenbergs. The reason, I believe, is that in the minds of the status-driven it is no special virtue to be more American than the Rosenbergs, but it is really something to be more American than Dean Acheson or John Foster Dulles—or Franklin Delano Roosevelt. The status aspirations of some of the ethnic groups are actually higher than they were twenty years ago—which suggests one reason (there are others) why, in the ideology of the authoritarian right-wing, anti-Semitism and such blatant forms of prejudice have recently been soft-pedaled. Anti-Semitism, it has been said, is the poor man's snobbery. We Americans are always trying to raise the standard of living, and the same principle now seems to apply to standards of hating. So during the past fifteen years or so, the authoritarians have moved on from anti-Negroism and anti-Semitism to anti-Achesonianism, anti-intellectualism, anti-nonconformism, and other variants of the same idea, much in the same way as the average American, if he can manage it, will move on from a Ford to a Buick.

Such status-strivings may help us to understand some of the otherwise unintelligible figments of the pseudo-conservative ideology—the incredibly bitter feeling against the United Nations, for instance. Is it not understandable that such a feeling might be, paradoxically, shared at one and the same time by an old Yankee-Protestant American, who feels that his social position is not what it ought to be and that these foreigners are crowding in on his country and diluting its sovereignty just as "foreigners" have crowded into his neighborhood, and by a second- or third-generation immigrant who has been trying so hard to de-Europeanize himself, to get Europe out of his personal heritage, and who finds his own government mocking him by its complicity in these Old-World schemes?

Similarly, is it not status aspiration that in good part spurs the pseudo-conservative on toward his demand for conformity in a wide variety of spheres of life? Conformity is a way of guaranteeing and manifesting respectability among those who are not sure that they are respectable enough. The non-conformity of others appears to such persons as a frivolous challenge to the whole order of things they are trying so hard to become part of. Naturally it is resented, and the demand for conformity in public becomes at once an expression of such resentment and a means of displaying one's own soundness. This habit has a tendency to spread from politics into intellectual and social spheres, where it can be made to challenge almost anyone whose pattern of life is different and who is imagined to enjoy a superior social position—notably, as one agitator put it, the "parlors of the sophisticated, the intellectuals, the so-called academic minds."

Why has this tide of pseudo-conservative dissent risen to such heights in our time? To a considerable degree, we must remember, it is a response, however unrealistic, to realities. We do live in a disordered world, threatened by a great power and a powerful ideology. It is a world of enormous potential violence, that has already shown us the ugliest capacities of the human spirit. In our own country there has indeed been espionage, and laxity over security has in fact allowed some spies to reach high places. There is just enough reality at most points along the line to give a touch of credibility to the melodramatics of the pseudo-conservative imagination.

The kind of vigilantism demanded of and by superpatriots tends to be placed above the law—the means are justified by the ends. Restrictions on personal liberty can be imposed just as effectively by a band of terrorists or patriotic zealots as they can by government. To be smeared for holding contrary views has been an all-too-frequent occurrence in the political climate that developed in America in the 1950's. Regardless of truth or falsity, charges so made tend to become a matter of record. The recent rash of loyalty oaths, a direct outgrowth of the deteriorating political climate, has created a storm of controversy as more and more public employees and organizations using public facilities are affected. Recently an attorney in a California community was honored by being appointed a fire commissioner, a nonpaying appointment. When confronted with the loyalty oath, he reneged, saying, in the Lockean-Jeffersonian tradition, that he could not in all honesty sign such an oath since he might want to overthrow the government someday!

It is difficult for a people to remain free. Many external forces endanger our liberty, from International Communism to the European Common Market. Government is established to safeguard our freedom from this kind of danger and Bills of Rights are instituted both to protect the State internally from its government, and its citizens from each other. Government, then, provides the order essential to group existence, but order can be far-reaching. The American idea of the proper balance between freedom and order emphasizes freedom. Those who truly cherish civil liberties are reluctant in any way to suspend the legal rights of any dissenting individual or group because of the reciprocal nature of civil liberties; to foreshorten any man's right is to do likewise to one's own.

The topic of civil liberties is one of the most prominent and most confused among contemporary issues. "Freedom Riders," "Fifth Amendment Communists," Little Rock, "Minutemen" and the right to bear arms, and wartime relocation of the Japanese are all specific instances of controversy in this area, contributing to the cloudiness of the subject.

The virtue of determining the *principle* of civil liberty, rather than citing specific instances, lies in the fact that such a principle will serve as the standard by which specific civil liberties can be explained and limited. Unless they are to be regarded as sacred, civil liberties have a reason, and are rights only insofar as they satisfy that reason. The principle of civil liberty rests on the assumption that government in general has a function which sets limits to its proper exercise, or defines the line between the use and the abuse of its powers. This principle has meaning only in a political philosophy, such as democracy, in which it is affirmed that government, instead of being an end in itself, is under obligation to benefit its citizens. The civil liberties thus embrace those rights whose destruction or prevention causes government to lose its excuse for existence, and forfeit its claim to obedience.

The effect of the Bill of Rights is to write into law the individualistic premises of the democratic political philosophy. Civil liberty thus becomes a form of legal liberty. As a result there are two systems of law: the Constitutional law, which embodies the minimum liberties that government is pledged to respect; and the statutory and administrative law by which the government uses its powers, thus limited, to raise the liberties of individuals to an optimum.

The principle of civil liberty, however, implies a tendency of government to defeat its legitimate end, and to abuse rather than use its power. The State serves its purpose by use of force; to secure liberty it must possess and use power to negate liberty. Government can be considered, therefore, a threat to liberty, and many a battle has been fought against it. This suspicion or fear of government is deeply rooted in the American tradition.

There are three ways in which government may become the enemy of liberty: by tyranny—deviation from public function; by excess—paternalism; and by inefficiency. Civil liberties set limits to the government in power. Their justification is that the government in power tends, unless restrained, to tyranny, paternalism, and inefficiency. If so, the civil liberties are not immutable and self-evident truths, but are subject to revision on the basis of social good. By this criterion, old civil liberties may be abolished and new ones added by procedures which the fundamental law provides for change. An intermediate zone within which the right decision is difficult and doubtful is unavoidable, but there is only one fundamental principle in this matter: the total system of law should take as its end, and so far as possible promote, the reciprocal liberties of all individuals.

Civil liberties cases are not always as weighty as desegregation. Sometimes they can be picayune to the point of low comedy. Several years ago in a subdivision known as Westlake, located south of San Francisco— a community noted for its symmetry and architectural conformity—there occurred a curious dispute called the "Westlake Ivy Controversy." It seems that a resident had tried without success to grow a lawn in his tiny front yard. After much costly replanting, spraying, and other landscaping techniques, the hapless homeowner decided to try an ivy ground-cover. Immediately he was requested by the attorney for the Westlake Subdivision Improvement Association "to return your premises to the condition in which they were prior to the changes made by you, that is to say, to replace the lawns as they were originally." Taken literally this would include the fungus that had infested the lawn in its "original condition." It seems that the nonconformist allegedly was bound by a restrictive covenant requiring permission from the "association" for such a change. With $300 invested in ivy, and fortified with the belief that "a man's home is his castle," he decided to fight the "association." Other

Westlake residents had unsuccessfully resisted the neighborhood organization. Two had planted Bishop pines in their front lawns, but capitulated when the attorney for the association sternly remonstrated: "I want to see exactly the same thing in exactly the same place when I look down that street." [21]

The outcome of this test case is not presently known. The point is that little rights as well as big rights are important and the same principle and criterion apply—the reciprocal liberties of all must be protected.

THE INTERRELATION OF AMERICAN INSTITUTIONS

As we near the end of this study it must be remembered that the configuration of institutions in American society is not static. A process of replacement of old institutional patterns by new forms is constantly taking place. For this reason the process of disintegration, with its consequences for the individual, has been an important factor in our understanding of behavior. As each form of community is replaced by a newer one, the institution which integrates the pattern is subject to change. As communities in traditional society decline, so does the integrative character of the family. In urban communities the new integrative force is the economic institution but this has changed, too, with the metropolitan explosion after 1940. Local governments, because of their multiple nature and limited power, have not contributed to the integration of society.

There does appear to be a marked trend toward the integration of American institutions around the State. In fact, our history for the last three or four generations defines this trend: the failure of the city to integrate American life; the compulsive growth of bigness in business and government; and our involvement in the affairs of an interdependent world. Let us look at a few examples of the interrelations between the State and other institutions.

1. The most obvious is that of the State and the economic institution, a long-standing relationship often obscured. A major reason for obscurity was, as Don Martindale has suggested, the insistence by *laissez-faire* economists upon a distinction between economy and society.[22] This separation hid the ecopolitical fact that businessmen, voicing their belief in free enterprise, sought government aid and control when beneficial to them. In the discussion of the ideologies of the moguls this point was illustrated in reference to tariffs and railroads. The relation has continued in the oil and coal industries which sought government control in 1933 as a consequence of the depression.[23] Farm subsidization is

another persistent example, although there are differences among farmers regarding the wisdom of continuing the program. Congressmen from areas such as the Ohio Valley glass and pottery industry continue to seek protective tariffs. Federal subsidization of airlines and shipping interests has become a well-guarded source of income. Even the medical profession has received grants-in-aid to medical students, and subsidies for research projects. Governmental regulation of other areas of the economy is so common today it hardly appears to be related to the State. The Pure Food and Drug Administration, the Department of Public Health, the Bureau of Weights and Measures, the National Labor Relations Board, the Departments of Labor, Commerce, Agriculture, and Health, Education and Welfare are examples of this development.

The close interrelations between State and economy mean that the economy has ceased to operate solely on a local or regional level. Stimulated by better means of transport, a new technology, and new sources of power, the economy has become national in scale.[24] Big business appropriately fits that scale. The nature of the economic decisions, however, changes under such conditions. Not the conditions of the market alone, but also bargaining between the State as one source of power and the economy as a countervailing source, becomes a major factor in economic decision-making.[25] This was illustrated, in 1962, when the steel industry increased its prices. President Kennedy exerted the prestige of his office, raised the threat of action by the Justice Department, and aroused public opinion to create an unfavorable climate for the steel industry's action. One by one the companies lowered their prices to the former level.

Government has become an arbiter of the economic system. The State no longer merely protects the economy as in the nineteenth century; it functions, instead, through its regulatory powers as a balancing agent of the economy. This began on a large scale in the New Deal, but continued into the post-Second World War era. The Atomic Energy Act of 1946 granted government monopoly over all nuclear devices and products. The Taft-Hartley Act of 1947 regulated unions. The exercise of its 80-day injunction clause by President Truman during a steel strike, and his threat to have the railroads operated by the army during a labor dispute in the railroad industry, as well as the Justice Department indictment, during the Eisenhower Administration, of equipment manufacturing executives for price fixing, indicate the active participation of government in the economy.

The State and the economy do not exist, then, as separate, distinct entities surrounded by mysterious, invisible forces. Their reality can be assessed only as they are viewed in relation to one another as two systems of power.

2. With increasing frequency the State is becoming interrelated with higher education, beginning in the field of economics with Franklin Roosevelt's "Brain Trust." Other presidents and governmental departments have relied on academic talent for a variety of functions: labor relations; agriculture; governmental reorganization; and armed forces testing and training programs.

During and after the Second World War programs of nuclear research expanded the areas of relationship between government and higher education, resulting in the growth of a bureaucratically organized, scientific enterprise. The faculty roster of a university physics department engaged in nuclear research does not begin to reveal the network of persons involved. Research associates—often more numerous than the teaching faculty—technicians, engineers, draftsmen, computer teams, mathematicians, chemists, electricians, carpenters, and maintenance crews form the complex force devoted to the research.

One of the effects of this relationship has been to create, to paraphrase C. Wright Mills, the academic entrepreneur.[26] Knowledge becomes a commodity to be sold. The price is not wealth but a research facility that his own university could not afford, the opportunity to be an executive with prestige in an institution where executives are traditionally scorned, and the opportunity to produce original research and influence a generation of graduate students. As a consequence, wrote Mills, "some academic careers are becoming dependent upon the traits of the go-getter in business and the manager in the corporation." [27]

Another effect of the relation between the State and higher education has been the appearance within colleges and universities of those pressures and stresses upon individual freedom and creativity which follow the concern for security. This has been a problem in the physical sciences since the inception of the Manhattan Project, which manufactured the atomic bomb. The epoch of Congressional investigation, beginning prior to the Second World War and seldom actually reaching into academic halls, has apparently created an atmosphere of apprehension [28] among those professors who feel the necessity of asserting their position through statements of political and social policy. Knowledge, freely acquired, becomes politicized.

3. The last example is the relation between the State and the family. In societies under a monistic, absolute State, the family was considered

the central institution to be nurtured by the State. The family was the foundation of taxation, the origin of armies, the essence of the labor force, and the source of State loyalty. The power of the family was curtailed in favor of political and military policies.

In American society, under a democratic ideology, there has also been a close relation between the State and the family. Restrictions on the family have been instigated for reasons of welfare rather than political or military policy.[29] This is indicated by federal legislation for health, welfare, and education of children. Child Labor laws restricting hours and conditions of work, compulsory school attendance laws, required vaccinations and health examinations for enrollment in public schools, the establishment of welfare agencies, and special youth courts are examples of the greatly increased responsibility for children now assumed by government. Laws requiring marriage tests, prenatal examination, birth registration; laws to determine child neglect; laws regulating divorce and the division of property—all function to limit the arbitrary power of the family.

If law has restricted the family, it has also created opportunities for many families which they might not have otherwise known. Security for old age has increased with the Social Security Act of 1935 and supplemental legislation. The Federal Housing Authority and the G. I. Bill of Rights made home ownership possible for millions of families. The G. I. Bill, through provisions for education and apprenticeship, opened the way for hundreds of thousands to receive higher education or specialized training. This increased economic opportunities to the direct benefit of their families.

The greater responsibility of the State for family welfare is a consequence of a number of social and cultural changes in America. The concentration of population in cities and the parallel decline of rural communities weakened the hold of the mores, making the ideal of self-sufficiency difficult to achieve. The rapidity with which change and growth have taken place in America has made obsolete many early institutional forms. The Church has declined as a welfare agency. The "little red schoolhouse" is inadequate.

The question remains: how far shall the State extend its control, a question which becomes more important in light of the establishment by the State of a large and permanent military. The nature of the military in American society, and the vested interests it has developed is the subject of the next chapter.

Notes

1. Cf., Max Savelle, "Nationalism and Other Loyalties in the American Revolution," *American Historical Review*, Vol. LXVII, July 1962, pp. 901–923.
2. This was done by Marshall in the face of attacks by Congress upon the Judiciary during Jefferson's second administration. Some federal judges were dismissed and Supreme Court Justice Chase was nearly impeached. Cf., Harold Faulkner, *American Political and Social History*, New York: Appleton-Century-Crofts, 1957, 7th Ed., p. 192.
3. Cited in Samuel Eliot Morison and Henry Steele Commager, *The Growth of the American Republic*, New York: Oxford University Press, Vol. II, 1950, 4th Rev. Ed., p. 913.
4. Cf., Fletcher M. Green, "Cycles of American Democracy," *Mississippi Valley Historical Review*, Vol. XLVIII, June 1961, pp. 3–23.
5. Cf., Hans Kohn, *American Nationalism*, New York: The Macmillan Company, 1957; Don Martindale, *American Society*, Princeton: D. Van Nostrand, 1960, pp. 240 ff.; Frederic Paxson, *A History of the American Frontier*, Boston: Houghton Mifflin, 1924; and Oscar Handlin, *The Uprooted*, New York: Universal Library, 1951.
6. Cf., David A. Shannon, ed., *The Great Depression*, Englewood Cliffs, N.J.: Spectrum Books, 1960.
7. United States Department of Commerce, *Historical Statistics of The United States from Colonial Times to 1957*, p. 70.
8. Robert Nisbet, *The Quest for Community*, New York: Oxford University Press, 1953, p. 49.
9. Boyd Shafer, "Toward a Definition of Nationalism," *Nationalism and International Progress*, Urban Whitaker, Jr. (ed.), San Francisco: Chandler Publishers, 1959, rev., pp. 4 ff. See, also, David Potter, "The Historian's Use of Nationalism and Visa Versa," *American Historical Review*, Vol. LXVII, July 1962, pp. 924–950.
10. C. P. Snow, *Science and Government*, Cambridge: Harvard University Press, 1961, p. 83.
11. This is one of the possible consequences of bureaucracy that led to the formulation of Parkinson's Law: "Work expands so as to fill the time available for its completion" (C. Northcote Parkinson, *Parkinson's Law*, Boston: Houghton Mifflin Company, 1957, p. 2), and Parkinson's Second Law: "Expenditure rises to meet income." (*The Law and the Profits*, Boston: Houghton Mifflin Company, 1960, p. 5.)
12. See Chapter 23 for a discussion of the continuing war economy.
13. Daniel Bell, *The End of Ideology*, Glencoe, Ill.: The Free Press, 1960, p. 375.
14. David Lilienthal, *Big Business*, New York: Pocket Books, Inc., 1956. See Chapter 15 for an excerpt from this work. John Kenneth Galbraith, *American Capitalism* (Sentry Edition), Boston: Houghton Mifflin Company, 1962.
15. In the House of Representatives, 87th Congress, Second Session, 1962, the Southeastern states of Arkansas, Georgia, Kentucky, North Carolina, Tennessee, and Virginia had 63 representatives and 9 Chairmanships of the 20 House Standing Committees (including Rules, Ways and Means, Interstate and Foreign Commerce, Banking and Commerce, Armed Services, and Agriculture). The five most populous states; California, Illinois, New York, Ohio, and Pennsylvania, with 150 representatives have only 5 Chairmanships. The situation in the Senate

532   The Quest for Community

was even more exaggerated. Alabama, Arkansas, Georgia, Louisiana, Mississippi, South Carolina, and Virginia had 9 Chairmen of 15 Standing Committees and California, Illinois, New York, Ohio, and Pennsylvania had none!

16. Senator Stephen M. Young, "Danger on the Right," *Saturday Evening Post,* January 13, 1962, p. 6.

17. Robert Welch, *The Blue Book of the John Birch Society,* Belmont, Mass.: 1961, p. 9.

18. Welch's choice of Emerson is curious in light of Emerson's questionable relationship to Brook Farm, a "collective" and an escape, albeit abortive, from reality.

19. Welch, *op. cit.,* p. iii.

20. "We must halt and rout these organized forces of evil—or help mightily to do so —before we can get on with our positive and constructive program. And it is difficult to discuss the future improvement of the landscape and gardens around a beautiful home while a vicious enemy is throwing incendiary bombs at the house." Welch, *op. cit.,* p. 161.

21. *San Francisco Chronicle,* December 12, 1960, p. 3.

22. Martindale, *op. cit.,* pp. 337 f.

23. *Ibid.*

24. *Ibid.,* Chapter 14, *et passim.*

25. John Kenneth Galbraith, *American Captialism,* Boston: Houghton Mifflin, 1962, pp. 144–145, and Chapter VII.

26. *White Collar,* New York: Oxford Galaxy Books, 1956, p. 132.

27. *Ibid.,* p. 134.

28. Paul Lazarsfeld and Wagner Thielens, Jr., *The Academic Mind,* Glencoe, Ill.: The Free Press, 1958.

29. Joseph K. Folsom, *The Family and Democratic Society,* New York: John Wiley and Sons, Inc., 1943, p. 96. See, also, Eric Erickson, *Childhood and Society,* New York: W. W. Norton, 1956.

Selected Readings

Bell, Daniel, ed., *The Radical Right,* Garden City: Doubleday & Company, Inc., 1963.

*Blankston, George. *The Economic Basis of Politics.* New York: Random House, 1960.

Hook, Sydney. *Political Power and Personal Freedom.* New York: Criterion Press, 1959.

*Kohn, Hans. *Nationalism.* Princeton: Anvil Books, 1955.

*Mills, John Stuart. *On Liberty.* New York: Liberal Arts Press, 1956.

*Roosevelt, Theodore. *The New Nationalism.* Englewood Cliffs: Spectrum Books, 1961.

Shafer, Boyd C. *Nationalism.* New York: Harcourt, Brace, 1951.

*Wilson, Woodrow. *The New Freedom.* Englewood Cliffs: Spectrum Books, 1961.

* Paperback edition.

Chapter 23

The Military
in the National Scene

The English Bill of Rights of 1689 contained a clause placing the military under the control of Parliament. This was Parliament's reply to the Stuarts, who had attempted to create a standing army as an instrument of tyranny. Thus, the British bequeathed a heritage of antimilitarism to the colonies of the New World.

This heritage was reinforced by life under the military governors in the late colonial period and by America's geographical isolation. The "Boston Massacre" of 1770 in which four Bostonians were killed grew out of antagonisms aroused by tightening of military reins to end the "salutary neglect" of the colonies as well as make mercantilism pay following the close of the costly French and Indian War in 1763. Action and reaction culminated in open conflict at Lexintgon and Concord. At each step toward war with England, the colonials were adversely impressed by military government. Even after the war began, the thought of a standing army was repugnant to Americans. It was not until the latter part of 1776 that the militia began to yield to the idea of a Continental Army, but by the end of hostilities in 1781 the Army was not much more than legislation. After Yorktown, Washington pleaded in vain for appropriations and enlistments. The war went on, officially, for two more years, with the British once again in command of the seas, occupying all major ports, and with a large, experienced army on our shores.

The vastness of these shores, coupled with great geographical distances, posed an almost insurmountable problem in logistics. Great Britain was also distracted from complete attention to its "civil war" by internal politics and war on several European fronts, enabling America to carry off a successful revolution with little regard for military "reality." The War of 1812, which served to maintain our independence, mirrored the favorable circumstances of the Revolution. In short, with very little military capacity young America emerged victorious, employing casual troops and casual attitudes against a superior force, an important obstacle

533

to the creation of a militaristic attitude in nineteenth-century America.
Until the First World War, the inspired military leaders like Washington, Jackson, Grant, and Theodore Roosevelt—so effective politically
and socially as well as militarily—were drawn largely from civilian life.
Beginning with the First World War leadership shifted to the professional soldier. Captain Alfred Thayer Mahan's *The Influence of Sea
Power Upon History* in 1890 marks the beginning of the movement from
antimilitarism to nonmilitarism; that is, from a position hostile to the
idea of a standing army to a tolerance of, but not active support of, an
enlarged military establishment. The Mahan philosophy of extending
America's manifest destiny beyond our shores through sea power came
at the time when American industry began to seek new markets. That
Mahan's theories should have found so ready an audience has led some
historians to view this phenomenon as latter-day mercantilism.[2] Whatever his purpose, Mahan's writings were to have a profound effect on the
United States and on "navalism" throughout the world. He was to become "the Clausewitz of naval warfare."[3]

Since 1940 the United States has been at war—hot or cold. Military
involvement on a scale unparalleled in history has caught up the United
States in a militaristic posture at odds with tradition, yet little recognized. Dressed often in mufti, the new militarism absorbs much of our
time, talent, and resources. Military academy curricula are broadened to
include the humanities and the social sciences, and there is the dignity
of affiliation with the great scientists and scholars of the nation. Yet,
as Morris Janowitz has said: "To believe that the military have become
integrated with other leadership groups into a monolithic national
political establishment is to commit a sophisticated error. But to believe
that the military are not an effective pressure group on the organs of
government is to commit a political error."[4]

Nourished by the "balance of terror" that has existed since the Soviet
Union exploded her first nuclear device in 1949, the new militarism has
become a voracious bureaucracy which, at the level of contemporary
military technology, threatens to consume not only great portions of our
resources, but also effective political control of the military establishment. Oskar Morgenstern stated the problem succinctly:

*
"In this time of peril we find distressing confusion wherever we look: one
day we are assured that this country is so strong that no one will dare to

* From *The Question of National Defense*, p. 4, by Oskar Morgenstern. Copyright
1959 by Oskar Morgenstern. Reprinted by permission of Random House, Inc.

attack it; the next day we are told that we are in mortal danger. Some of our military and political leaders tell us that the plans and provisions to cope with hostile intents are entirely satisfactory; others, equally competent and also highly placed, deny this vigorously. The system of defense has become so complicated and involved that even some of those who make it their profession to study it become confused and cannot evaluate our strength in the light of the capabilities of the enemy. The power to participate in any detail in the processes of political and military decision vanishes to practically zero for the ordinary citizen, a serious matter for the survival of a living and meaningful democracy. The complicated nature of the defense organization also gives rise to the familiar belief that anything so complicated must certainly have been thought out carefully, a view that is nurtured by whoever is in charge of the establishment."

TOWARD THE GARRISON STATE

The implications of militarism for democracy have been observed repeatedly. Alexander Hamilton, supporting ratification of the Constitution, wrote in The Federalist: "The perpetual menacings of danger oblige the government to be always prepared to repel it; its armies must be numerous enough for instant defense. The continual necessity for their services enhances the importance of the soldier, and proportionately degrades the citizen. The military state becomes elevated above the civil." [5] Hamilton felt that Congressional control of the purse strings, as vested by the Constitution, was a sufficient safeguard against militarism. This feeling was justified in practice for generations; but with our entry into the Second World War, Congress found itself pressured by international conditions, calling for commitments of longer range than the traditional annual appropriations. Still operating under annual appropriations, the Department of Defense has been permitted by Congress, through tacit agreement, to enter into long-range commitments and to "carry-over" unexpended funds to succeeding budgetary periods. In effect, this has amounted to wider latitude for independent decision by the Defense Department, the Joint Chiefs, and the individual services.

We are not faced with Prussianism, the dashing, monocled, saber-scarred German professional militarism of generations, but rather total militarism, extending beyond the professional soldiery into every phase of national life. According to Arthur A. Ekirch, Jr., this can lead to the "Garrison state" where distinctions are blurred between civil and military, and contrast and conflict between the two become less apparent.

* To support the largest peacetime military establishment in American history approximately one-third the federal budget, or some twelve billion dollars, was appropriated directly for the army and navy in 1947. Such vast military expenditures naturally gave the armed forces increasing influence within the government, and top military men moved into key positions in federal agencies. Admiral William D. Leahy stayed on at the White House as President Truman's personal military adviser or private chief of staff. General Marshall replaced James Brynes as Secretary of State, and the department itself came more and more under military control. Abroad in overseas posts, General Walter B. Smith, United States Ambassador to Russia, General Lucius Clay, High Commissioner of the American Occupied Zone in Germany, and General Douglas MacArthur, Supreme Allied Commissioner for Japan, gave a militarist cast to our postwar policy. At home, unification of the armed forces in a single department and establishment of the National Security Council enabled the Secretary of National Defense to work with the State Department in determining foreign policy.

The practical results of the new integration of American foreign and military policy was the continued acceptance of the doctrine of peace through strength. . . .

American military commitments and responsibilities of such a vast scope could not fail to have important effects at home as well as abroad. Military control of American foreign policy, as a wide variety of critical observers pointed out, involved not only a sharp break with the American past but also posed a strong threat to peace and democracy. The military's lifelong identification with the use of force and contempt for the workings of diplomacy was viewed in the long run as likely to lead the United States into war. Even if such a contingency were avoided, there was the danger that the almost exclusive reliance on armed power in the conduct of American foreign relations would go far to stifle the workings of democracy at home. Centralization of authority, military control over the economy, and conscription of manpower were looked upon as probable results of a policy of peace through strength.

Opponents of militarism were disturbed to see the armed forces' new role in foreign affairs paralleled by increasing military encroachments into other civilian areas, both public and private. In the important field of atomic energy, for example, military leaders were only barely defeated in their attempt to take control from the hands of the civilian commission headed by David Lilienthal, former chairman of the Tennessee Valley Authority. Even so, the concentration of the work of the commission upon the problem of

* From *The Civilian and the Military* by Arthur A. Ekirch, Jr. Oxford University Press, 1956. Reprinted by permission.

producing atomic bombs insured a preponderant military influence in the future development of nuclear power. . . .

Military predominance over science and industry extended also into the realm of culture. American higher education, for example, became dependent to a great extent upon military funds. A large proportion of university research activities in the sciences was subsidized by the army and navy. The armed forces also offered attractive scholarships to the better students and greatly expanded the size and activities of their prewar R.O.T.C. program. In the immediate postwar years, veterans under the G.I. aid bill crowded the campus, while a number of military men, led by General Dwight D. Eisenhower as President of Columbia University, gained influential positions in American colleges and universities.

Underlying these specific instances of the extension of military power into civilian fields, and an even greater threat to civil supremacy, was the growing ability of the military to influence both public and Congressional opinion. Flourishing in the atmosphere of perpetual crisis and war hysteria pervading Washington, the military expert with his argument of military necessity usually took first rank at Congressional hearings. Utilizing their new-found prestige, the armed services also conducted effective lobbying campaigns and spent large sums on public relations. Much of the military office's propaganda had as its object the enactment of some system for the compulsory peacetime training of all American youths. Such a measure, whether in the form of military training or a universal service law, was calculated to give the army virtual control of American manpower. This, together with the direction already exercised over industrial production, would bring the United States to the edge of the total mobilization for war so long desired by militarists within and outside the armed services. . . .

In the United States, official thinking, though by no means unaware of the danger of a war waged with atomic weapons, continued to advance the thesis of preparedness to prevent war. This point of view which, of course, had never won acceptance by pacifists or antimilitarists, was subjected to increasing re-examination as the costs of the United States armaments burden rose and as it appeared that Russia also had been able to produce an atomic bomb. Conservatives, by no means friendly to Soviet Russia, joined liberals and pacifists in voicing a concern over America's military program. Former President Hoover, in an address in the summer of 1949, pointed out that the average citizen must work thirty-five days a year in order to pay the taxes to cover the costs of past or future wars. Later in the year, the Committee for Economic Development, a nonpartisan busines group, made public a report attacking the nation's defense program as a threat to individual freedom and civil supremacy in government. The widespread publicity given the C.E.D. Report was paralleled by expressions on the part of thoughtful and influential journalists of concern over United States militarism and arms expenditures.

The reviving American interest in disarmament was brought to the attention of Congress early in 1950 in the important speeches made by Senators Brien McMahon of Connecticut and Millard Tydings of Maryland. Senator McMahon's remarks were inspired by President Truman's decision directing the Atomic Energy Commission to continue its work on the hydrogen bomb, a weapon theoretically without limit in its destructive capacity. Accepting the decision as a necessary substitute for unilateral disarmament, Senator McMahon nevertheless argued that the United States must take the lead in a new moral crusade for peace and disarmament. The only alternative, he warned, was an intensification of the cold war and a degree of military spending that would add significantly and perhaps fatally to the "restrictions on freedom already brought about by the atomic bomb and by its pressures upon us to accept loyalty checks, espionage counter measures, and widening areas of official secrecy."

Going beyond Senator McMahon, who called for a system of international inspection to outlaw atomic and hydrogen bombs, Senator Tydings stressed the need for "disarmament all the way down the line to rifles." Otherwise, the Senator pointed out, just as soon as a war started with conventional weapons, international inspection would cease, and each belligerent would immediately resume building atomic or hydrogen bombs. Noting that the United States was already spending, out of a total budget of forty-two billion dollars, some thirty billions for war—past, present, or future—Senator Tydings again urged the President to heed his repeated resolutions calling for a disarmament conference. Assailing the State Department for its "mountainous . . . defeatism" in committing the United States to a policy of continued cold war with Russia, Tydings warned that the significance of Dr. Albert Einstein's remark that "Annihilation of any life on earth is within the range of technical possibilities" had been overlooked by American policymakers. "Like Nero," he concluded, "we seem to show a willingness to fiddle while our world burns. . . ."

By the spring of 1950, leaders of American foreign policy were showing a new concern over charges of United States militarism. John Foster Dulles, adviser to the State Department and subsequently Secretary of State, in his book *War or Peace* pointed out that while "military needs are important, and a strong military establishment is a necessity . . . we shall fail in our search for peace, security, and justice unless our policies, in reality and also in appearance, give priority to the hopes and aspirations for peace of the peoples of the world." Afraid that "as a result of excessive zeal to give the military whatever they professionally suggest, we have let it appear that we have gone militaristic," Dulles urged the United States not to yield its moral birthright as a peaceloving and antimilitaristic nation.

In his Memorial Day address at Arlington National Cemetery, General George C. Marshall emphasized the need for the United States to lead the way to world peace through the United Nations. Opposed to a policy of weakness as inviting aggression, Marshall warned that "we should not place complete dependence on military and material power." Walter Lippmann saw Marshall's words as an attempt to counteract the growing feeling that "the Administration's foreign policy has during the past year created the impression here and abroad that it places virtually complete dependence on military and material power." Believing that the United States seriously weakened itself in world opinion "by explaining that everything we do, every decision we take, is based on a strategical calculation about war," Lippmann concluded: 'This damnable obsession has gotten to the point where we can hardly send milk to babies abroad with explaining that this is an important action in our cold war with Russian communism.'

Before this movement for disarmament could achieve any tangible results, war broke out in Korea and other parts of the Far East. The United States decision to defend South Korea resulted in new calls for combat troops and a defense budget approximating that of the World War II years. In the 1950's the armed forces exceeded three million men, with half that number stationed abroad in hundreds of bases. Congress, upset over inadequacies in the American military machine despite the fifty billion dollars already spent in the four years of the cold war, approved new annual appropriations to almost that amount for each single year throughout the early '50s. After the Korean War, it passed a special law to permit General George C. Marshall to become Secretary of Defense, making an exception to the rule that a civilian secretary should be over the armed services. Marshall, as well as Generals MacArthur and Eisenhower, was again discussed as a possible nominee for the Presidency, and in 1952 Dwight D. Eisenhower, despite his refusals four years earlier, was elected to the nation's highest office.

Top professional soldiers were often less militaristic than military-minded civilians, and Eisenhower's victory at the polls was due as much as anything to public feeling that he could terminate the unpopular Korean War. Though this was accomplished by the truce agreement of 1953, the heavy costs of the Korean struggle added to those of World War II, and the continued cold war in Asia and Europe gave the American people little hope of any sudden return to real peacetime modes of living. Whether American democracy would be able indefinitely to survive a perpetual war economy or garrison-type state was an unanswered question. But peace or war, dictatorship or democracy, it was difficult to believe that the society of the future would be governed by the antimilitarist traditions that had guided three centuries of American history. Even if such a prospect were not accepted as evidence of a decline in American and world civilization, it pointed to one of the grave problems and tragedies of our time. Two world wars, instead of lessening the dangers of militarism and war, had only brought the Western world closer to catastrophe. . . .

Between the two World Wars thoughtful American scholars had alluded to the danger that the United States, with the passing of the frontier and the end of the relative isolation of the nineteenth century, might become an aggressive imperialist and militarist power. While Frederick Jackson Turner, the historian of the frontier, felt it "inconceivable that we should follow the evil path of Europe and place our reliance upon triumphant force," his associate Frederic Logan Paxson posed the problem of whether the United States would turn to true internationalism, or: "Shall we, in the foreign field, develop our nationality, take advantage of our growing wealth, and become the world menace of the next century—for no imperial power has ever stopped itself thus far. . . ." Writing after American entrance into the war, Charles A. Beard, the leading American philosophic historian, raised the question of whether the United States would embrace the militarism of the totalitarian states of Europe and resort to a war economy to avert a postwar depression.

Thus by mid-century, the American people faced a future clouded with uncertainty. The age of the common man seemed limited in its achievement to the guarantee of temporary material comforts, while the progress of science had culminated in the hydrogen bomb. Everywhere there was the overshadowing specter of war and the tremendous reality of vast military establishments. The new-style, perpetual mobilization for war made all the more imperative the return of that general world peace which alone could restore any vestige of normal civil life. Only in such an atmosphere could the American tradition of antimilitarism, peace, and democracy flourish and continue to be a vital, living force for the future.

Others believe that militarism is already encroaching on us. Fred J. Cook suggests that the Welfare State has been replaced by the "Warfare State," an expression based in part on President Eisenhower's farewell address in which he warned against "the acquisition of unwarranted influence, whether sought or unsought, by the military-industrial complex"; and in part on a speech made by General Electric's Charles E. Wilson in 1944, in which he suggested an "alliance of Big Business and the Military in 'a permanent war economy,'" where the role of Congress would be reduced to voting the necessary funds.[6]

THE NEW CIVIL-MILITARY RELATIONS

Whether we are nonmilitaristic or militaristic may be difficult to determine by definition, or by our inability to assess contemporary history. But the size of current military commitments and expenditures, and the difficulty of comprehending modern military technology, suggest a change of relationship in the civilian and military spheres. The Pentagon, the largest building in the world, is the symbol of this change. The War Department, organized by Henry Fox in 1790 under George Washington, with a secretary, one clerk, and 5000 soldiers, is in sharp contrast to the 25,000 employees of the Pentagon—and the 8,000,000 servicemen, civilians, and reserves who compose the Department of Defense.

Viewing traditional civilian control as a moot question, in light of the blurring of civilian and military roles, Gene M. Lyons analyzes, in the following article, the changes occurring in the civilian-military relationship as a result of the tremendous demands for specialization.

*

Historically the character of civil-military relations in the United States has been dominated by the concept of civilian control of the military. This has largely been a response to the fear of praetorianism. As recently as 1949, for example, the first Hoover Commission asserted that one of the major reasons for strengthening the "means of exercising civilian control" over the defense establishment was to "safeguard our democratic traditions against militarism." This same warning was raised in the report of the Rockefeller Committee on defense organization in 1953. While the overriding purpose of the committee's recommendations was to provide "the Nation with maximum security at minimum cost," the report made it clear that this had to be achieved "without danger to our free institutions, based on the fundamental principle of civilian control of the Military Establishment." Finally, during the debate on the reorganization proposals of 1958, senators and congressmen used the theme of a "Prussianized" military staff to attempt to slow down the trend towards centralization in the military establishment.

Despite this imposing support, the concept of civilian control of the military has little significance for contemporary problems of national security in the United States. In the first place, military leaders are divided among themselves, although their differences cannot be reduced to a crass contrast between dichomatic [sic] doctrines. Air Force leaders who are gravely concerned over the need to maintain a decisive nuclear retaliatory force are by now acknowledging the need to develop a limited war capability. At the same time, Army leaders are quite frank to admit that "flexible response" requires both strategic and tactical power of sizable strength, although they are particularly committed to developing a large tactical force. If these differences appear to be only differences in emphasis, they are nonetheless crucial

* From Gene M. Lyons, "The New Civil-Military Relations," *The American Political Science Review*, Vol. LV, March 1961, pp. 53–63. Reprinted by permission of the author and the American Political Science Association.

in a political process within which priorities must be established and choices must be made. Without firm agreement on priorities, there is little reason to expect that the military can control government policy even if civilian authorities abdicate responsibility for basic decisions. The most that can result is a compromise between different military positions. Commonly, military disagreement, if exposed, is an invitation for civilian intervention.

Secondly, the concept of civilian control of the military ignores two other factors that complicate civil-military relations. On the one hand, the military themselves accept the principle of civilian supremacy; on the other, they have been thrown into a political role in the formation of policy. The resignation of General Gavin over the budgetary restrictions of the "New Look" strategy is a case in point. The General disagreed with the judgment of his civilian superiors but, like General Ridgway before him and General Taylor after him, held his most violent fire until he was out of uniform and freed from the limits of professional restrictions. His case dramatically illustrates the dilemma of the military as they move into the center of defense policy-making. Here they have to struggle between the non-partisan tenets of their creed and the requirements of effective participation in the political process. Their advice as experts is not only used by the Executive to bolster its case, but is eagerly courted by Congress and the public as a basis for testing the caliber of executive action. In one respect the political role of the military tends to dilute their own professionalism. But in another, it affords them more than one opportunity to maintain a balance between their professional code and the individual conscience. The nature of the American political system thus provides an outlet for frustration which, in other settings, has been the catalyst to set off an outburst of militarism.

In its broadest sense, the concept of civilian control of the military means military responsiveness to the policies of politically responsible government. But this too needs to be reinterpreted in the light of revolutionary changes that have greatly complicated the formation of defense policy. Preparedness is as much the product of civilian expertise in science and engineering and of civilian decisions on the allocation of national resources as it is of military planning. At the same time, it is very often the military who put defense policy to the test of political accountability by exposing the bases for decisions to congressional and public inquiry. As a result, there is a constant reversal of traditional roles, a situation that has brought civilians and military into a new set of relationships. These relationships have been reflected only in a limited way in recent organizational changes that have strengthened the central agencies of the defense establishment. To appreciate their full significance, it is also necessary to understand changes in the character of both civilian and military leadership in defense affairs. Civilians are becoming "militarized" and the military "civilianized" and it is these changes that reflect more clearly than organization alone, a fundamental break with tradition in the evolution of civil-military relations.

Like many institutions in American political life, a highly centralized, civilian dominated Pentagon has developed in response to changing forces and conditions. Had the Joint Chiefs of Staff been able to function as a collegial unit rather than as a divided group of service representatives, it is possible that reorganization trends might have taken different directions. Centralization, however, was probably inevitable in one form or another.

Increasing defense costs made centralized budgeting and programing a necessity. The bite of military expenditures in the total federal budget makes it impossible to ignore the impact of defense on the national economy, the government's tax program and the whole range of complex problems of resources allocation. The impact of technology has also been a centralizing factor. Indeed, work on the military applications of atomic energy had already been centralized in the Atomic Energy Commission. But work on missiles had been left in the separate services and the duplication of effort in three competitive programs brought on demands for greater coordination in propulsion programs in the late 1950's. Finally, both these areas of financial management and of research and development require skills that are "civilian," in essence, and are not yet possessed by many high ranking military officers. Thus it might be argued that "civilianization," as well as centralization, was inevitable given the nature of the problems that needed to be solved. . . .

The strides taken in recent years to develop new modes of government administration have largely been forced by the demands of technology. The scientific programs during the Second World War and the industry-based programs of the Air Force in the postwar years established precedents for government contracting in areas that now extend beyond technological projects to projects in the social and behavioral sciences. Each of the services has created a "think" organization to which it can farm out problems—the RAND Corporation of the Air Force, the Operations Research Office of the Army and the Operations Evaluation Group of the Navy. Within the Department of Defense a variety of advisory panels are available to the Secretary and his assistants—on research and development, on psychology and the social sciences and on education and manpower. In addition, the Institute of Defense Analyses has been established "to create machinery for putting a segment of the nation's intellectual resources more effectively at the disposal of the national security effort." Originally established in connection with the evaluation of competing weapons systems, the scope of the Institute now encompasses broad areas of military strategy where the support for judgments on weapons evaluation is very often to be found. Indeed the close connection with strategic issues has been the link that has extended research on military operations into the far reaches of national policy.

These innovations in administration project the professionalization of civilian leadership in defense far beyond the confines of government itself. That they extend as widely as they do is, in many ways, an indication of the response of industry, science, and private scholarship to the problems of national security. . . .

. . . It seems safe to predict that these trends will continue to gain momentum—the "depoliticalization" of appointive posts, the influence of career executives, innovations in government administration, and an interest in military affairs among writers, scientists, and scholars. They are also bound to contribute to a growing professionalization of civilian leadership in military affairs and, in turn, this professionalization will have important repercussions on the nature of civil-military relations.

The significance of the professionalization of civilian leadership cannot be judged without some consideration of the changing character of military leadership. When General Maxwell Taylor retired in mid-1959, a veteran Washington reporter commented that this marked "the point at which the Old Army is drawing to the end of its mission—and even of its relevance." He called Taylor "the last great captain of the old hunters . . ." and his successor, General Lyman Lemnitzer, "an intellectual, a staff officer of vast experience, a kind of professor of the new kind of war." The contrast is perhaps overdrawn, for it is difficult to think of the military without its "heroic leaders," left to the impersonal calculations of the "military managers." It nevertheless catches the essence of a fundamental change in the character of military leadership.

Military leadership is changing under the impact of two forces: the revolutionary developments in weapons technology; and the close relationship between military programs and foreign and economic policies. The management of a missile program or a test range, the constabulary duties of an overseas assignment, the pseudo-diplomatic function of a military assistance advisory group, the planning involved in a Pentagon or a NATO slot—these are the tasks for which the military must prepare the officers of the future. At the same time, the threat of war, total, nuclear, limited or conventional, and the demands that open hostilities make on military leadership, are ever present. Thus the old attributes of "heroic leaders," the qualities of discipline, courage, and command ability, cannot be forgotten. In this respect, the new responsibilities of military leaders have not so much altered their fundamental make-up as they have added new dimensions to their character and made them more complex human beings. This new complexity is being reflected in a number of changes in the military profession. Three of these are particularly important: the broadening base for officer recruitment; the development of higher military education; and new policies for selection and promotion to higher rank.

To a large extent, the broadening base for officer recruitment is a matter of arithmetic. In recent years the services have had to draw in more than 40,000 new officers every year, with a good percentage of these needed on a career basis. At the same time, the service academies graduate only about 1500 new lieutenants and ensigns. At a result, the services have had to look to other sources for career officers, particularly civilian colleges and universities. This development has more than quantitative significance, however; it is also qualitative. The broadening recruitment base for young officers is bringing into the services men with new outlooks and new areas of technical competence that serve to meet the widening range of military responsibilities.

The elaborate structure of higher military education is also responding to the broadening character of military responsibility. Curriculum changes in undergraduate programs at the service academies and in military programs in civilian colleges and universities are moving in two directions: first, they are incorporating new material to expose the students to the expanding technology that is making such an impact on military life; and, second, undergraduate courses are becoming less vocationalized and are taking the form of preprofessional education to lay a solid intellectual base for future career development. At the post-commissioning schools—from the command and staff colleges through the service war colleges to the Industrial College of the Armed Forces and the National War College—there is an increased emphasis on the problems of international politics, the dilemmas of war and peace brought on by nuclear weapons, the impact of defense on the national economy and the complexities of life in a world of allies, international organizations and uncommitted nations. There are still weaknesses in military education: there is a tendency to be highly technical and vocational, even in dealing with social science material; service-organized programs also tend to be parochial, emphasizing the narrow views of the service itself; and the image of the world scene that is projected in military teaching is static and over-simplified. The advancements in the last fifteen years have nevertheless been striking and have taken education far beyond the traditional emphasis on "loyalty, precedent, specific technical skill, and a gentlemanly code of conduct."

Traditions, however, die hard. In the transition from one generation of military leaders to another, the qualities of the "heroic leader" continue to have primary importance and significance for those older officers who grew up in the "old Army," in the "black-shoe Navy" or even in the "propeller-driven Air Force." These are the officers, moreover, who control the machinery for selection and promotion. Here the struggle between the old and the new takes place.

. . . However "civilianized" military officers may become, the profession itself will continue to be anchored in the distinct nature of its trade, the process that has so succinctly and meaningfully been called the "management of violence" by Harold Lasswell. And, in the fulfillment of their mission, the military will continue to be highly influenced by the particular tools of their craft. Indeed, without this distinction what is the meaning of the military profession as a separate group in society? And what do military leaders have to offer that physicists, engineers, diplomats and economists cannot do to meet the requirements of national security? The answer, obviously, is nothing. At the same time, within the framework of its primary and unique contribution, the military profession is dramatically changing. At the moment, it is in a state of transition from the old to the new with the dimensions of the new still unformed, still taking shape, still resembling the contours of an earlier day.

The nature of civil-military relations is thus being changed through the strengthening of central organization in the Department of Defense, through the professionalization of civilian leadership and through the broadening character of the military profession. These trends might also be expressed as the "militarization" of civilians and the "civilization" of the military. When extended to their logical conclusion, they suggest new relationships between civilians and military based on a more complex division of labor than has heretofore existed. These relationships, however, are responsive to the new shape of national security in which military affairs are no longer a monopoly of the military and a clean-cut division between matters of war and peace, between foreign and military policies, is a false and misleading notion.

If the question of civilian control of the military in the traditional sense is moot, the problem of coordinating the diverse and far-flung activities of our military establishment is certainly not moot. At the head of the largest organization of any kind in the world, the President, through his Secretary of Defense, is responsible for combining the myriad facets of our defense structure into a smoothly integrated network of military bases, supply lines, men, and matériel to achieve the protection of the United States. Is it reasonable to assume that this is possible? We know that lack of coordination fosters the growth of autonomy and empire building which may or may not harmonize with over-all objectives. On the other hand a highly integrated organization of the present magnitude requires a rigid bureaucracy, replete with highly disciplined bureaucrats. Such a structure, although easily coordinated, lacks flexibility to meet rapid changes in the adversary. The scope of this problem will be discussed in the section below.

If "professionalization of civilian leadership" is equivalent to the militarization of civilians, where is the line between the militarized civilian and the civilianized militarist? If clear-cut divisions between war and peace, foreign and military policies, civilian and military interests, no longer exist, do we have Ekirch's garrison state, or Cook's warfare state?

THE PENTAGON AND THE ECONOMY

To the eight million servicemen, civilians, and reserves who compose the Department of Defense must be added the nearly four million persons directly employed in defense industries. Deducting the reserves as part-time employees, there remain 7.5 million Americans, 10 per cent of the labor force, depending directly on the military for their jobs. Indirect military spending in service industries augments this figure considerably. Precise data are elusive, but it has been estimated that in Los Angeles "fully half the jobs are dependent, either directly or indirectly, on the continuance of the arms race—and arms spending." [7]

The magnitude of defense spending provides not only individuals but also whole communities with vested interests in the continuation of that spending. Although short-sighted from a national standpoint, lobbying by local Chambers of Commerce, unions, and industries to maintain military bases or defense contracts may be viewed in a different light; when the life of a community is at stake, arguments about the national interest go unheeded. As Harold Laski pointed out:

> Anyone who thinks for one moment of the effort involved in building the atomic bomb will not find it difficult to realize that, in the new warfare, the engineering factory is a unit of the army, and the worker may be in uniform without being aware of it. The new militarism may clothe itself in civilian uniform; and, if the present relations of production are maintained, it may be imposed upon a people who see in its development no more than a way to full employment. [8]

Responsible for $160 billion worth of equipment and bases scattered throughout the world, the Department of Defense spends approximately 60 cents of every tax dollar. It controls 32 million acres of land in the United States and 2.6 million acres abroad—larger than the states of Rhode Island, Delaware, Connecticut, New Jersey, Massachusetts, Maryland, Vermont, and New Hampshire combined. These assets are "three times as great as the combined assets of United States Steel, American Telephone and Telegraph, Metropolitan Life Insurance, General Motors and Standard Oil of New Jersey. The paid personnel of the Defense Department is triple the number of employees of all of these great corporations, whose influence on affairs of state have so often worried observers." [9]

Government involvement to this extent must affect the economy. The threat of disengagement should peace be negotiated poses interesting economic and philosophic problems. California, for example, receives nearly one-quarter of all defense contracts allocated and would suffer severe economic hardship should disarmament arrive. Other sections of the country, jealous of these lucrative contracts, lobby vigorously for their share. This could lead to a sectional split with serious political repercussions on a scale not seen since the gold-silver controversy of the late nineteenth century.

One school of thought advocates the award of defense contracts on a purely competitive basis; another views defense spending as a means of relieving chronic unemployment in depressed areas; still another sees spending solely as a political device—a means for establishing a good record in Congress by securing contracts for a Senator's state or a Representative's district. The fact remains that the far western states currently are receiving 32.6 per cent of all prime military contracts. In addition to Los Angeles, San Diego, Sacramento, and Seattle depend heavily on these contracts—so much so that such terms as "the Senator from Boeing" have been coined by critics.[10]

The dilemma appears insoluble: contract-rich communities fail to work at attracting more diversified industries; nondefense employment is not keeping pace with an increase in the labor force.

Benicia, California, a city of 6000, was threatened with near-extinction by the impending deactivation of the Benicia Ordnance Arsenal. Burdened with municipal debt incurred when Benicia built a new sewage plant far in excess of local needs without the arsenal, and faced with the loss of sales, gas, and beverage taxes when 2400 arsenal workers would be terminated, the civic leaders were unsuccessful in a protracted attempt, through their Congressmen, to prevent "a major catastrophe." They tried desperately to promote this "sleepy, isolated town"—which they said, optimistically, now had "a chance to wake up." [11]

Construction on the West Coast's largest naval air base was begun in 1959 in Kings County, California. On the strength of that fact, speculating contractors subdivided large tracts of farm land and constructed hundreds of new homes for the influx of Naval personnel. The influx came but the Navy, claiming the tract homes were too expensive, built 1300 homes on the base for married personnel. At last count, the two cities of Hanford and Lemoore, California, with a combined population under 15,000, had 1300 new, vacant homes priced between $11,000 and $16,000.[12]

Should disarmament come, the pressure for continuing government spending at the present rate would remain strong.

* There is now no shortage of goods and services at the prevailing market price. During the last ten years the privately owned firms have proved incapable of providing employment to the growing labor force. Between 1953 and 1959, the people available for jobs have increased by about 5,500,000, but employment has increased by only 3,500,000.

Broadly speaking, we are already producing all of the goods and services that are profitable to private industry. Therefore a necessary condition for giving useful employment to men who are now in military work is a major expansion of government initiative into areas where the needs of society cannot be satisfied by private businessmen who are operating for private gain.

For some years, the United States has been indulging in a major ideological prohibition against any sort of economic initiative other than by private business management. However, effective handling of the peace race clearly requires attention to the public sector of community life as an area for organizing alternatives to a military economy. The important military contracting firms have been a sort of twilight zone between public bodies and private firms. Once a lead is given by government in preparing for peace, much of the experience of military contractors in serving government requirements can be turned to account for peaceful purposes. Thus, the very tradition of serving a public market may make the military-producing firms amenable to operating within a public sector of a prosperous and peaceful economy.

Seymour Melman's foregoing suggestion is based on the eventuality of disarmament, devoutly to be wished, but not yet in sight. There are many writers who feel that disarmament is impossible because the only kind of enduring peace we can hope for is based on the "balance of terror." Oskar Morgenstern, for example, has said that *"war has to become technologically impossible in order to be stopped."* The failure of moral or religious considerations to stop wars has left only the "absolute technical certainty of immediate self-destruction for those nations who start a war" as the deterrent to war.[13] This condition, which is still to be reached, would preclude disarmament.

Morgenstern's position has been supported by Charles J. Hitch and Roland N. McKean of the Rand Corporation, provided nuclear deterrence is supplemented by the power to meet limited aggression with more advanced conventional weapons. "If it is clear that the aggressor too will suffer catastrophic damage in the event of his aggression, he then has strong reason not to attack, even though he can administer great damage.

* Reprinted from *The Peace Race* by Seymour Melman with the permission of the publisher, George Braziller, Inc. Copyright 1961 by Seymour Melman.

A protected retaliatory capability has a stabilizing influence not only in deterring rational attack, but also in offering every inducement to both powers to reduce the chance of accidental war." [14]

Herman Kahn, also supporting the deterrence position, commented on its cost:

*

A common fear, that raising our expenditures by some significant amount would just help the communists by weakening us economically, is probably baseless if we exercise reasonable prudence in how we raise the money. Lenin is often quoted to the effect that it would be a good Soviet strategy to force the United States to bankrupt itself by overspending on military items. The quotation seems to be erroneous; a careful search of Soviet literature and all the known writings of Lenin has failed to disclose the existence of any remark of that type. In fact, Marxist beliefs tend to go in the other direction. They argue that large military expenditures are essential to the capitalist nations to maintain their prosperity. This view is also held by many non-Marxist opponents and even by some adherents of capitalism. I do not believe that spending money on munitions is a good way to maintain prosperity. I believe the opposite; that except for idiosyncracies of the business cycle, such expenditures tend to reduce our current standard of living and our rate of economic growth. But I also believe that, if necessary, we can afford such expenditures.

I do not think we should become a militaristic society, nor do I believe that serious questions with regard to the long-run effects of inflation and the demoralizing and dislocating effects of high taxes are not important. But even if the defense budget climbs to somewhat higher levels we should be able to handle inflationary pressures and the impact of the new taxes, at the same time preserving what will look to all the world, including us, like a predominantly civilian and rather comfortable society. We are still not at the stage of making really hard economic choices.

We have no right to be indignant if it turns out that we cannot eat our cake and have it too. Security may come at a higher price than we have been accustomed to paying. It may, for example, include a willingness to incur casualties in limited wars just to improve our bargaining position moderately. This is a high price to pay. However, the monetary part of the price for security still runs low, so low in terms of percentage of our gross national product, that a responsible policy probably would not require a cutback in current standards of living—just a cutback in the rate at which they *increase*. If we include in this concept of security an increase in the rate of capital investment, then in the long run it might even mean an increase in our

* Reprinted from On *Thermonuclear War*, pp. 566–567, second edition, by Herman Kahn, by permission of Princeton University Press. Copyright 1961 by Princeton University Press.

standard of living, though it may involve some reduction in the consumption of consumer goods for the next decade or so.

It is apparent that whatever the route, disarmament or deterrence, the effect on the economy will be massive. Kahn's tacit belief that we could maintain massive deterrence without becoming militaristic is difficult to accept, but the likelihood of the balance of terror continuing is the more plausible of the choices at this point in history.

THE CONSTABULARY CONCEPT

Given the kind of nuclear stalemate both sides appear to be striving for, the possibility of limited and "brush-fire" war rather than "broken-back" war is enhanced. The preventive nature of such action calls for a redefinition of the military role, which Janowitz calls the *constabulary concept*. "The military establishment becomes a constabulary force when it is continuously prepared to act, committed to the minimum use of force, and seeks viable international relations, rather than victory, because it has incorporated a protective military posture. The constabulary outlook is grounded in, and extends, pragmatic doctrine." [15]

The constabulary concept is offered as a means of meeting the challenge of Soviet aggression while still permitting an optimum degree of civilian control.

*
In the early history of the United States, the Army, as an internal police force, was called on to enforce the authority of the central government. As the authority of the central government became paramount, after the Civil War, the internal police activity of the Army was required to enforce laws strained by opposing social and economic groups—strikes and race tension, in particular. In modern times, the Army has been reluctant to become involved in such disputes, except as the ultimate source of sanctions. Such intervention, which often involves the Army in short-run political conflict, is seen as detracting from its ability to perform as a guardian of the nation. When called on to intervene in support of the Supreme Court decisions on desegregation of the public school system, the Army found itself relatively unprepared for such police work. While, as a public servant, the military automatically and vigorously complied with orders, such duty ran counter to their self-conceptions. The constabulary concept does not refer to police functions in this historical role. On the contrary, extensive involvement of the military as an internal police force—except as the reserve instrument of

ultimate legitimate force—would hinder the development of the constabulary concept in international relations.

The officer in the constabulary force is particularly attuned to withstand the pressure of constant alerts and tension. He is sensitive to the political and social impact of the military establishment on international security affairs. He is subject to civilian control, not only because of the "rule of law" and tradition, but also because of self-imposed professional standards and meaningful integration with civilian values. Moreover, civilian control over the military, as it moves in the direction of a constabulary force, cannot be based on outmoded assumptions that it must merely prod the military into modernization or prevent a Bonapartist uprising.

Instead, the problems of civilian control consist of a variety of managerial and political tasks. As a requisite for adequate civilian control, the legislature and the executive must have at their disposal both criteria and information for judging the state of readiness and effectiveness of the military establishment in its constabulary role. The formulation of the standards of performance the military are expected to achieve are civilian responsibilities, although these standards cannot be evolved independent of professional military judgment. In this respect, the conventional aspects of warfare and military activities at the lower end of the destructive range present difficult problems for civilian leaders. The adequacy of forces for strategic deterrence and the conditions for atomic inspection and control have come to be posed as scientific questions over which the military have no monopoly of professional expertise, a fact which they recognize. The adequacy of limited war forces facilities, the management of military assistance, and the conduct of irregular warfare are questions over which segments of the military seek to perpetuate an exclusive professional jurisdiction.

Until the constabulary concept is firmly established, civilian authorities must also be prepared to respond to the pressures generated by the military definition of international relations. In varying degree, military responsibility for combat predisposes officers toward low tolerance for the ambiguities of international politics, and leads to high concern for definitive solutions of politico-military problems. Military management—of strategic deterrence or limited war—involves risk-taking according to one set of premises; conflict resolution, nuclear test suspension, and arms inspection involve risk-taking based on another calculus.

Finally, civilian control of the constabulary must be fashioned in terms of the kind of military service required of the citizen population. Three alternatives are available: First, citizen service could be eliminated by relying on a complete professional and voluntarily recruited military force. Second, a system of universal public service could be enacted in which military service was but one alternative to civilian defense, community service, or human and natural resources conservation duty. Third, the present mixed system of a predominately professional armed force and a limited system of selective service, which must necessarily operate without equality or clarity, could be continued. All three arrangements are compatible with the constabulary force conception, although each presents different problems of political supervision.

While one may argue that a system of universal public service is most appropriate for the consensus of a political democracy, there is no reason to assume that a completely professionalized constabulary force would necessarily be incompatible with democratic political institutions. The technological necessities of warfare weaken the citizen-soldier concept, at least in its traditional form. The constabulary officer corps must be composed of highly-trained personnel, ready for immediate operations. Citizen reservists must be organized on a stand-by basis. Short-term, active-duty officers will be more and more replaced by men who are available for periods of five to ten years of professional service. Longer and more continuous service will be required for enlisted personnel as well. The trend is toward a military force of career professionals, although strong arguments, both military and political, can still be offered against such a development.

. . . The constabulary concept would be facilitated by an effective unification of the military and organization of the military establishment along more functional lines. The present military organization does not permit adequate appraisal of the relative allocation of resources on the various tasks of strategic deterrence, versus limited warfare, versus the management of international security affairs. But in developing unification, each service faces a different set of problems in moving toward the constabulary concept. . . .

The pressure of the differing military doctrines has operated as a form of countervailing power. During the decade 1950–1960, while the American military posture became more absolutist, public criticism by pragmatic military leaders was extensive, and not without real effect. However, if these political activities of the military served national interests, they did not necessarily contribute to the strengthening of civilian control. In the next decade the pressure from the military is more likely to oppose pragmatic trends in civilian political leadership. To strengthen the civil service concept of anonymity, discretion, and subservience to political direction does not deprive the military of an active policy-recommending role.

By the same token, the effectiveness of the constabulary concept, during a period of active diplomacy, does not depend on ill-conceived and exaggerated "psychological warfare." The growing sense of frustration which leads the military to a search for a comprehensive ideology also contributes to the belief that the professional soldier should be a self-appointed publicist. The military establishment must have an active public information role—both domestic and foreign. To remain completely silent is to invite confusion. However, the constabulary concept, especially as it relates to strategic deterrence, rests on a self-conception of the older naval tradition of the "silent service. . . ."

On the basis of a professional redefinition toward the constabulary concept, new devices of civilian control become feasible. Foremost would be a congressional review of the adequacy of its own procedure of legislative oversight. In the executive branch changes would center around a stronger notion of a permanent higher civil service, and a system of longer tenure for political appointees seems in order. But the formulation by both Congress and the executive branch of acceptable limits for pressure group activities and domestic public information activities of the armed forces is not unimportant. Bold experimentation in the political education of the officer corps is also required. It is impossible to isolate the professional soldier from domestic political life, and it is undesirable to leave the tasks of political education completely to the professionals themselves, even though they have been highly responsible in this assignment. The goal of political education is to develop a commitment to the democratic system and an understanding of how it works. Even though this task must rest within the profession itself, it is possible to conceive of a bipartisan contribution by the political parties.

The political control of the military cannot be separated from the control of the activities of the Central Intelligence Agency, especially since Congress has avoided any such supervision. In 1959 a report of the Senate Foreign Relations Committee, concerning the views of retired senior foreign service officers, included the following statement: "It is true that there is little accurate information available, but every senior office of the Foreign Service has heard something of the C.I.A.'s subversive efforts in foreign countries, and probably most of them have some authentic information of this nature in some particular case. Unfortunately, most of these activities, if not all of them, seem to have resulted to the disadvantage of the United States and at times in terrible failure."

Ultimately, political control of the military profession hinges on the answer to the question why do officers fight. In a feudal society political control is civilian control only because there is an identity of person and interest between aristocratic groups and military leaders. The officer fights because he feels that he is issuing the orders. Under totalitarian control, the officer fights because he has no alternative. As they emerge into power, totalitarian political leaders make temporary alliances with military leaders, but, finally, they destroy the autonomy of the military profession.

Political democracies assume that officers can be effectively motivated by professional ethics alone. The officer fights because of his career commitment. The strain on democratic forms under prolonged international tension raises the possibility of the garrison state under which the military, in coalition with demagogic civilian leaders, wield unprecedented amounts of political and administrative power. In the garrison state the officer fights for national survival and glory.

But the constabulary force is designed to be compatible with the traditional goals of democratic political control. The constabulary officer performs his duties, which include fighting, because he is a professional with a sense of self-esteem and moral worth. Civilian society permits him to maintain his code of honor and encourages him to develop his professional skill. He is amenable to civilian political control because he recognizes that civilians appreciate and understand the tasks and responsibilities of the constabulary force. He is integrated into civilian society because he shares its common values. To deny or destroy the difference between the military and the civilian cannot produce genuine similarity, but runs the risk of creating new forms of tension and unanticipated militarism.

CONCLUSION

The stresses of international tension, the growing difficulty of military technology, and the sheer size of our military effort have brought us face to face with an undesirable and undemocratic product—militarism. That civilian control has proved inadequate and contradictory in many respects is understandable in the light of the unprecedented circumstances. But the vacuum left in the absence of civilian control not only encourages an extension of the tasks and power of the military élite, but also may make this mandatory.[16]

President Eisenhower's farewell address pointed to the changing nature of the military establishment: "The total influence—economic, political, even spiritual—is felt in every city, every state house, every office of the Federal Government. We recognize the imperative need for this development. Yet we must not fail to comprehend its grave implications. Our toil, resources, and livelihood are all involved, so is the very structure of our society." [17] This is a significant warning from a career soldier.

Through his Secretary of Defense, Robert S. McNamara, the late President Kennedy reaffirmed the importance of civilian authority over the military. Acting to curb the tremendous exposure of the military mind to the public view,[18] the Department of Defense undertook a program of correlating the statements of officers with official policy. This program, called by its critics "military censorship," came into prominence following the "admonishment" of Major General Edwin A. Walker for publicly accusing various national figures of communist affiliations. Charges of following a "no-win policy" were leveled at the Kennedy administration following General Walker's resignation.

The extremist tendencies of some active and retired military leaders, although not widespread, are perhaps symptomatic of the state of *anomie* of certain members of the military as a result of technological change, military consolidation, and contradictory civilian control. The essential conservatism of the officer corps is heightened by the kinds of frustration aggravated by the above changes.[19] That men who have known little else than the "socialized" military life should be so militant in their political and economic conservatism is a paradox. But the old-style soldier was accustomed to simple, clear-cut issues.

Political demagogues also relish the simple, clear-cut issue, creating distinctions where none exist. Charges of a "no-win policy" or a "sell-out" in the Departments of State and Defense make for ringing oratory but seldom tell the whole story. Oversimplification of the cold war is dangerous when innocently conceived; concocted for political gain it could prove fatal. The delicate balance in the world today wavers with every brush-fire war, every Berlin Corridor incident; with each irresponsible statement made by political leader, military attaché, or Peace Corps volunteer. The difficulty of coordination requires every member to give his utmost in skill to the objective of an honorable peace.

Recent experience indicated that there are no winners in large-scale wars, and the gentlemanly, restricted, winner-take-all combat of the Middle Ages begins to take on an irrefutable logic. The weary soldier's comment in *All Quiet on the Western Front* that the leaders should get in the ring and fight it out was wisdom born of experience. Morgenstern has said that "the probability of a large thermonuclear war occurring appears to be significantly larger than the probability of it not occurring." [20]

One of the real dangers of living with anxiety is that we learn to accommodate to it. The value of tension, if it does not immobilize our efforts, is to keep us alert to danger. But like the "boy who cried, 'Wolf,' " a protracted cold war, with repeated alarms, can become routine. And as we adjust, it is very possible that we might come to assume that we can take whatever the enemy has to deliver.

> Once the people are convinced that they can survive the present state of the art of killing, a broad and significant new habit pattern will have been introduced and accepted, one grotesquely different from any we have known for thousands of years—that of adjusting ourselves to

the idea of living in holes. From that time onward it will be simple to adjust ourselves to living in *deeper* holes." [21]

The question of the compatibility of militarism and democracy is frequently, perforce, subordinated to the question of survival as a guiding principle. It should not be forgotten that this, too, may prove defeating. Militarism and civil liberties are basically antagonistic. Can we truly survive unless they are made compatible?

Notes

1. Christopher Ward, *The War of the Revolution*, Vol. I., New York: The Macmillan Company, 1952, pp. 208–209.
2. See Walter LaFeber, "A Note on the 'Mercantilistic Imperialism' of Alfred Thayer Mahan," *The Mississippi Valley Historical Review*, Vol. XLVIII, March 1962, pp. 674–685, for a refutation of this notion.
3. Barbara Tuchman, *The Guns of August*, New York: The Macmillan Company, 1962, p. 93.
4. Morris Janowitz, *The Professional Soldier*, Glencoe, Ill.: The Free Press, 1960, p. vii.
5. Quoted from Fred J. Cook, "Juggernaut: The Warfare State," *The Nation*, Vol. 193, October 28, 1961, p. 285.
6. Cook, *op. cit.*, pp. 300, 278, 285.
7. Cook, *op. cit.*, p. 282.
8. Harold J. Laski, *Liberty in the Modern State*, New York: The Viking Press, 1949, p. 20.
9. Cook, *op. cit.*, p. 281.
10. *San Francisco Sunday Chronicle*, August 12, 1962, pp. 1, 10.
11. Cook, *op. cit.*, p. 302, and *San Francisco Sunday Chronicle, op. cit.*, p. 17.
12. *San Francisco Sunday Chronicle*, "This World" supplement, August 12, 1962, pp. 4–5.
13. Oskar Morgenstern, *The Question of National Defense*, New York: Random House, 1959, pp. 295–296.
14. Charles J. Hitch and Roland N. McKean, *The Economics of Defense in the Nuclear Age*, Cambridge: Harvard University Press, 1960, pp. 350, 354.
15. Janowitz, *op. cit.*, p. 418.
16. Janowitz, *Sociology and the Military Establishment*, New York: Russell Sage Foundation, 1959, p. 97. Janowitz calls this "unanticipated militarism."
17. Quoted in Waldemar A. Nielsen, "Huge, Hidden Impact of the Pentagon," *New York Times Magazine*, June 25, 1961, p. 36.
18. "Defense spokesmen, both military and civilian, make about six times as many speeches involving foreign-policy matters as officials of the Department of State; similarly they issue about six times as many articles bearing on foreign policy." *Ibid.*, p. 34.
19. See Janowitz, *The Professional Soldier*, Chapter 12, for a discussion of military conservatism.
20. Morgenstern, *op. cit.*, p. 296.
21. Harrison Brown and James Real, *Community of Fear*, Santa Barbara: Center

for the Study of Democratic Institutions, 1960, pp. 31–39, as quoted in *Issues of the Sixties*, Leonard Freedman and Cornelius P. Cotter, eds., San Francisco: Wadsworth Publishing Company, Inc., 1961, pp. 352–353.

Selected Readings

Andrzejewski, S. *Military Organization and Society*. London: Routledge and Kegan Paul, 1954.

Barnett, Richard. *Who Wants Disarmament?* Boston: Beacon Press, 1961.

Bernardo, C. J. and Eugene Bacon. *American Military Policy*. Harrisburg; Military Service Publishing Company, n.d.

Dupy, R. E. *The Compact History of the United States Army*. New York: Hawthorn Press, 1956.

*Gareau, F. H. *Balance of Power and Nuclear Deterence*. Boston: Houghton Mifflin, 1962.

Mills, C. Wright. *The Power Elite*. New York: Oxford University Press, 1956.

* Paperback edition.

Chapter 24

Conclusion

This book has demonstrated the value of the social sciences in analyzing existing institutions and their elements. It has also shown how these sciences may serve as aids in choosing courses of action when traditional solutions to social problems fail.

By developing its materials around several crucial processes of social life—socialization, urbanization, industrialization, specialization, secularization, and rational social organization—the book has made possible a unified study of change, both in individuals and institutions. These processes are not frozen, nor are they wholly unconnected. They are subject to constant modification, with each influencing the others and being influenced, in turn, by them. The means and speed of socialization of the individual, for example, can influence the rate and direction of urban, industrial, institutional, and bureaucratic development. Conversely, these other processes affect the way in which the child is inducted into society.

Besides emphasizing these key processes as basic themes, we have illustrated some of the social consequences of their interaction—that is, integration, disintegration, and disorganization. These appear in examples of what they have wrought, namely, alienation, stratification, the quest for community, and conformity and plurality in American life. Finally, the book has indicated how social institutions relate to each other by examining the development of major institutions which have come into being to meet specific needs created by changes in existing institutions. As Hertzler has said: "Institutions provide a society's profile. . . . The most comprehensive, revealing, and accurate way to envision the salient features of the social organization of any society under examination is to understand its major institutions and the relations between them." [1]

Behavior grows out of a combination of these several factors together with the inherited characteristics discussed in Chapter 2. A person who chooses, for example, to commute several hours each day to and from work in order to live on a tree-lined suburban street does so in response

559

to social processes, their consequences, institutional relationships, and perhaps an inherited predisposition toward suburban life. If all this—with the possible exception of DNA *—can be seen as a *social system in motion*, the importance of developing better understanding of the system and the desirability of applying intelligent direction to it can be appreciated. There is much to be done, however, before the social sciences can hasten the accomplishment of both.

SUMMARY

The growth of America has been the result of many different factors working in harmony. Their product has been the particular phenomenon that we call American civilization. Sheer physical expansion of the nation's territory has been one major source contributing to that civilization. The great diversity of the continent's physical environments has presented a continual challenge to adapt. Differences in environment, however, have given rise to sectional or regional snobbishness based on some very real differences in behavior—language, dress, and general style of life.

Accompanying the territorial expansion came the growth of America as a unique melting pot: somewhere in every American's background (Indians excepted) there is an immigrant. Today, even with decreases in immigration the population continues to grow through natural increase. In this respect America shares with other nations many problems springing from the population explosion.

As America matured, it had to tailor to its own dimensions the Western civilization from which it derived. English language and law, French social philosophy, German idealism, European concepts of trade and manufacture, European modes of dress, food habits, and manners, traditional systems of social status, and family and property relations all were adapted to conditions in the New World. Elements unique to the American scene, however, such as a greater range in temperature and topography than in Europe, the absence of feudal ties, and a highly mobile population mixed in urban areas, prompted changes in the European tradition. Besides, there was little agreement among those who settled the country on what European tradition really was. This was not only a reflection of diverse national backgrounds but also a consequence of the dispossessed, uprooted quality which had marked their lives in Europe.

As America developed its own civilization an ideological commitment

* See p. 18.

to capitalism as a philosophy of economics evolved. Ignored as much as it is observed, the ideology has nevertheless exerted continuous influence on American life. This is seen in the apparent contradiction of desiring to curb State interference in the economy while urging legislative action to regulate the economy in order to assure competition, the rights of property, and similar economic objectives.

There has also been present a growing, and often challenged, commitment to democracy. Some of the leading minds of the Revolution and the early days of the Republic were not, themselves, convinced of the democratic ideology. Jefferson's agrarian paternalism and his suspicion of the landless masses of America's cities illustrate the point. Democracy has been challenged as an ideology from time to time because it raises conflict over the rights of property. When the rights of property abuse the rights of individuals in a pure democracy, the State supports the people. This conflict becomes more complex as the nature of property ownership changes, particularly corporate ownership. It may very well be that the advocates of the rights of property are not always property owners but bureaucratic management which senses a threat to its position if the State forces changes on corporate organization.

An important element in the development of American civilization has been the shift from the traditional communities of an agrarian society to the urban communities of an industrial society. This transition has provoked some of the most profound changes in American life. Both the growth of a highly mechanized industrial order and a technological revolution in agriculture have led to new concentrations of population and urbanization of American communities. The adjustments required by this change—adjustments in property relations, law, production, occupational roles, statuses, and even family relations—have created a society vastly different from the eighteenth century.

In sum, current trends in American civilization reflect a generally increasing complexity of life. The question then becomes: in what specific ways has modern America grown more complicated?

First, the nature of the division of labor has changed. We are no longer a civilization of middle-class yeomen with feet planted in the soil. We have become a nation of professionals, managers, technicians, skilled and unskilled operatives, all massed in the enormous, endless task of producing goods and services for an affluent society. The vast division of labor has made possible both the affluence and productivity of American civilization. Yet the price of this division and its rewards has been the growth of subtle and intricate problems among individual personalities. In this sense the individual has suffered greater alienation from his social world. His possibilities of departing from accepted norms of behavior are so numerous that civilization finds itself in a constant state of flux.

Second, the industrial process and its division of labor have intensified the class structure. Ways of life have become more differentiated and economic opportunity has opened more doors than in the rural economy. The emergence of cities as the major form of community has brought an increase in life styles. Orbits of social space—from the slums to Park Avenue—provide visible evidence of these developments.

Third, modern America has seen the move toward bigness—in business, government, labor, military, education, and farming. Frequently viewed as a measure of progress, bigness more realistically represents increased efficiency under tight control. In a word, it signifies bureaucracy. Although possible within fairly small organizations, bureaucracy is essential in big organizations. But bureaucracy runs into stiff opposition when official policies and procedures counter the norms of informal social systems in large-scale organizations.

Fourth, all forms of social organization instill in their members those norms of conduct that are the basis of expected behavior. Can there, then, be a basic personality type in American civilization? Some social scientists answer this question affirmatively. But considering the pluralistic nature of American society, a single basic personality type is hardly likely. Most probably, a number of personality types exist in America. Differences in class and life style, insofar as they affect personality, certainly reinforce this conclusion.

In any event, American civilization cannot be summed up in a few generalizations. It must be seen in its entirety to grasp its reality.

INTERNAL CONFLICTS IN AMERICA

The complexity of America is heightened by the tendency to view conflicts as separate and unrelated. Race relations, crime, economic fluctuations, civil rights are often considered distinct forms of struggle. Let us look, instead, at some *areas* of conflict out of which these specific forms may arise.

The first area can be called the conflict between ends and means, based on the question: what do we want and how do we want to get it? In the field of economics the question is answered by the consumption dilemma of the American population. We want possessions: appliances, clothes, cars, houses, more efficient communication devices. How do we get them? Mass production and credit buying have been the answer. For the worker on the assembly line the answer is a contradiction. He, too, wants things, but the anxiety he can experience in his job is a high price to pay. The consumer is trapped in an endless cycle of purchasing sustained by newer, more stylish, and more efficient goods and services. Each new purchase is not a guarantee of satisfaction, nor the end of anxiety.

Means and ends also conflict in those institutions that state a concern for the individual, yet are faced with problems of overwhelming numbers. Corporations, government, and education are typical. Education is perhaps more affected than other institutions because, by its nature, education is an individual pursuit. Increasing enrollments, however, especially at the college level, have created conditions of mass activity reminiscent of the years immediately following the Second World War.

Means and ends may also conflict when secular and moral factors operate. This appears to be true in today's political and military institutions. A strong secular appeal for peace and survival as a nation is in conflict with the means by which these are to be ensured. There is the moral responsibility of maintaining peace and attempting to help the rest of the world, including the Soviet Bloc, to see the moral advantages of disarmament. At the same time there is the secular necessity of "keeping up" in the armament and space races. To expect consistent policy from a government committed to both courses is unrealistic.

The second area of conflict is between the ideal and the real, between what we *say* we believe and do, and what we *actually* believe and do. This is illustrated in many areas of institutional life. The contrast between the belief that America is a free-enterprise system, and its reality as a mixed economy, is an important example. The problems to which this belief has given birth are intensified by, first, the inability or unwillingness of apologists for free enterprise to understand that business has often sought State aid and intervention, and second, the inability to state clearly how far government can or should enter the economy.

Another important example of conflict between the ideal and the real is found in relation to the democratic ideology. The racial question in America, the cries of the pseudoconservatives, and the problems bearing on welfare legislation become interrelated here. The racial issue presupposes the principle of equality upon which the American nation-state was founded. The pseudoconservative issue is often reduced by them to the argument that America is not a democracy but a republic; therefore, government should represent property, not people. This question, of course, relates to both the racial issue and welfare legislation. If this nation was founded under God, as the pledge of allegiance indicates, then it is a nation which includes *all* of its citizens.

Culture lag provides another area of conflict, which grows out of the rapid advance of industry and of urbanization. These trends have made the ruralism of America's past the subject of romantic reminiscence. The "good old days," barbershop-quartet culture, and soda-fountain morality are constantly referred to, especially in the entertainment media, as the ideal period of American civilization. Culture lag develops insofar as attitudes, values, and beliefs from the rural past persist at a level inconsistent with the contemporary state of civilization. Conflict arises when effort is made to return to an earlier period in the civilization's development.

THE IMAGES OF AMERICA

America projects a many-sided image to the world, which is to be expected in light of its pluralistic nature. Whether it is possible or even desirable to present a uniform exterior to other nations is a question that has practical and philosophical implications beyond the scope of this book. On the other hand, it is quite clear that in the competition characteristic of the cold war—a struggle for the minds of men—we must be concerned with what the rest of the world thinks of us.

Regardless of the American's individual attitude toward his country's position of leadership, that leadership cannot be renounced, abdicated, or transferred except under pain of gross change in internal, as well as external, relationships. In other words, we are burdened with our greatness. It might be wise to examine, then, the ways in which our pluralism is projected to the world as contradiction. Once realized, a giant step will have been taken toward eliminating at least the more trivial and transitory clashes.

A major part of the confused, and thereby weakened, image often perceived by the European, Asian, or African comes as a result of the disparity between principle and practice. America is no exception to the habit of nations to stand for a principle and to implement in practice something quite different—for example, the dictatorship of the proletariat has long been a dictatorship of the Communist party élite, and there is still no sign of "withering" in the Communist State. But it should be apparent that were we to close the gap appreciably between principle and practice, there would be no guarantee that others' perceptions of us would necessarily be more accurate. The latter requires a conscious effort on our part.

There are several broad categories of sources of conflict in our exported image: political, economic, sociocultural, and ideological.

Political Conflict. Within the political category are diplomatic, military, and economic factors. Diplomacy is a craft dedicated to presenting the most favorable image of the diplomat's country to the host nation. Despite this over-riding purpose, an embassy or consulate is often one of the chief causes of confused and, hence, unfavorable images of America. From the inability of the ambassador to converse in the local tongue to the refusal of a visa on questionable grounds,[2] the diplomatic corps is in a key position to sabotage—certainly without malice—the best laid plans of an administration. *The Ugly American* by William J. Lederer and Eugene Burdick, a controversial novel about incompetence, high living, and dedication in the foreign service, has become generic for this variety of sabotage.[3]

Above the level of functionary stand the policy makers of the Executive Department, Congress, and the Central Intelligence Agency. Here, too, is fertile soil for confusion. From the XYZ Affair, the Tripolitanian Wars, and the Monroe Doctrine to the present, it is possible to chart contradiction between policies, and between policy and implementation. For example, the "New Imperialism," culminating in "spheres of influence" and the Spanish-American War, has been one of the more flagrant and lingering contributions to ill-will. Caught up in a cause-and-effect chain-reaction were the Philippine Insurrection; the Open-Door policy, and the Boxer Rebellion; the Platt Amendment and Cuba; the "Big Stick"; the Colombian "Revolution" and the Panama Canal; the Roosevelt Corollary to the Monroe Doctrine; "Dollar Diplomacy"; Pancho Villa; "Black Jack" Pershing and Mexican Confiscation; the "Good-Neighbor" Policy; "The Greater East Asia Co-Prosperity Sphere" of Japan and the Second World War; and Fidel Castro and the Alliance for Progress.

These are just a few of the high—and low—points of two strains which continually muddied diplomatic waters in our relationships with other nations. At least in part, they result from the internal contradictions of America, particularly between idealism and materialism. Idealism dictated the ameliorating Good Neighbor Policy, the Peace Corps, and the Alliance for Progress, while materialism was responsible for America's physical and economic high-handedness in Central America and Asia. Similarly, Wilson's Fourteen Points, Hoover's Belgian Relief, the Kellogg-Briand Peace Pact, the Marshall Plan, and Point Four Program, all examples of altruism, were offset by the isolationism of the twenties and thirties reflected in Congressional rejection of the League of Nations and the German treaty; by the failure to prevent reparations and the rise of Hitler; and by the vigorous support of "friendly" autocracies following the Second World War.

Even so great an achievement as the economic recovery of Europe, largely a result of the tremendous contribution of American aid through the Marshall Plan, Point Four, and subsequent aid programs, has had a peculiar reaction. We are at once pleased with, and fearful of, European recovery and the advent of the Common Market. Our response to this phenomenon, already complicated by competing considerations, could lead to further fuzziness of the American image, and even more important, wreck the unity of the West.

Militarily, the maintenance of a large standing army to protect the interests of the free world opens many opportunities for misinterpretation of our motives as well as for outright provocation, which fortunately has been held to a minimum. That we are the only nation to have exploded a nuclear device in war has made our protestations of peace and disarmament the easy target of Communist and neutralist criticism in a world supersensitive to the danger of nuclear annihilation.

Morison and Commager have pointed out that in the cold war the discovery was made by America's political leaders

*
. . . that the penalty of wealth and power was responsibility and trouble. The United States was expected to provide leadership, but not to exercise authority; to protect free peoples everywhere, but not to be militaristic; to provide limitless sums of money, but not to exact an accounting. It was impossible to satisfy all demands or meet all objections. If we financed the rebuilding of Taiwan or Vietnam, we were accused of backing the wrong governments. If we built airfields in Spain, we favored Fascism; if we helped Yugoslavia we were contributing to Communism. If we subsidized Pakistan we were hostile to India, and if we responded to the needs of Israel we were anti-Arab. When we poured billions into France, we subsidized a colonial power, but when we sided with Angola against Portugal we were fomenting revolution in a friendly state. When we spent money in Italy we were accused of buying elections; when we spent money in neutralist countries we were pouring money down the drain. If we stayed on good terms with a Trujillo or a Batista we were supporting dictatorships, but if we countenanced

* From *The Growth of the American Republic*, by Samuel Eliot Morison and Henry Steele Commager, Vol. 2, 5th ed., Oxford University Press, 1962. Reprinted by permission.

revolution—as in Guatemala—we were violating the principle of nonintervention. When we opposed the use of force in the Suez we betrayed our friends; when we ourselves used force in Lebanon we were imperialists.

Economic Conflict. In addition to governmental economic considerations, there is the area of foreign trade. Farmers, manufacturers, merchants, bankers, and labor all have special interests in the nature and extent of foreign trade. Frequently these interests are in conflict, causing pressure on tariff rates and in other ways altering stability of trade. The profit motive is sometimes opposed to political expediency, as the controversy over trade with Red China illustrates. The "dumping" of surplus grains in shortage areas for political gain, as well as for humanitarian reasons, has run repeatedly into farm-bloc opposition because this would be "robbing" the farmer of potential markets. Our overseas investments, reaching tremendous proportions in this century, have been the source of both a better standard of living and resentment in those nations where American corporations have established subsidiaries. The possibility of property confiscation and subsequent retaliation is heightened when investment is so extensive.

There is another source of economic conflict that is little appreciated: American importers who encourage the manufacture, particularly of specialty items, for an American market that can vanish overnight. To be burdened with equipment designed to produce a specialty item for the capricious American consumer has alienated a number of foreign producers. As other nations pull abreast of the United States in per capita wealth, however, these sources of conflict will diminish.

Sociocultural Conflict. A sense of superiority is always a source of trouble in relations between nations and it can appear in curious forms. An indiscreet—and snobbish—post card home almost destroyed the Peace Corps at the beginning of its career. As a secular mendicant order, the Peace Corps is a conscious effort at cultural diffusion, and as such, runs the risk of fomenting hostility. Some cultural groups believe "the old ways are the best ways." Hollywood has frequently been cited as a poor representative of America to the rest of the world; motion pictures and television undoubtedly have a profound effect upon the foreigner's perception. The mounting contact between hundreds of thousands of servicemen and tourists, and foreign nationals simultaneously increases the potential for hostility as well as fuller understanding.

Ideological Conflict. Much of the distortion of the American image abroad stems from the problem of "American rhetoric . . . the nation's ritualistic articulation of its principles to itself and to the world." [4] If the statement and carrying out of principle are not at variance, there is no problem. But the fact is that ideological discrepancies exist, both within and between ideologies. Our own ability to live with discrepancies between principle and practice and between the ideal and the material does not speak well for the possibility of presenting a uniform and appealing appearance to the world. Our sense of world mission, which frequently takes the form of a crusade, is predicated on a devotion to morals that can be very confusing to the outside observer. Our professed desire to see emergent peoples democratically determine their destinies has come into conflict with our own fear of the spread of communism. Because of our moralistic drive, we tend to extremes. We see issues as black and white; we tend to see as good nations those that agree with us and as bad nations those that disagree. In the past we have confused good order with good morals and have supported regimes that have not squared with democratic ideology.

Internally, the treatment of our minorities has left room for doubt about our protestations of liberty and justice for all. The inscription on the Statue of Liberty which reads in part, "Send me your tired, your poor, your huddled masses yearning to breathe free . . . " has been replaced by oriental exclusion and the quota system. The melting pot, in cooling, has left a residue of partially absorbed minorities, sometimes described as second-class citizens. The internment of 112,000 Japanese-Americans after Pearl Harbor and the continuing "problem of color" in America—North and South—is a reflection of still unsolved problems.

. . . .

We have cited throughout the book a number of ideological paradoxes that confuse the observer: we claim to be a nation of idealists—"the longest, lowest, most powerful," most material idealists in the world; we embrace peace but in the same breath proudly proclaim that we have never lost a war; we advocate free enterprise but scream for protection from countries employing "slave labor"; we claim to be a Christian nation but sat in judgment at Nuremberg.

The fact is that America must continually and critically examine and re-examine its weaknesses. So long as we hold a position of world leadership, America must offer the peoples of the world an example of the highest degree of freedom, order, and opportunity. When we look at the balance sheet we see that our assets outweigh our liabilities, but civilizations, like businesses, can become bankrupt and go into receivership if not assessed at frequent intervals, and corrected when warning signs are posted.

World trade is not merely economic, it is also a competition of ideas. We have much to export besides merchandise and military hardware. We have exportable ideas: a high material standard of living; an unusually high popular culture; technical skills in medicine, education, agriculture, communications, production, marketing, and the sciences; the striving for and maintenance of the rights of individuals in view of the demands of modern life, the heterogeneity of America, and the great numbers of "visible" minorities; and a sustained balance of freedom, order, and opportunity.

D. W. Brogan said recently that "the contest for the mind and heart of the world has not gone, is not going all one way. The generosity of the United States and of its people has not been unnoticed, even though the belief that the generosity was based exclusively on military and economic calculation of advantage has at times had a dangerous plausibility. But the great success of American policy, the salvation of Western Europe, has not only saved that treasure house from passing into the Soviet orbit but has made possible the reconstruction of a great economic power that in its turn is capable (if adequately led) of doing its part in saving the poorer regions of the world from despair and its temptations." [5]

It seems likely that this leadership will not be singular but will be collective in nature and that nationalism will perforce come to be subordinated to a community of nations. Whether America and other nations are yet mature enough for this more advanced political concept is currently being tested: "The United States, child of the Enlightenment, favored adolescent of the nineteenth century, powerful but erratic youth of the first half of the twentieth, must now confirm its maturity by acting from the present forward to see the values of the Enlightenment—or their equivalents in non-Western cultures—survive and dominate in the twenty-first." [6]

Notes

1. J. O. Hertzler, *American Social Institutions*, Boston: Allyn and Bacon, Inc., 1961, pp. 79–80.
2. Recently, a Fulbright Fellow, attempting to cement American-Finnish relations, invited a Finnish student to come to America to see for herself the glories that the Fulbrighter could only picture for her. To his chagrin she was subjected to what she described as an interrogation by an embassy official and was summarily

denied the visa. When the people-to-people diplomat advised certain parties that the young lady's father was chairman of the local Finnish-American Society, a *four-year* visa arrived posthaste. Although the young lady has come to America, her impressions of us have doubtless been conditioned by the affront she suffered at Helsinki.

3. William J. Lederer and Eugene Burdick, *The Ugly American*, New York: W. W. Norton & Company, Inc., 1958. See particularly "A Factual Epilogue," pp. 271–285. Curiously, the "Ugly American" was a good Samaritan but the label has been misapplied so often that it has stuck, becoming generic for boorishness.

4. W. W. Rostow, *The United States in the World Arena*, New York: Harper & Brothers, 1960, p. 480.

5. D. W. Brogan, *America in the Modern World*, New Brunswick: Rutgers University Press, 1960, pp. 112–113.

6. Rostow, *op. cit.*, p. 539.

Index

571